THE MCGRAW-HILL INVESTOR'S DESK REFERENCE

Ellie Williams

McGraw-Hill

New York   San Francisco   Washington, D.C.   Auckland   Bogotá
Caracas   Lisbon   London   Madrid   Mexico City   Milan
Montreal   New Delhi   San Juan   Singapore
Sydney   Tokyo   Toronto

For Mark and Nathan

Library of Congress Cataloging-in-Publication Data

Williams, Ellie.
  The McGraw-Hill investor's desk reference / by Ellie Williams.
    p. cm.
  ISBN 0-07-135945-1
  1. Investments—Handbooks, manuals, etc. I. Title.

  HG4527 .C585 2000
  332.6—dc21   00-040101

McGraw-Hill

*A Division of The **McGraw-Hill** Companies*

1 2 3 4 5 6 7 8 9 0   DOC / DOC   0 9 8 7 6 5 4 3 2 1 0

ISBN 0-07-135945-1

This book was set in Palatino by Carlisle Communications, Ltd.

Printed and bound by R.R. Donnelley & Sons Company/Crawfordsville.

This publication is designed to provide accurate and authoritative information in regard to the subject matter covered. It is sold with the understanding that the publisher is not engaged in rendering legal, accounting, or other professional service. If legal advice or other expert assistance is required, the services of a competent professional person should be sought.

> —From a declaration of principles jointly adopted by a committee
> of the American Bar Association and a committee of publishers.

McGraw-Hill books are available at special quantity discounts to use as premiums and sales promotions, or for use in corporate training programs. For more information, please write to the Director of Special Sales, Professional Publishing, McGraw-Hill, Two Penn Plaza, New York, NY 10121. Or contact your local bookstore.

This book is printed on recycled, acid-free paper containing a minimum of 50% recycled de-inked fiber.

Contents

Preface

In the last 20 years, the world of investing has changed tremendously. The biggest change is that most individuals now manage their own investments. Though many use a financial advisor for expert opinions, the days of investors blindly turning their money over to someone else are gone.

This book is written to aid investors who need a resource for financial terms, techniques, or ideas. Information provided here should help, whether you are looking for the rules on Roth IRAs, Warren Buffet's investment strategy, the best financial websites, or ways to hedge investments with options.

This book is not one of the many "how to invest" guides. Designed for the investor who has already begun the process, it is written in an encyclopedia style, organized by chapter topic, but in no particular sequence, so that you can pick and choose information pertinent to your current situation. Each subject is covered carefully and offers resources such as websites for further study.

Acknowledgments

Many thanks to Scotte Hardin for her tireless fact-finding work. Thank you to Bob Hockenhull of Moloney Securities (*www.stocktrader.com*) for sharing his expertise in the bond markets. Thank you to Chuck Butler of Everbank (*www.everbank.com*) for his insights into international economies and foreign currencies. Thank you to Craig Campbell, CPA of Anders, Minkler & Diehl, for being a resource on all things tax-related.

Thank you to Linda Bryant and Diane Pearl for their contributions to Moneywise and the books we co-authored. Thank you to Dani and Vickie Kunin, and as always, many thanks to my family.

Ellie Williams

Part 1

The World of Investing

The world of investing is the environment in which our investments are made. This environment changes constantly, and each change can affect the values and performance of different investments. Chapters 1 and 2 provide a background for understanding business cycles, economic indicators, interest rates, inflation, and currency values in a global economy. Chapters 3 and 4 concentrate on some of the practical aspects of the world of investing, covering securities exchanges and the indices used to track investment performance.

The U.S. Economy, Interest Rates, and Inflation

In any economy, there are periodic fluctuations in interest rates, inflation, unemployment, and economic output. Lawmakers in the United States have long attempted to lessen the severity of these fluctuations through fiscal and monetary policy. Fiscal policy strives to modify the economy through changes in government taxation and spending. Monetary policy uses manipulation of the money supply to affect output, unemployment, and inflation.

The Business Cycle

Changes in the level of economic activity tend to move in patterns called business cycles. These cycles may vary in length or severity, but typically contain four distinct stages: expansion, recession, depression, and recovery.

The strength of the economy parallels the levels of production and employment. In the expansion stage, levels of employment and output are high. When a period of economic expansion peaks and begins to move downward, the economy enters a recession, defined by six successive months of slower growth in output. If economic activity during a recession slows to a standstill, it becomes a depression; if it bottoms out and begins to increase, the economy may bypass the depression stage. A depression is usually a period of high unemployment that may be marked by a period of price deflation. Recovery is the stage immediately following recession or depression, in which output and employment growth increase.

Current Economic Cycle

In February 2000, the U.S. economy marked 107 months of expansion—the longest expansion phase ever—passing the 1961 to 1969 cycle that previously held the record. The recovery, which began slowly and unevenly in 1991, progressed with especially strong GDP growth of approximately 4% in the 1995 to 1998 period. During the same time and for the first time in 25 years, the unemployment rate fell below 4.5%, a rate many thought to be unattainable in the 1990s. All this has occurred as the core rate of inflation has fallen below 2%.

Conventional economic theory holds that as economic output increases, so does inflation. Higher output requires ever higher employment, and as employers vie for scarce workers they must pay them more. To recoup the costs of wage inflation, producers must charge more for goods and services, creating general price inflation. The current expansion, with its levels of high growth, high employment, and low inflation, is confounding traditional economists. The description often used is that of a "New Economy," in which productivity increases due to technological advances allow an increase in output without putting upward pressure on employment and wages. Those who argue for and against the existence of a new economy draw their conclusions from the interpretation of production, prices, interest rates, and employment data, called economic indicators.

Economic Indicators

Economic indicators are specific data reports that indicate levels of economic activity. The Conference Board publishes the most widely followed indices of economic indicators used to predict and evaluate the state of the economy. Leading indicators are those that tend to shift in direction in advance of the business cycle and thus have predictive value for future economic activity. Coincident indicators measure current economic activity. Lagging indicators change after the economy changes.

Conference Board Index of Leading Indicators

- Average weekly hours, manufacturing: Employers usually increase or decrease the average hours worked per week before making changes in their workforce. Therefore, the average hours worked per week can predict changes in employment.

- Average weekly initial claims for unemployment insurance: This average is inverted in the index because initial claims increase when layoffs rise. It leads the business cycle because the number of new claims for unemployment insurance is more sensitive than total unemployment to overall business conditions.

- Manufacturers' new orders, consumer goods and materials (reported in 1992 dollars): This inflation-adjusted indicator leads actual production of consumer goods and materials because new orders are placed after considering both unfilled orders and existing inventories.

- Vendor performance, slower deliveries diffusion index: This index measures whether industrial companies have received their deliveries of supplies faster, slower, or with no change from the previous month. This indicator leads the business cycle because slower deliveries are associated with increased demand for industrial supplies, which occurs in advance of actual increased production.

- Manufacturers' new orders, nondefense capital goods (in 1992 dollars): Similar to new orders for consumer goods, these lead the business cycle as orders precede production.

- Building permits, new private housing units: Building permits lead construction activity, which typically leads other types of production.

- Stock prices—the S&P 500: Changes in the index of stock prices reflect investor sentiment and interest rate activity, both good indicators of future economic activity.

- Money supply (in 1992 dollars): This figure is the inflation-adjusted measure of M2, which includes currency, demand deposits (checking accounts), other checkable deposits, traveler's checks, savings deposits, small-denomination time deposits (CDs), and balances in money market mutual funds. The money supply is a leading indicator, because when the money supply does not keep pace with inflation (i.e., real money supply falls) bank lending may fall in real terms. Bank lending is required for a growing economy.

- Interest rate spread, 10-year Treasury bonds less federal funds: This is a numerical measure of the yield curve, a graph of interest rates from short to long term. When short-term interest rates as measured by the federal funds rate (the overnight interbank borrowing rate) are higher than long-term, 10-year Treasury bond rates, the yield curve has a downward slope and is said to be inverted. Historically, this has been a strong indicator of recession.

- Index of consumer expectations: This index is based on a consumer confidence survey conducted by the University of Michigan's Survey Research Center. The survey asks for a positive, negative, or unchanged response for a consumer's expectation of (1) economic prospects for the family over the next 12 months, (2) economic prospects for the nation over the next 12 months, and (3) economic prospects for the nation over the next five years. This indicator leads the business cycle because consumer expectations affect future spending.

Conference Board Index of Coincident Indicators

- Employees on nonagricultural payrolls: Often called payroll employment, this number from the Bureau of Labor Statistics is one of the most closely watched indicators for evaluating the health of the economy. Changes in payroll employment reflect actual net hiring and firing of all but the very smallest firms in the nation except agricultural businesses and government agencies.

- Personal income less transfer payments (in 1992 dollars): This measure of personal income includes salaries and other income received less transfer payments such as Social Security. Income levels reflect the general health of the economy and determine aggregate consumer spending.

- Index of industrial production: This index compiles the physical output of all stages of production in the manufacturing, mining, gas, and electric utility industries, on a value-added basis. Although industrial production is only one sector of the economy, historically fluctuations in total output have been reflected in changes in this sector.

- Manufacturing and trade sales (in 1992 dollars): This index is an aggregate of sales for manufacturing, wholesale, and retail businesses. This level of spending moves with the business cycle.

Conference Board Index of Lagging Economic Indicators. Because lagging indicators tend to change direction after coincident indicators, their practical value is often discounted. The indicators in the Conference Board Index are the average duration of unemployment, the ratio of manufacturing and trade inventories to sales, the change in labor cost per unit of manufacturing output, the average prime rate, commercial and industrial loans outstanding, the ratio of consumer installment credit outstanding to personal income, and the change in the consumer price index for services.

Using Indices of Economic Indicators

Indices of economic indicators can provide a way to assess and predict economic activity, particularly recession. A general rule often quoted is that a decline in the Index of Leading Indicators for three consecutive months is a warning of impending recession. According to the Conference Board, publisher of the index, this rule produces too many false signals (at least one during four of the past five expansions). The Conference Board's rule for a more reliable recession prediction is a 1% decline in the leading index from its cyclical peak and concurrent declines in at least half of its 10 components.

Following Individual Economic Reports

In addition to using the Conference Board's Indices to evaluate the economy, you may want to follow individual economic reports as they are released. Although none can individually forecast the direction of the economy, announcements often have a profound effect on stock and bond markets. A summary list follows.

- Consumer price index for all urban consumers (CPI-U, or simply CPI): A measure of changes in the cost of a basket of goods and services for an urban consumer. This is the most common indicator of inflation. It is released on the tenth day of the business month by the Bureau of Labor Statistics and covers the prior month. Website: *http://stats.bls.gov/news.release/cpi.toc.htm*
- Durable goods orders: Tracks new orders of durable goods and is an indicator of manufacturing activity. It is released on the tenth business day of the month by the Commerce Department and covers the prior month. Website: *www.census.gov/ftp/pub/indicator/www/ m3/index.htm*
- Payroll employment: Part of the Index of Coincident Indicators, it measures the change in the number of individuals employed. It is released on the first Friday of every month by the Bureau of Labor Statistics and covers the prior month. Website: *http://stats.bls.gov:80/newsrels.htm*
- Gross domestic product (GDP): Lists the combined value of all goods and services produced in the United States. It is considered a coincident indicator, released quarterly on the twentieth business day of the month by the Commerce Department and covers the prior quarter. Website: *www.bea.doc.gov*
- Housing starts: Measures new residential construction started. Construction often leads other sectors of the economy. Similar to, but just following the building permits indicator used in the Conference Board Index. It is released on the fifteenth business day of the month by the Commerce Department and covers the prior month. Website: *www.census.gov/pub/const/www/c20index.html*

- Industrial production (IP): A coincident indicator used in the index, this measures production in manufacturing, mining, and utilities. It is released on the fifteenth business day of the month by the Federal Reserve and covers the prior month. Website: *www.bog.frb.fed.us/releases/G17*

- U.S. international trade: Provides monthly exports of U.S. goods and services, closely followed when there is concern about the value of the dollar. It is released during the third week of the month by the Commerce Department and covers activity two months prior. Website: *www.census.gov/foreign-trade/*

- Manufacturing NAPM report on business (NAPM): Provides a composite index of new orders, production, supplier deliveries, inventories, and employment. It is released on the first business day of the month by the National Association of Purchasing Management and covers the prior month. Website: *www.napm.org*

- Producer price index (PPI): A measure of the average domestic change in prices for wholesale producers of commodities. The PPI is a leading indicator of inflation because price increases at the producer level are often passed on to consumers. It is released on the tenth business day of the month by the Bureau of Labor Statistics and covers the prior month. Website: *stats.bls.gov/news.release/ppi.toc.htm*

- Retail sales: A measure of consumer spending on both nondurable and durable consumer goods. This coincident indicator of economic activity is released midmonth by the Commerce Department, covering the prior month. Website: *www.census.gov/svsd/www/advtable.html*

- Unemployment insurance claims: A leading indicator in the index, this number reflects initial claims for unemployment insurance. It is released every Thursday by the Department of Labor and covers the prior week through Saturday. Website: *www.dol.gov/dol/public/media/main.htm*

Inflation and Interest Rates

Inflation

Modern economies are based on a system of exchange between buyers and sellers of goods and services. The medium of exchange is money and the system that facilitates that exchange is price. In a textbook environment, price changes in an individual product or service are a result of changes in supply and demand for that item. However, many economies experience a general rise in prices, known as inflation, or a general decrease in prices, known as deflation.

Since 1925, the United States has experienced both inflation and deflation. The years 1926 to 1933 were deflationary, followed by an inflationary period which brought prices back to 1926 levels by 1945. Except for a postwar spike in 1946, the 1970s saw the highest inflation, with a monthly annualized peak of 24% in August 1973 and an annual peak of 13.3% in 1979. Inflation rates averaged about 5% in the 1980s and 3% in the 1990s. Compounded over the time period 1926 to 1998, annual inflation has been 3.1%.

The level of inflation or deflation is measured through changes in indices of prices for a basket of goods. The most common index followed is the consumer price index for all urban consumers (CPI-U, or simply CPI). Calculated each month by the Bureau of Labor Statistics, the CPI-U is a basket of goods and services thought to be typical of an urban consumer's current lifestyle. The basket includes food, apparel, housing, transportation, recreation, education, and health care. Because the food and energy components of the index are especially volatile, the CPI-U is also quoted excluding food and energy prices. Seasonal adjustments eliminate changes that normally occur at the same time every year, such as price changes resulting from climate, production cycles, model changes (automobiles), and holidays. An index of the CPI-U initiated at $1.00 at the end of 1925 grew to $9.14 by the end of 1998.

The producer price index (PPI), also tracked by the Bureau of Labor Statistics, calculates the cost of raw materials that are used to make products. The PPI is valued as an inflation predictor because when production costs rise, producers tend to pass along their increased costs to consumers in the form of increased consumer prices.

As the cost to purchase a basket of goods rises, inflation occurs. Armed with the same dollars in wages, consumers can buy less. Thus, the purchasing power of a dollar is eroded and rising wages, though they give the illusion of making more money, may be needed just to maintain an existing standard of living. See Figure 1–1 for CPI and PPI charts.

Effect of Inflation on Interest Rates

Irving Fisher first pointed out that when expected inflation rises, interest rates rise. The result, known as the Fisher effect, is due to shifts in the supply and demand curves for bonds. As expected inflation rises, the real cost of borrowing falls, because debt is repaid with cheaper dollars. When the real rate of interest, calculated by subtracting the rate of inflation from the

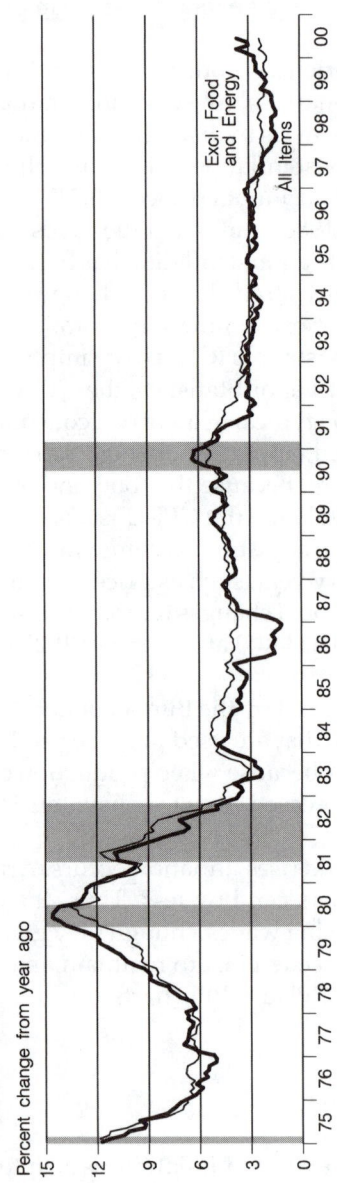
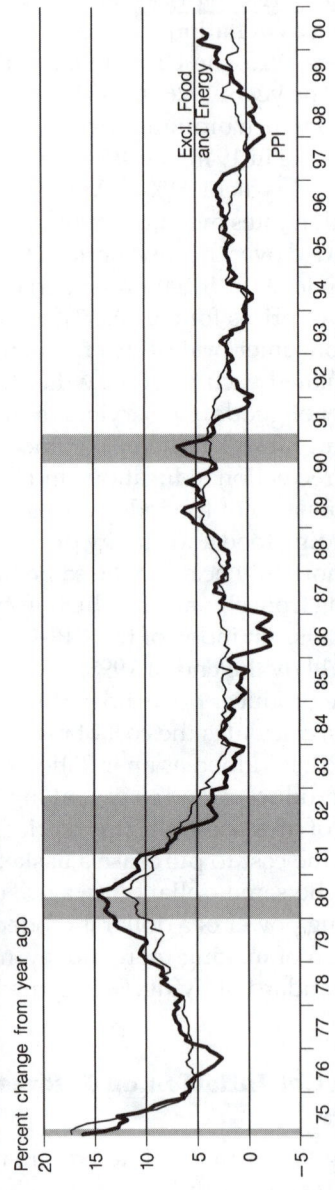

Figure 1-1. Consumer Price Index and Producer Price Index Charts
Source: Federal Reserve Bank of St. Louis.

nominal or stated rate of interest, is low, corporations borrow more, which increases the supply of bonds. As the expected return on bonds relative to real assets falls, demand for bonds falls. An increasing supply and decreasing demand for bonds means lower bond prices, which translate into higher interest rates.

Key Interest Rates

The term *interest rates* can be nebulous in its definition because, while different rates tend to move as a group, there are many distinct interest rates in the financial markets. Following is an explanation of several key interest rates.

Discount rate—The rate that the Federal Reserve charges banks that borrow funds. The announcement of a change in the discount rate is a key predictor of Federal Reserve monetary policy.

Federal funds rate—The rate that banks charge each other as they lend and borrow funds overnight in order to meet reserve requirements. Changes in this rate affect banks' willingness to lend money to the public and the rates at which they lend.

Prime rate—The interest rate that banks charge on loans to their most creditworthy borrowers. Many loans are based on the prime rate, with interest rates quoted relative to prime, such as "prime + 1." Although the prime rate is not set by any governing body, banks generally agree upon one prime rate. The prime rate affects the cost to businesses of borrowing for expansion, which in turn affects economic activity.

Residential mortgage rates—The interest rates charged on residential loans. Mortgage rates fluctuate based on the type and term of the loan and on other market interest rates. Changes in mortgage rates greatly affect the residential housing market, because monthly house payments of prospective home buyers change with every movement in the interest rate.

Long bond—The yield on the benchmark 30-year U.S. Treasury bond is highly sensitive to economic news and other market conditions. This rate generally moves more quickly than other rates, giving a fairly accurate picture of day-to-day changes in interest rate psychology.

Broker call rate—The rate charged on loans backed by marketable securities. The combination of margin requirements, (which is the amount that can be borrowed against securities) and the broker call rate (which is the basis of interest rates charged to borrow) affects levels of investor speculation. Lower margin requirements and a lower broker call rate decrease the cost of speculation, which encourages this activity.

Figure 1–2 provides an example of selected interest rates as reported in *Investor's Business Daily*.

Effect of Interest Rates on the Economy

A decrease in real interest rates lowers the cost of borrowing, which increases business expansion and consumer purchases of durable goods, such as cars and homes. At the same time, when lower real rates are combined with a healthy economy, banks may be more willing to lend money. The increased availability of credit, especially for the marginally creditworthy, borrowers may increase spending.

Lower real rates reduce the relative appeal of fixed income investments such as CDs and bonds. If inflation is at 9%, as it was in the late 1970s, a CD with an 8% rate has a negative 1% real rate of interest. Situations such as this send investors into real estate and common stocks, increasing their prices. Consumers who see the values of their stock portfolios and homes rise experience the wealth effect, which makes them willing to spend more because they feel wealthier.

In foreign exchange markets, lower real interest rates in the United States will reduce the value of the dollar in the short run, which lowers the prices of our exports and increases the prices of imports. This increases demand for domestic goods and services.

These increases in spending lead companies to increase production, which requires increased employment and business spending on capital goods for increased capacity. In turn, consumers spend more due to increased income received from higher levels of productivity and employment.

Investments

Interest rates and inflation affect investments in both market value and expectations for future returns, depending upon the characteristics of the investment. Bond, stock, and hard assets are all affected differently by interest rates and inflation.

Bonds

Real interest rates and bond prices are inversely related. As interest rates rise, the prices of existing bonds will fall, and vise versa, because investors have a choice of purchasing new bonds with higher rates or purchasing existing bonds with lower coupon rates. To make the return on an

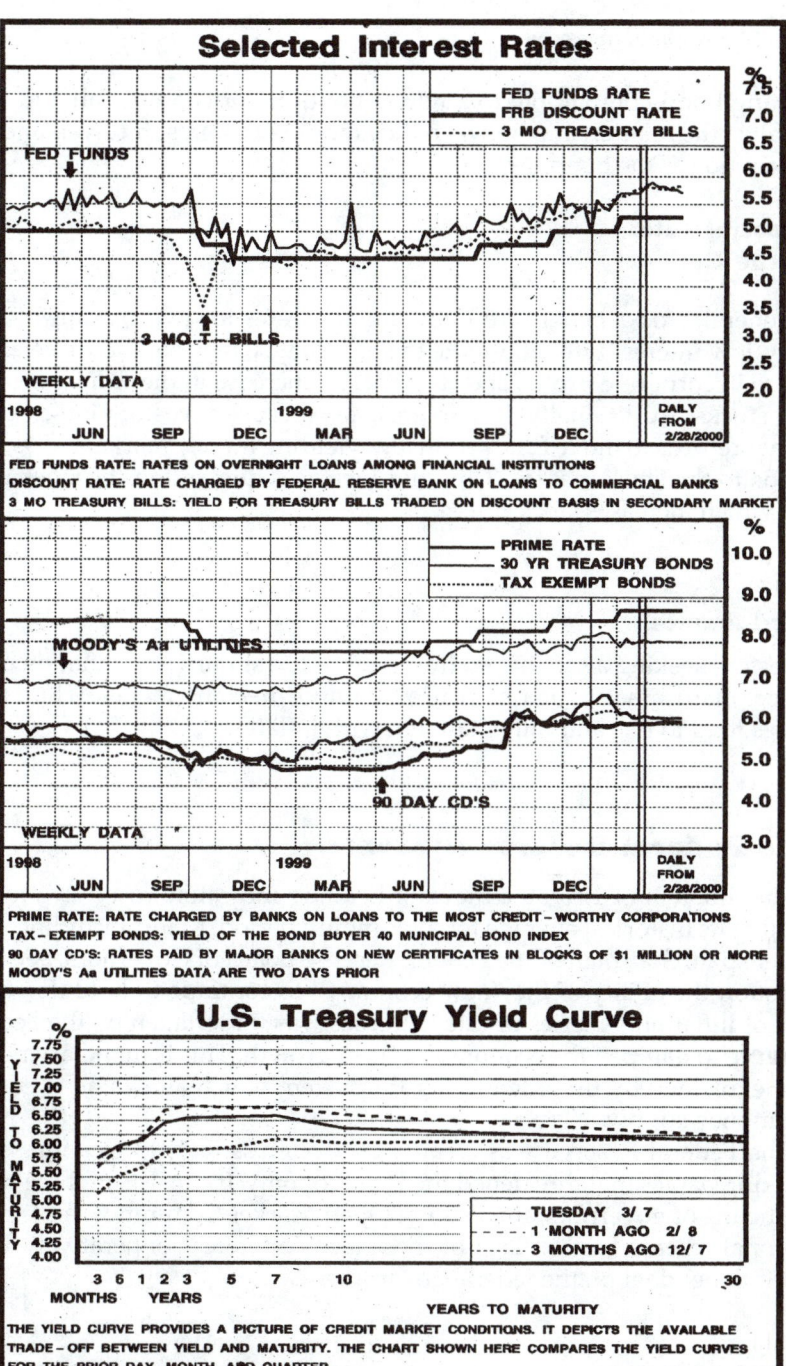

Figure 1-2. Selected Interest Rates
SOURCE: Investor's Business Daily.

existing bond comparable to a newer bond, its price must fall and thus equalize the relationship between the amount of interest received and the price paid for the bond.

Stocks

In general, stocks benefit from low interest rates for two reasons. Principally, low interest rates stimulate the economy, which should drive an increase in corporate profits and thus fuel an increase in the value of corporate stocks. Additionally, low interest rates cause investors in search of higher returns to move funds from low-yielding money markets, CDs, and bonds to the stock market. This shift increases demand in the stock market, which increases stock prices.

Hard Assets

Investors seeking a safe haven from high interest rates and inflation often choose hard assets, such as real estate and precious metals. Thus their prices tend to rise and fall in tandem with inflation.

The Federal Reserve System

In the first half of 1999, the Index of Leading Indicators rose 1.2%, nearly tripling its historical average for a six-month period. Many, including Alan Greenspan, chairman of the Federal Reserve Board of Governors, began to question the ability of the "new economy" to continue to hold down the rate of inflation. A series of rate increases was undertaken by the Federal Reserve to dampen the economy's rate of growth. This is monetary policy, best explained by first identifying the system which allows us to control the money supply.

The Federal Reserve was created by Congress in 1913 to address the banking panics that threatened the U.S. economy. It consists of three parts: the board of governors, the Federal Open Market Committee, and the 12 regional reserve banks. Each of these arms operates cooperatively with, but independent of, the federal government.

Board of Governors

The seven members of the Federal Reserve Board of Governors are appointed by the president of the United States and confirmed by the Senate to 14-year terms. The same process is followed as two board members are chosen to fill the 4-year terms of chairperson and vice chairperson. Staggered appointments and the length of terms preserve the political independence of the board by making it difficult for any one president to appoint a significant number of members.

The board of governors' primary responsibility is to set monetary policy through membership on the Federal Open Market Committee. In addition to setting monetary policy, the board supervises and regulates banks that are members of the Federal Reserve system, bank holding companies, international banking facilities in the United States, and the foreign activities of member banks.

The board of governors sets margin requirements, which limit the amount an investor can borrow against securities. The board also has responsibility for making, interpreting, and administering laws to protect consumers in lending and deposit transactions.

The board typically convenes biweekly, on Mondays and Wednesdays, in meetings which are either open or closed to the public in accordance with Title 5, Section 552b of the U.S. Code, known as the Government in the Sunshine Act. Notice of open board meetings is given seven days in advance and is available from the board's Freedom of Information and Public Affairs office, the Treasury Department Press Room, and the board meetings page of the Federal Reserve website at *www.bog.frb.fed.us/boarddocs/meetings/*. For a tape recording about open meetings, call (202) 452-3206, 24 hours. For information about agenda items, call Public Affairs at (202) 452-3204 between 9:00 A.M. and 5:00 P.M., Monday through Friday.

Closed meetings are announced on a schedule that varies due to the nature of the items being discussed. Such items include:

- Bank and bank holding company supervisory matters
- Monetary policy and any matters that could be used in financial speculation
- Personnel matters

Federal Open Market Committee

The Federal Open Market Committee (FOMC) has primary responsibility for engineering the Federal Reserve's monetary policy. Voting members of the FOMC are the seven members of the board of governors, the president of the Federal Reserve Bank of New York, and a rotating selection of four of the remaining eleven reserve bank presidents. The remaining seven reserve bank presidents participate in discussion but do not vote.

The FOMC typically meets eight times per year to discuss the U.S. economy and issue a directive to increase, decrease, or maintain the growth of the nation's money supply to maximize employment and output and minimize inflation. In February and July, the FOMC delivers Humphrey-Hawkins reports to Congress which discuss monetary policy in the context of current and expected economic performance.

The FOMC has three tools with which it can influence the growth of the money supply:

- The discount rate, which is the rate the Fed charges banks that borrow from it

- Member bank reserve requirements, which is the percentage of deposits that banks must hold on reserve with the Fed

- Open market operations, which are the buying and selling of Treasury securities to affect the federal funds rate

FOMC directives are generally issued immediately following the meeting in the form of an announcement about plans to use any or all of the tools available. In addition to stating current plans, the FOMC may provide a hint to future moves by announcing a policy bias toward easing, tightening, or remaining neutral. For example, a neutral bias signals that the Fed is unsure whether future rate changes are necessary and is prepared to move in either direction.

Federal Reserve Banks

Federal Reserve banks operate in three capacities: They serve as the bank of the U.S. Treasury, as a bank for banks, and as decentralized components of the Fed's policymaking bodies. The Federal Reserve bank system is divided into 12 districts, each with a regional reserve bank, which may have one or more branches (Table 1–1).

As banks for the U.S. Treasury, reserve banks sell U.S. Treasury securities, process the Treasury's payments, collect federal tax deposits, and implement cash management and investment activities.

As a bank for banks, each reserve bank supervises the commercial banks in its region. This responsibility includes acting as a lender of last resort for individual banks experiencing a shortage of funds. This lending occurs through the Fed's "discount window" and the interest rate charged is called the discount rate. Reserve banks also process and store currency and coins for banks, process checks, and provide electronic payment services. Electronic payments include funds transfer to other banks or the Fed and Automated Clearing House (ACH) transactions for paperless payments such as payroll direct deposits, electronic bill payments, and Social Security payments.

Table 1-1. Federal Reserve Banks

Federal Reserve Bank	Branches	Phone Number	Website
Atlanta	Birmingham Jacksonville Miami Nashville New Orleans	(404) 521-8020	*www.frbatlanta.org*
Boston	none	(617) 973-3989	*www.bos.frb.org*
Chicago	Detroit	(312) 322-5111	*www.frbchi.org*
Cleveland	Cincinnati Pittsburgh	(216) 579-3079	*www.clev.frb.org*
Dallas	El Paso Houston San Antonio	(214) 922-5254	*www.dallasfed.org*
Kansas City	Denver Oklahoma City Omaha	(816) 881-2683	*www.kc.frb.org*
Minneapolis	Helena	(612) 204-5255	*www.minneapolisfed. org*
New York	Buffalo	(212) 720-6134	*www.ny.frb.org*
Philadelphia	none	(215) 574-6115	*www.phil.frb.org*
Richmond	Baltimore Charlotte	(804) 697-8109	*www.rich.frb.org*
San Francisco	Los Angeles Portland Salt Lake City Seattle	(415) 974-2163	*www.frbsf.org*
St. Louis	Little Rock Louisville Memphis	(314) 444-8808	*www.stls.frb.org*

The role of reserve banks in contributing to the policymaking process involves monitoring the economies of their districts by gathering and analyzing data from diverse sources, such as financial and government institutions and business and community leaders. Much of this information is compiled in a report called the Beige Book, designed to help policymakers spot regional trends in economic activity and use them to predict the course of the national economy.

Monetary Policy

According to a 1977 amendment to the Federal Reserve Act, the goals of monetary policy are as follows:

- To promote maximum output and employment
- To promote stable prices (i.e., low inflation)

Maximum Output and Employment

The economy's level of output is the total dollar value of goods and services produced within the country, as measured by gross domestic product (GDP). The level of output is measured from quarter to quarter or year to year to determine whether the economy is growing at increasing rates (expansion) or decreasing rates (recession).

The Bureau of Labor Statistics measures employment by tracking the unemployment rate, which is the percentage of unemployed individuals looking for work as measured against the entire workforce (employed + unemployed).

Output and employment are usually positively correlated, as an increase in output—in the absence of productivity increases—requires an increase in employment. By the same token, increases in employment—in the absence of productivity decreases—bring increased output.

In the long run, maximum output and employment are not determined by monetary policy, but by productivity, technology, and individual preferences for saving and working. However, in the short run, monetary policy can alter business cycles which cause output and employment to differ from their long-run rates.

Tradeoff between Inflation and Unemployment

The Fed's two goals of maximizing employment and minimizing inflation are, according to economic theory, in conflict. The theory known as the Phillips curve shows in graphic form the inverse relationship between inflation and unemployment (Figure 1–3).

The logic behind this relationship is that as employment increases to the level of full employment, workers in tight job markets can demand higher wages. These higher wages increase the costs of creating goods and services, so firms will pass those costs on to consumers in the form of higher prices. Higher prices equal inflation. Higher wages also provide more disposable income to workers, prompting them to spend

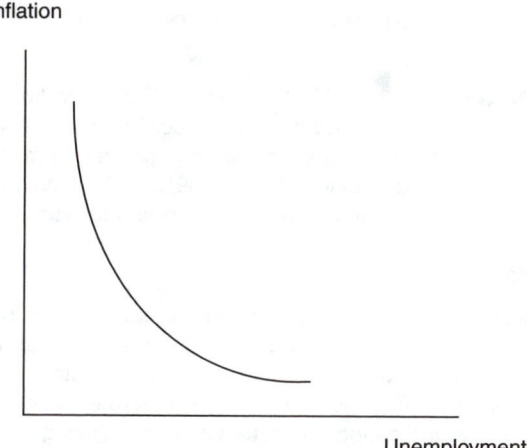

Figure 1–3. Phillips Curve

more, which increases demand for all output, requiring more hiring in a tight market, which prompts more wage inflation. Monetary policy strives to reach a balance between maximum output and employment and inflation.

Tools of Monetary Policy

The Fed cannot directly change inflation, output, or employment, but it can indirectly affect them with its ability to drive short-term interest rates. The tools it uses to affect interest rates are bank reserve requirements, the discount rate, and open market operations.

Reserve Requirements. Banks and other depository institutions are required to keep a certain percentage of the funds that depositors have placed in interest-bearing and noninterest-bearing accounts in reserve. Depending on the amount of funds held in the bank, between 3% and 10% of those funds must be held in cash in the vault or in reserve deposits with the Federal Reserve.

Reserve requirements affect interest rates through the federal funds market. The federal funds market is a private market through which banks may borrow or lend funds in order to comply with their reserve requirements. Because a bank's deposits change daily as consumers deposit and withdraw money, the amount of reserves they are required to hold changes daily also. On a short-term basis, a bank may need to borrow or may be able to lend excess funds in the federal funds market. The interest

---

ANATOMY OF A RATE INCREASE

On Tuesday, November 16, 1999, the Federal Open Market Committee announced a 1/4-point increase (to 5%) in the discount rate, a 1/4-point increase (to 5.5%) in the target for the federal funds rate, and a neutral policy bias. This was the third rate increase since June 1999 and Fed policymakers said it "should markedly diminish the risk of inflation going forward."[*]

The Days Before

The rate increase followed a 1/4-point federal funds target rate increase on June 30 and a 1/4-point increase in both the federal funds and discount rates on August 24. The previous rate increases were expected, as wage and job growth created inflationary pressures. The jobless rate for July was 4.3%, just above a 29-year low, indicating the potential for rising wages.

Economists were mixed in their expectations prior to the November rate hike. There was much talk of a Goldilocks economy—not too hot (inflationary), not too cold (recessionary), but a growth rate that was "just right." This attitude stemmed from the most recent productivity report which indicated a third-quarter gain in output of 5.7%; a 1.5% gain in the number of hours worked; a 4.2% gain in productivity, which is the increase in output per hour; and a 0.6% increase in unit labor costs.

Economists interpreted the productivity report: The 5.7% gain in output minus the 1.5% gain in number of hours worked equals a 4.2% gain in productivity. If the increase in unit labor costs of 0.6% does not exceed the gain in productivity, then the growth is not inflationary.

The Days After

Early reaction to the rate increase was mixed. Immediately after the Fed's announcement at 12:16 P.M. EST, the Dow Jones Industrial Average rose to 10,892 points, a 132-point gain for the day. Within moments, the entire 132-point gain was erased, then the markets again abruptly changed direction and rallied to the close. The Dow was up 171 points or 1.6%, the S&P 500 and NASDAQ indices set new highs, rising 1.8% and 2.3% respectively. Widespread interpretation of the Fed's move was that a rate increase would prevent future inflation and the neutral bias meant no further increases in the near future.

[*]"The Big Picture," *Investor's Business Daily* (November 17, 1999): A22.

---

paid or received on these transactions is called the federal funds rate. An increase in the reserve requirement increases the amount of money that banks must borrow. As demand increases, the price of funds (i.e., the interest rate) increases.

The Discount Rate. In addition to borrowing from each other through the federal funds market, banks can borrow directly from Federal Reserve banks to meet their reserve requirements. This procedure is called borrowing at the discount window and the rate charged is the discount rate. Because the Fed discourages this type of borrowing, the quantity of funds borrowed from the discount window is relatively small. Still, the discount rate is important because changes in the rate can signal changes in monetary policy. A higher rate can predict a more restrictive policy and a lower rate may signal a more expansionary policy. Thus, even though the discount rate might not actually affect interest rates directly, the announcement effect often causes interest rates in public markets to change.

Open Market Operations. Open market operations, the Federal Reserve's buying and selling of U.S. Treasury securities in the open market, are the primary tools of monetary policy. These transactions affect the level of reserves in the banking system and thus the funds available in the federal funds market. They are conducted by the Federal Reserve Bank of New York.

When the Fed's goal is to change interest rates through open market operations, it does not set the federal funds rate, as this rate is a function of market pressures. Rather, it sets a target rate and fine-tunes the purchase or sale of treasury securities so that the market interest rate for federal funds reaches the goal.

If the Fed wants interest rates to fall, it buys government securities from banks and pays for them by increasing the cash reserves held in the banks' accounts at the Fed. The selling banks then either have more reserves than they need, allowing them to lend in the federal funds market, or have less of a shortfall in reserves, allowing them to borrow less. This increases the supply of excess reserves in the federal funds market or decreases the demand, both of which act to decrease the price of funds, which is the federal funds interest rate.

If the Fed wants interest rates to rise, it reverses the process and sells government securities to banks. When the banks pay for the securities, their reserves are reduced, thus decreasing the excess reserves they have to lend or increasing the amount they must borrow.

Alan Greenspan

On August 11, 1987, Dr. Alan Greenspan was appointed by President Ronald Reagan to fill an unexpired term on the Federal Reserve Board of Governors. He was appointed as chairman at the same time. He was reappointed to the board for a full 14-year term on February 1, 1992, and began his third 4-year term as chairman on June 20, 1996. He was renominated to a fourth term by President Bill Clinton on January 4, 2000. Previous to his work with the Federal Reserve, Greenspan had been director of policy research for Richard Nixon's 1968 presidential campaign and chairman of Gerald Ford's Council of Economic Advisers.

During his tenure as chairman, Greenspan has earned the label "inflation hawk" for his commitment to combating inflation. He explained his viewpoint at his July 21, 1987, confirmation hearing, saying, "It is absolutely essential that our central focus be on restraining inflation," because "if that fails we have very little opportunity for sustained economic growth."[1]

Greenspan earned the title, "The Second Most Powerful Man in America," for his ability to move markets with a single comment. His rhetorical question, "How do we know when irrational exuberance has unduly escalated asset values?" rocked financial markets in 1996, sending the Dow Jones Industrial Average down 150 points. The question has become so famous that there is even a website, *www.getexuberant.com*, which bills itself as the unofficial Alan Greenspan fan club.

While Greenspan's nomination for a fourth term appears headed for an easy confirmation in light of the longest expansion in U.S. history and inflation rates under 3%, some people disagree with his policies. Several Senate Democrats, led by Iowa Senator Tom Harkin, tried to derail his confirmation in 1996. Harkin, in senatorial debate, accused Greenspan of "blind pursuit of inflation control" at the expense of growth and credited progress against inflation to global competition and mass marketing, not monetary policy.[2] During this writing, the United States is enjoying its ninth year of expansion and few would argue about the abilities of Alan Greenspan.

Fiscal Policy and Politics

Fiscal Policy

The government's attempts to affect the economy through changes in spending and taxation form its fiscal policy. Increases in government purchases of goods and services, such as defense spending, or decreases in taxes, such as corporate income or sales tax, act to influence aggregate demand and cause increases in the level of output. These are the tools that

---

[1]Steven K. Beckner, *Back from the Brink: The Greenspan Years* (New York: John Wiley & Sons, 1996), 27.

[2]Ibid., 417.

fiscal policy uses to combat recession, though the use of these tools to stabilize economic cycles has been largely discredited in favor of exercising monetary policy.

The Deficit and Crowding Out. One danger of high government spending is crowding out. This theory says that when government spending increases, the increased spending is not simply added to total spending. In the scenario in which total output remains the same and government spending increases, private spending (and investment) must decrease. Total crowding out is unlikely, because increased government spending generally increases the level of output, though not by the total amount of the spending. The result is partial crowding out.

In some cases, increased spending is financed by increasing the government's deficit. In deficit financing, the government sells Treasury bonds to pay for its spending. The availability of these bonds and the fact that the public invests in them consumes some public demand for investments and thus reduces the demand for private investments such as corporate bonds. With less financing available, corporations' plans to expand are reduced and privately fueled growth in economic output falls.

Politics

As the economic community has come to the agreement that monetary, not fiscal, policy should be used to fine-tune the economy, it should follow that politics has little to do with the state of the economy or the performance of investments. Robert J. Shapiro of the Progressive Policy Institute, a centrist Democratic think tank, voiced the opinion of most economists when he said, "The President can't control the business cycle, though he's often held politically accountable for it." He argues that the recession of 1990 to 1991, which helped sink George Bush's presidency, was the result of excesses built up before his tenure.[3]

Nevertheless, many claims are made by politicians and the public to place both credit and blame for economic conditions. In their 1996 reelection campaign, the Clinton administration claimed it had created 8 million jobs. Although the number of jobs in the United States was 8 million higher than in 1992, U.S. employment has been growing by an average of more than 2% per year since World War II. This, no matter who was in the White House.

A presidential election year is generally believed to be a positive year for stock prices. The theory is that the incumbent will do whatever he can to

---

[3]Rob Norton, "Reality Check/Economics; Presidents Don't Create Jobs," *Fortune* 133, no. 4 (March 4, 1996): 51.

Table 1–2. Return on the DJIA by Presidential Term

Republicans (President)	Term	Return on DJIA (%)
William McKinley/Theodore Roosevelt	1901–1904	−1.6
Theodore Roosevelt	1905–1908	23.8
William Howard Taft	1909–1912	2.0
Warren Harding/Calvin Coolidge	1921–1924	67.5
Calvin Coolidge	1925–1928	148.9
Herbert Hoover	1929–1932	−80.0
Dwight D. Eisenhower	1953–1956	71.1
Dwight D. Eisenhower	1957–1960	23.3
Richard M. Nixon	1969–1972	8.1
Nixon/Gerald Ford	1973–1976	−1.5
Ronald Reagan	1981–1984	25.7
Ronald Reagan	1985–1988	79.0
George Bush	1989–1992	53.9
Average		32.3
Post 1945 Average		37.1
Median		23.8

Democrats (President)	Term	Return on DJIA (%)
Woodrow Wilson	1913–1916	8.1
Woodrow Wilson	1917–1920	24.3
Franklin D. Roosevelt	1933–1936	200.2
Franklin D. Roosevelt	1937–1940	−27.1
Franklin D. Roosevelt	1941–1944	16.2
FDR/Harry S.Truman	1945–1948	16.4
Harry S. Truman	1949–1952	64.6
John F. Kennedy/Lyndon B. Johnson	1961–1964	41.9
Lyndon B. Johnson	1965–1968	8.0
Jimmy Carter	1977–1980	−4.0
Bill Clinton	1993–1996	95.3
Bill Clinton	1997–2000	Not Available
Average		106.3
Post 1945 Average		37.0
Median		16.4

SOURCES: *Investor's Business Daily, American Association of Individual Investors Journal.*

ensure a strong economy in order to win reelection for the party. Since 1952, the S&P 500 has posted a gain in 11 of 12 presidential election years. The exception was 1960, when Dwight D. Eisenhower (R) encouraged a round of inflation-fighting Federal Reserve Board rate increases before leaving office, the result of which was a recession and the election of John F. Kennedy (D).

During a presidential term there tends to be a pendulum pattern, in which the stock market has a definable up-down-up movement over the four-year period. Some explain this as resulting from initial excitement over a new president, subsequent disillusionment, then a rally in expectation that an unpopular president will be replaced or a popular one will be reelected.

Does a Republican or a Democrat president provide a better environment for the stock market? Draw your own conclusions as to whether it involved the president. Table 1–2 provides results of the Dow Jones Industrial Average during presidential terms after 1901. Although the individual terms vary, note the similarity of the average returns in the post–World War II era.

Summary

The economy provides a constantly changing environment for investing. Nearly all investments are affected by interest rates, business cycles, or inflation. Even those whose market values do not change will provide more or less in real (after inflation) returns when the economy fluctuates.

It is key for investors to understand economic cycles, their indicators, and the effect that they may have on a given portfolio. Fine tuning investments to take advantage of cycles is a worthwhile endeavor, yet it is not an exact science. Most prudent investors make periodic adjustments, yet hold a diversified mix of investments that will react differently to various economic conditions.

Appendix: Economic Indicators

The following figures illustrate some of the economic indicators discussed in this chapter. Found at the website of the Federal Reserve Bank of St. Louis, *www.stls.frb.org*, these indicators and their trends are used by policymakers to conduct the fine-tuning of the economy through monetary policy.

Real GDP Growth

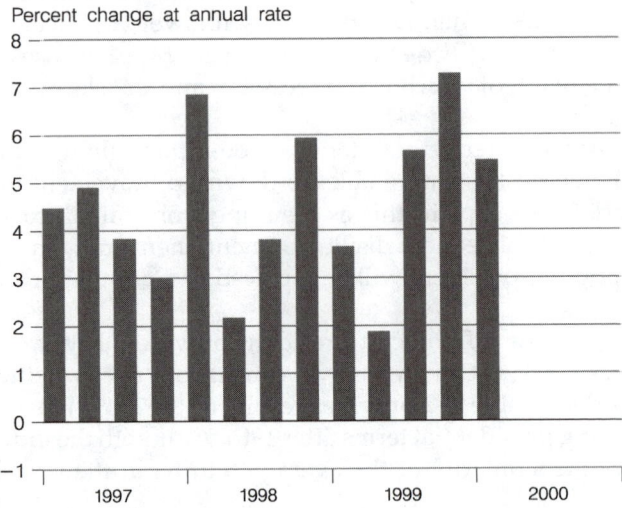

Figure A1-1. Real Gross Domestic Product (GDP) Growth
SOURCE: Federal Reserve Bank of St. Louis.

Industrial Production

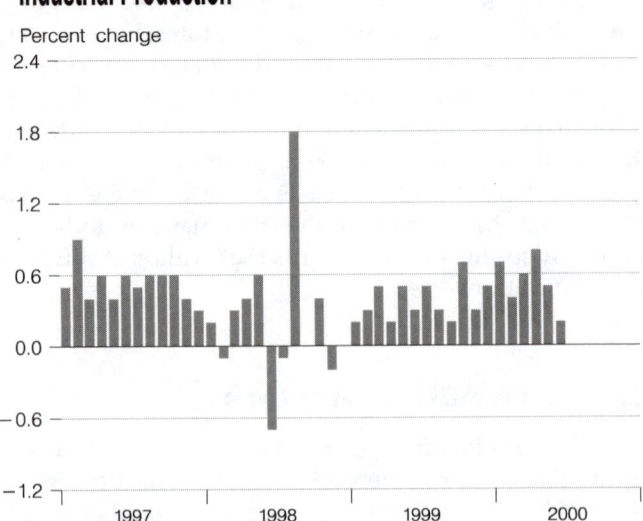

Figure A1-2. Industrial Production
SOURCE: Federal Reserve Bank of St. Louis.

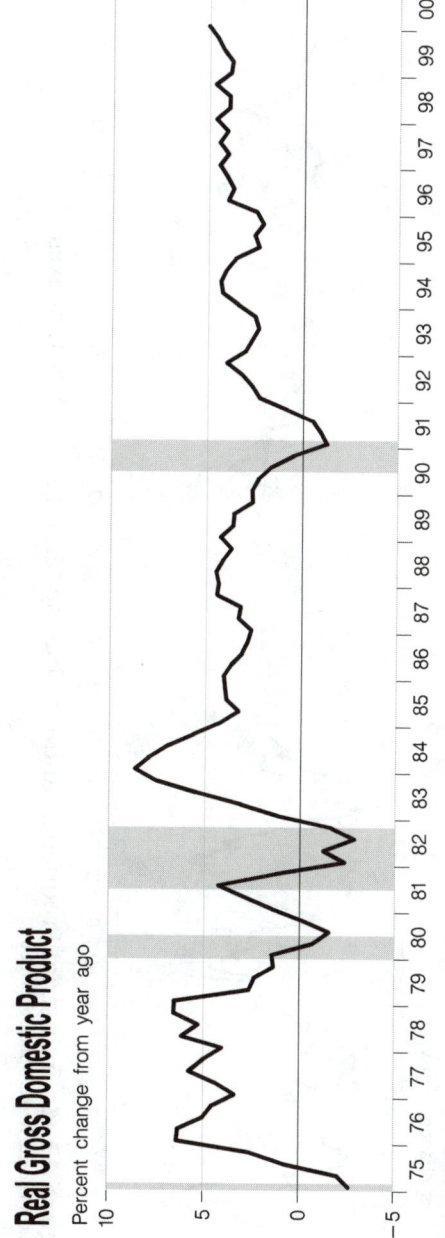

Figure A1-3. Real Gross Domestic Product

SOURCE: Federal Reserve Bank of St. Louis.

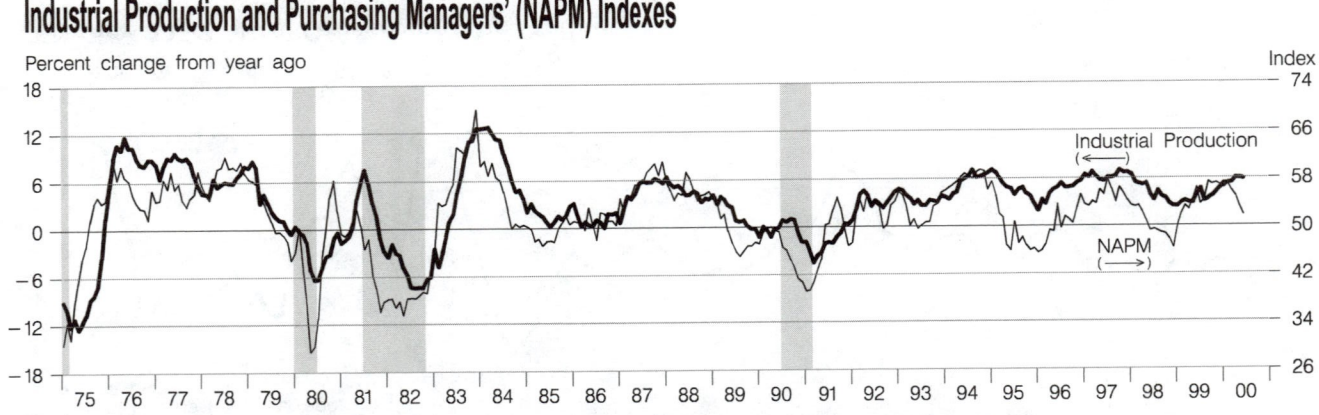

Industrial Production and Purchasing Managers' (NAPM) Indexes

Figure A1–4. Industrial Production and Purchasing Managers' (NAPM) Indexes
SOURCE: Federal Reserve Bank of St. Louis.

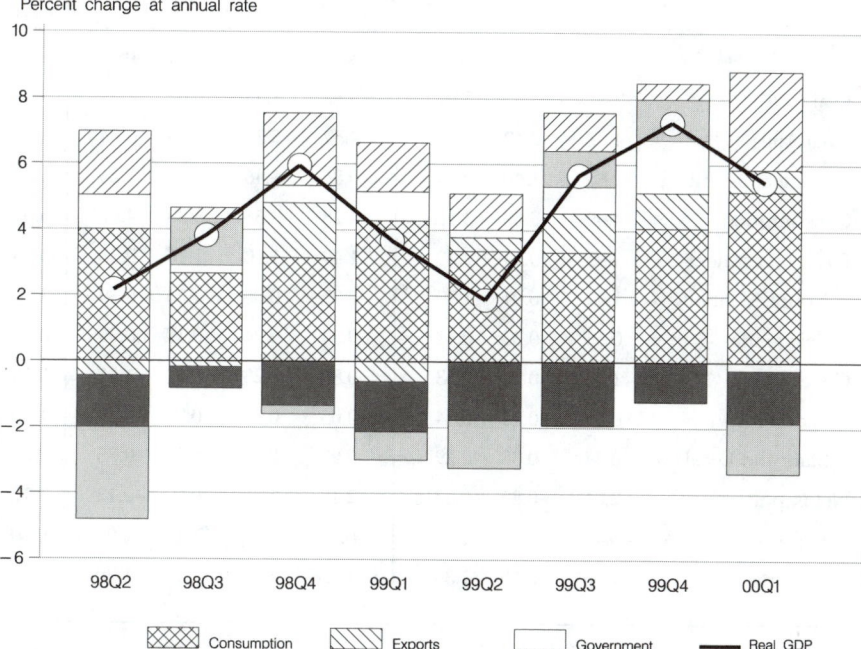

Figure A1–5. Contribution of Components to Real GDP Growth
SOURCE: Federal Reserve Bank of St. Louis.

Figure A1–6. Contributions to Real GDP Growth Rate

	1998			1999				2000
	2nd	3rd	4th	1st	2nd	3rd	4th	1st
Real GDP	2.17	3.82	5.94	3.67	1.88	5.67	7.28	5.40
Final Sales	4.97	2.42	6.20	4.52	3.34	4.58	6.04	6.83
Change in Inventory	−2.80	1.40	−0.26	−0.85	−1.46	1.09	1.24	−1.43
Consumption	4.00	2.67	3.14	4.28	3.36	3.33	4.07	5.02
Fixed Investment	1.95	0.34	2.20	1.49	1.10	1.16	0.48	3.13
Nonresidential	1.42	0.01	1.79	0.95	0.86	1.33	0.39	2.90
Residential	0.53	0.33	0.41	0.54	0.24	−0.17	0.09	0.23
Government	1.03	0.24	0.53	0.88	0.23	0.81	1.61	−0.20
Federal	0.69	−0.14	0.24	−0.03	0.13	0.26	0.87	−1.00
State and Local	0.34	0.38	0.29	0.91	0.10	0.55	0.75	0.80
Net Exports	−2.01	−0.82	0.33	−2.13	−1.35	−0.73	−0.12	−1.12
Exports	−0.45	0.17	1.67	−0.61	0.42	1.19	1.08	0.60
Imports	−1.56	−0.65	−1.34	−1.53	−1.77	−1.92	−1.20	−1.72

SOURCE: Federal Reserve Bank of St. Louis.

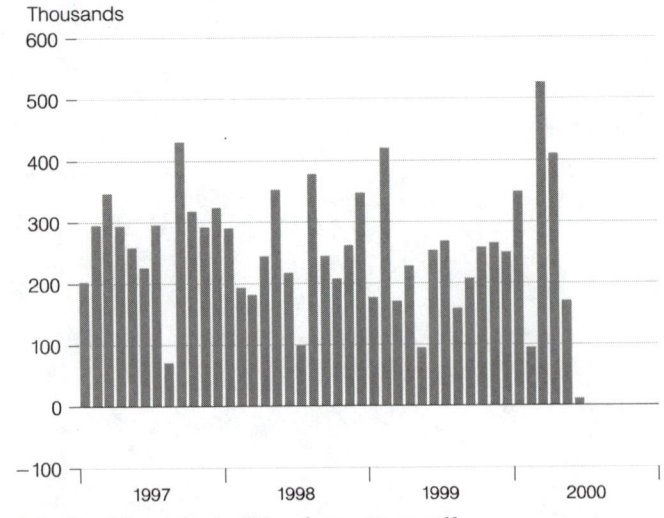

Change in Nonfarm Payrolls

Figure A1–7. Change in Nonfarm Payrolls
SOURCE: Federal Reserve Bank of St. Louis.

Unemployment Rate

Percent of labor force

Figure A1–8. Unemployment Rate
SOURCE: Federal Reserve Bank of St. Louis.

Employment

Percent change from year ago

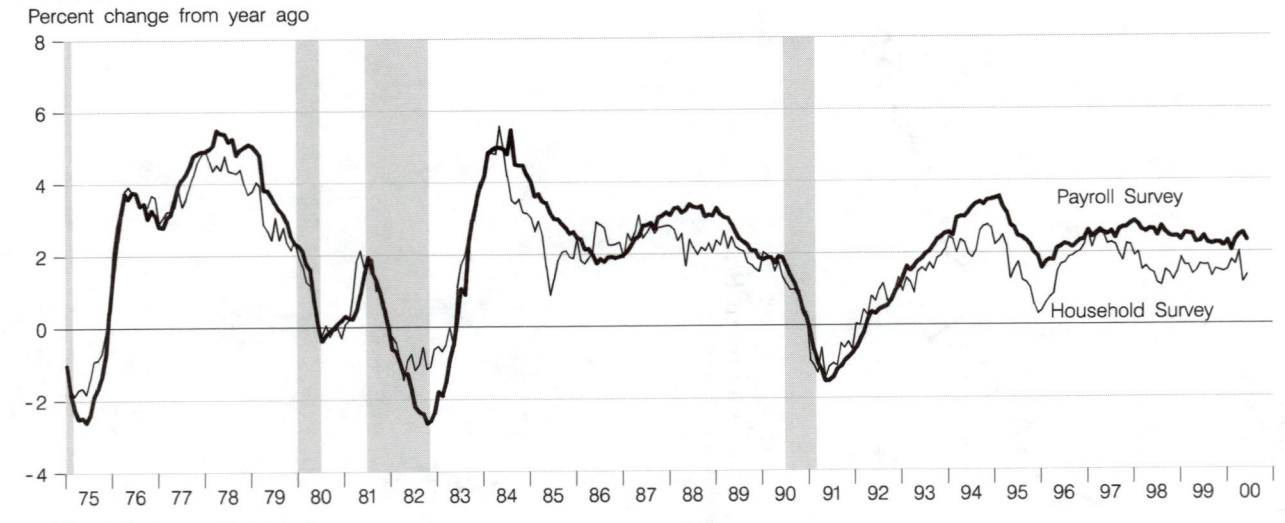

Figure A1–9. Employment
SOURCE: Federal Reserve Bank of St. Louis.

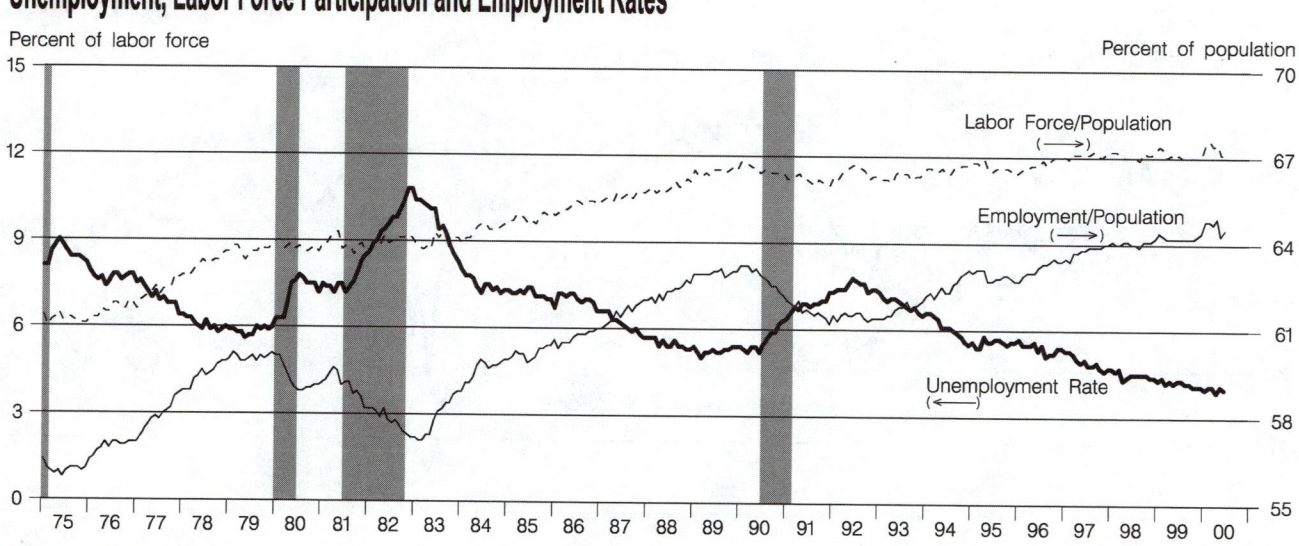

Unemployment, Labor Force Participation and Employment Rates

Percent of labor force

Percent of population

Labor Force/Population
(——→)

Employment/Population
(——→)

Unemployment Rate
(←——)

Figure A1–10. Unemployment, Labor Force Participation, and Employment Rates
SOURCE: Federal Reserve Bank of St. Louis.

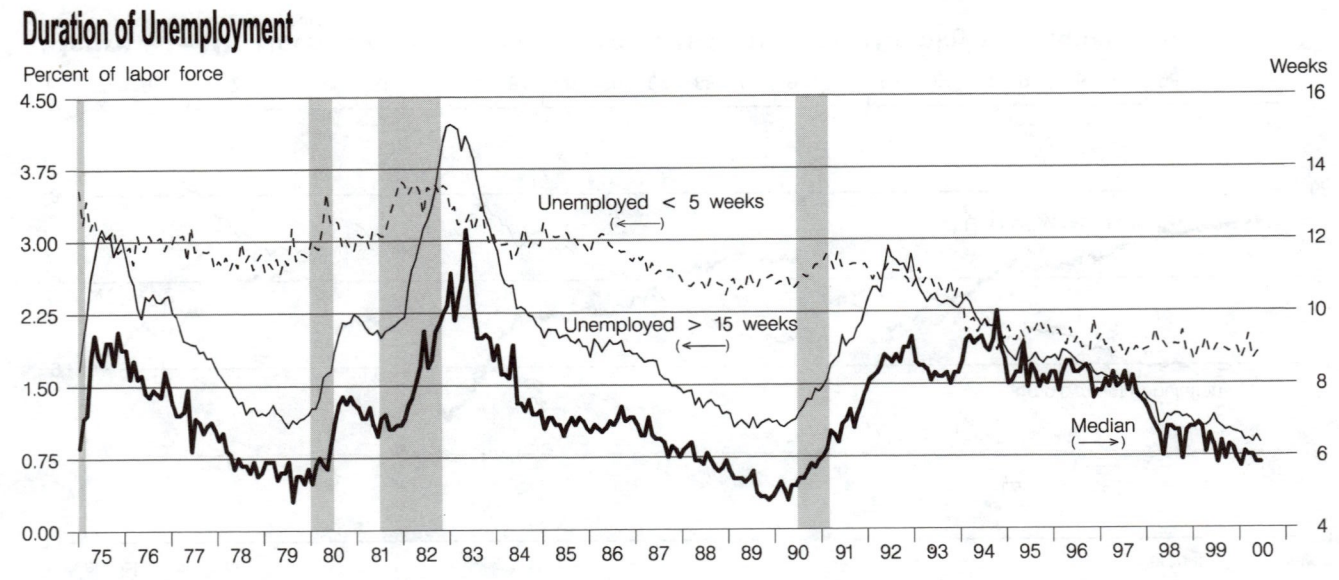

Figure A1-11. Duration of Unemployment
SOURCE: Federal Reserve Bank of St. Louis.

Consumer Price Index

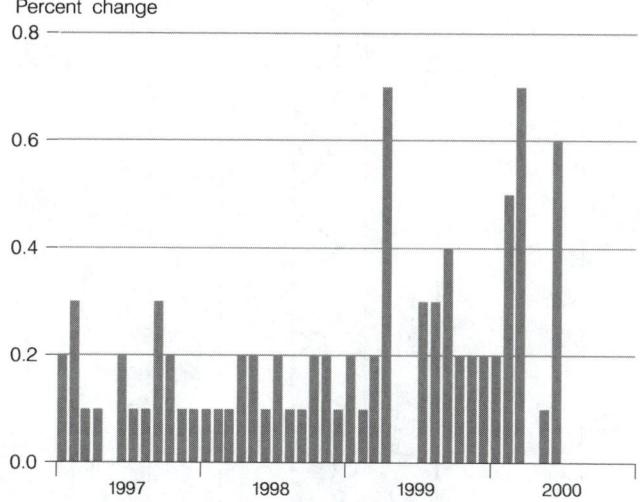

Figure A1–12. Consumer Price Index
SOURCE: Federal Reserve Bank of St. Louis.

Interest Rates

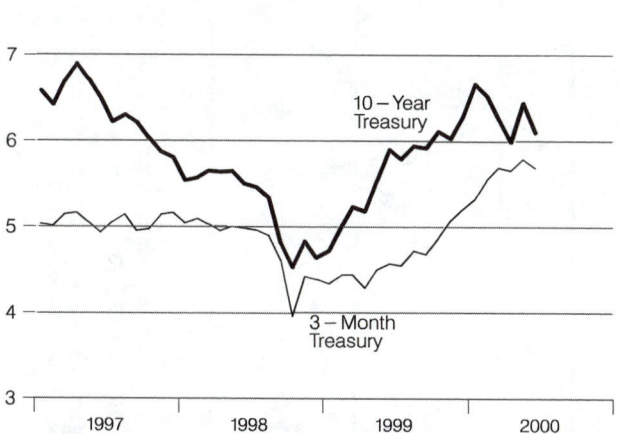

Figure A1–13. Interest Rates
SOURCE: Federal Reserve Bank of St. Louis.

Interest Rates

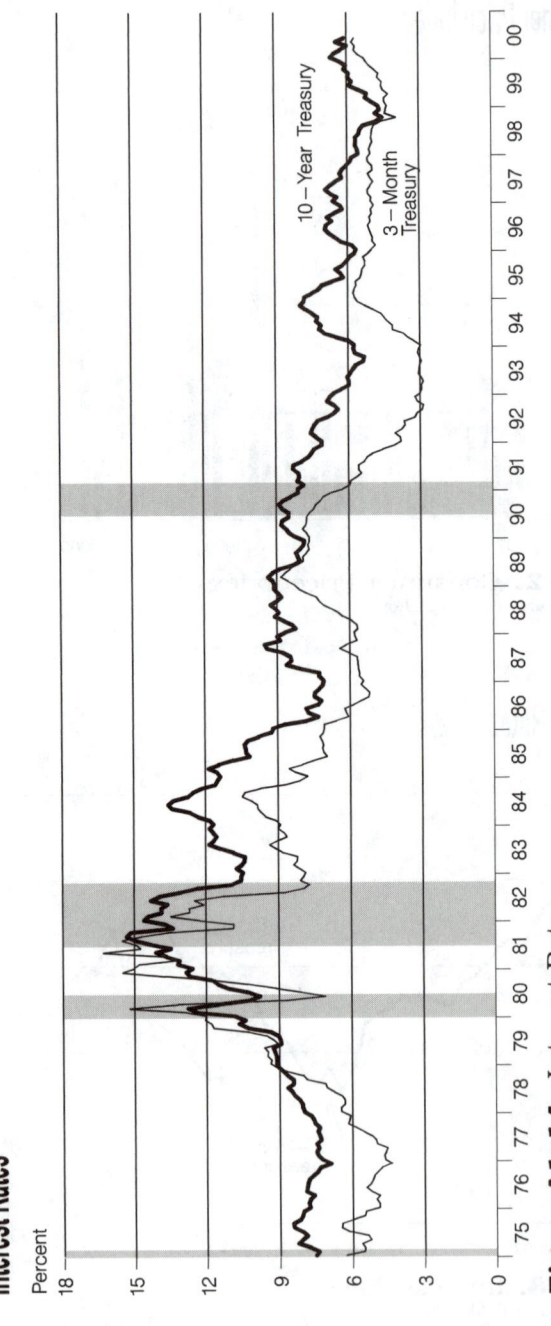

Figure A1-14. Interest Rates
SOURCE: Federal Reserve Bank of St. Louis.

Treasury Yield Curve

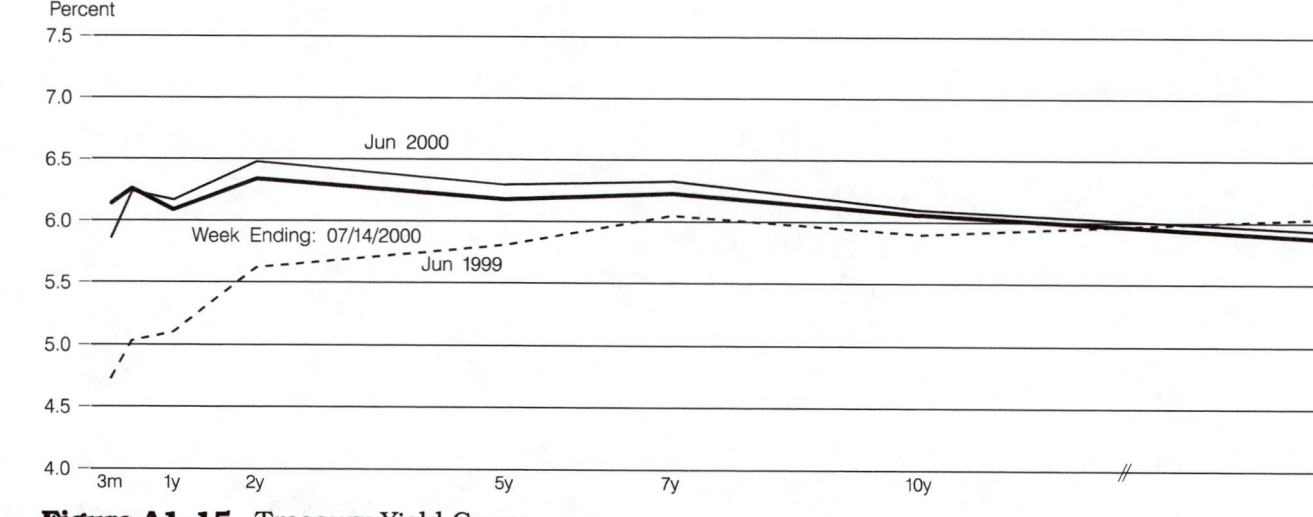

Percent

Figure A1-15. Treasury Yield Curve
SOURCE: Federal Reserve Bank of St. Louis.

2

The Global Nature of Finance

In the age of telecommunications, shared currencies, and international businesses, investing must be addressed from a global perspective. Even the stocks and bonds of U.S. corporations are not immune. Local businesses are affected by changes in their sales to consumers in other nations and by the cost of imported supplies. The prices of U.S. stocks and bonds reflect these business changes. Fluctuations in demand from the international investment community are also products of the relative strength of the dollar and the rate of inflation. This chapter will focus on the interaction of international economies as evidenced by currency exchange rates, plus a recent international financial development, the adoption of the euro. We will talk more about the specifics of investing internationally in Chapter 11.

The Interaction of International Economies

International Currencies

One measure of worldwide economic strength is the relative valuation of international currencies as measured by foreign exchange rates. Foreign exchange rates, which express the relationship between the monies of different countries, must exist for commercial transactions between individuals who use separate currencies. For example, if your business sold engine parts to manufacturers in Japan, you would insist on being paid in U.S. dollars, because Japanese yen are of no use in purchasing goods in the United States. The buyers in Japan must exchange the yen that they ordinarily use in order to pay you in dollars. The exchange rate defines how many yen will be exchanged for each dollar.

Balance of Payments and Currency Values. Exchange rates are the relative prices of different currencies and, like all prices, they are dictated by supply and demand. Demand for a currency comes from a combination of economic and speculative forces. The economic forces at work are derived from a country's balance of payments with other countries.

The balance of payments refers to the direction of transactions from one country to another. Are there more purchases from (imports) or sales to (exports) another country? For example, if the United States is buying the same value of goods from Japan that Japan is buying from the United States, then our balance of payments is in equilibrium. If, however, the United States imports more goods from Japan than it exports to Japan, then the relationship between the United States and Japan can be described as a trade deficit for the United States and a trade surplus for Japan.

In this case there will be a higher relative demand for the currency of Japan, because the U.S. buyers will have to sell their dollars to purchase Japanese yen in order to pay for their imports. Fewer transactions in the opposite direction mean less relative demand for dollars. When taken globally, differences in demand for currencies affect their relative prices, or exchange rates.

Other factors that may affect exchange rates include investors who exchange currencies to take advantage of higher interest rates elsewhere, a process called interest arbitrage. There are also many who trade currencies purely for speculation, and central banks that intervene in currency markets to maintain order.

In some cases, a balance of payments disequilibrium results in market forces that act to correct the balance. For example, if a country is importing more goods than it is exporting, lowered demand for its currency may cause the currency to lose value relative to other currencies. Having a weaker currency means that a country's exports are cheaper for those with stronger currencies and its imports are more expensive for its residents. The change in relative costs can act to increase exports and decrease imports, creating movement toward balance in payments.

What Does It Mean to Have a Strong or Weak Dollar? The dollar might be called strong when it is increasing in value against another currency or is high in value when compared with historical exchange rates. Currencies are measured individually against one another, so that on any given day, the dollar might be strong against the Mexican peso and weak against the Swiss franc. However, the tendency for the dollar to be strong against many other major currencies might lead to a general statement that we have a strong dollar.

When the dollar is strong, it takes more of a foreign currency to make an equal exchange for $1 than it did previously. This lowers the price of goods imported to the United States. For example, if the currency exchange ratio is now 5:1, meaning five foreign units equal $1, and the ratio used to be 4:1, U.S. citizens can now pay $1 for an import worth five foreign units where previously the cost was $1 for an import worth four foreign units. At the same time, prices for U.S. exports to citizens of the foreign country are increased. Before, they were paying four of their currency units for $1 worth of U.S. goods and now they will pay five units.

The effect of this change in relative costs acts to stimulate imports, which become relatively cheaper, and depress exports, which become relatively more expensive. For this reason, a strong dollar is expected to have a negative effect on domestic economic growth as U.S. corporations find sales depressed for two reasons:

- International customers will purchase less because the prices of U.S. goods are higher in their currencies.

- Domestic customers may switch to imported brands as they become relatively cheaper.

A weaker dollar, on the other hand, is expansionary for the opposite reasons.

A strong or weak dollar also affects inflation. When the dollar is strong, making imported supplies and industrial commodities cheap, manufacturers' production costs fall, enabling them to make more profit without raising prices. Additionally, the presence of cheap imported consumer goods makes the marketplace competitive, reducing manufacturers' ability to raise prices without losing sales. On the export side, a strong dollar increases the cost of U.S. exports to foreign consumers, which decreases overall demand for U.S. manufactured products. Lower worldwide demand reduces the likelihood that manufacturers will raise prices.

The relative strength or weakness of the dollar has an effect on stock prices due to the expansionary or recessionary effects of currency exchange rates. For example, a strong U.S. dollar versus the Japanese yen would be expected to boost Japanese stock prices due to the stimulus provided to its economy. It would be expected to depress the U.S. stock markets due to its recessionary effects. However, concurrently, a strong dollar has a positive effect on investment values and returns if it keeps inflation in check. If dollars returned from U.S. investments lose little value due to inflation, then demand for U.S. investments is higher. Additionally, if the dollar is expected to strengthen further, then investors can expect an enhanced return on their investment when they return to their own currency. (See Chapter 11 for a discussion of currency fluctuation and investment returns.) This expectation of higher returns makes U.S. stocks more attractive.

International Monetary Fund and Currency Crises

In some cases, natural market action does not rectify balance of payment problems, which puts pressure on the central banks of the countries involved. In an effort to help stabilize international monetary markets, the International Monetary Fund (IMF) was created at a 1944 United Nations conference, known as the Bretton Woods Conference after its host city in New Hampshire. Specifically, the IMF's mission is to monitor international currency exchange rates, provide short-term financing for member nations experiencing temporary balance of payment problems, create a forum for discussions about international monetary policies, and contribute technical assistance to member countries.

Until the mid-1970s, when the Organization of Petroleum Exporting Countries (OPEC) quadrupled the price of crude oil, the IMF's role as a lender was only tested sporadically. During the 1970s, the oil price shock, inflationary pressures, and higher interest rates put many nations into balance-of-payment difficulty as they paid more for oil imports while their exports dropped and the interest payments on their loans increased. The crisis culminated in 1982 when Mexico threatened to default on its loans and was bailed out by the IMF and the United States. Since that time, the IMF has played a major role in lending to countries in difficulty, most recently to the countries of Asia.

Does the IMF Help? There is much argument today as to whether the IMF's role in international monetary policy is a positive or negative force. According to proponents of IMF intervention, access to IMF financing prevents countries in financial trouble from adopting destructive policies, such as simply printing more money. Opponents suggest that the IMF could be more effective if it only acted to enhance the market discipline imposed by private capital flows. Those favoring IMF intervention accurately assess that it has much more influence on monetary policies when it places strict controls on the conditions under which it will lend. The question remains as to whether that influence is destructive or constructive.

The conditions of IMF bailouts include tight fiscal and monetary policy, currency devaluation, and market deregulation. It is a recipe for harsh medicine designed to prevent more pain later. The medicine of tight fiscal policy strives to reduce government spending, which in many cases means a reduction in aid to the poor and jobless. Tight monetary policy acts to increase interest rates with the expectation of attracting foreign investment, though at the same time it limits access to short-term capital, forcing many small businesses into bankruptcy. This can throw countries into recession, which lowers tax revenues and exacerbates the need for further IMF borrowing.

Asian Currency Crisis,
aka Asian Flu

The currency crisis of the late 1990s in the Asian countries of South Korea, Thailand, the Philippines, Malaysia, and Indonesia was widely reported in the United States, primarily from the perspective of its effect on U.S. corporations. The widespread concern throughout the U.S. economy and stock markets indicated that global U.S. businesses would be hurt by the loss of sales to consumers in Asian nations.

What exactly happened? As the developing countries of Asia grew, private businesses borrowed to finance their growth. Banks eager to be a part of emerging markets—and happy to charge the high interest rates associated with risky loans—lent aggressively. When it became apparent that some borrowers would default on their debts, players in international currency markets panicked. With a herdlike mentality, currency traders blindly rushed to sell Asian currencies, driving currency prices down. This devaluation of currencies made dollars more expensive to residents of the home nations, whose loans had to be repaid in dollars. Thus a situation which might have been merely tenuous became impossible as the cost to repay loans skyrocketed.

According to critics of the IMF, bailout packages to Asia have been counterproductive. The banks that recklessly lent money in risky ventures were not punished because they were repaid with IMF-lent money. The harsh-medicine policies required by the IMF instead hurt the populations of these countries. Recessionary monetary policies depressed wages and employment while tight fiscal policies cut aid to those in need. Foreign investors, anxious to avoid investing in this environment, withdrew more funds, further depressing currencies.

This advances the argument, faced on a national front by the Federal Deposit Insurance Corporation (FDIC), that the availability of a bailout creates a moral dilemma that perpetuates the problems it is designed to address. Banks earn high interest rates on loans to developing nations, which compensates them for the risk of lending. However, the existence of the IMF as a backup means that there is little real risk of default. Therefore, banks that have free insurance in the form of a bailout are encouraged to lend recklessly. The more reckless the lending, the more likely defaults will exist, creating a crisis that requires IMF intervention.

United States within a Global
Economy

Since 1991, the United States has enjoyed an unprecedented period of growth, high employment, and low inflation. Many of the forces responsible are easy to spot: technology-driven productivity increases, a Federal Reserve policy that carefully monitors inflation, low interest rates, and the wealth effect of a rising stock market. At the same time, global forces help to drive the U.S. economy by affecting (1) foreign investment here, (2) the prices of exported goods and services, and (3) the prices for imported goods and services.

In theory, strong economies—those with high employment and production— are good for the world, not just the inhabitants of their respective countries. The reason is prosperity creates consumers for the exports of other countries and productivity creates goods and services that international consumers desire. In some respects, however, recession in other countries has been positive for the United States.

For Americans, recent economic stagnation in Asia, Europe, Latin America, and Russia has meant cheap imported industrial commodities and finished goods, low commodity prices, and high levels of foreign investment. Cheap imports resulting from a strong dollar have kept manufacturing costs low and competition high, preventing both the need and the ability to raise prices. These are key ingredients in a U.S. expansion without high levels of inflation.

Foreign investment in the United States has resulted in a strong dollar and has played a significant role in our rising stock market. As other economies strengthen, providing investment opportunities overseas, investors, including those in the United States, will pull their money out of U.S. markets in search of high returns elsewhere. In addition to the obvious impact this will have on the stock market, it will send the value of the dollar down. The United States now runs a current account deficit of approximately $233 billion, as imports are greater than exports. The balance of payments is equalized by the approximately $237 billion of U.S. investment assets sold to international investors. If they pull their money out of U.S. investments, then U.S. balance of payments will be in disequilibrium, causing the value of the dollar to fall. To get back into equilibrium, the United States must either consume less or raise interest rates to attract investors. Either solution dampens economic growth.

The Euro

The most significant occurrence in recent monetary history is the adoption of the euro. The euro is the currency created by the European Union (EU) to replace the individual currencies of the European countries. The 15-member group of European Union countries consists of Austria, Belgium, Denmark, Finland, France, Germany, Great Britain, Greece, Ireland, Italy, Luxembourg, the Netherlands, Portugal, Spain, and Sweden.

Eleven of the 15 EU countries have voluntarily met the EU's requirements for adopting the euro. The voters of Great Britain, Denmark, and

Sweden have not agreed to participate. Greece did not meet entrance requirements. These requirements, called convergence criteria, are as follows:

- Price stability: A country may not have inflation above 1.5% over the three EU countries with the lowest inflation.
- Government budget deficits: A country's government borrowing as a percent of gross domestic product cannot be over 3%, unless it is declining and close to 3%.
- Total government debt: A country's gross government debt to GDP ratio cannot be over 60%, unless it is near 60% and continually decreasing.
- Interest rates: Nominal interest rates on long-term government bonds cannot be more than 2% greater than that of the three EU members with the lowest such rate.
- Exchange rate stability: A country's currency must be stable, trading with normal fluctuations.

The introduction of the euro involves three phases. In the first phase, phase A, which began May 1, 1998, the participating countries were determined and the European Monetary Institute became the European Central Bank, the equivalent of the U.S. Federal Reserve Bank.

In phase B, which began January 1, 1999, the euro became legal tender for book transactions under a "no compulsion, no prohibition" rule, which means that anyone could choose to use the euro but it was not a requirement. The term *book transactions* applies to any transactions that do not take place with currency or coin. They include checks, bank statements, accounting systems, and financial statements.

Phase C begins, at the latest, on January 1, 2002, and participating countries will each decide how long it will last, with a maximum of six months. In this phase, euro currency and coins will begin to be exchanged and will exist with national currencies. At the end of this phase, all transactions must take place with the euro, though banks will continue to exchange national currencies for euro currency indefinitely.

What the Euro Means to Investors

Investors can take advantage of the euro in three ways:

1. Purchase the stocks of international companies that do business with Euroland companies. (Euroland is the name for those countries adopting the euro.) Multinational corporations will find it much easier to do business with Euroland companies once the euro is fully in place. Theoretically, businesses that trade with many Euroland countries will benefit from reduced

exchange rate risk, lower transaction costs, and price transparency. Exchange rate risk is the risk that, in long-term transactions with an agreed upon price, the money received from a foreign customer will be worth less at the time of payment or the money paid to a foreign supplier will be worth more. If the euro is stable, this risk will be reduced. International companies hedge their risk in the currency futures markets, but these transactions have a cost and they are not readily available to smaller businesses. As the need to hedge is lessened or the number of individual currency hedges is reduced from 11 to a single currency, the cost of doing business will decrease. Simple transaction costs, such as fees for exchanging currencies, will also be eliminated. Price transparency, where prices in all Euroland countries are quoted in the same currency, is expected to reduce price discrimination and encourage consumers and businesses to compare prices across the continent.

2. Purchase the stocks of companies that will benefit from the transition process. Several industries are benefiting from the transition to the euro. Software engineers are in high demand as businesses reprogram their systems to reflect the new currency. Printers and graphic designers are needed as firms change their brochures, catalogs, and advertising to include new pricing. Accountants are indispensable as businesses change their accounting systems and prepare to deal with phase C, which includes transactions in two currencies, as are financial advisors and companies with expertise in large financial markets.

3. Purchase the stocks of businesses based in Euroland. The stocks of Euroland companies may be expected to thrive for two reasons. First, the fundamental prospects of many businesses can be expected to improve due to general economic prosperity, monetary stability, and the reduction of barriers to doing business. Second, financial markets immediately change from 11 fragmented markets subject to varied exchange rate risk to a single, deep market in which all financial instruments are denominated in one currency. This increases the demand for existing securities and makes more capital available for growth. The Dow Jones Euro Stoxx Index and FTSE Eurotop 300 have already been established to track Euroland stocks.

Summary

The globalization of world economies and markets means that investors can no longer ignore world events. Even investments in strictly U.S. corporations are affected by economic factors around the world, because they have an impact on the value of the dollar, the level of inflation, the strength of the U.S. economy, and the growth of the stock market. Though it may be difficult to follow international economies, exchange rates and the strength of the dollar provide a market-driven report on the relative health of international economies. Knowing how currency fluctuations affect the U.S. economy and investments can be of vital importance in assessing investment climates here and abroad.

Appendix: Visual Overview of Selected Topics

The following figures provide a visual overview of some of the topics covered in this chapter. They can be found at the website of the Federal Reserve Bank of St. Louis, *www.stls.frb.org.*

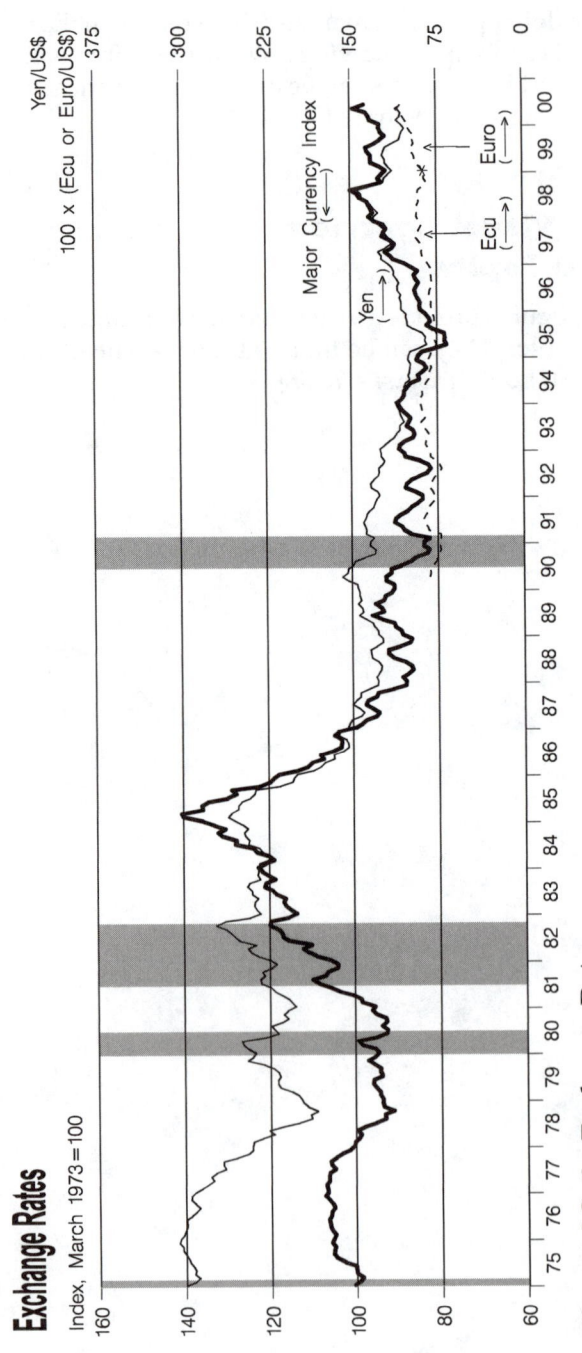

Figure A2-1. Exchange Rates

Source: Federal Reserve Bank of St. Louis.

Trade and Investment Income Balances

Billions of dollars, quarterly rate

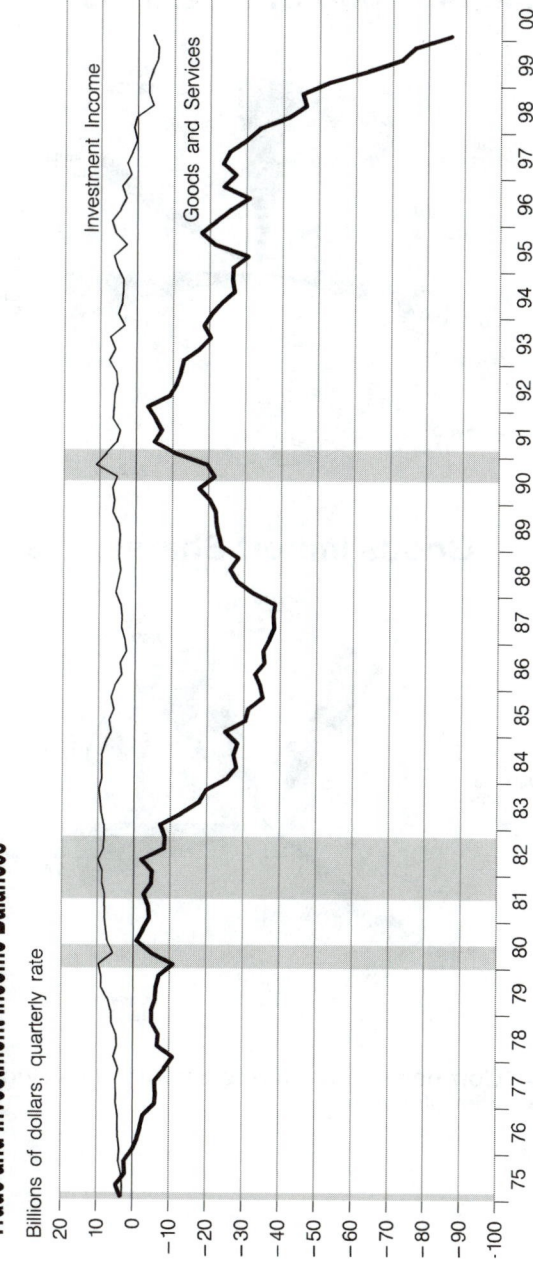

Figure A2–2. Trade and Investment Income Balances

SOURCE: Federal Reserve Bank of St. Louis.

Goods Export Shares, 1999

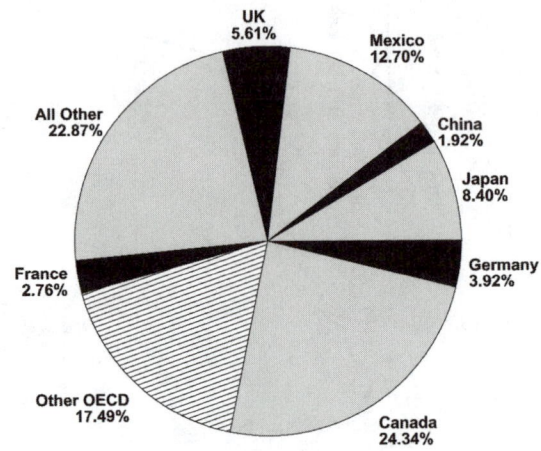

Goods Import Shares, 1999

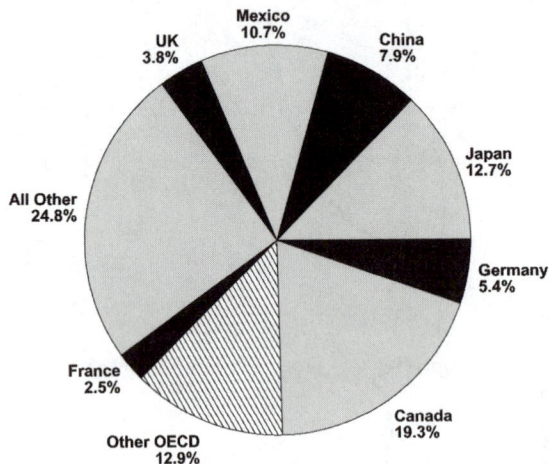

Figure A2–3. Comparison of Goods Exported to Goods Imported
SOURCE: Federal Reserve Bank of St. Louis.

Trade Balance

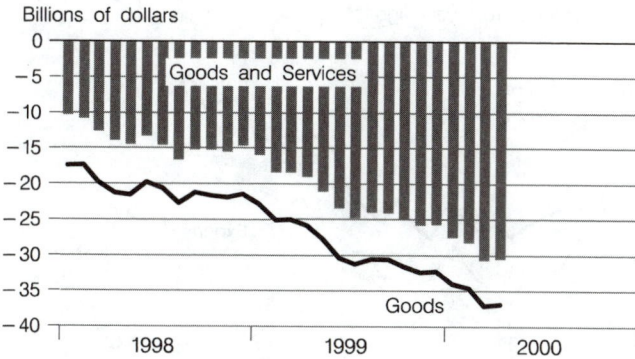

Figure A2–4. Trade Balance
SOURCE: Federal Reserve Bank of St. Louis.

Current Account Balance

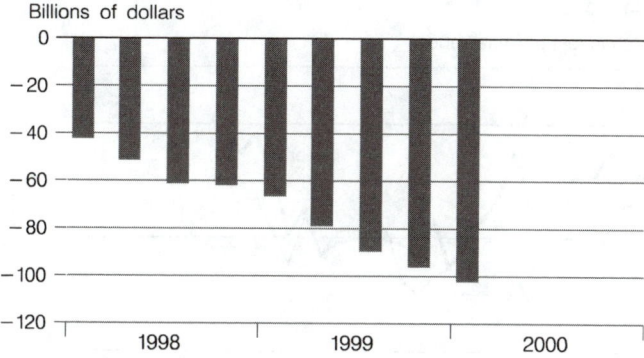

Figure A2–5. Current Account Balance
SOURCE: Federal Reserve Bank of St. Louis.

Goods Trade

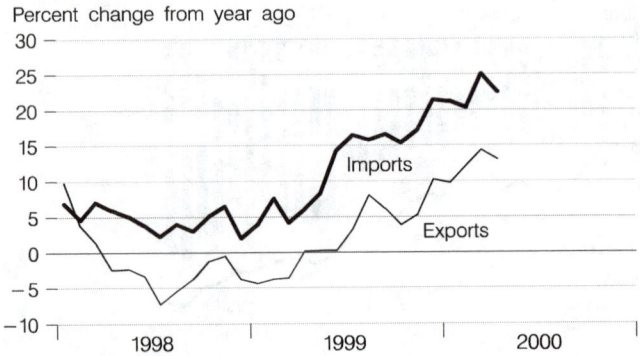

Figure A2–6. Goods Trade
SOURCE: Federal Reserve Bank of St. Louis.

Services Trade

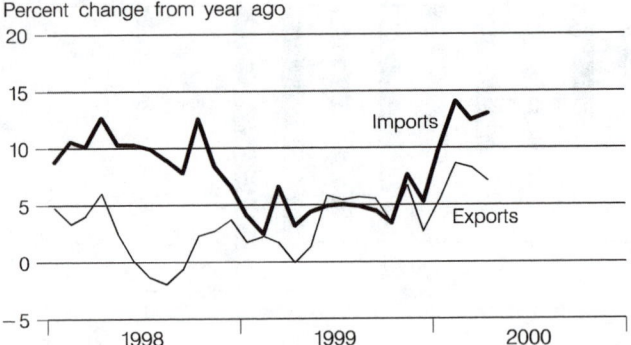

Figure A2–7. Services Trade
SOURCE: Federal Reserve Bank of St. Louis.

Real GDP Growth of Major Trading Partners

Percent change at annual rate

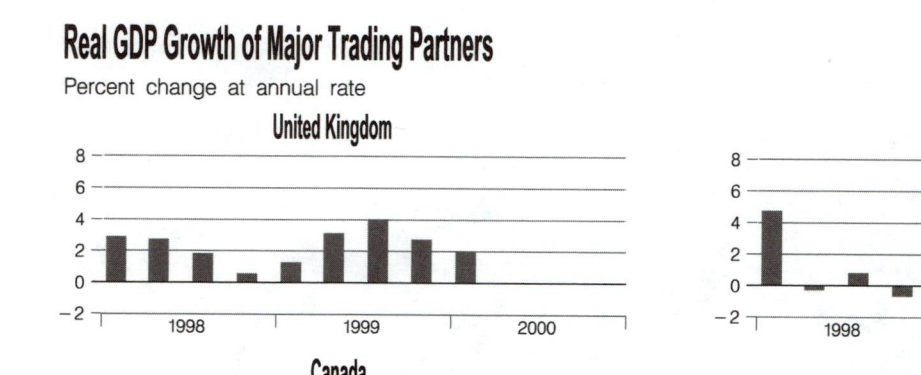
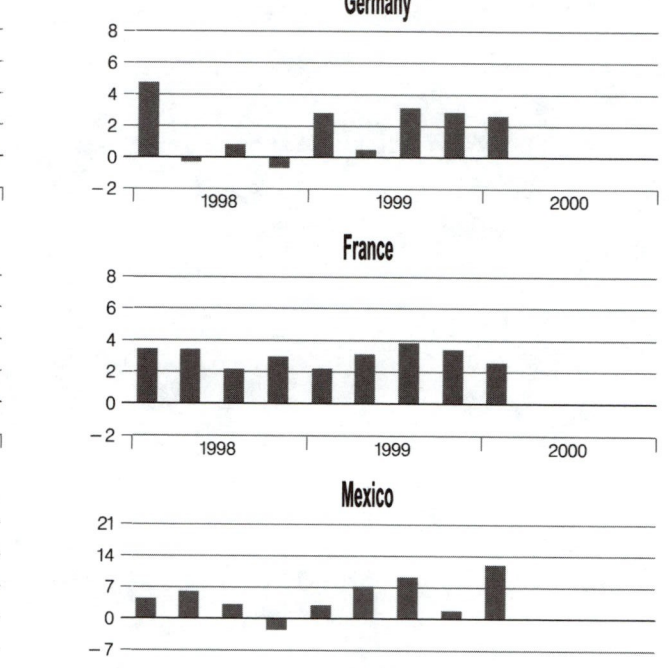

Figure A2–8. Real GDP Growth of Major Trading Partners
SOURCE: Federal Reserve Bank of St. Louis.

3

Financial Exchanges

For many years, stocks were traded at a central gathering place, known as a stock exchange, where buyers and sellers or their representatives met to transact business. The first organized stock exchange in the world was established in London in 1773; New York followed in 1792, Paris in 1802, Tokyo in 1818, and Sydney in 1872.

Now computerized networks have made possible trading by brokers and investors in separate places. What began as the over-the-counter (OTC) market—a dealer network for trading smaller stocks—is now the National Association of Securities Dealers Automated Quotation System (NASDAQ), a computerized network of brokers and dealers trading in some of the largest and most popular stocks of our time.

New York Stock Exchange

New York Stock Exchange

11 Wall Street

New York, NY 10005

212-656-3000

www.nyse.com

9:30 A.M. to 4:00 P.M., EST, Monday through Friday

The most famous stock exchange in the world, the New York Stock Exchange (NYSE), began unofficially in 1792, outdoors under a buttonwood tree on Wall Street. It was formally organized in 1817. The NYSE is an auction marketplace in which stocks are sold to the highest bidder and purchased from the lowest offerer. Average daily stock volume was 1.046 billion shares ($45.4 billion) traded through June 2000.

The NYSE lists 3,025 companies, comprising more than $16 trillion in market capitalization. Of those, 382 are based outside the United States. To

Table 3–1. Minimum Quantitative Standards: Distribution and Size Criteria

Round-lot holders	2,000 U.S.
Or:	
Total shareholders	2,200
... together with:	
Average monthly trading volume (most recent 6 months)	100,000 shares
Or:	
Total shareholders	500
... together with	
Average monthly trading volume (most recent 12 months)	1,000,000 shares
Public shares	1,100,000 outstanding
Market value of public shares	
Public companies	$100,000,000
IPOs, spin-offs, carve-outs	$60,000,000

SOURCE: New York Stock Exchange.

be listed, a company must meet certain qualifications, with particular attention given to (1) the degree of national interest in the company, (2) its relative position and stability in its industry, and (3) whether it is in an expanding industry, with prospects of at least maintaining its relative position.

More specific requirements for NYSE listing as of September 1999 are as shown in Tables 3–1 and 3–2.

NYSE transactions occur on a 36,000-square-foot trading floor. Around the perimeter of the floor are approximately 1,500 trading booths, which the exchange rents to securities firms. Traders on the floor of the NYSE must be part of a member firm that owns one of the 1,366 "seats" on the trading floor. The last seat traded in October 2000 sold for $1.65 million.

Floor brokers receive buy and sell orders from their brokerage firms' customers at the trading booths, either by telephone or electronically. The floor broker takes buy and sell orders to any of the 17 trading posts, which have designated locations for a particular company's stock. Each stock trades at only one location. At the trading post, the floor broker may trade with another floor broker or with a specialist. The specialist is a broker's broker, whose job is to maintain an orderly and efficient market in a particular stock. The specialist has four roles:

Table 3-2. Minimum Quantitative Standards: Financial Criteria

Earnings:

Aggregate pretax earnings over the last 3 years of $6.5 million achievable as:
Most recent year $2,500,000
Each of two preceding years $2,000,000
Or:
Most recent year (all 3 years must be profitable) $4,500,000
Or:
Operating cash flow
For companies with not less than $500 million in global market capitalization and
$20 million in revenues in the last 12 months:
Aggregate for the 3 years operating cash flow
(all years positive) $25,000,000

Or:

Global market capitalization:
Revenues for the last fiscal year $250,000,000
Average global market capitalization (most recent 6 months) $1,000,000,000
Stockholders' equity for REITs with less than 3 years operating history
$60,000,000
Net assets for funds with less than 3 years operating history $60,000,000

SOURCE: New York Stock Exchange.

- Auctioneer: It is the specialist's duty to show the best bids and offers and to transmit that information through the NYSE quote and other data systems for instant worldwide availability.

- Agent: The specialist may act as an agent in place of the floor broker when that broker leaves an order with instructions to execute it at a specific price. The specialist also acts as agent for SuperDot orders, which are electronically routed from brokerage firms, bypassing the floor broker.

- Catalyst: As an expert in a particular stock, the specialist becomes familiar with those who actively trade it. During times of imbalance in buy and sell orders, the specialist can contact interested parties in an effort to enhance trading activity.

- Principal: It is the specialist's responsibility to bridge temporary gaps in supply and demand by purchasing and selling stock for their own accounts. This buffer provides a cushion for stock price movements when supply overwhelms demand or vice versa.

NYSE Circuit Breakers and Trading Collars

In response to stock market volatility, the NYSE has implemented a series of thresholds at which trading is halted after a single-day decline in the Dow Jones Industrial Average. These thresholds, called circuit breakers, are set each quarter based on the DJIA average closing values of the previous month, rounded to the nearest 50 points. Set at 10%, 20%, and 30% decline levels, the circuit breakers for the third-quarter 2000 are:

- A 1,050-point decline in the DJIA that occurs before 2:00 P.M. will halt trading for one hour; between 2:00 P.M. and 2:30 P.M., it will halt trading for 30 minutes; and if occurring after 2:30 P.M., it will not halt trading.

- A 2,100-point decline in the DJIA that occurs before 1:00 P.M. will halt trading for two hours; between 1:00 P.M. and 2:00 P.M. it will halt trading for one hour; and at 2:00 P.M. or later, it will halt trading for the rest of the day.

- A 3,150-point decline in the DJIA will halt trading for the remainder of the day, regardless of its timing.

Trading collars restrict index arbitrage trading. Also calculated quarterly, they are set at 2% of the average closing value of the DJIA for the last month of the previous quarter, rounded down to the nearest 10 points. For the third-quarter 2000, the trading collar is triggered when the DJIA moves 210 points or more above or below its previous day's close. It is removed when the DJIA moves above or below the prior day's close by 100 points.

In the case of a decline in the DJIA of 210 points or more, all index arbitrage sell orders of S&P 500 stocks must be stabilizing, or sell plus, for the remainder of the day, unless the collar is lifted. In the case of an advance in the DJIA of 210 points, all index arbitrage buy orders of S&P stocks must be stabilizing, or buy minus, for the remainder of the day, unless the collar is lifted.

Visiting the NYSE

You can view trading on the NYSE from the Interactive Education Center, 20 Broad Street, New York. The center is open Monday through Friday, from 8:45 A.M. to 4:30 P.M., and admission is free. For general tour information, call (212) 656-5165. Reservations are required for groups of 10 persons or more, with a maximum of 25 persons. Call (212) 656-5168 for reservations. For directions to the exchange, complete with subway and street maps, see the NYSE website at *www.nyse.com*.

NYSE trading hours are 9:30 A.M. to 4:00 P.M., EST, Monday through Friday. The following days will be observed as holidays in the year 2001:

New Year's Day	January 1
Martin Luther King Jr. Day	January 15

Washington's Birthday	February 19
Good Friday	April 13
Memorial Day	May 28
Independence Day	July 4
Labor Day	September 3
Thanksgiving Day	November 22
Christmas	December 25

Other exchanges commonly follow the NYSE schedule.

American Stock Exchange

American Stock Exchange

86 Trinity Place

New York, NY 10006

212-306-1000

www.amex.com

9:30 A.M. to 4:00 P.M., EST, Monday through Friday

The New York Curb Exchange operated outdoors from 1842 to 1921 and changed its name in 1953 to the American Stock Exchange (Amex). The Amex is the second largest floor-based exchange in the United States, with 661 regular members (seats) and 824 companies listed. The average daily volume in May 2000 was 46.2 million. Listing guidelines for U.S. companies are shown in Table 3–3.

NASDAQ

NASDAQ (National Association of Securities Dealers Automated Quotation System)

NASD

1735 K. Street, NW, Eighth Floor

Washington, DC 20006

202-728-8000

www.nasdaq.com

Regular trading session: 9:30 A.M. to 4:00 P.M., EST, Monday through Friday

After-hours trading: 4:00 P.M. to 6:30 P.M., EST

Table 3–3. Amex Listing Guidelines

Regular Financial Guidelines	
Pretax income	$750,000 latest fiscal year or 2 of 3 most recent years
Market value of public float	$3,000,000
Stock price	$3
Operating history	—
Stockholders' equity	$4,000,000
Alternate Financial Guidelines	
Pretax income	—
Market value of public float	$15,000,000
Stock price	$3
Operating history	3 years
Stockholders' equity	$4,000,000
Distribution Guidelines	
Alternative 1:	
Public float	500,000
Public stockholders	800
Average daily volume	—
Alternative 2:	
Public float	1,000,000
Public stockholders	400
Average daily volume	—
Alternative 3:	
Public float	500,000
Public stockholders	400
Average daily volume	2,000

International market session: 3:30 A.M. to 9 A.M., EST
SelectNet pre-hours trading session: 9:00 A.M. to 9:30 A.M., EST
SelectNet after-hours trading session: 4:00 P.M. to 5:15 P.M., EST

The NASDAQ market is not a stock exchange like the NYSE or the Amex, where securities are traded in a particular location in an auction setting. Also known as the OTC or over-the-counter market, the NASDAQ market is a system of thousands of brokers and dealers who trade in stocks.

The NASDAQ has evolved from a dealer market into a hybrid market through the use of electronic trading. Retail orders for under 1,000 shares are guaranteed an execution at the best possible bid or offer through the Small Order Execution System (SOES). The Optimark Trading System™, integrated in 1999, matches large orders anonymously, as frequently as every two minutes. The SelectNet System is an electronic trading mechanism for large block orders, with a screen-based negotiation system. While still a dealer market system, it increases efficiency in large trades. In another effort to make the market more competitive, NASDAQ reduced its minimum quote increment to 1/16 from 1/8 on stocks priced $10 or more.

The NASDAQ is divided into two areas, the National Market System and the NASDAQ Smallcap Market, based on financial and distribution criteria. The smallest developing companies are traded on the OTC Bulletin Board (OTCBB), which has no minimum financial requirements.

The requirements for national market listing are as follows:

Alternative 1

Net tangible assets	$6 million
Market capitalization	—
Total assets	—
Total revenue	—
Pretax income (latest year or 2 of last 3)	$1 million
Public float	1.1 million shares
Operating history	—
Market value of public float	$8 million
Minimum bid price	$5
Shareholders (round lot)	400
Market makers	3
Corporate governance	yes

Alternative 2

Net tangible assets	$18 million
Market capitalization	—
Total assets	—
Total revenue	—
Pretax income (latest year or 2 of last 3)	—
Public float	1.1 million shares
Operating history	2 years
Market value of public float	$8 million
Minimum bid price	$5
Shareholders (round lot)	400
Market makers	3
Corporate governance	yes

In the first half of 2000, average daily NASDAQ volume was 1.7 billion shares per day. In 16 sessions, more than 2 billion shares were traded, with 2.88 billion on April 4, 2000, the heaviest trading day.

The NASD publishes several NASDAQ indices. The most widely watched index is the NASDAQ Composite. Others include the National Market System (NMS) Composite Index, the Bank Index, the Insurance Index, the Other Finance Index, the Transportation Index, the Utilities Index, and the Industrial Index. For more about indices, see Chapter 4.

Other U.S. Stock Exchanges

Arizona Stock Exchange (AZX)

Electronic exchange

To contact:

2800 N. Central, Suite 1575

Phoenix, AZ 85004

602-222-5800

www.azx.com

Boston Stock Exchange (BSE)

100 Franklin Street

Boston, MA 02110

617-235-2000

www.bostonstock.com

Chicago Stock Exchange (CHX)

440 LaSalle Street, Fifth Floor

Chicago, IL 60605

312-663-2980

www.chicagostockex.com

Cincinnati Stock Exchange

Electronic exchange

To contact:

Cincinnati Stock Exchange

440 LaSalle Street, Twenty-Sixth Floor

Chicago, IL 60605

312-786-8803
www.cincinnatistock.com

Pacific Stock Exchange (PSE)
301 Pine Street
San Francisco, CA 94104
415-393-4000

or

233 South Beaudry Avenue
Los Angeles, CA 90012
213-977-4500
www.pacificex.com

Philadelphia Stock Exchange (PHLX)
1900 Market Street
Philadelphia, PA 19103
215-496-5000
www.phlx.com

Options and Futures

Chicago Board of Trade
141 W. Jackson Boulevard
Chicago, IL 60604-2994
312-435-3500
www.cbot.com

Regular trading hours: Monday through Friday

Financial/Insurance	7:20 A.M. to 2:00 P.M., CST
Agricultural	9:30 A.M. to 1:15 P.M.
Equities (DJIA)	7:20 A.M. to 3:15 P.M.
Electricity	8:00 A.M. to 2:40 P.M.

Project A® electronic trading day session: Monday through Friday

Treasuries	5:30 A.M. to 2:00 P.M.

Project A® electronic trading afternoon session: Monday through Thursday

Financial Instruments	2:15 P.M. to 4:30 P.M.
Equities (DJIA)	3:30 P.M. to 4:30 P.M.

Project A® electronic trading overnight session: Sunday through Thursday

Financial Instruments	6:00 P.M. to 5:00 A.M.
Equities (DJIA)	6:00 P.M. to 5:00 A.M.
Agricultural	8:00 P.M. to 5:00 A.M.

In 1848, a group of 82 merchants formed the Chicago Board of Trade to facilitate the buying and selling of grain in Chicago. Standardized futures contracts were developed in 1865. Trading in futures and options on futures involves four product categories: financial, agricultural, equity index, and electricity.

Financial instruments include 30-year U.S. Treasury bonds, 10-year U.S. Treasury notes, 5-year U.S. Treasury notes, 2-year U.S. Treasury notes, municipal bond index, long-term (10-year) Fannie Mae benchmark and Freddie Mac reference notes.

Equity futures and options are those traded on the Dow Jones Industrial Average (DJIA). Agricultural instruments include corn, soybeans, wheat, soymeal, soybean oil, rough rice, and oats. Electricity instruments include futures and options on ComEd™ Hub Electricity and Tennessee Valley Authority Hub Electricity.

The Agricultural Visitors Center is open Monday through Friday, from 8:00 A.M. to 2:00 P.M. Explanations of the market are given every half hour, beginning at 9:00 A.M. Call (312) 435-3590 to make reservations for groups of 10 or more persons. The Financial Visitors Center is open Monday through Friday, from 8:00 A.M. to 2:00 P.M. Presentations on the markets are given at 9:15 A.M., 10:00 A.M., 11:00 A.M., 12:00 noon, and 12:30 P.M. Call (312) 435-3590 for reservations, required for groups of 10 or more persons. Both centers require that visitors be at least 16 years old.

Chicago Board Options Exchange

400 S. LaSalle Street

Chicago, IL 60605

1-800-OPTIONS

www.cboe.com

Regular trading hours:

Equity and narrow-based index options 8:30 A.M. to 3:02 P.M., CST
Broad-based index options (OEX, SPX, DJX, etc.) 8:30 A.M. to 3:15 P.M.

The Chicago Board Options Exchange (CBOE) was created in 1973 by the Chicago Board of Trade. It began by trading call options on 16 stocks. Put options were added in 1977. The CBOE, which merged with the Midwest Stock Exchange in 1980, now trades options on nearly 1,300 stocks.

In addition to puts and calls on stocks, the CBOE hosts trading in 201 equity LEAPS (Long-term Equity AnticiPation Securities™), 10 index LEAPS, 256 E-FLEX (Equity FLexible EXchange) options, 42 index options, and 17 structured product offerings. The CBOE website has an online tour called Virtual Visit at *www.cboe.com*.

Chicago Mercantile Exchange

30 South Wacker Drive

Chicago, IL 60606

312-930-1000

www.cme.com

Regular trading hours: 7:00 A.M. to 3:15 P.M., CST. Individual products have varied hours of trading. GLOBEX2, an electronic trading system, provides 24-hour trading availability.

The Chicago Mercantile Exchange, known simply as the Merc, began over a century ago as the Chicago Butter and Egg Board. From only two contracts, butter and eggs, the CME has grown into the home of trading for more than 50 futures and options products. The options and futures traded can be grouped into four categories: interest rates, indices, currencies, and agricultural commodities.

Interest rate contracts include three-month Eurodollars, one-month London Interbank Offered Rate (LIBOR), 13-week U.S. Treasury bills, one-year U.S. Treasury bills, Euroyen, one-month federal funds, the turn rate, the quarterly bankruptcy index, Brady bonds, 91-day Mexican CETES, 28-day Mexican TIIE, and 10-year Japanese government bonds.

Index futures and options include S&P 500, E-Mini S&P 500, NASDAQ 100, S&P Midcap 400, S&P 500/Barra Growth, S&P 500/Barra Value, Russell 2000, Nikkei 225, the Mexican IPC, and the Goldman Sachs Commodity Index.

Options and futures on many currencies and cross rates are traded, including the Australian dollar; Brazilian real; British pound; British pound/deutsche mark cross; Canadian dollar; deutsche mark; deutsche mark/Japanese yen cross; euro FX; euro FX cross with Japanese yen, British pound, and Swiss franc; French franc; Japanese yen; Mexican peso; Swiss franc; South African rand; New Zealand dollar; and Mexican CETES and TIIE.

Agricultural commodity futures and options include live cattle, feeder cattle, boneless beef, boneless beef trimmings, lean hogs, pork bellies, cheddar cheese, BFP milk, butter, random length lumber, oriented strand board, spot cheese (daily), spot butter (Fridays), and spot dry milk (daily). In addition, trading is based on the weather using the heating degree day index.

Reservations to visit the Merc are required for groups of 10 to 50 persons. Visit the website or call (312) 930-8249 for scheduling information. Presentations are available from 9:00 A.M. to 12:00 noon and are tailored to the type of group.

New York Mercantile Exchange (NYMEX) and Commodity Exchange (COMEX)

One North End Avenue

World Financial Center

New York, NY 10282-1101

212-299-2000

www.nymex.com

Regular trading hours:

NYMEX: 9:45 A.M. to 4:00 P.M., EST

COMEX: 10:00 A.M. to 2:45 P.M., EST

In 1872, a group of New York dairy merchants established the Butter and Cheese Exchange of New York, hoping to bring some order to the city's agricultural markets. Over the next decade many more products were added to the trading menu and the market's name was changed to the New York Mercantile Exchange (NYMEX).

The Commodity Exchange (COMEX) was established in 1933 by the merger of the National Metal Exchange, the Rubber Exchange of New York, the National Raw Silk Exchange, and the New York Hide Exchange. In 1994, the New York Mercantile Exchange and the Commodity Exchange merged to become the world's largest physical commodity futures exchange.

The NYMEX division trades futures and options on crude oil, heating oil, gasoline, natural gas, propane, platinum, and palladium. The COMEX division trades futures and options on gold, silver, copper, and the Euro-top 100 and 300 stock indices.

The museum located on the ground floor of the exchange is open Monday through Friday from 9:00 A.M. to 5 P.M. Visit the NYMEX website for directions by subway, bus, car, or ferry, or from airports.

Changes in U.S. Stock Markets

The late 1990s marked a period of dramatic changes for stock trading in the United States. These changes were driven by unprecedented increases in trading volume, advances in technology, and the advent of internet trading.

Industry Consolidation

Much has been said about the demise of traditional stock exchanges such as the NYSE and Amex as computer networks have rendered the central meeting place superfluous. In March 2000, the NYSE was reported to have approached the NASD about a NYSE/NASDAQ merger, which was rebuffed. In June 2000, the NASD and NASDAQ closed the first phase of a private placement. In it, the NASDAQ sold 24 million shares for $74 million, representing 40% ownership. The NASD raised $260 million by selling warrants that will be redeemable for more than 25 million NASDAQ shares.

U.S. Markets to Trade in Decimals

U.S. markets are the last in the world to trade in fractions instead of decimals. Several dates have been set, then suspended by the Securities and Exchange Commission (SEC), for the conversion; the current deadline is April 2001. A simple enough concept, this move has long been fought by brokerage firms that publicly decry the cost of software for conversion but privately fear that shrinking spreads between bid and asked prices will jeopardize profits. Most stocks currently trade in 1/8 ($0.125), 1/16 ($0.0625), or 1/32 ($0.03125) increments, a practice that stems from the 16th century method of chopping Spanish doubloons into eight pieces. For a market making firm, this spread between buy and sell transactions translates into profit on a trade.

Decimal trading may reduce the increment to $0.01. This move is better for the investor but worse for the market maker. Perhaps. Many industry analysts foresee a dramatic increase in trading volume from day traders as ever-smaller moves in a stock's price are required for a profitable trade. If this happens, firms may make up in volume what they lose on per-trade profit.

Expanded Trading Hours

As of this writing, talk of expanding the trading day continues. Most proposals are for specified times such as 6:00 P.M. to 9:00 P.M., EST, or 7:00 P.M. to 10:00 P.M., EST. Currently, expanded hours are possible for institutions through Instinet and for individual investors through the approximately 200 brokerage firms which trade with Island and other electronic communication networks (ECNs) that match NASDAQ NMS and Smallcap orders. Hours for Island are 8:00 A.M. to 8:00 P.M., EST; some others, such as NexTrade, never close.

A proposal for after-hours trading by Instinet would allow transactions to be placed through online brokers who have signed up for such trading. Proposals by Wit Capital and Eclipse Trading would allow individuals to place orders directly.

After-hours trading is expected to become a reality due to the demand from online traders. When trading after hours, consider the risks in trading in a market that may have little liquidity and is not manned by market makers with a responsibility to maintain an orderly market. Expect large spreads between bid and ask prices due to the smaller volume of participants. Place limit orders only. Thin markets can spell disaster for market orders.

World Securities Exchanges

While we have covered several of the largest United States exchanges, they are by no means the only places that stock trading takes place. Table 3–4 provides a listing of many stock exchanges worldwide.

Table 3–4. A Sampling of World Securities Exchanges

North American Exchanges			
Exchange	Symbol	Exchange	Symbol
New York	NYSE	Alberta	AE
NASDAQ	NASDAQ	Montreal	ME
American	AMEX	Toronto	TSE
Boston	BSE	Vancouver	VSE
Chicago Board of Options	CBOE	Winnipeg	WCE
Chicago Board of Trade	CBOT	International	ISE
Chicago Mercantile	CME	Kansas City Board of Trade	KCBOT
Chicago	CSE	Minneapolis Grain	MGE
Pacific	PSE	New York Cotton	NYCE
Philadelphia	PHLX	New York Mercantile	NYMEX

Table 3-4. A Sampling of World Securities Exchanges—*Cont.*

European Exchanges

Exchange	Symbol	Exchange	Symbol
UK London	FTSE	Frankfurt	DAX
Paris	CAC	Barcelona	BSE
Milan	Borsa	Madrid	MSE
Stockholm	SFB	Helsinki	HSE
Amsterdam		Greece	ASE
Switzerland	SWX	Dublin	IFOX

South American Exchanges

Exchange	Symbol	Exchange	Symbol
Bermuda	BSE	Rio de Janeiro	
Cayman Islands	CSX	Santiago	BCS
Bogota	BSE	Jamaica	JSE
Lima	LBVL	Trinidad Tobago	TTSE
Venezuela	BVC	Mexico	BMV

African Exchanges

Exchange	Symbol	Exchange	Symbol
Ghana	GSE	Johannesburg	JSE
South African Futures	SAFEX		

Asian Exchanges

Exchange	Symbol	Exchange	Symbol
Shanghai		Hong Kong	SEHK
India		Bombay	
Jakarta	BAP	Osaka	OST
Tokyo	TCO	Korea	KSE
Kuala Lumpur	BHD	New Zealand	NZSE
Pakistan		Singapore	SES
Taiwan	TSE	Thailand	SET

Middle Eastern Exchanges

Exchange	Symbol	Exchange	Symbol
Tel Aviv	TASE	Beirut	
Palestine	PSE	Istanbul	ISE

Summary

As with so many aspects of modern life, technology is changing the face of securities trading. The demise of the NYSE has been widely predicted, as its system of a central meeting place with middlemen (specialists) is hailed as expensive and outdated. While no one can predict the timing and exact outcome of the turf wars between physical exchanges and electronic networks, the consumer is sure to benefit from shrinking spreads and wider choices in convenience, service, and autonomy.

4
Indices

For many years those in the financial community have tracked groups of securities, calling them indices or averages, to measure general market trends and to provide a benchmark for investment performance. In recent years, more specialized indices have been created to track specific industries or types of stocks, bonds, and international investments.

U.S. Stock Indices

Dow Jones Averages

Charles Dow, one of the founders of Dow Jones Company and the first editor of *The Wall Street Journal*, created the first Dow Jones average in 1884. His intent was to express the general trend of the stock market. By 1896, he had split the average in two—the Dow Jones Industrial Average and the Dow Jones Railroad Average. The industrial average consisted of 12 general industrial stocks and the railroad average of 20 railroad stocks. As transportation changed, the railroad average was renamed the transportation average.

These two averages were the cornerstone of what is now known as Dow theory. Derived from Dow's writings in *The Wall Street Journal*, Dow theory follows the relationship between industrial companies and the transportation required to bring them raw materials and deliver finished products to their customers. Dow reasoned that by studying both sectors, he could more accurately determine the overall health of the economy.

Computing Dow Jones Averages. Initially, the Dow Jones averages were calculated by adding the closing prices of all stocks in the index and dividing the sum by the number of stocks. Over time, the divisor of each average has been mathematically adjusted due to stock splits and dividends. For example, the November 1, 1999, divisor of the Dow Jones Industrial Average (DJIA) was 0.197. If any stock in the average was down 3 points, you could divide 3 by 0.197 to find the number of points the DJIA would decline (15.228) as a result of the decline in that particular stock.

The biggest criticism of Dow Jones averages is that they are price-weighted, not market-value-weighted, averages. Under this method of calculating an index, which adds all the closing prices and divides by a divisor, a stock with a price of $100 has twice as much weight in the average as a stock with a price of $50. If a stock splits 2-for-1, its weight in the index is halved, as if its price had dropped in half, though the total market value of shares outstanding has not changed.

Dow Jones Industrial Average. As the most often quoted stock market barometer, the DJIA receives much attention when it reaches a 1,000-point milestone, two of which were crossed in 1999. While most investors agree that a few-point change in the level of the DJIA is of no great importance, the psychological impact on investors can be great when a barrier is crossed, either on the upside or downside. Table 4–1 provides a history of the DJIA.

The stocks in the Dow Jones Industrial Average change at the discretion of the Dow Jones Company, theoretically to better reflect American industry. In 1916, the industrial average was increased to 20 stocks and in 1928,

Table 4–1. Dow Jones Industrial Average Milestones

Milestone	Date	Time to Reach Milestone	Percentage Gain
1,000	November 14, 1972		
2,000	January 8, 1987	3,535 trading days	100
3,000	April 17, 1991	1,067 trading days	50
4,000	February 23, 1995	966 trading days	33
5,000	November 21, 1995	188 trading days	25
6,000	October 14, 1996	224 trading days	20
7,000	February 13, 1997	82 trading days	17
8,000	July 16, 1997	105 trading days	14
9,000	April 6, 1998	184 trading days	13
10,000	March 29, 1999	246 trading days	11
11,000	May 3, 1999	24 trading days	10

to 30, where it remains today. Some critics argue that poor-performing stocks are dropped as market leaders are added, thus artificially inflating index levels. On November 1, 1999, a major change took place in the DJIA as it added its first two NASDAQ stocks, Microsoft Corporation and Intel Corporation. Home Depot and SBC Communications were also added. Chevron Corporation, Goodyear Tire and Rubber Co., Sears, Roebuck & Co., and Union Carbide Corporation were dropped from the index. As of that date, stocks in the DJIA, ticker symbols in parentheses, were as follows:

AT&T Corp. (T)

Allied Signal, Inc. (ALD)

Alcoa, Inc. (AA)

American Express Co. (AXP)

Boeing Co. (BA)

Caterpillar, Inc. (CAT)

Citigroup, Inc. (C)

Coca Cola Co. (KO)

Walt Disney Co. (DIS)

DuPont E I De Nemours & Co. (DD)

Eastman Kodak Co. (EK)

Exxon Corp. (XON)

General Electric Co. (GE)

General Motors Corp. (GM)

Hewlett Packard Co. (HWP)

Home Depot, Inc. (HD)

Intel Corp. (INTC)

International Business Machines Corp. (IBM)

International Paper Co. (IP)

Johnson & Johnson (JNJ)

McDonald's Corp. (MCD)

Merck & Co., Inc. (MRK)

Microsoft Corp. (MSFT)

Minnesota Mining & Manufacturing Co. (MMM)

Morgan, J.P. & Co., Inc. (JPM)

Philip Morris Companies, Inc. (MO)

Procter & Gamble Co. (PG)

SBC Communications, Inc. (SBC)

United Technologies Corp. (UTX)

Wal-Mart Stores, Inc. (WMT)

Figure 4–1 tracks the level of the DJIA from the beginning of 1990 through the end of 1999.

Dow Jones Transportation Average. According to Dow theory, the Dow Jones Transportation Average (DJTA) is a predictor of economic activity and thus movement in the Dow Jones Industrial Average. Practitioners of Dow theory consider a buy or sell signal in the form of a new high or low for the DJIA or DJTA to be valid only if the other average follows shortly. The stocks in the Dow Jones Transportation Average, as of November 1, 1999, were as follows:

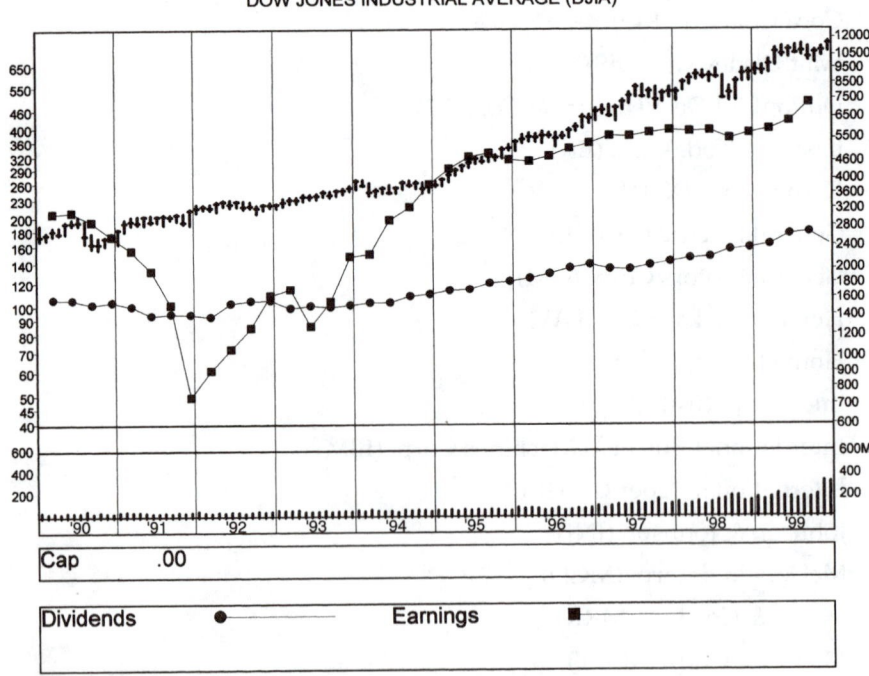

Figure 4–1. Dow Jones Industrial Average

SOURCE: Chart courtesy of Securities Research Company, 400 Talcott Avenue, Watertown, MA 02472.

Airborne Freight Corp. (ABF)

Alexander & Baldwin, Inc. (ALEX)

AMR Corp. (AMR)

Burlington Northern Santa Fe Corp. (BNI)

CNF Transportation, Inc. (CNF)

CSX Corp. (CSX)

Delta Air Lines, Inc. (DAL)

FDX Corp. (FDX)

GATX Corp. (GMT)

J.B. Hunt Transportation Services (JBHT)

Norfolk Southern Corp. (NSC)

Northwest Airlines Corp. (NWAC)

Roadway Express, Inc. (ROAD)

Ryder System, Inc. (R)

Southwest Airlines Co. (LUV)

UAL Corp. (UAL)

Union Pacific Corp. (UNP)

US Airways Group, Inc. (U)

USFreightways (USFC)

Yellow Corp. (YELL)

Dow Jones Utility Average. The Dow Jones Utility Average is a barometer for utility stocks. It began in 1929 with 20 utility stocks and today it has 15. As of November 1, 1999, its component stocks were as follows:

American Electric Power Co. (AEP)

Columbia Energy Group (CG)

Consolidated Edison, Inc. (ED)

Consolidated Natural Gas Co. (CNG)

Duke Energy Corp. (DUK)

Edison International (EIX)

Enron Corp. (ENE)

Reliant Energy (REI)

PECO Energy Co. (PE)

PG&E Corp. (PCG)

Public Service Enterprise Group (PEG)

Southern Co. (SO)

Texas Utilities Co. (TXU)

Unicom Corp. (UCM)

Williams Cos. (WMB)

Standard & Poor's Indices

Standard & Poor's Corporation, a division of McGraw-Hill Companies, Inc., tracks some of the most widely used indices in the investment world. Though the DJIA often gets the most media attention, throughout the investment community the S&P 500 is the standard benchmark for the performance of largecap U.S. stocks. The MidCap 400 and SmallCap 600 are highly regarded benchmarks for midsize and smaller stocks, respectively. In addition to these well-known indices, S&P tracks other more specialized indices.

Computing S&P Indices

S&P indices are base-weighted aggregate indices, which means that the level of each index is calculated using the total market value (stock price times shares outstanding) of the component stocks in the index relative to a particular base period. Using this method of calculation, a $1 stock price movement in a larger company will have a bigger impact on an index than a $1 price movement from a smaller company and stock splits, because they do not affect market capitalization and do not influence the index.

New companies are added to an S&P index only when other companies are removed for one of the following reasons: merger with or acquisition by another company, financial operating failure, lack of representation in the economy, or restructuring.

Companies are added with the following considerations in mind.

- Unless specialized, indices are diversified as to industry, generally reflecting the composition of the U.S. economy.
- Except for foreign averages, S&P indices consist of U.S. companies. A few non-U.S. companies have been in the S&P 500 since before this policy was in place; but new companies, despite having international operations, are all based in the United States.

- Market sector representation (technology, health care, transportation, etc.) should roughly mirror the general market.

- Only companies with sufficient trading liquidity are considered. This ensures that shares are available for investors to buy.

- The financial health of each company is important. Financial stability of index companies reduces index turnover due to insolvency.

Standard & Poor's 500 Index. The S&P 500 Index consists of 500 stocks which are chosen to be a representative sample of leading companies in leading U.S. industries. As a result, the S&P 500 is widely considered to be a benchmark for the stock market in general. The index's 500 largecap stocks from 25 different industries comprise about 80% of the total market value of the U.S. stock market. The 40 largest stocks in the index comprise more than half its market value. Standard & Poor's Corporation data about the S&P 500 Index, dated October 29, 1999, is given in Tables 4–2, 4–3, and 4–4.

Table 4–2. S&P 500 Industry Group Representation

	Number of Companies	Number of Companies as a Percent of 500
Industrials	376	75.2
Utilities	42	8.4
Financials	71	14.2
Transportation	11	2.2

SOURCE: Standard & Poor's Corp.

Table 4–3. S&P 500 Exchange Representation

	Number of Companies	Number of Companies as a Percent of 500
NYSE	455	91
NASDAQ	45	9
Amex	0	0

SOURCE: Standard & Poor's Corp.

Table 4–4. S&P 500 Statistics (market values in millions)

Total market value	$11,267,000
Mean market value	$22,534
Median market value	$7,932
Largest company's market value	$472,426
Smallest company's market value	$378
Median share price	$39.969
P/E ratio	33.23
Dividend yield	1.23%

SOURCE: Standard & Poor's Corp.

Figure 4–2 tracks the performance of the Standard & Poor's 500 Index from the beginning of 1990 through the end of 1999.

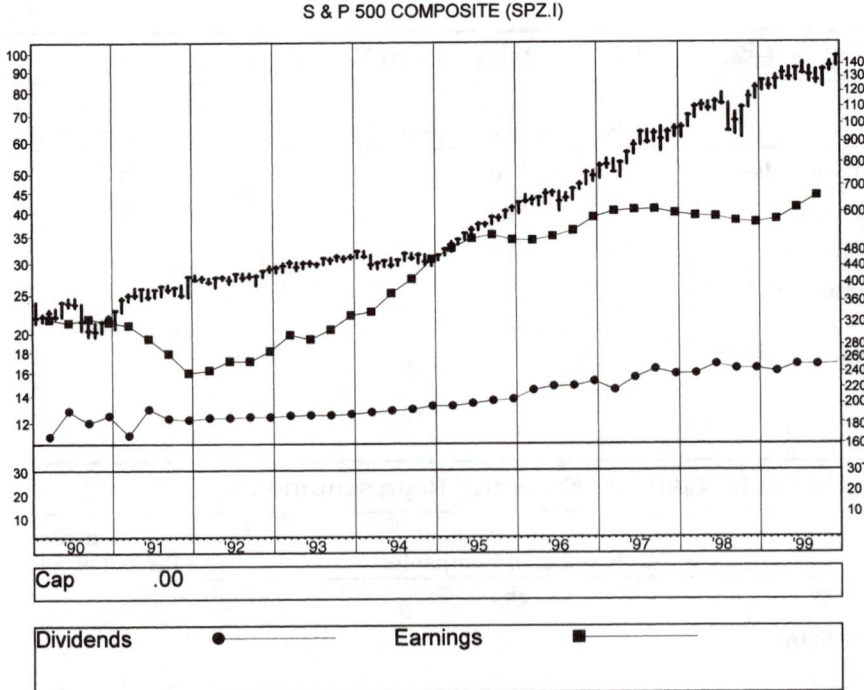

Figure 4–2. Standard & Poor's 500 Index

SOURCE: Chart courtesy of Securities Research Company, 400 Talcott Avenue, Watertown, MA 02472.

Standard & Poor's
MidCap 400 Index

The S&P MidCap 400 Index is an index of 400 stocks of midsize companies. The "cap" in MidCap stands for capitalization, which is the total market value of a company computed by multiplying the number of shares outstanding by current share price. Data about the S&P MidCap 400 Index as of October 29, 1999, are given in Tables 4–5, 4–6, and 4–7.

Table 4–5. S&P MidCap 400 Industry Group Representation

	Number of Companies	Number of Companies as a Percent of 500
Industrials	306	76.5
Utilities	40	10.0
Financials	43	10.7
Transportation	11	2.8

SOURCE: Standard & Poor's Corp.

Table 4–6. S&P MidCap 400 Exchange Representation

	Number of Companies	Number of Companies as a Percent of 500
NYSE	287	71.8
NASDAQ	106	26.5
Amex	7	1.7

SOURCE: Standard & Poor's Corp.

Table 4–7. S&P MidCap 400 Statistics (market values in millions)

Total market value	$854,000
Mean market value	$2,135
Median market value	$1,692
Largest company's market value	$18,375
Smallest company's market value	$195
Median share price	$24.875
P/E ratio	28.52
Dividend yield	1.20%

SOURCE: Standard & Poor's Corp.

Standard & Poor's SmallCap 600 Index

The S&P SmallCap 600 Index is a benchmark for the stocks of small companies. Because small-company stocks trade less frequently and in smaller amounts, careful attention is paid to liquidity in addition to market size and industry groups when choosing stocks for this index. Data about the S&P SmallCap 600 Index, as of October 29, 1999, is shown in Tables 4–8, 4–9, and 4–10.

Table 4–8. S&P SmallCap 600 Industry Group Representation

	Number of Companies	Number of Companies as a Percent of 500
Industrials	504	84.0
Utilities	24	4.0
Financials	52	8.7
Transportation	20	3.3

SOURCE: Standard & Poor's Corp.

Table 4–9. S&P SmallCap 600 Exchange Representation

	Number of Companies	Number of Companies as a Percent of 500
NYSE	321	53.5
NASDAQ	263	43.8
Amex	16	2.7

SOURCE: Standard & Poor's Corp.

Table 4–10. S&P SmallCap 600 Statistics (market values in millions)

Total market value	$326,000
Mean market value	$544
Median market value	$429
Largest company's market value	$3,078
Smallest company's market value	$18
Median share price	$18.000
P/E ratio	32.06
Dividend yield	0.78%

SOURCE: Standard & Poor's Corp.

Other U.S. Standard & Poor's Corporation Indices

- Standard & Poor's SuperComposite 1500 Index is a combination of the S&P 500, MidCap 400, and SmallCap 600 indices. Designed to be a broad market barometer, the SuperComposite 1500 represents 87% of the U.S. equity market by capitalization.

- Standard & Poor's 100 Index consists of 100 blue-chip stocks of diverse industries. It is a measure of large-company stock performance.

- Standard & Poor's/BARRA growth and value indices comprise each of the U.S. S&P indices. Companies within each index are divided into two groups based on their ratio of stock price to book value. Those with higher ratios are placed in the growth index and those with lower ratios in the value index. When combined, the S&P/BARRA 500 Growth Index and S&P/BARRA 500 Value Index equal the S&P 500 Index.

- Standard & Poor's REIT Composite Index, established in 1997, tracks 100 real estate investment trusts. The index covers more than 80% of the market for U.S. securitized real estate.

NASDAQ Indices

NASDAQ indices are different compilations of stocks that trade on the National Association of Securities Dealers Automated Quotation System. While stocks on the NASDAQ have historically been categorized as small-cap stocks, the popularity of the technology sector, most of whose stocks trade on the NASDAQ, has transformed these indices from compilations of unknown companies to high-performance benchmarks of hot technology stocks.

NASDAQ Composite. Not technically created as an index, the NASDAQ Composite is simply a market-capitalization weighting of the approximately 4,800 stocks listed on the NASDAQ market. It is a popular daily reporting benchmark, often given in contrast to the blue-chip DJIA as a performance measure of smaller cap and technology stocks. The 1990s were a record decade for the NASDAQ Composite, which showed a 685% rise—more than double the increases in the DJIA and the S&P 500. It is only fitting that the decade ended with a 1999 return of 85.6% (22% of which was earned in December alone). This compares with 1999 increases of 25.2% for the DJIA and 19.5% for the S&P 500. As hedge fund manager and TheStreet.Com favorite James Cramer put it, "The difference between the New York Stock Exchange and the NASDAQ is the difference between *Jeopardy* and *Who Wants to Be a Millionaire.*"[1]

The decade's rise, and particularly that of 1999, was fueled by the technology sector, featuring internet, telecommunications, and computer companies. Big winners of the decade include the following:

Cisco Systems, Inc.—up 125,000%

Dell Computer, Inc.—up 72,000%

CMGI—up 57,000%

For 1999, those on top are as follows:

Commerce One, Inc.—up 2,707%

Qualcomm, Inc.—up 2,618%

Verticlenet, Inc.—up 1,950%

Brocade Communication Systems—up 1,763%

Purchasepro.Com, Inc.—up 1,619%

Figure 4–3 shows a history of the NASDAQ Composite from the beginning of 1990 to the end of 1999.

NASDAQ 100 Index. An index of the 100 largest and most active non-financial stocks listed on the NASDAQ stock market, the NASDAQ 100 Index is a subset of the NASDAQ Composite. The technology-heavy NASDAQ 100 is led by names such as Microsoft, Cisco Systems, Dell Computer, MCI Worldcom, and Intel, which, given their large market capitalizations, comprise 40% of the index. In 1999, the NASDAQ 100 led the NASDAQ Composite, with a return of 102%.

Russell Indices

The Russell indices were developed jointly by the Frank Russell Company and the New York Futures Exchange (NYFE) to track investment grade securities. The capitalization-weighted indices are set each June from a list of the 3,000 largest publicly traded U.S. securities.

Russell 3000 Index. The Russell 3000 contains the 3,000 most actively traded U.S. stocks. It is divided into two subindices, the Russell 1000 and the Russell 2000.

---

[1]Joseph Nocera, "Broken Records: A Fitting Farewell to the Nasdaq Decade," *Fortune* (January 10, 2000): 210.

NASDAQ COMPOSITE INDEX (NCM.I)

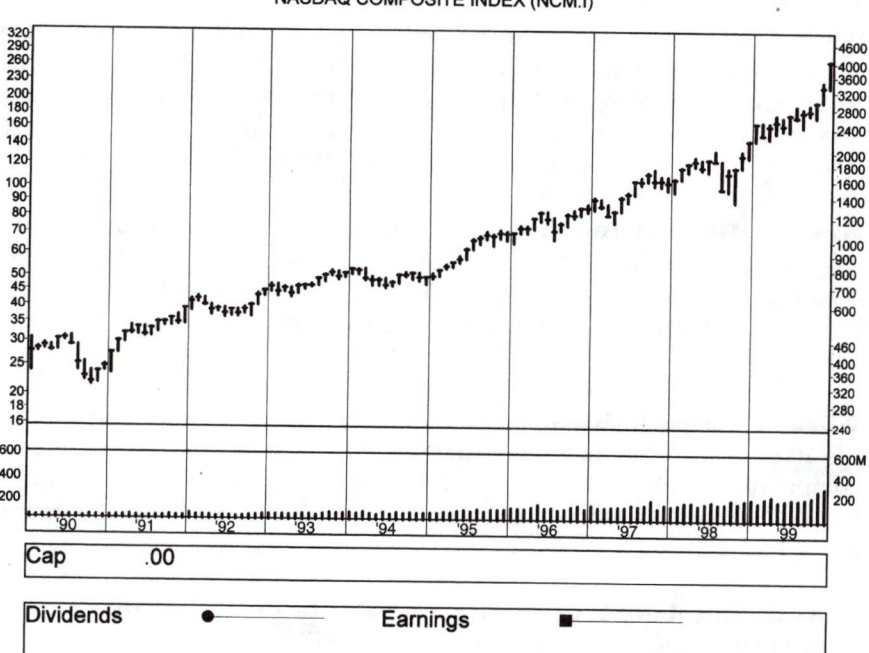

Figure 4–3. Nasdaq Composite Index

SOURCE: Chart courtesy of Securities Research Company, 400 Talcott Avenue, Watertown, MA 02472.

Russell 1000 Index. Companies in the Russell 3000 Index with market values greater than $300 million are represented in the Russell 1000 Index, with the remainder listed in the Russell 2000 Index. Approximately 90% of the market value of U.S. stocks is depicted in the Russell 1000 Index.

Russell 2000 Index. A widely followed benchmark for second-tier stocks, the Russell 2000 Index lists those with market values between $20 million and $300 million. The Russell 2000 Index tracks 8% to 9% of the market value of traded stocks. Though this index is often sited as being representative of small stocks and is used repeatedly as a benchmark for small-stock mutual funds, the narrowness of the stock rally in the past few years has made it less indicative of the market than one might think. While the index gained 19.6% in 1999, 56% of its stocks lost value. From June 30, 1999, (the index's latest revision) through February 11, 2000, the Russell 2000 appreciated 17%, but 51% of that gain came from only 13 companies.[2]

---

[2]Rhonda Brammer, "The Russell 13," *Barron's* (February 21, 2000): 40.

Wilshire Indices

Wilshire Associates, an investment advisor and money manager tracks one of the best-known total market indices, the Wilshire 5000. While the 5000 is the most popular, Wilshire tracks nearly 30 different market-capitalization weighted indices, which can be separated into three categories: Wilshire indices, Wilshire target indices, and Wilshire specialty indices.

Wilshire General Indices. There are 14 general Wilshire indices, including the Wilshire 5000. The Wilshire 5000 Total Market Index is the broadest index for tracking the performance of the U.S. equity market. It covers more than 7,000 stocks and compares to the S&P 500 as shown in Table 4–11.

Wilshire Target Indices. Formerly known as the Wilshire style indices, the 10 target indices track investment styles, such as growth or value, in combination with company size. Examples include the Wilshire Target Small Company Growth Index and the Wilshire Target Small Company Value Index.

Wilshire Specialty Indices. Three indices track specific market sectors. They are internet, real estate securities, and REIT.

Comparative Results for Selected U.S. Stock Indices

The news media primarily concentrate on the DJIA as "the stock market," but wide variations exist in the performance of the 30 Dow stocks and in stocks in general. Table 4–12 illustrates this observation by showing the annual returns for various U.S. stock indices.

Table 4–11. Wilshire 5000 versus S&P 500

Index Characteristics (market values in millions)	S&P 500	Wilshire 5000
Total market value	$11,300,000	$14,100,000
Mean market value	$22,543	$1,972
Median market value	$7,923	$110
Largest company's market value	$472,426	$472,426
Smallest company's market value	$378	Under $1 million
P/E ratio	30.2	31.7
Dividend yield	1.22%	1.17%
Market value of companies as a % of Wilshire 5000	77%	100%

SOURCE: Wilshire Associates, data as of October 31, 1999.

Table 4–12. Relative Performance of U.S. Stock Indices
1995–1999

Index	1995	1996	1997	1998	1999
DJIA	33.5%	26.0%	22.6%	16.1%	25.2%
S&P 500	34.1	20.3	31.0	26.7	19.5
NASDAQ Composite	39.9	22.7	21.6	39.6	85.6
Russell 2000	26.2	14.8	20.5	(3.5)	19.6

SOURCE: *Barron's,* January 3, 2000.

International Stock Indices

Multicountry Indices

Morgan Stanley Capital International (MSCI) World Index. The MSCI Index has approximately 1,482 international stocks. Those included trade on exchanges in the United States, Europe, Canada, Australia, New Zealand, and the Far East.

S&P Global 1200. An index of 1,191 international stocks, the S&P Global 1200 is a compilation of the S&P 500 Index, the S&P Euro Plus Index, the S&P/TSE 60 Index (Canada), the S&P/TOPIX 150 Index (Tokyo), the S&P Asia Pacific 100 Index, the S&P Latin America 40 Index, and the S&P United Kingdom 150 Index. To avoid double counting, the nine international stocks in the S&P 500 are omitted, as they are included in regional or country indices. This results in a total of 1,191 rather than 1,200 securities in the index.

Schwab International Index. Another multiple country index, the Schwab International Index has 350 of the largest stocks worldwide.

Morgan Stanley Capital International EAFE Index. This MSCI index has approximately 1,045 international stocks. Those included trade in 21 countries, on the exchanges of Europe, Australia, and the Far East (hence the EAFE).

Morgan Stanley Capital International Europe Index. This MSCI index has approximately 627 stocks from the 15 countries of Europe.

S&P Euro and Euro Plus Indices. The S&P Euro Index contains 160 stocks of the Eurobloc countries. It is a subset of the Euro Plus Index, which also includes 40 stocks from Denmark, Norway, Switzerland, and Sweden.

Financial Times Stock Exchange Eurotop 100 Index (FT-SE Eurotop 100). This index involves the 100 most-liquid stocks of the leading European companies.

Dow Jones Euro Stoxx 50 Index. This index involves 50 blue-chip stocks from the countries participating in the conversion to the euro.

Morgan Stanley Capital International Pacific Index. This MSCI index has approximately 418 stocks listed on the exchanges of Australia, New Zealand, Japan, Hong Kong, Singapore, and Malaysia.

S&P Asia Pacific 100 Index. This S&P index involves 100 stocks from the exchanges of Australia, New Zealand, Hong Kong, Korea, Malaysia, Singapore, and Taiwan.

S&P Latin America 40 Index. This S&P index involves 40 stocks from the countries of Mexico, Brazil, Argentina, and Chile.

A Sampling of Indices for Individual Countries

Austria
  Austrian Traded Index (ATX): An index of 22 Austrian companies traded on the Vienna Stock Exchange.

Belgium
  Belgian 20 Price Index (Bel 20): An index of 20 Belgian blue chips listed on the Brussels Stock Exchange.

Canada
  S&P/TSE 60 Index: An index of 60 largecap stocks listed on the Toronto Stock Exchange.

Czech Republic
  Prague Stock Exchange 50 Index (PX-50): An index of 50 companies listed on the Prague Stock Exchange. Listing in the index is based on market capitalization and trading volume.

Denmark
  Copenhagen Stock Exchange Index (KFX): An index of 21 Danish companies listed on the Copenhagen Stock Exchange. The index portfolio is

determined each November, based on highest trading volume and market capitalization.

Finland

Helsinki Stock Exchange 20 Share Prices Index (Hex-20): An index of the 20 most actively traded stocks on the Helsinki Stock Exchange. The companies in the index are determined twice a year.

Germany

Deutscher Aktiendindex (DAX): The leading German stock index, the DAX consists of 30 stocks listed on the German Stock Exchange. There is also a DAX 100, a MidCap index, the MDAX, and a composite DAX index (the CDAX).

Greece

Greece Stock Exchange Composite Index (ATG): The Greek Stock Exchange publishes nine indices, the Composite Index of 75 stocks, plus eight sector indices.

Hungary

The Budapest Stock Index (BUX): An index of 20 stocks listed on the Budapest Stock Exchange. The component stocks are updated semiannually.

Ireland

Irish Stock Exchange Equity Overall Index (ISEQ): An index of 76 stocks traded on the Irish Stock Exchange. Consists of the ISEQ General Index (73 stocks) and the ISEQ Financial Index (3 stocks).

Italy

Milan Italy Stock Exchange 30 Index (MIB-30): An index of the 30 most liquid and highly capitalized stocks listed on the Italian Stock Exchange, representing more than 70% of market capitalization and 75% of total trading volume. The composition of the index is revised semiannually.

Japan

Nikkei Stock Average: Japan's most widely watched stock index. The Nikkei is a price-weighted average, similar to Dow Jones averages, of 225 stocks listed on the Tokyo Stock Exchange.

Nikkei Stock Index 300: An index (market value weighted) of 300 stocks listed on the Tokyo Stock Exchange.

S&P/TOPIX 150 Index: An index of 150 stocks traded on the Tokyo markets.

The Netherlands

Amsterdam Exchanges Index (AEX): An index of 25 companies representative of the general trend of the Amsterdam Stock Exchange.

Norway

Oslo Stock Exchange Index (OBX): An index of the 25 companies on the Oslo Stock Exchange with the highest trading volume. The index is revised twice a year.

Sweden

Stockholm Stock Exchange SX-16 Index (SX-16): An index of the most frequently traded stocks on the Stockholm Stock Exchange.

Switzerland

Swiss Market Index (SMI): An index of 21 high-turnover stocks listed on the exchanges of Zurich, Geneva, and Basle.

United Kingdom

Financial Times Stock Exchange 100 Index (FT-SE 100): One of a family of indices jointly established by the *Financial Times,* the London Stock Exchange, and the Institute and Faculty of Actuaries. The FT-SE 100 tracks the 100 U.K. companies with the largest market value.

S&P United Kingdom 150 Index: An index of 150 stocks traded in the United Kingdom.

Bond Indices

Most bond indices measure total return for the bonds tracked; therefore, price appreciation or depreciation is added to interest income and computed as a percentage of the original investment. Some are market value weighted, so that the influence of a particular bond on the index is based on the percentage it represents within the market value of all bonds in the index. Following are examples of bond indices.

Lehman Brothers Aggregate Bond Index: A benchmark for performance of the bond market, this index is a compilation of the Lehman Brothers Government/Corporate Bond Index, the Mortgage-Backed Securities Index, and the Asset-Backed Securities Index.

Lehman Brothers Corporate Bond Index: An index of publicly issued, fixed-rate, nonconvertible, investment grade (BBB or better) U.S. corporate bonds.

Lehman Brothers Government Bond Index: An index of all publicly issued, nonconvertible, domestic debt of the U.S. government or any of its agencies. It also includes debt of quasi-federal corporations and corporate debt guaranteed by the U.S. government, but does not include flower bonds and mortgage-backed securities.

Lehman Brothers Intermediate Government Bond Index: An index of bonds included in the Lehman Brothers Government Bond Index that have maturities of more than 1 year but fewer than 10 years.

Lehman Brothers Government/Corporate Bond Index: An index of publicly issued debt of the U.S. Treasury and U.S. government agencies (excluding mortgage-backed securities); fixed-rate, nonconvertible, investment grade corporate debt; and U.S. dollar denominated, SEC registered, nonconvertible debt issued by foreign governments or international agencies.

Lehman Brothers Mortgage-Backed Securities Index: An index of 15- and 30-year fixed-rate bonds backed by the mortgages of the Federal National Mortgage Association (FNMA), the Government National Mortgage Association (GNMA), and the Federal Home Loan Mortgage Corporation (FHLMC).

Lehman Brothers Municipal Bond Index: An index of approximately 20,000 fixed-rate, investment-grade (BBB, Baa, or higher) tax-exempt bonds.

Merrill Lynch All-Convertible Bond Index: An index of U.S. corporate convertible securities with at least an original par value or current market value of $50 million.

Salomon/SB World Government Bond Index: An index that tracks the performance of the government bond markets of Australia, Austria, Belgium, Canada, Denmark, Finland, France, Germany, Ireland, Italy, Japan, the Netherlands, Portugal, Spain, Sweden, Switzerland, the United Kingdom, and the United States. There is also a non-U.S. index.

J.P. Morgan Overseas Government Bond Index Series: A series of indices for liquid government bonds of Australia, Belgium, Canada, Denmark, France, Germany, Italy, Japan, the Netherlands, Spain, Sweden, the United Kingdom, and the United States. There is a combined global index and a combined non-U.S. index.

First Boston High Yield Index: An index of publicly traded corporate bonds that are below investment grade (rated below BBB or Baa).

Dow Jones 20 Bond Average: This arithmetic average is similar to the Dow Jones stock averages, rather than a total return index like most bond indices. It is the unweighted average of the prices of 10 utility bonds and 10 industrial bonds. The average is quoted as a price, based on a percentage of par, just as bonds are quoted. A yield figure, the average yield for the bonds tracked, is also quoted.

Using Indices

Indices are most often used in one of three ways. First, they are valuable when used to track entire markets or smaller sectors of a market. Technical analysts watching stock markets pay close attention to market trends as measured by movements in particular indices, the breadth (number of issues in the index which are moving in the same direction) of the trends, and the volume of transactions during market movements. They also watch for indices to confirm price movements of one another. Investors watching bond market indices gain valuable information about price changes and yields in different sectors of the bond market. This information can be more informative of interest rate trends than the often-reported yield on T-bills or the 30-year Treasury bonds.

The second way investors find indices valuable is as a benchmark for comparing investment returns. Evaluating the investment return of a money manager, mutual fund, or even your own portfolio is easy with the number and diversity of tracking indices available. The key consideration is to use the right index for comparison. The criteria used to include stocks or bonds in the index should be the same as your investment objective. Comparing a balanced portfolio of 25% smallcap stocks, 45% largecap stocks, and 30% corporate and government bonds with the S&P 500 Index is like comparing apples to oranges. More logically, you should compare the return of the smallcap stocks with the Russell 2000 or the S&P Small-Cap 600, the largecap stocks with the S&P 500, and the bonds with the Lehman Brothers Government/Corporate Index. Be aware that it is difficult for actively managed portfolios to beat their comparable indices for the following reasons.

- An index does not have transaction costs. The obvious cost is commissions, but there are also less apparent trading costs, such as the spread. The spread is the difference between the bid and asked prices of a stock. A stock quoted at 20 by 20 1/8 means that a seller will sell for $20.00, a buyer will buy for $20.125, and the market maker will pocket

$0.125. If you bought and sold this stock when there was no movement in its price, you would lose $0.125 per share. Another cost is the effect of large transactions on market prices. The increase in demand caused by a large purchase order can drive up the price of a stock. Conversely, excess supply created by large sales orders drives down the price in a large sale.

- An index has no management fees. Both mutual funds and money managers charge a fee for their services, and the fee is generally deducted from total returns.
- Indices are not taxed. If you are paying taxes on income and capital gains out of your investment portfolio, your after-tax return will be significantly less than your pretax return.

The third way to use indices is to invest in them. You can invest in an index in two ways. One is through a mutual fund that tracks a particular index. These funds, described in detail in Chapter 12, purchase all the stocks in an index or a representative sampling of them. Another option is a relatively recent innovation in index investing, called index shares. Index shares are unit investment trusts that trade like a stock. The primary advantage of index shares over mutual funds is that they can be purchased and sold throughout the trading day. Open-end mutual funds can only be purchased or sold at the day's-end net asset value. In turbulent market times when it is not uncommon to see the DJIA move 200 points in one day, interday trading can be a real advantage. Some examples of index shares follow.

NASDAQ 100 Index Tracking Stock (symbol QQQ): Index shares based on the NASDAQ 100 Index and traded on the American Stock Exchange. Figure 4–4 shows a price performance graph of QQQ, whose nickname is Cubes.

Standard & Poor's Depositary Receipts (SPDRs) (symbol SPY): Known as spiders, SPDRs invest in the companies of the S&P 500 and trade on the American Stock Exchange.

MidCap SPDRs—Standard & Poor's MidCap 400 (symbol MDY): Index shares based on the S&P MidCap 400. Also traded on the Amex.

Diamonds (symbol DIA): An index that tracks the Dow Jones Industrial Average, designed to approximate 1/100 of the market value of the DJIA. Diamonds are traded on the Amex.

World Equity Benchmark Shares (WEBS) (various symbols): A series of country-specific index shares which track the country indices of Morgan

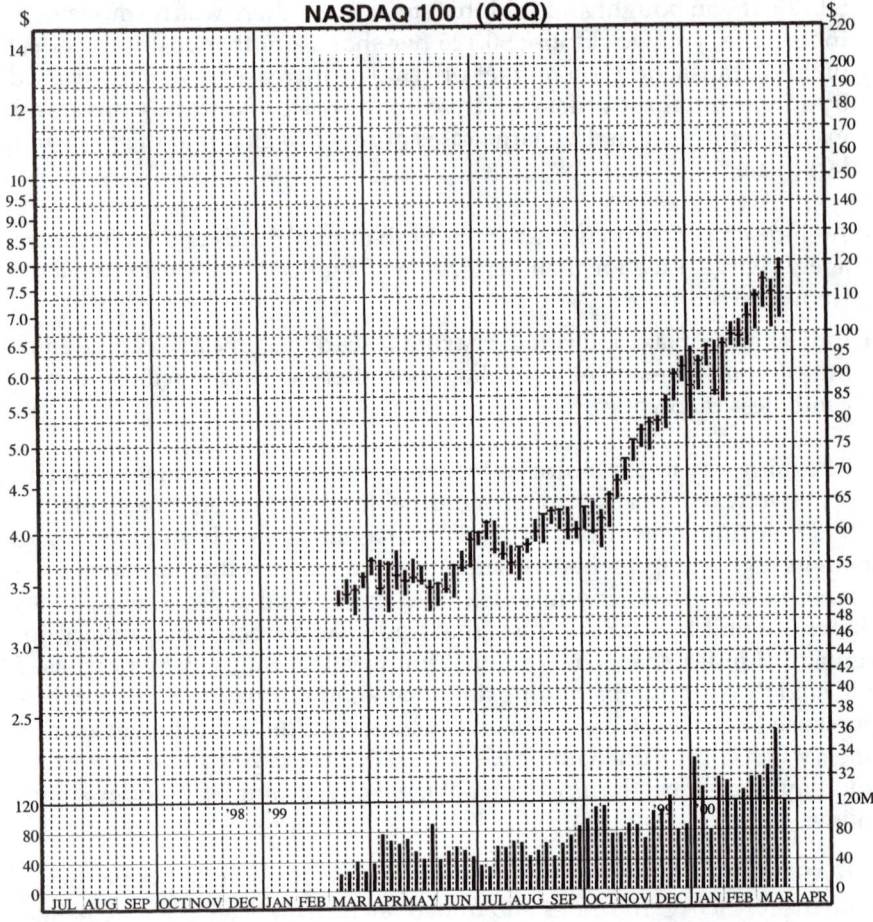

Figure 4–4. Price Performance of QQQ: March 1999 to March 2000

SOURCE: Chart courtesy of Securities Research Company, 400 Talcott Avenue, Watertown, MA 02472.

Stanley Capital International (MSCI). The shares are traded in U.S. dollars on the American Stock Exchange. The WEBS currently available are listed in Table 4–13.

For more information about index shares, visit the NASDAQ website, *www.nasdaq.com.* You can reach the index shares section by clicking on it at the bottom of the home page.

Table 4–13. World Equity Benchmark Securities (WEBS)

Country Tracked	WEBS Symbol
Australia	EWA
Austria	EWO
Belgium	EWK
Canada	EWC
France	EWQ
Germany	EWG
Hong Kong	EWH
Italy	EWI
Japan	EWJ
Malaysia (Free)	EWM
Mexico (Free)	EWW
The Netherlands	EWN
Singapore (Free)	EWS
Spain	EWP
Sweden	EWD
Switzerland	EWL
United Kingdom	EWU

Appendix: Performance of Various U.S. Industry Sector Indices

The following charts from StockMaster.com provide relative performance of different industry sectors.

Figure A4–1. Airline Index (I:XAL)
as of Tuesday, July 25, 2000

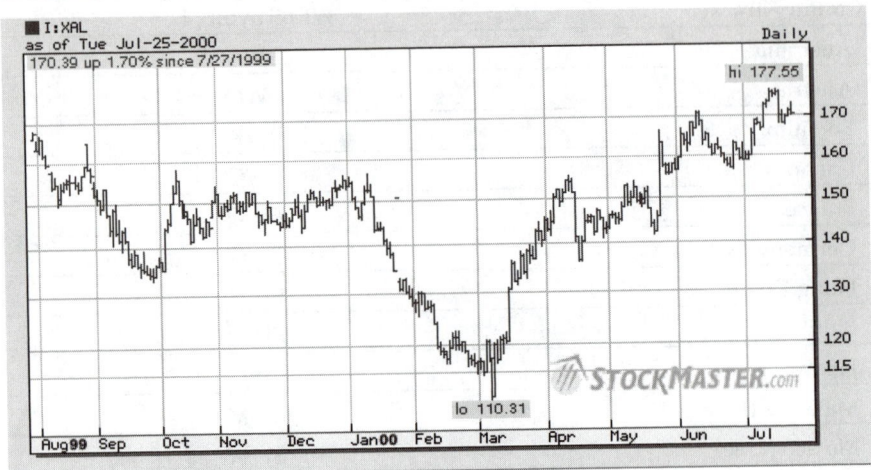

©2000 StockMaster.com

Figure A4–2. Automotive Index (I:AUX)
as of Tuesday, July 25, 2000

S&P 500
Daily

©2000 StockMaster.com

Figure A4–3. S&P Bank Index (I:BIX)
as of Tuesday, July 25, 2000

S&P 500
Daily

Figure A4–4. Biotechnology Index (I:BTK)
as of Tuesday, July 25, 2000

S&P 500
Daily

Figure A4–5. Broker/Dealer Index (I:XBD) as of Tuesday, July 25, 2000

S&P 500
Daily

Figure A4–6. S&P Chemicals Index (I:CEX) as of Tuesday, July 25, 2000

S&P 500
Daily

Figure A4–7. Morgan Stanley Consumer Index (I:CMR) as of Tuesday, July 25, 2000   S&P 500 Daily

Figure A4–8. Morgan Stanley Cyclical Index (I:CYC) as of Tuesday, July 25, 2000   S&P 500 Daily

Figure A4–9. Financial Index (I:IXF)
as of Tuesday, July 25, 2000

S&P 500
Daily

Figure A4–10. Gaming Index (I:GAX)
as of Tuesday, July 25, 2000

S&P 500
Daily

Figure A4–11. Gold and Silver Index (I:XAU) as of Tuesday, July 25, 2000

S&P 500 Daily

Figure A4–12. S&P Health Care Index (I:HCX) as of Tuesday, July 25, 2000

S&P 500 Daily

Figure A4–13. Morgan Stanley High-Tech
35 Index (I:MSH) as of Tuesday, July 25, 2000

S&P 500
Daily

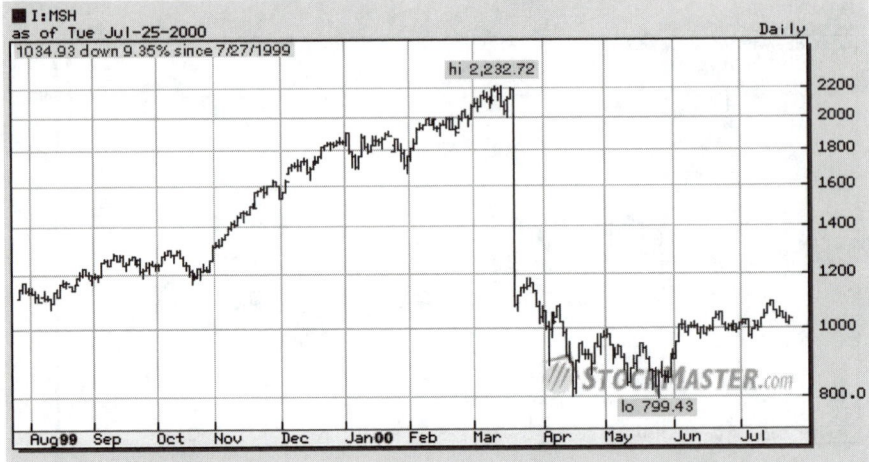

©2000 StockMaster.com

Figure A4–14. Inter@ctive Week Internet Index (I:IIX)
as of Tuesday, July 25, 2000

S&P 500
Daily

©2000 StockMaster.com

Figure A4–15. Oil and Gas Index (I:XOI)
as of Tuesday, July 25, 2000

S&P 500
Daily

Figure A4–16. Pharmaceutical Index (I:DRG)
as of Tuesday, July 25, 2000

S&P 500
Daily

Figure A4–17. S&P Retail Index (I:RLX) as of Tuesday, July 25, 2000

S&P 500
Daily

©2000 StockMaster.com

Figure A4–18. Telecommunications Index (I:IXTC) as of Tuesday, July 25, 2000

S&P 500
Daily

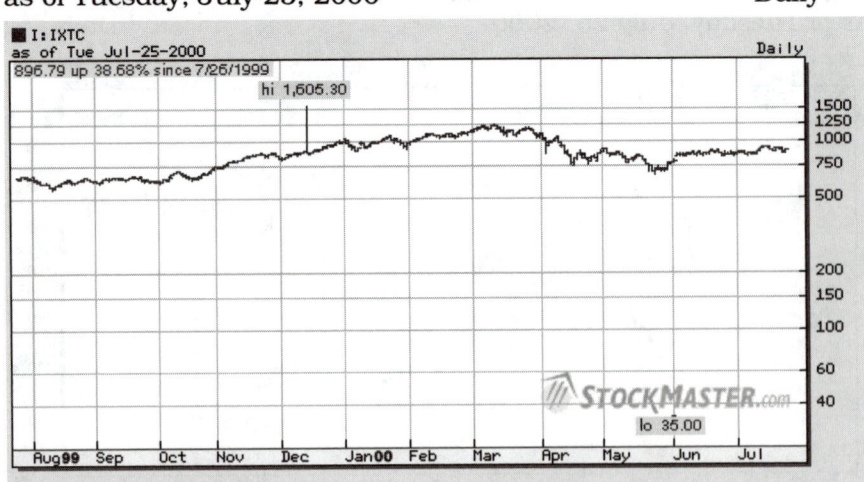

©2000 StockMaster.com

Figure A4–19. S&P Transportation Index (I:TRX) as of Tuesday, July 25, 2000

S&P 500 Daily

Figure A4–20. CBOE Technology Index (I:TXX) as of Tuesday, July 25, 2000

S&P 500 Daily

Part 2
Investment Concepts

Before spending a single dollar, each investor should be familiar with some tried and true investment concepts, discussed in the chapters of Part 2. Primary is the risk/reward tradeoff, which states that investment risk and expected return always go together. Chapter 5 outlines this truism and offers strategies for managing different types of investment risk. In Chapter 6, investing to reach a goal is presented, with a detailed discussion of retirement and college funding. Chapter 7 provides calculations and interpretations of formulas used in investing.

5
Managing Investment Risk

The number-one reason why individuals invest too conservatively or do not invest at all is fear of losing money. A healthy respect for the dangers of financial markets is essential to investing, but too much fear, often driven by a lack of understanding, can be debilitating. The key to investing is not avoiding risk, but managing it intelligently.

Types of Investment Risk

Business Risk

Business risk is the financial risk inherent in a particular company. Components of business risk include fluctuations in sales, cash flow, and earnings due to any multitude of causes, including poor management, economic downturns, or a highly competitive environment. The most extreme result of business risk is bankruptcy of the company in which investors receive partial or no payment of interest and principal on bonds and find their common stock worthless.

Investments subject to business risk are those based on corporations, such as common and preferred stocks and corporate bonds. Business risk may also be applied to municipal bonds, since the revenues of a municipality or a particular public project support payments of interest and principal. In a discussion about diversification, business risk is sometimes used to identify the risk of an individual security, regardless if it is based on a corporation.

There are two ways to guard a portfolio against business risk. The first measure applies whether a person has a single investment or 100 investments: Invest in financially stable companies with good records of increasing revenues, cash flow, and earnings. Watch for management that is able to meet new challenges and is willing to invest in new products for the future. The second way to guard against business risk is to diversify a portfolio. This technique is discussed in the next section.

Financial Risk

Financial risk relates to the level of debt used to finance a company. High levels of debt come with high obligations for principal and interest repayment. When business is good, these obligations may not be a burden, but there is risk that what would not ordinarily be a devastating downturn can cause insolvency for a company with large debt payments. Additionally, companies with bonds or bank loans, whose rates float with the prime or other interest rates, may be subject to huge increases in debt costs if interest rates increase. As with business risk, the most extreme result of financial risk is bankruptcy of the company.

Investments subject to financial risk are those based on corporations, such as common and preferred stocks and corporate bonds. Because financial risk is narrower than business risk, it may be easier to spot investments in danger by using financial ratios such as debt-to-equity or interest coverage ratios. In general, lower debt means less financial risk; however, some industries tend to be highly leveraged. Concern about financial risk should not necessarily keep you from investing, but should aid in comparing the relative risks of different investments. Compare financial ratios of a company to others in its industry and to industry averages to get a feel for relative financial risk.

Market Risk

Market risk is the result of momentum in the securities markets. These movements, or trends, are generally the result of changes in economic, political, or social conditions, or investor preferences. In many cases, though the business and financial risks and other prospects for a business do not change, market trends will affect the price of a security, sometimes drastically.

Nearly all marketable investments are subject to market risk. Stocks are subject to the market risk of the general stock market and to the current trend in investing styles, whether it is growth versus value or small versus large-company stocks. Bonds are subject to market risk, insofar as they may be sold prior to maturity, and market conditions can affect principal values at the time of sale. Investments in real estate and hard assets are subject to trends involving what is in and out of favor with the investment community as well.

Predicting the effect of market risk on a security is tricky, because it involves first predicting the volatility of a particular market and then its effect on the security. Beta is often used to predict movements in a stock's price based on movements in the stock market. It works like this: The beta of the stock market is 1.00. A stock with a beta above 1.00 will be expected to move more intensely than the market, in either direction. A beta of 1.5 predicts a 1.5% stock price movement for every 1.00% market movement, either up or down. Stocks with betas below 1.00 will be less volatile than the market. For example, a stock with a 0.85 beta should move 0.85% for every 1.00% market move. Though some in the investment community argue that beta cannot predict as it is simply derived from past price movements, it is still widely used in discussions of stock price volatility.

Purchasing Power or Inflation Risk

Purchasing power or inflation risk occurs when the dollars earned in interest or dividends and the principal returned on an investment have less purchasing power than those originally invested. In periods of rising prices, called inflation, it takes more money each year to purchase the same amount of goods and services. An investment that returns 5% during a period of 5% inflation essentially breaks even. The $0.05 in income plus $1.00 return of capital gives an investor $1.05 at the end of one year. With 5% inflation, it takes $1.05 to purchase what $1.00 would buy a year ago. Inflation any higher than the stated (nominal) investment return results in a real loss of purchasing power.

Investments subject to purchasing power risk are those that return a fixed amount of principal and provide a fixed return. These investments include bonds, certificates of deposit, and even cash on hand—anything whose principal is not expected to grow or whose income does not fluctuate with inflation or market interest rates. Also included to some extent are preferred stocks, which may increase in value but whose dividend rates are often fixed.

To the extent that some fixed-income investments (including cash) should be a part of every investment portfolio, a certain amount of purchasing power risk is unavoidable. Excessive purchasing power risk is most often seen in portfolios of the highly risk averse, those who are retired or who are otherwise living on the income from their investments. Fearing any kind of loss of principal which might occur in a growth investment, these investors maintain their principal in dollar terms, but often not in purchasing power. Table 5–1 illustrates what $1.00 could purchase after different time periods at various rates of inflation.

Interest Rate Risk

Interest rate risk is the risk that interest rates will change after the purchase of an investment. Any investment purchased for its income stream is subject

Table 5–1. The Purchasing Power of $1.00

Years	Inflation Rate					
	2%	3%	4%	6%	8%	10%
5	$0.91	$0.86	$0.82	$0.75	$0.68	$0.62
6	0.88	0.84	0.79	0.70	0.63	0.56
7	0.87	0.81	0.76	0.65	0.58	0.51
8	0.85	0.79	0.73	0.63	0.54	0.47
9	0.84	0.77	0.70	0.59	0.50	0.42
10	0.82	0.74	0.68	0.56	0.46	0.39
15	0.74	0.64	0.56	0.42	0.32	0.24
20	0.67	0.55	0.46	0.31	0.21	0.15
25	0.61	0.48	0.38	0.23	0.15	0.09
30	0.55	0.41	0.31	0.17	0.10	0.06
35	0.50	0.36	0.25	0.13	0.07	0.04
40	0.45	0.31	0.21	0.10	0.05	0.02
45	0.41	0.26	0.17	0.07	0.03	0.01
50	0.37	0.23	0.14	0.05	0.02	0.01

to interest rate risk. Included are bonds, marketable certificates of deposit, and stocks purchased mainly for their dividends. The two types of interest rate risk are risk to principal and reinvestment rate risk.

Risk to principal is the primary concern of interest rate risk. When interest rates rise, the prices of fixed-income investments fall, because investors have a choice between newly issued investments with higher rates of return or existing investments with lower rates of return. For the yield on these investments to be comparable, the price of lower-rate investments must fall. (For more discussion on this topic, see Chapter 9.) Risk to principal is not a problem for any investment with a fixed maturity date and price, as long as the investor does not need to sell it before maturity when the market value has fallen. It can be more of a problem with stocks purchased for their income or with income-oriented mutual funds which do not have a promised face value since they can remain below their purchase price indefinitely.

Reinvestment rate risk is an issue for income investors who make plans assuming that the income received from their investments can be reinvested at a particular rate, or that their principal, when it comes due, can be reinvested at similar rates. If interest rates fall, reinvestment of income may bring lower returns. More significantly for those who depend on the income from their investments, falling interest rates can reduce the amount of income received when certificates of deposit or bonds must be renewed or reinvested. For example, a $500,000 bond portfolio with an 8% average coupon rate would produce income of $40,000 per year. Reinvesting the bonds when they mature at an average rate of 6% decreases annual income to $30,000.

Liquidity Risk

Liquidity risk is the risk that an investment cannot be sold quickly at a reasonable price. In the event that you would need to raise cash for an emergency, selling investments with liquidity risk can cause significant losses in principal.

An investment with a promised maturity date and penalty for early withdrawal, such as a certificate of deposit, has liquidity risk, as do investments with high surrender charges, such as annuities and some mutual funds. Most stocks and bonds traded on major exchanges do not have liquidity risk, but stocks of very small companies or those with a small number of shares outstanding (referred to as thinly traded) may. A sell order for such a stock may be executed at a price much lower than the current market quote due to lack of buyers. Real estate, depending on its location, is usually quite illiquid.

Avoiding liquidity risk is as simple as keeping enough invested in liquid securities to cover an emergency. A good rule of thumb is six months' living expenses held in liquid investments.

Event Risk

Event risk is the risk of a single, unexpected event that would have a major impact on a company's financial condition. The impact may be an obvious negative, such as the FDA ban on silicone breast implants and the subsequent class-action lawsuits for Dow Corning; or the event may simply be a cloud over the share price, due to unknown outcomes, such as the U.S. government lawsuit against Microsoft.

Reducing Risk through Diversification

The best way to reduce exposure to any of the risks listed is through diversification, a term for not putting all your eggs into one basket. Diversification means buying many different securities to reduce the risk of any specific security. For example, if you invest $1,000 and the value of your investment drops by 50%, you will lose $500. If you invest $1,000 but divide it into two investments, one of which drops by 50%, you will lose $250. If you invest $1,000 but divide it into four investments, one of which drops by 50%, you will lose only $125 (see Table 5–2). This method of dividing your investment dollars reduces the effect of a catastrophe on your portfolio.

Statistically, you can reduce your business risk to nearly zero by investing in the stocks of 15 different companies. However, because you have a portfolio of common stocks, it may still be affected by market risk (see Figure 5–1).

Reducing the other types of risk through diversification means purchasing not only different stocks, but also stocks in different industries with different levels of debt, and purchasing different types of investments such as bonds, which will not all be vulnerable to the same types of risk. Ideally, by diversifying across industries and across investment products, you will see that the performance of different investments may even have an inverse relationship. In other words, when one does poorly, another

Table 5–2. Reducing Risk through Diversification

Invest	#1 Loses 50%	#2 No Change	#3 No Change	#4 No Change	Total Loss
$1,000	−$500				−$500
$500/$500	−$250	−$0			−$250
$250/$250/$250/$250	−$125	−$0	−$0	−$0	−$125

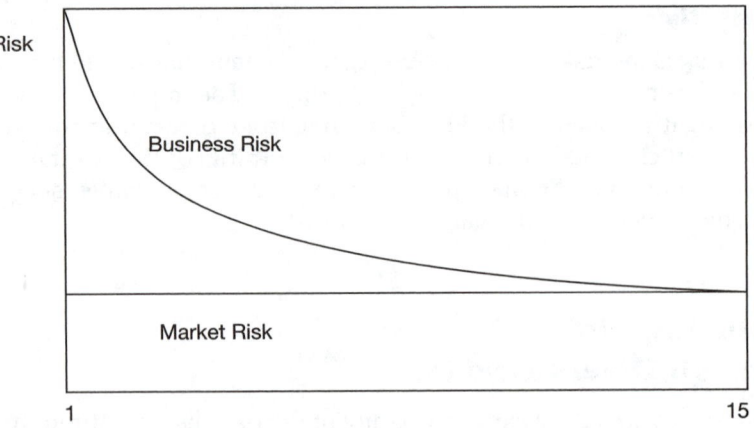

Figure 5–1. Business Risk, Market Risk, and Diversification

U.S. GOVERNMENT LAWSUIT AGAINST MICROSOFT

In a case that has lasted nearly a decade, the U.S. government's investigation of Microsoft has placed a dark cloud over the company's future. Beginning in 1990, the Federal Trade Commission investigated possible collusion between Microsoft and IBM. By 1998, after several years of wrangling over a consent decree that required the unbundling of Windows 95 and Internet Explorer, the Department of Justice and 19 states filed antitrust charges alleging that Microsoft used its market power to thwart competition.

In a December 1999 "finding of fact," U.S. District Judge Thomas Penfield Jackson stated that Microsoft was a monopoly which had harmed consumers and hindered innovation. Few were surprised when, on April 3, 2000, Judge Jackson ruled that Microsoft unlawfully tied its Internet Explorer web browser to its operating system in an effort to impede competition from Netscape Communications software.

As punishment, announced June 7, 2000, Judge Penfield ordered the giant software firm split into two pieces—one that makes Windows and another that produces applications such as Microsoft Office. As of this writing, Microsoft has appealed.

Prospects for the company and its stock remain uncertain as appeals are expected to last another year. Including a drop of over $15 on April 3, 2000, shares of Microsoft have fallen from a high of $119 at the beginning of 2000 to a low of $60 before rebounding to the low $70s in August 2000.

---

does well. For example, real estate and bond prices tend to move in opposite directions in times of high inflation and interest rates. Interest rate and inflation risk cause bond prices to fall, but inflation risk sends investors out of many investments into hard assets, such as real estate, sending those prices up. Statistically, the tendency for investment total returns to move together is called cross correlation. A cross correlation of 1.00 means the two investments move exactly in tandem. A low number means they do not tend to move together, and a negative number means that the two returns move in opposite directions. According to Ibbotson Associates' 1999 Yearbook, *Stocks, Bonds, Bills and Inflation,*[1] over the period 1926 to 1998, large-company stocks and small-company stocks had a cross correlation of 0.79. Large-company stocks had low correlations with long-term corporate bonds, long-term government bonds, intermediate-term government bonds, and U.S. Treasury bills, ranging from 0.12 for U.S. Treasury bills and increasing with the length of bond maturity to 0.32 for long-term corporate bonds. Small-company stocks showed little to negative correlations

---

[1] Ibbotson Associates, *Stocks, Bonds, Bills, and Inflation 1999 Yearbook,* Table 6-5, Serial and Cross Correlations of Historical Annual Returns, 130.

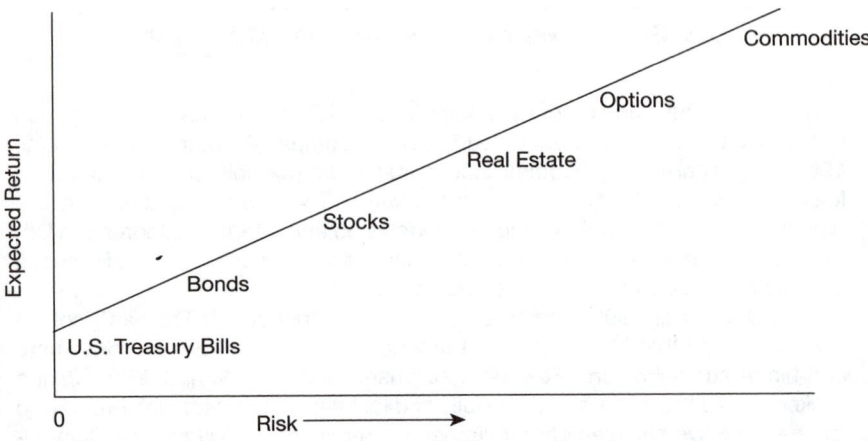

Figure 5–2. Risk-Return Relationship

with bonds, with a −0.06 correlation for U.S. Treasury bills increasing with bond maturity to 0.13 for long-term corporate bonds. Bonds generally showed high correlations with each other, especially in the intermediate- and long-term maturities (0.94 and above). Inflation had a negative correlation with all asset classes reviewed. Stocks were mildly negative at −0.08 for small-company stocks and −0.23 for large-company stocks, while bonds were all highly negative, at −0.54 to −0.75.

The Risk-Return Relationship

The amount of risk associated with an investment is directly related to its expected total return. This universal rule of investing means that if you want a higher level of return on your investment, then you will have to take more risk to get it. By the same token, if you are willing to take a higher level of risk, you should expect to be compensated by earning a higher rate of return. Figure 5–2 illustrates the risk-return relationship of various investment classes. Generally in an efficient market, most investments fall somewhere on the line and the hierarchy of assets is roughly as pictured. If you are promised investment results that vary greatly from the line depicted, such as very high expected return with low risk, then question the guarantees and the guarantor.

In addition to knowing intuitively that risk and expected return are related, you can measure the risk of investments numerically by equating volatility in total returns with risk. Standard deviation is a statistical measure of past volatility. It measures the extent to which numbers (in this case, total returns) differ from the arithmetic mean (average) of the series. The standard deviation has more meaning when you know that normally two-thirds of the returns will lie within one standard deviation of the mean. Ibbotson Associates tracks the standard deviations of five classes of investments, plus inflation from 1926 to 1998 in its 1999 Yearbook, *Stocks, Bonds, Bills and Inflation*.[2] According to Ibbotson, large- and small-company stocks have been more volatile than long-term corporate bonds, long-term government bonds, intermediate-term government bonds, U.S. Treasury bills, and inflation in each of the eight decades measured. For example, when comparing the volatility of large-company stocks with Treasury bills in the 1990s, two-thirds of the time the return on large-company stocks was within a 31.8% (+/−15.9% standard deviation) range while the return on Treasury bills varied by only 1% (+/−0.5% standard deviation). In each decade measured, the standard deviation of small-company stocks exceeded that of large-company stocks, but in the last two decades (1980s and 1990s) the margin of difference was relatively small. The annualized monthly standard deviation for small-company stocks was 22.5% and 18.9% for the 1980s and 1990s, respectively. For large-company stocks, it was 19.4% and 15.9%, respectively.

Although risk and real return do not correlate exactly (remember that risk and *expected* return always go together), there is an obvious relationship between the volatility of total returns as measured by standard deviation and actual annualized total returns. An Ibbotson Associates study[3] of compound annual rates of return by decade shows very few instances in which an asset class does not outperform other asset classes whose standard deviations are lower for the decade. Notable exceptions include the superior performance of large-company stocks over small-company stocks in the 1980s and 1990s, and the poor performance of large-company stocks in the 1970s as compared with bonds.

Asset Allocation

The concept of asset allocation, which seeks to diversify investments across asset classes, melds what is known about investment volatility, cross correlation, and the benefits of diversification. By combining asset classes that react differently to the same market conditions, asset allocation seeks to maximize returns while lowering volatility.

Most asset allocation models separate investors by age and stage of life or by risk tolerance. In 99 *Great Answers to Everyone's Investment Questions*, the Moneywise Partners divide life into four stages:[4]

1. Getting started—the first years of financial independence
2. Getting growing—buying a house, raising children

---

[2]Ibid., Table 6-1, Change in the Risk of Assets over Time, 112.

[3]Ibid., Table 1-1, Compound Annual Rates of Return by Decade, 19.

[4]Linda Bryant, Diane Pearl, and Ellie Williams, 99 *Great Answers to Everyone's Investment Questions* (Franklin Lakes, N.J.: Career Press, 1993) : 26–27.

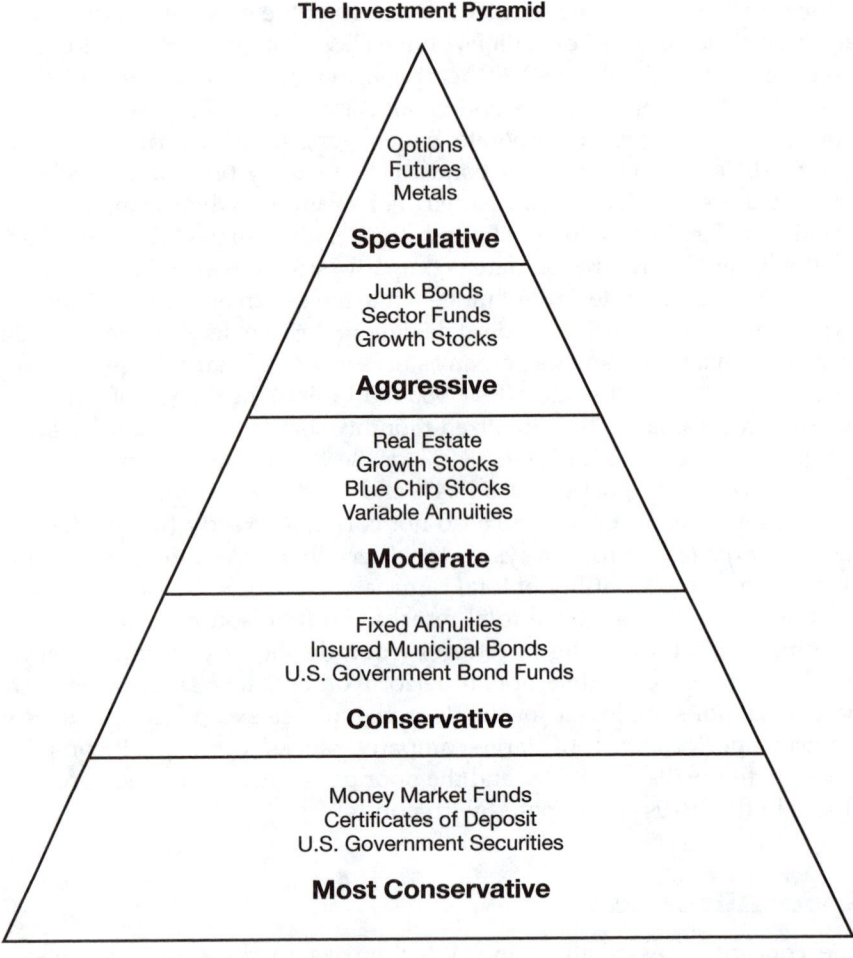

Figure 5–3a. Asset Allocation Using the Investment Pyramid and Four Financial Stages of Life

SOURCE FOR FIGURES 5–3a TO e: Linda Bryant, Diane Pearl, and Ellie Williams, *99 Great Answers to Everyone's Investment Questions* (Franklin Lakes, N.J.: Career Press, 1993).

3. Getting comfortable—high earning years and empty nest
4. Taking it easy—retirement

They provide recommended asset allocations for each stage based on a five-level investment pyramid in which expected return and risk increase with each level up the pyramid (see Figures 5–3a to e).

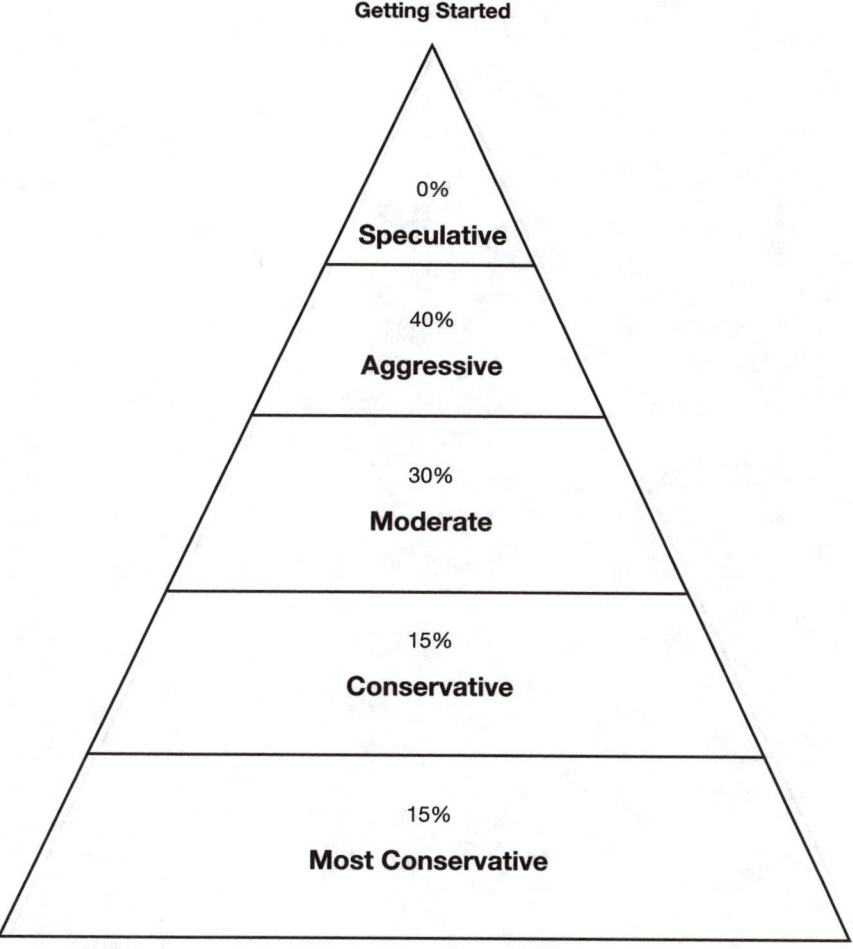

Figure 5–3b. Asset Allocation—Getting Started

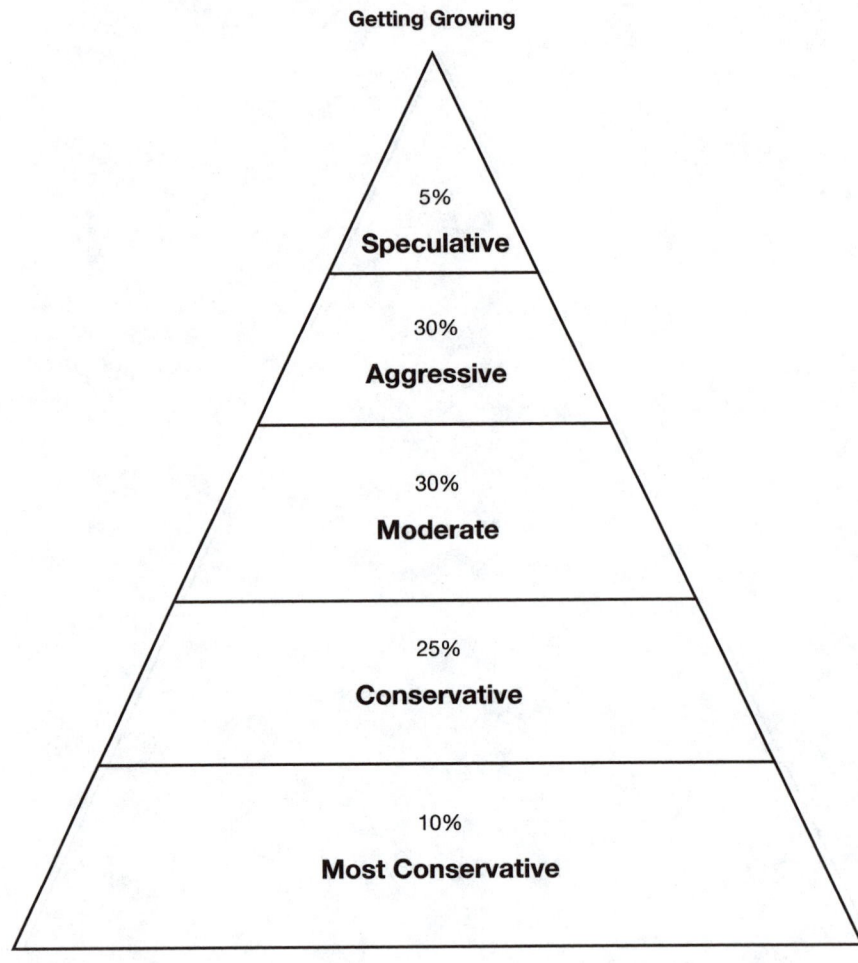

Figure 5–3c. Asset Allocation—Getting Growing

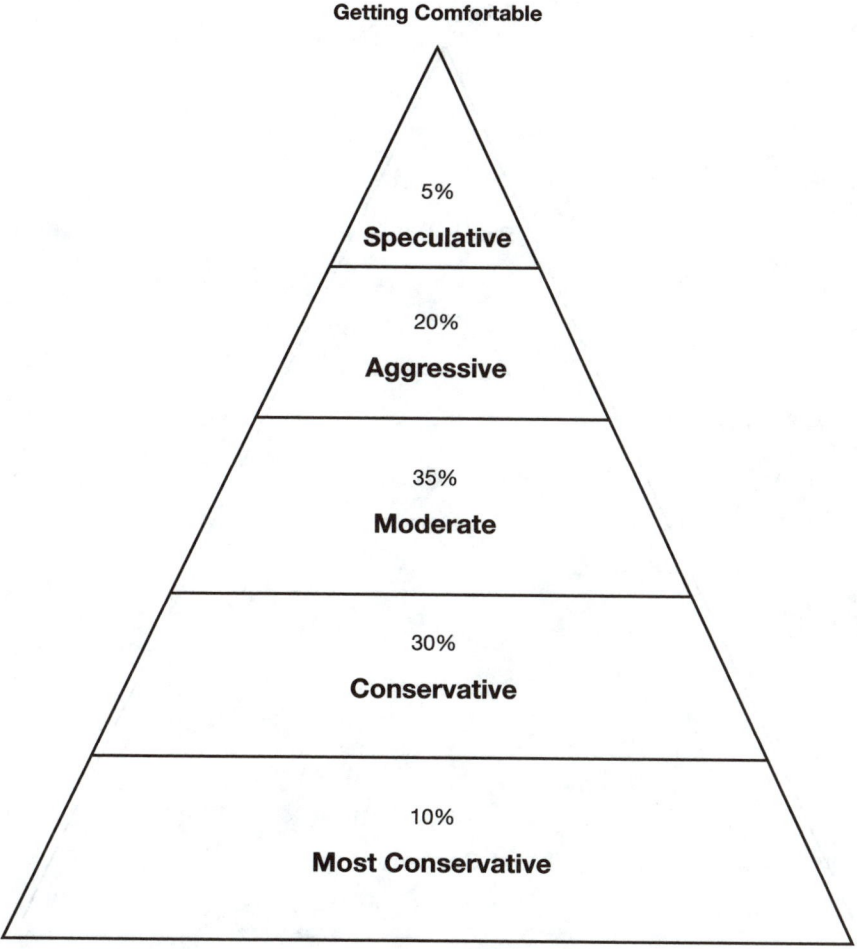

Figure 5–3d. Asset Allocation—Getting Comfortable

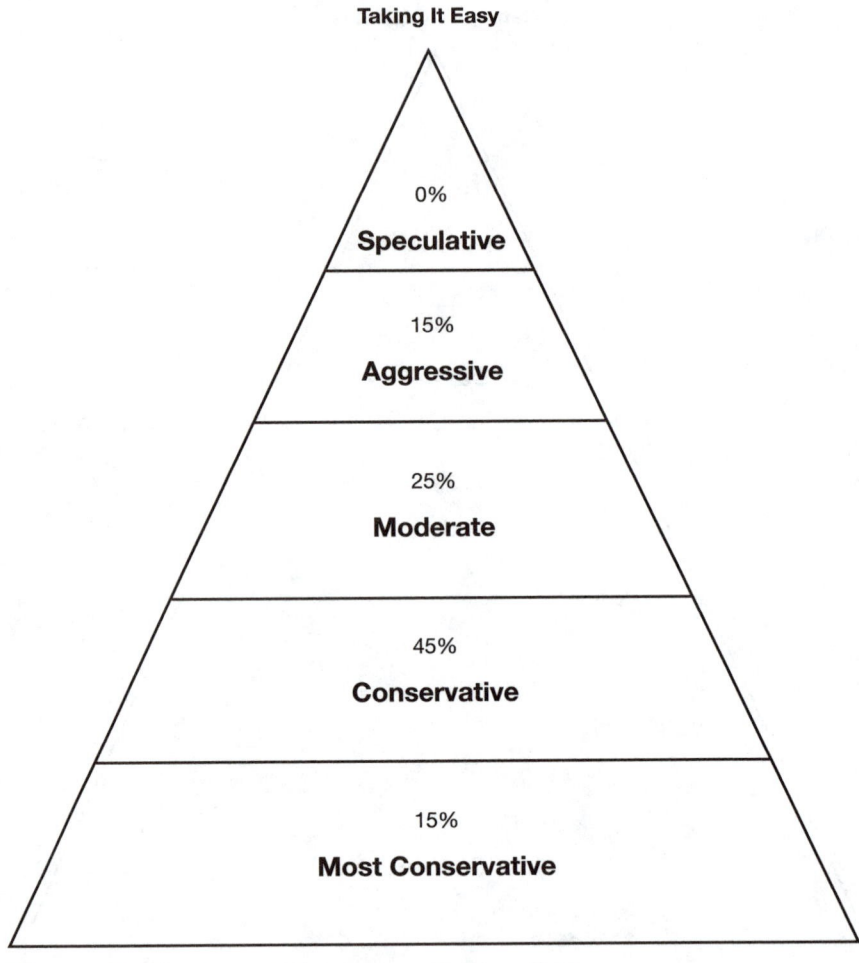

Taking It Easy

0%
Speculative

15%
Aggressive

25%
Moderate

45%
Conservative

15%
Most Conservative

Figure 5–3e. Asset Allocation—Taking It Easy

Another example of asset allocation might be to divide investors by risk tolerance into those seeking growth, balanced, or conservative investments as shown in Figures 5–4a to c.

It is important to consider the following when using asset allocation models.

- A range of + or –5% for each asset class is expected.
- Consider your own risk tolerance before strictly following a one-size-fits-all guide.

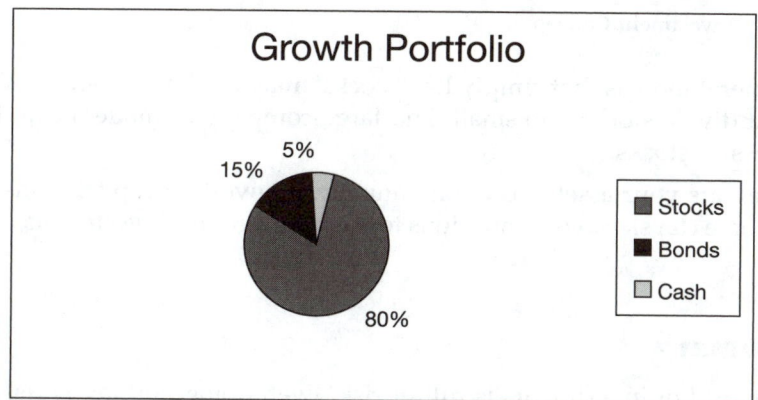

Figure 5–4a. Asset Allocation by Risk Tolerance (Growth)

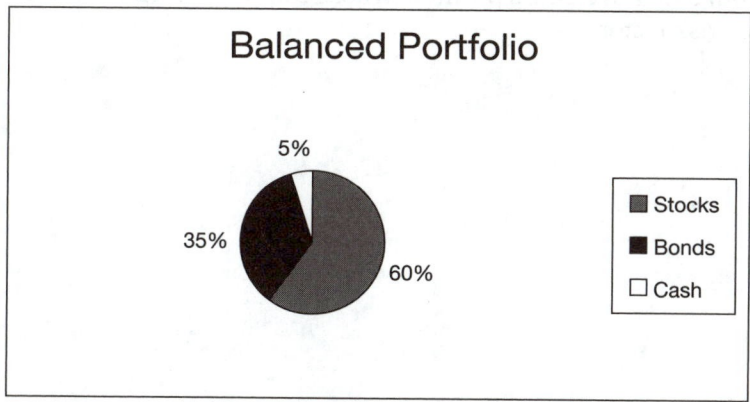

Figure 5–4b. Asset Allocation by Risk Tolerance (Balanced)

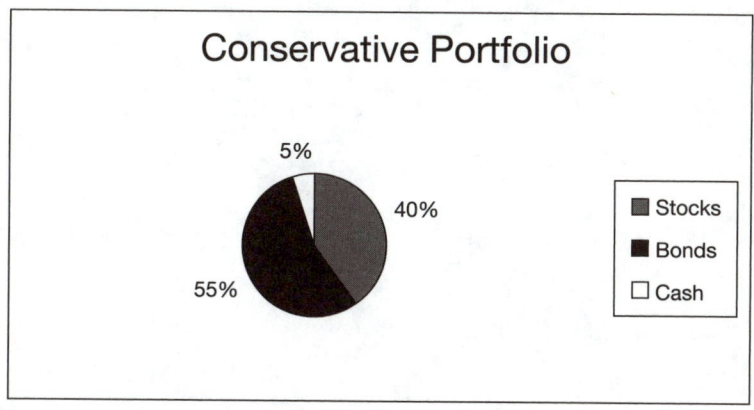

Figure 5–4c. Asset Allocation by Risk Tolerance (Conservative)

- General models that simply list "stocks" may not be as useful as those that divide stocks into small- and large-company or moderate and aggressive stocks.
- Evaluate your asset allocation annually. Reinvesting capital gains and income can skew concentrations toward high-return investments.

Summary

The world of investments is full of risk. Even doing nothing is risky, as funds left uninvested are exposed to the risk of inflation. The key to managing risk is being able to identify its sources and then diversify and allocate your assets to create a portfolio whose components react differently to various risk factors.

6

Investing for Special Purposes: Retirement and College Funding

Successful investing does not begin with choosing investments. It starts with getting a complete picture of what you have: all your investment accounts, your checking and savings accounts, retirement plans, and a clear idea of monthly income and expenses. The next step, before choosing the right investments, is to set goals—decide what you want your money to do for you. Those goals may include funding the purchase of a new home, paying for college educations, providing a comfortable retirement, or just setting aside an emergency fund. You may have several different goals, in which case you will want to segregate your assets and treat each subset accordingly. Set time horizons for each goal, because the long- or short-term nature of investments significantly affects the vehicles chosen. Then, unless you have unlimited funds, set priorities for your different goals. For example, many families are saving for retirement and children's college educations simultaneously. Never slight your retirement savings for education funds. If you run short on money for college, there are grants, loans, work-study programs, and a myriad of other ways to make up the difference. Such options are not available for retirees, who may or may not be able to continue to work.

Investing to Reach a Dollar Goal

You may be planning to buy a house, considering vacation property, or just looking to build a nest egg. No matter what the reason, going from zero to a large sum of money can be intimidating. This is where investment re-

Table 6-1. Reaching a Savings Goal at 5%

Savings Goal	At 5% Save This Much Each Month For		
	2 Years	5 Years	10 Years
$2,000	$79	$30	$13
5,000	199	74	32
10,000	397	147	65
20,000	794	294	129
30,000	1,191	441	193
40,000	1,588	588	258
50,000	1,985	735	322
75,000	2,978	1,102	483
100,000	3,971	1,471	644
200,000	7,941	2,941	1,288

turns and compounding come in. To save $20,000 by saving $1,000 per year would take 20 years if you deposited the first $1,000 at the end of year 1 and kept it all under a mattress. If you deposited each $1,000 in an account earning 6%, it would only take 13.5 years. Part of the difference is due to the 6% interest earned on the money you deposit and part of it is due to the interest earned on interest already earned.

To illustrate, after your first payment of $1,000 has been in the account for a year, you will have interest of $60 on it. This, added to your $1,000, gives you a balance of $1,060, which will in turn earn 6% interest or $63.60 the following year. In this manner, compounding increases the amount of interest you earn each year. Table 6-1 illustrates how much you would need to save each month at 5% in order to reach different savings goals. Table 6-2 undertakes the same illustration at 8%, and Table 6-3 illustrates the ending value of an account in which you saved $2,000 per year, given different rates of return.

These tables illustrate several concepts:

- Even a small amount of money is worth investing, if done regularly.

- The power of compounding is most valuable in long-term investments, so start early.

- A small difference in rate of return can make a large difference in dollars returned, so invest wisely.

Table 6–2. Reaching a Savings Goal at 8%

Savings Goal	At 8% Save This Much Each Month For		
	2 Years	5 Years	10 Years
$2,000	$77	$27	$11
5,000	193	68	27
10,000	386	136	55
20,000	771	272	109
30,000	1,157	408	164
40,000	1,542	544	219
50,000	1,928	680	273
75,000	2,982	1,021	410
100,000	3,856	1,361	547
200,000	7,712	2,722	1,093

Table 6–3. Saving $2,000/Year at Various Rates of Return

Years	Rate of Return				
	4%	6%	8%	10%	12%
5	$11,266	$11,951	$12,672	$13,431	$14,230
10	24,972	27,943	31,291	35,062	39,309
15	41,649	49,345	58,648	69,899	83,507
20	61,938	77,985	98,846	126,005	161,397
25	86,623	116,313	157,909	216,364	298,668
30	116,657	167,603	244,692	361,887	540,585
35	153,197	236,241	372,204	596,255	966,926
40	197,653	328,095	559,562	973,703	1,718,285

Investing for Retirement

How Much Will You Need?

Realistically, there is no way to know how much money you will need in retirement. There are too many variables, including the age at which you retire, how long you will live, your chosen retirement lifestyle, changes in the Social Security system, changes in the taxation of Social Security payments, changes in the Medicare system, the rate of inflation between now and your retirement, and income tax rates when you retire. Therefore, it is difficult to know how much you should be saving now, especially when you throw in the added variable of the return on your investments between now and retirement. Even with all these variables, it is worthwhile to compute how much you will need and how much to save now. Though the figures may not be completely accurate, they can provide a near-term goal and a benchmark to measure your progress.

Retirement Calculators

Your best bet in getting a handle on retirement figures is to try several of the retirement calculators available from investment firms. Many are available online. Be aware that many of the fields include default values which you may want to change. Try the Fidelity Investments calculator at *www.fidelity.com* for a comprehensive look. Click on the explanations for each question to reveal many helpful tips on making estimates. The Putnam Investments website at *www.putnaminv.com* provides results in both numeric and graphic form and gives you the opportunity to change several variables in order to meet your goal. The calculator at *www.quicken.com* considers taxes paid on the funds coming from retirement accounts, which can be a big issue when the bulk of your retirement assets are in 401(k) plans, ordinary IRAs, and annuities. Quicken's results page features a stoplight to tell you whether your current plan will meet your needs; then it lets you solve for certain variables, such as a realistic retirement age, given the other information you have entered.

You can improve the accuracy of your results by using actual figures rather than estimates wherever possible. For example, rather than using an estimate for your future Social Security income, call the Social Security Administration at 1-800-772-1213 for form SSA-7004-PC-OPC, Social Security Statement. Upon receipt of the completed form, the Social Security Administration will send you an estimate of your benefits with the reported earnings used to calculate them. It is important to do this every three years, because in the event that your income was underreported, you have only three years in which to correct the information. If you do not, it becomes part of your permanent record and your benefits will be calculated on an amount of income (and Social Security taxes paid) that is lower than it should be.

Part of the formula for retirement savings is based on the vehicles you use to save, because of the different tax treatments that various retirement vehicles receive. Depending on your situation, you may choose IRAs,

401(k) plans, 403(b) plans, keoghs, or annuities and accounts which are not retirement specific.

Individual Retirement Account

The individual retirement account (IRA) was designed by Congress to provide tax incentives for retirement savings. An ordinary IRA (as opposed to a Roth IRA, discussed in the next section) provides for tax-deferred growth of investments, and in some cases tax deductibility of contributions.

IRA Eligibility and Contribution Limits. If you are under 70.5 years of age, you can contribute a maximum of $2,000 per year to an IRA. You cannot contribute more than you have earned in income, except when spouses file jointly; then a nonearning spouse may contribute up to $2,000 as long as combined contributions do not exceed the earnings of the working spouse.

In an effort to stimulate retirement saving, the House of Representatives passed bill HR 1102 in July 2000. The bill, sponsored by Rep. Rob Portman, R-Ohio, increases maximum IRA contributions to $5,000 from $2,000 and maximum 401(k) contributions to $15,000 from $10,500 this year. However, at this writing, President Clinton had indicated that he would veto the bill.

Contribution Deductibility. For traditional and spousal (the nonearning spouse's) IRAs, you can deduct the full amount of your IRA contribution from your taxable income if neither you nor your spouse participated in a company-sponsored retirement plan, such as a 401(k) plan in the same year.

If you or your spouse contributed to a company-sponsored plan, then you can fully deduct your contribution if you are:

- Single and earned less than $31,000 in 1999; or
- Married, filing jointly, and earned less than $51,000 in 1999.

Contribution deductibility is subject to phaseouts for certain levels of income. This means that as you move from the lower level to the upper level of the range, less of your contribution will be deductible. If you or your spouse contributed to a company-sponsored plan, your contribution will be partially deductible if you are:

- Single and earned between $31,000 and $41,000 in 1999 (Deductibility is reduced by $10 for each $50 in income over $31,000); or
- Married, filing jointly, with joint income between $51,000 and $61,000 for 1999. (Deductibility is reduced $10 for each $50 in income over $51,000.)

You cannot deduct your contribution from taxable income if you contributed to a company-sponsored plan and you are:

- Single and earned over $41,000 in 1999; or
- Married, filing jointly, with joint income over $61,000 in 1999.

Withdrawing from an IRA. All withdrawals from a tax-deductible IRA are taxable as ordinary income. Withdrawals from nondeductible IRAs are taxable only to the extent that they exceed the amount contributed. In other words, only the investment earnings are taxed.

Rules restricting withdrawals from IRAs were designed to encourage their use as vehicles for retirement funding. Unless you meet certain exceptions, money withdrawn from an IRA before you reach the age of 59.5 is subject to a 10% IRS penalty, in addition to any income taxes owed. The exceptions to this rule, the first two of which were added with the Tax Reform Act of 1997, follow:

- The withdrawal will be used to pay for qualified higher education expenses for the taxpayer, the taxpayer's spouse, or any child (including stepchild) or grandchild of the taxpayer or taxpayer's spouse. A child is not required to be a dependent. See Internal Revenue Code 151(c)(3) for a full definition. Eligible expenses include tuition, fees, books, supplies, and other necessary equipment required to attend an eligible postsecondary educational institution. The expenses must be net of any tax-free benefits such as scholarships and grants. IRC 529(e)(3) and IRC 529(e)(5) provide exact IRS definitions of eligible expenses and institutions.

- The withdrawal, up to a lifetime limit of $10,000, will be used for a first-time home purchase. A first-time homebuyer is defined as anyone who has not had an ownership interest in a principal residence during the two-year period ending on the date of acquisition. If married, the homebuyer's spouse must also meet this condition.

- You become disabled as defined by the IRS.

- You die.

- You set up a schedule, based on your life expectancy, to take out substantially equal payments every year for the rest of your life. If you stop taking payments before five years or the age of 59.5, you will owe back penalties plus interest.

- Your unreimbursed medical expenses exceed 7.5% of your adjusted gross income.

- You use the withdrawal to pay for medical insurance while you are unemployed.

- You reinvest (roll over) the money into an IRA or other qualified plan within 60 days.

Rollovers and Transfers. Once you have chosen an IRA custodian, such as a bank, brokerage firm, or mutual fund, you are not locked into that decision for life. At any time, you may perform a custodian-to-custodian transfer, in which the funds are sent from your existing custodian to a new one, and you are never in possession of the funds. There is no limit to the number of transfers allowed and no IRS penalty or tax for a direct transfer; however, certain fees and commissions may be charged by the sending or receiving custodian.

An IRA rollover is a process in which you withdraw funds from an IRA or other qualified retirement plan, take possession of the money, and deposit it into the same or a different IRA. If you accomplish this within the 60-day time limit set by the IRS, you will not incur any taxes or penalties. The same money can only be rolled over once per year.

Required Withdrawals. You are required to begin withdrawals from your IRA by April 1 of the year following the year you turn 70.5. If you do not, the IRS will assess a penalty of 50% on what you should have withdrawn. The amount that you should withdraw is called your required minimum distribution (RMD). The RMD is applied to the aggregate amount of your IRAs and is calculated based on your life expectancy or the combined life expectancies of you and your beneficiary, as explained in IRS Publication 590. You may either calculate it once and continue to use that calculation every year or decide to recalculate it every year. You must make this choice with your initial withdrawal and once it has been made, you cannot change your method.

The Roth IRA

The Roth IRA, named for Senator William Roth of Delaware, is a relatively new (since 1998) wrinkle on retirement investing. There are key differences between ordinary IRAs and Roth IRAs. If you meet the income limits, contributions to an ordinary IRA are tax deductible and withdrawals are taxed as ordinary income. In contrast, contributions to a Roth IRA are never tax deductible; however, withdrawals from a Roth IRA are not taxable if certain conditions are met.

Eligibility Requirements for Contributing to a Roth IRA. To be eligible to make a Roth IRA contribution you must have earned income equal to or greater than the amount of your contribution, which cannot exceed $2,000 per year, less the amount of any contribution to an ordinary IRA. If you are married and filing jointly, either or both spouses can contribute, as long as one spouse has earned income equal to or greater than the combined total contribution. This allows a nonworking spouse to plan for retirement.

There is a limit to the amount of income you may earn and still be eligible to contribute to a Roth IRA. For single taxpayers, you may contribute $2,000 to a Roth IRA if your modified adjusted gross income (MAGI) is less than or equal to $95,000. Eligibility begins to phase out at MAGI of $95,000 and ends at $110,000. To phase out, reduce the allowable Roth IRA contribution by $10 for each $75 in income over $95,000. If you are married and filing jointly, you are eligible for a full $2,000 contribution with income of $150,000 or less. The phaseout begins at $150,000 with a $10 reduction in the allowable contribution for each additional $50 in income. You are completely ineligible at $160,000. For married taxpayers filing separately, the phaseout begins at $0 and ends at $10,000.

Withdrawing from a Roth IRA. Contributions to a Roth IRA can be withdrawn at any time without tax consequences or penalty, but the earnings withdrawn from the account are considered taxable income and may be subject to a 10% penalty if withdrawal requirements are not met. The requirements for tax-free, penalty-free withdrawals are as follows:

1. The Roth IRA has existed for more than five years, *and* either:

   - you are over age 59.5 years, *or*
   - it is for a qualified first-time home purchase (up to a lifetime limit of $10,000).

OR

2. The withdrawal is made due to death or disability.

Withdrawals for qualified higher education expenses (tuition, books, fees, and supplies—net of tax-free assistance such as grants and scholarships) can be made without penalty, but earnings withdrawn are taxable as income. For tax purposes, such withdrawals are treated as if all contributions are withdrawn first. If you have multiple Roth IRAs, but withdraw from just one, contributions to all accounts will be aggregated to determine whether any of the withdrawal is taxable. For example, if you had two Roth IRAs, the first of which had contributions of $4,000 and a market value of $5,500 and the second of which had contributions of $2,000 and a market value of $2,500, then you could withdraw up to $6,000 (the total of your contributions) before incurring any taxes. Even if you withdrew $5,000 from the first IRA—$1,000 more than was contributed to it—you would not owe any income taxes. The mandatory distribution requirement that applies to ordinary IRAs at age 70.5 does not apply to Roth IRAs.

Converting Ordinary IRAs to Roth IRAs. You may convert an ordinary IRA to a Roth IRA if your MAGI is less than or equal to $100,000. This applies to both single and joint filers, and in the case of married persons, they must file jointly to be eligible for conversion. Income taxes apply on the amounts converted, just as if they had been withdrawn from ordinary IRAs (no taxes are due on the contribution amounts from nondeductible IRAs) but the 10% IRS penalty for those under the age of 59.5 does not apply. The amount of the IRAs converted, although it is included in income for tax purposes, is not counted toward the $100,000 income limit for conversion eligibility.

Why convert your ordinary IRA to a Roth IRA? Consider an example in which you are 40 years old, have MAGI of less than $100,000, and have an IRA worth $50,000. Your combined federal and state taxes are 30%. If you convert this year, you will owe $15,000 ($50,000 × 30%) in income taxes. If you can pay the income taxes from other sources, you will have a Roth IRA worth $50,000 but $15,000 less in other assets that would have grown for you. If, over the next 20 years, your investments grow at an average rate of 10%, then the value of your Roth IRA will be $336,375.

The $15,000 paid in taxes would have grown to $100,905, given a 10% annual return. In the best case scenario, all growth would be capital gains, taxed at 20% at the end of 20 years. After paying $20,181 in taxes, the net value of the account would have been $80,724. Deducting the foregone gains on the $15,000 from the ending value of the Roth IRA yeilds a net value of $255,6451 ($336,375 − $80,724 = $255,651).

Compare this with leaving the $50,000 in the ordinary IRA, which, growing at 10%, would also be worth $336,375 after 20 years. Upon withdrawal, you would owe 30% in taxes, or $100,913, making your net $235,462. The advantage to converting to a Roth IRA is $20,189.

	Convert to Roth IRA		Keep ordinary IRA
%50,000 at 10% for 20 years		$336,375	$336,375
Tax on withdrawal		0	(100,913)
Net from IRA		336,375	235,462
Foregone value of $15,000	100,905		
Less 20% CG taxes	(20,181)		
Net foregone value		(80,724)	
Net value realized		255,651	235,462

The key in this example is the ability to pay income taxes with outside funds. This increases the amount deposited in the Roth IRA for tax-free growth and avoids the 10% penalty that would be assessed if you had to use IRA funds to pay the taxes. (Putting less in the Roth IRA than you withdrew from the ordinary IRA would constitute a withdrawal.)

Consider converting your ordinary IRA(s) if the following conditions exist:

- You do not plan to withdraw any IRA funds in the next five years (otherwise you will owe income taxes and possible penalties).
- You can pay the income taxes with outside funds.
- You expect your tax rate in retirement to be the same or higher than it is now.
- You have estate tax problems. Paying taxes on large IRAs now can reduce your taxable estate.
- Your heirs will be in the same or higher tax brackets.
- You would like to avoid mandatory distributions at age 70.5.

To find out whether converting makes sense for you, try one of the Roth IRA calculators at any of the following websites:

www.fidelity.com

www.strong-funds.com

www.vanguard.com

www.troweprice.com

Not all calculators are the same, so try a few before making your decision and read the fine print about the variables included. Make sure that the model includes the opportunity cost of outside funds used to pay taxes or the taxes and possible penalty for using IRA funds to pay taxes. Some calculators consider the fact that you are required to take minimum distributions from an ordinary IRA after age 70.5. Make sure the calculator you use includes this fact if you would prefer not to take IRA distributions (i.e., you have enough in other assets to support yourself). This is a significant advantage of the Roth IRA. If, however, you expect to take distributions in excess of the minimum, make sure the software allows you to input that data. If it uses only the minimum, the Roth will look better than it actually is. Table 6–4 shows the comparison between the ordinary IRA and the Roth IRA.

Simplified Employee Pension IRA

The simplified employee pension IRA (SEP-IRA) is for small businesses and sole proprietors. Contributions to SEP-IRAs are made pretax by the

Table 6–4. Comparing the Roth IRA to an Ordinary IRA

	Ordinary IRA	Roth IRA
Who is eligible?	Anyone under age 70.5 with earned income or whose spouse has earned income. No limit on income amount.	Anyone, regardless of age, whose earned income (MAGI) is below $110,000 for single filers and $160,000 for joint filers. Allowable contributions begin phaseout at $95,000 single and $150,000 joint.
Is the contribution tax deductible?	Yes, if neither spouse has a company-sponsored retirement plan. Income limits apply if you also contribute to a company-sponsored plan.	No.
Other tax benefits	Tax-deferred growth of investments. Taxes on investment growth are not due until withdrawal.	Tax-free growth of investments if the account is open over five years and owner is over 59.5 at withdrawal.
Penalties	Most withdrawals made prior to age 59.5 are subject to a 10% penalty, in addition to income taxes. Exceptions include first-time home purchases and the expenses of higher education.	Contributions may be withdrawn penalty-free at any time. Most other withdrawals prior to age 59.5 (except first-time home purchases and higher education expenses) are subject to a 10% penalty.
Mandatory distributions	Distributions must begin by age 70.5. Amounts are mandated by the IRS based on life expectancy. Noncompliance results in stiff penalties.	No minimum age or distribution amount.

employer and must be made at the same percentage of compensation for all eligible employees. Employer contributions do not reduce your taxable income unless you are a sole proprietor. The rules surrounding SEP-IRAs are the same as those for ordinary IRAs except that the contribution limit is significantly higher. The maximum contribution is the lesser of 15% of total compensation or $30,000.

Savings Incentive Match Plan for Employees IRA

The savings incentive match plan for employees IRA (SIMPLE-IRA) is a tax-deferred retirement plan for sole proprietors and businesses with fewer than 100 employees. The SIMPLE-IRA replaced the salary reduction SEP-IRA (SARSEP-IRA) for plans established on or after January 1, 1997, and in the same way allows employee contributions to the retirement plan.

Employee contributions are made pretax, up to a maximum of $6,000 (1999 rules). Employers can contribute either a 100% match for all employees, up to 3% of each employee's total compensation, or 2% of each employee's compensation regardless of employee contribution, up to a maximum of $3,200 per employee.

Keoghs

Keoghs are retirement plans for self-employed individuals or partners, including those who are incorporated. Keoghs are employer-contribution plans. The two types of Keogh plans, which may be used independently or together, are the profit sharing plan and the money purchase plan. The plans differ in their contribution limits and requirements to contribute every year.

Profit Sharing Plans. The profit sharing plan is the most flexible keogh because it allows you to vary the percentage of income that you contribute each year. You may also choose not to contribute in a given year. The maximum contribution allowed is the lesser of $30,000 or 15% of compensation. The maximum wage base for 1999 was $160,000, making the dollar maximum $24,000 except for circumstances in which key employees may receive more under a formula that integrates Social Security.

Consider a profit sharing plan if your income varies significantly from year to year and you do not want to be committed to an annual contribution.

Money Purchase Plans. Money purchase plans offer higher contribution limits, the lesser of $30,000 or 25% of compensation, but less flexibility. The percentage of each eligible employee's compensation to be contributed is set when the plan is established and cannot be changed each year. Consider a money purchase plan if your income is stable enough that you do not mind committing to an annual contribution and you would like to contribute as much as possible.

Combination Plans. Combining a profit sharing with a money purchase plan provides the most flexibility with the maximum tax deduction. Using two plans, you can establish a money purchase plan with a low required contribution, for example, 10% of employee compensation. In years of low profitability, this would be your only commitment. If you also establish a profit sharing plan, in which contributions are not required, you could choose to contribute more in years of high profitability, up to an additional 15%, not to exceed the $30,000 maximum per employee.

401(k) Plans

Company-sponsored retirement plans such as the 401(k) plan (named for the section of the IRS code which allows it) are fast becoming the primary method of retirement investing for many Americans. In a 401(k) plan, you direct your employer to deduct a percentage of your paycheck and deposit it into an investment account for you. You direct the investment of your funds from a range of investment choices. The amount you contribute is pretax, meaning that you do not pay current income taxes on the portion of your income contributed. In many cases, an employer will match a percentage of contributions with cash or with company stock, providing an immediate return on the money invested.

401(k) Plan Eligibility and Contribution Limits. The IRS does not place limits on personal income and eligibility for participation in 401(k) plans. Individual employer plans may require that you work full time or be employed for a certain amount of time, such as six months or one year, before you are eligible to participate.

The maximum allowable pretax contribution to a 401(k) plan is $10,500 for the tax year 2000. The House of Representatives passed a bill in July 2000 that increases the maximum 401(k) plan contribution to $15,000. As of this writing, the Senate had not voted on the bill and President Clinton had threatened to veto it. If your plan allows it, you may make additional after-tax (nondeductible) contributions. The combined company and personal contribution may not exceed the lesser of $30,000 or 25% of compensation. Other restrictions may apply to a small group of employees designated as "highly compensated."

Withdrawing Money from a 401(k) Plan. 401(k) plans are designed with restrictions similar to an IRA. That is, most distributions made before the age of 59.5 are subject to an IRS penalty of 10% and, as with pretax ordinary IRA contributions, withdrawals are taxable as current income. There are some exceptions to the penalty, including distributions for those who retire at age 55 or older. Required withdrawals must be made by April 1 following the year in which you turn 70.5 unless you are still working for the company that is sponsoring the plan. Then you are not required to begin withdrawals until April 1 of the year following the year in which you retire.

You can generally only withdraw from a 401(k) plan if you are terminated, separated from service, become disabled, or die. In certain instances, known as hardship distributions, you may withdraw funds from the plan; however, this does not alleviate the requirement to pay current income taxes or a penalty if you have not reached age 59.5.

Most plans offer the option of borrowing from your account, typically up to half of the account value, but not more than $50,000. Loans must be paid back within five years. Although this is generally preferable to taking a premature distribution, it can be risky in the instance that you quit or are terminated, as most plans require immediate repayment of the loan.

Leaving Your Job. If you leave your job, you may have two choices with respect to your 401(k) plan account. Some employers will allow you to maintain your existing account with the plan. Others require that you move the funds. If you must move your account, there are two ways to take your distribution:

- Direct transfer
- Distribution to you, subsequently reinvesting in another tax-advantaged account (rollover) or not

The preferred method for taking your distribution is the direct transfer, sometimes called a direct rollover. In this case you choose a custodian, either a new or existing IRA or a new employer's qualified retirement plan, and notify your 401(k) plan custodian to send the funds directly to the new account. There are no taxes or penalties due in this scenario.

If you choose to take your 401(k) distribution yourself, the IRS mandates that your employer withhold 20% of your account balance to pay taxes and penalties. If you are under age 59.5 and do not reinvest the proceeds into an IRA or other qualified account, you will owe current income taxes on the entire predistribution balance of the account, plus a 10% penalty. If you are over 59.5, or meet one of the exceptions, only the current income taxes will be due.

You have the option, after taking the distribution yourself, to avoid taxes and penalties by rolling your distribution over into another IRA or qualified plan. This can get tricky, however, because you will receive only 80% of your account value as your employer was required to withhold 20% for possible taxes and penalties. If you roll over the entire original value of the account, you will receive an IRS refund of the 20% withheld when you file your taxes the following year. In the meantime, you must make up the 20% from other funds in order to roll over the full account value.

For example, if you take distribution on an account worth $200,000, your employer will withhold 20% or $40,000. If you are under 59.5 and do not meet any exceptions, you must roll over a full $200,000 to avoid penalties, meaning that you must come up with $40,000 from other sources until you are reimbursed after filing your taxes. If you cannot, the $40,000 is considered a distribution and you will owe current income taxes and a 10% penalty on it.

There is an exception to the rule that you must pay current income taxes on a 401(k) distribution which applies when your account contains highly appreciated stock of your employer. In this case, upon distribution you owe current income tax only on the cost basis of the stock. When you sell the stock, the difference between its basis and its value on the day of distribution is treated as a long-term capital gain. You must hold it for one year after distribution for any further appreciation to qualify as a long-term gain.

For example, if your 401(k) plan has $200,000 worth of your employer's stock and your cost basis in the stock is $50,000, then you will pay current income taxes on $50,000 if you take a distribution in stock. At a 36% rate, this amounts to $18,000. If you later sell the stock for $200,000, then you will owe 20% capital gains tax on the appreciation of $150,000, for a tax of $30,000. Total taxes paid amount to $48,000. If you had paid at current income tax rates on the entire $200,000 balance it would have cost $72,000.

If you do not have a new employer or are not yet eligible for a new employer's plan, but would like to roll your 401(k) plan account into a new employer's plan at a later date, then open a new IRA for your distribution. The IRA will keep your funds tax protected, and using a new IRA will avoid commingling, which is the term for mixing funds from different sources. If you commingle your 401(k) distribution, you cannot subsequently roll it into another employer's plan.

Summary of 401(k) Plan Benefits

A summary of 401(k) plan benefits includes the following:

- Contributions are made pretax, thus saving current income taxes.
- Investments grow tax deferred.
- Contribution limits are high. The limit for tax year 2000 is $10,500.
- Payroll deduction is convenient and requires less discipline than writing a monthly check.
- Monthly investing results in dollar cost averaging.
- Investments are self-directed, within the limits of the choices offered by the plan.
- Penalties for early withdrawal reinforce the need to maintain a nest egg until retirement.

- Many plans allow loans in certain circumstances and early withdrawals in cases of hardship.

- Company matching provides an additional return, sometimes as much as 50% or 100%.

403(b) Plans

A 403(b) plan is a tax-deferred retirement plan for employees of certain tax-exempt organizations, such as educational institutions, hospitals, and nonprofit organizations. Except for some minor technicalities, 403(b) plans operate in the same way as 401(k) plans.

Annuities

Annuities, covered extensively in Chapter 13, are tax-deferred investment accounts offered by insurance companies. Funds invested are not tax deductible, but growth in the account is tax deferred until it is withdrawn. Similar to other retirement accounts, there is a 10% penalty for withdrawal before you reach age 59.5. Due to the high fees sometimes associated with annuities, consider them only if you are still interested in tax deferral after contributing the maximum allowed to 401(k)s and IRAs. Then invest only in no-load or low-load products.

Choosing Retirement Investments

Two main considerations when investing for retirement that may differentiate these investments from other possible investments are the long-term nature of retirement investments and the tax treatment of retirement accounts.

If you do not expect to use the assets in your retirement account for another 10 years, then you can afford to invest in securities that might be more volatile in the short term but are expected to offer greater long-term returns. Investments in stocks have greatly outperformed investments in bonds over the last 70 years. Therefore, if you have plenty of time, a good portion of your retirement funds should be in diversified stock investments.

The tax treatment of retirement accounts affects how they should be invested if they are part of a retirement strategy that includes funds not in tax-protected accounts. In Chapter 5 we discussed diversifying your investments across asset classes to reduce risk. So while you may want to concentrate retirement funds in equity investments, you will never want to put all your funds in the same asset class. As you diversify, you will include investments such as bonds or income-producing stocks, as well as stocks or funds whose returns are primarily capital gains.

Table 6–5. Investment Allocation of Tax-Deferred, Tax-Free, and Taxable Retirement Funds

Vehicle	Investments	Reason
Roth IRA	• Those with the highest expected returns.	• Tax-free income on the largest gains.
	• Growth portfolios with high turnover.	• No tax cost on gains from high turnover.
Retirement assets not held in a tax-protected account	• Those whose total return will come primarily from capital gains. • Opt for a buy and hold strategy or low turnover funds.	• Take advantage of the 20% capital gains tax rate. • Low turnover minimizes taxes.
Ordinary IRAs, 401(k)s, and annuities	• If your diversification plan includes income-producing investments, this is where they should be.	• Withdrawals will be taxed at ordinary income tax rates.

Which assets should be in the IRAs and 401(k)s and which outside? When capital gains were taxed as ordinary income, conventional wisdom said the highest returning assets belonged in tax-deferred accounts, to shelter the most income. This is no longer the case, now that capital gains are taxed at a maximum rate of 20% versus ordinary income tax rates that are as high as 36%. All investment gains in an ordinary IRA or 401(k) are taxed as current income when withdrawn, raising taxes due on capital gains by as much as 16%. Therefore, if you have a Roth IRA or retirement funds which will not be taxed when withdrawn in addition to ordinary IRAs and 401(k)s and you diversify to include some income-producing investments, allocate them as shown in Table 6–5.

Investing to Fund College Costs

Besides retirement, the biggest expense most investors face is funding college costs for their children. Although the rate of increase in college costs came down in 1999, it was still above the rate of overall inflation. According to the College Board, tuition and fees for the year 1999 to 2000 increased from the previous year by 3.4% and 4.6%, respectively, for four-year public and private colleges. This contrasts with an average increase of 6% to 8% in the 1980s. The full breakdown for 1998 to 1999 follows in Table 6–6.

Table 6–6. Average One-Year College Expenses for Undergraduates, 1998 to 1999

Type of College	Tuition, Fees, Books, and Supplies	Expenses Including Room and Board	Expenses Excluding Room and Board
Four-Year Public	$3,905	$6,553	$4,600
Four-Year Private	$15,175	$7,358	$4,195

SOURCE: The College Board. Trends in College Pricing, 1998.

You can find estimates for specific college costs at the College Board's website, *www.collegeboard.org.*

The cost of the college your child will attend is only one variable needed to determine how much to save today to be able to fund those costs in the future. Other variables include the following:

- The number of years until your child enters college
- The number of years you plan to pay for college costs
- The rate of increase of college costs between now and the time your child enters college
- The savings you have earmarked for college
- The rate of return you will receive on your savings and investments

Most brokerage firms and mutual fund companies have college savings calculators that combine these variables to give you either one-time, annual, or monthly savings goals. The key to making these tools useful is keeping them as accurate and as conservative as possible. (The 20+% stock market returns of the last few years are not likely to continue for the next 20 years.) Once you have decided how much you need to save, it is important to consider how your accounts are titled, to reap the maximum benefit from your money.

Custodial Accounts

A custodial account is established for the benefit of a minor. Depending upon the state in which you live, it is opened under either the Uniform Gift to Minors Act (UGMA) or Uniform Transfer to Minors Act (UTMA). A gift placed in a custodial account is irrevocable and must be used for the minor's benefit if used before the age of majority. At the age of majority, age 18 or 21 depending upon the law of your state, all funds in a custodial account become property of the minor. Until the minor reaches the age of majority, the custodian, who does not have to be the donor, has the authority to make investment decisions for the account.

The benefit of using a custodial account is the tax treatment of income and capital gains produced in the account. Children under the age of 14 pay no income tax on the first $700 of investment income and only 15% on the next $700 (1999 rules). Any additional income is taxed at the parents' highest marginal tax rate.

There are two disadvantages to using custodial accounts. The first is that, by law, all funds in the account become property of the minor at the age of majority. Should the child be less than financially responsible, the custodian cannot prevent that child from spending the money. If the child is a star scholar or athlete and receives a full-ride scholarship, the custodian cannot appropriate the unneeded money for personal retirement savings or college funds for a sibling. The second disadvantage is that custodial accounts may affect the child's ability to receive financial aid. Financial aid formulas generally assume that students can contribute 35% of their assets, which include custodial accounts, toward college expenses. If the same assets were held in their parents' names, only 5.6% of the assets would be considered available for college expenses.

Ordinary and Roth IRAs

Though not specifically designed for accumulating education funds, ordinary and Roth IRAs, can be used for education expenses. The 10% penalty for early withdrawal from an ordinary IRA is suspended for qualified higher education expenses. Income taxes are still due if contributions were tax deductible.

The penalty for early withdrawal on a Roth IRA is also suspended for qualified higher education expenses. If withdrawals exceed contributions, then income taxes will be due on earnings.

Education IRAs

Established by the same legislation that created the Roth IRA in 1997, the education IRA is not a retirement account at all, but a trust established to pay for higher education. Contributions to an education IRA are not tax deductible, but earnings accumulate tax free, and distributions used to pay for qualified higher education expenses such as tuition, fees, books, supplies, and certain room and board expenses may be withdrawn tax and penalty free.

Contributions. Annual contributions to a designated beneficiary's education IRA are limited to $500, but anyone may contribute provided their income is below $110,000 for single filers and $160,000 for married couples filing jointly. There is a phaseout of the allowable amount between $95,000 and $110,000 for single filers and $150,000 and $160,000 for joint filers. These contributions do not affect any ordinary or Roth IRA contributions that the contributor may make. Contributions may not be made to the account after the designated beneficiary reaches the age of 18. You may not contribute to both an education IRA and a qualified state tuition program in the same year.

Withdrawals. Distributions from an education IRA are not taxable as long as they do not exceed the beneficiary's incurred qualified higher education expenses in the same year. If the distribution is not used to pay for education expenses, the earnings portion of the distribution is taxable as income and is subject to a 10% penalty.

Any balance in the education IRA must be distributed by the time the beneficiary reaches the age of 30. If it is not used, the beneficiary may make a tax-free, penalty-free rollover of assets into the education IRA of an eligible family member as defined in IRC 529(e)(2).

Hope Scholarship Credit

The Hope Scholarship credit is not an investment vehicle, but its use and the use of the Lifetime Learning credit affect the decision to use an education IRA. The tax exclusion for a distribution from an education IRA cannot be taken in the same year, for the same student, as a Hope Scholarship credit or a Lifetime Learning credit; nor can the two credits be taken in the same year.

The Hope Scholarship credit is a credit against federal income taxes for qualified tuition and fees in a postsecondary or certificate program at an eligible institution. The student can be the taxpayer, the taxpayer's spouse, or a dependent and must be enrolled at least half time. The credit amounts to 100% of the first $1,000 in qualified tuition and fees, and 50% of the second $1,000, for a maximum of $1,500 per year, per student. It is available only for the first two years of postsecondary education. Beginning in 2002, the $1,500 limit will be indexed for inflation.

Eligibility for the credit phases out between $40,000 and $50,000 MAGI for single filers. The range is $80,000 to $100,000 for those married and filing jointly.

Lifetime Learning Credit

The Lifetime Learning credit is a credit against federal income taxes for 20% of qualified tuition and fees paid during the year. The student must be the taxpayer, the taxpayer's spouse, or a dependent and must be enrolled (no half-time requirement) at an eligible educational institution. The credit is computed per income tax return, not per student, and may be claimed for an unlimited number of years.

For expenses paid before January 1, 2003, up to $5,000 in tuition and fees may be claimed, resulting in a maximum credit of $1,000 per taxpayer return. For expenses paid after that date, up to $10,000 of tuition and fees are eligible, resulting in a maximum credit of $2,000.

Eligibility for the credit phases out between $40,000 and $50,000 MAGI for single filers. The range is $80,000 to $100,000 for those married and filing jointly.

Qualified Savings Tuition Plans

More often called Section 529 plans after the IRS code that authorizes their use, qualified savings tuition plans are tax-deferred savings plans for use in college funding. Similar to an IRA, you pay no federal or state income tax on earnings in the account until the funds are withdrawn. The plan is held in the donor's name, which is advantageous for financial aid calculations, but when the funds are withdrawn all earnings are taxed at the student's tax rate, which is presumably lower than the donor's rate.

The federal law allows each state to create a college savings plan. The plans, which differ by state, may allow contributions of up to $100,000 per child, with no income limitation on the donor, as in the education IRA. Contributions are not federally tax deductible, but some states give tax deductions for contributions (Missouri allows a deduction of up to $8,000 from taxable income). Additionally, some states do not tax withdrawals. Another tax benefit, especially for grandparents looking to reduce their taxable estate, is the suspension of federal gift tax for up to $50,000 per donor, because the law treats the gift as a series of five annual gifts of $10,000 and thus falls under the gift tax exclusion. No additional gifts may be made in the five-year period without triggering the gift tax.

Investments in 529 plans are not self-directed as with an IRA, but are invested by the plan's investment manager. In some cases you may have a choice between a conservative, fixed income investment and a blend of fixed income and equity investments.

Most plans allow withdrawals to be used for tuition and fees, plus some qualified expenses, which may include room and board. If the designated beneficiary does not use the money for college, the plan can be transferred to another family member. If the new beneficiary is of a younger generation, federal generation-skipping taxes may apply. If the donor chooses to withdraw the funds for other uses, there is a 10% penalty and income taxes will be due on investment earnings.

Each state's plan differs, but most have open residency requirements, meaning that you do not have to live in a particular state to invest in its plan nor do you have to choose a college in that state. One of the most popular plans is the UNIQUE College Investing Plan, a joint effort of Fidelity Investments and the State of New Hampshire, which is open to residents of all 50 states. The minimum UNIQUE contribution is $50 and maximum per donor is $50,000. Investments are made in portfolios that are tailored to the beneficiary's age; portfolios become more conservative as the time to use the money draws near.

To find out about your state's plan, log on to the College Savings Plan Network, an affiliate of the National Association of State Treasurers, at *www.collegesavings.org*. A map allows you to click on your state, sending you directly to your state's website. You may also reach the network at the following address and phone number.

College Savings Plan Network
P.O. Box 11910
Lexington, KY 40578-1910
(606) 244-8175
(606) 244-8053 fax
e-mail *cspn@csg.org*

Savings Bonds

The interest earned on EE or I series savings bonds, described in Chapter 9, can be excluded from taxable income if the following conditions are met:

- The bonds must be purchased after December 31, 1989.
- They must be issued in the name of a taxpayer who is age 24 or older.
- The bond proceeds must be used for educational expenses, such as tuition and fees of the taxpayer, his or her spouse, or dependent. Room and board and books are not qualified expenses.
- Married couples filing jointly may not have MAGI above $79,650 (1999 limit) to receive the full interest exclusion.
- Single filers may not have MAGI above $53,100 (1999 limit) to receive the full interest exclusion.

Choosing Investments
for College Funding

Investment decisions for college funding are similar to those for retirement, in both the long-term nature of the investments and the allocation between tax-advantaged and ordinary investment vehicles. If you use both custodial and noncustodial accounts, place any investments with current income in custodial accounts to benefit from preferred tax treatment. In general, plan a buy and hold strategy for stocks or pick mutual funds with low turnover whose total return is derived mainly from capital gains, to minimize realized returns.

Growth investments are generally most appropriate for long-term goals such as college funding. If you are very risk averse or just want to balance your portfolio, you may choose some income-producing investments. In that case, consider savings bonds, which have an education exclusion on interest taxation, or put investments into an education IRA, whose income is tax free if used for educational expenses.

Summary

Investing to reach a specific goal requires the consideration of multiple variables. In addition to evaluating the performance and risk of the particular investments chosen, you must contemplate the time horizon for the goal in question and the tax consequences of available investment vehicles. The longer the time horizon, the more impact each decision makes when compounded. Careful evaluation, especially in situations such as deciding between ordinary and Roth IRAs, can mean thousands of dollars difference.

7

The Mathematics of Investing

There is no getting around the fact that successful investing depends on mathematics. Whether you are computing interest earned, calculating total returns, assessing a yield to maturity, or interpreting risk from a standard deviation, formulas are everywhere. This chapter will provide many of the valuable formulas used in investing and explain what they mean. Some formulas are also included in context in their respective chapters. This chapter is primarily for quick reference.

Computing Interest

Types of Interest

There are several different types of interest that you may earn on an investment. Simple interest is interest paid on the initial investment. A $1,000 investment that earns simple interest of 5% would earn $50 in one year, calculated as follows:

$$\$1,000 \times 0.05 = \$50$$

Compound interest is computed by applying the stated interest rate to the sum of the initial deposit and any interest earned in each prior period. With each compounding period, you earn interest on the interest earned previously. To modify the previous example, a $1,000 investment that earns 5% interest, compounded semiannually, would earn $50.63 in one year, calculated as follows:

$$\text{First 6 months' interest} = \$1,000 \times 0.05 \times \tfrac{1}{2} = \$25.00$$
$$\text{Second 6 months' interest} = \$1,025 \times 0.05 \times \tfrac{1}{2} = \$25.63$$
$$\text{Total year's interest} = \$50.63$$

Note that you must multiply the interest formula by ½ to adjust for the semiannual format. Interest compounded quarterly would use ¼, and so on. The total interest earned through compounding is higher since during the second half of the year interest is calculated on a larger investment. Logically, the more frequent the compounding, the greater its benefit.

The stated rate of interest is called the nominal rate. In the previous examples, it is 5%. The effective rate of interest is the rate of return actually earned after the effect of compounding. It is computed as follows:

$$\text{Effective rate of interest} = \frac{\text{Actual interest earned in one year}}{\text{Amount initially invested}}$$

In the previous examples, the nominal and effective rates are the same for the investment whose interest is computed as simple interest. The interest earned is $50, which, divided by $1,000 invested, equals 5% (the nominal rate). In the compound interest example, the effective rate is computed by dividing the interest earned in one year, $50.63, by $1,000 invested, to equal 5.06%.

The effective interest rate of an investment will exceed the nominal rate by a greater amount as interest is compounded more often. Table 7–1 compares nominal rates of interest and effective rates, given different compounding periods.

Future Value of an Investment

The previous method used to compute compound interest becomes unwieldy over long time periods. You can use a future value formula or a financial calculator, but perhaps the easiest way to find out what an invest-

Table 7–1. Effective Interest Rates under Different Compounding Periods

Nominal Rate	Effective Rate, with Compounding				
	Annually	Semiannually	Quarterly	Monthly	Daily
4.00%	4.00%	4.04%	4.06%	4.07%	4.08%
5.00	5.00	5.06	5.09	5.12	5.13
6.00	6.00	6.09	6.14	6.17	6.18
7.00	7.00	7.12	7.19	7.23	7.25
8.00	8.00	8.16	8.24	8.30	8.33
9.00	9.00	9.20	9.31	9.38	9.42
10.00	10.00	10.25	10.38	10.47	10.52

ment will be worth in the future after it earns a particular rate of compound interest is to use a future value factor. To compute a future value, multiply the amount invested by the appropriate future value factor. To use the future value factors in Table 7–2, find the factor at the intersection of the row that contains the number of years involved with the column that contains the nominal interest rate. For example, the future value factor for a $10,000 investment earning 8% for 10 years is 2.159. Compute the future value of a $10,000 investment as follows:

$$
\begin{aligned}
\text{Future value} &= \text{Initial investment} \times \text{future value factor} \\
&= \$10,000 \times 2.159 \\
&= \$21,590
\end{aligned}
$$

If the compounding period is less than one year, the number of periods should be equal to the number of compounding periods. For example, with semiannual compounding, multiply the number of years by 2 to get the number of periods. Then divide the nominal interest rate by the compounding periods per year.

Future Value of a Series of Equal Investments

Using the same process, you can find the future value of a number of equal payments—for example, the deposit of $2,000 each year into an IRA. The difference is in the factor, which should be chosen from Table 7–3. The future value of 20 annual payments of $2,000 is calculated by multiplying $2,000 by the factor at the intersection of row 20 and the column for the rate of return earned. If the rate of return is 8%, this factor is 45.762. The future value of the investment is $91,524 ($2,000 × 45.762). Note that the use of the word *annuity* in the table title refers to a stream of equal payments, not a particular type of investment. To adjust for monthly payments, multiply the number of years by 12 to compute the number of periods and divide the stated rate of interest by 12 for the interest per period.

Present Value of a Future Sum

Because money earns interest, a dollar in hand today is worth more than a dollar that will be received 10 years from now, which is worth more than a dollar that will be received in 20 years. This concept is the basis of the time value of money. Using formulas that are the inverse of those used to calculate the future value of an investment with compound interest, we can also calculate the current value of a payment to be received in the future.

Table 7-2. Future Value Factors for $1 Compounded at k Percent for n Periods:

$$FV_{k,n} = (1 + k)^n$$

Compound Rate, k

Period, n	1%	2%	3%	4%	5%	6%	7%	8%	9%	10%	11%	12%	13%	14%	15%	16%	17%	18%	19%	20%
1	1.010	1.020	1.030	1.040	1.050	1.060	1.070	1.080	1.090	1.100	1.110	1.120	1.130	1.140	1.150	1.160	1.170	1.180	1.190	1.200
2	1.020	1.040	1.061	1.082	1.102	1.124	1.145	1.166	1.188	1.210	1.232	1.254	1.277	1.300	1.323	1.346	1.369	1.392	1.416	1.440
3	1.030	1.061	1.093	1.125	1.158	1.191	1.225	1.260	1.295	1.331	1.368	1.405	1.443	1.482	1.521	1.561	1.602	1.643	1.685	1.728
4	1.041	1.082	1.126	1.170	1.216	1.262	1.311	1.360	1.412	1.464	1.518	1.574	1.630	1.689	1.749	1.811	1.874	1.939	2.005	2.074
5	1.051	1.104	1.159	1.217	1.276	1.338	1.403	1.469	1.539	1.611	1.685	1.762	1.842	1.925	2.011	2.100	2.192	2.288	2.386	2.488
6	1.062	1.126	1.194	1.265	1.340	1.419	1.501	1.587	1.677	1.772	1.870	1.974	2.082	2.195	2.313	2.436	2.565	2.700	2.840	2.986
7	1.072	1.149	1.230	1.316	1.407	1.504	1.606	1.714	1.828	1.949	2.076	2.211	2.353	2.502	2.660	2.826	3.001	3.185	3.379	3.583
8	1.083	1.172	1.267	1.369	1.477	1.594	1.718	1.851	1.993	2.144	2.305	2.476	2.658	2.853	3.059	3.278	3.511	3.759	4.021	4.300
9	1.094	1.195	1.305	1.423	1.551	1.689	1.838	1.999	2.172	2.358	2.558	2.773	3.004	3.252	3.518	3.803	4.108	4.435	4.785	5.160
10	1.105	1.219	1.344	1.480	1.629	1.791	1.967	2.159	2.367	2.594	2.839	3.106	3.395	3.707	4.046	4.411	4.807	5.234	5.695	6.192
11	1.116	1.243	1.384	1.539	1.710	1.898	2.105	2.332	2.580	2.853	3.152	3.479	3.836	4.226	4.652	5.117	5.642	6.176	6.777	7.430
12	1.127	1.268	1.426	1.601	1.796	2.012	2.252	2.518	2.813	3.138	3.498	3.896	4.335	4.818	5.350	5.936	6.580	7.288	8.064	8.916
13	1.138	1.294	1.469	1.665	1.886	2.133	2.410	2.720	3.066	3.452	3.883	4.363	4.898	5.492	6.153	6.886	7.699	8.599	9.596	10.699
14	1.149	1.319	1.513	1.732	1.980	2.261	2.579	2.937	3.342	3.797	4.310	4.887	5.535	6.261	7.076	7.988	9.007	10.147	11.420	12.839
15	1.161	1.346	1.558	1.801	2.079	2.397	2.759	3.172	3.642	4.177	4.785	5.474	6.254	7.138	8.137	9.266	10.539	11.974	13.590	15.407
16	1.173	1.373	1.605	1.873	2.183	2.540	2.952	3.426	3.970	4.595	5.311	6.130	7.067	8.137	9.358	10.748	12.330	14.129	16.172	18.488
17	1.184	1.400	1.653	1.948	2.292	2.693	3.159	3.700	4.328	5.054	5.895	6.866	7.986	9.276	10.761	12.468	14.426	16.672	19.244	22.186
18	1.196	1.428	1.702	2.026	2.407	2.854	3.380	3.996	4.717	5.560	6.544	7.690	9.024	10.575	12.375	14.463	16.879	19.673	22.901	26.623
19	1.208	1.457	1.754	2.107	2.527	3.026	3.617	4.316	5.142	6.116	7.263	8.613	10.197	12.056	14.232	16.777	19.748	23.214	27.252	31.948
20	1.220	1.486	1.806	2.191	2.653	3.207	3.870	4.661	5.604	6.727	8.062	9.646	11.523	13.743	16.367	19.461	23.106	27.393	32.429	38.338
21	1.232	1.516	1.860	2.279	2.786	3.400	4.141	5.034	6.109	7.400	8.949	10.804	13.021	15.668	18.822	22.574	27.034	32.324	38.591	46.005
22	1.245	1.546	1.916	2.370	2.925	3.604	4.430	5.437	6.659	8.140	9.934	12.100	14.714	17.861	21.645	26.186	31.629	38.142	45.923	55.206
23	1.257	1.577	1.974	2.465	3.072	3.820	4.741	5.871	7.258	8.954	11.026	13.552	16.627	20.362	24.871	30.376	37.006	45.008	54.649	66.247
24	1.270	1.608	2.033	2.563	3.225	4.049	5.072	6.341	7.922	9.850	12.239	15.179	18.788	23.212	28.625	35.236	43.297	53.109	65.032	79.497
25	1.282	1.641	2.094	2.666	3.386	4.292	5.427	6.848	8.623	10.835	13.585	17.000	21.231	26.462	32.919	40.874	50.658	62.669	77.388	95.396
26	1.295	1.673	2.157	2.772	3.556	4.549	5.807	7.396	9.399	11.918	15.080	19.040	23.991	30.167	37.857	47.414	59.270	73.949	92.092	114.48
27	1.308	1.707	2.221	2.883	3.733	4.822	6.214	7.988	10.245	13.110	16.739	21.325	27.109	34.390	43.535	55.000	69.345	87.260	109.59	137.37
28	1.321	1.741	2.288	2.999	3.920	5.112	6.649	8.627	11.167	14.421	18.580	23.884	30.633	39.204	50.066	63.800	81.134	102.97	130.41	164.84
29	1.335	1.776	2.357	3.119	4.116	5.418	7.114	9.317	12.172	15.863	20.624	26.750	34.616	44.693	57.575	75.009	94.927	121.50	155.19	197.81
30	1.348	1.811	2.427	3.243	4.322	5.743	7.612	10.063	13.268	17.449	22.892	29.960	39.116	50.950	66.212	85.850	111.06	143.37	184.68	237.38
35	1.417	2.000	2.814	3.946	5.516	7.686	10.677	14.785	20.414	28.102	38.575	52.800	72.068	98.100	133.18	180.31	243.50	328.00	440.70	590.67
40	1.489	2.208	3.262	4.801	7.040	10.286	14.974	21.725	31.409	45.259	65.001	93.051	132.78	188.88	267.86	378.72	533.87	750.38	1051.7	1469.8
45	1.565	2.438	3.782	5.841	8.985	13.765	21.002	31.920	48.327	72.890	109.53	163.99	244.64	363.68	538.77	795.44	1170.5	1716.7	2509.7	3657.3
50	1.645	2.692	4.384	7.107	11.467	18.420	29.457	46.902	74.358	117.39	184.56	289.00	450.74	700.23	1083.7	1670.7	2566.2	3927.4	5988.9	9100.4

Table 7-2. $FV_{k,n}$ (Continued)

Compound Rate, k

Period, n	21%	22%	23%	24%	25%	26%	27%	28%	29%	30%	31%	32%	33%	34%	35%	40%	45%	50%	55%	60%
1	1.210	1.220	1.230	1.240	1.250	1.260	1.270	1.280	1.290	1.300	1.310	1.320	1.330	1.340	1.350	1.400	1.450	1.500	1.550	1.600
2	1.464	1.488	1.513	1.538	1.563	1.588	1.613	1.638	1.664	1.690	1.716	1.742	1.769	1.796	1.823	1.960	2.103	2.250	2.403	2.560
3	1.772	1.816	1.861	1.907	1.953	2.000	2.048	2.097	2.147	2.197	2.248	2.300	2.353	2.406	2.460	2.744	3.049	3.375	3.724	4.096
4	2.144	2.215	2.289	2.364	2.441	2.520	2.601	2.684	2.769	2.856	2.945	3.036	3.129	3.224	3.322	3.842	4.421	5.063	5.772	6.554
5	2.594	2.703	2.815	2.932	3.052	3.176	3.304	3.436	3.572	3.713	3.858	4.007	4.162	4.230	4.484	5.378	6.410	7.594	8.947	10.486
6	3.138	3.297	3.463	3.635	3.815	4.002	4.196	4.398	4.608	4.827	5.054	5.290	5.535	5.789	6.053	7.530	9.294	11.391	13.867	16.777
7	3.797	4.023	4.259	4.508	4.768	5.042	5.329	5.629	5.945	6.275	6.621	6.983	7.361	7.758	8.172	10.541	13.476	17.086	21.494	26.844
8	4.595	4.908	5.239	5.590	5.960	6.353	6.768	7.206	7.669	8.157	8.673	9.217	9.791	10.395	11.032	14.758	19.541	25.629	33.316	42.950
9	5.560	5.987	6.444	6.931	7.451	8.005	8.595	9.223	9.893	10.604	11.362	12.166	13.022	13.930	14.894	20.661	28.334	38.443	51.640	68.719
10	6.728	7.305	7.926	8.954	9.313	10.086	10.915	11.806	12.761	13.786	14.884	16.060	17.319	18.666	20.107	28.925	41.085	57.665	80.042	109.95
11	8.140	8.912	9.749	10.657	11.642	12.708	13.862	15.112	16.462	17.922	19.498	21.199	23.034	25.012	27.144	40.496	59.573	86.498	124.06	175.92
12	9.850	10.872	11.991	13.215	14.552	16.012	17.605	19.343	21.236	23.298	25.542	27.983	30.635	33.516	36.644	56.694	86.381	129.75	192.30	281.47
13	11.918	13.264	14.749	16.386	18.190	20.175	22.359	24.759	27.395	30.288	33.460	36.937	40.745	44.912	49.470	79.371	125.25	194.62	298.07	450.36
14	14.421	16.182	18.141	20.319	22.737	25.421	28.396	31.691	35.339	39.374	43.833	48.757	54.190	60.182	66.784	111.12	181.62	291.93	462.00	720.58
15	17.449	19.742	22.314	25.196	28.422	32.030	36.062	40.565	45.587	51.186	57.421	64.359	72.073	80.644	90.158	155.57	263.34	437.89	716.10	1152.9
16	21.114	24.086	27.446	31.243	35.527	40.358	45.799	51.923	58.808	66.542	75.221	84.954	95.858	108.06	121.71	217.80	381.85	656.84	1110.0	1844.7
17	25.548	29.384	33.759	38.741	44.409	50.851	58.165	66.461	75.862	86.504	98.540	112.14	127.49	144.80	164.31	304.91	553.68	985.26	1720.4	2951.5
18	30.913	35.849	41.523	48.039	55.511	64.072	73.870	85.071	97.862	112.46	129.09	148.02	169.56	194.04	221.82	426.88	802.83	1477.9	2666.7	4722.4
19	37.404	43.736	51.074	59.568	69.389	80.731	93.815	108.89	126.24	146.19	169.10	195.39	225.52	260.01	299.46	597.63	1164.1	2216.8	4133.4	7555.8
20	45.259	53.358	62.821	72.864	86.736	101.72	119.14	139.38	162.85	190.05	221.53	257.92	299.94	348.41	404.27	836.68	1688.0	3325.3	6406.7	12098
21	54.764	65.096	77.269	91.592	108.42	128.17	151.31	178.41	210.08	247.06	290.20	340.45	398.92	466.88	545.77	1171.4	2447.5	4987.9	9930.4	19342
22	66.264	79.418	95.041	113.57	135.53	161.49	192.17	228.36	271.00	321.18	380.16	449.39	530.56	625.61	736.79	1639.9	3548.9	7481.8	15392	30948
23	80.180	96.889	116.90	140.83	169.41	203.48	244.05	292.30	349.59	417.54	498.01	593.20	705.67	838.32	994.66	2295.9	5145.9	11222	23857	49517
24	97.017	118.21	143.79	174.63	211.76	256.39	309.95	374.14	450.98	542.80	652.40	783.02	938.51	1123.4	1342.8	3214.2	7461.6	16834	36979	79228
25	117.39	144.21	176.86	216.54	264.70	323.05	393.63	478.90	581.76	705.64	854.64	1033.6	1248.2	1505.3	1812.8	4499.9	10819	25251	57318	126765
26	142.04	175.94	217.54	268.51	330.87	407.04	499.92	613.00	750.47	917.33	1119.6	1364.3	1660.1	2017.1	2447.2	6299.8	15688	37876	88843	202824
27	171.87	214.64	267.57	332.95	413.59	512.87	634.89	784.64	968.10	1192.5	1466.6	1800.9	2208.0	2702.9	3303.8	8819.8	22747	56815	137706	324518
28	207.97	261.86	329.11	412.86	516.99	646.21	806.31	1004.3	1248.9	1550.3	1921.3	2377.2	2936.6	3621.9	4460.1	12347	32984	85222	213445	519229
29	251.64	319.47	404.81	511.95	646.23	814.23	1024.0	1285.6	1611.0	2015.4	2516.9	3137.9	3905.7	4853.3	6021.1	17286	47826	127834	330840	830767
30	304.48	389.76	497.91	634.82	807.79	1025.9	1300.5	1645.5	2078.2	2620.0	3297.2	4142.1	5194.6	6503.5	8128.6	24201	69348	191751	512803	*
35	789.75	1053.4	1401.8	1861.1	2465.2	3258.1	4296.7	5653.9	7424.0	9727.9	12720	16599	21617	28097	36648	130161	444508	*	*	*
40	2048.4	2847.0	3946.4	5455.9	7523.2	10347	14195	19426	26520	36118	49074	66520	89963	121392	163437	700037	*	*	*	*
45	5313.0	7694.7	11110	15994	22958	32860	46899	66749	94740	134106	189325	266579	374389	524464	732857	*	*	*	*	*
50	13780	20796	31279	46890	70064	104358	154948	229349	338443	497929	730406	*	*	*	*	*	*	*	*	*

Table 7-3. Future Value Factors for an Annuity of $1 Compounded at k Percent for n Periods:

$$FVA_{k,n} = \sum_{t=0}^{n-1}(1+k)^t = \frac{(1+k)^n - 1}{k}$$

Compound Rate, k

Period, n	1%	2%	3%	4%	5%	6%	7%	8%	9%	10%	11%	12%	13%	14%	15%	16%	17%	18%	19%	20%
1	1.000	1.000	1.000	1.000	1.000	1.000	1.000	1.000	1.000	1.000	1.000	1.000	1.000	1.000	1.000	1.000	1.000	1.000	1.000	1.000
2	2.010	2.020	2.030	2.040	2.050	2.060	2.070	2.080	2.090	2.100	2.110	2.120	2.130	2.140	2.150	2.160	2.170	2.180	2.190	2.200
3	3.030	3.060	3.091	3.122	3.152	3.184	3.215	3.246	3.278	3.310	3.342	3.374	3.407	3.440	3.472	3.506	3.539	3.572	3.606	3.640
4	4.060	4.122	3.091	4.246	4.310	4.375	4.440	4.506	4.573	4.641	4.710	4.779	4.850	4.921	4.993	5.066	5.141	5.215	5.291	5.368
5	5.101	5.204	5.309	5.416	5.526	5.637	5.751	5.867	5.985	6.105	6.228	6.353	6.480	6.610	6.742	6.877	7.014	7.154	7.297	7.442
6	6.152	6.308	6.469	6.633	6.802	6.975	7.153	7.336	7.523	7.716	7.913	8.115	8.323	8.536	8.754	8.977	9.207	9.442	9.683	9.930
7	7.214	7.434	7.662	7.898	8.142	8.394	8.654	8.923	9.200	9.487	9.783	10.089	10.405	10.730	11.067	11.414	11.772	12.142	12.523	12.916
8	8.286	8.583	8.892	9.214	9.549	9.897	10.260	10.637	11.028	11.436	11.859	12.300	12.757	13.233	13.727	14.240	14.773	15.327	15.902	16.499
9	9.269	9.755	10.159	10.583	11.027	11.491	11.978	12.488	13.021	13.579	14.164	14.776	15.416	16.085	16.786	17.519	18.285	19.086	19.923	20.799
10	10.462	10.950	11.464	12.006	12.578	13.181	13.816	14.487	15.193	15.937	16.722	17.549	18.420	19.337	20.304	21.321	22.393	23.521	24.709	25.959
11	11.567	12.169	12.808	13.486	14.207	14.972	15.784	16.645	17.560	18.531	19.561	20.655	21.814	23.045	24.349	25.733	27.200	28.755	30.404	32.150
12	12.683	13.412	14.192	15.026	15.917	16.870	17.888	18.977	20.141	21.384	22.713	24.133	25.650	27.271	29.002	30.850	32.824	34.931	37.180	39.581
13	13.809	14.680	15.618	16.627	17.713	18.882	20.141	21.495	22.953	24.523	26.212	28.029	29.985	32.089	34.352	36.786	39.404	42.219	45.244	48.497
14	14.947	15.975	17.086	18.292	19.599	21.015	22.550	24.215	26.019	27.975	30.095	32.393	34.883	37.581	40.505	43.672	47.103	50.818	54.841	59.196
15	16.097	17.293	18.599	20.024	21.579	23.276	25.129	27.152	29.361	31.772	34.405	37.280	40.417	43.842	47.580	51.660	56.110	60.965	66.261	72.035
16	17.258	18.639	20.157	21.825	23.657	25.673	27.888	30.324	33.003	35.950	39.190	42.753	46.672	50.980	55.717	60.925	66.649	72.939	79.850	87.442
17	18.430	20.012	21.762	23.698	25.840	28.213	30.840	33.750	36.974	40.545	44.501	48.884	53.739	59.118	65.075	71.673	78.979	87.068	96.022	105.93
18	19.615	21.412	23.414	25.645	28.132	30.906	33.999	37.450	41.301	45.599	50.396	55.750	61.725	68.394	75.836	84.141	93.406	103.74	115.27	128.12
19	20.811	22.841	25.117	27.671	30.539	33.760	37.379	41.446	46.018	51.159	56.939	63.440	70.749	78.969	88.212	98.603	110.28	123.41	138.17	154.74
20	22.019	24.297	26.870	29.778	33.066	36.786	40.996	45.762	51.160	57.275	64.203	72.052	80.947	91.025	102.44	115.38	130.03	146.63	165.42	186.69
21	23.239	25.783	28.676	31.969	35.719	39.993	44.865	50.423	56.765	64.002	72.265	81.699	92.470	104.77	118.81	134.84	153.14	174.02	197.85	225.03
22	24.472	27.299	30.537	34.248	38.505	43.392	49.006	55.457	62.873	71.403	81.214	92.503	105.49	120.44	137.63	157.41	180.17	206.34	236.44	271.03
23	25.716	28.845	32.453	36.618	41.430	46.996	53.436	60.893	69.532	79.543	91.148	104.60	120.20	138.30	159.28	183.60	211.80	244.49	282.36	326.24
24	26.973	30.422	34.426	39.083	44.502	50.816	58.177	66.765	76.790	88.497	102.17	118.16	136.83	158.66	184.17	213.98	248.81	289.49	337.10	392.48
25	28.243	32.030	36.459	41.646	47.727	54.865	63.249	73.106	84.701	98.347	114.41	133.33	155.62	181.87	212.79	249.21	292.10	342.60	402.04	471.98
26	29.526	33.671	38.553	44.312	51.113	59.156	68.676	79.954	93.324	109.18	128.00	150.33	176.85	208.33	245.71	290.09	342.76	405.27	479.43	567.38
27	30.821	35.344	40.710	47.084	54.669	63.706	74.484	87.351	102.72	121.10	143.08	169.37	200.84	238.50	283.57	337.50	402.03	479.22	571.52	681.85
28	32.129	37.051	42.931	49.968	58.403	68.528	80.698	95.339	112.97	134.21	159.82	190.70	227.95	272.89	327.10	392.50	471.38	566.48	681.11	819.22
29	33.450	38.792	45.219	52.966	62.323	73.640	87.347	103.97	124.14	148.63	178.40	214.58	258.58	312.09	377.17	456.30	552.51	669.45	811.52	984.07
30	34.785	40.568	47.575	56.085	66.439	79.058	94.461	113.28	136.31	164.49	199.02	241.33	293.20	356.79	434.75	530.31	647.44	790.95	966.71	1181.9
35	41.660	49.994	60.462	73.652	90.320	111.43	138.24	172.32	215.71	271.02	341.59	431.66	546.68	693.57	881.17	1120.7	1426.5	1816.7	2314.2	2948.3
40	48.886	60.402	75.401	95.026	120.80	154.76	199.64	259.06	337.88	442.59	581.83	767.09	1013.7	1342.0	1779.1	2360.8	3134.5	4163.2	5529.8	7343.9
45	56.481	71.893	92.720	121.03	159.70	212.74	285.75	386.51	525.86	718.90	986.64	1358.2	1874.2	2590.6	3585.1	4967.3	6879.3	9531.6	13203	18281
50	64.463	84.579	112.80	152.67	209.35	290.34	406.53	573.77	815.08	1163.9	1668.8	2400.0	3459.5	4994.5	7217.7	10435	15089	21813	31515	45497

Table 7-3 $FVA_{k,n}$ (Continued)

Compound Rate, k

Period, n	21%	22%	23%	24%	25%	26%	27%	28%	29%	30%	31%	32%	33%	34%	35%	40%	45%	50%	55%	60%
1	1.000	1.000	1.000	1.000	1.000	1.000	1.000	1.000	1.000	1.000	1.000	1.000	1.000	1.000	1.000	1.000	1.000	1.000	1.000	1.000
2	2.210	2.220	2.230	2.240	2.250	2.260	2.270	2.280	2.290	2.300	2.310	2.320	2.330	2.340	2.350	2.400	2.450	2.500	2.550	2.600
3	3.674	3.708	3.743	3.778	3.813	3.848	3.883	3.918	3.954	3.990	4.026	4.062	4.099	4.136	4.173	4.360	4.553	4.750	4.952	5.160
4	5.446	5.524	5.604	5.684	5.766	5.848	5.931	6.016	6.101	6.187	6.274	6.362	6.452	6.542	6.633	7.104	7.601	8.125	8.676	9.256
5	7.589	7.740	7.893	8.048	8.207	8.368	8.533	8.700	8.870	9.043	9.219	9.398	9.581	9.766	9.954	10.956	12.022	13.188	14.448	15.810
6	10.183	10.442	10.708	10.980	11.259	11.544	11.837	12.136	12.442	12.756	13.077	13.406	13.742	14.086	14.438	16.324	18.431	20.781	23.395	26.295
7	13.321	13.740	14.171	14.615	15.073	15.546	16.032	16.534	17.051	17.583	18.131	18.696	19.277	19.876	20.492	23.853	27.725	32.172	37.262	43.073
8	17.119	17.762	18.430	19.123	19.842	20.588	21.361	22.163	22.995	23.858	24.752	25.678	26.638	27.633	28.664	34.395	41.202	49.258	58.756	69.916
9	21.714	22.670	23.669	24.712	25.802	26.940	28.129	29.369	30.664	32.015	33.425	34.895	36.429	38.029	39.696	49.153	60.743	74.887	92.073	112.87
10	27.274	28.657	30.113	31.643	33.253	34.945	36.723	38.593	40.556	42.619	44.786	47.062	49.451	51.958	54.590	69.814	89.100	113.33	143.71	181.59
11	34.001	35.962	38.039	40.238	42.566	45.031	47.639	50.398	53.318	56.405	59.670	63.122	66.769	70.624	74.697	98.739	130.16	171.00	223.75	291.54
12	42.142	44.874	47.788	50.895	54.208	57.739	61.501	65.510	69.780	74.327	79.168	84.320	89.803	95.637	101.84	139.23	189.73	257.49	347.82	476.46
13	51.991	55.746	59.779	64.110	68.760	73.751	79.107	84.853	91.016	97.625	104.71	112.30	120.44	129.15	138.48	195.93	276.12	387.24	540.12	748.93
14	63.909	69.010	74.528	80.496	86.949	93.926	101.47	109.61	118.41	127.91	138.17	149.24	161.18	174.06	187.95	275.30	401.37	581.86	838.19	1199.3
15	78.330	85.192	92.669	100.82	109.69	119.35	129.86	141.30	153.75	167.29	182.00	198.00	215.37	234.25	254.74	386.42	582.98	873.79	1300.2	1919.9
16	95.780	104.93	114.98	126.01	138.11	151.38	165.92	181.87	199.34	218.47	239.42	262.36	287.45	314.89	344.90	541.99	846.32	1311.7	2016.3	3072.8
17	116.89	129.02	142.43	157.25	173.64	191.73	211.72	233.79	258.15	285.01	314.64	347.31	383.30	422.95	466.61	759.78	1228.2	1968.5	3126.2	4917.5
18	142.44	158.40	176.19	195.99	218.04	242.59	269.89	300.25	334.01	371.52	413.18	459.45	510.80	567.76	630.92	1064.7	1781.8	2953.8	4846.7	7868.9
19	173.35	194.25	217.71	244.03	273.56	306.66	343.76	385.32	431.87	483.97	542.27	607.47	680.36	761.80	852.75	1491.6	2584.7	4431.7	7513.4	12591
20	210.76	237.99	268.79	303.60	342.94	387.39	437.57	494.21	558.11	630.17	711.38	802.86	905.88	1021.8	1152.2	2089.2	3748.8	6648.5	11646	20147
21	256.02	291.35	331.61	377.46	429.69	489.11	556.72	633.59	720.96	820.22	923.90	1060.8	1205.8	1370.2	1556.5	2925.9	5436.7	9973.8	18053	32236
22	310.78	356.44	408.88	469.06	538.10	617.28	708.03	812.00	931.04	1067.3	1223.1	1401.2	1694.7	1837.1	2102.3	4097.2	7884.3	14961	27983	51579
23	377.05	435.86	503.92	582.63	673.63	778.77	900.20	1040.4	1202.0	1388.5	1603.3	1850.6	2135.3	2462.7	2839.0	5737.1	11433	22443	43375	82527
24	457.22	532.75	620.82	723.46	843.03	982.25	1144.3	1332.7	1551.6	1806.0	2101.3	2443.8	2840.9	3301.0	3833.7	8033.0	16579	33666	67233	132045
25	554.24	650.96	764.61	898.09	1054.8	1238.6	1454.2	1706.8	2002.6	2348.8	2753.7	3226.8	3779.5	4424.4	5176.5	11247	24040	50500	104213	211273
26	671.63	795.17	941.46	1114.6	1319.5	1561.7	1847.8	2185.7	2584.4	3054.4	3608.3	4260.4	5027.7	5929.7	6989.3	15747	34680	75751	161531	338038
27	813.68	971.10	1159.0	1383.1	1650.4	1968.7	2347.8	2798.7	3334.8	3971.8	4727.9	5624.8	6687.8	7946.8	9436.5	22046	50548	113628	250374	540862
28	985.55	1185.7	1426.6	1716.1	2064.0	2481.6	2982.6	3583.3	4302.9	5164.3	6194.5	7425.7	8895.8	10649	12740	30866	73295	170443	388081	865381
29	1193.5	1447.6	1755.7	2129.0	2580.9	3127.8	3789.0	4587.7	5551.8	6714.6	8115.8	9802.9	11832	14271	17200	43214	106279	255666	601527	*
30	1445.2	1767.1	2160.5	2640.9	3227.2	3942.0	4813.0	5873.2	7162.8	8730.0	10632	12940	15738	19124	23221	60501	154106	383500	932368	
35	3755.9	4783.6	6090.3	7750.2	9856.8	12527	15909	20188	25596	32422	41029	51869	65504	182636	104136	325400	987794	*		
40	9749.5	12936	17154	22728	30088	39792	52571	69377	91774	120392	158300	207874	272613	357033	466960	*				
45	25295	34971	48301	66640	91831	126382	173697	238387	326688	447019	610723	833058	*							
50	65617	94525	135992	195372	280255	401374	573877	819103	*											

There are several investment uses for calculating the present value of a payment to be received in the future. The value of any discounted security (one that is sold at a discount to face value, pays no interest, and pays face value at maturity) is computed using present value techniques. Examples include zero coupon bonds and U.S. Treasury bills. Another use of present value techniques is calculating how much you must invest now to have a particular lump sum later, perhaps for college or retirement.

Table 7–4 provides factors for calculating the present value of a lump sum to be received in the future. To find the present value of $10,000, in 10 years, given a 6% interest rate, follow the row for 10 periods to the column for 6%. At their intersection is the factor 0.558. Compute the present value as follows:

$$\begin{aligned} \text{Present value} &= \text{Future value (lump-sum payment)} \times \text{Present} \\ &\qquad \text{value factor} \\ &= \$10{,}000 \times 0.558 \\ &= \$5{,}580 \end{aligned}$$

Present Value of a Series of Equal Payments

You can also compute the present value of a series of payments, called an annuity, in a similar manner, using the factors in Table 7–5. Say, for example, that you won $20 million in the lottery and were given two choices: 20 payments of $1 million in each of the next 20 years, or a lump sum immediately. Disregarding tax issues, you would decide by estimating the return you can earn on your investments and using this interest rate to calculate the present value of the stream of 20 payments. If you choose 10%, the lump sum offered would have to be greater than $8,514,000 ($1,000,000 × 8.514) to be more valuable than the annual payments.

Bond Yields

When calculating interest on the investments in the previous sections, we assume that there would be no change in the value of the underlying investment and that interest earned on the investment could be added to the value of the investment for the purposes of compounding. These assumptions are accurate for a certificate of deposit or a savings account, but different methods must be used to calculate returns on a bond. Unless they are discounted securities, bonds pay interest semiannually in cash to the owner. Interest is not added to the principal of the bond. In addition to the interest received, you may incur a gain or loss on the principal of a bond if you purchased it at a price lower or higher than its face value.

Table 7-4. Present Value Factors for $1 Discounted at k Percent for n Periods:

$$PV_{k,n} = \frac{1}{(1+k)^n}$$

Discount Rate, k

Period, n	1%	2%	3%	4%	5%	6%	7%	8%	9%	10%	11%	12%	13%	14%	15%	16%	17%	18%	19%	20%
1	0.990	0.980	0.971	0.962	0.952	0.943	0.935	0.926	0.917	0.909	0.901	0.893	0.885	0.877	0.870	0.862	0.855	0.847	0.840	0.833
2	0.980	0.961	0.943	0.925	0.907	0.890	0.873	0.857	0.842	0.826	0.812	0.797	0.783	0.769	0.756	0.743	0.731	0.718	0.706	0.694
3	0.971	0.942	0.915	0.889	0.864	0.840	0.816	0.794	0.772	0.751	0.731	0.712	0.693	0.675	0.658	0.641	0.624	0.609	0.593	0.579
4	0.961	0.924	0.888	0.855	0.823	0.792	0.763	0.735	0.708	0.683	0.659	0.636	0.613	0.592	0.572	0.552	0.534	0.516	0.499	0.482
5	0.951	0.906	0.863	0.822	0.784	0.747	0.713	0.681	0.650	0.621	0.593	0.567	0.543	0.519	0.497	0.476	0.456	0.437	0.419	0.402
6	0.942	0.888	0.837	0.790	0.746	0.705	0.666	0.630	0.596	0.564	0.535	0.507	0.480	0.456	0.432	0.410	0.390	0.370	0.352	0.335
7	0.933	0.871	0.813	0.760	0.711	0.665	0.623	0.583	0.547	0.513	0.482	0.452	0.425	0.400	0.376	0.354	0.333	0.314	0.296	0.279
8	0.923	0.853	0.789	0.731	0.677	0.627	0.582	0.540	0.502	0.467	0.434	0.404	0.376	0.351	0.327	0.305	0.285	0.266	0.249	0.233
9	0.914	0.837	0.766	0.703	0.645	0.592	0.544	0.500	0.460	0.424	0.391	0.361	0.333	0.308	0.284	0.263	0.243	0.225	0.209	0.194
10	0.905	0.820	0.744	0.676	0.614	0.558	0.508	0.463	0.422	0.386	0.352	0.322	0.295	0.270	0.247	0.227	0.208	0.191	0.176	0.162
11	0.896	0.804	0.722	0.650	0.585	0.527	0.475	0.429	0.388	0.350	0.317	0.287	0.261	0.237	0.215	0.195	0.178	0.162	0.148	0.135
12	0.887	0.788	0.701	0.625	0.557	0.497	0.444	0.397	0.356	0.319	0.286	0.256	0.231	0.208	0.187	0.168	0.152	0.137	0.124	0.112
13	0.879	0.773	0.681	0.601	0.530	0.469	0.415	0.368	0.326	0.290	0.258	0.229	0.204	0.182	0.163	0.145	0.130	0.116	0.104	0.093
14	0.870	0.758	0.661	0.577	0.505	0.442	0.388	0.340	0.299	0.263	0.232	0.205	0.181	0.160	0.141	0.125	0.111	0.099	0.088	0.078
15	0.861	0.743	0.642	0.555	0.481	0.417	0.362	0.315	0.275	0.239	0.209	0.183	0.160	0.140	0.123	0.108	0.095	0.084	0.074	0.065
16	0.853	0.728	0.623	0.534	0.458	0.394	0.339	0.292	0.252	0.218	0.188	0.163	0.141	0.123	0.107	0.093	0.081	0.071	0.062	0.054
17	0.844	0.714	0.605	0.513	0.436	0.371	0.317	0.270	0.231	0.198	0.170	0.146	0.125	0.108	0.093	0.080	0.069	0.060	0.052	0.045
18	0.836	0.700	0.587	0.494	0.416	0.350	0.296	0.250	0.212	0.180	0.153	0.130	0.111	0.095	0.081	0.069	0.059	0.051	0.044	0.038
19	0.828	0.686	0.570	0.475	0.396	0.331	0.277	0.232	0.194	0.165	0.138	0.116	0.098	0.083	0.070	0.060	0.051	0.043	0.037	0.031
20	0.820	0.673	0.554	0.456	0.377	0.312	0.258	0.215	0.178	0.149	0.124	0.104	0.087	0.073	0.061	0.051	0.043	0.037	0.031	0.026
21	0.811	0.660	0.538	0.439	0.359	0.294	0.242	0.199	0.164	0.135	0.112	0.093	0.077	0.064	0.053	0.044	0.037	0.031	0.026	0.022
22	0.803	0.647	0.522	0.422	0.342	0.278	0.226	0.184	0.150	0.123	0.101	0.083	0.068	0.056	0.046	0.038	0.032	0.026	0.022	0.018
23	0.795	0.634	0.507	0.406	0.326	0.262	0.211	0.170	0.138	0.112	0.091	0.074	0.060	0.049	0.040	0.033	0.027	0.022	0.018	0.015
24	0.788	0.622	0.492	0.390	0.310	0.247	0.197	0.158	0.126	0.102	0.082	0.066	0.053	0.043	0.035	0.028	0.023	0.019	0.015	0.013
25	0.780	0.610	0.478	0.375	0.295	0.233	0.184	0.146	0.116	0.092	0.071	0.059	0.047	0.038	0.030	0.024	0.020	0.016	0.013	0.010
26	0.772	0.598	0.464	0.361	0.281	0.220	0.172	0.135	0.106	0.084	0.066	0.053	0.042	0.033	0.026	0.021	0.017	0.014	0.011	0.009
27	0.764	0.586	0.450	0.347	0.268	0.207	0.161	0.125	0.098	0.076	0.060	0.047	0.037	0.029	0.023	0.018	0.014	0.011	0.009	0.007
28	0.757	0.574	0.437	0.333	0.255	0.196	0.150	0.116	0.090	0.069	0.054	0.042	0.033	0.026	0.020	0.016	0.012	0.010	0.008	0.006
29	0.749	0.563	0.424	0.321	0.243	0.185	0.141	0.107	0.082	0.063	0.048	0.037	0.029	0.022	0.017	0.014	0.011	0.008	0.006	0.005
30	0.742	0.552	0.412	0.308	0.231	0.174	0.131	0.099	0.075	0.057	0.044	0.033	0.026	0.020	0.015	0.012	0.009	0.007	0.005	0.004
35	0.706	0.500	0.355	0.253	0.181	0.130	0.094	0.068	0.049	0.036	0.026	0.019	0.014	0.010	0.008	0.006	0.004	0.003	0.002	0.002
40	0.672	0.453	0.307	0.208	0.142	0.097	0.067	0.046	0.032	0.022	0.015	0.011	0.008	0.005	0.004	0.003	0.002	0.001	0.001	0.001
45	0.639	0.410	0.264	0.171	0.111	0.073	0.048	0.031	0.021	0.014	0.009	0.006	0.004	0.003	0.002	0.001	0.001	0.001	*	*
50	0.608	0.372	0.228	0.141	0.087	0.054	0.034	0.021	0.013	0.009	0.005	0.003	0.002	0.001	0.001	0.001	*	*	*	*

*Value is zero to three decimal places.

Table 7-4.

$PV_{k,n}$ (Continued)

Discount Rate, k

Period, n	21%	22%	23%	24%	25%	26%	27%	28%	29%	30%	31%	32%	33%	34%	35%	40%	45%	50%	55%	60%
1	0.826	0.820	0.813	0.806	0.800	0.794	0.787	0.781	0.775	0.769	0.763	0.758	0.752	0.746	0.741	0.714	0.690	0.667	0.645	0.625
2	0.683	0.672	0.661	0.650	0.640	0.630	0.620	0.610	0.601	0.592	0.583	0.574	0.565	0.557	0.549	0.510	0.476	0.444	0.416	0.391
3	0.564	0.551	0.537	0.524	0.512	0.500	0.488	0.477	0.466	0.455	0.445	0.435	0.425	0.416	0.406	0.364	0.328	0.296	0.269	0.244
4	0.467	0.451	0.437	0.423	0.410	0.397	0.384	0.373	0.361	0.350	0.340	0.329	0.320	0.310	0.301	0.260	0.226	0.198	0.173	0.153
5	0.386	0.370	0.355	0.341	0.328	0.315	0.303	0.291	0.280	0.269	0.259	0.250	0.240	0.231	0.223	0.186	0.156	0.132	0.112	0.095
6	0.319	0.303	0.289	0.275	0.262	0.250	0.238	0.227	0.217	0.207	0.198	0.189	0.181	0.173	0.165	0.133	0.108	0.088	0.072	0.060
7	0.263	0.249	0.235	0.222	0.210	0.198	0.188	0.178	0.168	0.159	0.151	0.143	0.136	0.129	0.122	0.095	0.074	0.059	0.047	0.037
8	0.218	0.204	0.191	0.179	0.168	0.157	0.148	0.139	0.130	0.123	0.115	0.108	0.102	0.096	0.091	0.068	0.051	0.039	0.030	0.023
9	0.180	0.167	0.155	0.144	0.134	0.125	0.116	0.108	0.101	0.094	0.088	0.082	0.077	0.072	0.067	0.048	0.035	0.026	0.019	0.015
10	0.149	0.137	0.126	0.116	0.107	0.099	0.092	0.085	0.078	0.073	0.067	0.062	0.058	0.054	0.050	0.035	0.024	0.017	0.012	0.009
11	0.123	0.112	0.103	0.094	0.096	0.079	0.072	0.066	0.061	0.056	0.051	0.047	0.043	0.040	0.037	0.025	0.017	0.012	0.008	0.006
12	0.102	0.092	0.083	0.076	0.069	0.062	0.057	0.052	0.047	0.043	0.039	0.036	0.033	0.030	0.027	0.018	0.012	0.008	0.005	0.004
13	0.084	0.075	0.068	0.061	0.055	0.050	0.045	0.040	0.037	0.033	0.030	0.027	0.025	0.022	0.020	0.013	0.008	0.005	0.003	0.002
14	0.069	0.062	0.055	0.049	0.044	0.039	0.035	0.032	0.028	0.025	0.023	0.021	0.018	0.017	0.015	0.009	0.006	0.003	0.002	0.001
15	0.057	0.051	0.045	0.040	0.035	0.031	0.028	0.025	0.022	0.020	0.017	0.016	0.014	0.012	0.011	0.006	0.004	0.002	0.001	0.001
16	0.047	0.042	0.036	0.032	0.028	0.025	0.022	0.019	0.017	0.015	0.013	0.012	0.010	0.009	0.008	0.005	0.003	0.002	0.001	0.001
17	0.039	0.034	0.030	0.026	0.023	0.020	0.017	0.015	0.013	0.012	0.010	0.009	0.008	0.007	0.006	0.003	0.002	0.001	0.001	*
18	0.032	0.028	0.024	0.021	0.018	0.016	0.014	0.012	0.010	0.009	0.008	0.007	0.006	0.005	0.005	0.002	0.001	0.001	*	*
19	0.027	0.023	0.020	0.017	0.014	0.012	0.011	0.009	0.008	0.007	0.006	0.005	0.004	0.004	0.003	0.002	0.001	0.001	*	*
20	0.022	0.019	0.016	0.014	0.012	0.010	0.008	0.007	0.006	0.005	0.005	0.004	0.003	0.003	0.002	0.001	0.001	*	*	*
21	0.018	0.015	0.013	0.011	0.009	0.008	0.007	0.006	0.005	0.004	0.003	0.003	0.003	0.002	0.002	0.001	*	*	*	*
22	0.015	0.013	0.011	0.009	0.007	0.006	0.005	0.004	0.004	0.003	0.003	0.002	0.002	0.002	0.001	0.001	*	*	*	*
23	0.012	0.010	0.009	0.007	0.006	0.005	0.004	0.003	0.003	0.002	0.002	0.002	0.001	0.001	0.001	*	*	*	*	*
24	0.010	0.008	0.007	0.006	0.005	0.004	0.003	0.003	0.002	0.002	0.002	0.001	0.001	0.001	0.001	*	*	*	*	*
25	0.009	0.007	0.006	0.005	0.004	0.003	0.003	0.002	0.002	0.001	0.001	0.001	0.001	0.001	0.001	*	*	*	*	*
26	0.007	0.006	0.005	0.004	0.003	0.002	0.002	0.002	0.001	0.001	0.001	0.001	0.001	*	*	*	*	*	*	*
27	0.006	0.005	0.004	0.003	0.002	0.002	0.002	0.001	0.001	0.001	0.001	0.001	*	*	*	*	*	*	*	*
28	0.005	0.004	0.003	0.002	0.002	0.002	0.001	0.001	0.001	0.001	0.001	*	*	*	*	*	*	*	*	*
29	0.004	0.003	0.002	0.002	0.002	0.001	0.001	0.001	0.001	*	*	*	*	*	*	*	*	*	*	*
30	0.003	0.003	0.002	0.002	0.001	0.001	0.001	0.001	*	*	*	*	*	*	*	*	*	*	*	*
35	0.001	0.001	0.001	0.001	*	*	*	*	*	*	*	*	*	*	*	*	*	*	*	*
40	*	*	*	*	*	*	*	*	*	*	*	*	*	*	*	*	*	*	*	*
45	*	*	*	*	*	*	*	*	*	*	*	*	*	*	*	*	*	*	*	*
50	*	*	*	*	*	*	*	*	*	*	*	*	*	*	*	*	*	*	*	*

*Value is zero to three decimal places.

Table 7-5. Present Value Factors for an Annuity of $1 Discounted at k Percent for n Periods:

$$PVA_{k,n} = \sum_{t=1}^{n} \frac{1}{(1+k)^t} = \frac{1}{k} - \frac{1}{k(1+k)^n}$$

Discount Rate, k

Period, n	1%	2%	3%	4%	5%	6%	7%	8%	9%	10%	11%	12%	13%	14%	15%	16%	17%	18%	19%	20%
1	0.990	0.980	0.971	0.962	0.952	0.943	0.935	0.926	0.917	0.909	0.901	0.893	0.885	0.877	0.870	0.862	0.855	0.847	0.840	0.833
2	1.970	1.942	1.913	1.886	1.859	1.833	1.808	1.783	1.759	1.736	1.713	1.690	1.668	1.647	1.626	1.605	1.585	1.566	1.547	1.528
3	2.941	2.884	2.829	2.775	2.723	2.673	2.624	2.577	2.531	2.487	2.444	2.402	2.361	2.322	2.283	2.246	2.210	2.174	2.140	2.106
4	3.902	3.808	3.717	3.630	3.546	3.465	3.387	3.312	3.240	3.170	3.102	3.037	2.974	2.914	2.855	2.798	2.743	2.690	2.639	2.589
5	4.853	4.713	4.580	4.452	4.329	4.212	4.100	3.993	3.890	3.791	3.696	3.605	3.517	3.433	3.352	3.274	3.199	3.127	3.058	2.991
6	5.795	5.601	5.417	5.242	5.076	4.917	4.767	4.623	4.486	4.355	4.231	4.111	3.998	3.889	3.784	3.685	3.589	3.498	3.410	3.326
7	6.728	6.472	6.230	6.002	5.786	5.582	5.389	5.206	5.033	4.868	4.712	4.564	4.423	4.288	4.160	4.039	3.922	3.812	3.706	3.605
8	7.652	7.325	7.020	6.733	6.463	6.210	5.971	5.747	5.535	5.335	5.146	4.968	4.799	4.639	4.487	4.344	4.207	4.078	3.954	3.837
9	8.566	8.162	7.786	7.435	7.108	6.802	6.515	6.247	5.995	5.759	5.537	5.328	5.132	4.946	4.772	4.607	4.451	4.303	4.163	4.031
10	9.471	8.983	8.530	8.111	7.722	7.360	7.024	6.710	6.418	6.145	5.889	5.650	5.426	5.216	5.019	4.833	4.659	4.494	4.339	4.192
11	10.368	9.787	9.253	8.760	8.306	7.887	7.499	7.139	6.805	6.495	6.207	5.938	5.687	5.453	5.234	5.029	4.836	4.656	4.486	4.327
12	11.255	10.575	9.954	9.385	8.863	8.384	7.943	7.536	7.161	6.814	6.492	6.194	5.918	5.660	5.421	5.197	4.988	4.793	4.611	4.439
13	12.134	11.348	10.635	9.986	9.394	8.853	8.358	7.904	7.487	7.103	6.750	6.424	6.122	5.842	5.583	5.342	5.118	4.910	4.715	4.533
14	13.004	12.106	11.296	10.563	9.899	9.295	8.745	8.244	7.786	7.367	6.982	6.628	6.302	6.002	5.724	5.468	5.229	5.008	4.802	4.611
15	13.865	12.849	11.938	11.118	10.380	9.712	9.108	8.559	8.061	7.606	7.191	6.811	6.462	6.142	5.847	5.575	5.324	5.092	4.876	4.675
16	14.718	13.578	12.561	11.652	10.838	10.106	9.447	8.851	8.313	7.824	7.379	6.974	6.604	6.265	5.954	5.668	5.405	5.162	4.938	4.730
17	15.562	14.292	13.166	12.166	11.274	10.477	9.763	9.122	8.544	8.022	7.549	7.120	6.729	6.373	6.047	5.749	5.475	5.222	4.990	4.775
18	16.398	14.992	13.754	12.659	11.690	10.828	10.059	9.372	8.756	8.201	7.702	7.250	6.840	6.467	6.128	5.818	5.534	5.273	5.033	4.812
19	17.226	15.678	14.324	13.134	12.085	11.158	10.336	9.604	8.950	8.365	7.839	7.366	6.938	6.550	6.198	5.877	5.584	5.316	5.070	4.843
20	18.046	16.351	14.877	13.590	12.462	11.470	10.594	9.818	9.129	8.514	7.963	7.469	7.025	6.623	6.259	5.929	5.628	5.353	5.101	4.870
21	18.857	17.011	15.415	14.029	12.821	11.764	10.836	10.017	9.292	8.649	8.075	7.562	7.102	6.687	6.312	5.973	5.665	5.384	5.127	4.891
22	19.660	17.658	15.937	14.451	13.163	12.042	11.061	10.201	9.442	8.772	8.176	7.645	7.170	6.743	6.359	6.011	5.696	5.410	5.149	4.909
23	20.456	18.292	16.444	14.857	13.489	12.303	11.272	10.371	9.580	8.883	8.266	7.718	7.230	6.792	6.399	6.044	5.723	5.432	5.167	4.925
24	21.243	18.914	16.936	15.247	13.799	12.550	11.469	10.529	9.707	8.985	8.348	7.784	7.283	6.835	6.434	6.073	5.746	5.451	5.182	4.937
25	22.023	19.523	17.413	15.622	14.094	12.783	11.654	10.675	9.823	9.077	8.422	7.843	7.330	6.873	6.464	6.097	5.766	5.467	5.195	4.948
26	22.795	20.121	17.877	15.983	14.375	13.003	11.826	10.810	9.929	9.161	8.488	7.896	7.372	6.906	6.491	6.118	5.783	5.480	5.206	4.956
27	23.560	20.707	18.327	16.330	14.643	13.211	11.987	10.935	10.027	9.237	8.548	7.943	7.409	6.935	6.514	6.136	5.798	5.492	5.215	4.964
28	24.316	21.281	18.764	16.663	14.898	13.406	12.137	11.051	10.116	9.307	8.602	7.984	7.441	6.961	6.534	6.152	5.810	5.502	5.223	4.970
29	25.066	21.844	19.188	16.984	15.141	13.591	12.278	11.158	10.198	9.370	8.650	8.022	7.470	6.983	6.551	6.166	5.820	5.510	5.229	4.975
30	25.808	22.396	19.600	17.292	15.372	13.765	12.409	11.258	10.274	9.427	8.694	8.055	7.496	7.003	6.566	6.177	5.829	5.517	5.235	4.979
35	29.409	24.999	21.487	18.665	16.374	14.498	12.948	11.655	10.567	9.644	8.855	8.176	7.586	7.070	6.617	6.215	5.858	5.539	5.251	4.992
40	32.835	27.355	23.115	19.793	17.159	15.046	13.332	11.925	10.757	9.779	8.951	8.244	7.634	7.105	6.642	6.233	5.871	5.548	5.258	4.997
45	36.095	29.490	24.519	20.720	17.774	15.456	13.606	12.108	10.881	9.863	9.008	8.283	7.661	7.123	6.654	6.242	5.877	5.552	5.261	4.999

Table 7-5. $PVA_{k,n}$ (Continued)

Discount Rate, k

Period, n	21%	22%	23%	24%	25%	26%	27%	28%	29%	30%	31%	32%	33%	34%	35%	40%	45%	50%	55%	60%
1	0.826	0.820	0.813	0.806	0.800	0.794	0.787	0.781	0.775	0.769	0.763	0.758	0.752	0.746	0.741	0.714	0.690	0.667	0.645	0.625
2	1.509	1.492	1.474	1.457	1.440	1.424	1.407	1.392	1.376	1.361	1.346	1.331	1.317	1.303	1.289	1.224	1.165	1.111	1.061	1.016
3	2.074	2.042	2.011	1.981	1.952	1.923	1.896	1.868	1.842	1.816	1.791	1.766	1.742	1.719	1.696	1.589	1.493	1.407	1.330	1.260
4	2.540	2.494	2.448	2.404	2.362	2.320	2.280	2.241	2.203	2.166	2.130	2.096	2.062	2.029	1.997	1.849	1.720	1.605	1.503	1.412
5	2.926	2.864	2.803	2.745	2.689	2.635	2.583	2.532	2.483	2.436	2.390	2.345	2.302	2.260	2.220	2.035	1.876	1.737	1.615	1.508
6	3.245	3.167	3.092	3.020	2.951	2.885	2.821	2.759	2.700	2.643	2.588	2.534	2.483	2.433	2.385	2.168	1.983	1.824	1.687	1.567
7	3.508	3.416	3.327	3.242	3.161	3.083	3.009	2.937	2.868	2.802	2.739	2.677	2.610	2.562	2.508	2.263	2.057	1.883	1.734	1.605
8	3.726	3.619	3.518	3.421	3.329	3.241	3.156	3.076	2.999	2.925	2.854	2.786	2.721	2.658	2.598	2.331	2.109	1.922	1.764	1.628
9	3.905	3.786	3.673	3.566	3.463	3.366	3.273	3.184	3.100	3.019	2.942	2.868	2.798	2.730	2.665	2.379	2.144	1.948	1.783	1.642
10	4.054	3.923	3.799	3.682	3.571	3.465	3.364	3.269	3.178	3.092	3.009	2.930	2.855	2.784	2.715	2.414	2.168	1.965	1.795	1.652
11	4.177	4.035	3.902	3.776	3.656	3.543	3.437	3.335	3.239	3.147	3.060	2.978	2.899	2.824	2.752	2.438	2.185	1.977	1.804	1.657
12	4.278	4.127	3.985	3.851	3.725	3.606	3.493	3.387	3.286	3.190	3.100	3.013	2.931	2.853	2.779	2.456	2.196	1.985	1.809	1.661
13	4.362	4.203	4.053	3.912	3.780	3.656	3.538	3.427	3.322	3.223	3.129	3.040	2.956	2.876	2.799	2.469	2.204	1.990	1.812	1.663
14	4.432	4.265	4.108	3.962	3.824	3.695	3.573	3.459	3.351	3.249	3.152	3.061	2.974	2.892	2.814	2.478	2.210	1.993	1.814	1.664
15	4.489	4.315	4.153	4.001	3.859	3.726	3.601	3.483	3.373	3.268	3.170	3.076	2.988	2.905	2.825	2.484	2.214	1.995	1.816	1.665
16	4.536	4.357	4.189	4.033	3.887	3.751	3.623	3.503	3.390	3.283	3.183	3.088	2.999	2.914	2.834	2.489	2.216	1.997	1.817	1.666
17	4.576	4.391	4.219	4.059	3.901	3.771	3.640	3.518	3.403	3.295	3.193	3.097	3.007	2.921	2.840	2.492	2.218	1.998	1.817	1.666
18	4.608	4.419	4.243	4.080	3.928	3.786	3.654	3.529	3.413	3.304	3.201	3.104	3.012	2.926	2.844	2.494	2.219	1.999	1.818	1.666
19	4.635	4.442	4.263	4.097	3.942	3.799	3.664	3.539	3.421	3.311	3.207	3.109	3.017	2.930	2.848	2.496	2.220	1.999	1.818	1.666
20	4.657	4.460	4.279	4.110	3.954	3.808	3.673	3.546	3.427	3.316	3.211	3.113	3.020	2.933	2.850	2.497	2.221	1.999	1.818	1.667
21	4.675	4.476	4.292	4.121	3.963	3.816	3.679	3.551	3.432	3.320	3.215	3.116	3.023	2.935	2.852	2.498	2.221	2.000	1.818	1.667
22	4.690	4.488	4.302	4.130	3.970	3.822	3.684	3.556	3.436	3.323	3.217	3.118	3.025	2.936	2.853	2.498	2.222	2.000	1.818	1.667
23	4.703	4.499	4.311	4.137	3.976	3.827	3.689	3.559	3.438	3.325	3.219	3.120	3.026	2.938	2.854	2.499	2.222	2.000	1.818	1.667
24	4.713	4.507	4.318	4.143	3.981	3.831	3.692	3.562	3.441	3.327	3.221	3.121	3.027	2.939	2.855	2.499	2.222	2.000	1.818	1.667
25	4.721	4.514	4.323	4.147	3.985	3.834	3.694	3.564	3.442	3.329	3.222	3.122	3.028	2.939	2.856	2.499	2.222	2.000	1.818	1.667
26	4.728	4.520	4.328	4.151	3.988	3.837	3.696	3.566	3.444	3.330	3.223	3.123	3.028	2.940	2.856	2.500	2.222	2.000	1.818	1.667
27	4.734	4.524	4.332	4.154	3.990	3.839	3.698	3.567	3.445	3.331	3.224	3.123	3.029	2.940	2.856	2.500	2.222	2.000	1.818	1.667
28	4.739	4.528	4.335	4.157	3.992	3.840	3.699	3.568	3.446	3.331	3.224	3.123	3.029	2.940	2.856	2.500	2.222	2.000	1.818	1.667
29	4.743	4.531	4.337	4.159	3.994	3.841	3.700	3.569	3.446	3.332	3.225	3.124	3.030	2.941	2.857	2.500	2.222	2.000	1.818	1.667
30	4.746	4.534	4.339	4.160	3.995	3.842	3.701	3.569	3.447	3.332	3.225	3.124	3.030	2.941	2.857	2.500	2.222	2.000	1.818	1.667
35	4.756	4.541	4.345	4.164	3.998	3.845	3.703	3.571	3.448	3.333	3.226	3.125	3.030	2.941	2.857	2.500	2.222	2.000	1.818	1.667
40	4.760	4.544	4.347	4.166	3.999	3.846	3.703	3.571	3.448	3.333	3.226	3.125	3.030	2.941	2.857	2.500	2.222	2.000	1.818	1.667
45	4.761	4.545	4.347	4.166	4.000	3.846	3.704	3.571	3.448	3.333	3.226	3.125	3.030	2.941	2.857	2.500	2.222	2.000	1.818	1.667
50	4.762	4.545	4.348	4.167	4.000	3.846	3.704	3.571	3.448	3.333	3.226	3.125	3.030	2.941	2.857	2.500	2.222	2.000	1.818	1.667

Current Yield

The current yield on a bond or any investment is computed as follows:

$$\text{Current yield} = \frac{\text{Actual interest earned in one year}}{\text{Current market price}}$$

The current yield takes into account only current income earned, not any changes in the value of the investment. For bonds purchased at a price different from their face value, a more accurate measure of return includes the gain or loss of principal. This yield is called yield to maturity.

Yield to Maturity

As stated in Chapter 9, if you pay $1,020 for a 10-year, 7% bond which pays back $1,000 at maturity, you will lose $20 in principal when you receive your face value. This loss reduces the $700 in income received over the life of the bond. Similarly, if you purchase a bond for $20 less than it returns at maturity, you can add that $20 to the interest income paid over the life of the bond. The formula for computing your approximate yield to maturity is shown in Figure 7–1.

Using our two previous examples, with 7% bonds purchased at either 102 ($1,020) or 98 ($980), approximate yields to maturity would be computed as shown in Figures 7–2a and b.

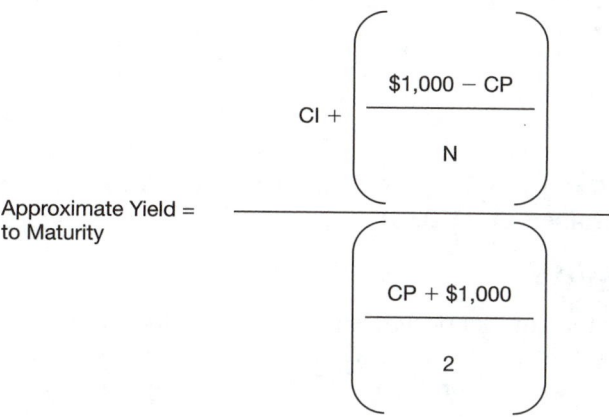

$$\text{Approximate Yield to Maturity} = \frac{CI + \dfrac{\$1,000 - CP}{N}}{\dfrac{CP + \$1,000}{2}}$$

CI = annual current interest income (coupon rate × $1,000)
CP = current price of the bond
N   = number of years until maturity

Figure 7–1. Formula for Computing Approximate Yield to Maturity

7% Bond purchased at a premium: $1,020

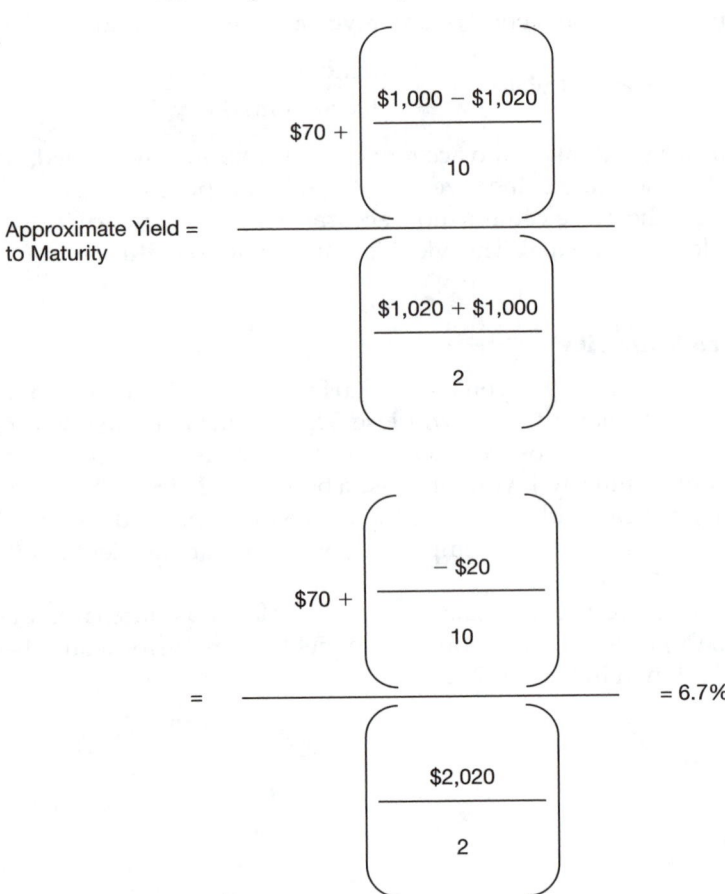

Figure 7–2a. Computing Approximate Yield to Maturity (7% Bond Purchased at $1,020)

Stock Splits

To calculate the number of shares you will own after a split, apply the fraction listed in the split to your shares. For example, if you own 500 shares of a stock that splits 3-for-2, you will own 750 shares after the split.

$$\frac{500 \text{ shares} \times 3}{2} = \frac{1,500}{2} = 750$$

To adjust all share-related numbers—such as the price per share, dividends per share, or earnings per share—multiply by the inverse, in this case 2/3. If the stock noted previously was trading at $90 before the split, it could be expected to begin trading at $60 ($90 × 2/3) immediately after the split.

7% Bond purchased at a discount: $980

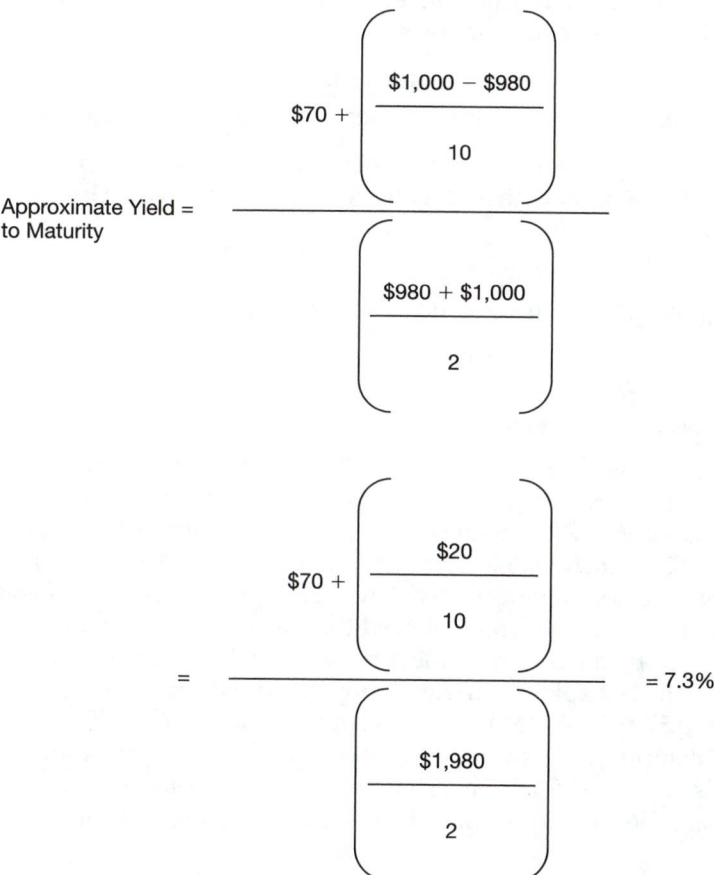

Approximate Yield to Maturity:

$$\text{Approximate Yield to Maturity} = \cfrac{\$70 + \cfrac{\$1{,}000 - \$980}{10}}{\cfrac{\$980 + \$1{,}000}{2}}$$

$$= \cfrac{\$70 + \cfrac{\$20}{10}}{\cfrac{\$1{,}980}{2}} = 7.3\%$$

Figure 7–2b. Computing Approximate Yield to Maturity (7% Bond Purchased at $980)

Tax-Related Formulas

Taxable Equivalent Yield

The taxable equivalent yield (TEY) is that which a taxable investment would need in order to provide the same after-tax return as a tax-exempt investment. The formula, using only federal income taxes, is as follows:

$$\text{Taxable equivalent yield} = \frac{\text{Tax-exempt yield}}{(1.00 - \text{Federal income tax rate})}$$

A municipal bond issued in the investor's home state is nearly always state income tax exempt. The taxable equivalent yield computation, including state income taxes, is as follows:

$$\frac{\text{Tax-exempt yield}}{1.00 - \{[(1.00 - \text{State tax rate}) \times \text{Federal tax rate}] + \text{State tax rate}\}}$$

If you are in a 31% federal income tax bracket and a 6% state income tax bracket, a municipal bond with a 5% coupon rate would have a TEY computed as follows:

$$\text{TEY} = \frac{0.05}{1.00 - \{[(1.00 - 0.06) \times 0.31] + 0.06\}} = \frac{0.05}{(1.00 - 0.35)} = 7.7\%$$

Capital Gains and Losses

Capital gains and losses are computed by subtracting an investment's cost basis from its sales proceeds, including commissions. For example, a purchase of 100 shares of XYZ Company at $50, with a $35 commission, yields a cost basis of $5,035. When selling the entire position, use the $5,035 basis regardless of splits or stock dividends that have subsequently occurred. If you sell a portion of the position, you will need the cost basis per share. In that case, divide $5,035 by the current number of shares in the entire position.

For example, if XYZ splits 3-for-2, you now have 150 shares. Your basis per share is $33.57 ($5,035/150). In the event that you sell only 50 shares, your gain is computed by subtracting $1,678.50 ($33.57 × 50) from the sales proceeds. If you sell for $45 per share and pay a $35 commission, your capital gain is $536.50 ($50 × $45 − $35 = $2,215. $2,215 − $1,678.50 = $536.50).

Financial Statements and Ratios

Balance Sheet and Income Statement

Ratios used to analyze stocks are derived from a company's balance sheet and income statement. The balance sheet is a statement of all that is owned and owed on a particular date. On one side (or the top) of the sheet are assets, or everything that is owned. Current assets are expected to be used within one year, and include cash and marketable securities, accounts receivable, and inventories. Noncurrent assets, called fixed assets, include property, plant, equipment, and any other long-term assets.

The opposite side (or the bottom) of the balance sheet begins with liabilities, which are debts of the company. Current liabilities are debts that will come due within the year, such as accounts payable, income taxes due, and the current portion of any long-term debt. Long-term liabilities include long-term bank debt and any bonds that have been issued. The excess of assets over total liabilities is stockholders' equity, which is theoretically what the stockholders would receive if the company were liquidated. A sample balance sheet is shown in Figure 7–3.

An income statement, also called a profit and loss statement, shows the income for a firm over a particular time period. It begins with revenues—the amount received for selling a product or service—and subtracts the expenses of the business to find the resulting profit. Several intermediate steps divide expenses as to type. For example, subtracting the cost of goods sold from revenues provides a figure known as gross profit margin. Selling, general, and administrative expenses are the overall costs of running the business. Included in those costs is depreciation, which is an accounting charge that allows a business to spread the cost of purchasing a fixed asset over the useful life of the asset. Though it is subtracted on the income statement to compute taxable income, depreciation is a noncash charge, because the asset was paid for at the time of purchase. Figure 7–4 contains a sample income statement.

When analyzing a company's financial performance and comparing it to that of other companies, investors often use financial ratios derived from the balance sheet and income statement. Consider some of the following ratios.

Liquidity Ratios

Liquidity ratios measure a company's ability to meet short-term obligations with current assets available.

The current ratio compares current assets with current liabilities. A common standard used for a desirable current ratio is 2.0, though industry norms vary. Current ratios of less than 1.0 can signal financial difficulty whereas very high current ratios can signal financial assets that could be invested more productively.

$$\text{Current ratio} = \frac{\text{Current assets}}{\text{Current liabilities}}$$

Figure 7-3. Balance Sheet

Consolidated Balance Sheet
December 31, 2000
Assets

Current Assets	
Cash and cash equivalents	$ 100
Accounts receivable	285
Inventory	440
Other assets	200
Total current assets	1,025
Long-term assets	
Property, plant and equipment, net of depreciation	2,875
Other long-term assets	800
Total long-term assets	3,675
Total assets	$4,700

Liabilities and Stockholders' Equity

Current liabilities	
Accounts payable	$ 620
Short-term debt and current maturities of long-term debt	400
Accrued expenses and other	525
Total current liabilities	1,545
Long-term liabilities	
Long-term debt, less current portion	1,275
Deferred taxes	460
Other	150
Total long-term liabilities	1,885
Stockholders' equity	
Common stock, including additional paid-in capital	360
Treasury stock at cost	(300)
Retained earnings	1,210
Total stockholders' equity	1,270
Total liabilities and stockholders' equity	$4,700

The quick, or acid test, ratio subtracts inventories from current assets in the current ratio equation. This stricter measure of liquidity is sometimes used because inventory may not be very liquid.

$$\text{Quick ratio} = \frac{\text{Current assets} - \text{Inventory}}{\text{Current liabilities}}$$

Figure 7-4. Income Statement

Income Statement	
Year Ended December 31, 2000	
Revenue	$7,750
Cost of goods sold	4,370
Gross profit margin	3,380
Selling, general, and administrative expenses	2,500
Operating income	880
Other income and expenses	10
Earnings before interest and taxes (EBIT)	870
Interest	90
Taxes	330
Net income	450

Asset Management Ratios

Asset management ratios seek to determine whether the levels of certain assets are appropriate in the context of the business. Excess funds tied up in assets such as accounts receivable and inventory could be used productively elsewhere, but levels that are too low may point to policies that hamper sales.

Days sales outstanding gives the average number of days that it takes to collect payment for sales. This measures the effectiveness of credit-granting and collection procedures. In general, a low ratio is best, because it indicates fast payment on sales and few uncollectible accounts. In some cases, however, too low a ratio may mean sales have been lost due to too-tight credit policies. Days sales outstanding is computed by dividing accounts receivable by sales per day, which is sales/365.

$$\text{Days sales outstanding} = \frac{\text{Accounts receivable}}{\text{Sales}/365}$$

Inventory turnover measures the number of times a company sells its inventory each year. High inventory turnover relative to a firm's peers signals efficient inventory management and a minimum of capital tied up in inventory.

$$\text{Inventory turnover} = \frac{\text{Cost of goods sold}}{\text{Inventory}}$$

Debt Management Ratios

Debt management ratios measure the leverage of a company and the risk that it faces from annual interest costs. There is a balance between using some debt to magnify earnings and using so much debt that the financial health of the company is compromised.

The debt to equity ratio measures the relationship of debt financing to equity financing. Debt levels vary widely by industry, generally running higher in capital-intensive industries such as manufacturing.

$$\text{Debt to equity} = \frac{\text{Total debt}}{\text{Stockholders' equity}}$$

Times interest earned measures the ratio of earnings before payment of interest and taxes to the amount of interest payments due. A higher multiple means less danger of defaulting on interest payments, should earnings fall short of current levels.

$$\text{Times interest earned} = \frac{\text{Earnings before interest and taxes (EBIT)}}{\text{Annual interest costs}}$$

A more comprehensive measure of a firm's ability to meet its obligations includes the cost of long-term lease obligations and preferred dividends. Lease expenses are added to both the numerator and denominator, and the after-tax cost of preferred dividends is added to the denominator in fixed charges coverage.

$$\text{Fixed charges coverages} = \frac{\text{EBIT} + \text{Leased expenses}}{\text{Interest} + \text{Leased expenses} + \text{Preferred div} [1/(1 - \text{tax rate})]}$$

Profitability Ratios

Profitability ratios measure a firm's ability to generate a profit, given its level of sales, assets, and equity.

Gross profit margin is the ratio of gross profits (revenue – cost of goods sold) to revenue. This measures the profitability of the company in producing its products, without the other costs of running the business.

$$\text{Gross profit margin} = \frac{\text{Gross profit}}{\text{Revenue}}$$

Net profit margin is the ratio of net income to revenue. This ratio shows total profitability of the firm. Both gross and net profit margins should be compared within a firm's peer group as industry norms vary widely.

$$\text{Net profit margin} = \frac{\text{Net income}}{\text{Revenue}}$$

Return on total assets is a measure of a firm's ability to earn a profit given its available assets. A higher ratio shows efficiency of management in using its asset base to generate profits. Some financial managers call this ratio return on investment (ROI), and some use only fixed assets in the denominator rather than total assets.

$$\text{Return on assets} = \frac{\text{Net income}}{\text{Total assets}}$$

Return on equity (ROE) is a measure of the profitability of the company given the amount of stockholders' equity employed. Since high debt results in lower relative equity, ROE should always be viewed in conjunction with debt management ratios. A high ROE resulting from excessive debt is not a sign of profitability, but of operating leverage.

$$\text{Return on equity} = \frac{\text{Net income}}{\text{Stockholders' equity}}$$

Market Ratios

Market ratios are not related to a company's financial health as are the preceding ratios, but to the price/value relationship exhibited by the stock's market price per share. The price/earnings (P/E) ratio measures how much investors are willing to pay for a dollar in earnings per share (EPS). All other things being equal, a lower P/E means a better value.

$$\text{Price/earnings ratio} = \frac{\text{Current share price}}{\text{Earnings per share}}$$

The price/earnings/growth (PEG) ratio measures the relationship of the P/E ratio to the rate of earnings growth. Investors are willing to pay a higher price for stocks whose earnings are growing rapidly, because EPS, the denominator of the P/E ratio, is expected to increase quickly, effectively reducing the real P/E. A PEG of 1.00 is generally considered to be a fair value.

$$\text{Price/earnings/growth ratio} = \frac{\text{P/E ratio}}{\text{Growth rate in EPS}}$$

The ratio of a stock's price to its book value per share measures how much investors are willing to pay for the theoretical liquidation value of the company. Book value per share is the assets of the company, less liabilities, divided by the number of shares outstanding. A higher price to book value ratio signals a good value, but may also be a sign that investors do not believe that management adds much value to the business in its operation.

$$\text{Price to book value per share} = \frac{\text{Current share price}}{\text{Book value per share}}$$

The dividend yield of a stock is the investment return derived from dividends paid. If the dividend is not in danger of being cut, a high dividend yield can provide a floor for the stock price by attracting investors (buying demand) who are purchasing for current return. Generally, stocks with a high dividend yield are those without significant growth prospects.

$$\text{Dividend yield} = \frac{\text{Annual dividend per share}}{\text{Current price per share}}$$

Part 3

Investment Vehicles

Investment vehicles are the nuts and bolts of investing. Chapters 8 through 16 cover the specific features of investment products, how they work and some of the arguments for and against buying them. Look here for details on cash equivalents, bonds, stocks, international investments, mutual funds, life insurance and annuities, options, real estate, and precious metals.

8
Investing in Cash Equivalents

What is cash? Ordinarily, cash refers to dollar bills (fives, tens, twenties), but in the investment world, cash is short for cash equivalent. A cash equivalent is any security that can be exchanged for cash quickly and easily. A necessary part of our financial system, cash equivalents can be used to (1) meet daily living expenses, (2) accumulate funds for large purchases, (3) supply a cushion for unexpected expenses or opportunities, and (4) provide a "time out" between other investment decisions.

Checking, Savings, and Money Market Deposit Accounts

The most common cash equivalent is the checking account. Offered by financial institutions such as banks, saving and loans, and credit unions, a checking account is a demand deposit. This means that the funds deposited into the account are available on demand, with the demand being a check. Regular checking accounts offered by commercial banks pay no interest and are often free with a minimum balance of $500 to $1,000.

Negotiable order of withdrawal (NOW) accounts are checking accounts that pay interest. They often have minimum balance requirements or interest rates that increase as the account balance increases.

Savings accounts and money market deposit accounts (MMDAs) offered by financial institutions pay interest monthly and generally allow a limited number of checks or interaccount transfers, usually three to six. Additional transfers may be available for a fee and a minimum balance is often required to avoid a monthly service charge. The interest rates paid on savings and money market deposit accounts are usually slightly higher than those paid on a NOW account.

Money Market Mutual Funds

Money market mutual funds (MMMFs) are mutual funds that invest in short-term marketable securities, such as U.S. Treasury securities, corporate commercial paper, commercial bank securities, and the debt of various government agencies. The fund pools the money of many small investors, offering shares to be purchased and redeemed at $1.00, with a variable rate of interest paid monthly. Some money market mutual funds require minimum balances of as much as $2,000 to avoid a fee. Many MMMFs offer check-writing privileges, which may be limited in the number per month allowed and minimum dollar value of each check.

All MMMFs are not alike. For example, Alliance Capital offers more than 13 different money market funds, each with its own distinct characteristics. Although 13 choices may be more than the norm, most mutual fund companies will offer at least a standard money market fund, a government money market fund, and a municipal money market fund.

The standard money market fund, as discussed, suits the needs of most investors. However, if you are interested in higher levels of safety or tax advantages, a government or municipal fund may be the right choice.

Government funds invest only in U.S. government securities, repurchase, and reverse-repurchase agreements for those securities. The yield on a government money market fund is generally lower than that of a standard money market fund, because higher-yielding investments such as bank CDs are not allowed. On the other hand, risk to principal is lower in government securities due to the direct guaranty of the U.S. government. Government money market funds may yield from 0.05% to 0.30% less than standard money market funds, depending on the interest rate environment.

Municipal money market funds fall into two categories: general portfolio and state-specific portfolio. The general portfolio contains short-term municipal securities from various states. Its dividends are exempt from federal income tax. State-specific portfolios contain municipal securities from just one state. Dividends from these funds are both federal and state tax exempt for investors living in that state. While stated yields of municipal money market funds are much lower than those of standard money market funds, taxable equivalent yields (see Chapter 7) are comparable.

Certificates of Deposit

Certificates of deposit, commonly referred to as CDs, are time deposits with a financial institution. In return for a rate of interest that is generally higher than that offered on an MMDA, investors must promise to keep their funds on deposit for a specified amount of time, anywhere from seven days to several years. Although you may withdraw the principal invested prior to maturity, a substantial interest penalty usually results.

In addition to purchasing CDs directly from the issuing financial institution, you may purchase them from a stockbroker. In this transaction, the brokerage firm identifies CDs with attractive rates and purchases them in bulk from financial institutions. The firm then parcels out the CDs, identified as brokered CDs, to its customers in smaller pieces. Often the investor will not see a commission charged for this transaction. It may be paid by the issuing financial institution or may be reflected in a difference in the price the brokerage firm pays for the CDs and the price at which it resells them to customers. Benefits of brokered CDs include slightly higher interest rates than those offered in the direct market and the availability of a secondary market. The secondary market allows the investor to sell prior to maturity without incurring a penalty, though changes in interest rates may cause a loss in principal.

If you live in a metropolitan area, bank online, or are willing to bank by mail, you can take advantage of websites that offer to find the best rates on checking, savings, CD, and money market accounts. At *www.bankrate.com,* you can search for the best rates and lowest fees in the following categories: auto loans, credit cards, checking/ATM fees, savings, money market, credit unions, home equity loans, and online banks. Results provide telephone numbers and may be sorted according to several different criteria. Survey dates differ, so make sure you are looking at a recent survey.

A listing of the 100 largest U.S. banks, ranked by total assets, is provided in Figure 8–1.

Commercial Paper

Commercial paper is a short-term (generally less than six months) debt security issued by banks and corporations. For corporations, commercial paper provides a direct short-term borrowing opportunity that circumvents banks. For individual investors, commercial paper from highly rated corporations offers a yield slightly higher than other money market instruments, without a significant amount of additional risk.

Figure 8–1. Top 100 U.S Banks, Ranked by Total Assets

No.	Bank	City	State	Total Assets
1	Bank of America NA	Charlotte	NC	$563,226,000
2	Citibank NA	New York	NY	312,608,000
3	Chase Manhattan Bk	New York	NY	299,390,000
4	First Union NB	Charlotte	NC	220,674,000
5	Morgan Guaranty Tr Co of NY	New York	NY	160,563,541
6	Bank One NA	Chicago	IL	85,926,780
7	Wells Fargo Bk NA	San Francisco	CA	85,711,000
8	Fleet NB	Providence	RI	80,475,000
9	Keybank NA	Cleveland	OH	74,594,984
10	BankBoston NA	Boston	MA	71,541,323
11	US Bk NA	Minneapolis	MN	70,449,952
12	PNC BK NA	Pittsburgh	PA	67,060,670
13	Wachovia Bk NA	Winston-Salem	NC	61,841,288
14	Bank of New York	New York	NY	60,242,491
15	State Street B&TC	Boston	MA	50,196,389
16	Republic NB of NY	New York	NY	49,190,234
17	Bankers Trust Co	New York	NY	47,804,000
18	Southtrust Bk NA	Birmingham	AL	42,374,181
19	Regions Bank	Birmingham	AL	40,904,896
20	Mellon Bk NA	Pittsburgh	PA	39,422,437
21	Washington MSB	Seattle	WA	34,325,893
22	HSBC Bank USA	Buffalo	NY	34,158,353
23	Chase Manhattan Bk USA NA	Wilmington	DE	33,988,747
24	Norwest Bk MN NA	Minneapolis	MN	33,772,482
25	National City Bk	Cleveland	OH	33,204,860
26	Union Planters NB	Memphis	TN	32,514,110
27	Union Bk of CA NA	San Francisco	CA	32,204,442
28	Bank One NA	Columbus	OH	31,565,638
29	Summit Bk	Hackensack	NJ	30,999,134
30	Comerica Bk	Detroit	MI	30,424,234
31	Firstar Bk NA	Cincinnati	OH	30,318,105
32	Branch Bkg&TC	Winston-Salem	NC	29,351,209

Figure 8–1. (*Continued*)

No.	Bank	City	State	Total Assets
33	Lasalle Bank NA	Chicago	IL	$28,873,999
34	Northern Trust Co	Chicago	IL	28,836,113
35	Huntington NB	Columbus	OH	28,771,882
36	Bank One Texas NA	Dallas	TX	28,193,487
37	Fleet Bk NA	Jersey City	NJ	28,172,000
38	MBNA America Bk NA	Wilmington	DE	27,086,386
39	Crestar Bk	Richmond	VA	25,659,253
40	Chase Bank of TX NA	Houston	TX	24,331,455
41	Bank One MI	Detroit	MI	23,022,937
42	Bank One Arizona NA	Phoenix	AZ	22,939,683
43	First American NB	Nashville	TN	21,936,271
44	Amsouth Bk	Birmingham	AL	21,201,519
45	Manufacturers & Traders TC	Buffalo	NY	21,163,174
46	Suntrust Bk	Atlanta	GA	20,700,992
47	Mercantile Bk NA	St Louis	MO	20,376,500
48	Harris T&SB	Chicago	IL	19,010,405
49	First USA Bk NA	Wilmington	DE	18,783,630
50	First Tennessee Bk NA	Memphis	TN	18,220,462
51	Compass Bk	Birmingham	AL	17,724,715
52	First Security Bk NA	Ogden	UT	17,609,253
53	Old Kent Bk	Grand Rapids	MI	17,432,637
54	Banco Popular De PR	San Juan	PR	17,399,000
55	National City Bk MI/IL	Bannockburn	IL	17,026,968
56	Allfirst Bk	Baltimore	MD	16,816,858
57	Greenwood TC	Greenwood	DE	16,472,270
58	Bank One NA	Indianapolis	IN	15,786,920
59	Greenpoint Bk	New York	NY	15,462,326
60	Hibernia NB New Orleans	New Orleans	LA	15,048,581
61	European American Bk	New York	NY	14,799,107
62	Fifth Third Bk	Cincinnati	OH	14,521,254
63	Citibank South Dakota NA	Sioux Falls	SD	13,573,383
64	Bank of Hawaii	Honolulu	HI	13,152,836
65	National City Bk of PA	Pittsburgh	PA	13,051,271
66	Bank One LA NA	Baton Rouge	LA	12,960,000

(Continued)

Figure 8–1. (*Continued*)

No.	Bank	City	State	Total Assets
67	American Express Centurion	Midvale	UT	$12,436,578
68	National City Bk Indiana	Indianapolis	IN	11,854,330
69	North Fork Bk	Melville	NY	11,837,204
70	Norwest Bk TX NA	San Antonio	TX	11,443,504
71	American NB&TC	Chicago	IL	11,291,833
72	Citibank-New York State	Pittsford	NY	11,273,181
73	Bank of America NA USA	Phoenix	AZ	11,254,984
74	M&I Marshall & Ilsley Bk	Milwaukee	WI	10,872,091
75	Michigan NB	Farmington Hills	MI	10,751,436
76	Norwest Bk Colorado NA	Denver	CO	10,719,240
77	Colonial Bk	Montgomery	AL	10,624,845
78	Providian NB	Tilton	NH	10,453,171
79	National City Bk	Louisville	KY	10,111,885
80	Peoples Bk	Bridgeport	CT	10,077,932
81	Firstmerit Bk NA	Akron	OH	9,923,911
82	Bank of The West	San Francisco	CA	9,515,266
83	Commerce Bk NA	Kansas City	MO	9,273,461
84	First-Citizens B&TC	Raleigh	NC	8,934,739
85	Sanwa Bk California	San Francisco	CA	8,883,074
86	Centura Bk	Rocky Mount	NC	8,774,520
87	Suntrust Bk Central FL NA	Orlando	FL	8,619,106
88	Provident Bk	Cincinnati	OH	8,541,728
89	Bank One WI	Milwaukee	WI	8,479,524
90	Hudson City Svgs Bk	Paramus	NJ	8,367,942
91	Capital One Bk	Glen Allen	VA	8,028,254
92	Banco Santander PR	Hato Rey	PR	8,010,699
93	Civitas Bk	St Joseph	MI	7,779,505
94	Roslyn Svgs Bk	Roslyn	NY	7,745,914

Figure 8–1. (Continued)

No.	Bank	City	State	Total Assets
95	Firstar Bk-Milwaukee NA	Milwaukee	WI	$7,643,387
96	Hudson United Bk	Mahwah	NJ	7,201,450
97	Zions First NB	Salt Lake City	UT	7,168,971
98	First Hawaiian Bk	Honolulu	HI	7,139,358
99	Wells Fargo Bk TX NA	Houston	TX	7,032,346
100	City NB	Beverly Hills	CA	6,924,060

As of September 30, 1999, all dollars in thousands.

Reprinted with permission, Sheshunoff Information Services, a Thomson Financial Company.

Banker's Acceptance

Created to facilitate international trade, banker's acceptances are bank drafts, similar to a check, issued by a firm and "accepted" or guaranteed by a bank for future payment. The firm is required to deposit funds to cover the draft with the bank, which accepts responsibility for making payment. In international trade, the use of banker's acceptances reduces the risk that a firm will not meet its financial obligations. Once issued, banker's acceptances can be sold in the secondary market.

Repurchase Agreements

Repurchase agreements (repos) are short-term loans (often overnight, usually less than two weeks) collateralized by U.S. Treasury bills. Investors often use repos when they have excess funds available for a short period of time. In the transaction, the investor buys U.S. Treasury bills from a bank, which agrees to repurchase them at a slightly higher price in the future.

U.S. Treasury Securities

The U.S. government finances much of its debt ($5,744,560,824,206 on March 9, 2000) by selling Treasury securities to the public in the form of U.S. Treasury bills, notes, and bonds. Although these securities have a stated maturity date, an active secondary market means they are nearly as liquid as cash, though it is possible to lose money on the investment if interest rates have risen since the time of purchase. Most brokerage firms offer next-day availability of the cash from the sale of a U.S. Treasury security. You will have to pay a brokerage commission to sell.

U.S. Treasury bills, or T-bills, are issued with three-month (13-week), six-month (26-week), and one-year (52-week) maturities. Treasury bills are sold on a discounted basis in minimum denominations of $1,000, followed by increments of $1,000. (Some brokerage firms may have higher minimums.) When you purchase a discounted security, the interest is equal to the difference between the price paid and the value at maturity. For example, you might pay $9,892 for a three-month T-bill with a maturity value of $10,000. The $108 difference paid at maturity would be the interest. This is a bond-equivalent yield of 4.65%.

Treasury notes have a term of more than 1 year, but not more than 10 years. Treasury bonds are issued with a term of more than 10 years. Treasury notes and bonds can be purchased in increments of $1,000. They have a stated rate of interest, which is paid semiannually.

Inflation-indexed U.S. Treasury securities pay interest semiannually at a stated rate, but the principal amount by which the coupon rate is multiplied changes according to inflation. The index used to measure inflation is the consumer price index for urban consumers (CPI-U). In indexing, the CPI-U number used incorporates a three-month lag and is called the reference CPI-U. To calculate inflation-adjusted principal for a particular date, multiply the face value of the security by a ratio of the current date's reference CPI-U divided by the reference CPI-U for the security's issue date. For example, say you purchased a $1,000 note on January 15 with a 4% coupon rate. To make the math easy, say the CPI-U was 100 on that date. If inflation was 1% in the first quarter, the reference CPI-U for the July 15 interest payment would be 101 (100 + 1% change through March; there is a three-month lag). Your inflation-adjusted principal would then be $1,000 × 101/100 = $1,010. Your semiannual interest payment would be ($1,010 × 4%)/2 = $20.20.

At maturity, inflation-indexed securities are redeemed at the greater of their inflation-adjusted principal value or their face value.

Purchasing Treasury Securities

Treasury securities are sold at auctions held throughout the year. Information about auctions is available from Federal Reserve banks or the Bureau of the Public Debt. Many newspapers also report auction schedules.

Weekly auctions for the three- and six-month bills are announced every Thursday. The bills are auctioned the following Monday and are issued on the Thursday following the auction. One-year bills are offered every four weeks. The auction is announced every fourth Thursday; the bills are auctioned the following Tuesday and are issued the following Thursday.

Two-year notes are issued once a month. The auction is generally announced near the middle of the month and takes place one week later. Notes are issued on the last day of the month (or on the first day of the following month if the last day is a weekend or holiday).

Five- and 10-year notes and 30-year bonds are usually auctioned during the second week of February, May, August, and November. Auctions are announced on the first Wednesday of the month and notes are issued on the fifteenth day of the month.

Inflation-indexed notes and bonds are usually auctioned during the second week of January, April, July, and October. They are announced on the first Wednesday and issued on the fifteenth day of the month.

Once an auction is announced, investors may submit one of two types of bids.

- Noncompetitive bid: The competitive bidders set the rate of return. The investor agrees to accept this rate and is guaranteed a security. Most individual investors choose this type of bid.

- Competitive bid: Investors submit a bid, also called a tender, which specifies the minimum discount rate (for a bill auction) or a yield (for a note or bond auction) that they are willing to accept. The Treasury Department accepts bids beginning with the lowest up until the entire offering is placed. An investor will be awarded a security if the bid falls within the accepted range, but the bid will be rejected if it does not. Although there may be many different bids within the accepted range, all investors are awarded securities at the price equivalent to the highest rate or yield (lowest price) accepted.

Noncompetitive bids may be made over the internet, by phone, or on paper. Competitive bids must be submitted on paper. Paper tender forms, available from the nearest Federal Reserve bank or most commercial banks, can be mailed to the nearest Federal Reserve Bank Servicing Office or the Bureau of the Public Debt's Capital Area Servicing Center. See the appendix at the end of the chapter for addresses, or use the automatic locator at the Bureau of the Public Debt Online at *www.publicdebt.treas.gov.*

If you would like to purchase Treasury securities by phone or online, the Treasury Department has a service called TreasuryDirect which maintains accounts to hold marketable Treasury securities. An account will be established by TreasuryDirect for new purchasers who complete PDF 5381, Treasury Bill, Note & Bond Tender, with their purchase. You may establish an account without purchasing a security by submitting a PDF 5182, New

Account Request. This form is available from your Federal Reserve Bank Servicing Office listed in the appendix. You may also obtain it with an e-mail request to *OSAS-DCS@bpd.treas.gov* or you can download it at *www.publicdebt.treas.gov/sec/secform1.htm*.

By providing the appropriate information about a checking, savings, or share account at a financial institution, you may then purchase securities through TreasuryDirect and have the cost directly debited from your account. To make a transaction, request a statement or pay your annual fee ($25 for accounts with a par value in excess of $100,000):

- Dial 1-800-943-6864 (outside the United States, 1-304-480-7955); or
- Visit the Virtual Lobby at *www.treasurydirect.gov/sec/sectdes.htm*.

Treasury securities can also be purchased through commercial banks and brokerage firms. These dealers may purchase at auction or offer one of many securities already outstanding in the secondary market. Although you will pay a commission, it may be worthwhile as the secondary market provides a much wider selection of maturities. Once purchased, securities are held in the commercial book-entry system, which means they will appear on your account statement from your securities firm rather than being issued in certificate form. Most Treasury securities can be transferred between the commercial book-entry system and TreasuryDirect accounts.

Taxation of Treasury Securities

State and local authorities do not tax the interest paid on U.S. Treasury bills, notes, and bonds.

U.S. Savings Bonds

Series EE savings bonds, formerly called series E bonds, are the bonds to which most people refer when they say "savings bonds." Due to the name change, these bonds are often called E/EE bonds. They are backed by the full faith and credit of the U.S. government and can be purchased through payroll deduction plans or most banks and financial institutions for as little as $25.

Series E/EE bonds are accrual securities, meaning they are issued at a discount and interest is paid when they are cashed. The rate of interest paid is variable, with adjustments made every six months. There is no stated maturity date for E/EE bonds. The higher the rate of interest earned, the less time it takes for the bond to reach its face value, which is double its purchase price.

Savings Bond Interest

Bonds issued before May 1995 have a guaranteed minimum rate of return, as shown in Table 8–1. They are entitled to market-based yields (85% of the average of five-year Treasury yields) if the market yield is higher and the bond has been held for more than five years.

Bonds issued on or after May 1995 do not have a guaranteed minimum rate. Bonds issued from May 1995 through April 1997 earn short-term market-based rates for the first five years and long-term market-based rates after five years.

Bonds issued on or after May 1997 earn interest at 90% of the average yields of five-year Treasury securities for the preceding six months. New rates for all bonds are announced each May 1 and November 1.

The interest on series E/EE bonds is not paid by check but accrues until the bond is cashed or it reaches final maturity.

Table 8–1. Minimum Rates of Return Series E/EE bonds

Bonds Issued on These Dates	Earn a Guaranteed Minimum Rate of
Series E	
12/61–5/65	
11/73	
9/74–2/78	6%
Series EE	
1/80–4/81	
9/81–2/83	
9/87–2/93	
Series E	
9/59–11/61	
6/65–11/65	
9/69–10/73	
12/73–8/74	
3/78–6/80	4%
Series EE	
5/81–8/81	
3/83–8/87	
3/93–4/95	

SOURCE: Bureau of the Public Debt Online.

Taxation of E/EE Bond Interest

During the time of accrual, you have the choice of reporting the accrued interest each year on your federal income tax return or of deferring interest reporting. Although most investors choose to defer reporting, you might decide to report annually if you anticipate a rising tax bracket or hold the bonds in the name of a child. For children under age 14, only interest and dividend income in excess of $1,400 is taxed at the parents' rate in 1999. For children 14 or older, income is taxed at the child's rate. If you decide to report interest annually, use Public Debt Form 3501 to determine how much interest you have earned. You can begin reporting annually at any time, even if you have been deferring interest reporting. However, you will need to report all interest earned to date in the year you begin annual reporting and you must continue annual reporting for all savings bonds you own and any you acquire. You must get approval from the IRS to change from annual reporting back to deferred reporting.

Savings Bond Maturity

Though they can be redeemed at any time past six months after their issue date (a three-month interest penalty applies to bonds redeemed during the first five years), all series E/EE bonds have two maturity dates. The first, original maturity, is the maximum amount of time it will take for the bond to reach face value (see Table 8–2). After the original maturity date, a bond does not stop earning interest. It automatically enters an extension period, during which it earns a market-based yield. (Bonds issued before 1995 will earn the greater of the market-based yield and a guaranteed minimum

Table 8–2. Original Term: The Maximum Amount of Time for Series E/EE Bonds to Reach Face Value

Issue Date	Original Term
1/80–10/80	11 years
11/80–4/81	9 years
5/81–10/82	8 years
11/82–10/86	10 years
11/86–2/93	12 years
3/93–4/95	18 years
5/95–present	17 years

SOURCE: Bureau of the Public Debt Online.

yield.) At the end of the extension period, bonds reach final maturity and stop earning interest. Final maturity for series E/EE bonds is 30 years from the date of issue and for series HH bonds is 20 years from the date of issue.

Series HH Bonds

You cannot buy series HH bonds. They can only be acquired in exchange for series E/EE bonds and savings notes or by reinvesting the proceeds of matured series H bonds. Sold in multiples of $500, series HH bonds pay interest every six months at a rate which is set on the purchase date. Since March 1, 1993, the rate has been 4%. On the tenth anniversary of the bonds' issue date, rates may be reset.

Exchanging Series E/EE Bonds for Series HH Bonds

You can exchange series E/EE for series HH bonds by completing form PDF 3253. The series E/EE bonds must be:

- At least six months old
- Worth at least $500 in current redemption value
- Not older than one year past final maturity.

You can add cash to the transaction or receive cash if the redemption value of the bonds being exchanged is not in even multiples of $500; however, receiving cash may have tax consequences. If you have been deferring reporting interest on your E/EE bonds, you may continue to defer reporting the accrued interest as long as you hold the series HH bonds. When the series HH bonds are cashed, reach final maturity, or are reissued in another name, you must pay income tax on any deferred series E/EE accrued interest. If you receive cash in an exchange, some or all of the cash payment may be considered interest, which you must report in the year it is received.

Series I Bonds

Series I bonds are accrual securities whose interest rate is indexed to inflation. They are issued at face value for as little as $50 and increase in value every month with interest compounded semiannually. There is no guaranteed level of earnings. As with series E/EE bonds, the I bond can be redeemed after the first six months, but a three-month interest penalty applies to bonds redeemed during the first five years.

The earnings rate of an I bond is the sum of a fixed rate of return and a semiannual inflation rate. The fixed rate, announced each May and November by the U.S. Treasury, applies to all I bonds issued during the six-month period following the announcement. The fixed rate remains the same for the life of each bond.

The semiannual inflation rate, announced at the same times, is a measure of inflation based on the CPI-U. This rate is added to the fixed rate of an I bond to determine the bond's earnings rate for the next six months.

Education Tax Exclusion

The savings bond education tax exclusion permits qualified taxpayers to exclude from federally taxable income some or all of interest earned on series EE or I bonds. The following conditions must be met.

- The bonds must be purchased after December 31, 1989.
- They must be issued in the name of a taxpayer who is age 24 or older.
- The bond proceeds must be used for qualified educational expenses, which include tuition and fees of the taxpayer, a spouse, or dependent. Room and board and books are not qualified expenses.
- Married couples filing jointly may not have MAGI above $79,650 (1999 limit) to receive the full interest exclusion.
- Single filers may not have MAGI above $53,100 (1999 limit) to receive the full interest exclusion.

If you intend to claim the education tax exclusion, use IRS Form 8815, which contains instructions and a worksheet. To substantiate your claim, make a record of serial numbers, face amounts, and issue dates and retain receipts or canceled checks for educational expenses.

If you have already purchased bonds in your children's names or do not qualify under the required income levels, consider reporting interest annually. As mentioned, for children under age 14, only income in excess of $1,400 per year is taxed at the parents' rate (1999 rules).

Computing the Value of Savings Bonds

Several resources are available for managing your savings bond inventory and determining the value of the bonds you own. The Bureau of the Public Debt (*www.publicdebt.treas.gov*) provides a Windows® application for download, which allows you to maintain an inventory of your bonds. It will also determine current redemption values and earned interest. Available at the same website is a set of tables called Bond Earnings Reports. They show redemption values, six-month earnings as an annual yield, and yield from issue date for series EE/E bonds, series I bonds, and savings notes based on $100 denominations.

The Federal Reserve Bank of New York's website at *www.ny.frb.org* offers an online savings bond redemption calculator. You can use it to calculate your bonds' worth online.

How Safe Is Your Money?

Cash equivalent investments are considered the safest available, but slight variations exist in the risk to your principal. These variations and differences in liquidity, account for the discrepancies in yields which may be earned.

The safest investment, in terms of getting your money back, is a U.S. Treasury security. Backed by the full faith and credit of the U.S. government, Treasury securities—savings bonds included—will only default if the U.S. government defaults on its obligations, which is not likely, given the fact that the U.S. government has the ability to print money.

Federal Deposit Insurance

The banking crisis of the 1980s and early 1990s saw 1,300 savings and loans fail and 1,617 commercial banks fail or receive financial assistance from the Federal Deposit Insurance Corporation (FDIC). The existence of federal deposit insurance and Congress' willingness to step in when the Federal Savings and Loan Insurance Corporation (FSLIC) ran out of money prevented a nationwide banking failure such as that seen in the 1930s.

Today, 99% of commercial banks, savings and loans, and savings banks and 90% of credit unions are federally insured by U.S. government agencies such as the FDIC. Three private deposit insurance funds cover many credit unions that are not covered by federal insurance.

Maximizing Your FDIC Insurance Coverage. The stated amount of FDIC insurance per depositor is $100,000; however, different categories of legal ownership qualify for separate coverage. You can increase your coverage by carefully titling different accounts. Categories of ownership for which separate insurance applies are single ownership, joint ownership, testamentary, irrevocable trust, and retirement accounts.

Single Ownership Accounts. A single ownership account is owned by an individual. Such accounts include those in the owner's name, those established for the benefit of the owner, and those titled to a business that is a sole proprietorship. Accounts established under the Uniform Gift to Minors Act are single ownership accounts of the minor. Revocable living trust accounts are insured as single ownership accounts of the grantor, unless the trust qualifies as a testamentary trust. If the revocable living trust has been established by more than one grantor, funds will be divided equally and insured as single ownership accounts of each grantor. All single ownership accounts in a financial institution are combined to determine insurance coverage, the limit of which is $100,000.

Joint Ownership Accounts. Joint accounts are insured separately from single ownership accounts provided that the following occur.

- All co-owners are natural persons (no corporations).
- Each co-owner has the same rights of withdrawal.
- Each co-owner has signed a signature card (not required for CDs).

Each person's share in a joint account is considered equal, unless it is stated otherwise on the deposit records. The maximum $100,000 coverage applies to the sum of the interests of an individual in all joint accounts in a financial institution. For example, if Jane and Tom had a joint account for $150,000 and Jane and Steve had a joint account for $120,000, Jane's interest in joint accounts would be $75,000 + $60,000 = $135,000. Of Jane's funds, $100,000 would be insured and $35,000 would be uninsured.

Testamentary Accounts. A testamentary account provides that the funds will belong to a named beneficiary upon the death of the owner. Sometimes known as tentative or "Totten" trust accounts, revocable trust accounts, or payable-on-death accounts, testamentary accounts belong to a separate legal ownership category and therefore are insured independently of single and joint ownership accounts.

To qualify as a testamentary account, the following conditions must be met.

- The beneficiary(ies) must be named specifically in the deposit records of the financial institution.
- The named beneficiary(ies) must be the owner's spouse, child, grandchild, parent, brother, or sister.
- The owner's intention to give the funds, upon his or her death, to the beneficiary must be indicated in the account title. Commonly accepted terms include "in trust for," "as trustee for," and "payable on death."

If these requirements are met, a testamentary account is insured up to $100,000 per qualifying beneficiary. If any beneficiary does not qualify (for example, a niece), funds are divided equally among beneficiaries and the nonqualifying beneficiary's share is added to the owner's single owner-ship funds for determining insurance limits.

Irrevocable Trusts. The interest of each beneficiary of an irrevocable trust is insured separately from other accounts of the grantor, trustee, or beneficiary up to $100,000. The following requirements must be met.

- The trust must be valid under state law.

- The deposit account records of the financial institution must disclose the existence of the trust.

- The interests of the beneficiaries must be ascertainable from the deposit account records of the financial institution or from the records of the trustee.

- The value of each beneficiary's interest must be determinable.

A beneficiary is insured separately for interests in trusts established by different grantors, but interests in separate trusts established by the same grantor are added together for determining insurable values.

Retirement Accounts. Self-directed retirement account funds, such as IRA, Roth IRA, Keogh, and 457 plan accounts, are insured separately from single ownership funds but are combined as a group for determining in-surance limits. IRA and Keogh time deposits (CDs) made before Decem-ber 19,1993, are not combined as a group until the deposits mature, roll over, or are renewed. An education IRA is not considered to be an IRA by the FDIC. Instead, it is treated as an irrevocable trust.

Pension and profit sharing plans generally receive pass-through insur-ance, meaning that each participant's interest in the group deposit is in-sured up to $100,000. The rules, however, are complicated. If your pension or profit sharing plan is held in a federally insured institution, check with your plan administrator to make sure that your interest receives pass-through insurance.

FDIC Insurance and Mergers

The rampant consolidation of the banking industry can create problems for depositors who use several banks to maximize their insurance cover-age. If you have funds in two financial institutions that merge, your de-posits are separately insured for six months from the date of the merger. Certificates of deposit are separately insured until the first maturity date after the six-month period. Those that mature during the six-month pe-riod and are renewed for the same dollar amount and term are separately

Figure 8-2. Largest Financial Institution Mergers since 1993

No.	Buyer: Name	Buyer: State	Target: Name	Target: State	Completion Date	QPA Target: Total Assets ($000)
1	Travelers Group Inc.	NY	Citicorp	NY	10/07/1998	330,414,000
2	NationsBank Corporation	NC	BankAmerica Corporation	CA	09/30/1998	265,436,000
3	Deutsche Bank AG	FF	Bankers Trust Corp.	NY	06/04/1999	156,267,000
4	Chemical Banking Corporation	NY	Chase Manhattan Corporation	NY	03/31/1996	118,756,000
5	Bank One Corporation	OH	First Chicago NBD Corporation	IL	10/01/1998	114,804,000
6	Norwest Corporation	MN	Wells Fargo & Company	CA	11/02/1998	94,820,000
7	Fleet Financial Group Inc	MA	BankBoston Corporation	MA	10/01/1999	73,513,000
8	Wells Fargo & Company	CA	First Interstate Bancorp	CA	04/01/1996	58,071,000
9	HSBC USA, Inc.	NY	Republic New York Corp.	NY	12/31/1999	50,453,034
10	First Chicago Corporation	IL	NBD Bancorp, Inc.	MI	12/01/1995	48,050,694
11	First Union Corporation	NC	CoreStates Financial Corporation	PA	04/27/1998	47,591,000
12	Washington Mutual, Inc.	WA	H.F. Ahmanson & Company	CA	10/01/1998	46,678,752
13	NationsBank Corporation	NC	Barnett Banks, Inc.	FL	01/09/1998	44,005,071
14	Washington Mutual, Inc.	WA	Great Western Financial Corp	CA	07/01/1997	42,874,572
15	NationsBank Corporation	NC	Boatmen's Bancshares, Inc.	MO	01/07/1997	40,682,558

All dollars in thousands.

QPA = Quarter prior to announcement.

Reprinted with permission, Sheshunoff Information Services, a Thomson Financial Company.

insured until the first maturity date after the six-month period. Figure 8–2 lists recent mergers of large financial institutions.

Mutual Fund Safety

Money market mutual funds, even when purchased through a bank-owned brokerage firm, are not insured by the FDIC. However, they may be insured by the Securities Investor Protection Corporation (SIPC) if they are held in an account at an investment firm. The general limits of SIPC insurance are $500,000 in securities and $100,000 in uninvested cash. For SIPC purposes, a money market mutual fund is considered a security, not cash.

How Much Cash Should You Keep?

There are many ways to decide how much of your investible funds should be in cash. The first issue to consider is how large a cushion you need for emergencies. A good rule of thumb is to keep six months' living expenses (not income) in cash or securities that can easily be converted to cash. If this amount is not large enough to handle an emergency, it will give you enough time to consider how and when to best liquidate other holdings. The second issue to consider is large purchases, such as a home, which loom on the near horizon. You never want to be in the position of having to sell stocks or mutual funds when they are depressed in order to fund a purchase. After you have covered the cash you will need for emergencies and purchases, it is time to decide what percentage of your investible portfolio should be in cash. Recommendations vary, but 10% to 15% is a good place to start, depending on your stage of life and risk tolerance.

Summary

The best choice for investing in cash equivalents depends on your time horizon, your risk aversion, and your tax situation. Given that these variables change, you may find that it takes several cash equivalent vehicles to meet your needs. Daily living expenses may be best kept in a checking account, short-term savings in a money market mutual fund, cash for a home purchase or next year's vacation in a CD or Treasury bill, and funds for a child's college education in savings bonds.

For all the reasons noted in this chapter, cash equivalents have a place in every investor's portfolio. Caution should be taken, however, that the very risk averse do not place much emphasis in this area. While cash equivalents are the least risky investment available in terms of getting your principal back, inflation hits these investments hardest. Losing purchasing power in times of even moderate inflation affects a fixed portfolio just as if there had been a loss of principal. See Chapter 5 for a more detailed discussion on avoiding the dangers of inflation.

Appendix: Federal Reserve Bank Servicing Offices

If Your Zip Code Begins with . . .	This Is Your Federal Reserve Bank Servicing Office	Address	Phone Number
006 thru 009 066 068 thru 079 088 thru 139	FRB New York	FRB New York Federal Reserve P.O. Station New York, NY 10045-0001	212-720-6619 or 212-720-5823 (recording)
010 thru 065 067	FRB Boston	FRB Boston P.O. Box 2076 Boston, MA 02106-2076	617-973-3800 (recording)
080 thru 087 166 thru 199	FRB Philadelphia	FRB Philadelphia P.O. Box 90 Philadelphia, PA 19105-0090	215-574-6680 or 215-574-6580 (recording)
140 thru 149	FRB Buffalo	FRB Buffalo P.O. Box 961 Buffalo, NY 14240-0961	716-849-5000 or 716-849-5158 (recording)
150 thru 165 260 439	FRB Pittsburgh	FRB Pittsburgh P.O. Box 867 Pittsburgh, PA 15230-0867	412-261-7802 or 412-261-7988 (recording)
200 thru 209 220 thru 223	Capital Area Center	Capital Area Servicing Center Bureau of the Public Debt Department N Washington, DC 20239-1500	202-874-4000 or 202-874-4026 (device for hearing impaired)
210 thru 219 254 255 thru 268	FRB Baltimore	FRB Baltimore P.O. Box 1378 Baltimore, MD 21203-1378	410-576-3300 or 410-576-3500 (recording)
224 thru 253 225 thru 259	FRB Richmond	FRB Richmond P.O. Box 27622 Richmond, VA 23261-7622	804-697-8372 or 804-697-8355 (recording)
300 thru 319 373 thru 374	FRB Atlanta	FRB Atlanta P.O. Box 662 Atlanta, GA 30301-0662	404-521-8653 or 404-521-8657
320 thru 329 335 thru 338 342 344 346 thru 347	FRB Jacksonville	FRB Jacksonville P.O. Box 2499 Jacksonville, FL 32231-2499	904-632-1179 or 904-632-1178 (recording)

If Your Zip Code Begins with . . .	This Is Your Federal Reserve Bank Servicing Office	Address	Phone Number
330 thru 334 339 thru 340 349	FRB Miami	FRB Miami P.O. Box 520847 Miami, FL 33152-0847	305-471-6497 or 305-471-6257 (recording)
350 thru 364 367 thru 368	FRB Birmingham	FRB Birmingham 1801 Fifth Ave. N. Birmingham, AL 35203-2104	205-731-8708 or 205-731-8702 (recording)
365 thru 366 369 390 thru 396 700 thru 708 713 714	FRB New Orleans	FRB New Orleans P.O. Box 52948 New Orleans, LA 70152-2948	504-593-3200 or 504-593-5839 (recording)
380 thru 383 386 thru 389 397 723 thru 724	FRB Memphis	FRB Memphis P.O. Box 407 Memphis, TN 38101-0407	901-523-7171 Ext. 423 or 901-523-9380 (recording)
400 thru 402 406 420 thru 424 427 474 thru 479	FRB Louisville	FRB Louisville P.O. Box 32710 Louisville, KY 40232-2710	502-568-9238 or 502-568-9240 (recording)
403 thru 405 407 thru 418 425 thru 426 450 thru 457 470 472 thru 473	FRB Cincinnati	FRB Cincinnati P.O. Box 999 Cincinnati, OH 45201-0999	513-721-4794 Ext. 334
430 thru 438 440 thru 449 458	FRB Cleveland	FRB Cleveland P.O. Box 6387 Cleveland, OH 44101-1387	216-579-2000 or 216-579-2490 (recording)
460 thru 469 500 thru 509 512 thru 514 520 thru 528 530 thru 539 541 thru 543 549	FRB Chicago	FRB Chicago P.O. Box 834 Chicago, IL 60690-0834	312-322-5369 or 312-322-2202 (recording)
600 thru 619 625 627			
480 thru 497	FRB Detroit	FRB Detroit P.O. Box 1059 Detroit, MI 48231-1059	313-964-6157 or 313-964-6140 (recording)

If Your Zip Code Begins with . . .	This Is Your Federal Reserve Bank Servicing Office	Address	Phone Number
270 thru 299 498 thru 499 540 544 thru 548 550 thru 599	FRB Minneapolis	FRB Minneapolis P.O. Box 291 Minneapolis, MN 55480-0291	612-204-6650
510 thru 511 515 thru 516 680 thru 693	FRB Omaha	FRB Omaha Securities Department P.O. Box 3958 Omaha, NE 68103-0958	402-221-5636 or 402-221-5638 (recording)
620 thru 624 628 thru 639 650 thru 652 654 thru 658	FRB St. Louis	FRB St. Louis P.O. Box 14915 St. Louis, MO 63178-4915	314-444-8703
540 thru 648 653 660 thru 679	FRB Kansas City	FRB Kansas City P.O. Box 419033 Kansas City, MO 64141-6033	816-881-2883 or 816-881-2767 (recording)
370 thru 372 376 thru 379 384 thru 385 710 thru 712 750 thru 754 756 thru 769 790 thru 794	FRB Dallas	FRB Dallas P.O. Box 660657 Dallas, TX 75266-0657	214-922-6100 or 214-922-6700 (recording)
716 thru 722 725 thru 729 755	FRB Little Rock	FRB Little Rock P.O. Box 1261 Little Rock, AR 72203-1261	501-324-8272 or 501-324-8274 (recording)
730 thru 731 734 thru 741 743 thru 749	FRB Oklahoma City	FRB Oklahoma City P.O. Box 25129 Oklahoma City, OK 73125-0129	405-270-8652 or 405-270-8660 (recording)
770 thru 778	FRB Houston	FRB Houston P.O. Box 2578 Houston, TX 77252-2578	713-652-1621 or 713-652-1629 or 713-652-1688 (recording)
779 thru 789	FRB San Antonio	FRB San Antonio P.O. Box 1471 San Antonio, TX 78295-1471	210-978-1305 or 210-978-1330 (recording)
797 thru 799 878 thru 884	FRB El Paso	FRB El Paso P.O. Box 100 El Paso, TX 79999-0100	915-521-8272 or 915-521-8295 (recording)

If Your Zip Code Begins with . . .	This Is Your Federal Reserve Bank Servicing Office	Address	Phone Number
800 thru 816 820 thru 831	FRB Denver	FRB Denver P.O. Box 5228 Denver, CO 80217-5228	303-572-2470 or 303-572-2475 (recording)
832 thru 834 836 thru 837 840 thru 847 893 898	FRB Salt Lake City	FRB Salt Lake City P.O. Box 30780 Salt Lake City, UT 84130-0780	801-322-7882 or 801-322-7844 (recording)
835 838 970 thru 979 994	FRB Portland	FRB Portland P.O. Box 3436 Portland, OR 97208-3436	503-221-5932 or 503-221-5931 (recording)
850 thru 865 870 thru 877 890 thru 891 900 thru 935	FRB Los Angeles	FRB Los Angeles P.O. Box 512077 Los Angeles, CA 90051-0077	213-624-7398
894 thru 897 936 thru 969	FRB San Francisco	FRB San Francisco P.O. Box 7702 San Francisco, CA 94120–7702	415-974-2330 or 415-974-3491 (recording)
980 thru 993 995 thru 999	FRB Seattle	FRB Seattle P.O. Box 3567 Seattle, WA 98124-3567	206-343-3605 or 206-343-3615 (recording)

SOURCE: Bureau of the Public Debt Online.

9

Investing in Bonds

When you buy a bond, you lend money. If everything goes as planned, you receive interest while it is outstanding and get your principal back at maturity. For the issuer, whether it is the U.S. government, a city, a state, or a corporation, selling bonds is a way to borrow money from the public.

Bond Basics

All bonds have a par value and a maturity date. Most bonds have a coupon interest rate, and some bonds have call dates and/or sinking funds. A quick explanation of these terms will simplify our upcoming discussion about investing in bonds.

The amount that the bond will pay at maturity is the *face,* or *par value,* of the bond, generally $1,000. If you purchase a bond on its initial offering from the issuer, you will likely pay a price equal or close to par value. If you purchase later, in the secondary market, the price you pay may be higher or lower than par value. Regardless of the price paid for a bond, the par value is the amount you will receive if you hold the bond until maturity and is the amount upon which interest payments are calculated.

The coupon rate, stated on the face of the bond and usually fixed for the life of the bond, is the interest rate that the issuer pays to borrow the money. The rate is stated in percentage terms and is generally paid semiannually. For example, a $1,000 par value bond with a coupon rate of 6.75% would pay its owner $67.50 in interest each year, most likely in two equal payments of $33.75.

Every bond has a maturity date, upon which the issuer must repay the par value to bondholders. Bonds generally mature within 30 years and can be categorized according to their expected life span:

- Short-term notes: up to 4 years
- Medium-term notes/bonds: 5 to 12 years
- Long-term bonds: more than 12 years

In addition to the maturity date, some bonds have one or more call dates, on which the issuer may (but is not required to) repay principal to some or all bondholders. The issuer will commonly call bonds when interest rates have dropped since the bonds were issued. This enables the issuer to reduce the interest costs by selling new bonds at the prevailing, lower interest rates. Of course, this is not good for the bondholder, who must replace high-yielding bonds with the lower-yielding securities that are currently available. In many cases, the issuer compensates the bondholder for the risk of an early call by paying a slightly higher coupon rate and paying more than face value if the bonds are called early.

Similar in some ways to a call, a sinking fund provision in a bond indenture (the contract that the issuer has with bondholders) requires that a certain portion of the bonds issued be retired periodically, before maturity. On the positive side, this regular debt retirement reduces the issuer's total debt outstanding, which makes repayment of remaining debt less risky. Also, in times of rising interest rates (falling bond prices), many firms will meet their sinking fund requirements by buying bonds on the open market. This added demand may support bond prices. The negative side of sinking funds is that bondholders can receive a call at par when interest rates have fallen and existing bonds are priced well above par in the secondary market.

Bond Prices

Bonds are priced at a percentage of face value or par. A bond price of 101 equals 101% of par or $1,010 for every $1,000 bond. Likewise, a bond price of 96 is 96% of par or $960 for every $1,000 bond. A bond selling at a price over par is said to be selling at a premium. Conversely, a bond selling below its par value is said to be selling at a discount.

Yields

If all bonds were sold at par, it would be easy to determine the yield on investment because it would be equal to the coupon interest rate paid. However, if you purchase a bond at a price other than par, you should know your yield to maturity (YTM) and, in cases of callable bonds, your yield to call (YTC). The YTM combines the income received in interest and the principal gained or lost at maturity. Logically, bonds purchased for more than par value will have a YTM less than their coupon rate. If you pay $1,020 for a 10-year, 7% bond which pays back $1,000 at maturity, you will lose $20 in principal, which reduces the $700 in income received over the life of the bond. Similarly, a bond purchased for $20 less than it returns at

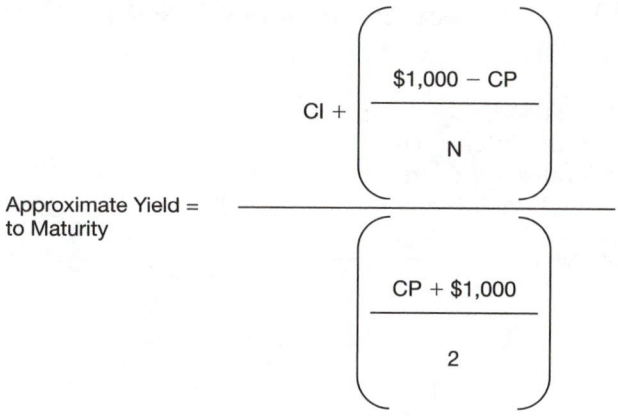

CI = annual current interest income (coupon rate × $1,000)
CP = current price of the bond
N = number of years until maturity

Figure 9–1. Formula for Computing Approximate Yield to Maturity

maturity will have a yield greater than its coupon interest rate when you add the $20 difference in purchase and maturity price to the income you have received. The formula for computing approximate yield to maturity is shown in Figure 9–1.

Using the two previous examples, with 7% bonds purchased at either 102 ($1,020) or 98 ($980), approximate yields to maturity are shown in Figures 9–2a and b.

The Relationship between Bond Prices, Yields, and Interest Rates

When a bond is issued, its coupon interest rate is set until maturity. However, over the next 10 to 30 years, market interest rates can fluctuate greatly, making a particular bond completely out of step with what newly issued bonds are paying. In the secondary market, the great equalizer is prices. When prevailing interest rates rise, the prices of existing bonds fall and when interest rates fall, the prices of existing bonds rise.

Say, for example, that you purchased a corporate bond last year, which had a coupon rate of 8%. Since then, new bonds of comparable quality and years until maturity are being issued with coupon rates of 9%. If you wanted to sell your bond to someone who had the choice of newly issued 9% bonds or your 8% bond, what would you have to do? Lower the price

7% Bond purchased at a premium: $1,020

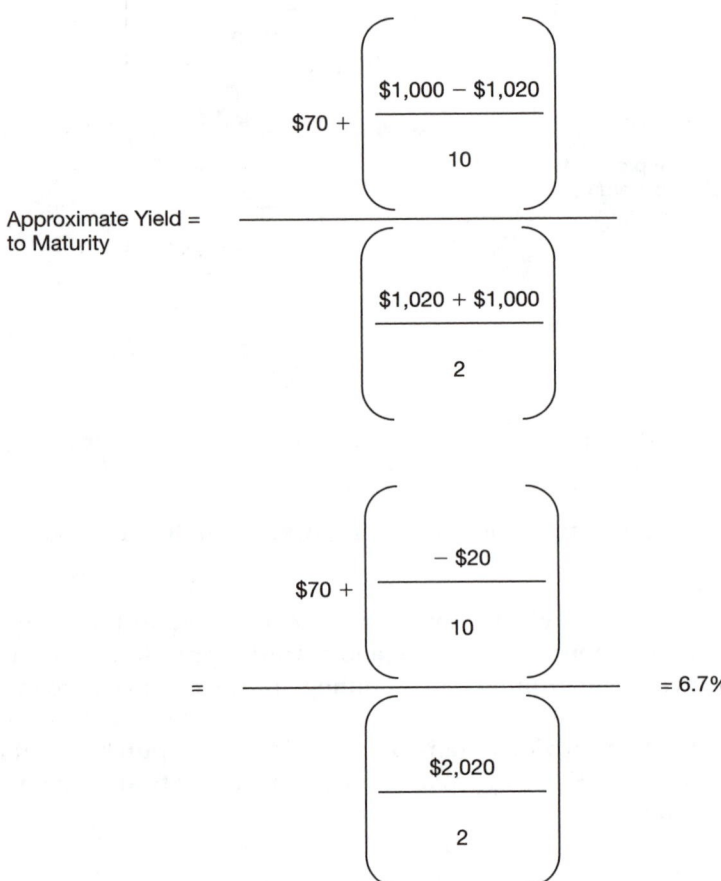

Figure 9–2a. Computing Approximate Yield to Maturity (7% Bond Purchased at $1,020)

until the yield to maturity was competitive. Conversely, if interest rates had fallen recently, you could charge more than par for your bond, because you would be offering a higher coupon than otherwise available.

The Relationship between Yields and Maturities: The Yield Curve

Interest rate changes such as the ones illustrated do not affect all bonds equally. The longer it takes for a bond to reach maturity, the more time there is for interest rates and the bond's price to fluctuate and for the credit

7% Bond purchased at a discount: $980

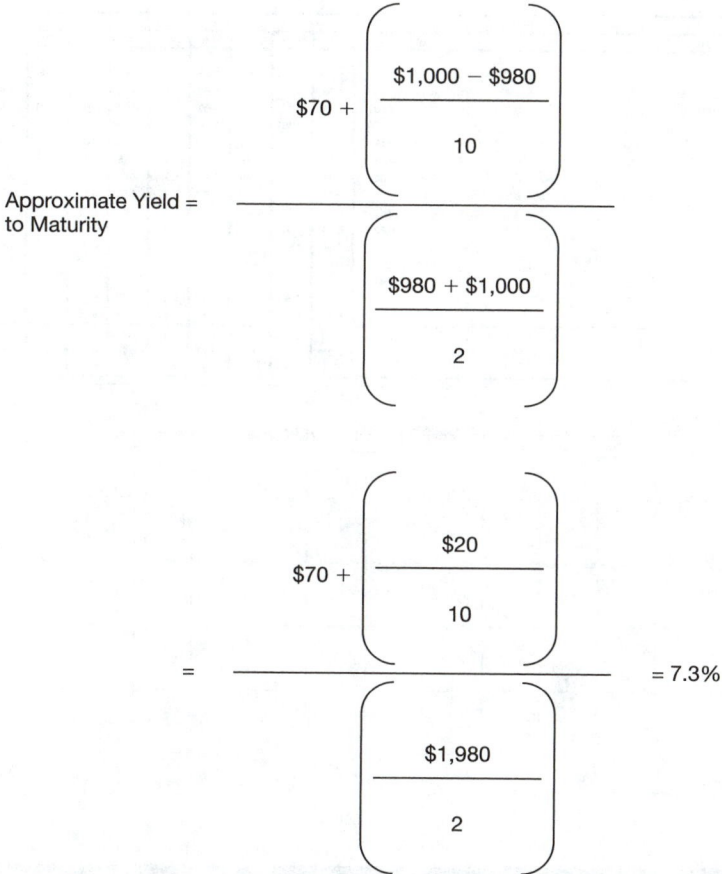

$$\text{Approximate Yield} = \frac{\$70 + \dfrac{\$1,000 - \$980}{10}}{\dfrac{\$980 + \$1,000}{2}}$$

$$= \frac{\$70 + \dfrac{\$20}{10}}{\dfrac{\$1,980}{2}} = 7.3\%$$

Figure 9–2b. Computing Approximate Yield to Maturity (7% Bond Purchased at $980)

quality of the issuer to deteriorate. Because of this higher risk, investors will demand a higher yield on longer-term bonds. This link between maturity and yield can best be illustrated by drawing a yield curve, which is a line between the yields of similar securities with different maturities, from shortest to longest.

Although a yield curve works for any type of bond, it is most often used in the U.S. Treasury market, where bond quality is identical and securities of every maturity are available. Figure 9–3 shows the yield curve on March 24, 2000, in numerical and graphical form. The curve column shows the day's Treasury yields for different maturities ranging from the discount

The "CURVE" column shows Treasury yields at futures close today.
The "MATRIX" shows spreads between various maturities of Treasuries.
All bonds are compared to Treasuries of similar maturities for relative value.

Maturity	YLD	90	180	2YR	3YR	5YR	10YR	15YR	20YR	30YR	1999	1998	1997	1996	1995	1994	1993	1992	1991	1990	1989
CURVE						TREASURY MATRIX									YEAR END						
PRIME	9.00										8.50	7.75	8.50	8.25	8.50	8.50	6.00	6.00	8.50	10.00	10.50
DISC	5.50	0.41	0.66	1.12	1.10	1.00	0.69	0.91	0.85	0.50	4.75	4.50	5.00	5.25	4.75	3.00	3.00	3.50	6.50	7.00	
FUNDS	6.00	-0.09	0.16	0.62	0.60	0.50	0.19	0.41	0.35	0.00	5.00	4.75	6.50	7.00	5.50	6.00	3.00	4.43	7.31	8.45	
90 DAY	5.91		0.25	0.71	0.69	0.59	0.28	0.50	0.44	0.09	5.32	4.46	5.35	5.20	5.10	5.70	3.06	3.15	4.12	6.01	7.64
180 DAY	6.16			0.46	0.44	0.34	0.03	0.25	0.19	-0.16	5.71	4.54	5.44	6.31	5.17	6.48	3.30	3.38	4.16	6.76	7.45
YEAR	6.28			0.34	0.32	0.22	-0.09	0.13	0.07	-0.28	5.96	4.53	5.49	5.48	5.17	7.15	3.58	3.59	4.38	7.05	7.72
2 YR	6.62				-0.02	-0.12	-0.43	-0.21	-0.27	-0.62	6.24	4.53	5.65	5.86	5.17	7.69	4.25	4.56	5.03	7.31	7.78
3 YR	6.60					-0.10	-0.41	-0.19	-0.25	-0.60	6.29	4.65	5.62	6.00	5.21	7.78	4.53	5.05	5.39	7.47	7.27
4 YR	6.53					-0.03	-0.34	-0.12	-0.18	-0.53	6.36	4.69	5.72	6.10	5.30	7.81	4.87	5.65	5.79	7.60	7.76
5 YR	6.50						-0.31	-0.09	-0.15	-0.50	6.34	4.54	5.71	6.20	5.39	7.84	5.21	6.04	6.19	7.73	7.75
7 YR	6.48						-0.29	-0.07	-0.13	-0.48	6.54	4.71	5.77	6.33	5.50	7.83	5.36	6.40	6.89	8.00	7.85
10 YR	6.19							0.22	0.16	-0.19	6.44	4.66	5.74	6.42	5.50	7.82	5.00	6.63	7.09	8.08	7.84
15 YR	6.41								-0.06	-0.41	6.80	5.02									
20 YR	6.35									-0.35	6.83	5.38	6.07	6.65	6.12	7.99	6.40				
30 YR	6.00										6.48	5.09	5.93	6.64	5.95	7.87	9.36	7.40	7.70	8.24	7.90
90D-30Y	0.09										1.16	0.03	0.58	1.44	0.85	2.17	4.25	3.58	1.43	0.26	
2Y-30Y	-0.62										0.24	0.56	0.26	0.78	0.78	0.18	2.11	2.84	2.67	0.03	0.12
90D-10Y	0.28										1.12	0.20	0.39	1.22	0.48	2.32	2.74	3.54	2.97	1.27	0.20

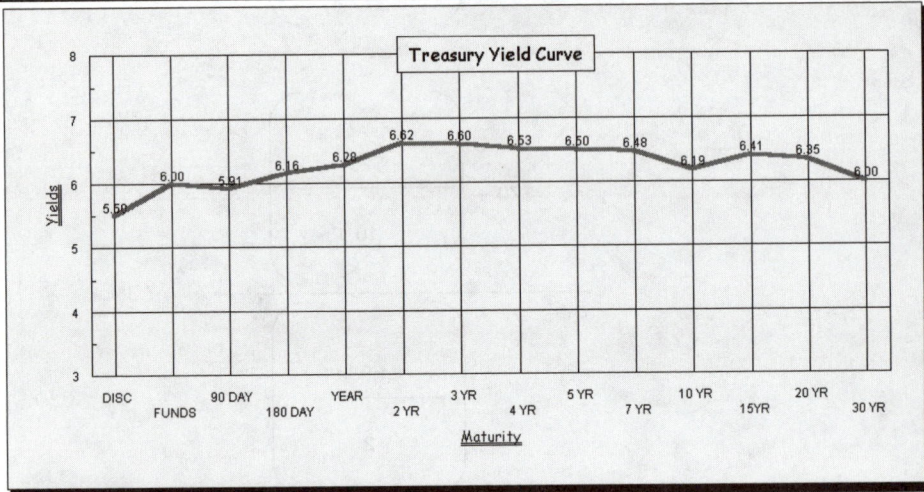

Figure 9-3. The Yield Curve
SOURCE: Moloney Securities at *www.stocktrader.com.*

rate to the 30-year bond. The prime rate is shown at the top for comparison. The treasury matrix shows the spreads between Treasury securities with different maturities. Year end shows rates at the end of the last 10 years for different maturities. The Treasury yield curve shows the day's Treasury yields graphically.

The slope of the yield curve offers a consensus opinion of where interest rates are headed. A positively sloped yield curve is considered normal (see Figure 9–4), with higher yields at longer maturities compensating investors for increased interest rate and price fluctuation risk. The curve may be flat, with little additional yield reward in longer-term securities (see

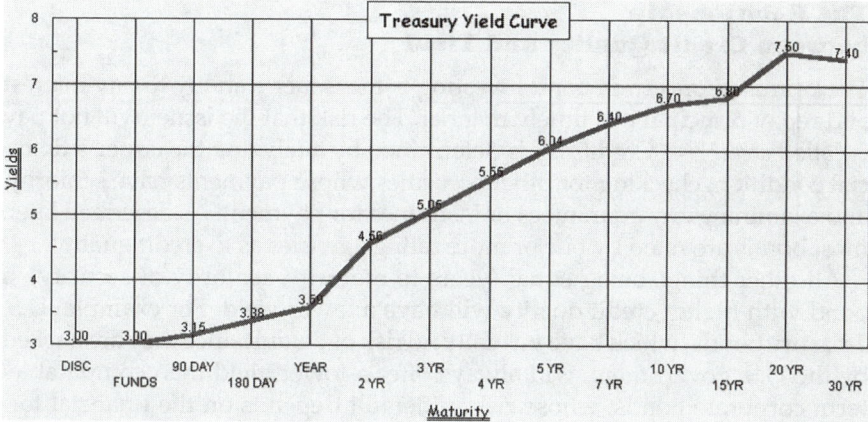

Figure 9–4. Positive Yield Curve
SOURCE: Moloney Securities at *www.stocktrader.com.*

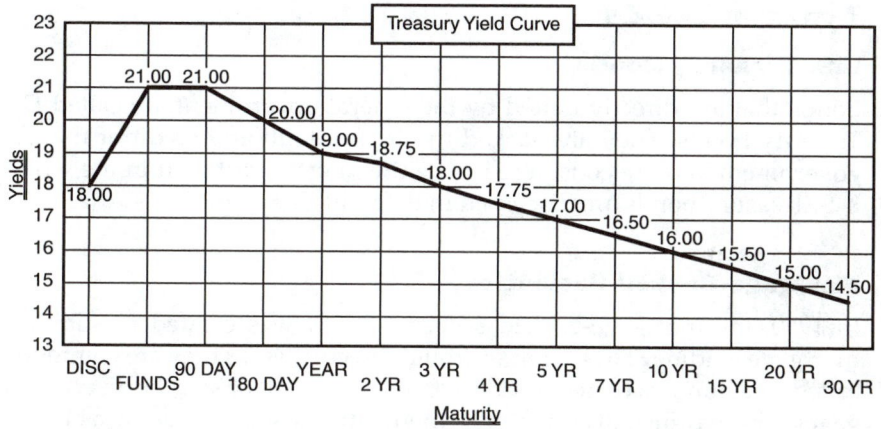

Figure 9–5. Inverted Yield Curve
SOURCE: Moloney Securities at *www.stocktrader.com.*

Figure 9–3). A flatter yield curve generally means that investors expect interest rates to remain steady. If investors expect declining interest rates, they may be willing to accept lower yields on longer-term securities in an effort to lock in rates. This results in a negatively sloped or "inverted" yield curve (see Figure 9–5 for an inverted yeild curve from the early 1980s). You can find yield curves in *The Wall Street Journal, Investor's Business Daily,* or on many financial websites. Moloney Securities has good yield curves at *www.stocktrader.com.*

The Relationship
between Credit Quality and Yield

The primary concern in bond investing is the issuer's ability to pay interest and repay principal in a timely manner. The risk that the issuer will not pay is called *credit risk*. Credit risk is determined by analyzing the issuer's financial condition, checking for other securities whose payments have seniority, and examining any guarantees or insurance for payment. As described later, most bonds are rated by one or more rating agencies as to credit quality.

All other things being equal (years to maturity, seniority of security), a bond with higher credit quality will have a lower yield. For example, U.S. Treasury bonds, which have virtually no risk of default since they are backed by the U.S. government, will always offer a lower yield than comparable-term corporate bonds, whose risk of default depends on the financial fortunes of the issuing corporation. Bonds with low credit quality have higher yields, to compensate investors for the additional risk taken.

Types of Bonds

U.S. Treasury Bonds

Bonds that are directly issued by the federal government are called U.S. Treasury bonds. They are backed by the full faith and credit of the U.S. government and are considered to be the safest investment in the world. U.S. Treasury bonds are discussed in detail in Chapter 8.

Mortgage-Backed Securities

In 1970, the mortgage-backed security (MBS) was created to stimulate mortgage lending. These "pass-through" securities, as they are commonly called, are bundles (usually $250,000 to $1,000,000) of standardized mortgages whose principal and interest payments are guaranteed by a government agency. Agencies include the Federal National Mortgage Association (FNMA, or Fannie Mae), the Government National Mortgage Association (GNMA, or Ginnie Mae), and the Federal Home Loan Mortgage Corporation (FHLMC, or Freddie Mac). When individuals make their mortgage payments, the issuing financial institution passes the payments through to the owner of the security in a single payment.

Risks Specific to Mortgage-Backed Securities. The risk of repayment, or credit risk, on a government agency-backed security is negligible. Ginnie Maes have the explicit guarantee of the U.S. government, as do U.S. Treasury securities. Fannie Maes and Freddie Macs do not have an explicit guarantee, but one that is implied.

Though credit risk is not a problem, other risks are associated with mortgage-backed securities. The first, commonly discounted by financial professionals but often a problem for the unsophisticated investor, is not understanding the structure of the security. Just as your mortgage payments consist of principal and interest, so do payments of a MBS. Similarly, at the end of payments, the balance of the security is zero. The investor who treats all income received as interest receives a rude awakening at maturity, when there is no principal left to reinvest.

The second risk specific to mortgage-backed securities is prepayment/extension risk. Unlike ordinary bonds which may be prepaid only on specified call dates, mortgages may be prepaid at any time. If investors prepay the mortgages underlying the MBS, the security holder may receive principal faster than anticipated (prepayment risk). This generally happens in periods of declining interest rates, when borrowers refinance mortgages to take advantage of lower rates available. In times of increasing rates, borrowers are happy with the low-rate loans they have and refinance less, which may extend the expected life of the security (extension risk). In both cases the investor is at a disadvantage. When interest rates fall, rather than being happily locked into a high-rate security, the investor begins to get principal back quickly with only current, low-rate options for reinvestment. When interest rates rise, the investor is locked into a low-rate security which may last even longer than originally expected.

Collateralized Mortgage Obligations. In 1983, in an effort to reduce some of the prepayment risk associated with ordinary mortgage-backed securities, collateralized mortgage obligations (CMOs) were created. CMOs take a mortgage-backed security such as a Fannie Mae or Freddie Mac and divide it into tranches (the French word for *slices*) intended to appeal to investors with different maturity preferences. Each tranche has a stated maturity, a stated interest rate, and different payment seniority within the structure. Additionally, each tranche is given an assumed maturity range, as opposed to the stated maturity range, that is calculated based on possible changes in interest rates.

CMO tranches are organized as to their priority on interest and principal repayments and their risk for prepayment or extension. The most conservative tranches are planned amortization classes (PACs) and targeted amortization classes (TACs). They are first in line to receive regular interest and principal repayments, and have a well-defined maturity and low prepayment/extension risk. Because they are the most predictable, their yields are lower than those of other types of CMOs.

Simultaneously with the PACs and TACs, another type of CMO must exist to absorb the risk taken out of those tranches. Called *companion* or *support bonds,* they take the prepayment shocks by receiving prepayments first and protect cash flow by receiving regular interest and principal repayments after the PACs and TACs have been paid. Due to their higher risk, these tranches carry higher yields.

Another tranche, designed to diffuse some interest rate risk, is the floater. Similar to an adjustable rate mortgage, its interest rate is reset periodically. Floaters generally have no annual ceiling on interest rate changes and have a higher lifetime cap than adjustable rate mortgages (ARMs).

Z bonds are accrual bonds which pay no interest during the life of the bond, but instead pay all interest at maturity. As are all types of zero coupon bonds, Z bonds are vulnerable to interest rate risk.

Table 9–1 outlines the differences between CMO tranches.

Although the basic characteristics of each type of tranche are helpful in choosing among them, thousands of individual tranches are available in the market at any given time, all with different maturities, payment priorities, coupon rates, and collateral characteristics. Two organizations conduct complex analysis to provide volatility ratings for CMOs. They are Fitch Investors Service (5 Hanover Square, New York, NY 10004) and Bloomberg Financial Markets (100 Business Park Dr., Princeton, NJ 08542). Volatility ratings assess potential prepayment risk and price volatility by simulating price, total return, and cash flow performance for a tranche under a range of interest rate conditions.

Corporate Bonds

Corporate bonds are the debt of corporations. Rather than borrowing from a bank, a corporation can borrow from the public by issuing bonds. As with any bond, the coupon interest rate, maturity date, and call provisions are important features. Other additional features of corporate bonds which have not been an issue in our discussion of government-backed bonds are discussed here.

Table 9–1. CMO Tranches

	PAC or TAC	Companion	Floater	Z Bond
Yield	Low	High	Moderate	High
Prepayment risk	Low	High	Moderate	High
Extension risk	Low	High	Moderate	Low
Interest rate risk	Low	High	Low	High

Table 9–2. Corporate Bond Ratings by Moody's, Standard and Poor's, Fitch, and Duff & Phelps (D&P)

Rating Moody's	S&P, Fitch, D&P	Description	Examples of Corporate Bonds in 1999
Aaa	AAA	Highest quality	BellSouth
Aa	AA	High quality	AT&T, Mobil Oil, Eli Lilly
A	A	Upper medium grade	Chase Manhattan Bank, Ford Motor Co., IBM
Baa	BBB	Medium grade	Delta Air Lines, Dole, Safeway
Ba	BB	Lower medium grade	Sequa
B	B	Speculative	Stone Container, CompUSA
Caa	CCC, CC	Poor	TWA
Ca	C	Highly speculative	Service Merchandise
C	D	In default	

Credit Quality. While the ability to repay is not a consideration in purchasing a U.S. Treasury bond, it may be the most important issue in evaluating a corporate bond. The issuer's promise to pay interest on time and repay principal at maturity is only as good as its ability to do so. Fortunately, several services help evaluate the financial strength of companies that issue bonds: Standard & Poor's Corporation, Moody's Investors Service, Fitch Investors Service, and Duff & Phelps Credit Rating Company all grade the credit quality of bonds, as outlined in Table 9–2.

Bonds rated BBB or higher by Standard & Poor's, Fitch, and Duff & Phelps or Baa or higher by Moody's are considered to be "investment grade." This label means that they are of high enough quality that a prudent investor might purchase them.

Bonds rated BB (S&P, Fitch, Duff & Phelps), Ba (Moody's), or lower are called high-yield or junk bonds. These bonds are speculative investments that yield higher interest rates to compensate investors for additional risk taken. The high yield may come from a high coupon rate for a bond whose risks were apparent at the time of issue (see Stone Container in Table 9–3), or high yield may result from a low price for bonds whose risk factors surfaced after they were issued (see Fruit of the Loom in Table 9–3). Higher risk comes from financial factors such as those found in new, start-up

Table 9–3. High Yield or Junk Bonds

Rating	Bond	Coupon	Maturity Date	Current Yield	YTM	Closing Price
B–	StoneC	10.75%	04/02	10.8%	10.8%	100
BB–	FruitL	7.0%	03/11	15.9%	19.3%	44

companies, companies with financial problems, those in competitive or volatile industries, or companies whose business practices and reporting may be in question.

While it may appear that the corporation's financial strength receives the rating, it is the individual issue being rated. A corporation may have bonds outstanding with several different ratings due to the structure and seniority of each individual issue.

Bond Security and Seniority. If a corporation goes out of business, there is a certain order in which claims against the business are paid (lawyers and the IRS are at the top of the list). Bondholders are paid before stockholders, but some bondholders have a higher claim than others depending on the terms of their particular bonds. A higher claim translates into lower credit risk, which generally means a lower yield on the bond.

Secured Bonds. Secured bonds are those in which the issuer has pledged specific assets or collateral that may be sold to pay the bondholders, if necessary. Following are several types of secured bonds.

- Mortgage bonds, most often issued by public utilities, are bonds for which real estate or other physical property has been pledged as collateral. Many mortgage bonds have a rank (first, second, and so on) which designates the priority of the claim on the particular asset. Higher priority denotes higher safety.

- Collateral trust bonds are those in which the collateral, often other securities, is placed in a trust in order to back the bonds.

- Equipment trust certificates enable such businesses as airlines and railroads to pay for new equipment with bonds. Similar to the way a bank holds title to a car during an auto loan, a trustee holds title to equipment to secure the trust certificates until the certificate holders are paid off. The equipment may be sold to pay investors if the company defaults.

- Guaranteed bonds exist when a corporation other than the issuer guarantees payment of a bond's interest and principal. This is common in cases of a subsidiary's bonds being guaranteed by the parent company or a joint venture's bonds being guaranteed by the related corporations.

Unsecured Bonds. Unsecured bonds are backed only by the issuer's general capacity to pay interest and repay principal. They come in two types:

- Debenture bonds, the most common corporate bonds, are unsecured. Debentures are generally in line for repayment after secured bonds, unless they were issued first. In that case they may have a negative pledge provision. This provision prohibits the issuing of new debt with a priority over the debenture's claim on assets. Subordinated debentures have a priority below all senior debentures and secured bonds.

- Income bonds, also unsecured, are generally issued in the reorganization of a company that is in financial trouble. They require interest to be paid only to the extent that it is earned by the corporation. Similar to dividends on preferred stock, unpaid interest may be cumulative, requiring that any interest not paid on time be paid in the future if it is earned.

Convertible Bonds. A corporate convertible bond is a stock and bond hybrid in which the owner of a bond has the option to exchange the bond for common stock at any time. The number of shares received for each $1,000 bond is the conversion ratio. The face value of the bond ($1,000) divided by the conversion ratio is the conversion price.

For example, XYZ Corporation's bonds are convertible into 25 shares of common stock; therefore, the conversion ratio is 25. Dividing $1,000 by 25 yields a conversion price of $40. Purchasing a bond for $1,000 and converting it into 25 shares of stock would be the equivalent of paying $40 per share for the stock. Typically on the date that bonds are issued the conversion price is set about 20% higher than the stock price, making immediate conversion unprofitable. XYZ convertible bonds might be issued with a conversion price of $40 when XYZ stock is trading around $33.

Investors are generally willing to accept a lower coupon rate for convertible bonds in exchange for the option of participating in stock price appreciation. What is good for the investor is also good for the corporation, as lower coupon rates reduce interest costs.

Valuing Convertible Bonds. The value of a convertible bond is the greater of its bond value and its conversion value. Its bond value is what the bond is worth as a bond, taking into account the creditworthiness of the issuer, the coupon interest rate, prevailing interest rates, and years until maturity. The bond value is the floor price of a convertible bond.

The conversion value is the conversion ratio multiplied by the current stock price. In the previous bond example, if XYZ Corporation's stock price rose to $45, then the conversion value would be 25 × $45 = $1,125. In an open market, the bond's price will immediately rise to this level. If not, investors would buy the bond, convert it, and sell the stock and pocket the difference. (This process is called arbitrage.)

While most convertible bonds are callable at a premium, this price may be much lower than conversion value if the stock price has risen greatly. After a call is issued, the owner generally has a brief period (usually 30 days) in which to convert bonds.

Municipal Bonds

Municipal bonds, often called munis, are the debt of states, cities, counties, and other governmental entities. Money borrowed through municipal bonds will fund projects for the public good, such as hospitals, highways, schools, sewer systems, and convention centers. Bonds are usually sold to finance long-term capital projects, although short-term notes may be used to raise money in anticipation of future revenues until long-term financing can be arranged. Municipal bonds are most often issued as serial obligations, meaning that an issue is divided into a series of smaller issues, each with its own maturity date and coupon rate. Thus, rather than having one large issue that matures in 20 years, a bond may have a series of multiple maturity dates over the next 20 years.

General Obligation Bonds. General obligation (GO) bonds are voter-approved debt, supported by the full faith and credit of the issuer. As such, they are usually supported by the issuer's ability to tax. The general obligation bond is similar in concept to a corporate debenture.

Revenue Bonds. Revenue bonds are issued to fund particular projects, such as highways, bridges, hospitals, airports, and sewer or water treatment plants. The principal and interest payments are secured by revenues derived from charges or rents paid by the users of the facilities. The issuer of a revenue bond is only required to pay principal and interest if a sufficient level of revenue is generated from the project. For this reason, revenue bonds are considered riskier than general obligation bonds and usually carry a higher yield.

Tax Advantages of Municipal Bonds. The feature that draws most investors to municipal bonds is the treatment of interest payments under federal and state tax law. Under current federal law, interest income from municipal bonds is not federally taxable. In most states, municipal bond income is not taxable to investors who reside in that state.

The effect of a municipal bond's tax advantage is most apparent through example. Let us say you have $20,000 to invest. You are married, filing jointly, and earn $130,000 a year. This puts you in the 31% federal tax bracket for 1999. Your state income tax rate is 6%. If we allow for the federal tax deductibility of state income taxes, your effective marginal federal tax rate becomes:

$$\text{Effective federal tax rate} = (1 - \text{State tax rate}) \times \text{Federal tax rate}$$
$$= (1 - 0.06) \times 0.31$$
$$= 0.29$$

You have three alternatives: a tax-exempt municipal bond issued in your state with a 5% coupon interest rate, a U.S. Treasury bond with a 6.6% coupon interest rate, and a taxable corporate bond with a 7% coupon interest rate. If you purchase the municipal bond, interest on your $20,000 will be $1,000 ($20,000 × 0.05) annually. No federal or state taxes will be due. If you purchase the U.S. Treasury bond, interest on your $20,000 will be $1,320 ($20,000 × 0.066) annually. The interest on a U.S. Treasury security is state tax exempt, but you will owe $409 ($1,320 × 0.31) in federal taxes, bringing your after-tax return to $911, or a 4.56% return ($911/$20,000). If you purchase the corporate bond, your annual interest will be $1,400 ($20,000 × 0.07). You will owe $406 ($1,400 × 0.29) in federal taxes and $84 ($1,400 × 0.06) in state taxes. After paying the taxes, your net return will be only $910. This is an after-tax return of 4.55% ($910/$20,000). In this case, the municipal bond provides the best after-tax return. See Table 9–4 for a comparison between taxable and tax-exempt securities.

Table 9–4. Comparing Taxable and Tax-Exempt Securities

	Municipal Bond	U.S. Treasury Bond	Corporate Bond
Investment	$20,000	$20,000	$20,000
Coupon interest rate	5%	6.6%	7%
Annual interest	$1,000	$1,320	$1,400
Federal income tax at 31%	0	($409)	
Effective federal tax at 29%			($406)
State tax at 6%	0	0	($84)
Net return	$1,000	$911	$910
After-tax yield	5%	4.56%	4.55%

Another way to compare taxable and tax-exempt securities is to use a taxable-equivalent yield (TEY). The TEY is the yield that a taxable investment would need to provide in order to match the return of a tax-exempt investment on an after-tax basis. The formula for the taxable equivalent yield is as follows:

$$\frac{\text{Tax-exempt yield}}{1.00 - \{[(1.00 - \text{State tax rate}) \times \text{Federal tax rate}] + \text{State tax rate}\}}$$

Using the numbers from our previous example, the taxable equivalent yield for the 5% municipal bond is 7.7%, computed as follows:

$$\frac{0.05}{100 - \{[(1.00 - 0.06) \times 0.31] + 0.06\}}$$

The corporate bond would need to have a pretax yield of 7.7% to provide an equal after-tax return.

For investors residing in states without income tax, the formula is simply:

$$\frac{\text{Tax-exempt yield}}{(1.00 - \text{Federal tax rate})}$$

For the taxable-equivalent yields at various tax-exempt rates and tax brackets (federal only), see Table 9–5.

Credit Quality. As with any bond, the most important part of the investment decision is the issuer's ability to pay interest and repay principal. For municipal bonds, it is much more difficult for an individual investor to determine credit quality than it is with the bonds of public corporations, whose financial records are not only public, but also often analyzed by several different brokerage firms. For this reason, municipal bond investors rely heavily on rating services that evaluate the financial strength of issuers. Standard & Poor's Corporation, Moody's Investors Service, and Fitch Investors Service all grade the credit quality of municipal bonds in much the same way as they grade corporate bonds (see Table 9–6).

As with corporate bonds, those rated Baa by Moody's or BBB by Standard & Poor's and Fitch are considered investment grade. Those with lower ratings are called high-yield or junk bonds.

Municipal Bond Insurance. As a backup to the issuer's ability to collect taxes or revenues, several insurance companies insure the timely payment of interest and principal on municipal bonds. Bonds insured by Ambac Assurance Corporation (AMBAC), MBIA Insurance Corporation (MBIA), and Financial Guaranty Insurance Company (FGIC), among

Table 9–5. Taxable Equivalent Yields

Filing Single	Taxable Income in 1999					
	$0–$25,750	$25,751–$62,450	$62,451–$130,250	$130,251–$283,150	$283,151 & over	Sample effective
Filing Jointly	$0–$43,050	$43,051–104,050	$104,051–158,550	$158,551–283,150	$283,151 & over	marginal income rate/high
Tax bracket	15%	28%	31%	36%	39.6%	41%
Tax-Exempt Yields (%)	Taxable Equivalent Yields (%)					
2.0	2.35	2.78	2.90	3.12	3.31	3.39
2.5	2.94	3.47	3.62	3.91	4.14	4.24
3.0	3.53	4.17	4.35	4.69	4.97	5.08
3.5	4.12	4.86	5.07	5.47	5.79	5.93
4.0	4.71	5.56	5.80	6.25	6.62	6.78
4.5	5.29	6.25	6.52	7.03	7.45	7.63
5.0	5.88	6.94	7.25	7.81	8.28	8.47
5.5	6.47	7.64	7.79	8.59	9.11	9.32
6.0	7.06	8.33	8.70	9.37	9.93	10.17
6.5	7.65	9.03	9.42	10.16	10.76	11.02
7.0	8.24	9.72	10.14	10.94	11.59	11.86
7.5	8.82	10.42	10.87	11.72	12.42	12.71
8.0	9.41	11.11	11.59	12.5	13.25	13.56

Table 9–6. Municipal Bond Ratings by Moody's, Standard & Poor's, and Fitch

	Rating		
Moody's	S&P	Fitch	Description
Aaa	AAA	AAA	Highest quality
Aa	AA	AA	High quality
A	A	A	Upper medium grade
Baa	BBB	BBB	Lower medium grade
Ba	BB	BB	Speculative
B, Caa	B, CCC,CC	B, CCC, CC, C	Very Speculative
Ca, C	D	DDD, DD, D	Default

others, receive AAA or Aaa ratings from the major rating agencies. This benefits both the issuer and the investor. Issuers benefit because insured, AAA/Aaa rated bonds can be sold with a lower coupon rate than uninsured, lower rated securities. Lower coupon interest rates mean lower borrowing costs. Investors benefit because insurance alleviates safety concerns about a bond.

In general, the yield on insured bonds is lower than comparable, lower rated uninsured bonds but higher than true AAA/Aaa rated bonds. A true AAA/Aaa bond is one that receives this rating without insurance. Any AAA/Aaa bond will nearly always yield less than a similar AA/Aa or lower rated bond since a higher rating means less risk to the investor. The yield difference between AAA/Aaa insured bonds and true AAA/Aaa bonds is obviously not due to a rating difference, but more often attributed to the perception that the insured bond is riskier because the issuer had to get insurance to achieve its high rating.

Alternative Minimum Tax. In 1978, the alternative minimum tax (AMT) was established to prevent taxpayers from reducing their taxable income to near zero through the use of tax-sheltered investments. Under AMT, taxpayers compute both their regular tax liability and their AMT formula tax liability and pay whichever is higher.

The AMT computation taxes the first $175,000 of income at 26% and income over $175,000 at 28%. There are no personal exemptions or standard deductions, only an exemption of $45,000 for married taxpayers filing jointly and $33,750 for single taxpayers. These exemptions phase out for joint filers earning more than $150,000 and single filers earning more than $112,500.

The AMT formula adds "tax preference" items to your taxable income to calculate your AMT income. These are normally deductible or tax-exempt items such as state and local income taxes, real estate taxes, the profit on incentive stock options, and the tax on some municipal bond interest. Municipal bonds subject to the AMT add-back are private purpose muni bonds, including many housing, industrial development, pollution control, airport and student loan bonds. A bond subject to ANY should be identified as such and often carries a yield that is about 10 basis points higher than a non-AMT municipal bond.

Zero Coupon Bonds

Zero coupon bonds are accrual securities, sold at a discount to face value, which pay all their interest at maturity. The term *zero coupon* refers to the bond's structure; the underlying bond may be issued by the U.S. government, a corporation, or a municipality. U.S. Treasury zero coupons go by several acronyms, including CATS (Certificates of Accrual on Treasury

Securities) and STRIPS (Separate Trading of Registered Interest and Principal of Securities).

For example, in October 1999, you could purchase a $1,000 U.S. Treasury zero coupon bond due in November 2009 for $511.25. At maturity, you would receive the full face value of $1,000. The $488.75 difference between the price that you paid and the face value you would receive is your interest. The yield in this case is 6.78%.

Although interest is not paid on a zero coupon bond each year, it is implied in changes in the value of a bond. This implied interest is called *accretion* and is the amount by which the bond increases in value in a given time period.

Taxation of Zero Coupon Bonds. Because zero coupon bonds do not make any interest payments, it might be logical to assume that no annual income taxes are due and the difference between the purchase price and a sale or maturity value would be treated as a capital gain; however, this is not the case. The rate of return on a zero coupon bond is set at purchase (in the previous example, it is 6.78%). Each year, for tax purposes, the value of the bond is accreted in accordance with the original rate of return. Unless the bond is a municipal, this amount is taxable income to the bondholder who will receive a 1099-OID (Original Issue Discount) detailing the amount of interest to report, from the bond custodian. Each year, after adding implied interest, the new bond value is called the current accreted value, or CAV. If you hold your zero coupon bond until maturity, you will owe taxes on nothing other than the last year's implied interest when the bond matures. If you sell prior to maturity, the current year's accreted interest is considered ordinary income and the difference between the sale price and your bond's CAV will be a capital gain or loss.

Price Volatility of Zero Coupon Bonds. As long as you hold your bond until maturity and the credit of the issuer is not in question, you can be assured that you will receive face value for your bonds. However, should you decide to sell a zero coupon bond before it matures, you may see wide price swings. Zero coupon bonds are subject to much more price volatility than ordinary bonds, in the face of the same interest rate changes, because all interest is compounded at the same rate for a zero coupon bond.

When you own ordinary bonds, the coupon rate is set at issue, but each interest payment received must be reinvested at current interest rates. For example, if you own an ordinary 7% coupon bond and market interest rates rise to 8%, you are locked into the 7% on your principal, but at least you can reinvest interest payments at higher current rates. For a zero coupon bond, all interest is compounded at 7%, which makes the bond less valuable than the ordinary bond. Conversely, if interest rates fall to 6%, you must reinvest the interest payments on an ordinary bond at lower current rates while the zero coupon bonds keeps compounding at 7%, making it more valuable than the ordinary bond. Thus, when interest rates rise, the value of a zero coupon bond falls more than that of an ordinary bond, and when interest rates fall, a zero coupon bond increases in value more than an ordinary bond.

Benefits of Buying Zero Coupon Bonds. Investors purchase zero coupon bonds rather than ordinary bonds for the following reasons.

- By purchasing at a discount, investors can buy a larger face value with a smaller amount of money.

- Zeros make good planning tools for events that require a specific amount of money on a particular date in the future. Many investors use them for college education or retirement planning.

- Price sensitivity to interest rate swings is higher with accrual securities than with ordinary bonds. Those betting on declining interest rates will see the largest price gains in long-term zeros.

Buying Bonds

The government, corporate, and municipal bond markets are large and liquid, with billions of dollars of bonds trading daily on both the New York Stock Exchange (NYSE) and the over-the-counter (OTC) market. To purchase a corporate bond, you must use a broker, who will charge either an explicit commission or a markup, but not both. Commissions are more often charged on small transactions and are shown separately on the confirmation. The concept of a markup is similar to paying retail when buying from someone who paid wholesale. The dealer or brokerage firm adds its profit to the price paid in order to give a price to the consumer. The markup is measured in "points" with each point being 1% of the face value of the bond, or $10 per $1,000 bond. The amount of the markup will vary, generally increasing with length of maturity and difficulty of obtaining the bond in question. Markups are generally higher for retail (small dollar amount) customers and lower for institutional customers and individuals who buy frequently and in large amounts. Markups for government bonds fall in the 0.5- to 2-point range ($5 to $20 per bond), and for municipals and corporates, in the 0.5- to 3-point range ($5 to $30 per $1,000 bond).

Because markups are hidden from the buyer, it may be difficult to be sure that you are getting a good price for your bonds. Following are several ways to double-check, once a broker has quoted you a price.

- Call several other brokers for a price on the same security. Be sure to provide the same dollar amount on the transaction, as this will affect the price.

- Financial newspapers such as *The Wall Street Journal, Investor's Business Daily,* or *Barron's* provide tables of U.S. government and corporate bond prices and yields for many different issues. Transactions quoted are generally for lots of $1 million, so your price may vary.

- The Bond Market Association's website, *www.investinginbonds.com,* provides price and yield information daily for more than 1,000 actively traded municipal bonds.

- A service jointly provided by Standard & Poor's and The Bond Market Association will price 25 bonds for $9.95 + applicable state taxes. Call 1-800-BONDINFO (1-800-266-3463) with the CUSIP number of your bond and a credit card. You can also get a brochure outlining the service at this number.

Reading Bond Tables in the Newspaper

Reading the newspaper can be a convenient way to keep tabs on the bond market. The difficulty for most investors who are accustomed to finding their stocks each morning is that they may not be able to find their bonds in the newspaper. There are millions of outstanding bonds in the U.S. Treasury, municipal, and corporate bond markets. Although these markets are highly liquid, the reporting of bond prices may be limited by space constraints in a particular newspaper. Most financial papers, such as *The Wall Street Journal* and *Investor's Business Daily,* print daily transactions in the U.S. Treasury market. In Figure 9–6, the first bond listed has a coupon interest rate of 5.5% and a maturity date of January 2003. The bid price is the price at which you could sell to a dealer.

Figure 9–6. Reading Bond Tables in the Newspaper

Coupon	Maturity	Bid	Asked	Bid Chg.	Yield
5.50	Jan 03	98.19	98.21	−0.02	5.95
6.25	Feb 03	100.23	100.25	−0.03	5.99
5.50	Mar 03	98.15	98.17	−0.02	5.97

It is quoted in 32nds thus, 98.19 means a price of 98 19/32 or 98.594% of par. This translates to $985.94 per $1,000 bond. The asked price—the price at which you might buy from a dealer—is 98 21/32 or 98.656 ($986.56 per $1,000 bond). The day-to-day change in prices is computed on the bid price and is 2/32 or 0.0625. The yield to maturity is 5.95%. NYSE-traded corporate bonds are generally listed in the same manner and a sampling of municipals may be listed as well. In many cases the best you can do is find a bond of comparable quality, coupon, and maturity and expect that yours will react in a similar manner to changes in market and interest rate environments.

Summary

Bonds, with their fixed interest rates and promised return of principal, have a place in nearly every investor's portfolio. Though they may not be exciting in years when the S&P 500 returns 30%, they provide stability and a sure return in the inevitable bear markets. Key to investing in bonds is staggering maturity dates to avoid the necessity of selling at an inopportune time. This approach also tempers exposure to interest rate fluctuations, as funds are locked in and come due at different times.

Although bonds are generally purchased for their presumed safety, there is a significant inflation risk for portfolios that lean too heavily on bonds. At the other end of the spectrum, investors who venture into the junk bond arena leave safety behind as they search for higher returns. Prudent investors buy bonds for the balancing benefit that they provide to a diversified portfolio.

10

Investing in Stocks

A share of common stock represents ownership of a company and gives the shareholder a proportional piece of profits, assets, liabilities, dividends, and voting power. Shares of stock may be issued by any corporation, and those that are available for purchase or sale on a stock exchange or public market are referred to as publicly traded. At last count, more than 69 million Americans owned common stocks, either directly, through a mutual fund, or in a retirement plan.[1]

Ownership and Rights

The ownership represented by shares of stock is residual ownership, meaning stockholders have a claim on assets, but only after other claims have been satisfied. These claims may include debts owed to the IRS, bondholders, banks, and any other creditors. In the event of bankruptcy, the common stockholders are the last to be paid if there is any money left.

As partial owners, stockholders have voting rights in some decisions of the corporation, including elections to the board of directors and mergers and acquisitions. Generally, each share is allowed one vote, so that shareholders with a larger percentage of ownership have a proportionately larger voice in matters. Some corporations may issue shares labeled "A" and "B" which have different voting rights. This may be done to keep more power in the hands of the original owners or it may be used in a poison pill situation. Poison pills can be used to ward off unfriendly takeovers by putting shares with extraordinary voting power into friendly hands.

[1]New York Stock Exchange, "Shareownership 1998," Table 1: Total Number of Shareowners (millions), 1989–1995.

Shares may be voted at stockholders' meetings, which take place annually unless extenuating circumstances require more frequent meetings. Shareholders may vote their shares without attending a meeting by signing a proxy that assigns their voting rights to another person and indicates how they would like to vote.

Basic and Diluted Shares Outstanding

Firms report two different numbers of shares outstanding with their financial statements. Basic shares outstanding is the number of shares actually in the hands of investors. This equals all shares that have been issued, less any treasury shares (shares that the company has repurchased). Diluted shares outstanding equals all basic shares plus the shares potentially outstanding due to the exercise of stock options or the conversion of any bonds, notes, or other securities which may be exchanged for common stock. The figure for diluted shares represents the most shares that could be outstanding under current circumstances.

Preferred Stock

Stock may be issued as common or preferred shares. The term *preferred* relates to the right of preference in payment of dividends when funds are scarce and preference in payment in the event of bankruptcy. In exchange for these preferences, the preferred shareholder generally accepts a fixed dividend as opposed to a common dividend which may increase as company profits increase. When a company is unable to pay dividends for several periods on cumulative preferred stock, all unpaid dividends must be paid before any common dividends may be paid. The voting rights of preferred stockholders may not be the same as those of common stockholders.

Dividends

Dividends are paid to stockholders in cash or in the form of additional stock. Cash dividends are the most common and are generally paid on a quarterly basis to shareholders of record on a particular date, known as the record date. The amount of dividends paid is decided by the board of directors. Dividends are essentially a sharing of a corporation's profit with its stockholders, but it is not necessary for the company to be profitable in order to pay a dividend, as dividends may be paid from cash reserves. Logically, however, a company cannot do this indefinitely.

A common measure of the amount of dividends paid on a stock is its dividend yield, a measure of the value of the dividend relative to the price per share of stock. This amount is computed as follows:

$$\text{Dividend yield} = \frac{\text{Annual dividends per share}}{\text{Market price per share}}$$

Using this formula, the relative value of a $2 dividend on a $100 per share stock is the same as the value of a $0.50 dividend on a $25 per share stock. Both $2/$100 and $0.50/$25 equal 2%.

Stock dividends are occasionally paid in place of or in addition to cash dividends. When paid in place of cash dividends, it is often when the company is short of cash but wishes to pay a dividend. If the dividend is in shares of the same company (paying in shares of a subsidiary is called a spin-off which will be discussed later), it is of no real value to shareholders. Each shareholder receives a prorated amount based on current ownership, thus total percentage ownership does not change. For example, if a company declares a 10% stock dividend, each holder of 100 shares will receive 10 additional shares. However, because ownership of the company whose total value has not changed is now divided into 10% more shares, the value of each share will decline proportionately and thus leave each shareholder with the same total value in shares. Two exceptions apply here: (1) If investors bid the stock up after a stock dividend is announced for the illogical reason that they like stock dividends, stockholders will benefit. (2) If the stock pays a cash dividend whose rate stays the same or increases, investors will receive more in the form of cash dividends when they have more shares.

Dividend-Paying Stocks versus Nondividend-Paying Stocks

Some stocks pay a dividend because they have profits that are available for payout. Others operate at a loss and have no funds to pay. In addition to the ability to pay are some nuances to the decision to pay a dividend, depending on the company and its point of view.

Dividend-Paying Companies. Companies that pay a dividend usually fall into one of three categories, whose stocks are listed in order of descending dividend yield: income stocks, blue-chip stocks, and established growth stocks. Shareholders buy income stocks because they pay dividends. These companies often do not have a high-return opportunity for reinvesting cash flow into their business. Blue-chip stocks pay dividends because many investors like a bird-in-the-hand form of total return. A 2% dividend can cushion the loss in years in which the stock price falls. For both types of stock, the dividend yield acts to limit price declines, because as stock prices fall the dividend yield increases. As the yield increases, more investors buy the stock for its income and this demand acts to increase or at least stabilize the price. Note that this only works when investors believe that a company will not cut or eliminate its dividend. Established growth stocks often pay investors a minimal dividend that does not affect total returns greatly.

In addition to the obvious cash benefit of a dividend is the information content of dividends. Dividends are set by the board of directors—a group of insiders who know more about the financial prospects of a company than anyone else. Therefore, an increase in a dividend rate sends the message that prospects for the future are rosy. A decrease in the dividend rate or the elimination of dividends implies the opposite. This applies not only to absolute increases in the dividend, but also to changes in the rate of dividend growth for a company that habitually increases its dividend.

Nondividend-Paying Companies. Many companies do not pay a dividend. These companies either do not have enough cash flow to pay dividends or they believe that investors will be better off if they retain the funds within the company. Some companies are growing at such high rates that it makes more sense for them to reinvest profits in their business. Theoretically, a company that reinvests funds at high rates of return rather than paying a dividend will see an increased stock price.

Other companies are aware that under a tax code which taxes capital gains at lower rates than dividends, stockholders are better off without dividends. This is best illustrated by an example. Say you own 1,000 shares of XYZ Company, which you purchased at $40 per share. Its market price is $50. You would like $1,000 in income from your stock. For the sake of argument, you have the choice of either obtaining it through a $1 per share dividend or selling 20 shares of stock. Assume the following:

- Your internet broker will charge a $10 commission.
- Your marginal income tax rate is 31%; the capital gains tax rate is 20%.
- Stock prices generally fall by the amount of dividends paid, as that much cash has left the company, reducing its value.

See Table 10–1 for a comparison between receiving and not receiving a dividend. In this example you are ahead by $262 if your company does not pay a dividend.

Table 10–1. The Tax Consequences of Paying a Dividend

	XYZ Pays a Dividend	No Dividend/ Sell 20 Shares
Initial value: 1,000 shares × $50	$50,000	$50,000
$1 per share dividend	$1,000	
Sell 20 shares ($10 commission)		$990
Income tax on dividend at 31%	($310)	
Capital gains tax on $190 gain*		($38)
Stock value 1,000 shares × $49	$49,000	
Stock value 98 shares × $50		$49,000
Total net value	$49,690	$49,952

*Gain = sale amount of $990 less basis of $40 × 20 shares or $800

Types of Stock

There are many different ways to categorize individual stocks, ranging from the investment objective of those who buy them to the size of the underlying company. Because the methods differ, much overlap occurs. For example, a stock can be a largecap, blue-chip, cyclical stock. Following are brief definitions of different classifications of stock.

Classification by Investment Objective

Blue-Chip Stocks. Blue-chip stocks (named for the most valuable chips in a poker game) are those of high-quality, financially stable companies with long and mostly uninterrupted records of increasing earnings and dividends. Such household names include General Electric, Anheuser-Busch, Coca Cola, Disney, and McDonalds. Investors buy blue-chip stocks when they are in search of a high-quality investment with a decent dividend yield and respectable growth potential. The quality of financials and the existence of a nice dividend are expected to provide some protection against downside risk. Blue-chip stocks are generally purchased as long-term investments for their dependable rates of return.

Growth Stocks. Growth stocks are based on companies whose revenues and earnings are growing rapidly and are expected to continue that pace.

A good growth stock might exhibit a sustained rate of growth in earnings of 15% to 20% or more. Current examples include Microsoft (43%, five-year EPS growth) and Intel (21%, five-year EPS growth). These stocks often pay little or no dividends because rapid growth requires that all earnings be reinvested in the company. Investors buy growth stocks for their capital appreciation potential, with little concern for current income.

Because many investors favor growth stocks, these generally sell at high P/E ratios. The price/earnings growth (PEG) ratio discussed in the next section can be a good way to tell whether a high P/E is warranted. It is also common for growth stocks to have high betas, possibly a result of their high P/Es, as P/Es often expand in a bull market and contract in a correction or bear market.

Value Stocks. Value stocks represent companies that are out of favor with investors and appear undervalued when measured by such ratios as price/earnings, price/book value, and current yield. Often good value stocks have experienced a one-time problem with earnings that is expected to reverse in the near-term future. Examples might include inability of a supplier to provide enough of a key component or temporary labor issues that have been resolved.

Investors buy value stocks with the expectation of capital appreciation when they return to normal market valuations. Dividends paid provide current return during the wait.

Income Stocks. Income stocks are those whose appeal is based on the dividends that they pay. These companies have a stable level of earnings and cash flow suitable for funding a steady or increasing dividend. They are often in mature industries where large reinvestments in the company are not necessary.

Investors buy income stocks for their current income, with little expectation of capital appreciation. They expect that dividends will increase over time, keeping with or exceeding the pace of inflation. This increasing payout is an advantage of income stocks over bonds and similar fixed-income investments. Look for stocks whose current yield exceeds that of the average blue chip but is not so high that it signals risk. A current yield out of line with the market, such as 15%, usually indicates belief that the dividend will be cut or eliminated.

Speculative Stocks. Speculative stocks are for gamblers or anyone with a little play money. Most speculative stocks have an idea, a patent, or a product but have not yet been able to implement it into a business that makes money. Biotech stocks whose discoveries are still in clinical trials are a good example. If the product passes the trials, it could be the next blockbuster cure, but if it fails, it is worthless.

In the past speculative stocks were primarily penny stocks, those whose prices are under $5. Now, with the internet phenomenon, some speculative stocks sell for $300 per share. Often these companies have no earnings, only the prospect of being first in a market category that is growing exponentially and is therefore expected to produce exceptional earnings someday.

Classification by Sensitivity to the Business Cycle

Cyclical Stocks. Stocks whose price movements are inclined to follow the business cycle are said to be cyclical. When the economy is in an expansionary stage, the prices of cyclical stocks generally increase, whereas during an economic contraction, prices fall. Cyclical stocks tend to be found in basic industries. For example, an increase in new home starts is typical of an expansionary economic phase, so companies related to home-building, such as steel and lumber, can be expected to profit. The auto industry is also typically cyclical as good economic times with high employment encourage consumers to buy new cars.

Defensive Stocks. Defensive stocks are those whose prices are not expected to be affected by fluctuations of the business cycle. They may be income stocks, whose price is primarily determined by their dividend yield or they may be stocks in industries which do not suffer greatly in an economic downturn. For example, the stocks of food and beverage or household goods companies are relatively impervious to cyclical swings, because consumers do not change their spending on these products in relation to the economy.

Some companies are lucky (or smart) enough to position themselves to be attractive to investors who are looking for both cyclical and defensive stocks. Home Depot is a good example. In an economic expansion, it benefits from new home building and during a recession from the do-it-yourselfers who renovate because they cannot afford new homes.

Classification by Market Capitalization

Market capitalization refers to company size. A company's market cap is figured by multiplying its current share price by the number of shares outstanding. For example, a company whose stock price is $75 and has 10 million shares outstanding has a market cap of $750 million. The market cap is essentially what the investing public believes the company is worth,

Table 10–2. Market Capitalization Classifications

Category	Market Capitalization
Microcap	Less than $100 million
Smallcap	$100 to $500 million
Midcap	$500 million to $5 billion
Largecap	$5 billion +

because that is what it would cost to purchase all the outstanding shares. Most segregations by market capitalization are similar to those in Table 10–2.

In some respects, classifying by market cap has similar results to using speculative, growth, and blue-chip labels, since stocks that fit these descriptions tend to be naturally grouped by size. High-growth and speculative stocks have historically been smallcap, and blue-chip stocks have historically been largecap, but there are notable exceptions that cross these lines. Microsoft, one of the growth stock darlings of the 1990s, has a market cap of $370 billion (July 2000), making it a largecap stock. Many internet stocks, considered speculative, are also in the largecap category. For example, Ariba, whose market cap was $29 billion (July 2000), was not operating at a profit.

Mutual funds often use market capitalization in their investment guidelines as an indication of the type of portfolio that they intend to build. However, due to the difficulty in categorizing one segment as more or less conservative, pay close attention to other statements within the investment objective, in addition to capitalization limits.

Key Measures of Stock Performance and Value

Fundamental analysis is the analysis of quantitative and qualitative data about a corporation in order to determine its investment value. This contrasts with technical analysis, which measures trading price and volume patterns. The measures we will discuss here are fundamental. Some aspects of technical analysis are addressed in Chapter 18.

Revenue

Revenue, also called sales, is the amount a company receives from selling its products or services. By itself, this number may not be particularly valuable, as there are plenty of companies with revenue but no profits. However, revenue growth, or lack of it, can be very telling when used with profit figures. When profits, as measured by earnings per share (EPS), grow without a corresponding increase in revenue, it is a signal for further investigation. Increased earnings without increased revenues may be the result of cost cutting or of one-time gains, which, although positive, cannot keep expanding EPS indefinitely. Growing profit margins are good, but revenues must grow as well. The level of revenue growth should be comparable with the rate of EPS growth and the historic revenue growth rate.

Revenues derived from a few key customers or key products tend to be volatile. Annual and 10-K reports should detail dependence on a small number of customers or products.

In some industries order backlogs can be an indicator of future revenues. The order backlog is the value of contracts signed whose work has not yet been delivered. Larger-than-normal backlogs signal higher future revenue as sales are completed.

Price to Sales Ratio. The price to sales ratio (PSR) measures the dollars in stock price paid for every dollar of sales generated. The quick version of this formula is market price per share divided by sales per share. A more conservative use of the formula includes long-term debt, using the logic that if you were to buy the whole company, you would pay market price for all the shares outstanding, plus you would be responsible for paying the company's long-term debt. Using this point of view, it is easier to work on an entire company framework than on a per share basis.

To find the market price of the entire company, called the market capitalization, multiply the market price per share by the number of shares outstanding; then add long-term debt. Divide this number by sales from the most recent (called trailing) 12 months to compute the PSR, as follows:

$$PSR = \frac{(\text{Share price} \times \text{Shares outstanding}) + \text{Long-term debt}}{\text{Trailing 12 months' sales}}$$

The PSR computation for a company whose share price is $20, has 10 million shares outstanding, $200 million in long-term debt, and sales of $200 million is

$$PSR = \frac{(\$20 \times 10{,}000{,}000) + \$200{,}000{,}000}{\$200{,}000{,}000}$$

$$= \frac{\$400{,}000{,}000}{\$200{,}000{,}000}$$

$$= 2$$

As with other valuation ratios such as P/E, a lower PSR is better. Value investors often look for a PSR of 1 or lower to find stocks that the market has undervalued. PSRs should be used in comparison with industry averages and may be useful in calculating whether a firm's sales are being given a lower value than its peers.

The recent phenomenon of internet stocks has revived the use of the PSR. Many of these firms have no earnings, making P/E ratios useless. In such cases, the PSR is one of the few income-related methods for comparing and valuing these companies.

Earnings

The earnings of a company, also called net income or profits, are its bottom line. After paying all expenses, earnings equal the money left from the revenues collected. Earnings are measured on a per share basis, using the term earnings per share (EPS). They are computed as follows:

$$\text{EPS} = \frac{\text{Net profit after taxes} - \text{Preferred dividends paid}}{\text{Diluted shares outstanding}}$$

Preferred dividends are subtracted from profits because they must be paid before any cash is available to the common stockholders. Diluted shares outstanding are used in order to be the most conservative. If a firm reports income from continuing operations before subtracting or adding items such as income/loss from discontinued operations or cumulative effect of accounting changes, use the income from continuing operations as profit in the EPS calculation, because investors are interested in profits generated from the primary, ongoing business. By definition, one-time charges or gains are not ongoing.

Measure EPS growth on a quarterly and annual basis, comparing it with historic and peer group rates of growth. The stock tables in *Investor's Business Daily* show an EPS rating for each stock listed, which is a valuable resource for analyzing EPS growth. In computing the rating, they compare the two most recent quarters' earnings with the same quarters' earnings a year ago for a short-term measure. Then they examine the long-term history (three to five years) for earnings growth and stability. The results are compared with all other companies in the database and ranked from 1 to 99, with 99 being the best. An EPS rating of 95% would mean that the company outperformed 95% of the other companies in the database.

Price/Earnings Ratio. The price/earnings (P/E) ratio tells how many dollars in stock price are being paid for each dollar of EPS generated. The P/E ratio is computed as follows:

$$P/E \text{ ratio} = \frac{\text{Share price}}{\text{Trailing 12 months' EPS}}$$

Using this formula, a stock selling for $50 per share whose last 12 months' EPS was $2 would have a P/E of 25. The P/E ratio is helpful in comparing two stocks with different prices and EPS. For example, the $50 stock just noted has the same valuation, using a P/E comparison, as a stock selling for $75, whose EPS is $3 ($75/$3 = 25 P/E ratio).

Obviously, all else being equal, a lower P/E ratio is better. This is one of the mantras of value investors, who often screen stocks for low P/E ratios, searching for those that are undervalued relative to their earnings power. How then do we explain the $100 stock whose EPS is $2 alongside the $50 stock whose EPS is $2? The P/E of the first is 50, while the P/E of the second is 25. Why would anyone pay $100 for the first stock? The answer is the expectation of EPS growth. If an investor expects the EPS of the first stock to quickly reach $4, its P/E would then be 25, as is the P/E of the second stock. This leads us to the next ratio, the PEG. Before you go there, note that if the investor is wrong and EPS does not quickly grow to $4, then for the valuation of the two stocks to be the same, the price of the first would have to drop to $50.

Price/Earnings Growth Ratio. The price/earnings growth (PEG) ratio is a comparison of a stock's P/E ratio with its rate of EPS growth. It is computed by dividing the P/E ratio by the estimated rate of future earnings per share growth. For example, a stock with a P/E of 50, whose two- to five-year earnings growth forecast is 45%, has a PEG of 50/45 = 1.11.

An investing rule of thumb is that a stock's P/E ratio should be approximately equal to its rate of EPS growth. Using this general rule, a fully valued stock has a PEG near 1. A PEG below 1 indicates an undervalued stock, while a PEG above 1 indicates an overvalued stock. This ratio provides some rationale to high P/E growth stocks and a method for determining how much high growth is worth.

Price/Book Value. The book value of a corporation is theoretically what it would be worth if it were liquidated. Book value is computed by subtracting liabilities and preferred stock from assets. The result is what would be available to distribute to common stockholders if all the assets were sold for cash and all obligations were paid. Book value per share is the corporation's book value divided by the diluted number of shares outstanding. For example, if a company had $100 million in assets, $50 million in liabilities, no preferred stock, and 10 million shares outstanding, its book value per share would be as follows:

$$\text{Book value per share} = \frac{\$100 \text{ million} - \$50 \text{ million}}{10 \text{ million}}$$

$$= \$5 \text{ per share}$$

The ratio of price to book value is the market price of a share of stock divided by its book value per share. All else being equal, lower is better. Value investors often look for stocks whose ratio is less than 1. They also look at the quality of the assets involved. For example, cash is the most prized asset in a book value equation, because its value is undisputed. Accounts receivable that may not be collectible or assets such as outdated machinery deserve further scrutiny. On the other hand, fully depreciated assets which still have real value may be hidden treasures.

Long-Term Debt to Stockholders' Equity Ratio

The long-term debt to stockholders' equity ratio is not a valuation measure but a measure of financial health for a corporation. The ratio is calculated as follows:

$$\text{Debt to equity ratio} = \frac{\text{Total long-term debt}}{\text{Stockholders' equity}}$$

High debt loads raise the possibility that interest payments could strangle a business in an economic or industry downturn; therefore, a high debt to equity ratio means more financial risk. Debt to equity ratios differ widely by industry and depend greatly on how capital intensive a business is. Compare with the peer group and look for major changes. As noted in the Chapter 15 discussion on real estate investment trusts (REIT), long-term assets should be financed by long-term debt. Become concerned when significant amounts of debt are short term, as long-term financing at a later date may become more expensive or unavailable.

Interest Coverage Ratio. One way to see the financial effect of debt is to compute an interest coverage ratio. This ratio takes either profits or cash flow and divides by total interest payments to compute how safe the interest payments are.

Return on Equity

Return on equity (ROE) tells how efficiently a company used its investment of stockholders' equity to produce profits. The formula is as follows:

$$ROE = \frac{Profit}{Stockholders'\ equity}$$

As with other profitability measures, higher is better and increasing is better. Compare with historic figures and the peer group. ROE should always be analyzed with the debt/equity ratio, because a corporation's capital structure affects ROE. Companies are generally financed with a combination of debt and equity, which, when added together, equal total assets. So, as debt goes up, equity goes down, and vice versa. Because equity is the denominator in the ROE equation, less equity makes for a higher resulting ROE but less equity means higher debt. Therefore, it is a good idea when comparing the ROE of two companies to check whether their debt levels are similar. A higher ROE may simply be the result of higher debt levels.

Return on Assets

Return on assets (ROA) measures a company's profit in relation to the assets it had available to make that profit. It is conceptually similar to ROE, without the issue of capital structure. The formula is as follows:

$$ROA = \frac{Profit}{Total\ assets}$$

Compare ROA to previous years' levels and to the ROA of peer group stocks.

Beta

The beta of a stock is a measure of past price volatility relative to market averages and is used to predict future volatility. Computed through statistical analysis of price movements, the beta seeks to measure how a stock's price will change when general market levels change. A beta of 1 means that a stock can be expected to move in the same percentage increments as the market, usually measured by the S&P 500 Index. Therefore, if the S&P 500 rose (or fell) by 20%, and a stock had a beta of 1, the stock's price could be expected to rise (or fall) by 20%. If the stock had a beta of 1.5, then the movement in its price, either up or down as the index moved, could be expected to be 30%. This is computed by multiplying the beta by the market movement ($1.5 \times 20\% = 30\%$). A stock with little market sensitivity might have a beta of 0.8. Its price movements relative to the market index should be expected to be less extreme ($0.8 \times 20\% = 16\%$).

You can find the beta of a stock in most market research reports. There is some disagreement as to whether this tool, garnered from past price changes, has any value as a predictor, but it is still widely used.

Initial Public Offerings

When a company first sells its stock to public shareholders, it is called an initial public offering (IPO). In the late 1990s, IPOs generated unprecedented levels of excitement as many new offerings increased by 300% or more on the very first day of trading.

The IPO Process: Going Public

When a company decides to go public, it prepares a business plan and financial statements and enlists an investment bank or a team of investment banks to perform the offering. Together they create a brochure, called a prospectus, for investors which is full of financial information, descriptions of company officers, and a discussion of how the proceeds will be used. This preliminary prospectus (often called a red herring because the words "Preliminary Prospectus" are stamped in red across it) is filed with the SEC and the NASD.

Next the lead underwriter assembles a syndicate of other investment banks to help it sell the offering. The company's management must go on a tour, called a road show, to convince these major players that the company has good prospects. After the road show, a final prospectus is printed and the underwriter decides on the offering price. The offering price is a balance, ideally positioned slightly below what investors believe the company is worth. It is priced below so that investors who buy the offering will see some initial price appreciation; but not too far below, because the company wants to raise as much money as possible. The internet IPO business has changed this model somewhat, as a huge run-up in price on the initial day of trading is desirable for the publicity it creates.

Once the final prospectus is available for investors and a targeted price range has been decided (the actual price is set at the last moment), investors can place their orders with brokers participating in the underwriting. Popular offerings may have many more investors who wish to buy than shares available. This situation is termed an oversubscribed offering. To buy shares in a popular offering, you generally must be a good customer of a broker in the syndicate, though recently, small allocations of IPOs have been available through some online brokers, such as Fidelity, E-Trade, Charles Schwab, and Wit Capital.

On the first day of trading, investors who received shares in the offering pay the final set offering price, which may have little to do with the first public transactions. Trading in the stock begins with a price based on supply and demand. The first few days' stock price may fluctuate widely as speculators trade in and out of a popular issue.

The targeted price range, actual offering price, and first day's trading of a real stock are illustrated in a news story from Reuters on February 3, 2000: "Wireless communications company Alamosa PCS Holdings Inc. (APCS), part of the Sprint PCS Group (PCS), saw its shares more than double when opening for trade on Thursday after raising $182.1 million in its initial public offering. The stock jumped as high as $34 before settling back with a gain of 15 points to trade at $32. Alamosa offered 10.714 million shares at a price of $17, above the targeted price range of $13 to $15."[2]

Information about IPOs

There are many sources of information about IPOs. Most internet financial sites include an IPO calendar and several sites are dedicated to IPOs, such as Hoover's IPO Central at *www.ipocentral.com*. IPO Express at *www. ipoexpress.com* is part of EDGAR Online, the online service operated by the SEC. There you can find calendars of IPOs, search for specific companies, and read prospectuses. Linkups to IPO companies' sites are also available.

Begin your research by reading the prospectus, which you can get online from IPO Central or IPO Express or from any firm in the syndicate. The prospectus is always heavy on risk factors to protect the company from being sued for misleading investors with an overly optimistic outlook. Much of this is boilerplate, but read it anyway, then look for some positive signs.

In addition to the requisite financial hurdles of increasing revenues, profits, and profit margins are other positive signs sprinkled throughout a prospectus. One is a well-known underwriter with a good performance history. The name at the bottom of the prospectus should be recognizable, and if you really want to do your homework, research how well the company's IPOs have performed. This is known as betting on the jockey when you do not know the horse.

Look for shares in the offering to come from the company rather than selling stockholders. The company receives no money from shares that stockholders sell and if a company's prospects are strong, existing investors will not want to sell.

[2]Reuters Limited, "Sprint's Alamosa doubles in stock debut" (February 3, 2000).

It is good to see a specific section on use of proceeds. Check for forward-looking statements of intended activity rather than the payoff of existing debt or previous stockholders.

Read the management descriptions carefully, looking for both experience and compensation. A management team that is experienced in comparable public companies and is compensated in part with stock options should have both the ability and the desire to drive the stock price upward.

Direct IPOs

In 1999, the online brokerage firm W.R. Hambrecht & Co. tried a new system for allocating IPOs with the intent of leveling the playing field between retail and institutional investors. Traditional IPOs generate huge fees for investment banks and the hot offerings are doled out to their favorite clients, often large institutions such as mutual funds. W.R Hambrecht & Co. at their website, Open IPO, (*www.openipo.com*), performed an IPO that was sold directly to the public through a process called a Dutch auction.

In the Dutch auction, investors place secret bids for the number of shares they would like and the maximum dollar they are willing to pay. All bids are tallied with the highest taken first, until the entire offering is placed. The price of the last bid taken (lowest price) is the price at which the entire offering sells. In a simplified example, a company that wanted to sell 1 million shares might have the bids shown in Table 10–3.

In this example, once the bidding reached $10, the cumulative number of shares for which there were bids reached the amount the company wished to sell. This set the offering price at $10. All investors who bid above $10 received their allocations at the $10 price. Those who bid $10 received 50% of their requested allocation, because by allocating half of the shares bid at $10, the cumulative number of shares bid equaled the goal of 1 million. Anyone who bid below $10 did not receive shares. The company received $10 million (1 million shares × $10 per share).

Table 10–3. Bids in a Sample Dutch Auction

Number of Shares	Cumulative Shares	Price per Share	Shares Allocated	Cumulative Shares Allocated
200,000	200,000	$13	200,000	200,000
100,000	300,000	$12	100,000	300,000
500,000	800,000	$11	500,000	800,000
400,000	1,200,000	$10	200,000	1,000,000
200,000	1,400,000	$9	0	1,000,000

To date, W.R. Hambrecht has brought three offerings public: Ravenswood Vinyards (RVWD), a California winery; Salon.com (SALN), an online magazine; and Andover.Net (ANDN), owner of *www.slashdot.org*, a Linux open-source software site. The first two began trading at levels similar to their Dutch auction prices, validating the fairness of the market pricing system. Andover.Net surged 252% in its first day of trading, raising questions about the process; but in an interview, Bruce Twickler, Andover.Net's chief executive officer, called the IPO a success. He noted that traditional investment bankers were not willing to undertake the offering and that W.R. Hambrecht brought it to market very quickly.[3] Andover.Net has since agreed to be purchased by VA Linux Systems for approximately $1.04 billion.

Lockup

Lockup is the term for the agreement that prevents insiders from selling stock for a period of time (usually six months) after the IPO. The end of a lockup period can be a serious negative for the price of an IPO stock as some insiders rush to cash in and the increased supply of shares hangs over the market.

Penn State University finance professors Laura Field and Gordon Hanka studied 3,217 IPOs over 10 years and found that the average price drop for a stock in the week that lockup ends is 1.8%. More recently, between 1994 and 1996, the average drop rose to 2.5%. On average, trading volume increases 75% on the day after lockup expires, and price declines are more severe in high-tech and venture-capital-backed companies.[4]

According to Field and Hanka's research, and conventional logic, it may be a good idea to avoid buying shares in a recent IPO immediately before the lockup expires. To find a calendar of lockups soon to expire, visit FreeEDGAR's IPO Express lockup page at *www.edgar-online.com/ipoexpress/lockup.asp*. Try IPOLockup.com at *www.ipolockup.com* for a chronological list of expiring lockups with pertinent information such as the number of shares to be released from lockup, lockup shares as a percentage of total shares outstanding, average trading volume, and the number of trading days it would take to absorb lockup shares. Once lockup has expired for a company, the site reports closing prices from four days before lockup expiration to four days after.

---

[3]Dick Satran, "NetTrends: Andover's 'Community IPO'," *Reuters Limited* (January 26, 2000).

[4]Alex F. McMillan, "Be Wary of IPO Lockup End," CNNfn (January 21, 2000).

IPO Performance

Hoover's Online reported the following statistics for IPOs in 1999.

- Approximately 75% of all IPOs raise $100 million or less.
- The 12 largest offerings raised about half of the total raised for the year.
- One in 10 IPOs rose by 500% by year-end.
- About 25% of IPOs had year-end prices below their offering prices.

Interestingly, no overlap occurs in the 10 IPOs with the biggest first-day gains and the 10 IPOs with the best returns for the year. These results are found in Tables 10–4 and 10–5.

The all-time list of first-day gainers includes theglobe.com, inc., which went public in November 1998. Its first-day gain from an offering price of $9 to a closing price of $63.50 was 606%. Since 1999, Avanex Corporation, which debuted in February 2000, was offered at $36 and closed at $172 for a gain of 378%.

Stock Splits

Investors love stock splits. Why not? In a 2-for-1 split, you receive a new share for every share you already have, doubling the number of shares that you own. However, under closer scrutiny, a split is merely an accounting

Table 10–4. Biggest First-Day IPO Gains in 1999

Company	Offer Price	Closing Price	Percent Increase
VA Linux Systems, Inc.	$30	$239.25	698%
Foundry Networks, Inc.	25	156.25	525
FreeMarkets, Inc.	48	280.00	483
Cobalt Networks, Inc.	22	128.13	482
MarketWatch.com	17	97.50	474
Akamai Technologies, Inc.	26	145.19	458
CacheFlow Inc.	24	126.38	427
Sycamore Networks, Inc.	38	184.75	386
Finisar Corporation	19	86.88	357
Crossroads Systems, Inc.	18	78.72	337

SOURCE: Hoover's Online.

Table 10–5. 1999 IPOs with the Best Returns Through Year-End

Company	Offer Price	Closing Price	Percent Increase
Internet Capital Group, Inc.	$12	170.00	2,733%
Commerce One, Inc.	21	196.50	2,707
VerticalNet, Inc.	16	164.00	1,950
Brocade Communications Systems, Inc.	19	177.00	1,763
Purchase Pro.com Inc.	12	137.50	1,619
Vignette Corporation	19	163.00	1,616
Liberate Technologies	16	257.00	1,506
Redback Networks, Inc.	23	178.00	1,443
Ariba, Inc.	23	177.38	1,442
Red Hat, Inc.	14	211.25	1,409

SOURCE: Hoover's Online.

exercise similar to trading a dime for two nickels. When a stock splits 2-for-1, investors will have twice as many shares, but everything related to those shares is cut in half, including the dividend per share, earnings per share, and the stock's price. The same happens in a 3-for-2, 3-for-1, or 4-for-1 split, only the ratios change.

Why Companies Split Shares

The main reason companies split their shares is to make the shares more affordable for the individual investor. Investors generally like to buy stocks in 100-share lots and a 100-share lot of a $90 stock is quite expensive, at $9,000. If the company splits 2-for-1, the share price would be $45, bringing a 100-share lot to a more affordable level of $4,500. An obvious question here is, why does the company care? There are several reasons why a company wants individual investors to buy its shares. One is that the added demand of investors who now find the stock affordable may cause an increase in its price. Another reason is that individual investors are more likely to be long-term investors than institutional traders, so that a large individual ownership leads to less price volatility. Finally, for companies that sell consumer products, individual ownership leads to brand loyalty as a consumer.

Companies also split their shares to call attention to the fact that their stock prices have risen to lofty levels. Splitting implies that the board of directors expects the stock to stage a repeat performance and encourages new investors to take part.

Why a Stock Price Rises after a Split Is Announced

We have already established that there is no intrinsic value to a stock split, yet it is common knowledge that a stock's price often rises after a split is announced. According to the *Right Line Report*, a newsletter published by professional trader Roger Perry, stocks that split outperform stocks that do not by an average of 8% in the year following the split.[5] This is generally due to increased demand for the stock arising from the announcement. Demand may come from investors who fail to realize they are not getting something for nothing and from investors who hope to cash in on increased demand when the stock is more affordable. Other investors may realize that certain stocks have a pattern to their splits and the board of directors usually announces a split during a period of strong earnings, which nearly guarantees good postsplit performance.

Not all experts agree that a split is good for stock prices. Some maintain that companies that split their stock too frequently run the risk of having too large a supply of available stock. A large supply requires ever higher levels of demand for positive price movements.

At several financial websites, including Quicken.com at *www.quicken.com,* you can register to receive e-mail alerts of stocks that have announced a split. The *Right Line Report* uses a proprietary model to uncover and analyze stock split candidates. You can subscribe to receive it by e-mail at *www.rightline.net.*

Reverse Splits

A reverse split is a process by which companies reduce their number of shares outstanding. The math is the opposite of a split. As the number of shares are reduced, all per share data is increased. For example, a stock that has a 1-for-10 reverse split would see its stock price and EPS increase 10 times as each investor would now have a share for every 10 shares previously owned.

Reverse splits are an effort to increase the price and perceived value of a low-priced stock, however, a reverse split is not an effective way to increase stock prices over the long term. A study noted in the October 1999

---

[5]Paul Cherney, "Performance," the Right Line Report, *www.rightline.net* (February 2000).

issue of *American Association of Individual Investors Journal* found "substantial negative price performance" both during and after a reverse split.[6]

Mergers and Spin-Offs

Depending on the industry and the current corporate wisdom, companies go through periods of consolidation in which they merge with or purchase other companies, and through periods of divestiture in which they focus on their core business by spinning off or selling unrelated divisions.

Mergers

Mergers and acquisitions fall in two general categories. One type of merger is that which combines two companies whose businesses have little potential for synergy and is undertaken as a diversification. Current wisdom says that while this may reduce volatility in the returns of the individual company, it provides no value to the investor, who can diversify in the same way by holding the stocks of different companies. Mergers more in favor currently are those that combine complementary technologies or customer bases or that provide economies of scale in operations. Recently, the banking and technology industries have been fertile grounds for these combinations.

In 1999, the telecom and cable industries were hotbeds of merger activity as companies scrambled to combine different aspects of telephone service, television programming, and internet access. The largest mergers of 1999 by dollar amount are listed in Table 10–6.

As an investor, you may be affected by mergers in several ways. If you are a stockholder in a company involved in a merger, you will be asked to vote on it. If your company is being acquired, you may receive shares of the acquiring company, cash, or a combination of the two.

The decision of whether to hold stock in the combined company is often a difficult one. The $184 billion purchase of Time Warner Inc. by America Online (market value $286 billion), announced January 10, 2000, is a good example. There was general applause in the investment community as to the strategy behind the combination, which brings together giants of information and entertainment delivery and content. Still, disagreement remains about the expected performance of the stock price. Though AOL, unlike many internet companies, makes a profit, it inhabits a world where

---

[6]Wayne A. Thorp, and John Bajkowski, "Frequently Asked Questions About Financial Statements," *American Association of Individual Investors Journal* (October 1999).

Table 10-6. The Largest Mergers of 1999 (by dollar amount)

Acquirer	Target	Value (in billions)	Status
Vodafone Airtouch	Mannesmann	$135	Pending
MCI Worldcom	Sprint	115	Pending
Pfizer	Warner-Lambert	80	Pending
Olivetti	Telecom Italia	58	Completed
AT&T	MediaOne	58	Completed
Vodafone	Airtouch	55	Completed
Qwest	U.S. West	48	Completed
TotalFina	Elf Aquitaine	44	Completed
Viacom	CBS	37	Pending
Monsanto	Pharmacia & Upjohn	27	Pending

SOURCE: Morningstar.

stocks are priced at a multiple of revenues and Time Warner exists in a world where stocks are priced at a multiple of earnings. It remains to be seen whether the markets will give the new company an internet valuation, an ordinary valuation, or something in between.

Spin-Offs

In a spin-off, a corporation makes a previously owned subsidiary independent and distributes (spins off) shares in the new, independent company to its shareholders. Shareholders in the original corporation then have shares of two distinct corporations. The value is essentially the same, because the businesses have not changed, just separated. For tax purposes the parent corporation will issue a statement providing a basis per share for each share of the spin-off corporation.

On the first day of trading you can expect the stock price of the parent company to drop by roughly the market value of the spin-off, taking into account the ratio of shares distributed. For example, if you had a company priced at $90 per share and it spun off 1 of 10 equal divisions on a 1-for-1 share basis, you might expect the first-day trading price to be approximately $81 for the parent company and $9 for the spin-off company.

Like a stock split, spin-offs have no real intrinsic value. In the marketplace, however, the sum of separate parts is often worth more than the previous whole (a concept called breakup value). In some cases this is due to a fast-growing division which can now be priced on its own merits rather than be disregarded as a small part of a more slow-growing parent. In other cases, theory has it that management of newly independent companies behaves differently without the deep pockets of a parent company overhead. With their own capital at risk in the form of company stock, independents become more cost-conscious and take more strategic risks.

Tracking Stocks

Tracking stocks are similar to spin-offs in that they are issued to shareholders, and their financial statements reflect a particular division or subsidiary of the parent company. The key difference between tracking stocks and spin-offs is that tracking stocks are not independent corporations; their stock is merely set up to track the fortunes of the subsidiary. This difference is reflected in the control of the company. As a shareholder of a tracking stock, you will probably not be able to vote for the stock's board of directors, which will be put in place by the parent company. This board is more likely to put the parent company's interests first.

Tracking stocks are often issued because a subsidiary could be expected to command a higher price if it were not a portion of a larger company. For example, Donaldson, Lufkin & Jenrette sold tracking stock in its online trading subsidiary DLJdirect in 1999, because valued separately as an internet stock, it was worth much more. Of the 25 tracking stocks now in existence, 6 were issued in 1999 and 5 of those were internet related.

Direct Investing and Dividend Reinvestment Plans

Direct investing and dividend reinvestment plans (DRIPs) offer a way to bypass a broker and buy shares of stock directly from a corporation, with either a minimal or no fee charged. Direct plans refer to those that allow you to purchase shares of stock directly from the corporation. DRIPs are those in which the dividends paid on your stock are reinvested in shares of the same stock. You generally must obtain your first share(s) through a broker, but may make subsequent purchases directly. Some brokerage firms now offer DRIP plans in which you pay a commission on your initial purchase, but the brokerage firm purchases additional shares with the dividends received at no charge.

The advantages of direct and DRIP investing are the minimal fees charged, the ability to invest small amounts of money, the ability to purchase fractional shares, and the easy method of dollar cost averaging. The characteristics of DRIPs differ somewhat depending on the plan, but unless the DRIP is managed by your brokerage firm, most plans require that the initial purchase of stock be registered in your name (not street name). This stipulation can add to your costs if you trade through a broker that charges to register and deliver securities. Most DRIPS automatically reinvest quarterly dividend payments into the stock at current market prices. Some plans also allow additional cash contributions on schedules that vary from any time to once a year. Some will even debit your bank account for you, just like automatic purchase plans at many mutual funds. There is often a fee of $5 to $10 associated with cash contributions.

Securities purchased through a DRIP are held in an account for you. You will receive a statement periodically and if you wish to sell the shares you must sell them through the DRIP. Although you do not receive cash dividends when they are reinvested using a DRIP, they are still taxable income in the year in which they were paid. The reinvestment is treated as two separate transactions: a payment of cash dividends and a subsequent purchase of stock.

There are many sources of information about direct investing and DRIP plans. Two websites are Drip Advisor at *www.dripadvisor.com* and Netstock Direct at *www.netstockdirect.com.* Both provide education about DRIPs and lists of companies that offer direct investing. There are also clubs and cooperatives that exist to help investors obtain the first share of a company so that they can participate in a DRIP. First Share at *www.firstshare.com* is one of these, but with an annual membership fee of $24 plus transaction fees of $5 to $10, it may be cheaper to go to a deep discount broker.

Stock Repurchases and Insider Activity

Why Companies Repurchase Shares

Periodically companies announce that they plan to repurchase some of their outstanding shares. Everyone who knows the equation for earnings per share realizes that this is a good thing for investors. If EPS = profit/shares outstanding and shares outstanding is reduced, then EPS will increase. Or, from a conceptual standpoint, if a company is a pie and each share is a piece of that pie, cutting it into fewer pieces means that each piece can be a little bigger. So, share repurchases are good for investors because they increase EPS and decrease dilution (the number of pieces of pie).

There are still other reasons for shareholders to applaud, one of which is shares repurchased by a corporation no longer require the payment of dividends. This provides an ongoing cash flow savings. Another issue involves float—the number of shares outstanding which are available in the market. A smaller float means a smaller supply of shares for purchase. Because stock prices are determined by supply and demand, a decrease in supply may result in a higher stock price. In fact, many companies that split their shares announce repurchases at the same time, due to concerns of oversupply.

A repurchase announcement also involves some information content. Repurchasing shares implies that management believes that shares are undervalued. Why else would they take cash reserves that are perhaps needed later to repurchase shares? They would not, unless they believed that in the event the company needed the cash they could resell those shares at a higher price.

Stock repurchases do increase stock price according to a study by university professors David Ikenberry, Josef Lakonishok, and Theo Vermaelen.[7] The study followed 1,290 companies that announced stock repurchases between 1980 and 1990 and found that these companies outperformed others by 2.04% over one year, 5.16% over two years, and 12.60% over three years.

Companies That Repurchase

Companies that repurchase their shares generally fall into two categories. The first is companies with good cash flow that do not have excellent opportunities to reinvest in their business (or whose cash flow exceeds those opportunities). Rather than build up high levels of cash, which could make them a target for a hostile takeover, they choose to return the cash to investors. They could do this by paying cash dividends or by repurchasing shares. The repurchase makes more sense because it increases EPS and creates a taxable event only for those stockholders who choose to sell. A cash dividend would be taxed to all stockholders as current income at their marginal income tax rate. In a repurchase scenario, if the stockholders who choose to sell have held their shares longer than 12 months, they will pay taxes at a capital gains rate rather than current income tax rates.

The other category of company that may announce a repurchase program is one that has just experienced an earnings disappointment. The program is intended to help prop up the stock price for all the previous reasons and to underscore management's belief that the stock is undervalued.

The area titled "Stock Buybacks" on the Online Investor site at *www.theonlineinvestor.com/buyback.shtml* provides a calendar and details of

---

[7]Ian Mount, "Buy on the Buybacks," SmartMoney.com (July 28, 1999).

recent stock repurchase announcements. The Buyback Letter, found in the Stock Advisors section at the INVESTools site, *www.investools.com*, is an entire newsletter devoted to choosing stocks based on share repurchases. It offers current announcements plus model buyback portfolios.

Insider Activity

Insiders, classified by the SEC as anyone who has access to nonpublic, material, insider information, are generally considered to be officers and directors of a company, plus anyone who owns more than 10% of the shares outstanding. Given their access to nonpublic information, insider actions can tell a story that has yet to hit the news.

Insiders are required to report their purchases and sales of a company's stock to the SEC, and the SEC makes this information public. It is illegal for insiders to trade on the basis of significant nonpublic information, such as a pending merger or a devastating loss that has not yet been announced. (In 1986, Dennis Levine was charged by the SEC with using inside information to make nearly $13 million in profits over a six-year period.)

Different from the illegal insider trading, reported trading of insiders can be useful to investors since officers and directors of a company should be closely attuned to the intrinsic value of their stock and its merits as an investment. Purchases are the most valuable indicator as they illustrate the belief that the stock will increase in price and show the willingness to put personal capital at risk. Records of stock sales by insiders can be less valuable since there may be several different causes. Insiders may sell because they believe either the prospects for the company are not good or the stock has become overvalued. However, they may also sell to collect on stock options, an increasingly common form of executive compensation; to diversify their investments; or to fund the purchase of a new home or a child's college education.

Find out about insider transactions in a Value Line Investment Survey report, on the SEC's website at *www.freeedgar.com* or at *http://insiders.mw.cnation.com*. InsiderSCORES.com at *www.insiderscores.com* identifies insiders whose purchases or sales have predicted price moves in their stock. Those with the best track records are listed as all-stars. Insider Trader at *www.insidertrader.com* offers daily screens of insider activity and a weekly commentary.

Buying and Selling Stock

Types of Orders

The type of order you place with your broker can greatly affect the price at which you buy or sell and whether the transaction takes place at all. Being well versed in your choices can prevent surprises.

Market Orders. A market order to buy or sell is an instruction to your broker to make your transaction at the best price available in the current market, which means the lowest price for a buy and the highest price for a sale. When you place a market order, you are assured of an execution but have no guarantees on the price. For example, if you place a market order for Apple Computer after the market closes today, you might expect it to be executed near today's closing price of $60 when the market opens tomorrow morning. However, there is no guarantee that the market will open tomorrow where it closed today. If Apple announces an incredible earnings increase at the end of the day, the stock could begin trading at $65 tomorrow. A market order to buy would be executed at $65, not $60.

If you trade with a deep discount broker, you should be aware that many of them are able to charge minimal commissions because they are paid for order flow. This means that the broker might receive a payment of $2 for placing your order with a particular market maker. In this case the incentive to shop your order for the very best price is greatly minimized.

If you receive quotes that are delayed by 15 or 20 minutes, always get a real-time quote before placing a market order. Much can happen in 15 minutes in a volatile market.

Limit Orders. A limit order places an upper limit on the price you will pay for a purchase and a lower limit on the price you will accept for a sale. You are not guaranteed that your order will be executed when you place a limit order. If you place a buy limit order below the current market price or a sell limit order above it, trading may never reach your limit.

You can place a limit order for one day only and it will be automatically canceled at the end of the trading day or you may place a good-'til-canceled (GTC) order which will remain in place until you cancel it. You may also place an all-or-none (AON) restriction on your order, which states that you only want the transaction executed if the entire order can be executed and are not willing to accept partial executions. Without stating this specifically, you may receive a partial execution of your order. Different brokers have varying rules regarding such restrictions as GTC and AON.

Be aware when placing limit orders on NASDAQ stocks that in a dealer market you buy or sell from a market maker who then takes a spread before buying or selling to someone else. For example, if a stock is trading with a bid price of $21 and an asked price of $21.125, you can buy from a market maker at $21.125 or sell to a market maker at $21. If you see a transaction reported at $21.125 and you have a limit order to sell at that price, it does not necessarily mean your order will be executed. If that transaction was a purchase, you must wait until the bid increases to $21.125 for your order to be executed.

Market Order versus Limit Order. The investor should consider the proper time to place either a market order or a limit order.

Place a market order when:

- The market is open and you have a real-time quote.
- The stock price is not volatile.
- You want the transaction executed immediately, regardless of price.

Place a limit order when:

- The market is currently closed.
- You are trading in an after-hours or otherwise thin market.
- You are trading with a deep discount broker.
- The stock price is highly volatile.
- You are placing a particularly large order, relative to the bid and ask sizes or daily volume in the stock.
- You are willing to let the stock reach your price before you buy and sell.
- It is okay if the transaction is not executed.

Stop-Loss Orders. A stop-loss order is one that becomes a market order when trading in a stock reaches a specified price. A sell stop-loss order is designed to limit losses by placing a price below the current market to trigger an order to sell. For example, if you owned a stock currently trading at $80 but would like to limit your losses should it drop, you might place a sell stop-loss order at $70. This order would become a market order to sell once trading reached $70 or any price below it. In this scenario you are not guaranteed an execution at $70. If, for example, the stock were trading at $72 when poor earnings were announced and the next trade took place at $65, your order would immediately become a market order to sell, garnering a price near $65.

To prevent this occurrence, in which you sell at a price radically different from your stop-loss price, you can place a stop-limit order. The stop-limit order becomes a limit order as soon as the stock trades at the stop-loss price (or below it for a sell, above it for a buy). In our case, you would not sell because you would have a limit order at $70 and the stock is now trading at $65. While this would keep you from selling at a price below $70, it would not protect you from further losses should the stock continue to drop.

Buy stop-loss and buy stop-limit orders operate in the opposite way. A buy stop-loss price is placed above current prices for anyone who wants to be sure to buy when a stock begins to make an upward move or for short sellers who want to limit their losses if a stock's price rises.

Be aware that you cannot always place a stop-loss order. NASDAQ does not officially accept stop-loss orders, though some brokers will execute them on their own systems.

Timing Purchases and Sales

Record Date and Ex-Dividend Date. When companies announce a dividend, it is generally worded as follows: "XYZ Company declared a dividend of $1.00 per share, payable to shareholders of record on January 22, 2001." In this example, January 22, 2001, is the record date. Anyone who owns the stock on that date is entitled to the dividend.

The first day upon which anyone who buys the stock is not entitled to the dividend is the ex-dividend date. Logically, this might be the day following the record date, but it is not because stocks are purchased and sold with a three-day settlement procedure. Under a three-day settlement, you actually own a stock three business days after the purchase transaction, when you are required to pay for it. This is the first day that you are the shareholder of record. Therefore, the ex-dividend date, the date upon which the seller is entitled to the dividend and the buyer is not, is two days before the record date. Generally a stock's price will drop by the amount of the dividend per share on the ex-dividend date, because it is less valuable to the buyer by the amount of the dividend not received.

One difficulty with record dates and dividend payments is the lag time in updating the list of shareholders on a company's records. This means that, in many transactions that take place just before the ex-dividend date, the wrong person gets the dividend. For example, if you purchase stock in the week before the ex-dividend date, you are entitled to the upcoming dividend. However, if the company's records are not changed to reflect your ownership by the time the dividend is paid, then it will go to the seller. The seller, who is not entitled to it, must repay any dividend received in error.

Due Bill Split. A due bill split is not unlike the scenario in which dividends are paid to the wrong party. If you sell stock just prior to the ex-dividend date on a split, you may receive split shares from the company if it has not had time to update the records. These shares must be returned in order to go to the buyer of your shares. The easy way to tell whether you are entitled to split shares is if you sold at a presplit or postsplit price. If you sold at a presplit price, you are not entitled to split shares.

Buying on Margin

Buying stocks on margin means borrowing from your broker in order to buy stocks. Once you have opened a margin account (with some financial requirements), you can borrow up to 50% of the transaction amount when purchasing a marginable stock. A marginable stock is generally defined as one that trades at a price above $5, but each brokerage firm may set its own limits. Some firms have set stricter limits on the amount that you may borrow to purchase certain classes of highly volatile stocks, such as internet stocks.

The brokerage firm charges interest on the amount borrowed at a rate based on the broker call rate, which you can find in most financial newspapers. Often this rate declines as the margin loan balance increases. If your firm charges 8.5% on margin balances, in order to make money using margin, then you must expect a return on the stock above 4.25%, disregarding taxes (8.5% interest on half the purchase price equals 4.25% on the entire principal amount).

Effect of Using Margin on Investment Returns. Investors buy on margin to make a profit using money that they do not have. The amount you have invested is reduced by buying on margin. Because this is the denominator of the return on investment formula (profit/amount invested), ROI is magnified by investing on margin, whether to the upside or downside.

Table 10–7 is a comparison between the purchase of stock paid for in full and the purchase of stock on 50% margin (you pay half down and borrow the rest from the brokerage firm). The initial investment is 100 shares of Merck & Co. at $70 per share. You can either pay the full $7,000 cost ($70 × 100 shares) or buy on margin and pay only $3,500 ($7,000 × 0.5) and borrow the remaining $3,500.

In the event that the price of Merck & Co. increases to $90 in the next year, your return on investment (profit divided by the amount invested) when you paid in full would be 29%. With margin, where the amount you have invested is cut in half, your return on investment rises to approximately 49%. If the stock's price drops to $50, your return on investment without margin is –29% and with margin is –66%.

Dangers of Using Margin. In a scenario when the stock price drops, a margin purchase magnifies the negative return on investment; however, you always have the option of waiting until it comes back to your purchase price. The two negatives to this approach when you have purchased on margin are (1) you will continue to pay or accrue margin interest while you wait; and (2) in the event that the stock price drops by a large amount, the

Table 10-7. Buying on Margin

Results of Investing in 100 shares of Merck & Co. (with and without using margin)

	Without Margin	With Margin
Amount invested	$7,000	$3,500
Amount borrowed		$3,500
Total cost (100 shares @ $70)	$7,000	$7,000
Merck & Co. Rises to $90, Sell Stock		
Sell 100 shares at $90	$9,000	$9,000
Less interest on $3,500 at 8.5%		($298)
Less total cost	($7,000)	($7,000)
Net profit	$2,000	$1,702
Return on investment calculation	$2,000/$7,000	$1,702/$3,500
Return on investment	29%	49%
Merck & Co. Drops to $50		
Sell 100 shares at $50	$5,000	$5,000
Less interest on $3,500 at 8.5%		($298)
Less total cost	($7,000)	($7,000)
Net loss	($2,000)	($2,298)
Return on investment calculation	($2,000)/$7,000	($2,298)/$3,500
Return on investment	(29%)	(66%)

brokerage firm may feel uncomfortable about the shrinking value of its collateral given the size of the loan. Firms outline this relationship by setting a maintenance requirement, which is a percentage of equity that you must maintain in the account. If your equity drops below this figure, you will receive a margin call, which is a request to reduce the size of your loan by selling stock or depositing more cash into the account.

As an example, say you purchased $10,000 of stock using $5,000 cash and $5,000 margin borrowed from the brokerage firm. The brokerage firm has a maintenance requirement of 25%. If the value of your stock dropped to $6,000, the equity in your account would be $1,000 ($6,000 value of stock –$5,000 loan balance = $1,000 equity). As a percentage, the equity in your account would be 17% ($1,000/$6,000 = 17%). The firm would issue a margin call, requesting that you either sell some stock or deposit $500 into the account to bring your equity up to 25%. Your loan balance would be $4,500 after paying off $500. Your equity would be $1,500 ($6,000 − $4,500 = $1,500) and your equity percent would be 25% ($1,500/$6,000 = 0.25 or 25%).

Selling Short

In the majority of stock transactions an investor buys a stock and then later sells it, hoping to profit from the fact that the sale price is higher than the purchase price. Short selling reverses the order of the buy and sell transactions, allowing an investor to profit from falling stock prices.

Selling short is selling a stock that you do not own with the expectation that its price will fall, thus allowing you to purchase it later (called *covering*) at a lower price. To sell a stock that you do not own, you must borrow it from someone who does own it, in order to deliver it to the buyer.

Short selling occurs in a margin account and there are limits as to how much stock you can borrow. Generally, you may borrow twice the value of stock or cash in your account. For example, if you had $5,000 in stock in your account, you could borrow $10,000 of stock to sell short. Your broker will charge interest on your short position for as long as it is outstanding and you must pay the amount equal to any dividends that the stock pays to the owner of the shares you borrowed. There are minimum maintenance requirements in which equity must be a minimum percentage (usually 30%) of the value of the short position.

Risks of Selling Short. One reason why many respected investment experts, including Peter Lynch and Warren Buffet, never sell short is the risks are unlimited, but the return is limited. The maximum return you can realize on a short sale is the amount of the stock sale, less any margin interest paid. This could only occur if the stock were to become worthless. However, the upward potential of the stock price is unlimited, making the amount you can lose unlimited as well. For example, if you shorted 1,000 shares of a $25 stock, you would realize $25,000 on the sale. This, less any margin interest paid, is the upper limit on your return. However, in an era in which Qualcomm, Inc. increased in price by 2,618% in 1999, the upper end of your losses can spell disaster.

A dangerous situation for short sellers is known as a short squeeze. Short squeezes occur when stocks have a high number of shares which have been borrowed and shorted relative to the total number of shares outstanding. This ratio is known as the short interest. When a stock that has been heavily shorted rises in price, traders who have shorted it rush to buy in order to cover their positions and limit their losses. The additional demand caused by short covering increases the stock price even more, making it more attractive to long (ordinary) buyers and creating more of a scramble by the short sellers who are still holding out.

Due to the possibility of a short squeeze, short interest can be a contrarian indicator. This means that stocks with a high short interest may have a tendency to rise, as a result of the pent-up demand of short sellers who must eventually cover their positions. Short interest and the number of trading days at average trading volume required to cover all short positions are reported periodically in financial newspapers such as *The Wall Street Journal* and *Investor's Business Daily*.

The Financial Web at *www.financialweb.com* has a column called the Daily Screen, which often sorts for stocks with high short interest so that long investors can profit from a short squeeze. Bear Tracker, which can be reached through the Financial Web or at *www.beartracker.com* offers educational articles about short selling, a two-year history of NASDAQ short interest, and columns such as Bear of the Month (a recommended short) and Cub Scouting (summaries of overvalued stocks).

Taxation of Stock Transactions

Dividends

All dividends paid on stock holdings are considered ordinary income and are taxable at ordinary income tax rates. Occasionally, a stock (perhaps a REIT) will pay what appears to be a dividend except that a note with the payment indicates that a portion of the payment is a return of principal. In that case, the payment is not taxable as ordinary income; it reduces your cost basis when you eventually sell the stock.

Capital Gains and Losses

The purchase price of a stock, including commissions, is called its cost basis. The difference between a stock's cost basis and its sale price, including commissions, is a capital gain if you made money and a capital loss if you lost money. Calculate your gains and losses on the total amount that you paid rather than the per share price to eliminate complications in adjusting for stock splits.

For example, if you purchase 100 shares of ABC Company for $60 per share and pay a commission of $35, your basis on ABC is $6,035 (100 × $60 + $35). If you sell the stock for $70 and pay a commission of $35, your net sales proceeds are $6,965 (100 × $70 − $35). The capital gain on your sale is computed by subtracting your net sales proceeds from your basis, for a gain of $930.

If you have owned the stock for more than one year, the gain or loss is classified as long term. Anything owned for a year or less produces a short-term gain or loss. Long-term capital gains are eligible for a tax rate of 20%. For taxpayers in the 15% tax bracket, the rate is 10%.

Capital losses in any amount can be used to offset capital gains. If your capital losses exceed your capital gains, up to $3,000 can be used to reduce other income. Excess losses over $3,000 can be carried forward into future tax years.

Wash Sales

A certain IRS rule is designed to prevent taxpayers from taking a loss on stock that they intend to continue holding. The rule says that selling a security for a loss and purchasing the same security within 30 days constitutes a wash sale, making the taxpayer ineligible to take the loss. Purchases within 30 days before or after the sale count. The wash sale rule applies to securities which are essentially the same; for example, bonds or warrants that are convertible into shares of stock are considered essentially the same as shares of stock.

Sources of Information on Stocks

Annual Reports

Publicly held companies publish annual reports that detail financial performance and provide information about corporate activities. Though it is akin to a sales brochure for the stock, the annual report can be a good place to get a feel for the business. You will generally find a letter from the CEO at the beginning of each report that encapsulates the year's performance and tells investors what management expects in the following year. In reports from companies that have had a difficult year, look for an acknowledgment of management's role in poor performance or at least a plan for turning things around.

A CEO's letter that is eagerly awaited by both shareholders and non-shareholders is Warren Buffet's annual letter to the shareholders of Berkshire Hathaway. Anyone can read it at the company website at *www.berkshirehathaway.com*. Buffet acknowledged his stock's poor performance record in his 1999 letter, saying, "Even Inspector Clouseau could find last year's guilty party: your Chairman. What most hurt us during the year was the inferior performance of Berkshire's equity portfolio—and the responsibility for that portfolio, leaving aside the small piece of it run by Lou Simpson of GEICO, is entirely mine."[8]

The annual report also provides detailed financial data for the previous time period and those before it. Statements provided should include a balance sheet, income statement, cash flow statement, and statement of changes in shareholders' equity, plus numerous supporting statements called notes to financial statements. This is where you can find data for financial analysis. For a sample balance sheet and income statement, see Chapter 7. The difficulty with annual reports is that they are only annual and are generally not available until several months after year-end. Quarterly reports are provided in the interim but are usually not as comprehensive in their information.

If you are a shareholder, you will automatically receive a company's annual report. If you are not, call the company and ask someone in shareholder services or investor relations to send you one. You may also be able to request one or download it at the company's website. You can order annual reports on more than 3,600 participating companies from the Public Register's Annual Report Service at *www.prars.com*.

The 10-K report is a company's filing of financial data with the SEC. This is an all-business report, as opposed to most firms' glossy picture-filled annual reports. For financial data, in addition to what you can find in an annual report, obtain a 10-K from the company. You may also be able to access it at EDGAR Online at *www.freeedgar.com*.

Independent Financial Data

The internet has quickly become the main source of financial data for most investors. Not only is it easy to access internet reports, but costs, even to subscription sites, are much lower than most printed information. Best of all, data is frequently updated. For websites that provide financial data, see Chapter 21.

If you prefer a hard copy, many companies still publish financial data. Chapter 20 covers periodicals and newspapers, plus two of the big purveyors of company data, Standard & Poor's Corporation and Value Line Investment Survey.

Stock Prices in the Newspaper

Although you may ordinarily check your stocks' prices online, at times the newspaper is more convenient or provides additional information.

---

[8]Warren Buffet, "Chairman's Letter," Berkshire Hathaway, Inc. 1999 Annual Report: 3.

Figure 10–1 is an excerpt from the March 23, 2000, *Investor's Business Daily*. The first stock listed in the column is McGraw-Hill, publisher of this book. Bold type identifies it as one of the day's relevant market performers. Moving from left to right, an 88 earnings per share rating means its EPS growth exceeds 88% of other stocks. The 26 relative price strength rating means its price has outperformed on 26% of other stocks in the last 12 months. An industry group relative strength of C places the industry group's stock price performance in the middle 20%. Sales + profit margins + ROE rating of A places it in the top 20% of stocks. An accumulation/distribution rating of E indicates heavy selling.

McGraw-Hill's 52-week high is $63.125. A small, bold **c** means the CEO has been there less than two years; the **5** means it is in the S&P 500. The ticker symbol is MHP. Its closing price was $47.4375, an increase of $1.625

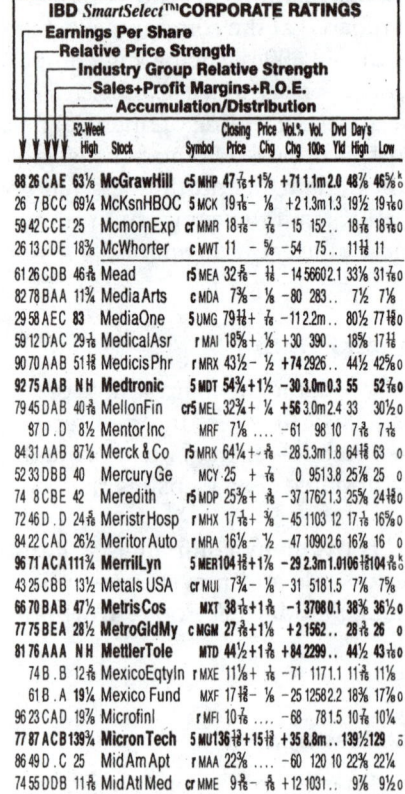

Figure 10–1. Stock Tables

SOURCE: *Investor's Business Daily* (March 23, 2000). Reprinted with permission.

from the previous day's close. Trading volume was up 71% at 1.1 million shares. The dividend yield on the stock is 2.0%, and the trading range for the day was $48.875 high to $46.625 low. The small *k* indicates that earnings will be reported in the next four weeks and the *o* indicates that there are options traded on the stock.

Summary

Investing in stocks is a complex topic, and this chapter barely scratches the surface with explanations of basic concepts. For more discussion about how to choose the right stocks, see Chapter 18 for the thought process behind different investment theories; and Chapter 19 explains how those theories are put into practice.

11
International Investments

Our discussion on business and market risk in Chapter 5 concluded that while business risk can be effectively diversified away, market risk is inevitable. If you are willing to invest in international securities, this may not be true. In many cases, international markets have a low correlation with the U.S. stock markets, meaning they tend to move independently. For example, in 1987, U.S. stocks were up 3%, stocks in the United Kingdom gained 35%, and German stocks were down 25%. For a comparison of world stock market indices from April 1999 through March 2000, see Figure 11–1. Differences in returns may be due to many factors. Local economic climates have a major effect on a country's securities markets and a recession in one area can affect economies worldwide. Relative currency valuations also play a part, as do investor interpretations of political environments (see Chapter 2).

Issues in Choosing International Investments

If investing internationally can reduce market risk, why is it often considered speculative? Most likely, because additional risk factors associated with international investments are not inherent in most domestic securities. These serve to illustrate that diversification when purchasing foreign investments is just as important—maybe more—as diversification in U.S. investments.

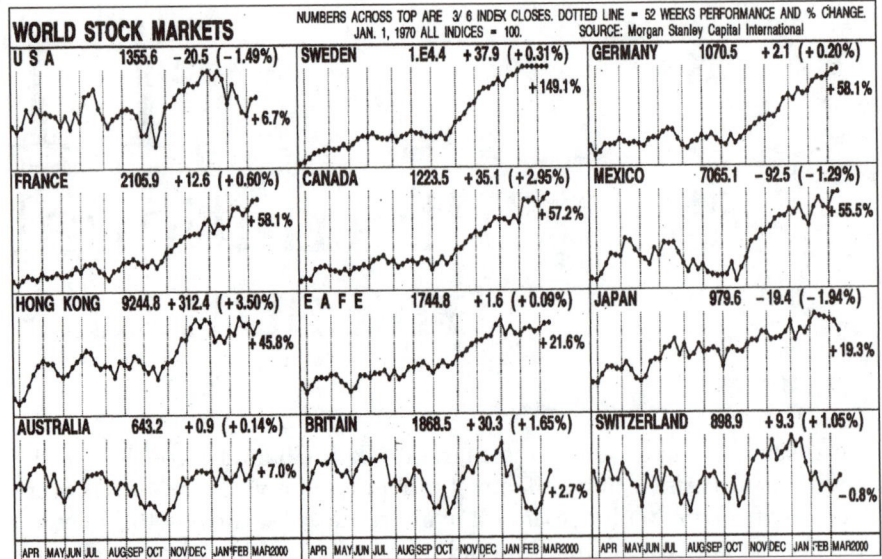

Figure 11-1. Comparative World Stock Market Returns
SOURCE: *Investor's Business Daily*, March 8, 2000. Reprinted with permission.

Volatility

The returns in international markets are notoriously volatile and difficult to time. Buying in only one geographic region, at the wrong time, with a short-term horizon, can be devastating. Take for example the markets of 1993 and 1994. In 1993, overseas stock markets had outstanding returns. *Hulbert Financial Digest*, a periodical that tracks the returns of investment newsletters, found the average gain of international emerging growth newsletter portfolios to be 30.6%. World equity mutual funds tracked by Lipper Analytical returned 43.0%. In 1994, however, a reversal of fortunes brought an average 3.7% loss to emerging growth newsletter portfolios and an average 3.9% loss to world equity mutual funds. Investors who expected a repeat of 1993 returns were highly disappointed.

Fluctuations in Currency Exchange Rates

Currency exchange rates define the relative value of different currencies. As addressed in Chapter 2, exchange rates are dictated by a combination of economic and speculative forces. Simply put, demand for a country's currency drives its price up. Demand is created when individuals in other countries wish to buy goods and services or investments from a country and must exchange their currency into that of the exporting country to pay. A country that exports and/or draws more foreign investment than it imports has a trade surplus and experiences strong demand for its currency. Speculators who buy a country's currency with the expectation that it will strengthen (become relatively more valuable) or sell a currency with the expectation that it will weaken often intensify currency movements.

Fluctuations in currency exchange rates can be positive or negative for the international investor. Returns are enhanced for an investment denominated in a currency that is appreciating against the dollar, because at the end of the investment period, the foreign currency will be exchanged for more dollars. Returns are decreased on investments denominated in a currency depreciating against the dollar, because the foreign currency will buy fewer dollars (see Table 11–1).

To calculate the return on an investment denominated in a foreign currency, you must combine the currency gain or loss with the total return on the investment (change in price plus dividends or interest) as earned in the foreign currency. The formula is as follows:

$$\text{Return} = \left(\frac{\text{Ending value of currency in U.S. \$}}{\text{Beginning value of currency in U.S. \$}} \times \frac{\text{Ending value of investment} + \text{Dividends or interest in foreign currency}}{\text{Beginning value of investment in foreign currency}} \right) - 1.00$$

The reason for using an ending value in the formula, then later subtracting 1.00, is to calculate the currency gain or loss on the principal and the investment return. In the following example, outlined in Table 11–2, we calculate the return on a Brazilian investment which appreciates by 15% (no dividend paid) while the Brazilian currency, the real, falls in value by 10%.

Table 11–1 Currency Fluctuations and Investment Return

Dollar	Foreign Currency	Effect	Investment Return
Weakens	Strengthens	Foreign currency buys more dollars	U.S. investors' return is increased
Strengthens	Weakens	Foreign currency buys fewer dollars	U.S. investors' return is decreased

Table 11–2. A U.S. Investment in Brazil

	Cost of One Brazilian Real in U.S. Dollars	Price of Brazilian Stock in Brazilian Real
Beginning of Period	$0.60	100.00
End of Period	$0.54	115.00

$$Return = \left(\frac{\$0.54}{\$0.60} \times \frac{115.00}{100.00}\right) - 1.00$$
$$= (0.90 \times 1.15) - 1.00$$
$$= 1.035 - 1.00$$
$$= 3.5\%$$

In this example, a return on investment of 15% is reduced to 3.5% when the foreign currency falls in value by 10%. Table 11–3 outlines the effects of currency fluctuations on investment returns using this formula.

Information Risk

Information risk refers to the fact that it is sometimes difficult to obtain comprehensive financial data on businesses overseas, especially small

Table 11–3. Effect of Currency Fluctuations on Investment Returns

Investment Total Return in Foreign Currency	Change in Value of Foreign Currency vs. U.S. Dollar						
	+15%	+10%	+5%	0%	−5%	−10%	−15%
20%	38	32	26	20	14	8	2
15%	32	27	21	15	9	4	−2
10%	27	21	16	10	5	−1	−7
5%	21	16	10	5	0	−6	−11
0%	15	10	5	0	5	−10	−15
−5%	9	5	0	−5	−10	−16	−19
−10%	4	−1	−6	−10	−15	−19	−24
−15%	−2	−7	−11	−15	−19	−24	−28
−20%	−8	−12	−16	−20	−24	−28	−32

companies or companies in emerging markets. Add to this the sometimes questionable quality of information reported under less stringent accounting practices than those we have become accustomed to in the United States. The result may be investment decisions made with little, late, and/or inaccurate data.

Economic and Political Climate

Investing in international markets often takes a top-down approach in which prices move based on the country or region more than on the specifics of the investment. The tendency for economics and politics to play a big role in stock values is inversely related to an area's economic and political stability. Consider the United States as an example of high political stability. The political party elected to hold the office of president and the majority party elected to Congress rarely have a great impact on the stock market due to the effectiveness of our three-branch system. At the other end of the spectrum, elections in Russia may have a large impact on securities values.

When considering an investment in a foreign market, look at the government's relationship with business; issues such as tax incentives for businesses and the regulatory environment help define a pro- or antibusiness stance. Pay attention to a government's fiscal responsibility as this will affect currency values. Check past volatility for currency exchange rates and the government's commitment to supporting their currency at certain levels. Learn about upcoming elections, which parties are expected to prevail, and worst-case scenarios.

Diversification

Investing overseas is all about diversification. Experts recommend not more than 20% of your total portfolio be invested in foreign markets. Those who invest a major portion of their assets internationally are stepping into the speculative arena.

Purchasing one or two international investments with a short-term time horizon is risky. Purchasing a diversified portfolio of international investments with a long-term horizon using careful research or the professional management of a mutual fund is not. In fact, it can reduce your market risk over time.

Plan to invest in several different areas within a region and several different global regions to reduce your exposure to political or economic disaster. If the cost and commitment in dollars invested make this prohibitive, consider a mutual fund.

Vehicles for Investing Internationally

Multinational U.S. Stocks

An easy, low-risk way to invest internationally is through U.S.-based companies that derive significant portions of their revenues and profits overseas. These companies will benefit from strong economies in the regions that buy their products and will suffer during economic downturns just as individual foreign stocks would. However, there are several buffers which reduce downside risk and limit upside potential.

Multinational companies have a built-in diversification from the fact that they derive revenues and profits from several areas, including the United States. Currency risk exists in multinational companies because their businesses are exposed to it; however, most global operations are adept at hedging currency risk. This reduces potential losses, but since hedging has a cost, it also reduces potential gains. Information risk for U.S. multinational companies is eliminated from financial reporting, though it may exist in assessing the political and economic environment of overseas business areas.

One difficulty of this approach is finding out which corporations have international operations and how large a part these operations play in the business. Often this information is not detailed in standard reports available on the internet. In many cases, the best resource is a corporation's annual report. Finding prospects can be as simple as targeting a few large, obviously multinational corporations or asking a broker; or it may take a little more work, possibly thumbing through investment research reports from Value Line Investment Survey or a similar source.

Stocks on Foreign Exchanges

Though buying stocks on foreign exchanges seems an obvious way to invest internationally, for the nonprofessional investor it is probably the least common method used, since transaction costs tend to be high and the risks noted are highest in individual stocks. If you choose to buy stocks directly on foreign exchanges, it is essential to have the assistance of a globally connected brokerage firm for both transaction execution and research.

A good resource for financial reports on foreign stocks is Wright Investors, whose website is *www.wisi.com*. The Research Center provides a Wright Quality Rating, a company profile, research report, analysis summary, sales analysis, and earnings analysis for each of 18,000 companies in 50 countries. A feature that makes comparisons easier converts all figures into the currency of your choice. For the latest on European markets, go to European Investor.com at *www.europeaninvestor.com*. You will find results for each European market, exchange rates, and news on international stocks.

American Depositary Receipts

American depositary receipts (ADRs), introduced in the 1920s, are an alternative to purchasing shares of stock directly on international exchanges. An ADR is a security issued by a U.S. commercial bank (the depositary) and priced in U.S. dollars, which represents shares listed on a foreign stock exchange. ADRs trade like ordinary domestic stocks on the NYSE, Amex, or NASDAQ.

An ADR closely tracks the foreign security represented, though not always on a one-to-one ratio. Each ADR has a conversion ratio that indicates the number of shares represented. For example, Telefonos de Mexico has a 1:1 ratio, whereas British Steel has a 10:1 ratio, meaning that each ADR represents 10 shares of the underlying stock.

Following are benefits to using ADRs as a means to invest internationally.

- ADRs tend to be the largest capitalization stocks of a foreign market, which means they are usually established, stable companies.

- High capitalization also makes them highly correlated with the country's market index return. They can be a proxy for investing in the market of a particular country.

- ADRs are highly liquid.

- Since they are securities on U.S. exchanges, ADRs are regulated by the SEC.

- The depositary bank converts dividends into U.S. dollars and distributes them. It also provides annual reports.

There are several resources available to the ADR investor, in addition to those that provide information about any U.S. listed stock. Worldlyinvestor.com at *www.worldlyinvestor.com* has daily articles covering different international regions and sectors. The ADR Screener allows you to screen ADRs according to performance, country, and sector. J.P. Morgan's website at *www.adr.com* is full of international investment information, including a bar chart comparison of the day's international regions and their best- and worst-performing country indices.

International Mutual Funds

One of the most popular ways to invest internationally is through mutual funds, because they offer professional management and diversification. There are several categories of international mutual funds from which to choose, thus providing a fit for most investment objectives. You can usually obtain performance data and screen for international funds at any website that offers mutual fund screening. The Offshore Fund Screener at worldlyinvestor.com (*www.worldlyinvestor.com*) allows you to screen by country, asset type, investment objective, and currency. Some of the major categories of international mutual funds are discussed next.

Global Funds. Global funds may include stocks from all over the globe, including the United States. Relative weightings of different countries depend on current economic and market conditions, so the recent strength of the U.S. stock markets has enticed many global fund managers to overweight domestic stocks. Consider your investment objective and plan accordingly if your international fund is heavily invested in U.S. stocks.

International Funds. International funds usually invest in a variety of non-U.S. stocks. Fund managers are given a fairly free hand in deciding which regions and sectors are attractive, though the prospectus of an international fund may place limits on the percentage of the portfolio that can be invested in a single country or region. Due to their broad approach, global and international funds can be a good one-stop way to add some international diversification to an investment plan.

Index Funds. International index funds invest in the stocks of international indices or in a representative sample of those stocks. Some investors favor index funds which naturally have low turnover because transaction costs in international investing can be high. Others in the investment community note that while it is difficult for an active U.S. investment manager to beat index funds over a long period of time, the international arena can be different. The varied availability of information from international sources can often create inefficient markets, giving active managers the opportunity to produce returns well above index averages. For a list of international indices and index funds, see Chapter 4.

Small-Company Funds. Most international funds focus on largecap stocks, using a top-down approach that begins with assessing a region's economic and political climate. Small-company international funds search for individual companies with outstanding growth prospects in much the same way as U.S. small-company funds do. In many cases, the region becomes either a secondary benefit or a risk to be added to the equation.

Regional Funds. Regional funds invest in securities from a defined group of countries, such as those in the Pacific Rim or Latin America. While stocks in one region will tend to move together due to economic influences, differences in currencies and governments can provide some diversification. When comparing regional funds, check the list of countries included. For example, some funds labeled Asian or Pacific Rim include Japanese securities, while others do not.

Single-Country Funds. Mutual funds that invest only in the securities of a particular country are the most concentrated and therefore the riskiest. You can win big or lose big, as illustrated by the 63% fall (from 38,916 to 14,309) of Japanese stocks from December 1989 to August 1992.

Emerging Markets. Emerging markets funds are concentrated in the stocks of small countries that are seeing high growth. Examples might include countries recently emerging from communist rule, now busy privatizing state-owned industries. Emerging markets funds may be well diversified regionally or highly concentrated.

Brady Bonds

Brady bonds are named after U.S. Treasury Secretary Nicholas Brady, who together with the IMF and the World Bank, sponsored the permanent restructuring of the debt of emerging market countries in the late 1980s. The countries originally involved were Argentina, Brazil, Bulgaria, Costa Rica, Dominican Republic, Ecuador, Mexico, Morocco, Nigeria, Philippines, Poland, and Uraguay. In the restructuring, debtor countries had their principal, interest, and interest arrears (interest they had been unable to pay but still owed) reduced. The bank debt was exchanged for Brady bonds, whose principal is collateralized by U.S. Treasury zero coupon bonds. Interest is guaranteed on a rolling basis, in which 12 or 18 months' interest is covered. As each interest payment is made, the collateral guarantees the next successive unsecured coupon payment. In the event of a default in which the collateral is used, there is no requirement that it be replaced.

In October 1999, Ecuador became the first country to default on its Brady bonds with a failure to make $45 million in interest payments. Initial concern that this would affect the markets for Latin American Brady bonds has dissipated. Ecuador has only about $6 billion in outstanding Brady bonds compared with the more than $200 billion total Brady bond debt, two-thirds of which is owed by Mexico, Brazil, and Argentina.

Several websites provide market and pricing information on Brady bonds. MaxEMG.com at *www.maxemg.com* features price and volume data and graphs for Brady and other global bonds. Two levels of subscription services are offered: basic and premium; premium service includes up-dated intraday prices on actively traded bonds. BradyNet Pro at *www.bradynet.com* provides news and market data for international bond markets. News and discussion boards are free; basic service includes bond descriptions, historical charting, research, and analysis. Premium service adds real-time prices and intraday charting.

Foreign Currencies

Individuals who are not engaged in international trade become involved in foreign currency markets either to hedge risk or to speculate. You might hedge risk when planning a European vacation a year in advance. If you are on a tight budget and expect the euro to appreciate relative to the dollar (or do not want to take the chance that it might), you could exchange the amount you expect to spend on the trip for euros right now. Place it in an interest-bearing account so fluctuations in the exchange rate will have no effect on your ability to vacation comfortably. This small hedging transaction takes place in an entirely different marketplace from those that speculate on the relative changes in currency values.

Speculating on currency works under the same premise as any other speculation: Plan to buy low and sell high. The price of currency is its exchange rate, and there are several different ways to quote it. The spot rate for currency is the current rate, also called the cash price, denominated in the trader's home currency. The cross rate is the exchange rate between two currencies but does not include the trader's home currency. For example, a U.S. citizen interested in the relationship between the deutsche mark and the yen will look at the deutsche mark/yen cross rate. A forward rate is the expected exchange rate between two currencies at 30, 60, or 90 days into the future. A table of spot and forward exchange rates from *Investor's Business Daily* can be found in Figure 11–2.

To speculate on movements in exchange rates through the foreign currency market, you may buy and sell the currencies of other countries. Once purchased, you can place the foreign currency in a money market account or certificate of deposit, or buy a government bond or other security denominated in the foreign currency. Buying a bond adds interest rate risk to the investment, should you decide to liquidate the position before the bond matures. You can trade in foreign currencies at many banks and brokerage firms. Most require a minimum investment of $250,000, more for illiquid currencies. Currency trading costs are not explicitly charged fees like stock commissions. Rather, they are like the cost to buy or sell bonds, in which the fee is added to the purchase price when you buy and is sub-

Foreign Exchange Rates

Currency	Currency In U.S. $ 3/7	3/6	U.S. $ in Currency 3/7	3/6
I–Argent (Peso)	1.0002	1.0005	.9998	.9995
Australia (Dollar)	.6038	.6021	1.6562	1.6609
Austria (Schilling)	.0697	.0699	14.349	14.315
c–Belgium (Franc)	.0237	.0238	42.15	42.07
Brazil (Real)	.5730	.5729	1.7452	1.7455
Britain (Pound)	1.5793	1.5741	.6332	.6353
30-day fwd	1.5763	1.5721	.6344	.6361
60-day fwd	1.5749	1.5707	.6350	.6367
90-day fwd	1.5738	1.5696	.6354	.6371
Canada (Dollar)	.6876	.6885	1.4543	1.4525
30-day fwd	.6874	.6877	1.4547	1.4541
60-day fwd	.6870	.6872	1.4557	1.4552
90-day fwd	.6865	.6867	1.4567	1.4562
y–Chile (Peso)	.001984	.001988	504.05	503.00
China (Yuan)	.1208	.1208	8.2785	8.2789
Colombia (Peso)	.000508	.000509	1967.50	1964.50
c–CzechRep (Koruna)	.0270	.0270	36.99	37.03
Denmark (Krone)	.1288	.1291	7.7630	7.7442
Dominican (Peso)	.0627	.0627	15.95	15.95
z–Ecudr (Sucre)	.000040	.000040	25000.00	25000.00
d–Egypt (Pound)	.2911	.2911	3.4350	3.4350
Euro (Euro)	.95760	.95900	1.0443	1.0428
30-day fwd	.95910	.96110	1.0426	1.0405
90-day fwd	.96300	.96400	1.0384	1.0373
Finland (Mark)	.1613	.1617	6.1999	6.1854
France (Franc)	.1460	.1462	6.8486	6.8414
Germany (Mark)	.4897	.4902	2.0420	2.0399
Greece (Drachma)	.002865	.002876	348.98	347.70
Hong Kong (Dollar)	.1285	.1285	7.7836	7.7832

Currency	Currency In U.S. $ 3/7	3/6	U.S. $ in Currency 3/7	3/6
Hungary (Forint)	.0037	.0037	267.50	266.84
y–India (Rupee)	.0230	.0230	43.560	43.550
Indnsia (Rupiah)	.000134	.000134	7465.00	7450.00
Ireland (Punt)	1.2177	1.2206	.8212	.8193
Israel (Shekel)	.2499	.2483	4.0018	4.0280
Italy (Lira)	.000495	.000495	2021.58	2019.47
Japan (Yen)	.009420	.009300	106.16	107.53
30-day fwd	.009475	.009347	105.54	106.99
60-day fwd	.009514	.009384	105.11	106.56
90-day fwd	.009561	.009430	104.59	106.04
Jordan (Dinar)	1.4075	1.4075	.71048	.71048
Lebanon (Pound)	.000663	.000663	1507.50	1507.50
Malaysia (Ringgit)	.2632	.2632	3.8000	3.7995
z–Mexico. (Peso)	.107759	.107331	9.2800	9.3170
Nethrlnd (Guilder)	.4343	.4351	2.3028	2.2983
N. Zealand (Dollar)	.4830	.4820	2.0704	2.0747
Norway (Krone)	.1187	.1191	8.4245	8.3990
Pakistan (Rupee)	.0193	.0193	51.89	51.88
y–Peru (New Sol)	.2932	.2931	3.411	3.412
z–Philpins (Peso)	.0244	.0245	41.04	40.82
Poland (Zloty)	.2427	.2433	4.12	4.11
Portugal (Escudo)	.004784	.004795	209.05	208.56
a–Russia (Ruble)	.0350	.0350	28.5500	28.5800
SDR (SDR)	1.33790	1.34060	.7474	.7459
Saudi Arab (Riyal)	.2667	.2667	3.7502	3.7502
Singapore (Dollar)	.5820	.5797	1.7183	1.7250
SlovakRep (Koruna)	.0230	.0230	43.43	43.48
So. Africa (Rand)	.1532	.1538	6.5295	6.5005
So. Korea (Won)	.000894	.000894	1118.50	1119.10

Figure 11–2. Foreign Exchange Rates
SOURCE: *Investor's Business Daily*, March 8, 2000. Reprinted with permission.

tracted from the sales price when you sell. This differential is known as the spread. On a liquid (actively traded) currency, transaction costs might run 0.50% to 0.75%. On an illiquid currency, transaction costs are higher, more likely 1% to 1.25%.

Another way to play the currency market is through futures, which are contracts for future delivery of a currency. Futures offer leverage, whereby you can spend a relatively small amount to control a large amount of currency. Their drawback is the future delivery date, which can result in a loss when you are right about the direction of the currency but wrong about the timing. If you cannot afford to actually take delivery of your contract, you might be forced to close it out during a market dip. Owning the actual currency allows you more flexibility in timing. (For more on futures, see Chapter 14.)

Regardless of the vehicle used, you can profit when currencies fluctuate based on the reasons noted earlier in this chapter and in Chapter 2. To keep abreast of the market for foreign currencies visit these helpful websites: Everbank Brokerage at *www.everbank.com* has an excellent daily commentary on the foreign exchange markets called A Pfennig for Your Thoughts (call

314-567-9055 x202 for a recorded version). Bloomberg.com at *www.bloomberg.com* provides spot rates on currencies plus a currency calculator that will determine the exchange rate between any two world currencies. Worldlyinvestor.com at *www.worldlyinvestor.com* provides fewer currency quotes but more columns and news stories about countries and regions around the world.

Remember that there are many risks involved in trading foreign currencies; speculative currency trading is for experienced investors. Commit your principal cautiously and only with a trusted financial advisor.

Summary

Used correctly, international investments can provide a way to reduce market risk and enhance investment returns. Investors should be aware of the risks involved in international investing, such as currency exchange rate fluctuations, poor availability of information, and unpredictable economic and political climates. Diversification—whether through investing in different regions of the world or different types of instruments, such as currencies, mutual funds and stocks, or ADRs—is key to minimizing risks and realizing the most benefit from foreign investments.

12
Mutual Funds

A mutual fund is an investment company that pools the funds of many investors in a large portfolio. Each investor who purchases shares of the mutual fund owns a portion of a professionally managed, diversified investment portfolio. As the prices of the investments in the portfolio change, the shares will fluctuate in value.

The two types of mutual funds available are open- and closed-end funds. Open-end funds, the largest category, continuously sell shares to the public and redeems shares for anyone wishing to sell. In contrast, closed-end funds sell a fixed number of shares in an initial offering and all subsequent buying and selling of shares takes place in the secondary market between shareholders. Unless otherwise noted, all reference to mutual funds will be to open-end funds.

Benefits of Mutual Fund Ownership

Professional Management

In today's complex, volatile investment environment, many individuals feel overwhelmed by the prospect of making investment decisions, but do not want to hire expensive professionals. Mutual funds can solve this problem. With an investment as small as $250, you can leave the buy and sell decisions to the trained professionals who are supported by extensive research staffs.

Diversification

Diversification means buying many different securities to reduce the risk of any specific security.

As discussed in Chapter 5, dividing your investment dollars reduces the effect of a catastrophe on your portfolio. As you continue to diversify across investment type and industry, your risk decreases. This investment-specific risk is called business risk. In a diversified portfolio you can still have market risk, which is the risk of a stock market or economic collapse that would affect a variety of different investments.

While the theory of diversifying to reduce risk is widely accepted, it can be time consuming and expensive in terms of commissions to own a large portfolio of different investments. Mutual funds can invest with much lower commissions due to their large dollar volume of trading and can spread out the work required to follow a large portfolio.

Convenience in Buying and Selling Shares

Mutual fund shares are easy to buy and sell. You may use a broker or purchase shares directly from the investment company by mail, or by phone or internet if you have an established account. The share price of any purchase or sale transaction is based on the net asset value (NAV) of each share. The NAV is computed at the end of each trading day by taking the total value of the portfolio at the day's closing prices and dividing it by the number of mutual fund shares outstanding. Purchases may take place at NAV (no-load funds) or NAV plus a commission (load funds).

Sales of open-end mutual funds are called redemptions, because the shares are returned to the fund. Most funds allow redemption requests to be made in writing or by telephone, and many will allow requests over the internet. Redemption requests must generally be made by the close of regular trading for the New York Stock Exchange (NYSE) at 4:00 P.M. (EST) in order to receive that day's closing NAV. Brokerage firms may have earlier deadlines so they have time to relay instructions to the mutual fund company.

Low Initial Investments

Initial investments in many mutual funds are as low as $1,000, with minimums for subsequent investments often in the $250 range. Many companies have lower minimums for IRA purchases, typically $250 to open an account and $50 thereafter. Automatic investment programs, in which you invest periodically through an electronic funds transfer from your bank, may have even lower minimum investment amounts, some beginning at $25.

Variety and Flexibility in Choosing Investment Objectives

Mutual funds have become such a popular investment vehicle that thousands of different funds are now available, with investment objectives that run the entire range of possibilities. Stated investment objectives usually include both the risk level of the portfolio and the types of securities that can be included.

Mutual fund companies that operate many different individual funds are called fund families. They generally provide benefits for investors who spread their assets among several funds in the family. These benefits include breakpoints (lowered commissions for larger dollar amounts invested), the ability to move assets from one fund to another by telephone (often without a fee), reinvestment of dividends and capital gains into another fund within the family, and consolidated statements. The 30 largest U.S. mutual fund companies are listed in Table 12–1. Addresses, phone numbers, and websites for many fund companies can be found in the appendix.

Regulation

Mutual funds are regulated by the Securities and Exchange Commission (SEC), which requires that investors receive a prospectus when purchasing a fund. The SEC also regulates much of the information provided in the prospectus and requires that it be presented in a standardized format. When disclosing annual returns, funds must give 1-, 5-, and 10-year annual returns which include dividends, capital gains, and changes in net asset value. This prevents a fund company from presenting only the attractive information to entice investors to buy.

Closed-End Mutual Funds

As previously noted, closed-end mutual funds issue a fixed number of shares initially and then any later trading takes place on an exchange just like shares of stock. You must purchase shares through a broker and pay a commission to do so.

There are several perceived benefits to purchasing closed-end funds. One is that managers of closed-end funds may invest all of their available funds without leaving a cash cushion for investor redemptions. Another is that the price of a closed-end fund may vary significantly from its NAV.

Table 12-1. Largest U.S. Mutual Fund Companies

Mutual Fund Management Company	Net Assets in Millions	No. of Funds
Fidelity Management & Research Co.	$810,449.5	388
Vanguard Group Inc.	544,614.8	104
American Funds Distributors Inc.	331,628.8	31
Putnam Investment Management Inc.	257,900.8	207
Janus Capital Corp.	219,674.5	27
Merrill Lynch Asset Management L.P.	216,004.2	325
Franklin/Templeton Worldwide	165,630.2	238
AIM Advisors Inc.	151,604.3	165
SSB Citi Fund Management Inc.	124,584.5	219
Morgan Stanley Dean Witter Advisors	120,155.2	225
T. Rowe Price Associates	119,905.3	81
Charles Schwab Investment Mgmt. Inc.	111,853.9	44
Oppenheimerfunds Inc./Centennial	107,212.4	188
American Century Investments Inc.	106,452.8	117
Federated Investors	105,823.2	223
Dreyfus Corp.	103,239.0	307
IDS Mutual Fund Group	100,379.5	126
MFS Investment Management	94,089.4	218
Alliance Capital Management L.P.	91,123.6	191
Banc Of America Advisors	81,098.1	268
Evergreen Investment Services	78,809.6	257
Goldman Sachs & Co.	69,651.1	146
Prudential Investment Fund Mgmt L.L.C	66,956.7	251
Banc One Investment Adv.	64,085.1	159
Pimco Advisors L.P.	60,368.6	187
Wells Fargo Bank	57,468.4	131
Van Kampen Investment Adv. Corp.	53,523.1	148
Zurich Kemper Investments Inc.	53,315.4	160
Chase Manhattan Bank	49,948.7	123
Paine Webber/Mitchell Hutchins	49,466.6	124

As of 2/29/00.
SOURCE: Lipper, Inc.

While NAV is the primary determining factor in a fund's share price, it is not the only factor. Investor perceptions play a role, creating prices which may be at a premium (over) or a discount (under) to NAV. Traditionally, closed-end funds trade at a discount to NAV. The Herzfeld closed-end average, published in *Barron's*, showed an average discount to NAV which ranged from –6% to –13% in 1999. Funds trading at premiums tend to be those with outstanding returns or country-specific funds in hot areas. In October 1999, the Thai Fund was trading at an 82.8% premium to NAV and the Indonesia Fund at a 29.7% premium. For the lucky/smart investor, a shrinking discount or increasing premium combined with the fund's market return can provide returns in excess of those available elsewhere. Most closed-end funds offer dividend reinvestment, usually at the market price, which is an advantage when a fund is trading at a discount to net asset value.

Market prices, NAVs, premiums or discounts, and market returns are available daily in *The Wall Street Journal's* interactive edition at *http://wsj.com* or weekly in *Barron's*, which also offers free annual or semi-annual reports for some closed-end funds through its Annual Reports Club at 1-800-965-2929, fax 1-800-747-9384.

Unit Investment Trusts

Unit investment trusts (UITs) are mutual funds whose holdings are set at inception. Once the portfolio is established, whether it is bonds or stocks, the UIT cannot purchase new securities or sell existing ones except in extreme situations, such as the impending default of a bond. As such, UITs only make sense for portfolios that do not require active management.

Unlike mutual funds, UITs have a stated maturity date, which may range from 1 to 30 years. During the life of the UIT, the trustee collects and distributes interest and dividends to investors and pays principal when bonds mature. If investors want to sell their units, the trustee must redeem them at NAV. When the UIT reaches maturity, any unpaid principal is distributed by the trustee.

You can purchase UITs from a broker with commissions that range from 2.75% to 5% on the initial offering. Management fees are negligible, as there is no active management and annual maintenance costs are approximately 0.2%.

Stock portfolios with a strict discipline, such as Dogs of the Dow (buying the 10 highest yielding stocks in the Dow Jones Industrial Average), or those that follow a particular index are good candidates for UITs. UITs containing municipal bonds appeal to investors who want predictable income but want to invest less than it would take to buy individual bonds. Because the portfolio is set at inception, the income is locked in for the life of the UIT unless a bond is called, in contrast to municipal bond mutual funds that have fluctuating yields.

Index share UITs follow a stock index in a manner similar to index mutual funds. For example, Diamonds (symbol DIA) is a UIT that follows the Dow Jones Industrial Average and trades on the American Stock Exchange. An advantage to the UIT over index mutual funds is that it collects dividends and pays them monthly. Another advantage, in volatile stock markets where the DJIA may swing 200 points in a day, is index shares can be traded throughout the day, while index funds can only be bought or sold at the day's closing price. For more on index shares, see Chapter 4.

The risks in stock UITs can be high, as portfolios are concentrated and set for the life of the UIT. Some stock UITs, such as Dogs of the Dow portfolios, expire annually in order to reset their portfolios. While this practice may make investment sense, it generates annual capital gains, so these investments are best held in a retirement account. Due to the risks and fees associated with UITs, compare carefully with mutual funds to find the best value.

Dollar Cost Averaging

The convenience of regular purchasing is one hallmark of mutual fund investing. Most mutual funds have automatic investment plans that allow you to provide a schedule, a dollar amount, and a bank account to debit and then to sit back and relax while the fund handles the transactions. Minimum purchases are usually low ($25 to $50) and you can purchase fractional shares so that all your money goes to work.

Convenience is not the only benefit at work here. Regular purchases in the same amount create a result called dollar cost averaging, in which your average share cost is lower than the average share purchase price, because you purchase more shares when prices are low and fewer shares when prices are high.

Table 12–2 provides an example of $200 invested in the Janus Fund on the first business day of each month of 1999. In January, when the share price was lowest, at $33.62, you would have purchased the most shares (5.949) with $200. In December, at the highest price ($44.84), you would have purchased the fewest shares (4.460) with $200. At year-end, after investing $2,400 you would have an average share cost of $38.35, while the average of the monthly share prices was $38.57.

In addition to providing a lower share cost, dollar cost averaging provides two helpful disciplines. The first is that of regular saving and investing. There is no amount too small to invest and a habit of regular investing means that you always pay yourself first. The second discipline is avoiding the temptation to invest more at market peaks, when prices are high, and less in bear markets, when all the news is bad. Although this is a natural tendency, the obvious but difficult strategy is to do the opposite. Dollar cost averaging takes the emotion out of the timing decision.

The caveat to dollar cost averaging is a false sense of security. It is better to buy more shares of a volatile investment when prices are down, but do not be lulled into thinking that falling prices on a poor investment will always rise.

Table 12–2. Dollar Cost Averaging

Date of Purchase	Amount Invested	Share Price	Shares Purchased
January 4	$200	$33.62	5.949
February 1	$200	$36.68	5.453
March 1	$200	$34.87	5.736
April 1	$200	$37.82	5.288
May 3	$200	$38.20	5.236
June 1	$200	$36.95	5.413
July 1	$200	$40.46	4.943
August 2	$200	$38.86	5.147
September 1	$200	$39.02	5.126
October 1	$200	$39.42	5.074
November 1	$200	$42.08	4.753
December 1	$200	$44.84	4.460
Total	$2,400	$462.82	62.578

Average share price = $462.82/12 = $38.57.

Average share cost = $2,400/62.578 = $38.35.

Tax Issues

Annual Tax Considerations

You might think that if you reinvest all your dividends and do not sell any shares, you could avoid thinking about taxes on your mutual funds; but this is not the case. Mutual fund companies pay out dividends and capital gains realized by their portfolios. Funds differ as to their schedules; some pay dividends monthly, some quarterly, some semiannually, and some annually. Capital gains are more often paid semiannually or annually. Even if you choose to reinvest these distributions, they are taxable in the year paid. Dividends are taxable as current income. Capital gains will be reported as long term or short term; long-term capital gains are taxed at a 20% rate and short-term capital gains are taxed as ordinary income.

If your funds are not in a tax-deferred account, such as an IRA, the tax liability on annual capital gains distributions can significantly reduce your total return. Because a fund only incurs capital gains when it sells an appreciated security, funds whose style is to buy and hold generate fewer capital gains than those that trade furiously. You can check a fund's turnover ratio, found in its prospectus and in most fund research reports such as Morningstar Mutual Funds and Value Line Mutual Funds, to determine into which camp your fund falls. Turnover is measured as a percent and tells you what dollar amount of the portfolio is sold and replaced in one year's time. A turnover ratio of 100% means that the fund replaces its whole portfolio (or the equivalent dollar amount) in a given year. Ratios vary widely by fund and by fund type; for example, in October 1999, Morningstar reported average turnover for small value domestic stock funds of 58% and average turnover for technology stock funds of 345%.[1] Look for turnover under 100% if you are concerned about capital gains.

In addition to the turnover ratio, you can check a fund's tax efficiency rating. This number is the percentage of total return that a fund retains after taxes. It is computed by taking pretax total return less maximum taxes on distributed dividends, short-term capital gains, and long-term capital gains and dividing it by pretax total return. Not usually available in the prospectus or annual reports (Vanguard Group is an exception), you can find the tax efficiency rating in a Morningstar report, which also provides pretax and after-tax returns. What is a reasonable number? A study of 10-year performances of 530 U.S. stock funds by KMPG found that efficiencies ranged from 51% to 100%, with an average of 83%.[2] Several funds (56 by Morningstar's latest count[3]), called tax-managed funds, strive to keep shareholder taxes low by holding stocks for the long term and trying to match gains and losses.

Turnover ratios and tax efficiency ratings are best used as a secondary consideration in choosing a mutual fund. Once the field has been narrowed to several funds chosen for their investment objectives and performance, differences in tax efficiency can break a tie. Tax efficiency and turnover are also helpful in deciding which funds to place in retirement accounts and which to hold in taxable accounts.

At the end of 1999, Quicken listed the funds shown in Table 12–3, from the 50 largest mutual funds, as the most tax efficient over the previous decade.

Timing of Purchases

Rising markets can be tax traps for investors who want to buy top-performing mutual funds near year-end. Most growth mutual funds distribute dividends and capital gains to their shareholders late in the calendar year. When a fund distributes dividends and capital gains, its NAV drops by the amount of the distribution because the cash that is paid out is no longer in the portfolio. Consider the following scenario: In November

---

[1] "Benchmark Averages," *Morningstar Mutual Funds* (October 21, 1999): S8.

[2] Peter McKenna, "Quick, How Tax Efficient Are Your Funds?" *Investor's Business Daily* (June 17, 1999).

[3] Ibid.

Table 12–3. Most Tax-Efficient Large Mutual Funds in the 1990s

Mutual Fund	Tax Efficiency
AIM Constellation A	96.1%
Legg Mason Value	95.1
Vanguard U.S. Growth	94.0
Vanguard 500 Index	93.9
American Century Ultra	93.8

SOURCE: *Quicken.com.*

you purchase shares of ABC Fund for $20 a share. On December 31, the share price of ABC Fund is still $20 and it declares dividends of $0.25 a share and long-term capital gains of $2.50 a share. Immediately, the NAV drops by $2.75 to $17.25. No problem. You have a check (or reinvested shares) for $2.75 per share. However, you owe current income taxes on the dividends at your marginal rate of 31% and taxes at 20% on the long-term capital gain. Taxes due are $0.25 × 0.31 = $0.08 on the dividends + $2.50 × 0.20 = $0.50 on the long-term capital gain. Now you have shares worth $17.25 and cash worth $2.17 after taxes for a net value of $19.42. Why is this only an issue for investors who purchase near year-end? Investors who purchase during the year and see their NAVs rise due to capital gains in the fund's portfolio are still likely to be ahead, even after paying taxes.

Selling of Shares

For years it was the investor's responsibility to keep track of different share prices for dividend reinvestment and automatic investment programs in order to compute the tax basis of fund shares. While you still have the option of doing this if you would like to use the specific identification or first-in first-out (FIFO) methods, most mutual funds will now calculate the average cost basis for your shares using one of two methods.

The single category method combines all shares owned, multiplies them times their various purchase prices, and divides them by the number of shares owned to arrive at an average cost. Reinvested dividends and capital gains are added in as if they were separate purchases. For example, if you bought 100 shares of ABC Fund on January 1, 1998, for $20, then 100 shares on July 1, 1998, for $22, then 100 shares on January 1, 1999, for $25, and 100 shares on July 1, 1999, for $26 and you received dividends of $1 per share (reinvested) and long-term capital gains of $1 per share (reinvested) on December 31, 1998, you would calculate your average cost using the single category method, as shown in Table 12–4.

Table 12–4. Single Category Method of Computing Mutual Fund Cost Basis

Date	Transaction	Number of Shares	Price per Share	Cost
1/1/98	Purchase	100	$20	$2,000
7/1/98	Purchase	100	$22	$2,200
12/31/98	Div $1/sh	8	$25	$200
12/31/98	LTCG $1/sh	8	$25	$200
1/1/99	Purchase	100	$25	$2,500
7/1/99	Purchase	100	$26	$2,600
		416		9,700

Average cost basis = $9,700 / 416 = $23.32.

Some fund families use the double category method, which segregates long-term and short-term holdings. On November 1, 1999, the long-term holdings (over 12 months) in Table 12–4 would have an average cost of $2,000 + $2,200 + $200 + $200 = $4,600 divided by 216 = $21.29. Short-term shares would have a cost of $2,500 + $2,600 = $5,100 divided by 200, or $25.50 a share.

Fund Rating Services

Several rating services compile mutual fund data and results and report them in a way that makes comparisons easy. The best known service is Morningstar Mutual Funds, 225 W. Wacker Drive, Chicago, Illinois 60606 (312-696-6000, *www.morningstar.com*). Morningstar tracks more than 1,700 mutual funds and is known for its five-star rating system. The star ratings are risk-adjusted performance ratings which are assigned in a bell curve according to broad investment groups. A sample report is shown in Figure 12–1.

Lipper, Inc., a division of Reuters (908-273-2772 or 303-534-3472, *www.lipperweb.com*), is known for its extensive performance data on more than 47,000 mutual funds. Its quarterly performance analysis provides an overall rank for each of the funds covered.

The Value Line Mutual Fund Survey, 220 East 42nd Street, New York, New York 10017-5891 (1-800-833-0046) provides an overall rank and a risk rank for each fund evaluated. The ranking system goes from 1 (highest) to 5 (lowest).

Published October 7, 1999. Reprinted by permission of Morningstar.

Fidelity Magellan

	Ticker	Load	NAV	Yield	Total Assets	Mstar Category
	FMAGX	Closed	$122.02	0.5%	$92,187.0 mil	Large Blend

Prospectus Objective: Growth

Fidelity Magellan Fund seeks capital appreciation.

The fund invests primarily in common stocks and convertible securities, with up to 20% of assets invested in debt securities of all types and qualities. It features domestic corporations operating primarily in the United States, domestic corporations that have significant activities and interests outside the U.S., and foreign companies. No limitations are placed on total foreign investment, but no more than 40% of assets may be invested in companies operating exclusively in one foreign country.

The fund closed to new investment in 1965 and reopened in 1981. It closed again in 1997.

Historical Profile

Return	Above Avg
Risk	Average
Rating	★★★★★ Highest

| 81% | 84% | 93% | 93% | 79% | 95% | 96% | 97% |

Investment Style
Equity
Average Stock %

▼ Manager Change
▽ Partial Manager Change

Fund Performance vs. Category Average
■ Quarterly Fund Return
+/− Category Average
— Category Baseline

Performance Quartile
(within Category)

1988	1989	1990	1991	1992	1993	1994	1995	1996	1997	1998	09-99	History
48.32	59.85	53.93	68.61	63.01	70.85	66.80	85.98	80.65	95.27	120.82	122.02	NAV
22.77	34.58	−4.51	41.03	7.02	24.66	−1.81	36.82	11.69	26.59	33.63	6.96	Total Return %
6.16	2.90	−1.39	10.54	−0.60	14.60	−3.13	−0.71	−11.26	−6.76	5.05	1.59	+/− S&P 500
5.57	3.16	−0.43	8.56	−1.18	14.92	0.54	−0.83	−9.87	−6.71	4.58	2.48	+/− Wilshire Top 750
2.24	2.60	1.42	2.46	1.93	1.22	0.18	0.88	1.41	1.57	0.72	0.19	Income Return %
20.52	31.98	−5.93	38.57	5.09	23.43	−1.99	35.94	10.28	25.03	32.91	6.77	Capital Return %
10	7	63	13	54	4	60	16	98	60	3	17	Total Rtn % Rank Cat
0.90	1.24	0.83	1.30	1.25	0.75	0.13	0.59	1.10	1.25	0.67	0.23	Income $
0.00	3.82	2.42	5.43	8.82	8.50	2.64	4.69	12.85	5.21	5.15	7.19	Capital Gains $
1.14	1.08	1.03	1.06	1.05	1.00	0.99	0.96	0.92	0.64	0.61	0.60	Expense Ratio %
1.33	2.13	2.54	2.47	1.57	2.11	1.07	0.39	0.95	1.75	0.77	0.66	Income Ratio %
101	87	82	135	172	155	132	120	155	67	34	37	Turnover Rate %
6,971.1	12,699.6	12,325.7	19,257.1	22,268.9	31,705.1	36,441.5	53,702.3	53,988.7	63,766.2	83,552.1	92,187.0	Net Assets $mil

Portfolio Manager(s)

Robert E. Stansky, CFA. Since 6-96. '78 Nichols C.; MBA'83 New York U. Stansky joined Fidelity Management & Research in 1983 as a portfolio manager. Funds previously managed: Fidelity Growth Company (04-87 - 06-96), Fidelity Emerging Growth (12-90 - 04-91).

Performance 09-30-99

	1st Qtr	2nd Qtr	3rd Qtr	4th Qtr	Total
1995	8.44	15.77	10.60	−1.46	36.82
1996	1.79	1.00	1.67	6.85	11.69
1997	−0.56	16.55	9.67	−0.40	26.59
1998	14.22	3.37	−11.05	27.22	33.63
1999	7.39	5.93	−5.97	—	—

Trailing	Total Return%	+/− S&P 500	+/− Will Top 750	% Rank All Cat	Growth of $10,000
3 Mo	−5.97	0.27	0.59	77 39	9,403
6 Mo	−0.40	−0.77	0.03	58 66	9,960
1 Yr	36.08	8.29	8.36	15 8	13,608
3 Yr Avg	24.58	−0.51	−0.05	5 14	19,333
5 Yr Avg	22.33	−2.69	−2.22	7 32	27,399
10 Yr Avg	17.06	0.25	0.82	6 7	48,319
15 Yr Avg	19.70	1.73	2.22	3 1	148,409

Tax Analysis	Tax-Adj Ret%	%Rank Cat	%Pretax Ret	%Rank Cat
3 Yr Avg	22.58	18	91.9	32
5 Yr Avg	19.49	35	87.3	54
10 Yr Avg	13.85	22	81.2	57

Potential Capital Gain Exposure: 39% of assets

Risk Analysis

Time Period	Load-Adj Return %	Risk %Rank¹ All Cat	Morningstar Return Risk	Morningstar Risk-Adj Rating
1 Yr	32.00			
3 Yr	23.32	66 57	1.98 0.88	★★★★
5 Yr	21.59	73 84	1.48 0.94	★★★★
10 Yr	18.71	71 72	1.62 0.94	★★★★★

Average Historical Rating (166 months): 4.7★s

¹1=low, 100=high

Category Rating (3 Yr)

① ② ③ ④ ⑤
Worst — Best

Return: Above Avg
Risk: Average

Other Measures	Standard Index S&P 500	Best Fit Index S&P 500
Alpha	−0.6	−0.8
Beta	1.02	1.02
R−Squared	94	94

Standard Deviation	21.72
Mean	24.58
Sharpe Ratio	1.01

Portfolio Analysis 03-31-99

Share change since 09-99 Total Stocks: 343

	Sector	PE	YTD Ret%	% Assets
⊕ General Elec	Industrials	39.7	17.35	4.17
⊕ Microsoft	Technology	63.8	30.60	4.10
⊕ MCI WorldCom	Services	NMF	0.17	2.37
⊕ America Online	Technology	NMF	33.84	2.34
⊕ Home Depot	Retail	53.2	12.36	2.22
⊖ Cisco Sys	Technology	NMF	47.74	2.03
⊕ Merck	Health	28.3	−11.00	2.01
⊕ Citigroup	Financials	24.9	34.04	1.71
⊕ Wal−Mart Stores	Retail	42.9	17.19	1.67
⊖ Time Warner	Services	NMF	−1.98	1.55
⊖ AT & T	Services	18.4	−12.70	1.49
⊖ Intel	Technology	35.1	25.45	1.40
⊕ American Intl Grp	Financials	28.1	12.64	1.37
⊕ Tyco Intl	Industrials	NMF	36.97	1.18
⊕ Texas Instruments	Technology	73.4	92.55	1.14
⊖ Bristol−Myers Squibb	Health	40.2	2.20	1.11
⊕ Schering−Plough	Health	33.6	−20.40	1.08
⊕ Fannie Mae	Financials	21.2	−14.30	1.07
⊕ Johnson & Johnson	Health	38.0	10.51	1.06
⊕ Chase Manhattan	Financials	14.5	7.76	1.04
⊖ EMC/Mass	Technology	79.3	67.94	1.04
⊖ American Home Products	Health	27.5	−25.40	1.02
⊕ Philip Morris	Staples	13.7	−33.80	1.01
⊕ Dayton Hudson	Retail	27.5	11.25	1.01
⊕ Bank of America	Financials	—	—	0.98

Current Investment Style

Style: Value Blend Growth
Size: Large Mid Small

	Stock Port Avg	Relative S&P 500 Current	Rel Cat
Price/Earnings Ratio	36.6	1.02 1.15	1.11
Price/Book Ratio	8.6	0.96 1.12	1.12
Price/Cash Flow	25.1	1.04 0.99	1.11
3 Yr Earnings Growth	20.7	1.27 1.41	1.17
1 Yr Earnings Est%	20.6	1.13 —	1.18
Med Mkt Cap $mil	70,670	1.0 1.3	1.55

Special Securities % assets 03-31-99

Restricted/Illiquid Secs	0
Emerging−Markets Secs	Trace
Options/Futures/Warrants	Yes

Composition % assets 03-31-99

		Market Cap	
Cash	6.6	Giant	57.3
Stocks*	93.4	Large	32.9
Bonds	0.0	Medium	9.4
Other	0.0	Small	0.4
		Micro	0.0
*Foreign (% stocks)	4.1		

Sector Weightings

	% of Stocks	Rel S&P	5-Year High Low
Utilities	0.3	0.1	9 0
Energy	6.4	1.0	25 1
Financials	14.2	1.0	17 7
Industrials	11.2	0.9	31 11
Durables	3.4	1.5	16 3
Staples	4.3	0.5	10 0
Services	16.7	1.2	17 10
Retail	10.8	1.8	11 2
Health	11.1	1.0	15 2
Technology	21.7	0.9	42 4

Analysis by Scott Cooley 07-29-99

For Fidelity Magellan Fund, $100 billion is just another number.

In July, this fund received a lot of press attention as it crossed the $100 billion mark, but Bob Stansky has not changed the way he runs the portfolio. Long before the fund crossed that milestone, he had altered the fund's style to accommodate its girth. For example, he likes to buy stocks on weakness, hold them for the long term, and then sell them on strength. Recently moderate cash inflows have helped him stick to this steady approach.

Given Stansky's opportunism, some observers predicted that he would bulk up the fund's tech stake during the sector's second quarter sell-off, but that did not happen. Stansky says that he likes tech's long-term earnings prospects, but worries about its lofty valuations. It is worth noting, too, that the recent tech correction was neither as long nor as severe as 1998's, when Stansky presciently hiked the fund's exposure to the sector. He

does like companies that can benefit from the explosion of data and Internet traffic, so firms like MCI WorldCom, AT&T, and Lucent Technologies dot the fund's top 10.

The fund has continued to put up strong returns in 1999, edging the S&P 500 for the year to date through July 27. Underweightings in financials and electric utilities have boosted the fund, as rising interest rates have hurt both areas. But the main factor that has helped the fund is solid stock-picking. Only two stocks in the choppy financials sector (Citigroup and AIG) make the fund's top 15, for example, and both have notched 1999 gains north of 20%.

Given that the fund now has an S&P 500–ish market cap and sector weightings, Stansky is unlikely to leave his rivals or the index in the dust. Indeed, the fund's returns since early 1997 are roughly in line with the index's. But with small sector bets and good stock-picking, he can likely add enough value to make this fund an above-average long-term holding.

Address:	82 Devonshire Street Boston, MA 02109 800−544−8888	Minimum Purchase: Min Auto Inv Plan: Sales Fees: Management Fee: Actual Fees: Expense Projections: Avg Brok Commission:	Closed Closed 3.00%L 0.30%+0.52% max./0.27% min.(G)+(−)0.20%P Mgt: 0.43% Dist: — 3Yr: $493* 5Yr: $635* 10Yr: $1051* Income Distrib: Semi−Ann,	Add: $250 IRA: — Add: $100
Web Address: Inception: Advisor: Subadvisor:	www.fidelity.com 05-02-63 Fidelity Management & Research FMR (U.K.)/FMR (Far East)			
NTF Plans:	Muriel Siebert	Total Cost (relative to category):	—	

M**ORNINGSTAR** Mutual Funds

Figure 12–1. Morningstar Mutual Funds Report at *www.morningstar.com.*

Reprinted by permission of Morningstar.

Mutual Funds Update is published monthly by CDA/Wiesenberger, 1455 Research Boulevard, Rockville, Maryland 20850 (1-800-232-2285, *www.cda.com*). In addition to total returns, it contains up-market and down-market rankings and a Wiesenberger rating.

Weiss Ratings' Guide to Mutual Funds, P.O. Box 109665, Palm Beach Gardens, Florida 33410 (800-289-9222) provides three ratings for each fund in addition to standard total return figures. It rates each fund from A to E with an overall rating, a performance rating, and a risk rating.

The Investment Company Institute, 1401 H Street N.W., 12th Floor, Washington, D.C. 20005 (202-326-5800, *www.ici.org*), provides the *Directory of Mutual Funds*, with names and addresses of more than 7,000 mutual funds, and the *Mutual Fund Fact Book*, with performance and risk ratings for more than 7,000 mutual funds. Both are available in PDF format for download from the website.

The American Association of Individual Investors (AAII), 625 N. Michigan Avenue, Suite 1900, Chicago, Illinois 60611 (800-428-2244, *www.aaii.com*) prints the *Individual Investor's Guide to Low-Load Mutual Funds*, which is an annual analysis of more than 900 low-load mutual funds, and the *Quarterly Low-Load Fund Update*.

Charles Schwab & Co., 101 Montgomery Street, San Francisco, California 94104 (800-435-4000, *www.schwab.com*) prints the *Mutual Funds Performance Guide*, which includes performance data and ticker symbols.

See Chapter 21 for websites that provide mutual fund data. More on the subscription services of Morningstar and Value Line can be found in Chapter 20.

Choosing Mutual Funds

Choosing the right mutual fund involves evaluating many different variables to find the fund which best fits your goals. The following topics include some, but certainly not all, criteria you may want to consider.

Investment Objectives

In November 1999, the AIM Value Fund had a three-year annualized total return of 23.93%. On the same date, the Fidelity Target Timeline 2001 had a three-year annualized total return of 6.33%. Which fund would you rather have? The choice is not as easy as picking the fund with the highest return.

Before you can compare returns you must be sure you are comparing apples to apples. This means comparing funds whose investment objectives are the same. While categories may differ among fund companies and rating agencies, the criteria are generally the same. Bond funds are separated by type: government, municipal, corporate, and corporate convertible; by maturity: short term, intermediate term, and long term; and by risk: high quality or high yield. Stock funds are separated by stock/bond mix or investment strategy: growth, value, growth and income, balanced, and asset allocation; by risk: aggressive growth, capital appreciation, and emerging growth; by industry: health sciences, technology, and so forth; by geographic area: international growth, emerging markets (Europe, Asia, Latin America, etc.), and specific countries; and by market capitalization (size of companies in the portfolio): small company, midcap, and large company.

A fund's investment objective may seem apparent from its name, but a fund labeled "growth" may fit into a wide range of risk parameters. Learn more by checking its largest holdings. Read the prospectus carefully to determine its goals. The SEC now requires that mutual fund prospectuses be written in plain language. Many are still difficult to read, but a few, such as those of the IPS Funds—managers of IPS Millenium and New Frontier—are refreshingly blunt. Their risk disclosures include the following statements.

> We buy scary stuff. You know, Internet stocks, small companies. These things go up and down like Pogo Sticks on steroids. . . . Many of the companies we buy are growing really fast. . . . Many of them also don't make any money, although they may be relatively large companies. That means they have silly valuations by traditional valuation techniques. We don't know what that means any more than you do, because we have never seen anything like the Internet before. So we might overpay for these companies, thinking we are really smart and can get away with it because they are growing so fast. It doesn't take a whole lot for these companies to drop 50 percent or more, because nobody else knows what they are worth either.[4]

Choose your objective first, then compare funds within that objective so that you can find the best one. If you look more closely at the two funds noted at the beginning of this section, both have five-star ratings (the highest) from Morningstar and rank in the top 10% of funds within their investment objective. The choice depends on whether you are in search of the capital appreciation found in a largecap stock fund (AIM Value) or the income provided by an intermediate bond fund (Fidelity Target).

Investment Total Return

The bottom line for most investors is performance. Though past performance does not necessarily predict future performance, it is the most widely

[4]George Benigno, "IPS Funds Jolts Investors with Plain-Talk Risk Disclosure," *Financialweb.com.*

used indicator. There are several common ways of measuring returns, the best of which is total return. Total return is the sum of current income and change in share value. It is measured on an annual basis as a percentage of the amount invested.

$$\text{Percentage total return} = \frac{\text{Annual interest or dividends} + \text{Change in share price}}{\text{Amount invested}}$$

For example, if you purchased a share of ABC Company for $10 on January 1, received a $0.20 dividend, and on December 31 the share was worth $11, your total return would be $0.20 + $1 = $1.20. To get a percentage, divide $1.20 by the amount you invested, $10, for a 12% total return.

Current return, or current yield, widely used in fixed income investing, considers only current income as a percentage of the amount invested. In the previous example, compute the current yield by dividing the $0.20 dividend by the $10 invested. Your current yield is $0.20/$10 = 2%. The inadequacy of current yield computations is that they do not take the whole picture into account. If you were using current yield to compare the previous investment with XYZ Corporation, a $10 investment that paid a dividend of $0.60 (current yield of 6%) but whose share value did not increase, you might conclude that you would make more money on XYZ. This is especially dangerous in the case of an investment that pays high dividends at the expense of its share price. A bond fund that owns bonds priced at a premium is a prime example. High-priced bonds pay above-market rates of interest, allowing the fund to pay high current dividends, but as the bonds mature at par, the NAV of the fund will drop. You must subtract the capital loss from a high current yield to find the true total return. Table 12–5 shows that the fund MAX fits this description.

When evaluating total returns for mutual funds in volatile markets, it is most valuable to consider performance over several years as compared with market averages and a group of the fund's peers. You most often hear comparisons to the Standard & Poor's 500 or the Dow Jones Industrial Average, but fund rating services and the funds themselves more accurately choose a benchmark that most closely represents the fund's holdings. Sam-

Table 12–5. Current Yield and Total Return

Investment	Price Jan. 1	Price Dec. 31	Change in Value	Dividend Paid	Current Yield	Total Return
ABC	$10	$11	$1	$0.20	2%	12%
XYZ	$10	$10	$0	$0.60	6%	6%
MAX	$10	$9.75	($0.25)	$0.80	8%	5.5%

ple benchmark indices follow. More detailed information on the composition of these indices can be found in Chapter 4.

Bond Indices

Lehman Brothers Aggregate Bond Index

Lehman Brothers Municipal Bond Index

Lehman Brothers Government Bond Index

Lehman Brothers Corporate Bond Index

First Boston High Yield Index

Lipper Money Market Fund Average

Lipper Tax Exempt Money Market Fund Average

Merrill Lynch All-Convertibles Index

Lipper Convertible Securities Funds Average

Salomon Brothers World Government Bond Index

Stock Indices

Standard and Poor's (S&P) 500 Index

S&P Midcap 400 Index

Russell 2000 Index

Russell Midcap Index

NASDAQ Industrial Index

Morgan Stanley Capital International (MSCI) World Index

MSCI EAFE (Europe, Australia, and Far East) Index

Indices give you a backdrop for comparison and using several can be especially valuable. For example, a small stock fund might compare its returns with the S&P 500 as a benchmark for the stock market in general and also a more specific index, such as the Russell 2000, for companies with market values from $25 million to $275 million.

An even more specific, and therefore valuable, comparison is to a fund's peers. Mutual fund rating companies make this easy by classifying a fund and indicating its relative performance against other funds in the class. The percentage total return difference between the fund and its peer average, and a percentile ranking within the peer group, are usually provided.

Peer rankings can differ greatly depending on a fund's classification. Many funds' investment objectives are vague and the portfolios of others do not match their stated objectives, leaving classification choices up to the rating service. Lipper, Inc. made two notable changes in their classification system in 1999. The first was to add a category called multicap funds for mutual funds holding stocks of diversified capitalization or whose capitalization weightings change according to market opportunities. (Capitalization refers to the total market value of the company, as derived by multiplying shares outstanding by current share price.) The second was to institute the 75% rule, which states that regardless of the stated objective, to be classified as largecap, midcap, or smallcap, a fund must have at least 75% of its equity investments in stocks of the appropriate size.

The performance of a sampling of mutual fund sectors followed by Morningstar Mutual Funds can be found in Table 12–6.

Returns for a year and cumulative returns for 5 and 10 years of the 25 largest equity and fixed income mutual funds, ranked by net assets, are listed in Table 12–7.

Fees

Front-End Loads. The most obvious (and most onerous) mutual fund fee is a sales charge or commission, also called a load, paid in most part to the broker who sells a mutual fund. Commissions are paid as a percentage of the amount invested, either at the time of purchase or upon liquidation.

Commissions paid at purchase are known as front-end loads. Mutual fund shares with front-end loads are usually called A shares. By law, sales charges may be as high as 8.5%, but most are much lower, in the 4% to 6% range for standard funds and 2% to 4% range for those labeled "low load." Of the commission charged, typically 80% to 90% of that is paid to the firm of the selling broker, in a dealer reallowance. The brokerage firm then splits this amount with the salesperson.

The price at which an investor may purchase shares of a load fund is the offering price, which is simply the NAV plus the commission charged. When a commission percentage is quoted, it is as a percentage of the offering price.

For example, on November 1, 1999, the NAV of Putnam Voyager A Fund was 26.38. The offering price for purchases of less than $50,000 was 27.99, which includes a sales commission of 5.75% calculated as a percentage of the offering price. If you purchased $20,000 of Putnam Voyager A Fund on that date, you would have bought 714.541 shares at $27.99. If you wrote a $20,000 check for this investment, $1,150.41 in commission would have been paid up front and your beginning account balance would have been $18,849.59

Table 12–6. The Morningstar Benchmark of Mutual Fund Performance, 1999

Category	Annualized Total Returns			
	1 Year	3 Year	5 Year	10 Year
Domestic Stock Total	27.16	21.13	22.32	15.42
Large Value	6.59	14.73	19.31	13.95
Large Blend	19.47	22.63	23.90	15.71
Large Growth	38.60	31.34	28.46	18.63
Midcap Value	6.71	10.74	16.09	12.19
Midcap Blend	17.06	16.54	19.25	13.97
Midcap Growth	60.14	28.53	25.89	17.55
Small Value	4.91	7.31	13.46	11.60
Small Blend	22.29	13.67	16.90	12.44
Small Growth	66.10	25.02	22.98	18.58
S&P 500 Index	21.04	27.55	28.54	18.20
S&P Midcap 400	14.72	21.80	23.04	17.31
Russell 2000	21.26	13.08	16.70	13.40
International Stock Total	50.95	15.26	13.30	9.61
Europe Stock	24.93	20.26	20.70	10.77
Latin America Stock	60.84	6.86	5.17	—
Emerging Markets	71.79	5.69	4.70	7.60
Pacific Stock	92.96	8.28	6.27	7.19
Pacific Stock –ex Japan	72.12	–0.58	2.70	5.16
Japan Stock	113.90	25.04	9.02	–0.99
Foreign Stock	44.31	18.65	15.11	10.23
World Stock	37.77	19.74	18.19	11.36
MSCI EAFE	26.96	15.74	12.83	7.01
MSCI World	24.93	21.61	19.76	11.42
MSCI Emerging Mkts	66.18	1.76	–0.42	3.45
Hybrid Total	11.23	12.97	15.33	11.38
Domestic Hybrid	8.76	12.92	15.61	11.37
Convertible	29.60	17.49	17.53	13.57
International Hybrid	20.82	10.47	11.25	6.55
Bond Total	–0.41	4.81	6.64	7.00
Long-Term Bond	–2.76	4.59	7.42	7.66
Intermediate-Term Bond	–1.37	4.78	6.83	7.21
Short-Term Bond	2.14	4.91	6.09	6.43
Ultrashort Bond	4.74	5.19	5.62	5.82
Lehman Bros Aggregate	–0.83	5.73	7.73	7.70
U.S. 90-Day Treasury	4.87	5.07	5.25	5.10

SOURCE: Morningstar Mutual Funds. Reprinted with permission.

Table 12–7. Performance of the Largest Mutual Funds

Net Assets $ Millions	Mutual Fund	Cumulative Performance		
		1 Year	5 Year	10 Year
100,818.6	Fidelity Magellan Fund	17.74%	201.41%	488.87%
98,617.3	Vanguard 500 Index;Inv	14.74	217.67	440.61
53,350.2	Investment Co Of America	14.84	174.75	356.88
46,545.7	Fidelity Contrafund	22.32	228.05	689.53
46,217.3	Janus Fund	41.01	287.49	615.06
44,091.0	Washington Mutual Inv	–2.26	141.33	304.53
43,135.5	Janus Worldwide	70.54	330.28	NA
42,337.1	Fidelity Gro & Inc	6.46	174.12	442.27
42,158.4	Amer Cent:AC Ultra;Inv	31.79	260.85	856.63
37,589.4	Fidelity Growth Company	107.92	422.37	936.66
37,460.0	Europacific Growth	51.41	175.2	359.35
37,216.3	Janus Twenty	35.71	511.73	1,041.85
33,825.2	New Perspective Fund	38.06	192.95	402.12
33,288.4	Growth Fund Of America	58.92	285.31	581.49
28,261.0	Fidelity Blue Chip Growth	22.14	211.86	670.95
27,866.7	Vanguard Instl Indx;Ins	14.85	219.66	NA
26,869.1	Putnam Voyager;A	62.22	292.38	751.65
23,844.3	PIMCO:Total Return;Inst	1.53	45.79	139.31
21,978.5	Fidelity Aggr Growth	98.65	502.47	NA
21,963.9	Vanguard Wellington Fund	1.43	99.74	228.32
21,858.4	Vanguard PRIMECAP	57.52	317.43	744.74
21,748.8	Putnam New Oppty;A	85.99	345.45	NA
21,546.8	Fidelity Puritan	0.79	94.28	249.82
21,458.9	Vanguard Windsor II	–10.64	120.49	269.13
20,379.6	Fidelity Adv Gr Opp;T	2.1	136.52	424.18

All data as of 3/16/00.
Excludes money market funds.
SOURCE: Lipper, Inc.

Breakpoints. Front-end loads generally decrease according to the amount invested. The points at which the percentage drops are called breakpoints. The levels vary from fund to fund, but Table 12–8 provides a general format. If an investment is over a particular breakpoint, the entire investment qualifies for the lower percentage sales charge.

Many funds will combine all accounts with the same Social Security number, such as individual, joint, and retirement accounts, for the purposes of reaching a breakpoint. This is commonly referred to as a right of accumulation. Additionally, most funds will charge a lower breakpoint fee to an investor who signs a letter of intent indicating the plan to purchase shares over the breakpoint amount within the next 12 or 13 months.

Table 12-8. Typical Mutual Fund Breakpoints

Amount Invested	Sales Charge (%)
$0 – $24,999	5.75
$25,000 – $49,999	5.25
$50,000 – $99,999	4.50
$100,000 – $249,999	3.75
$250,000 – $499,999	3.00
$500,000 – $999,999	2.00
$1,000,000 +	0.00

Back-End Loads. The contingent deferred sales charge (CDSC), commonly known as a back-end load, is a sales charge due when shares are redeemed. Shares subject to a CDSC are called B shares. Most CDSCs decline over time. A typical CDSC schedule is shown in Table 12-9.

Funds will generally not impose a CDSC on shares acquired through the reinvestment of dividends and capital gains. When processing a partial liquidation (the sale of some, but not all of your shares), funds will redeem reinvested shares first, so as to minimize fees charged. Additionally, the CDSC is typically computed on the lesser of the original purchase price or the current market value. In other words, you will not pay a sales commission on the increase in value of your shares, and if they decrease in value, you will only pay commission on the reduced market value, not your original purchase amount. At the end of the holding period in which the CDSC declines to zero, B shares are generally converted into A shares.

Load versus No-Load. Most load mutual funds and many rating services now report total returns with and without including commissions to help investors compare between load and no-load funds. The maximum sales charge is applied as if front-end load funds had been purchased at the beginning of the period measured and back-end load funds had been liquidated at the end. For an investor looking to purchase a new fund and

Table 12-9. Typical Schedule of Contingent Deferred Sales Charges

Year	1	2	3	4	5	6	7+
Charge	5%	4%	3%	3%	2%	1%	0%

wishing to compare load and no-load funds, it is helpful to have load-adjusted returns available. Those who own front-end load funds and have already paid the commission may prefer to see returns at NAV since the commission is a sunk cost and will not be paid again.

There is much argument as to whether load funds are worth the commission paid. Many load funds outperform no-load funds after commissions, but many do not. The key is to realize what you are buying with a load. A commission pays a broker for time spent in advising you. If you need someone to help set goals, to educate you about investments, to provide recommendations, to handle the paperwork, or to encourage you to jump in, you must pay for it. You can do this by working with a fee-only planner or by paying commissions on your transactions. On the other hand, if you make all your own investment decisions and do all your own work, save yourself some money by investing in no-load funds.

12b-1 Fees. In 1980, the SEC allowed mutual funds to begin charging 12b-1 fees to recover their advertising and distribution costs. The 12b-1 fees are levied annually as a percentage of a shareholder's total assets in a fund. These fees range from 0.15% ($0.15 per $100 in assets) to more than 1% ($1.00 per $100 in assets) per year. They may be charged on load and no-load funds alike. Load funds typically pay some or all of the 12b-1 fee to the selling brokerage firm in what is called a trailer. No-load funds use the fee to fund the costs of answering phone calls, mailing prospectuses, and advertising.

Mutual fund total returns are calculated after the expense ratio, which includes 12b-1 fees. In some cases the total return for A (front-end load) and B (back-end load) shares will be different even when they are not adjusted for sales commissions, because many companies charge a higher 12b-1 fee for B shares than for A shares. For example, a company may charge 0.25% annually for A shares and 0.35% for B shares.

Management Fees. Running a mutual fund is a business and the way fund companies make money is through management fees. These fees are charged as a percentage of assets under management, which rewards the managers for good performance. Both increasing the value of shareholder accounts and performance that is good enough to attract more investors will result in higher fees. Management fees generally range from 0.5% to 0.8% and are included in a fund's expense ratio.

Expense Ratios. The expense ratio, expressed as a percent of assets, includes 12b-1 fees, management fees, and other fund expenses. Borne equally by all shareholders, the expense of running the fund is not charged explicitly to shareholder accounts, but reduces total returns. For example,

Table 12–10. Average Expense Ratios

Number of Funds	Category	Average Expense Ratio (%)
3,933	Domestic Stock	1.43
1,521	International Stock	1.91
565	Specialty Stock	1.65
870	Hybrid	1.38
656	Specialty Bond	1.37
949	General Bond	0.92
534	Government Bond	1.09
1,836	Municipal Bond	1.05

SOURCE: Morningstar.

a fund which had a real total return of 12% and an expense ratio of 1% would report a total return to shareholders of 11%.

Expense ratios can be found in the fund prospectus or in reports by any of the mutual fund rating services. Usually, the expense ratio of a stock fund will be higher than that of a bond fund and international portfolios have the highest expenses. Average expense ratios for different categories of funds as reported by Morningstar on October 21, 1999, are given in Table 12–10.

The SEC's website at *www.sec.gov* has a mutual fund cost calculator in its Investor Education section which allows you to compare the costs of different mutual funds. The program provides for input of front-end sales charges, deferred sales charges and expense ratios, the amount invested, expected holding period, and expected rate of return. The answer computed shows the total cost in fees and foregone earnings on fees paid and gives the value of the investment at the end of the holding period. This type of computation can be valuable for comparing load and no-load funds or for deciding between A shares, which have a front-end load, and B shares, which have a deferred load but higher 12b-1 fees. Remember that the results of the computation are highly dependent on the predictions of your holding period and the funds' annual rates of return.

Management

Two management issues must be considered when evaluating the past performance of a mutual fund. The first, and easiest to track, is to identify the manager(s) whose decisions were responsible for past performance. Credentials and tenures of fund managers are available in a fund's prospectus. Morningstar notes manager changes and partial manager changes in its historical profile. The second issue is how much of a fund's performance is due to the performance of the portfolio's asset class as defined in the fund's investment objectives and how much is due to the skill of the manager. Morningstar notes that in the mid to late 1990s, when largecap stocks greatly outperformed smallcap stocks, many more largecap funds had four- and five-star ratings.[5] Did these funds earn higher ratings due to superior management or because their market cap was in favor? In an effort to answer this question, Value Line Mutual Funds calculates a manager rating, which seeks to measure the value that the manager adds or detracts by comparing performance against a narrow peer group. Managers must have been at the fund for 24 months and the peer group must contain at least five funds for a fund to obtain a manager rating.

Special Situations

Index Funds

Index funds are passively run portfolios that track specific benchmarks such as the S&P 500 Index. These funds have become popular because actively managed funds have such a poor track record in beating the market consistently. Index funds exhibit the following characteristics.

- Performance is predictable. Index funds track their benchmark by investing in all the securities in the target index or a large sampling of them.

- Expenses are low. A buy and hold strategy cuts transaction costs, and passive management means low management fees. While the average expense ratio for domestic stock funds is approximately 1.4%, many index funds have expense ratios of only 0.2%, in part due to low commission costs. In addition to savings on explicit costs, index funds save on the hidden costs of trading. Some of these include the spread (difference between the bid and asked price of securities, often $0.125) and the market impact of large transactions in which a large purchase order drives prices upward and a large sell order drives prices downward. See Table 12–11 to find out how much different expense ratios cost the investor over time.

    For a truly low-cost index fund, visit StockJungle.com at *www.stockjungle.com*. In November 1999, StockJungle.com launched an S&P 500 Index fund with an expense ratio of zero. According to the prospectus, all fees

---

[5]"Seeing Beyond the Stars: Using Morningstar Ratings Effectively," *Morningstar Mutual Funds:* 18.

Table 12-11. The Cost of High Fund Expenses

	Number of Years			
	5	10	20	30
Future value of $10,000 at 10% before expenses	$16,105	$25,937	$67,625	$174,494
Loss in value with expense ratio of:	$	$	$	$
0.20%	-146	-468	-2,405	-9,271
0.25%	-182	-583	-2,993	-11,513
0.50%	-363	-1,155	-5,859	-22,291
0.75%	-542	-1,715	-8,603	-32,378
1.00%	-719	-2,264	-11,231	-41,817
1.25%	-895	-2,801	-13,746	-50,649
1.50%	-1,069	-3,328	-16,155	-58,912
2.00%	-1,412	-4,348	-20,665	-73,867
2.50%	-1,749	-5,327	-24,796	-86,944

SOURCE: *AAII Journal*, "The Index fund Advantage: Low Cost Passive Investing" (May 1999).

and expenses on the fund are waived. The minimum investment is $5,000 and the maximum, to keep institutional investors out, is $100,000.

- Funds in an index mutual fund are fully invested. Actively managed mutual funds often keep 5% to 10% of their portfolios in cash as a cushion for buying opportunities and redemptions, sometimes more when markets look uncertain. In a market with an upward bias (on average, 7 of every 10 years), this creates a drag on performance. Index funds strive to be fully invested at all times.

- Annual taxes are low. Index funds have very low turnover because the only reason they have to sell securities is to remove one that has been dropped from the benchmark or to meet redemption requests. Because turnover is what creates capital gains, index funds are very tax efficient.

- Funds have style consistency. Actively managed funds often suffer from "style drift" in which the manager moves away from the fund's stated objectives toward what is currently in favor in search of higher returns.

Because index funds do not stray from their target benchmarks, a manager's change in style cannot affect your asset allocation.

Before you invest in an index fund, it is important to realize the differences between a fund's performance and its target index and the differences among funds that track the same index. Following are some of these differences.

- A fund may invest in the entire index or in a representative sample. With "complete replication" such as you would find in a large S&P 500 Index fund, the fund would invest in all 500 companies and weight them as they are in the index. However, smaller funds or those tracking very large indices, such as the Wilshire 5000, invest in a sample chosen from the index. The sample chosen determines how funds perform relative to the benchmark and each other.

- Funds with the same stated objectives may use different target benchmarks, resulting in significantly different returns. For example, a small-cap index fund might track the Russell 2000 Index, the S&P Smallcap 600, the Schwab Smallcap Index, the Wilshire Smallcap Index, or the CRSD Index 10.

- An index, by definition, has no expenses. Therefore, a managed portfolio must outperform its benchmark to stay even after expenses. Expense ratios on index funds are often the primary reason for performance differences. All else being equal, an index fund with a higher expense ratio will underperform its benchmark and its peers.

- A fund's ability to handle cash flow also affects performance. "Cash drag" occurs when new money to the fund is not invested in a timely fashion, resulting in stocks being purchased at higher prices. In a rising market even a one-day delay can impact returns. Funds with multiple distribution channels are likely to be affected by cash drag.

The general consensus among market experts is that index funds are best used in markets that are efficient, such as largecap stocks and high-quality bonds, where it is difficult for active fund managers to add value after expenses. A listing of index funds is found in Table 12–12.

Bond Funds

Investors buy bond funds for some of the same reasons that they buy other types of mutual funds: professional management, diversification, and the ability to purchase in small amounts. However, in some situations, individual bonds might be a better choice. If you are buying high-quality

Table 12–12. Index Mutual Funds

Fund (Symbol)	Index Followed
Stock Funds	
Aon Funds: S&P 500 Index (ASPYX)	S&P 500
Dreyfus Index Funds: S&P 500 Index (PEOPX)	S&P 500
Fidelity Spartan Market Index (FSMKX)	S&P 500
Galaxy Funds II: Large Company Index (ILCIX)	S&P 500
Northern Stock Index (NOSIX)	S&P 500
S&P 500 Index, CCM Partners (SPFIX)	S&P 500
Schwab S&P 500/Inv (SWPIX)	S&P 500
Scudder S&P 500 Index (SCPIX)	S&P 500
SsgA: S&P 500 Index (SVSPX)	S&P 500
Strong Index 500 (SINEX)	S&P 500
T. Rowe Price Equity Index 500 (PREIX)	S&P 500
USAA S&P 500 Index (USSPX)	S&P 500
Vanguard 500 Index (VFINX)	S&P 500
Vanguard Growth Index (VIGRX)	S&P 500/BARRA Growth
Vanguard Value Index (VIVAX)	S&P 500/BARRA Value
Dreyfus Index Funds: Midcap Index (PESPX)	S&P Midcap 400
S&P Midcap Index, CCM Partners (SPMIX)	S&P Midcap 400
Galaxy Funds II: Small Company Index (ISCIX)	S&P Smallcap 600
Schwab Smallcap Index Fund/Inv (SWSMX)	Schwab Smallcap 1000
Rydex Srs Tr: OTC Fund/Inv (RYOCX)	NASDAQ 100
Vanguard Smallcap Index (NAESX)	Russell 2000
Vanguard Extended Market Index (VEXMX)	Wilshire 4500
Fidelity Spartan Total Market Index (FSTMX)	Wilshire 5000
Vanguard Total Stock Market Index (VTSMX)	Wilshire 5000
Vanguard Balanced Index (VBINX)	60% Wilshire 5000/40% Lehman Aggregate Bond
Galaxy Funds II: Utility Index (IUTLX)	S&P Utilities
Guinness Flight Wired Index Fund (GFWIX)	*Wired* Index of Hot Tech Stocks
American Century: Global Gold/Inv (BGEIX)	FTSE Gold Mines
Aon Funds: REIT Index (AREYX)	Morgan Stanley REIT
Vanguard REIT Index (VGISX)	Morgan Stanley REIT
International Funds	
Vanguard Total International (VGTSX)	MSCI EAFA + MSCI Emerging Markets Free
Vanguard Emerging Markets Stock Index (VEIEX)	MSCI Emerging Markets Free
Vanguard European Stock Index (VEURX)	MSCI Europe
Vanguard Pacific Stock Index (VPACX)	MSCI Pacific
Schwab International Index/Investor (SWINX)	Schwab International

(Continued)

Table 12–12. Index Mutual Funds—*Cont.*

Fund (Symbol)	Index Followed
Bond Funds	
Galaxy Funds II: U.S. Treasury Index/Ret A (IUTIX)	Galaxy U.S. Treasury
Schwab Total Bond Market Index (SWLBX)	Lehman Aggregate Bond
Vanguard Total Bond Market Index (VBMFX)	Lehman Aggregate Bond
Vanguard Intermediate-Term Bond Index (VBIIX)	Lehman Fund Intermed (5–10) Govt/Corp
Vanguard Long-Term Bond Index (VBLTX)	Lehman Fund Long (10+) Govt/Corp
Schwab Short-Term Bond Market Index (SWBDX)	Lehman Fund Short (1–5) Govt/Corp
Vanguard Short-Term Bond Index (VBISX)	Lehman Fund Short (1–5) Govt/Corp

bonds or bond funds, rated BBB/Baa or higher and often insured bonds, the value added with diversification is slight because there is little risk that a highly rated bond will default. If you are buying highly rated bonds or funds with no intention of trading for short-term gains, there is little need for professional management. Through a bond fund you will get diversification and professional management that you may not need and you will pay for it with an average expense ratio near 1.00%. Thus, you will sacrifice 1.00% of your total return for unnecessary "advantages."

If you purchase bond funds because you can buy in small dollar amounts, there is certainly value added when purchasing a fund. Still, compare open-ended funds to UITs which may have front-end loads but lower annual expenses.

If you purchase bond funds, especially U.S. government bond funds, for their safety of principal be aware that if interest rates rise the prices of the bonds held in the fund's portfolio will fall, causing your NAV to fall. The same thing can happen if you buy individual bonds; but if you hold them until maturity, you will receive your par value and not lose principal. Because a bond fund never matures, you do not have this guarantee of getting your principal back. As NAVs fall, investors may rush in to redeem their shares, causing the fund to liquidate bonds, thus locking in the loss in principal.

Who Owns Mutual Funds?

The typical mutual fund investor, according to the Investment Company Institute's *1998 Profile of Mutual Fund Shareholders*, is an average American: middle-aged, married, and concerned about saving for retirement.[6] The survey of more than 1,400 financial decision makers conducted by the Investment Company Institute uncovered the following characteristics of mutual fund investors.[7]

- The median age of the primary decision maker in households that own mutual funds is 44 years; 68% are married and 50% have college or higher degrees.

- The median household income of mutual fund investors is $55,000 and median level of financial assets is $80,000. Of those financial assets, the median amount invested in mutual funds is $25,000.

- The typical mutual fund investor owns four different funds, in two different fund families.

- 62% own mutual funds inside employer-sponsored retirement plans and 54% own funds outside such plans, while 77% of all owners consider retirement to be their primary financial goal.

Top Stock Mutual Funds of the 1990s

The close of 1999 brought a rush to compile a list of the best investments of the decade. Table 12–13 lists diversified stock funds, excluding sector-specific funds, as provided by Lipper, Inc. Data is for total returns (dividends reinvested) for the period from December 31, 1989, to December 31, 1999. When multiple classes of shares of a fund made the list, only the top performer is included.

Summary

Mutual funds have a place in nearly every investor's portfolio. If you are just getting started, they offer diversification for a low minimum investment. Using an automatic investment plan makes it easy to get in the habit of paying yourself first and provides the added benefit of dollar cost

---

[6]Investment Company Institute, "1998 Profile of Mutual Fund Shareholders."
[7]Ibid.

Table 12–13. Top 25 Stock Mutual Funds of the 1990s

Fund	Cumulative Total Return (%)	Annualized Total Return (%)
Putnam New Opportunities*	1,240	32.06
RS Emerging Growth	1,130	28.52
Van Kampen Emerging Growth A	1,073	27.92
Janus Twenty	982	26.88
Spectra Fund	939	26.38
MFS Emerging Growth B	826	24.93
United New Concepts A	817	24.80
Managers Capital Appreciation	807	24.68
American Century Ultra	791	24.44
Fidelity Advisors Equity Growth	775	24.22
Putnam OTC Emerging Growth	775	24.22
INVESCO Dynamics	764	24.07
Dreyfus/Founders Discovery F	757	23.96
Harbor Capital Appreciation	739	23.70
Fidelity Growth Company	734	23.63
PBHG Growth	732	23.60
Janus Venture	730	23.57
IDEX JCC Growth T	713	23.32
AIM Aggressive Growth A	695	23.04
Fidelity OTC	684	22.86
Oppenheimer Mainstay Growth & Inc. A	666	22.58
Fidelity Contrafund	653	22.38
Mainstay Capital Appreciation B	639	22.15
Pilgrim Small Cap Opportunity T	637	22.11
Putnam Voyager A	635	22.08
Average All Funds	342	15.39

*From inception date 8/31/90.
SOURCE: Lipper, Inc.

averaging. For the established investor who may enjoy managing a portfolio of stocks and bonds, mutual funds can still be useful. They provide professional management for forays into international markets and can be a good way to diversify an investment style.

Professional management is one advantage of mutual funds, but a wide disparity exists in the performance of different funds. Buy and hold is a good rule of thumb, but not if your fund consistently underperforms its peer group. Evaluate returns at least annually, using benchmarks from Morningstar Mutual Funds and Lipper, Inc. as well as the appropriate indices.

Consider costs when evaluating mutual funds. Some high-cost funds may have exceptional performance over the short term, but long-term, high costs are a drag on investment returns. Always consider the cost of commissions when analyzing mutual funds. A commission is there to pay for the advice of a financial planner. If you need assistance, advice, and ideas, then expect to pay for them. If you handle your own research and transactions, then buy no-load funds; the absence of a commission is payment for your time spent.

Appendix: Contact Information for Large Mutual Fund Companies

Contact information for many popular fund companies follows.

AIM Advisors

P.O. Box 4739

Houston, TX 77210-4739

800-959-4246

800-AIM-LINE (246-5463)
  Automated Investor Line

www.aimfunds.com

Alliance Capital

P.O. Box 786003

San Antonio, TX 78278-6003

800-221-5672 or 201-553-3300
  Monday through Friday, 8:30 AM
  to 8:00 PM, EST

800-251-0539 Alliance Answer, 24
  hours, 7 days a week

www.alliancecapital.com

American Century

P.O. Box 419200

Kansas City, MO 64141-6200

800-345-2021 Individual or IRA
  Investors

888-345-2431, extension 4545
  Rollover IRA Accounts

800-345-8765 Automated Account
  Information

www.americancentury.com

American Funds

Regional Service Centers:

East:

P.O. Box 2280

Norfolk, VA 23501-2280

Eastern Midwest:

P.O. Box 6007

Indianapolis, IN 46206-6007

Western Midwest:

P.O. Box 659522

San Antonio, TX 78265-9522

West:

P.O. Box 2205

Brea, CA 92822-2205

800-421-0180, extension 23

714-671-7000 collect from outside
  the United States

www.americanfunds.com

Berger Funds
P.O. Box 219958
Kansas City, MO 64121-9958
800-551-5849
800-333-1001 Literature Requests
www.bergerfunds.com

Calamos Asset Management
1111 East Warrenville Road
Naperville, IL 60563-1593
800-323-9943
www.calamos.com

Charles Schwab
Use branch locator at website for
nearest office
800-225-8570
www.schwab.com

Delaware Capital Management
1818 Market Street
Philadelphia, PA 19103
800-523-1918
800-362-FUND (800-362-3863)
Automated Account Information

Dodge & Cox Funds
c/o Boston Financial Data Services
P.O. Box 9051
Boston, MA 02205-9051
800-621-3979
www.dodgeandcox.com

Dreyfus Service Corporation
144 Glenn Curtiss Boulevard
Uniondale, NY 11556
800-782-6620 Mutual Fund Sales
Representatives
800-472-5990 Market
Commentaries
800-645-6561 Automated Account
Information
www.dreyfus.com

Eaton Vance Distributors
The Eaton Vance Building
225 State Street
Boston, MA 02109
800-262-1122
www.eatonvance.com

Federated Investors
Federated Investors Tower
Pittsburgh, PA 15222-3779
800-341-7400
www.federated.com

Fidelity Investments
Brokerage Services:
P.O. Box 770001
Cincinnati, OH 45277
Mutual Fund Services:
Retirement:
P.O. Box 660602
Dallas, TX 75266-0602

Non-Retirement:

P.O. Box 193

Boston, MA 02101-0193

800-544-6666 Account Information and Service

800-544-4774 Retirement Specialists

800-544-5650 Rollover Specialists

800-544-2442 Annuity Specialists

www.fidelity.com

Founders Funds

P.O. Box 173655

Denver, CO 80217-3655

800-525-2440

www.founders.com

Franklin-Templeton

P.O. Box 2258

Rancho Cordova, CA 95741-2258

800-632-2301

www.franklintempleton.com

Gabelli Asset Management

One Corporate Center

Rye, NY 10580

800-872-5365 Open-End Mutual Funds

800-336-6983 Closed-End Mutual Funds

www.gabelli.com

Harbor Funds

c/o Harbor Transfer, Inc.

P.O. Box 10048

Toledo, OH 43699-0048

800-422-1050

www.harborfunds.com

IDEX Investor Services

P.O. Box 9015

Clearwater, FL 33758-9015

888-233-4339

www.idexfunds.com

INVESCO Funds

P.O. Box 173706

Denver, CO 80217

800-675-1705

www.invescofunds.com

Janus

P.O. Box 173375

Denver, CO 80217-3375

800-525-3713 Monday through Friday 8:00 AM to 8:00 PM, Saturday 10:00 AM to 4:00 PM, EST

888-979-7737 Automated Account Information

www.janus.com

Kaufmann Fund

140 East 45th Street, 43rd Floor

New York, NY 10017

800-922-0555

www.kaufmann.com

Kemper Funds

P.O. Box 219151

Kansas City, MO 64141-6151

800-621-1048 Monday through
Friday 7:00 AM to 6:00 PM,
Saturday 8:00 AM to 3:00 PM, CST

800-972-3060 Automated Account
Information

www.kemper.com

Legg Mason

100 Light Street, 7th Floor

P.O. Box 1476

Baltimore, MD 21203-1476

800-822-5544

www.leggmason.com

Liberty Funds Services

P.O. Box 1722

Boston, MA 02105-1722

800-799-7526 Transaction Department

800-345-6611 Automated Account
Information

www.libertyfunds.com

Lord, Abbett & Co.

767 Fifth Avenue

11th Floor

New York, NY 10153

800-874-3733

www.lordabbett.com

Mainstay Funds

300 Interpace Parkway, Building A

Parsippany, NY 07504

800-624-6782

www.mainstayfunds.com

Managers Funds

40 Richards Avenue

Norwalk, CT 06854

800-835-3879

www.managersfunds.com

Marsico Funds

Sunstone Financial Group

P.O. Box 3210

Milwaukee, WI 53201-3210

888-860-8686

www.marsicofunds.com

MFS

P.O. Box 2281

Boston, MA 02107-9906

800-637-2929 Product
Information

800-MFS-TALK (800-637-8255)
Automated Account Information

www.mfs.com

Neuberger Berman Management Inc.

Attn: Retail Services

605 Third Avenue

2nd Floor

New York, NY 10158-0180

800-877-9700

www.nbfunds.com

PBHG Funds

P.O. Box 219534

Kansas City, MO 64121

800-433-0051 Representatives available Monday through Friday 8:00 AM to 7:00 PM, EST, Automated 24 hours, 7 days

www.pbhgfunds.com

PIMCO (Pacific Investment Management Company)

840 Newport Center Drive

Newport Beach, CA 92660

800-927-4648

www.pimco.com

Pioneer Investments

60 State Street

Boston, MA 02109

800-225-6292

800-622-0176 Retirement Plans

800-225-4321 Automated Account Information

www.pioneerfunds.com

Putnam Investor Services

P.O. Box 41203

Providence, RI 02940-1203

888-4PUTNAM (888-478-8626)

800-225-1581

www.putnaminv.com

Scudder Funds

P.O. Box 2291

Boston, MA 02107-2291

800-SCUDDER Representatives available Monday through Friday 8:00 AM to 7:00 PM, EST, Automated 24 hours, 7 days for a free prospectus

www.scudder.com

Stein Roe Mutual Funds

P.O. Box 8900

Boston, MA 02205-8900

800-338-2550

www.steinroe.com

Strong Funds

P.O. Box 2936

Milwaukee, WI 53201

800-359-3379 Investor Services

800-359-3329 Fund Literature

800-588-4472 Retirement Assistance

800-362-6275 Automated Account Information

www.estrong.com

T. Rowe Price

P.O Box 17630

Baltimore, MD 21297-1630

800-225-5132 Monday through Friday 8:00 AM to 10:00 PM, weekends 8:30 AM to 5:00 PM, EST

800-922-9945 Retirement information, Monday through Friday 8:30 AM to 10:00 PM, EST

800-638-2587 Automated Information Line

www.troweprice.com

TIAA-CREF

730 Third Avenue

New York, NY 10017-3206

800-223-1200

www.tiaa-cref.com

United Funds/Waddell & Reed

P.O. Box 29217

Shawnee Mission, KS 66201-9217

888-923-3355

www.waddell.com

The Vanguard Group

P.O. Box 1110

Valley Forge, PA 19482

888-285-4563 Monday through
Friday 8:00 AM to 10:00 PM,
Saturday 9:00 AM to
4:00 PM EST

800-662-6273 Automated
Information Line

www.vanguard.com

Van Kampen Investor Services

7501 Tiffany Springs Parkway

Kansas City, MO 64153

800-341-2911

www.vankampen.com

Warburg Pincus Funds

P.O. Box 9030

Boston, MA 02205-9030

800-WARBURG (800-927-2874)

www.warburg.com

13

Life Insurance and Annuities

Disagreement abounds in the financial community about whether life insurance should be used as an investment and whether the advantages of annuities outweigh the disadvantages. This chapter will cover the basics of both products and touch on each side of the argument.

Life Insurance

Who Needs Life Insurance?

Life insurance, even when it is not purchased for its investment characteristics, is still a part of planning for financial security. In its simplest application, if anyone depends upon your income, then you need life insurance. Additionally, if you have debts, such as a mortgage, which would be a burden to those left behind, you need life insurance. Other applications of life insurance include its use for estate tax payment, the buyout of a closely held business, and charitable contributions.

Those who do not need life insurance include children, because they do not have dependents. At most, they need enough for burial costs. Retired persons without estate tax problems should reassess their life insurance needs. If they are living on the proceeds of investments that will be passed on to a surviving spouse, there may be no need for life insurance.

How Much Life Insurance Is Necessary?

There are hundreds of insurance formulas or calculators available on the internet. QuickenInsurance offers one at *www.insuremarket.com*. It takes about five minutes to complete and includes funeral expenses, debts and loans, household bills, mortgages, the ages of your children, public or private college tuition, income taxes for the year of your death, legal fees, other obligations, and an emergency fund of your choice. It also takes into account present family income, existing life insurance benefits and current retirement savings.

When making a decision about how much life insurance you need, consider some of the following issues.

- This is not a lottery for your family. Plan to buy enough insurance to provide for their needs, not a windfall to make them wildly rich. You may live to a ripe old age and would be much better served buying reasonable amounts of insurance and investing other available funds so that you and your family can use them.

- Periodically evaluate not only who is dependent upon your income, but also how dependent they are. For example, your insurance needs at the age of 30, with a nonworking spouse and three small children are much different than your needs at 50 with a spouse who is ready to return to the workforce and three children on the brink of becoming self-sufficient. A formula might calculate the same insurance requirement for both scenarios if it simply considers four dependents.

- Remember that you have other assets available to support your family. Avoid the trap of deciding how much they will need, then buying a policy with this amount as the death benefit.

- Plan to cover any family debts, especially a mortgage, so that your spouse will not be burdened. Periodically reevaluate this amount as you pay down your mortgage.

- Consider the values you would have if you were alive (which you probably will be). If you had planned for your children to pay for half of their college educations, then plan to fund just half of college costs with life insurance, not all of it as many formulas do. Since chances are that you will be around when they are in college, investing the premium dollars saved could fund half the expenses, or more.

If you use a formula or calculator, view the results with a good dose of common sense and enlist the aid of a financial professional for complicated issues such as estate tax planning, charitable giving, or the buyout of a business partnership.

Types of Life Insurance

Once you know that you need life insurance and have decided how much you need, you are ready for the hard part: deciphering the many policies available.

All life insurance policies have the following:

- An owner: the person who pays for the policy
- An insured: the person whose death is covered
- Premiums: the cost of the insurance, in one or more payments
- A death benefit: the amount that will be paid if the insured dies while the policy is in force
- A beneficiary: the person(s) who receives the death benefit

Life insurance can be divided into two categories, term and cash value, depending on whether the policy is pure insurance or insurance plus an investment.

Term Life Insurance. Term life insurance is pure insurance protection for a specified period of time. The death benefit, also called the face amount, is payable upon the insured person's death, if it occurs before the policy's maturity date, assuming all premiums have been paid. Premiums are the periodic payments for the insurance, and are based on the policy's death benefit and the insured's age. Logically, the younger you are, the lower your premiums will be because there is less risk that the insurance company will have to pay the death benefit. When compared with cash value policies, term life insurance offers the highest death benefit for the lowest premium.

One drawback of term insurance is that at the end of the term, you must qualify for insurance again (called providing evidence of insurability) in order to get another term policy. Two options, whose inclusion will increase premium amounts, offer protection in the event that health problems would prevent you from qualifying. They are:

- Renewability is the right to renew term insurance on the renewal (maturity) date without evidence of insurability. This does not lock in a premium, which will be based on your age at renewal.
- Convertibility is the right of the insured to convert a term policy to a permanent (cash value) policy without evidence of insurability. The premium for a converted policy is based on your age at conversion.

Types of Term Insurance. The three types of term insurance are level, decreasing, and increasing term insurance. Following is a brief discussion of each.

- Level term insurance has a death benefit of the same amount from the effective date of the policy through the maturity date (see Figure 13–1). Premiums do not change over the life of the policy.

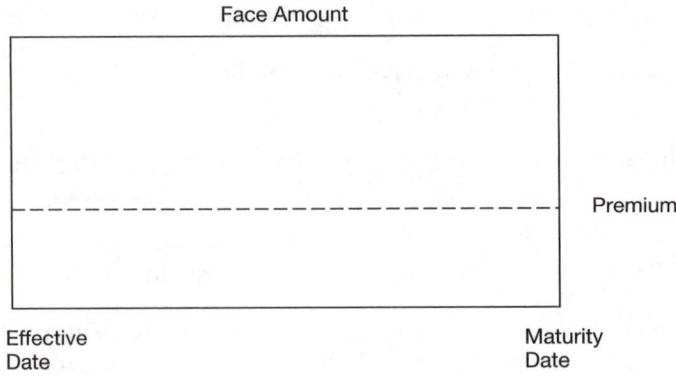

Figure 13–1. Level Term Insurance

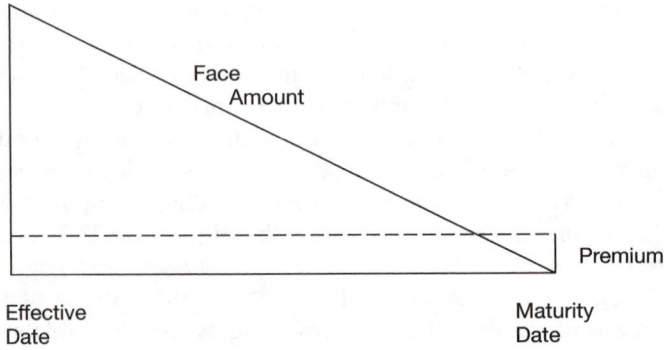

Figure 13–2. Decreasing Term Insurance

- Decreasing term insurance has a death benefit which decreases from the effective date through the maturity date (see Figure 13–2). Premiums stay the same, at a lower level than a comparable level term policy. This type of insurance might be used when insuring against the burden of a mortgage. As time passes and the mortgage is paid down, the amount of insurance necessary to cover the debt decreases. Decreasing term insurance is generally the lowest cost term insurance because the amount of the death benefit decreases as the risk that it will be paid increases.

- Increasing term insurance has a death benefit which increases from the effective date of the policy through the maturity date (see Figure 13–3). This type of insurance might be considered by a young person who expects family obligations to grow but wants to lock in a low premium.

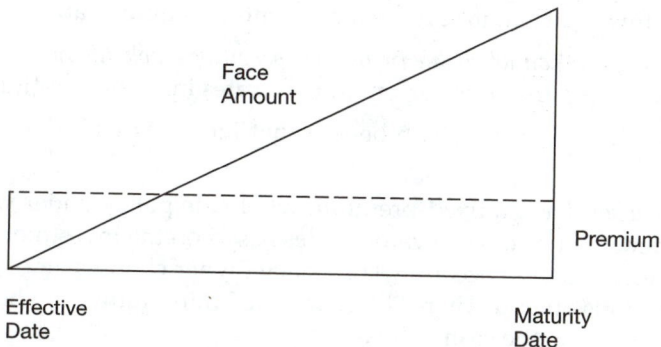

Figure 13–3. Increasing Term Insurance

Cash Value Life Insurance. Cash value life insurance, also called permanent life insurance, promises to protect you for your entire life, not just a stated number of years. Cash value policies combine pure insurance with an investment account, funded by a premium paid in excess of the actual cost of insurance. This accumulation account has a cash value and grows each year, tax deferred. If the accumulation account grows quickly enough, your annual premiums may decrease or disappear entirely as the interest earned on the accumulation account pays them. Subject to the conditions of the policy, you may borrow against the cash value of the account. The cash value in the account, less any surrender charges and outstanding loans, is available should you terminate (surrender) the policy.

Whole Life Insurance. Whole life insurance offers permanent protection while building cash value in an accumulation account managed by the insurance company. Several different types of whole life insurance exist; all have fixed premiums but differ in the timing and amount of premiums paid.

- *Straight life* (also called continuous or ordinary life) has level premiums over the life of the insured.

- *Limited payment* has higher annual premiums paid over a shorter period of time. Toward the end of the policy, which might likely be during retirement, no premiums are paid.

- *Single premium whole life* has an initial lump-sum premium payment, which creates an immediate cash value.

- *Modified life* has premiums in the first three to five years that are lower than straight life and later premiums that are higher than straight life.

- *Graded-premium whole life* has premiums that begin at less than 50% of straight life and increase annually for 5 to 20 years, then remain level thereafter.

- *Indeterminate premium* has premiums that may vary according to investment returns but cannot exceed a maximum premium cap.
- *Current assumption whole life* or *interest sensitive whole life* has indeterminate premiums and uses current interest rates in its assumptions.
- *Indexed whole life* has a death benefit that increases with the consumer price index.
- *Variable whole life* is a fixed-premium whole life policy under which the death benefit and/or cash value varies based on the investment returns of the accumulation account. The policy owner chooses among investment options offered. There is a guaranteed minimum death benefit but no guarantee on the cash value.

Universal Life Insurance. Universal life policies offer the policyholder some flexibility in both premiums and the policy's face amount or death benefit. Within limits, the policyowner can decide how much to pay in premiums. The premiums on universal life policies are not guaranteed as in whole life and term policies, but are projected based on assumptions of the returns on the policy's accumulation account and the ability of those returns to subsidize premium payments. Actual premiums required may be higher or lower depending on the returns of investments in the accumulation account. Subject to insurability, the death benefit may be increased or decreased as the owner chooses. Market returns can vary greatly over the life of a policy, making universal life policies more risky than whole life and term policies due to the possibility that premiums may be higher than initially projected.

The accumulation accounts of straight universal life policies earn market rates with a guaranteed minimum: accumulation accounts of variable universal life policies earn interest based on investment choices that are like individual mutual funds, similar to variable whole life policies. As the owner of a variable universal life policy, you may choose investment accounts with different combinations of stocks and bonds. Variable universal life offers the flexibility of universal life but without the guarantee of minimum cash values or investment returns.

Table 13–1 displays features of the different life insurance policies.

Taxation of Insurance

Part of the appeal of insurance products is their tax treatment. The death benefit on life insurance is not included in the income of the beneficiary for tax purposes. As the accumulation account of cash value policies grows, it grows tax deferred, meaning that current income taxes are not due as they would be on an ordinary investment.

Table 13–1. Features of Life Insurance Policies

Type of Policy	Flexible Premium	Flexible Death Benefit	Choice of Investment Accounts	Guaranteed Minimum Return
Term life	No	No	N/A	N/A
Whole life	No	No	No	Yes
Variable whole life	No	No	Yes	No
Universal life	Yes	Yes	No	Yes
Variable Universal life	Yes	Yes	Yes	No

The cash value of a policy can be withdrawn tax free until the withdrawals exceed the amount of premiums that have been paid into the policy. Note, however, that these withdrawals reduce the policy death benefit by the amount of cash withdrawn.

Evaluating Insurance Companies

The promise of a death benefit or return of your cash value is only as good as the financial solvency of the company standing behind it. Several well-known services evaluate the insurer's ability to pay future claims to policyholders and publish ratings for the consumer. Check ratings by contacting any of the following:

A.M. Best

Ambest Road

Oldwick, NJ 08858

(908) 439-2200

www.ambest.com

Top ratings: A++, A+, A

Duff & Phelps Credit Rating Company

17 State Street, 12th Floor

New York, NY

(212) 908-0200

www.dcrco.com

Top ratings: AAA, AA+, AA

Standard & Poor's Insurance Rating Services

25 Broadway

New York, NY 10004

(212) 208-8000

www.standardandpoors.com

Top ratings: AAA, AA+, AA

Moody's Investor's Service

99 Church Street

New York, NY 10007

(212) 553-0300

www.moodys.com

Top ratings: Aaa, Aa1, Aa2

Weiss Ratings Hotline	(800) 289-9222
P.O. Box 109665	*www.weissratings.com*
Palm Beach Gardens, FL 33410	Top ratings: A, B

Only consider insurers that have been rated by at least two rating companies and consistently receive ratings in the top three categories. Check your insurer's ratings annually. Most insurers will provide ratings or you may check with the rating companies, often online. Many independent, informational websites, such as Insure.com (www.insure.com), provide insurance company ratings. This site provides insurance company financial profiles and ratings from Standard & Poor's and Duff & Phelps.

Insurance as an Investment

The argument for using insurance as an investment hinges upon the tax deferral of growth in the accumulation account. Also key is the ability of the policyholder to borrow or withdraw cash value should the need arise. The argument can only be rationally considered in the case that insurance is necessary. Due to the cost of the insurance (i.e., cost to the insurance company of providing a death benefit, which is called mortality cost), it will never make sense to purchase insurance purely as an investment.

If you need life insurance, should you buy term insurance, which is much cheaper than cash value insurance, and invest the difference? There are several issues to consider.

- Your ability to pay premiums. First, determine how much insurance you need. Then check the premium cost for both term and cash value policies. If you can only afford the term policy, go term. Never skimp on the amount of the death benefit.

- Your tax bracket, both federal and state. The benefit of tax deferral is only as valuable as the amount of taxes you would be deferring. The higher your tax bracket the more valuable it is.

- The possibility that you might not be able to qualify for insurance later. Some people use this argument to insure children, who should never be insured if you can afford burial costs. As an adult with potential health issues, it may be more of a concern. If it is, compare guaranteed renewable term with permanent cash value policies.

- Your willingness to shop for no-load (i.e., no commission) insurance policies. Unless you buy no- or low-load insurance policies, the costs of cash value policies drag down returns so much that it almost always makes more sense to buy term and invest the difference.

- Your investing discipline. Buying term and investing the difference between cost of a term and a cash value policy requires that you be disciplined enough to actually invest the difference. If your nature is such that you will pay monthly life insurance premiums but will not always make monthly payments to a mutual fund, consider a cash value policy even if the returns are lower than buying term and investing in a mutual fund. An investment with mediocre returns is better than no investment at all.

Shopping the Internet for Insurance

If you have decided on life insurance, either term or cash value, the internet is a great place to comparison shop. Two types of sites are available, aggregators and online insurance companies. The aggregators provide one-stop shopping for insurance quotes. They promise to shop for the best-priced policy, given your chosen parameters. Online insurance companies include both direct companies, such as Progressive and GEICO which once operated by 800 numbers, and mail and agent-driven companies, such as State Farm and Travelers which use the sites as an alternative distribution or to generate leads for their agents. Gomez Advisors, at *www.gomez.com,* is a market research and analysis firm in Lincoln, Massachusetts, that ranked online insurance sites in the winter of 1999. The top 20 for overall performance are listed in Table 13–2.

Table 13–2. Insurance Websites

Company	Website
1. Insweb	*Insweb.com*
2. QuickenInsurance	*quickeninsurance.com*
3. AIGdirect.com	*aigdirect.com*
4. State Farm Insurance	*statefarm.com*
5. Electric Insurance Company	*electricinsurance.com*
6. Quotesmith.com	*quotesmith.com*
7. Progressive Insurance	*1.progressive.com*
8. Prudential Insurance	*prudential.com*
9. GE Financial Network	*gefn.com*
10. Youdecide.com	*youdecide.com*
11. Amica	*amica.com*
12. Liberty Mutual	*libertymutual.com*
13. 1stQuoteNetwork	*1stquote.com*
14. QuickQuote	*quickquote.com*
15. 4freequotes.com	*4freequotes.com*
16. SecureLife	*securelife.com*
17. AccuQuote	*accuquotelife.com*
18. GEICO Insurance	*geico.com*
19. IntelliQuote.com	*intelliquote.com*
20. Fidelity Investments Life Insurance	*Personal400.fidelity.com*

SOURCE: Gomez Advisors at *www.gomez.com.*

Annuities

An annuity is a tax-deferred investment packaged within an insurance product. Contributions to an annuity are not tax deductible, but the earnings in the investment account are not subject to income taxes until they are withdrawn. There are penalties for withdrawing the funds invested in an annuity before reaching age 59.5.

An annuity has two distinct phases, accumulation and distribution. You contribute funds to the annuity during the accumulation phase and the money invested grows, tax deferred. During the distribution phase, you withdraw money, either in one lump-sum payment or in a stream of payments, called an annuity. The annuity payments can come either over a specified time period or over the rest of your life.

Annuities are purchased for several reasons:

- Their ability to defer taxes while investment returns are compounding

- The option of annuitizing for a life term, which will provide certain payments for the rest of your life during retirement

- The unlimited amount of money which can be put to work tax deferred, after retirement plan limits have been reached

- An offer of a guaranteed death benefit, in which the insurer promises to pay beneficiaries the greater of the premiums paid in or the value of the account

Annuity Choices

You can choose from many different features when purchasing an annuity, some of which are discussed here.

Investment Style: Fixed or Variable. A fixed annuity offers a set return, similar to a certificate of deposit. Periodically, the rate comes up for renewal, based on current interest rates. You can choose to lock in your rate for different time periods.

A variable annuity allows you to choose among subaccounts, similar to mutual funds, to invest your money. Investment objectives range from money market accounts to aggressive stock funds. Most companies will allow you to choose a combination of different accounts and to switch between accounts at least four times per year.

Money Returns: Deferred or Immediate. Most annuities are deferred annuities, meaning that during an extended accumulation phase, contributions are made to the annuity, before annuitization begins. An immediate annuity begins paying right away.

Payout Options: Life or Period Certain. Several payout options are available, in addition to a lump-sum distribution. They are all variations of life income payments or payments over a certain time period.

- Life income or straight life: Annuity payments are made as long as the owner lives.

- Temporary annuity certain: The annuity is payable for a fixed amount or fixed time period, whether the owner lives or dies. If the annuitant dies, payments are made to a beneficiary.

- Life income period certain: The annuity is payable over the owner's life, with a minimum period. For example, "life income, 10 years certain" means that if the owner dies after 5 years, a beneficiary will continue to receive payments until the tenth year. If the owner lives past 10 years, payments will continue throughout, but will not exceed the owner's lifetime.

- Life income with refund: The annuity is payable over the owner's lifetime. If the owner dies before receiving an amount equal to payments made into the plan, a beneficiary will receive the balance.

- Life income joint and survivor: The annuity is payable to two or more people while they are living. Upon the death of the first, payments will continue, sometimes at a reduced rate.

- Joint life: The annuity is payable to two or more annuitants while both are living. Payments stop upon the death of either annuitant.

Fees

The main reason not to invest in annuities is the fees charged. In many cases, high fees outweigh the benefits of tax deferral. Fees are often quoted in basis points instead of percentage points. To convert, place a decimal in front of the last two numbers. For example, 125 basis points equals 1.25% and 60 basis points equals 0.60%. Some fees to note are as follows:

- Sales commissions: Often running as high as 7% of the amount contributed, commissions are not explicitly charged to the account. However, the money has to come from somewhere. Often it shows up in the form of higher asset charges.

- Mortality and expense/asset charges: Similar to the cost of insurance in a cash value life insurance policy, this is the cost of providing guaranteed death benefits and guaranteed lifetime payments to those who outlive their life expectancy. This fee may also include some general expenses, such as the cost of paying agents' commissions. According to the National Association of Variable Annuities (NAVA), the industry average is 1.15%.

- Management fees: The cost of managing each subaccount, management fees are also charged by mutual funds and differ depending on the particular subaccount chosen. According to NAVA, the industry average is 0.82%. This figure is greatly dependent on the type of securities held in the account. As with mutual funds, expect lower management fees on index and bond funds, and higher fees on actively managed stock funds.

- Annual contract charge: A maintenance fee ranging from $20 to $40 per account is typically charged.

- Surrender charges: On many annuities substantial penalties apply if you cash out in the first few years. Most surrender charges work the same way that a contingent deferred sales charge (CDSC) applies to a mutual fund sale, typically lasting for seven years, beginning at 7% and declining by 1% each year.

Taxation of Annuities

Taxes during the Accumulation Phase. As already noted, the primary attraction for investing in annuities is the favorable tax treatment of growth during the accumulation phase. In contrast to other investments held outside of an IRA, a retirement plan, or insurance contract, growth in the value of an annuity is not taxable as income until it is withdrawn, at which time it is taxable as ordinary income.

During the accumulation phase, funds may be transferred among different annuity subaccounts without taxation. In investments such as mutual funds or stocks, transferring money from one to another is a taxable event, in which the difference between the sales price and cost basis of the security sold is taxable as a capital gain or loss.

Taxes on Withdrawals. When money is withdrawn or paid out of an annuity, the amount of premiums paid in is treated as a return of capital and is not taxable. The gain in the account (difference between the account value and premiums paid) is taxable as ordinary income. Partial withdrawals are treated as if all interest or growth is withdrawn first. For example, if you took a $20,000 partial withdrawal from an annuity with a cost basis (premiums paid in) of $100,000 and a current value of $120,000, the full $20,000 would be taxable as ordinary income.

In a full surrender (withdrawal), the excess of the account value over premiums paid in would be taxable as ordinary income. In both cases, the withdrawals might also be subject to surrender charges and a 10% penalty tax, depending on their timing.

Penalty Taxes. If you make a partial or full withdrawal before reaching the age of 59.5, the IRS charges a 10% penalty on growth in the annuity's value. This penalty does not apply if

- the contract owner has died;
- the recipient has become disabled, as defined by federal law;
- the withdrawal is part of the annuitization process; or
- the annuity was purchased by an employer for an employee and held by the employer until the employee separates from service.

Taxes during the Distribution (Annuitization) Phase. During annuitization, a pro rata portion of each payment is considered ordinary income, based on the ratio of the growth in the account (computed as the account value less total premiums paid) to the entire account value. For lump-sum distributions, all growth is taxable as ordinary income. Lump-sum distributions carry the additional tax consideration that a large sum might push you into a higher tax bracket.

Premium Taxes. A few states tax the premiums paid into an annuity. Except for South Dakota, which taxes premiums when the contract is issued, taxes are levied when you surrender the policy or begin annuitization. The percentages differ based on whether the account is qualified or nonqualified. Qualified means the premiums were contributed pretax in an IRA or retirement plan; nonqualified means premiums were paid with money that had already been taxed. Table 13–3 provides a list as of March 2000 of state taxation of annuities.

Table 13–3. State Taxation of Annuities

State	Qualified (%)	Nonqualified (%)
California	0.5	2.35
Kentucky	2.0	1.9
Maine	0.0	2.0
Nevada	0.0	3.5
South Dakota	0.0	1.25
West Virginia	1.0	1.0
Wyoming	0.0	1.0

SOURCE: Annuity Net/State Tax Summary from ALCI.

Inheritance. Annuities do not receive favorable tax treatment upon the owner's death. The growth in the annuity account is taxed as ordinary income to heirs. In contrast, the appreciation of an ordinary mutual fund account escapes income taxes at death because heirs receive a "stepped-up" basis, meaning their cost basis is the value of the account at the time of death, rather than the previous owner's original cost basis.

1035 Exchanges. If you are not pleased with the performance of an annuity, you are not locked in until retirement. In a 1035 exchange (named for the section of the federal tax code that allows it), you can liquidate an annuity without owing taxes or penalties so long as you exchange it for another annuity. To be eligible for special treatment, the transaction must take place between the two insurance companies. You may still owe surrender charges to the insurance company.

Ordinary Income Tax versus Capital Gains Tax. All gains in the value of an annuity are taxed at ordinary income tax rates, which range as high as 39.6%. This is in contrast to gains on a mutual fund or stock investment which, if they are increases in the share price of the security, are taxed at capital gains rates of 20% if held for more than one year. This difference in taxation of an annuity's investment gains may cancel out any benefit of tax-deferred growth for investment accounts whose returns are derived primarily from capital appreciation.

Summary of Advantages and Disadvantages of Annuities

Advantages
- Growth in the account value is tax deferred.
- Transfers between subaccounts are not taxable events.
- Having a guaranteed death benefit means heirs will receive at least as much as was paid in premiums.
- A lifetime annuitization option means that payments will never run out.

Disadvantages
- Gains are treated as ordinary income rather than capital gains for tax purposes.
- The IRS imposes a 10% penalty for withdrawal before the age of 59.5.
- The IRS method for taxing withdrawals is interest first, principal second.

- High surrender charges often begin at 7% and last for seven years.
- Mortality and expense charges generally add 1% to fees found on comparable mutual funds.
- At death, growth in the account is taxable to heirs as ordinary income.

Annuities as an Investment

The overwhelming opinion of the investment community (excluding those in the business of selling annuities) is that the additional fees, tax treatment of proceeds, and lack of liquidity outweigh the benefit of tax deferral. That said, annuities may make sense under the following conditions.

- You have contributed the maximum allowable to your IRA and 401(k). Both of these avenues of retirement saving provide tax deferral without the additional expenses of annuities. Take maximum advantage of these before investing in annuities. Note: Do not buy an annuity in your IRA. There is no reason to pay the extra fees when the IRA provides tax deferral already.
- Your time horizon is at least 15 years and preferably 20 years, during which time you will gain significant benefit from tax deferral and will not be subject to high surrender charges.
- You expect your tax bracket to be lower in retirement.
- Your preferred investment funds have high turnover or high levels of income, which would result in a stiff tax bill for ordinary mutual funds.
- You are willing to search out no-load, low expense annuities. Consider annuities without a death benefit. Unless you make terrible investment choices, this is an expense without much value.
- You are not terribly concerned with leaving assets to your heirs, as they will have to pay income taxes on the growth of the account.
- You would like the peace of mind of knowing that lifetime annuitization means you will not outlive your payments.

Insure.com at *www.insure.com* has partnered with Morningstar to provide variable annuity performance reports online. Its VA performance tool's general search provides a report on requested annuities and the subaccount performance search sorts for variable annuities by star rating, investment objective, investment style, and annualized total returns, ranging from 3 months to 10 years.

Sources for no-load variable annuities are listed in Table 13–4.

Table 13-4. Sources for No-Load Variable Annuities

Policy Name or Annuity Distributor	Phone
Ameritas No-Load Variable Annuity	800-255-9678
John Hancock MarketPlace	888-742-6262
Janus Retirement Advantage	800-504-4440
Schwab Variable Annuity	800-838-0650
Scudder Horizon Plan	800-225-2470
T. Rowe Price No-Load Variable Annuity	800-469-6587
USAA Life Variable Annuity	800-531-6390
Vanguard Variable Annuity Plan	800-523-9954
Jack White Value Advantage	800-622-3699

Summary

As a general rule, life insurance and annuities are not good investments. The fees associated with cash value life insurance make it difficult for an insurance policy to beat the returns of buying term and investing the difference. The fees, lack of liquidity, tax treatment of gains, and taxation to heirs usually outweigh the benefits of tax deferral in an annuity.

However, there are instances in which insurance products can make sense as part of an investment portfolio. If you are considering using insurance or annuities as an investment, find no-load or low-load policies and carefully analyze the guaranteed and past (not illustrated) returns, as well as the financial status of the insurance company. If you already own insurance products with high fees or poor performance, consider a 1035 exchange into a more attractive policy.

If you have questions about life insurance or annuities, call the National Insurance Consumer Helpline (NICH) at 800-942-4242. Your state department of insurance should also be able to handle questions. You can find phone numbers at Insure.com.

14

Leveraging and Hedging with Options and Futures

Few investments occupy such a wide range of risk as options and futures. At the very low risk end of the spectrum, options and futures can be used to hedge or reduce the risk of loss in other investments. At a midpoint, they can be volatile, but the amount invested is the maximum loss. At the high end of the risk spectrum, losses can be unlimited. The strategy employed, not the instrument, is responsible for the risk involved. This chapter will outline the mechanics of options and futures and cover some common strategies and the risks and rewards involved.

Options

An option is a contract that gives its owner the right, but not the obligation, to buy or sell a security at a specific price within a designated time frame. The contract is generally for 100 shares of stock, usually expiring within eight months. More than 1,700 actively traded stocks and many indices have options based on them.

Puts and Calls

A call option gives its owner the right to buy (call away) 100 shares of stock. For example, a Dell Computer March 40 call gives its owner the right to buy 100 shares of Dell Computer at $40 per share, regardless of its current market price, at any time through its expiration date in March. The buyer of the call option is its owner. The initial seller, known as the writer of the call option, has the obligation to sell the shares of stock to the call owner if the owner chooses to exercise the option and buy them.

A put option gives its owner the right to sell 100 shares of stock. For example, a Dell Computer March 50 put gives its owner the right to sell 100 shares of Dell Computer at $50 per share, regardless of its current market price, at any time through its expiration date in March. The initial seller, known as the writer, of the put has the obligation to buy the shares if the put option owner chooses to exercise the option and sell them.

Each option contract has the following key components.

- Underlying security: The stock controlled by the option. In the previous examples, it is Dell Computer.

- Strike price: The price named in the option at which the call owner may buy or the put owner may sell the underlying security. On our Dell Computer March 40 call, the strike price is $40. Strike prices are set at 2 1/2-point (dollar) intervals for strike prices under $25, 5-point intervals when the strike price is between $25 and $200, and 10-point intervals when the strike price is above $200. Strike prices are adjusted for stock splits, so that when a stock splits 2-for-1, its strike prices are adjusted to one-half their former values.

- Expiration date: The last date upon which the option may be exercised. Options expiration dates are standardized so that all options expiring in a given month expire on the same day. This day is the Saturday following the third Friday of the month. The last day to buy or sell an expiring option is the Friday before it expires. Options are generally available for two near-term months plus two additional months from a quarterly cycle (January, April, July, October / February, May, August, November / March, June, September, December).

What Is an Option Worth?

The price paid for an option is called the premium. Options prices are quoted per share even though each contract controls 100 shares. For this reason, the premium quoted must be multiplied by $100 to obtain the actual contract price. Therefore, an option with a price of $4 would cost $400 per contract.

Initially, the premium goes to the writer of the contract as compensation for giving up control over the investment. After that transaction, the owner of the contract may sell it in the open market. It may change hands many times before expiration, with the premium each time going to the previous owner rather than the original writer.

The premium has two components:

- The intrinsic value (if any) of the option
- The time value of the option

The intrinsic value is the value you would receive if you exercised the option immediately (disregarding commissions for the sake of clarity). For a call, it is the amount by which the strike price of the option is less than the market price of the underlying security. For a put, it is the amount by which the strike price of the option is greater than the market price of the underlying security. If the strike price of the call is not less than the market price of the underlying security or the strike price of the put is not greater, the option has no intrinsic value. For example, if you purchased a Coca Cola February 55 call when the stock was trading at $60, the intrinsic value of the call would be as follows:

Market price of Coca Cola	$60.00
Less call option strike price	−$55.00
Intrinsic value	$5.00

In this case, if you were to exercise the option to purchase at $55, then immediately sell the stock at $60, you would realize a gain of $5 per share.

If you purchased a Coca Cola February 65 put when the stock was trading at $60, the intrinsic value of the put would be as follows:

Put option strike price	$65.00
Less market price of Coca Cola	−$60.00
Intrinsic value	$5.00

In this case, if you were to purchase the stock at $60, then immediately exercise your option to sell the stock at $65, you would realize a gain of $5 per share.

Options with intrinsic value are said to be "in the money." Those without intrinsic value are "out of the money." Options whose strike price is equal to the underlying security's market price are "at the money."

The intrinsic value is not the full story of what an option is worth. In January 2000, Coca Cola was trading at $60. The February 55 call had a price of $6.75 and the February 65 put had a price of $5.75. The intrinsic value of each was $5. The difference in the intrinsic value of an option and its market price is called its time value. This is the amount traders are willing to pay for the possibility that the underlying security will move in a favorable direction before the option expires. It is based on a combination of three factors:

- The amount of time remaining before the option expires

- The volatility of the underlying security
- The bias (expected direction) of both the underlying security and the market

The time value of an option decreases as it nears expiration. The time value of an in-the-money option will diminish until, at expiration, it trades at its intrinsic value. An out-of-the-money option, whose premium is entirely composed of time value, is worthless at expiration.

Using the previous two examples, time value of the call can be computed as follows:

Market price of Coca Cola	$60.00
Less call option strike price	−$55.00
Intrinsic value	$5.00
Call premium (price)	$6.75
Less intrinsic value	−$5.00
Time value	$1.75

And the time value of the put:

Put option strike price	$65.00
Less market price of Coca Cola	−$60.00
Intrinsic value	$5.00
Put premium (price)	$5.75
Less intrinsic value	−$5.00
Time value	$.75

The difference in the time value for the put and call implies an expectation that the price of Coca Cola is more likely to rise than fall.

Reading the Options Page

You can find daily listings of options transactions in *The Wall Street Journal* and *Investor's Business Daily*. An example of *Investor's Business Daily*'s January 10, 2000, listing for closing prices on January 7, 2000, is shown as Figure 14–1.

Underlying stock issues are listed in boldface with their closing prices to the right. Below, calls are listed first, in ascending strike price order, denoted by a *c* before the strike price. Puts are listed after calls, also in ascending strike price order, denoted by a *p* before the strike price. The next six columns are the volume (number of contracts traded) and closing price for the option on three different expiration dates. Open interest is the number of outstanding contracts of that strike price and expiration.

A24 Investor's Business Daily

Call (C) Put (P) Strike Price	Jan Vol.	Jan Last Price	Feb Vol.	Feb Last Price	Vol.	Last Price
eBay		Close 134¾				**Apr**
c120	251	18	3	2¼	no	tr
c130	114	12	3	17¾	14	25⅞
c140	255	7⅝	26	13½	8	20⅞
c150	146	5	105	12	46	18¼
c155	100	3⅝	4	9	no	tr
c160	220	2¾	6	7¾	21	17¼
p100	110	⅞	no	tr	1	8
p110	332	1 13/16	no	tr	no	tr
p115	119	3⅛	no	tr	5	12¾
p120	122	3⅞	1	9¾	no	tr
p125	144	5½	3	12⅝	1	17¾
p130	164	8⅜	no	tr	3	21
p135	120	11	1	17	no	tr
eToys		Close 21 9/16				**May**
c25	605	1	164	3⅛	no	tr
c30	185	⅜	261	1½	112	4
c35	614	3/16	53	13/16	no	tr
c40	52	⅞	116	9/16	12	2⅝
c65	no	tr	no	tr	260	1
p20	107	1¼	3	2 9/16	22	5

Call (C) Put (P) Strike Price	Jan Vol.	Jan Last Price	Feb Vol.	Feb Last Price	Vol.	Last Price
c120	155	⅛	552	9/16	3136	2¼
c140	no	tr	no	tr	155	1 5/16
p40	44	⅛	no	tr	113	15/16
p45	112	1/16	no	tr	150	1 13/16
p47½	270	3/16	no	tr	19	2 7/16
p50	840	1/16	no	tr	38	2⅞
p52½	608	5/16	no	tr	15	3¼
p55	187	⅜	no	tr	83	4¼
p57½	213	⅝	no	tr	107	5⅛
p60	4685	¾	786	3	262	5¾
p62½	1770	1 1/16	no	tr	105	6¾
p65	1350	1½	328	4¾	322	7¾
p67½	494	2⅜	no	tr	31	9⅛
p70	2476	3⅛	548	6	417	9¾
p72½	1169	4⅛	no	tr	418	11⅜
p75	1200	6	728	9⅛	849	12⅜
p77½	159	7½	no	tr	52	14⅛
p80	919	8⅞	117	13	605	15¾
p85	869	13½	170	16⅜	no	tr
p90	131	19¼	69	20⅜	no	tr
p100	364	29	90	29	16	31⅞

Call (C) Put (P) Strike Price	Jan Vol.	Jan Last Price	Feb Vol.	Feb Last Price	Vol.	Last Price
c20	251	1/16	524	½	no	tr
p17½	167	9/16	80	1⅛	2	1½
BaxterIntl		Close 67¼				**May**
c70	5	¾	368	2⅜	15	5⅛
Beckman		Close 54⅜				**Apr**
p55	no	tr	200	2¾	no	tr
BellAtlantic		Close 58⅝				**Apr**
p60	182	2 9/16	10	3¾	no	tr
BellSouth		Close 45				**Apr**
c45	81	1¾	183	2 13/16	6	3⅝
BergenBru		Close 9 3/16				**Mar**
c10	217	⅜	10	7/16	113	15/16
BestBuy		Close 57 7/16				**Mar**
c50	333	8½	21	10⅜	64	12⅛
c55	766	5	214	7¼	151	9⅜
c60	782	2⅝	102	5⅛	51	7½
c65	424	1⅛	no	tr	22	5¼
c70	162	9/16	no	tr	61	4
p45	244	⅜	100	1 7/16	no	tr
p50	107	1 5/16	34	2 13/16	29	4
p55	124	2¼	no	tr	17	6¼

Figure 14–1. Reading the Options Table in the Newspaper
SOURCE: *Investor's Business Daily*, January 10, 2000.

Options Strategies

Using Options for Leverage. Using a call option to buy shares or a put option to sell shares is called exercising the option. This is one choice that option buyers have, but more often buyers of options purchase them with the intent of reselling at a higher price. However, if you know that part of an options price (the time value) will decrease as time passes, it may seem more logical to buy shares of the underlying stock, whose value is fairly straightforward. The reason for buying options is leverage, in which a small amount of money can control a large amount of stock. This is best shown by comparing the purchase of 100 shares of XYZ Company with the purchase of one call option for XYZ Company (see Table 14–1). When the stock is $60, you can purchase 100 shares for $6,000 or a March 60 call for $5, with a total cost of $500. If the price of XYZ rises to $80 before the March expiration, you could sell your 100 shares for $80 or your call for at least $20 (its intrinsic value). Leverage results in a 300% return when buying the option versus a 33% return when buying the stock.

There are two ways to look at the risk in purchasing options. On the positive side, the most you can lose is the amount of the premium paid. On the negative side, your percentage loss can be as high as 100% and you do not have the ability to wait out price corrections. Using the previous example, if the price of XYZ Company falls to $50, selling your stock would result

Table 14–1. The Leverage of Options

	XYZ Company	
	Buy a March 60 Call Option for $5	Buy 100 Shares for $60
Purchase amount	($500)	($6,000)
Sale amount	$2,000	$8,000
Profit	$1,500	$2,000
Percentage return	300%	33%

in a 17% return, expiration of your options, a –100% return, as shown in Table 14–2.

If you did not sell the stock and it subsequently rose, you could end up making money on the stock. This is where the time constraint of options can cost you money when you are right about the ultimate direction of a stock's price but wrong about the timing.

Hedging with Put Options. In many cases investors use options not for speculation, but to limit their possible losses. This process is known as hedging. For example, you might own a stock (or want to buy one) that you expect will rise in price, but within a year you would like to make a down payment on house. Conventional wisdom says that you should begin to liquidate your stock holdings because they could drop in value. An alternative, which would cost you money but allow you to participate in

Table 14–2. The Risk of Options

	XYZ Company	
	Buy a March 60 Call Option for $5	Buy 100 Shares for $60
Purchase amount	$500	($6,000)
Sale amount	$0	$5,000
Profit (loss)	($500)	($1,000)
Percentage return	–100%	–17%

the upside potential of the stock while limiting your downside risk, is to hedge by buying puts.

For example, on January 7, 2000, Cisco Systems closed at $105.875 and its April 100 put closed at $7.75. Assuming you could purchase both at the closing prices and disregarding commissions, you could purchase 100 shares of stock and one put for $11,362.50. Through the April expiration, you could always sell for $100 a share, making your maximum loss $1,362.50. Your upside potential would be reduced by the cost of the put, or $775. See Table 14–3 for your results given different moves in Cisco Systems's stock price both with and without the hedge.

Another instance in which you might hedge is when your employer matches your 401(k) contributions with company stock. If you are unable to sell your stock but anticipate either a general downturn in the stock

Table 14–3. Hedging with Put Options

	100 Shares	100 Shares + 1 Put
Purchase 100 Cisco Systems	($10,587.50)	($10,587.50)
Purchase 1 April 100 put		($775.00)
Total cost	($10,587.50)	($11,362.50)
Minimum sale price	$0	$10,000.00
Maximum loss	($10,587.50)	($1,362.50)
Cisco Systems drops to $60.00		
Sell 100 shares at $60	$6,000.00	
Exercise April 100 put		$10,000.00
Less total cost	($10,587.50)	($11,362.50)
Loss	($4,587.50)	($1,362.50)
Cisco Systems drops to $98.00		
Sell 100 shares at $98	$9,800.00	
Exercise April 100 put		$10,000.00
Less total cost	($10,587.50)	($11,362.50)
Loss	($787.50)	($1,362.50)
Cisco Systems rises to $150		
Sell 100 shares at $150	$15,000.00	$15,000.00
Less total cost	($10,587.50)	($11,362.50)
Profit	$4,412.50	$3,637.50

market or a drop in your company's stock price, you might buy puts on the stock. In that case, if the stock's price dropped, you would expect to sell them for a profit, rather than exercise them. While the taxes paid on any profit make this a less than perfect hedge, it can be an effective way to reduce your exposure to a highly concentrated retirement plan.

Puts and calls are available with expirations of up to eight months, but continually renewing these short-term options can become expensive. Those interested in hedging strategies should consider the more than 200 stocks that trade options with expirations as far out as three years. These options are called LEAPS®, short for Long-Term Equity AnticiPation Securities and will be discussed later in this chapter.

Generating Income by Writing Covered Calls. The writer, or original seller, of an option receives the premium for undertaking an obligation to either sell or buy shares of stock. This is a purely speculative strategy similar to selling short for a call writer who does not own the stock. If the market price of the stock skyrockets, the owner must purchase the security at any price to be able to deliver it upon exercise of the option. This is a very risky undertaking.

Writing covered calls, a call-writing strategy of writing calls when you own the underlying stock, has limited risk. A rising stock price means only that you will lose out on the appreciation of your stock, not that you must take a loss to purchase it in the open market.

When you write a covered call, you sell someone else the option to buy your stock at a specific price through the option's expiration date. This income-producing strategy is employed by investors who believe that the price of the underlying stock will not change perceptibly. It is a bad strategy if the stock either rises or falls significantly. A covered call writer will not be able to benefit from a rise in stock price, because the stock will be called away at the strike price if the market price rises above it. If the stock falls greatly in price, by more than the premium received, the covered call writer loses less than if he had held the stock and not written the call, but loses more than if he had just sold the stock. Table 14–4 provides an example of covered call writing with the results given different movements in the underlying stock price.

For example, on January 7, 2000, Johnson & Johnson closed at $96.625 and its April 105 call closed at $3.50. Assuming you could purchase the stock and sell the call at the closing prices and disregarding commissions, you could purchase 100 shares of stock for $9,662.50 and sell one April call for $350. Your net cost for the stock would be $9,312.50, which, divided by 100, is your breakeven sale price of $93.125. Through the April expiration, you would be obligated to sell the stock for $105 a share, should the call be exercised, making your maximum gain $1,187.50 plus any dividends paid during the period.

Table 14–4. Covered Call Writing

	Buy 100 Shares	Buy 100 Shares + Sell 1 Call
Purchase 100 Johnson & Johnson	($9,662.50)	($9,662.50)
Sell 1 April 105 call		$350.00
Net cost	$9,662.50	$9,312.50
Breakeven sale price per share	$96.625	$93.125
Maximum sale amount	Unlimited	$10,500.00
Maximum gain	Unlimited	$1,187.50
Johnson & Johnson stock price does not change; hold stock		
No sale, no assignment	$0	$0
Premium on call		$350.00
Profit	0	$350.00
Johnson & Johnson drops to $75; sell stock		
Sell 100 shares at $75	$7,500.00	$7,500.00
Cost of stock	($9,662.50)	($9,662.50)
Premium received on call		$350.00
Loss	($2,162.50)	($1,812.50)
Johnson & Johnson rises to $120; sell stock, call assigned		
Sell 100 shares at $120	$12,000.00	
Call is assigned at $105		$10,500.00
Cost of stock	($9,662.50)	($9,662.50)
Premium received on call		$350
Profit	$2,337.50	$1,187.50

Selling Cash-Secured Puts. Selling cash-secured puts is a strategy for the investor who would like to purchase a security but is willing to wait for it to drop to a particular price. Usually investors who feel this way would place a limit order to buy at the desired price. In the same situation, an investor selling a cash-secured put would receive the put premium for accepting the obligation to buy the stock chosen at the preferred price.

Selling a cash-secured put means selling the put and depositing enough money to purchase the stock at the brokerage firm. The brokerage firm requires this in order to ensure that funds will be available should the put be assigned to you (the account receiving the exercise of an option is said to be assigned). This situation will occur if the stock price drops below the strike price of the put. If not, you may keep the premium and continue waiting for the stock to reach your price, during which time you may sell another put.

For example, on January 7, 2000, General Electric closed at $150. Suppose you would like to buy General Electric but are not willing to pay more than $145 per share. On that day the closing price of the April 150 put was $7.625. The following examples compare placing a limit order at $145 with selling the April 150 put, given three different scenarios.

- The price of General Electric rises above $150, staying there until expiration. The put is not assigned.

Limit order to buy 100 GE at $145	Sell 1 GE April 150 put at $7.625
No stock purchased	No stock purchased
	Keep premium of 7.625 = $762.50

- General Electric drops below $150, but remains above $145 by expiration. The option is assigned.

Limit order to buy 100 GE at $145	Sell 1 GE April 150 put at $7.625
No stock purchased	Purchase 100 GE at $150
	Less put premium of $7.625
	Own 100 GE at net price of $142.375

- General Electric drops below $145 by expiration. The option is assigned.

Limit order to buy 100 GE at $145	Sell 1 GE April 150 put at $7.625
Purchase 100 GE at $145	Purchase 100 GE at $150
	Less put premium of $7.625
	Own 100 GE at net price of $142.375

Covered Combinations. A covered combination, also known as a double up/double down strategy, is the combination of the sale of a covered call and a cash-secured put. It is used when you would like to generate some income from an existing or new stock position *and* would be willing to purchase more if the price drops. With this tactic, you purchase half of the stock you are willing to own and sell a call whose strike price is above the current price and a put whose strike price is below the current price. If the stock price remains between the two strike prices, you profit from the premiums of selling the put and call. If the stock price rises above the call strike price, your stock will be called away at a profit, plus you will profit on the premiums received from selling the options. If the stock price falls below the put strike price, you will purchase more stock, but your net cost will be reduced by the premiums received.

Investors most often use covered combinations for stocks whose prices they do not expect to change much (in place of just selling a covered call) or for highly volatile stocks whose long-term prospects they like. Let us look at an example of the latter, using an internet stock, Amazon.com.

In this example, you are an investor who is willing to purchase 200 shares of Amazon.com. You are concerned that its price might drop before it rises, but you do not want to completely miss out if it does not drop. On January 7, 2000, Amazon.com closed at $69.5625. Using a covered combination, you purchase 100 shares at $69.5625 and sell an April 80 call for $11.125 and an April 60 put for $10. Your net cost is $4,843.75 or $48.4375 per share. Table 14–5 outlines the example under three different scenarios for movement in the price of *Amazon.com*.

Index Options

Options on individual equities give the investor the opportunity to bet on the direction of a stock price or to hedge an investment; index options allow a bet or hedge on entire markets or individual industries, through their comparable indices. The primary concepts behind index options are the same as those discussed thus far, but with a few key differences.

Cash-Settled Options. The first difference between equity and index options is that index options are cash settled. Whereas equity options are settled by delivery of a particular stock when they are exercised, the exercise of an index option results in a delivery of cash which is equal to the intrinsic value of the option. For example, if you owned an S&P 500 Index (SPX) call with a strike price of 1,450 and exercised it when the index was 1,462 at the end of the trading day, you would receive the difference between the strike price of the call (1,450) and the closing index value (1,462), times 100. Thus you would receive $1,462 - 1,450 = 12 \times 100 = \$1,200$.

European- and American-Style Options. An American-style option may be exercised by its owner at any time before its expiration date. Equity (individual stock) options traded on U.S. exchanges are American-style options, as are some index options, notably the S&P 100 (OEX) options, traded on the Chicago Board Options Exchange (CBOE). European-style options can only be exercised at maturity. The S&P 500 (SPX) and DJIA (DJX) options, both traded on the CBOE, are European-style options.

The style of the option is not really an issue with option buyers, who may always sell their option prior to maturity; however, a seller of an American-style option may find it assigned prior to maturity.

Table 14–5. A Covered Combination

	Buy 100 Shares	Buy 100 Shares + Sell 1 Call & 1 Put
Purchase 100 Amazon.com at $69.5625	($6,956.25)	($6,956.25)
Sell 1 April 80 call at $11.125		$1,112.50
Sell 1 April 60 put at $10		$1,000.00
Net cost	($6,956.25)	($4,843.75)

Amazon.com rises to $85 by expiration. Sell stock/assign call, put expires

Sell stock at $85	$8,500.00	
Call assigned at $80		$8,000.00
Cost of stock	($6,956.25)	($6,956.25)
Premium received on call		$1,112.50
Premium received on put		$1,000.00
Profit	$1,543.75	$3,156.25

Amazon.com drops to $55 by expiration; put is assigned, call expires

Put assigned: purchase 100 shares at $60		($6,000.00)
Original purchase of 100 shares	($6,956.25)	($6,956.25)
Premium received on call		$1,112.50
Premium received on put		$1,000.00
Net cost of shares	($6,956.25)	($10,843.75)
Number of shared owned	100	200
Net cost (breakeven) per share	$69.5625	$54.219

Amazon.com price does not change; hold stock

No sale, no assignment	$0	$0
Premium received on call		$1,112.50
Premium received on put		$1,000.00
Profit	$0	$2,112.50

Using Index Options. Call options on an index allow the investor/trader to participate in a rising market. You might purchase index call options if you expect a rising market and one or more of the following descriptions apply.

- You have a feel for the market as a whole or even a particular segment, but prefer not to make bets on individual stocks.

- You are fairly certain about the time frame of your expectation.
- You want to leverage your investment (see "Using Options for Leverage" earlier in the chapter).
- You want to participate in the stock market but are unwilling to take the unlimited downside risk of investing funds which will be needed in the near term (college funding, retirement, down payment on a home). The maximum loss on an option is the price of the option.

Index put options provide a general hedge against market downturns or segments falling out of favor with the investing public. You might buy index put options if one or more of the following descriptions apply.

- You own a diversified portfolio of stocks, whose price movements, in aggregate, tend to follow one of the popular indices.
- You are unwilling to sell your stocks because:

    You have significant unrealized capital gains; and/or

    You are not sure of a downturn, just uneasy.
- You are bearish enough that you do not own any stocks and would like to profit from a falling market by owning puts.
- You do not want to sell stocks short due to the unlimited risk of that strategy.

Index options may be traded on a variety of market indices, such as the S&P 500 and S&P 100, the DJIA, the NASDAQ 100, the Russell 2000, and the Amex Major Market, as well as individual industries and sectors. The following list includes many of the index options available for trading.[1]

Broad-Based Index Options

Amex Institutional Index (also LEAPS®)

Amex Major Market Index

Dow Jones Industrial Average

GSTI™ Composite Index

Morgan Stanley Consumer Index

Morgan Stanley Cyclical Index

NASDAQ 100 Index

New York Stock Exchange Composite Index

Russell 2000 Index (also Reduced-Value LEAPS®)

---

[1] Chicago Board Options Exchange and the American Stock Exchange.

S&P 100 Index

S&P Midcap Index (also LEAPS®)

S&P 500 Index

S&P 500/BARRA Growth Index

S&P 500/BARRA Value Index

Options Based on the Dow Jones Averages

Dow 10 Index (also LEAPS®)

Dow Jones Equity REIT Index

Dow Jones Industrial Average

Dow Jones Internet Commerce Index (also LEAPS®)

Dow Jones Transportation Average (also LEAPS®)

Dow Jones Utility Average (also LEAPS®)

CBOE Sector Index Options

Automotive Index

Computer Software Index

Gaming Index

Gold Index

Internet Index (also Reduced-Value LEAPS®)

Oil Index

Technology Index (also Reduced-Value LEAPS®)

Amex Sector Index Options

Airline Index

Biotechnology Index

Morgan Stanley Commodity Related Equity Index

CSFB Technology Index

The Computer Hardware Index

Computer Technology Index

Deutsche Bank Energy Index

Disk Drive Index

Inter@ctive Week Internet Index

de Jager Year 2000 Index

Morgan Stanley High Technology 35 Index

Natural Gas Index

Networking Index

Oil Index

Pharmaceutical Index

Securities Broker/Dealer Index

The Street.com E-commerce Index

The Street.com E-finance Index

Standard & Poor's Sectors Index Options

S&P Banks Index

S&P Chemical Index

S&P Health Care Index

S&P Insurance Index

S&P Retail Index

S&P Transportation Index

Goldman Sachs Technology Index Options

GSTI™ Hardware Index

GSTI™ Internet Index (also Reduced-Value LEAPS®)

GSTI™ Multimedia Networking Index

GSTI™ Semiconductor Index

GSTI™ Software Index

GSTI™ Services Index

GSTI™ Composite Index

International Index Options

Eurotop 100 Index

Hong Kong Option Index (also LEAPS®)

IPC™ Index

Japan Index

Latin 15 Index™

Amex Mexico Index

CBOE Mexico Index (also Reduced-Value LEAPS®)

Nikkei 300 Index

Long-Term Options

LEAPS®, the acronym for Long-Term Equity AnticiPation Securities, are long-term options. They expire in two to three years from the date of initial listing, up to a maximum of 39 months. LEAPS® follow the general rules of standard options and, as their maturity nears, they roll into the standard option associated with the underlying security. Both equities and indices have LEAPS® options, though LEAPS® do not exist on all securities that have standardized options.

Strategies for trading LEAPS® are similar to those for trading standardized options. The key difference is in the premium components of intrinsic value and time value. Due to their long-term nature, a newly issued LEAPS® option will have much of its premium composed of time value.

FLEX Options

In 1993, a new type of options security was developed to allow options traders to customize their contracts. FLEX® (FLEXible exchange index) options, which are a variation of standard index options, and E-FLEX® (Equity FLEXible exchange) options, which are a variation of standard equity options, give traders the ability to choose expiration date, exercise style, and strike price.

FLEX® and E-FLEX® options were designed for sophisticated investors and institutions and have very high minimum trading limits. To trade in an open or existing series, the minimum transaction for FLEX® options is $1 million and for E-FLEX® options is 100 contracts, unless it is a closing transaction of the trader's entire position.

Learning More about Options

Several of the options exchanges offer educational material about options. The Chicago Board Options Exchange (CBOE) has an excellent education center, at *www.cboe.com*, where you can learn basic definitions and advanced trading strategies. Register there for the Options Toolbox, a free interactive, educational CD-ROM covering equity options, index options, and LEAPS®.

The Philadelphia Stock Exchange provides good basic information about options at its website, *www.phlx.com*. The American Stock Exchange, at *www.amex.com*, provides quotes on equity and index options plus an educational area with definitions and trading strategies.

Futures

A futures contract is an agreement on a transaction to take place at a specific date in the future, with a designated price, quantity, and quality of the underlying product or commodity. Futures contracts differ from options contracts in that both the buyer and seller of a futures contract are bound to the transaction. In the options market, only the seller of the contract is obligated to carry through on the contract.

Early futures contracts developed in the market for agricultural commodities as both sellers (farmers) and buyers (manufacturers of food products) tried to reduce price volatility in their transactions. The farmer who contracts for the future delivery of his grain eliminates the risk of a price decline. The buyer of the grain contract eliminates her risk of a price increase. Both are bound by the contract, so that the farmers whose crops fail must purchase grain in the open market to deliver it in order to satisfy the contract. The buyer must pay the contractual price even if there is a subsequent price decline and she could buy in the open market at a lower price.

Futures markets exist in many commodities in addition to agricultural products. Industrial products, such as metals, have active futures markets as manufacturers strive to manage costs. Financial futures, based on instruments such as Treasury bonds or the S&P 500 Index, provide a measure of management for interest rate or stock market volatility.

While futures markets may have developed to protect those who intend to physically exchange a commodity, only a small percentage of futures contracts are actually delivered. The rest are settled by engaging in an equal but offsetting contract. Therefore, if you begin with a contract to buy coffee, you may settle the contract either by buying the coffee or by contracting to sell coffee. Market participants who do this to make a profit are called speculators. Corporations, banks, insurance companies, and mutual fund managers trying to reduce their exposures to particular risks are known as hedgers. Both have a valuable place in the market, as the speculators provide liquidity by increasing the number of available buyers and sellers.

Trading Futures

As with options contracts, each futures contract is based on a specific underlying instrument. Futures may be based on a commodity, a currency, a security, or an index. Each contract has a fixed expiration date and a detailed description of the underlying instrument, along with specifications as to the quality range which may fulfill the contract. Also specified are the terms of physical delivery, if possible, or cash delivery in the case of stock index or similar nondeliverable futures.

The buyer of a futures contract is said to be long and the seller of a contract is short. At the time of the transaction, both the buyer and seller must deposit funds, called margin, with the brokerage firm. The margin amount is typically less than 10% of the value of the item underlying the contract, but may fall anywhere between 5% and 18%. Gains and losses on a contract are computed daily by comparing the actual market price of the underlying item and the price designated in the futures contract. Losses on a contract are posted each day to the brokerage account and may result in a margin call, the request for a deposit of additional funds.

Because futures contracts entail obligation on both the buyer and seller's part, they will never expire worthless as an option contract may. You must always close out a futures position, long or short, to avoid being required to take or make delivery of the underlying item. Closing out the position involves placing an order exactly opposite to your existing position.

Hedging with Futures. Farmers often use futures to hedge against falling agricultural prices. For example, a soybean farmer might want to hedge his crop against the possibility of falling soybean prices. Expecting a crop over 10,000 bushels, he sells two November soybean futures contracts, each worth 5,000 bushels at $6.25 per bushel. After the harvest in September, soybean cash and futures prices have fallen. The farmer sells his crop for $5.72 per bushel. He offsets his hedge by buying two November soybean futures at $5.95. The gain on the futures transaction offsets the lower price received on the crop[2]. Table 14–6 shows the results on a per bushel basis.

Speculating with Futures. When speculating with futures, it is not necessary to venture into the cash markets; speculators simply buy and sell the same contract with the intent of making a profit. There is no requirement that the purchase come before the sale, only the goal that its price be lower. A speculator betting on interest rates might buy and sell Treasury

---

[2] From "Action In The Marketplace," a Chicago Board of Trade publication.

Table 14–6. Hedging with Futures

		Cash Market Only	Cash and Futures Markets
June	Cash price for soybeans is $6.00,		
	Sell 2 Nov. contracts at $6.25		$6.25
Sept	Sell soybeans at $5.75	$5.75	$5.75
	Buy 2 Nov. contracts at $5.95		($5.95)
	Net per bushel received	$5.75	$6.05

bond futures. Because futures move nearly in tandem with cash prices, you can expect bond futures to fall if interest rates rise. A speculator expecting rising interest rates would sell bond futures with the hope of making an offsetting purchase later, at a lower price.

Due to the unlimited risks inherent in futures trading, it is only for the sophisticated investor. Such investors should trade futures only with a reputable brokerage firm and only after studying the marketplace to obtain an understanding of the risk involved. Many books and self-study courses are available in futures trading. Good places to gain knowledge are the Chicago Board of Trade (CBOT) and the Futures Industry Institute.

The CBOT offers educational materials for sale and worthwhile descriptive information on its website. Sale materials can be ordered there, and several free publications can be viewed directly or downloaded.

Chicago Board of Trade
141 W. Jackson Boulevard
Chicago, IL 60604-2994
312-435-3500
www.cbot.com

The Futures Industry Institute is the nonprofit educational organization established by the Futures Industry Association. Its website provides information and courses that target industry professionals and the "Introduction to the Futures and Options Markets," an online tutorial for the beginner.

Futures Industry Institute
2001 Pennsylvania Avenue, N.W.
Suite 600
Washington, DC 20006-1807
202-223-1528
www.fiafii.org

The National Futures Association (NFA) is a self-regulatory organization for the futures industry. You may order educational materials and publications about arbitrating disputes by phone or from the website. You may also download many documents at the website in PDF format.

National Futures Association
200 West Madison Street, Suite 1600
Chicago, IL 60606
312-781-1300
www.nfa.futures.org

Summary

There is no doubt that options and futures are tools for the sophisticated investor. The markets move quickly and the leverage involved magnifies percentage losses as well as gains. However, there are many strategies, some of which are outlined in this chapter, that can be used as part of a prudent investment program. The key is to have a clear objective and understand the downside risk before committing any investment dollars.

15

Real Estate and Real Estate Investment Trusts

Investors often turn to real estate as a diversification for investment portfolios consisting of stocks and bonds. As discussed in Chapter 5, real estate and other hard assets often have a low or even negative correlation to other investment classes, meaning their values will react differently to economic and market conditions. In general, real estate values are expected to rise as inflation rises, at the same time the value of bonds and other fixed-income investments should fall.

Key to investing in real estate is being aware that different properties or trusts can be as different as individual stocks. Location and industry can make a world of difference in property values and income generation. For example, good economic times should increase values of office buildings as thriving companies expand, but might decrease the value of low-rent apartment buildings as tenants are able to move to more expensive apartments or homes.

This chapter will touch on some of the reasons and methods of analysis for buying both individual properties and real estate investment trusts (REITs) which are professionally managed portfolios of properties. The discussion of investing in individual properties is designed only to introduce concepts. For those considering buying individual properties, there are entire books devoted to the subject and there is no substitute for the advice of a trusted accountant or lawyer. We will also cover the reverse mortgage, a method for pulling equity out of your home.

Investing in Real Estate

Buying real estate in the form of a home may be the largest investment you ever make. Though ideally your home will appreciate in value, its use as an investment is rarely the primary consideration in a purchase. Therefore, our discussion about investing in real estate refers only to real estate that is purchased for profit.

There are three ways to profit from real estate investments:

1. Cash flow from rents, which may

   - pay some or all of the mortgage, thus reducing the cost of ownership
   - provide free cash flow in excess of mortgage payments and operating expenses
2. Appreciation in the value of the property
3. Tax shelter provided by depreciation

In the 1970s, a period of high inflation, real estate's investment potential was most often realized through capital appreciation. In the 1980s, real estate syndications utilized tax shelter benefits until the Tax Reform Act of 1986. In the 1990s and beyond, a period marked by relatively low inflation to date and fewer real estate tax benefits, real estate's appeal as an investment more often relies on its ability to produce cash flow and the diversification it offers an investment portfolio.

Valuing Real Estate

Many types of real estate are purchased with the expectation that they will produce income. Possibilities include single-family rental homes, apartment buildings, mobile home parks, office buildings, parking lots, and any other building or property occupied by tenants. The primary method of appraising value for such property is the income, or capitalization, approach. In this method, annual net income is divided by a capitalization rate to produce a present value for the property. The formula is as follows:

$$\frac{\text{Annual net income}}{\text{Capitalization rate}} = \text{Value}$$

To compute annual net income, begin with potential gross income at 100% occupancy and deduct for an average vacancy rate and credit losses for nonpaying tenants. Add in any incidental income, such as that earned from laundry facilities to derive gross effective income—the income the property is realistically expected to produce. Subtract from that figure fixed expenses such as property insurance, taxes, permits, and licenses. Then subtract variable operating expenses, which are those that will vary with occupancy, such as supplies, maintenance, utilities, and property management. Then subtract a replacement reserve, which is money set aside for large expenditures on items such as hot water heaters, dishwashers, pavement, or roofs. The resulting figure is net operating income.

Note that mortgage payments are not included so that all properties, whether owned free and clear or with a substantial mortgage, are set on the same footing. Also not included is depreciation, as it is a noncash expense.

To complete the formula, you must divide net operating income by a capitalization rate, which is a rate of return generally comparable to what investors are earning on similar properties. The rate is not only affected by similar properties, but also by differences in perceived risk of loss and by relative liquidity. As discussed in Chapter 5, a higher risk requires a higher expected return. Low liquidity is a risk, as it implies loss of principal in a quick sale. See Table 15–1 for an example.

Table 15–1. Computing Annual Net Operating Income and Value through Capitalization

Property: A 100-Unit Apartment Complex with Rents of $500 per Month per Unit		
Potential gross income: 100 × $500 × 12		$600,000
Less vacancy and credit loss (6%)		(36,000)
Plus other income		8,000
Gross effective income		$572,000
Less operating expenses		
Fixed expenses:		
Property insurance	9,800	
Property taxes, licenses, & permits	38,600	($48,400)
Variable expenses:		
Maintenance	$42,000	
Utilities	39,000	
Supplies	6,400	
Advertising	2,500	
Legal and accounting	7,500	
Wages and salaries	36,000	
Property management	26,000	($159,400)
Replacement reserve		($10,000)
Total expenses		$217,800
Annual net operating income		$354,200
Value with 12% capitalization rate (354,200/0.12)		$2,951,667

Tax Benefits of Owning Commercial Real Estate

Owning commercial real estate involves three primary tax benefits, the first two of which are not available on ownership of a primary residence. They are the tax deductibility of:

- Operating expenses
- Depreciation
- Interest on the mortgage

Similar to the expenses of running a business, the expenses of operating investment property are tax deductible. This is in contrast to the expenses of holding personal property, such as a home, which are not tax deductible. In the previous example, the expenses deducted to reach net operating income are all tax-deductible expenses.

Tax depreciation is a provision of the tax law that allows a property owner to recover the cost of an asset over its useful life through a business deduction for annual depreciation. Depreciation is computed on the value of buildings, not on the land beneath them, and is an arbitrary procedure that may be taken even if the property is appreciating in value.

The two depreciation schedules for real estate are set by the Tax Reform Act of 1986 and the Revenue Reconciliation Act of 1993. They set the life of real estate at 27.5 years for residential property and 39 years for nonresidential property. Depreciation must be taken on a straight-line basis, meaning that, each year, the owner of a single-family rental home can deduct 1/27.5 of the home's value (not including the land) as a depreciation expense.

In general, the amount of investment expenses claimed, including depreciation, cannot exceed a property's income, meaning you cannot use the noncash loss of depreciation to shelter other income. For example, if your income on a property is $25,000 this year, but you have $32,000 in expenses, you can claim only $25,000 in expenses, for a net income/loss of $0 this year. The excess loss of $7,000 can be carried forward to other years. Some exceptions apply to investors who manage their own property and have income under certain limits.

In addition to the deduction for depreciation, owners of investment property may deduct mortgage interest paid when computing their taxable income. To see how these deductions benefit a property owner, we return to the example in Table 15–1. There we had a purchase price for the property of approximately $2,950,000. This price includes the land underneath the building, so we must separate the building and land costs to calculate depreciation. If we assign 15% of the value to land, the building is worth $2,507,500. Using straight-line depreciation over 27.5 years, the annual depreciation ($2,507,500/27.5) is $91,182. If mortgage interest in the first year is $188,087 and net operating income after expenses is $354,200, then the net taxable income is computed as follows:

Net Operating Income	$ 354,200
Less: Interest	−188,087
Depreciation	−91,182
Net Taxable Income	$ 74,931

In a 28% tax bracket, the $91,182 depreciation deduction, which is a non-cash expense, saves you $25,530 in federal income taxes.

Real Estate Investment Trusts

Real estate investment trusts (REITs) are corporations that own, lease, or lend money for real estate. They are similar in concept to closed-end mutual funds. The REIT pools the funds of many individuals in order to invest in real estate, such as office buildings, apartments, shopping centers, or hotels. Their shares trade on the stock exchanges at whatever value investors believe they are worth. The benefits to an investor of purchasing REIT shares rather than individual properties include the ability to invest and diversify holdings with relatively small amounts of money and the much higher liquidity of REIT shares.

Established by Congress in 1960, REITs receive favorable tax treatment under Internal Revenue Code Sections 856–858, which classify them as conduits of income for their shareholders, a designation that allows them to avoid corporate income tax. This is a benefit for shareholders whose ordinary stock holdings are taxed first at the corporate level on corporate profits and again at the personal level when dividends are paid or capital gains are realized.

The following tests must be met to qualify as an REIT.

- The company must have at least 75% of its assets invested in real estate, through direct ownership or lending.

- At least 75% of its income must be derived from real estate activities such as lending, leasing, or both.

- It must distribute 95% (90% after January 1, 2001) of its taxable income to shareholders each year.

- It must have a minimum of 100 shares and no more than 50% of its shares may be owned by five or fewer shareholders.

The main categories of REITs are equity and mortgage REITs, plus a hybrid category that includes some of both. Equity REITs earn profits through direct investment in income-producing real estate, whereas mortgage REITs earn profits through interest income on mortgages secured by real estate. According to the National Association of Real Estate Investment Trusts (NAREIT), there were 203 publicly traded REITs at the end of 1999, with a market capitalization of $124,261,900,000. Of those, 167 or $118,232,700,000 were equity REITs, 26 or $4,441,700,000 were mortgage REITs, and 10 or $1,587,500,000 were hybrid REITs.

The investor's total return on an REIT consists of the dividends paid out plus any change in share price. Because REITs are required to pay out 95% (90% after January 1, 2001) of their income, they are generally high-yield investments. Yields in 1999 were commonly in the 7% to 9% range. The share prices of REITs can and do fluctuate widely. Share prices change in response to interest rate changes as do other yield-based investments such as bonds. They also change due to concerns over the financial situation of a particular REIT real estate portfolio or due to the financial state of real estate markets in general. So even though current yields tend to be high, total returns may vary significantly from year to year, as illustrated by total return figures provided by NAREIT for 1993 and 1999 (see Table 15–2).

Long-term returns for different classes of REITs can be found in Table 15–3.

Investing in REITs

Several key REIT characteristics, such as the type and diversity of the underlying properties, financial leverage, and the general financial health of the company, drive share value.

Underlying Properties. Similar to the way that securities in a stock portfolio dictate the value of a mutual fund, the individual properties or properties upon which mortgages are based affect the value of an REIT. REITs

Table 15–2. Volatility of REIT Total Returns

	Total Return (%)		
Year	Equity REITs	Mortgage REITs	Hybrid REITs
1993	19.65	14.55	21.18
1999	–4.62	–33.22	–35.90

Table 15–3. REIT Compound Annual Returns

Sector	Compound Annual Returns (%)*					
	1 Year	3 Year	5 Year	10 Year	15 Year	20 Year
All	–6.48	–3.37	7.70	8.10	6.81	10.28
Equity	–4.62	–1.82	8.09	9.14	9.77	12.34
Mortgage	–33.22	–21.12	3.88	1.41	0.07	4.27
Hybrid	–35.90	–22.34	–5.71	0.90	0.30	6.15

*For periods ending December 31, 1999.

© 2000 National Association of Real Estate Investment Trusts. Used with permission.

can be segmented into major industry groups such as residential (apartments, mobile home parks), health care (nursing homes, hospitals, medical office buildings), travel and recreation (hotels, restaurants, golf courses, amusement parks), retail (shopping centers), and commercial/industrial (office buildings, industrial facilities). Some REITs include several major industry groups. They may be geographically concentrated in one area or diversified in location.

The value of an REIT will tend to move with the financial fortunes of its industry and its geographic region. Residential properties may perform much differently than nursing home properties in the same area. While office properties in one geographic area may prosper, those in an economically depressed region may fall vacant. As with a stock portfolio, diversification reduces risk. Across industries and geographic areas, diversification reduces the risk that an economic downturn in one type of real estate or in a particular region will torpedo the entire REIT. On the other hand, it also reduces the possibility that a booming market or region will increase values significantly.

Look specifically at the individual properties owned or mortgaged by the REIT and consider the quality of tenants. A strong anchor tenant with a long-term lease greatly reduces the risks of a shopping center. The same is true for office buildings. Diversification is valuable, as dependence on a few major tenants increases risk.

Financial Leverage. REITs take the funds provided by a stock offering to either purchase real estate (equity REITs) or to lend to others to purchase real estate (mortgage REITs). Additionally, many REITs use leverage, meaning they borrow to either purchase more or have more funds available to lend. During a market boom, an REIT may borrow to acquire more properties, thus adding interest expenses. As long as the economy expands, this strategy is profitable; however, if a recession hits and reduces rents or affects occupancy rates, revenues may fall as expenses remain high. Check the debt/equity ratio of an REIT against the same ratio in past years and against the REIT's peers. Lower debt/equity means less risk.

In addition to the debt/equity ratio, which checks for the level of long-term debt, note levels of short-term debt. Long-term assets such as real estate should be financed with long-term debt. Although REITs may be tempted to finance with short-term debt because those interest rates are usually lower, doing so involves two risks. One is at refinancing time, when interest rates may have greatly increased. In this case, long-term rates locked in at the original time of financing would have resulted in lower costs. An even more dangerous possibility is that when it is time to refinance short-term debt, the REIT may not be able to get long-term financing.

General Financial Health: FFO, Payout Ratios, and Dividends. A standard measure of the financial health of an REIT is the trend in funds from operations (FFO). Earnings per share are not as valuable a sign of financial well-being with an REIT as they are for many companies, due to high noncash charges for depreciation. These charges result in stated earnings which may be much lower than cash flow. FFO is the cash flow available for repairs and payout to shareholders. The payout ratio of dividends to FFO is calculated as follows:

$$\frac{\text{Dividends per share}}{\text{FFO per share}}$$

A ratio above 100% cannot be sustained for long, because the REIT is dipping into capital in order to pay shareholders.

In addition to the obvious test of whether an REIT can continue to pay dividends at its current level is the predictive value that changes in dividends or the absence of any changes can provide. Dividend payout levels are set by a board of trustees that has access to public and private financial information. Increases in dividends signal confidence in growth of FFO. Conversely, a stagnant dividend, or even a slower rate of growth, signals a board which is less sanguine about the REIT's prospects.

Red Flags. Avoid REITs that exhibit the following characteristics.

- A yield that is much higher than its peers. Higher yield signals higher perceived risk.
- A yield that is too good to be true. A stratospheric yield indicates widespread expectation that the dividend will be cut.

- Debt/equity ratio higher than its peers. Higher debt increases risk.
- Increasing amounts of short-term debt. A short-term perspective keeps current interest costs down at the risk of higher costs later.
- A dividend that has not increased in the last 12 months. An increasing dividend is the surest sign that those who know (the board of directors) have a positive outlook.
- Concentration in both sector and geographic distribution. Diversification reduces risk in the downturn of a particular sector or geographic region.

REIT Mutual Funds

Because REIT investing can be tricky, many investors turn to mutual funds for some of the advantages they provide. Professional management and diversification top the list of reasons to buy REITs through a mutual fund. While some REITs offer diversification as to property type or geographic region, many are highly concentrated in a particular industry and/or area. Professional management leaves the prediction about which sectors will outperform to someone with experience in the industry. The many different REITs owned in each fund portfolio allow for diversification when the individual securities do not.

Other advantages of mutual funds investing are related to the advantages that an institutional investor has over the ordinary individual investor. Mutual funds have the ability to invest in attractive IPOs that might not be offered to the individual investor. They may be able to trade with much lower commissions than an individual who creates a diversified portfolio.

A disadvantage of buying REITs through mutual funds is the additional costs involved due to management fees and sales charges. Of the 74 real estate funds listed in a January 2000 screen of Morningstar's database of 8,051 mutual funds, 30 were no-load funds, 23 had contingent deferred sales charges (back-end loads), and 21 had front-end sales charges (one of which also had a CDSC). Expense ratios ranged from very low for the Aon REIT Index Fund (0.2%) and the Vanguard REIT Index (0.3%) to very high for the U.S. Global Investors Real Estate Fund (3.2%).

Learning More about REITs

Information about REITs is generally available from the same sources as information about other publicly traded stocks. As mentioned, the National Association of Real Estate Investment Trusts (NAREIT) is an industry association that provides general information about REITs for both real estate professionals and investors. Its website includes total return statistics for different time frames and REIT categories, a listing of publicly traded REITs and the exchanges on which they trade, and an excellent FAQs (Frequently Asked Questions) area.

National Association of Real Estate Investment Trusts (NAREIT)
1875 Eye Street N.W.
Washington, DC 20006
202-739-9400
800-3-NAREIT
www.nareit.org

Reverse Mortgage

Most popular with senior citizens looking to supplement their income, the reverse mortgage is a way to access home equity built over time. In a process that is opposite of an ordinary mortgage, the reverse mortgage lender pays the homeowner. As the borrower, you put up a home whose mortgage is fully paid (or nearly so) in order to receive either a lump-sum cash payment or a monthly stream of payments. During the life of the reverse mortgage, the loan balance increases and equity decreases. The loan balance on a reverse mortgage does not have to be repaid until the borrower moves out of the home, sells it, or dies.

Payment Plans

You can take your payments on a reverse mortgage in several different ways.

- Lump-sum payments are typically paid at the time the mortgage is initiated. They may be used for home repairs, to pay down a small existing mortgage, or to invest.
- Credit-line payments provide available funds in amounts and timing determined by the homeowner. Generally, you can write a check to draw on the line of credit and you have the option, but not the obligation, of making payments on the credit line.
- Monthly payments provide a dependable amount of additional income every month.

Types of Reverse Mortgages

In addition to a choice of payment plans, you may choose the structure of a reverse mortgage from the following three categories.

- Tenure loans. This type of loan provides for a guaranteed amount to be loaned, based on the value of the home. For a credit-line tenure loan, a specific upper limit sets the amount that may be borrowed. For a monthly payment tenure loan, payments are set based on the value of the home and the life expectancy of the homeowner. If the owner is a married couple, both must be at least age 62 to qualify and the life expectancy will be based on the younger of the two. If the homeowner(s) outlives the stated life expectancy, it is unlikely that the lender will advance more than the original amount agreed upon, unless the home has appreciated in value.

- Lifetime annuity loans. Called a reverse annuity mortgage, these plans use the equity in a home to purchase an annuity that promises to make a monthly payment for the rest of the homeowner's lifetime. The payment amount is computed from the value of the home and the life expectancy of the homeowner, but there is no danger of outliving payments, should the owner exceed his or her life expectancy.

- Term loans. A term loan, whether it is lump sum or in the form of monthly payments, has a specified date for repayment, typically in 5 or 10 years. This is in sharp contrast to other types of reverse annuities which require repayment only upon permanent relocation, sale of the home, or death. Because of the risk of being forced out of the home when the loan is due, this type of loan is generally used only for borrowers who are over 90 years old or for those who plan to move into a smaller home at a later date.

Obtaining a Reverse Mortgage

Senior citizens (at least age 62) who have substantial home equity and are in need of either a lump-sum payment or additional monthly income, might consider a reverse mortgage as an alternative to selling their home. Due to high origination fees, this option makes the most financial sense for those who plan to remain in their homes for at least five years. Note that reverse mortgages are only available on a principal residence, which is defined as a home that you live in at least six months per year.

Check with your tax advisor before taking out a reverse mortgage. While payments received in a reverse mortgage are not considered taxable because loan proceeds are not taxable, some annuity proceeds may be taxable if the lifetime annuity structure is chosen.

The Federal Housing Administration (FHA), the Federal National Mortgage Association (FNMA, or Fannie Mae), and the Financial Freedom Plan are the three leading lenders in reverse mortgages according to real estate expert Robert Bruss.[1] These companies are sources of the loans, but banks and mortgage bankers originate them. To find Fannie Mae reverse mortgage lenders, call 800-7FANNIE; for GMAC lenders, call 888-737-4622; and for Financial Freedom Plan lenders, call 800-500-5150.

To learn more about reverse mortgages, visit *www.reverse.org*, the website of the National Center for Home Equity Conversion (NCHEC), an independent, not-for-profit organization for reverse mortgage consumer information and analysis. The site includes a good FAQs area and a calculator to determine the cash available from a reverse mortgage and the costs involved.

Summary

As noted in our chapter introduction, real estate can be a good diversification for an investment portfolio of stocks and bonds. Both individual properties and REITs can accomplish this goal; the choice between the two depends on the amount of capital available and the level of involvement desired. For investors with a small amount of capital to employ, an REIT can be a good way to obtain the diversification of real estate. Those with significant amounts of capital can consider whether they want to manage their investment actively or passively. The owner of an apartment building can expect an occasional midnight tenant's phone call and will likely spend time making property decisions, even if a professional manager is employed. In contrast, an REIT causes no more trouble than any other stock in the portfolio, however, the REIT holder's return is reduced by the amount required to pay the managers who handle the headaches.

[1] Robert Bruss, "Backing into Reverse Mortgages," Inman News Feature, on *CBSmarketwatch.com*, July 8, 1999.

16

Precious Metals

Precious metals are among the oldest investments known to civilization. As such, investing in gold, silver, platinum, and palladium has an aura all its own. Metals are known as hard assets, a category of investments that applies to items that you can actually touch, such as gold, art, or real estate, as opposed to investments in which a certificate represents a portion of ownership (stock) or a contract to pay (bond or certificate of deposit).

Hard assets are purchased for a myriad of reasons. In the short term, many investors use the futures markets for speculation in hard assets. In the long term, many buy hard assets as an inflation hedge or for the fact that these assets retain value in a catastrophic situation such as war or extreme currency devaluation. Those who are concerned with the latter favor precious metals because they are portable and highly liquid, and in bullion or bullion coin form their value is easily determined.

Gold

Gold has been a monetary standard since the beginning of civilization, and only in recent history has paper money in the United States not been backed by gold. Until the fall of the gold standard on March 18, 1968, the price of gold was dictated by the government and individuals were prohibited from owning gold. The last official price was $42 an ounce, which is still the price at which the U.S. Treasury values its gold. Today, the price of gold is dictated by supply and demand.

Supply and Demand for Gold

Gold Buyers. The annual demand for gold is estimated to be about 3,500 tons per year. The world's jewelry manufacturers are the largest buyers of gold. Investors are the next largest group of gold buyers, followed by industrial manufacturers. They use gold's superior conductivity in computer circuits and electronic products and its reflective powers in satellite shields, medical lasers, and energy efficient windows. Additionally, some modern medicines, particularly arthritis cures, contain gold. About 60 tons each year are used for dentistry, 200 tons for official gold coins, 35 tons for medallions and gold medals, and another 60 tons for decorative purposes.

Gold Supply. The world's gold supply has three primary sources:

- Mining production
- Secondary sources, meaning gold recycled from other uses
- Sales by government central banks

According to data reported by the Gold Institute, South Africa leads the world in gold production, with 14.4% of world production. The United States and Australia follow in second and third with 11.4% and 9.9%, respectively.[1]

Currently, world consumption of gold exceeds its production from mining sources by about 1,000 tons per year. Much of the difference has been made up in recent years by governments selling portions of the estimated 35,000 tons held in central bank vaults around the world. Some sales come from Third-World countries in need of funds and from countries that find it difficult to justify keeping large amounts of wealth in a noninterest-bearing asset.

Gold Prices

The last 20 years have been hard on gold investors, who have seen a steady drop in prices due to both excess supply and reduced demand. From 1980 to 1999 gold declined from $875 an ounce to $255 an ounce, a 70% loss in value. Prices recovered to above $300 an ounce in the winter of 2000, then fell to the mid $270s in the summer.

On the supply side, gold has been plentiful, with a seemingly endless supply coming from the coffers of central banks. In the late 1990s, the Central Bank of Switzerland announced it would sell 54% of its reserves; the Netherlands, Australia, and Argentina all sold reserves; and President Clinton was quoted as urging the International Monetary Fund to sell gold reserves to pay its debts.[2]

---

[1] The Gold Institute, *www.goldinstitute.com*, data from 1998.

[2] Joseph Weber, "Why Goldbugs Feel So Squashed," *Business Week* 385 (June 28, 1999): 106.

At the same time, steadily falling gold prices enticed mining companies to sell futures in order to lock in current prices. Futures sales are contracts to sell gold in the future at a specified price. These sales of nonexistent gold, which are later covered with gold production, create additional current supply and further depress prices. The process by which the cure (locking in current prices to avoid lower prices later) becomes part of the cause (excess supply) creates a self-fulfilling prophecy.

On the demand side, gold's attractiveness as an investment is based on a combination of the level of interest rates, the strength or weakness of the dollar, and the expectation of future inflation. *Interest rates* refers to the level of "real" interest rates, which are the combination of nominal or stated rates and inflation. The formula is as follows:

$$\text{Real interest rate} = \text{Nominal interest rate} - \text{Expected inflation}$$

If nominal rates are high, but expected inflation is also high, the real rate of interest may be low or even negative. This fact makes gold attractive, because the real interest lost by having funds invested in a noninterest-bearing asset is minimal. If nominal rates are high and expected inflation is low, or nominal rates are low and expected inflation is much lower, the real rate of interest is high. When the real interest rate is high, investors move out of gold in favor of interest-bearing investments.

The success of the Federal Reserve Board in keeping inflation under control has had a major effect on gold's price. In addition to its role as part of the real interest rate equation, inflation affects the price of gold because hard assets tend to increase in value when prices rise. In situations of moderate inflation, gold can be expected to keep pace with rising prices. In situations of extreme inflation, increases in the value of gold may surpass the rate of inflation as worried investors flock to inflation-hedging assets.

The relative strength or weakness of international currencies and the U.S. dollar also affects the price of gold. In general, the dollar and the price of gold move in opposite directions. A strong dollar means weak gold prices and vice versa. Many investors expected the currency crisis in Asia to bring support to gold prices, but this was not the case. Worried investors, who might have rushed into gold as a safe store of value, instead flocked to the U.S. dollar. See Figure 16–1 for a chart of gold's price history.

Silver

As a precious metal, silver shares many characteristics with gold, including its status as a monetary standard. Like gold, silver has historically been

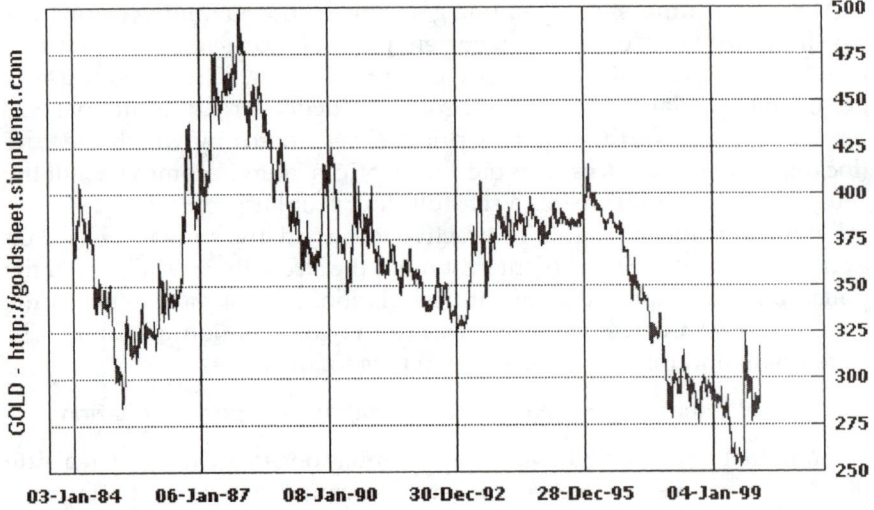

Figure 16–1. The Price of Gold
SOURCE: *http://goldsheet.simplenet.com.*

used for coins and to back paper money in the form of silver certificates, which were issued by the U.S. Treasury from 1933 to 1963. In the early 1960s, a few years before the fall of the gold standard, the Treasury began printing Federal Reserve notes that could not be cashed for silver and reduced the silver in U.S. coins when their market value in silver was worth more than their face value as a coin.

Supply and Demand for Silver

Silver Buyers. The demand for silver has a much larger industrial base than the demand for gold; according to the Silver Institute, industrial uses command about 65% of silver consumed.[3] This demand is led by the photographic industry, which accounts for about 28% of total silver use. While photographic companies continue to reduce the amount of silver used in film and its development, growth in industry volume has kept total demand from falling. Other industrial uses of silver include electrical contacts and conductors, brazing alloys and solders, batteries, and electronic-plated wire. Investors in silver comprise the next largest group of silver

---

[3]Andrew Serwer, "Burned by Gold," *Fortune* 137, no. 5, (March 16, 1998): 92.

buyers. Silver jewelry forms a relatively small portion of the total silver market.

Silver Supply.   Mining production of silver accounts for approximately half of the world's annual silver supply. In contrast to gold, platinum, and palladium, silver mining is rather evenly distributed around the globe, with the largest representations found in North, South, and Central America; Russia; and Australia.

Secondary supplies of silver from industrial recycling and melting coins, flatware, and scrap comprises nearly the rest of silver supply today, though selling from the U.S. Treasury stockpile was a large part of the market in the 1960s. During that decade, the national stockpile went from over 2 billion ounces to under 200 million ounces as the government sometimes disposed of 2 million ounces of silver a week. Lawmakers continue to argue the logic of holding silver in the U.S. Treasury, but the opposing interests of mining companies and industrial users have effectively deadlocked the issue.

Silver Prices

Movement in the price of silver tends to track the price of gold, responding to the same factors that affect gold's value as an investment. Silver's price is often considered more volatile, perhaps due to the numerous attempts to manipulate it. No discussion of silver as an investment would be complete without mentioning the Hunt brothers, Nelson Bunker and Herbert, and their ill-fated attempt to corner the silver market in 1979 and 1980. In a carefully orchestrated plan, the Hunts purchased so many silver futures contracts that a request for delivery on those contracts (something possible, but not usually done) would have cornered the entire silver market. After several attempts to diffuse the situation, the New York Commodity Exchange (COMEX) ruled that no one but the wholesale operators who controlled the COMEX could buy silver on the exchange. As silver's price plunged, the Hunts and many other investors who were along for the ride, lost billions of dollars.

See Figure 16–2 for a chart of silver's price history, and Figure 16–3 for a history of the ratio between the prices of silver and gold.

Platinum and Palladium

Platinum and palladium are the best known members of the platinum group of metals, which also includes rhodium, ruthenium, iridium, and

Silver Bullion

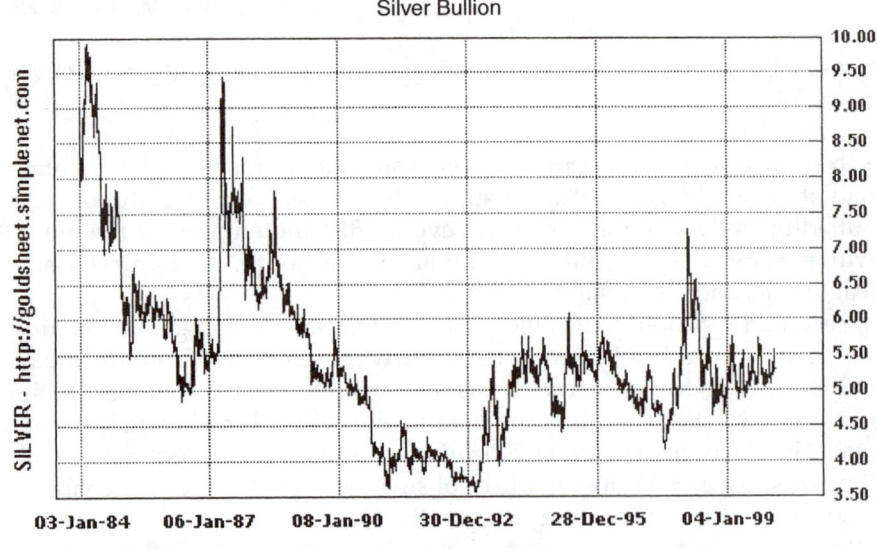

Average price = $5.45

Figure 16–2. The Price of Silver

SOURCE: *http://goldsheet.simplenet.com.*

Gold-to-Silver Ratio

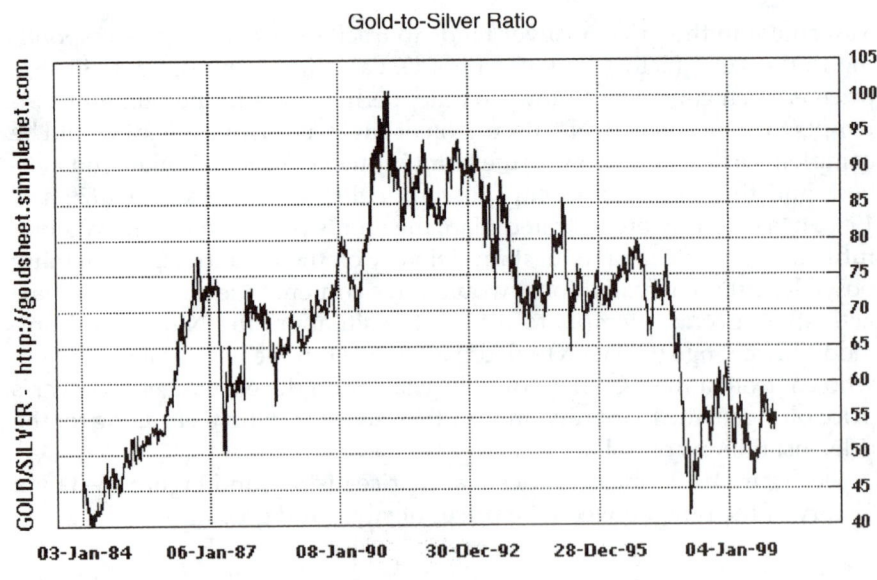

Average ratio = 68.8
Below average — silver is expensive relative to gold
Above average — silver is inexpensive relative to gold

Figure 16–3. The Gold-to-Silver Ratio

SOURCE: *http://goldsheet.simplenet.com.*

osmium. Only since the 1980s have these two metals been actively traded by investors. Today, they are still less commonly quoted than gold and silver.

Supply and Demand of Platinum and Palladium

Platinum and Palladium Buyers. Due to their strength, durability, and resistance to corrosion, platinum and palladium are prized industrial metals. They are much harder than gold and silver, have a higher melting point, yet are still malleable. The United States is the largest user of these two metals and the U.S. auto industry is key in that demand. Platinum and palladium are used in catalytic converters, which are required by law for pollution control in automobiles. Platinum jewelry enjoyed a resurgence in popularity in the late 1990s, though palladium's use in jewelry is relatively rare. Palladium is often used in electronic components. Investor demand for platinum and palladium is low when compared with that of gold and silver.

Platinum and Palladium Supply. Platinum and palladium are much rarer than gold and silver. It takes 4 tons of ore to produce 1 ounce of gold, but 10 tons of ore to produce 1 ounce of platinum. South Africa supplies about 70% of the world's platinum and Russia about 70% of the world's palladium. Each country ranks second as a producer of the other metal. This concentration of production has much greater effect on the overall market than the concentration in gold mining, due to limited strategic stockpiles of both metals. Since neither has ever been used as a monetary metal, there are no central bank vaults full of excess reserves.

Platinum and Palladium Prices

Throughout the 1970s and 1980s the relative prices of platinum and gold fluctuated many times, generally moving together, with platinum most often the higher of the two. Palladium most often traded at a price roughly one-third that of platinum. As the 1990s drew to a close, platinum and palladium commanded significant price premiums over gold with palladium pulling well ahead of platinum.

Due to their high use as industrial metals, investor concerns such as inflation have less effect on platinum and palladium prices than on gold prices. More often, concerns about industrial demand and unstable supply sources affect these volatile markets. For example, in the week ended

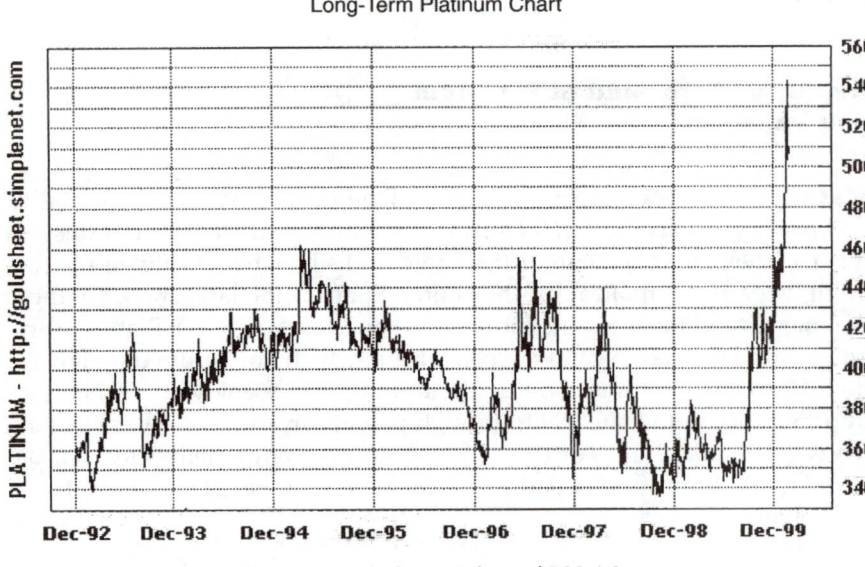

Average platinum price = $390.16

Figure 16–4. The Price of Platinum

SOURCE: *http://goldsheet.simplenet.com.*

February 18, 2000, platinum closed at a price of $503.20 an ounce after fluctuating in a $40 range and palladium closed at $701.25, with a $145 trading range. The two largest factors affecting the markets were an announcement by General Motors that it intended to reduce its use of both metals next year and a stall by Russia in signing an export agreement.

See Figures 16–4 and 16–5 for price histories of platinum and palladium, and Figures 16–6 and 16–7 for the platinum/palladium ratio and the platinum/gold spread.

Vehicles for Precious Metals Investing

There are many different ways to invest in precious metals, each with unique characteristics and appeal. This section covers the most common ways to invest in precious metals.

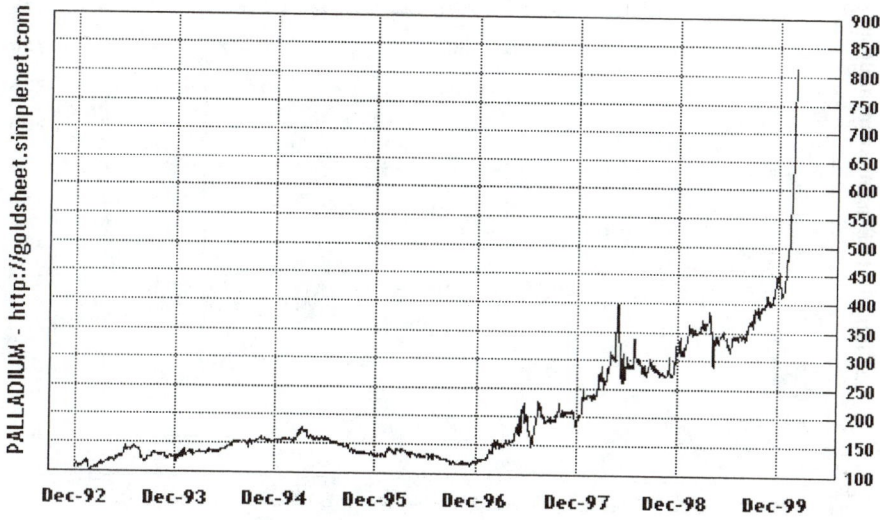

Average palladium price = $193.24

Figure 16–5. The Price of Palladium
SOURCE: *http://goldsheet.simplenet.com.*

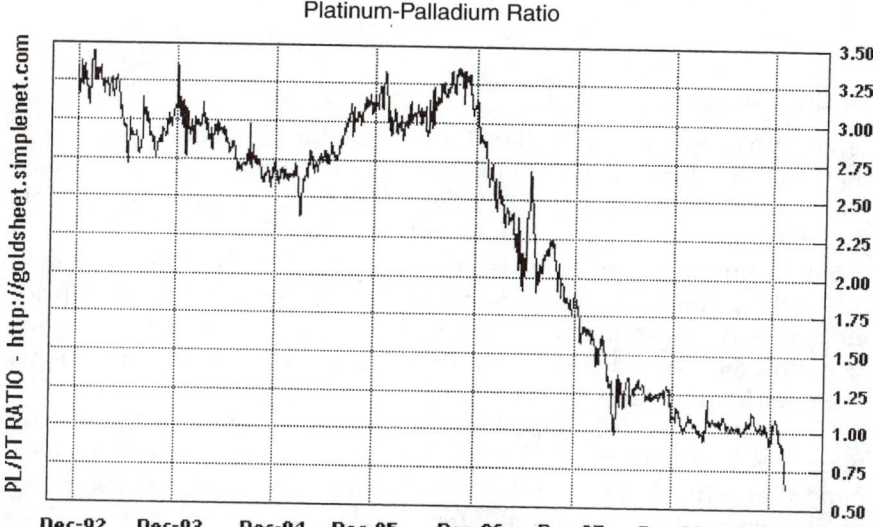

Average platinum-palladium ratio = 2.49

Figure 16–6. Platinum to Palladium Ratio
SOURCE: *http://goldsheet.simplenet.com.*

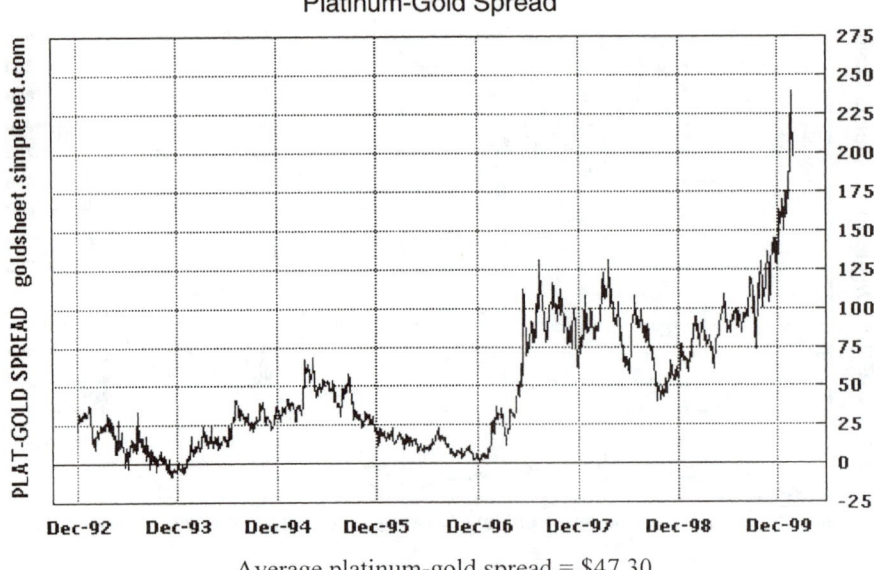

Average platinum-gold spread = $47.30

Figure 16–7. Platinum to Gold Spread
SOURCE: *http://goldsheet.simplenet.com.*

Bullion Bars

Buying precious metals in bullion form means buying a chunk of the metal that has been formed into a block. Bullion is measured in troy ounces, which are slightly larger (1.0971102 to 1.002) than a standard U.S. (avoirdupois) ounce and come 12 ounces to 1 troy pound.

Similar to other commodities, it is cheaper to buy precious metals in bulk, with a minimum of packaging. This makes bullion bars a very price-efficient way to own metals, as there is little cost involved in forming bars as opposed to coins. For the same reason, it is more cost effective to own one large bar than the same amount in several small bars or ingots.

Each bullion bar is stamped with a registration number, the number of ounces, and the percentage of purity, as well as the name of the company that refined and fabricated it. This name is the hallmark; recognizable names include Credit Suisse, Englehard, and Johnson Matthey. Similar to respected brand names of other products, a well-known hallmark implies quality. With a known hallmark, it is not likely that you would ever have to pay for a chemical test, called an assay, to prove that the metal is pure.

When buying precious metals in bullion form, you have the option of taking delivery or asking the dealer to store your metal. There are fees for delivery and annual costs for storing your metals at the dealer in addition to commissions on the transaction. Consider the costs involved, the frequency with which you expect to buy and sell, and the reputation of the dealer (see "Risks in Precious Metals Investing" later in the chapter) when deciding whether to take physical possession.

Coins

Precious metal coins fall into two categories: bullion and numismatic. Bullion coins are those whose value is strictly related to their metal content. In contrast, the value of numismatic coins depends primarily on their condition and appeal as rare or historical coins. Some investors include a hybrid category, the seminumismatic coin. These coins are not as rare as numismatic coins and their prices depend on a combination of their metal value and a premium for rarity.

Bullion Coins. Bullion coins appeal to investors who buy precious metals in small amounts, usually 1 troy ounce and above, although smaller denominations are available. They also appeal to those buying metals as a final store of value in the event of worldwide disaster as they are easily portable and divisible.

Bullion coins are sold at a slight premium to their pure metal or meltdown value, partially due to the fabrication process as mentioned and partially due to the fact that different bullion coins carry varying levels of investor appeal. This appeal is due to liquidity, purity, politics, and marketing. For example, on February 18, 2000, when the spot price of gold was $305.20, Numismatic Properties, an internet dealer at *www.numismaticproperties.com,* offered to sell 1-ounce gold coins in quantities of less than 20 at the following prices:

American Gold Eagles	$314.20
Austrian Philharmonic	$322.20
Canadian Maple Leaf	$314.20
South African Krugerrands	$314.20
Chinese Pandas	$328.70

The Krugerrand, minted in South Africa, was the first-made bullion coin in the 1960s. In 1979, Canada introduced the Maple Leaf, with the intention of taking the market share of antiapartheid investors. The United States ventured into the market in the early 1980s with American Arts

Gold Medallions, then later with Gold Eagles. Political preferences play a part in the relative popularity of gold coins as do preferences for the composition of the coins. For example, Canadian Maple Leafs and South African Krugerrands both contain 1 troy ounce of gold, but the Maple Leaf is pure gold and the Krugerrand has added copper to make the coin harder and more resistant to damage.

Silver bullion coins, including Chinese Silver Pandas and 2000 American Silver Eagles, are an inefficient investment. For a low-cost coin, the premium for minting and shipping, when compared with actual silver value, is quite high in percentage terms.

Most nonnumismatic silver coins are bought and sold in bullion bags, a term for bags full of pre-1965 U.S. silver coins, which are 90% silver. The bags contain $1,000 worth of coins as measured by their actual monetary face value. For example, a silver bullion bag of quarters would contain 4,000 quarters. The price of these bags is based on the silver value of the coins, although theoretically the coins' face value provides a floor of $1,000. Although this floor is not significant for 90% silver coins trading for more than $3,000 a bag, it does provide a measure of risk protection for a small group of silver bullion bags known as Kennedy clads or 40% halves. These Kennedy half-dollars issued between 1965 and 1970 are 40% silver. At 0.148 ounces of silver each, a 2,000 coin bag contains 296 ounces of silver. Since the face value of a bag is $1,000, an ounce of Kennedy clad silver cannot fall below $3.38 ($3.38 x 296 = $1,000).

A latecomer to the market, platinum bullion coins became available first in Great Britain, with the issue of the 1-ounce British Noble (not counting Russian platinum coins available in the early 1800s). American Platinum Eagles are now widely available in denominations of 1 ounce, 1/2 ounce, 1/4 ounce, and 1/10 ounce.

Numismatic Coins. Numismatic coins are rare coins which trade on their value as collector items. The prices of individual coins are based on their rarity, quality, and popularity among collectors. For very rare coins, their metal or bullion value is relatively unimportant. Seminumismatic coins, those of lesser rarity, fluctuate in price based on a combination of their metal value and collector value.

The rare coin business can be complicated, because establishing the worth of a coin is somewhat subjective. While trading markets are fairly active and information on recent transactions is easy to obtain, all 1882-S Morgan dollar coins are not worth the same amount as are all shares of General Motors Corporation. This is due to differences in condition, called a coin's grade. Grading a coin is a method of categorizing its condition, which is important, because tiny scratches that are barely visible can make hundreds of dollars of difference in a coin's price. The grade of a perfect coin, if it exists, would be MS-70 (MS refers to "mint state"). Most investment grade, uncirculated coins have grades such as MS-63, MS-65, or MS-67.

Because a coin's grade is an opinion of the grading expert, there is room for error or fraud. Dishonest dealers may undergrade coins they purchase and overgrade those they sell in order to make more money. Always buy rare coins from a reputable dealer with an unqualified guarantee that you can get your money back or exchange the coin if other experts do not agree with its grade. Always consult guidebooks and shop several dealers to make sure that the price quoted for a specific coin of a particular grade is reasonable.

For more information about rare coins, contact the nonprofit American Numismatic Association (ANA) at 818 North Cascade Avenue, Colorado Springs, Colorado 80903-3279, 719-632-2646 or *www.money.org*. Its website provides educational information, numerous guidebooks of current coin prices, and a search feature for finding ANA member dealers in your area.

Certificate Plans

A precious metals certificate plan is a way to purchase metals without taking delivery of them. Rather than receiving the coin or bullion, you receive a certificate which indicates how much you own and where it is stored. This is similar to purchasing a metal and having it stored by your dealer, except that you do not have to pay delivery charges and there are often other benefits.

Plans differ but usually include minimum purchase amounts, commissions for transactions, and storage charges. Some allow you to purchase by phone, and most allow you to invest by dollar volume rather than by number of ounces. Many provide automatic investment programs to take advantage of dollar cost averaging. Investor holdings in certificate plans may be segregated or nonsegregated, meaning that it may be set aside with your name on it or you may have a percentage ownership in a large vault of that particular metal. While some investors believe that segregated storage is safer, it is actually more important to make sure you are dealing with a large, reputable dealer that keeps its metals in a third-party, separately insured, periodically audited facility.

Precious Metals Mining Company Stocks

Purchasing bullion, coins, or certificates are pure ways to invest in precious metals; however, another way to benefit from changes in the value of a precious metal is through investing in companies that mine it. Buying stock in mining companies is easy, but choosing the right companies for investment can be complicated.

Among other things, the value of mining companies is based on the price of the metal(s) mined, the management of the company, the amount of proven reserves owned, the company's extraction costs, and the company's financial strength. Additionally, for the many mining stocks not based in the United States, issues of currency risk, political stability, and availability of financial information affect values. Many financial websites' screening tools allow you to screen by industry, which can provide a list of precious metals mining stocks. Goldsheet, at *http://www.goldsheet.simplenet.com*, is dedicated to precious metals. In addition to historical pricing and charts, you can find lists of mining companies with descriptions and links.

The following list of considerations can help you choose mining stocks.

- Consider the metal being mined. Even the best company's stock will come under pressure when the price of its metal falls. Buy the stock of gold-mining companies only when you expect the price of gold to rise.

- Research the company. Insist on respected management; scandal follows some mining executives. Buy companies that have proven reserves, not those that simply plan to explore attractive areas. Require a strong balance sheet that is not heavy on debt. Low-cost producers will be able to withstand bear markets in their metal and still remain profitable. High-cost producers may provide proportionately higher increases in stock price as metals prices rise and they move from unprofitable to profitable.

- Use regional politics to your advantage. The precious metals reserves of a mining company in a politically stable region are worth more to investors than those in a country whose government might seize assets or ban all exports on a whim. Your strategy, whether safety or speculation, dictates whether you are looking for a bargain or are willing to pay more for stability. Consider investing in companies whose operations provide an alternative to production from politically unstable areas. In metals with concentrated geographic production, such as platinum and palladium, disruption in the principal mining countries of Russia and South Africa could instantly increase the value of producers elsewhere. For example, part of the appeal of the Australian mining company, Delta Gold, is that it owns a 33% share in the Hartley Project, the largest platinum deposit outside of politically volatile South Africa.

- Diversify to reduce risk. Combine mining stocks from different areas of the world to lessen your exposure to political risk and currency fluctuations.

- Avoid penny stocks. Issues priced under $5 are notoriously subject to market manipulation. Add the sometimes sketchy financial information available on foreign mining stocks, for an especially risky investment. If you want to reduce risk, stick with the larger capitalization mining stocks.

Precious Metals Mutual Funds

If you are interested in precious metals but would like to leave the choice of specific investment vehicles to a professional, then consider precious metals mutual funds. These funds, of which gold funds are the most common, invest in a combination of bullion, mining stocks, bonds and preferred stocks convertible into mining shares, and cash.

In general, you can expect the returns of precious metals funds to be affected by rising or falling metals prices; however, there is discretion in the particular investments owned, and returns can vary widely. For example, a CBS MarketWatch Mutual Fund Profile on February 18, 2000, which ranked the top 25 U.S. gold oriented mutual funds, showed significant differences in the returns of the funds ranked. Franklin Gold Fund A was the top performer for one-year returns at 24.3% and Midas Fund R was ranked twenty-fifth with a –15.6% return, a range of nearly 40%. Given the bear market in gold of recent years, it is not surprising that none of the funds listed had a positive three-year return and 21 were down in double digits, four of them over 30%.

When investing in precious metals funds, compare the following characteristics, in addition to previous total returns relative to the peer group.

- Country weightings: Gold funds can generally be divided into North American and global funds. Consider that the political atmosphere in foreign countries and currency fluctuations will affect returns on global funds depending on where they are invested.

- Portfolio composition: Stocks of mining companies, which have established operations, are less risky than stocks of exploration companies, which require little capital and hope to hit it big with a discovery. Weightings in bullion differ widely, and some gold funds also invest in silver and platinum bullion. Bullion values move in a one-to-one relationship with metals prices, while stocks tend to feel a multiplier effect from metals prices, making them more volatile.

- Expense ratios: Expenses as a percentage of assets vary widely in precious metals funds. While reported returns are net of expense ratios, it is difficult for a fund with high expenses to outperform its peers over the long term.

- Dividend yield: Most investors purchase precious metals investments for their potential capital gains; however, some funds pay a dividend that is worth noting.

Futures

Precious metals are commodities, and as such, contracts for future delivery can be traded on the futures exchanges. Mining companies and large industrial users buy and sell futures to reduce the risk that prices will fall (for mining companies) or rise (for industrial manufacturers). The existence of this market creates an opportunity for those who would like to speculate on the direction of metals prices.

Futures trading is only for experienced investors, as the risks involved can exceed the amount invested. For more information about futures, see Chapter 14.

Risks in Precious Metals Investing

Precious metals investing involves plenty of risk, as the price of the metal in question could fall, causing you to lose money. In bullion and coin investing, however, an additional risk not associated with many modern investments is risk of fraud. Although most metals dealers are honest, the industry is rife with shady characters. To avoid trouble, read the following set of rules for precious metals investing provided in literature from the Canadian Better Business Bureau (CBBB).[4]

- Always check the background of a metals dealer. Ask for bank references and call them. Check the local branch of the Better Business Bureau, state securities commission, and attorney general. The Industry Council for Tangible Assets (ICTA) is a national trade association for coin and precious metals dealers that urges its members to subscribe to a program of binding arbitration. They can be contacted at 666 Pennsylvania S.E., Washington DC 20003.

- Do not buy precious metals advertised at "below spot prices." Spot prices are metals prices fixed on major exchanges. Dealers who sell below the market price cannot make money if they actually purchase the metal when it is ordered. Instead, they often wait, hoping to profit by buying the metal at a later date, when the spot price has dropped.

- Avoid precious metals dealers who are willing to pay you to keep the metal in their vault. This can signal a classic Ponzi scheme in which the same metal is sold to different customers. By the same token, beware the dealer who refuses to make a timely delivery of your purchase.

[4]Canadian Better Business Bureau, "Steps Investors Can Take to Protect Themselves," *Gold and Silver Investments.*

- The safest way to guarantee delivery is to use a bank draft which is only payable upon delivery of the metal to your bank. Do not send a check in the mail, assuming the dealer will deliver.

- To avoid counterfeiting, stick with known hallmarks on bullion.

- Metals certificates and warehouse receipts, with which you never take possession of the metal, are only as good as the name of the seller. Deal only with reputable banks or brokerage firms.

Summary

With the exception of a small group of doomsdayers and goldbugs, few investment professionals recommend any significant purchase of precious metals for most portfolios. The markets for both bullion and rare coins are volatile and best left to speculators (bullion) and educated collectors (rare coins). If you choose to invest or speculate, do so only through reputable dealers after careful study.

Part 4
The Mechanics of Investing

Once an investor understands how investments work, it is time to formulate a personalized investment strategy. Each is as different as the family situation and goals it is designed to benefit. The following chapters provide insight into different approaches. Chapter 17 outlines the differences among brokerage firms and the pros and cons of full service or deep discount, plus the gray area in between. Chapter 18 defines many common investment strategies, such as growth and value investing and the methodology used to follow each technique. Chapter 19 outlines the investment strategies of a wide range of experts, providing insight into their analysis and showing how they effectively combine some of the methodologies discussed in Chapter 18.

17
Where to Trade

The choice of a particular broker can affect your investment results significantly, whether the difference is in quality of advice, ease of executions, range of products, or cost in commissions and fees. This chapter will outline some of the differences among brokers, provide sources of information for finding and rating brokers, and discuss taking action when there is a dispute.

Choosing a Broker

At one time there existed a clear delineation between full-service and discount brokerage firms. Full-service firms offered investment advice, research, and an experienced advisor on the other end of the phone line each time you called. For these perks, the investor paid with higher commissions. Discount brokerage firms, on the other hand, offered only execution of transactions for investors who made their own decisions. Commissions were low because the personnel handling the orders were simply taking down transactions—there were no salesperson commissions or research department salaries to pay. While some definitions of full-service and discount brokerage firms may still be correct, the line separating the two has blurred as many full-service firms race to join the internet trading explosion and discount firms incorporate a multitude of value-added services, including research and retirement planning.

Full-Service Brokerage

If you want to work with a financial planner who will assess your assets, and help you with a financial plan for reaching your goals, then expect to pay for the service. You may pay through commissions on your transactions or you may pay on a fee basis. Most full-service firms offer both options; individual planners may only offer one. No one should charge both a fee and a commission without disclosing that fact.

Fee-Only Financial Planners and Investment Advisers

Many investors prefer fee-only planners to commission planners because they have no bias toward unnecessary trading. Fee-only planners generally charge either by the hour or as a percent of assets under management. A planner who charges by the hour may be the more cost-effective choice if you need a few specific questions answered or would like an objective second opinion on the investments in your portfolio. These planners charge you for their time only when you ask them to.

A planner who charges as a percentage of assets under management is expected to continuously monitor your investments. Given the payment arrangement, these planners have a financial incentive to increase the value of your portfolio, as this will increase management fees. Brokerage firms often call this arrangement a wrap account; it may be either fee-only or a combination of a fee and reduced transaction fees.

Commission-Based Financial Planners

Commission-based planners are those who you pay by placing transactions. They earn a percentage of the commission you pay on each trade. For active traders, this can get expensive, but if you have a buy and hold outlook, this may be a cost-effective way to obtain investment advice. Many full-service firms have several commission levels, which are based on activity or account value. Although commissions are higher than at discount firms, they are generally negotiable. If you have a large portfolio and/or trade actively, ask for a discount.

Many full-service firms now offer discount online trading. Most have account minimums in the $50,000 to $100,000 range and wrap fees from 0.2% to 2.25% of assets. The fee pays for advice, research, and sometimes perks such as bill paying and estate planning. These arrangements can make sense if you trade often and would like advice, research, and customer service.

Keep in mind that there is an inherent conflict of interest in commission-based advice, whether it is the inclination to recommend a higher- rather than lower-commission investments or the tendency toward high rates of activity, which produce higher levels of commissions. Check out commission-based brokers with the National Association of Securities Dealers (NASD), a self-regulating body for the financial industry. Through its public disclosure program, you can find information about individual brokers, including current and past employment and any complaints filed against them. Call the direct toll-free hotline at 800-289-9999 or access the website at *www.nasdr.com*.

Working with a planner employed by a well-known firm provides some comfort, because these planners are subject to supervision of the firm. If you choose one of many planners who operate independently of major brokerage firms, then ask for credentials such as securities licenses and any professional designations (e.g., certified financial planner, CFP). To be designated a CFP, a planner must take a series of tests and be subject to a set of ethics and standards set out by the CFP Board of Standards. Note that a planner with a CFP designation may operate either as a fee-only or a commission-based planner. For help in finding a planner in your area who has advanced credentials, contact one of the following professional organizations.

American Institute of Certified Public Accountants, Personal Financial Planning Division
800-862-4272 or *www.aicpa.org*
Contact the AICPA for a list of CPAs who are designated as personal financial specialists.

Certified Financial Planner Board of Standards
888-237-6275 or *www.cfp-board.org*
Contact the CFP board to confirm that a planner has achieved this designation.

Financial Planning Association
800-322-4237 or *www.iafp.org*

This organization was created by the January 1, 2000, merger of the Institute of Certified Financial Planners and the International Association for Financial Planning. FPA is in the process of merging the databases of the two organizations. The PlannerSearch application at its website provides lists of CFP professionals by city, state, or zip code.

National Association of Personal Financial Advisors
888-333-6659 or *www.napfa.org*
Contact NAPFA for a list of fee-only financial planners in up to five states.

Some financial planners are registered as investment advisers with the Securities and Exchange Commission (SEC), a designation that requires extensive reporting of investment activities. Registered investment advisers generally have account minimums of $1 million or more. To find an adviser in your area, try the following directories.

Directory of Registered Investment Advisers
800-446-2810 or
www.mmdaccess.com
This directory includes more than 11,000 SEC- registered investment advisors. In addition to names and addresses, the directory includes some basic information about assets under management, investment style, client composition, fee structure, and minimum

account size. You may order online or by phone. Cost is $450.

Money Manager Review Online
415-386-7111 or
www.slip.net/~mmreview
The website for Money Manager Review provides performance information about more than 800 top money managers. The site allows you to find a particular manager, rank money managers

using different criteria, track the performance of different managers, and compare them with one another. A one-year subscription is $295.

Nelson's World's Best Money Managers
800-333-6357 or *www.nelnet.com*
Published quarterly from the Nelson Investment Manager Database,

the World's Best Money Managers ranks more than 1,500 investment managers on more than 4,500 portfolios. There are 200 ranking reports, based on performance time frame and asset type. The printed version is $260 but access to the reports is free at the website with registration.

Choosing among the Many Firms

Choosing a full-service brokerage firm depends largely on the individual investment broker and on the range of services and costs set by the firm. In November 1999, *SmartMoney Magazine* conducted a ranking of full-service brokers, based on performance in six categories: services and products, stock research, mutual funds, commissions and fees, online services, and staying out of trouble. Because this ranking involved full-service firms, it double-weighted the results in the categories of services and products and stock research. The resulting rankings were as follows:

1. Merrill Lynch
2. A.G. Edwards
3. Fidelity Investments
4. Charles Schwab
5. Edward Jones
6. PaineWebber
7. Prudential

Key to note in their findings is that none of the firms dominated the rankings. Only two (Schwab and Fidelity) won more than one category, making it clear that you should decide which attributes are most important and evaluate firms based on those criteria. For help, you can sort the results by any one category, online at *www.smartmoney.com/si/brokers/fullserv/*.

Discount and Online Brokerage

Discount brokerage firms arrived on the scene in 1975, with the end of fixed commission rates. In the beginning, these firms simply took orders, executing stock transactions for investors who found their information elsewhere. As competition increased, the range of products and services also increased, until some discount firms, notably Charles Schwab and Fidelity Investments, fit into either the full-service or discount category. Although not all discounters offer the level of services that these two provide, you can likely find just the right balance of cost and service among those available. Discount/online brokers can vary considerably in commission rates, products offered, level of service, and reliability.

The Investor Protection Trust of the Securities Division of the Washington State Department of Financial Institutions is a nonprofit group dedicated to educating investors about online investing. Their website is *www.investingonline.org*.

When choosing a particular firm, ask the following questions.

- Are investor accounts insured and by how much? The Securities Investor Protection Corporation (SIPC), a government-sponsored organization, covers $100,000 in cash plus $400,000 in securities. If your account value will be higher, make sure that the firm carries additional insurance. Not all firms do.

- Does it offer all the investment alternatives that you need? Not all deep discounters offer IRAs and a wide range of mutual funds. Check into the availability of bonds, foreign stocks, and options if they are part of your investment plan. If you want dividend reinvestment for your stocks, make sure it is offered.

- Can you trade the way you want and will alternatives cause costs to skyrocket? Most online brokerage firms offer internet and touch-tone trading and many provide a live broker, but transaction costs may be different for each option. Be sure the costs that draw you to the firm are for the type of trading you tend to do. If you normally trade on the internet but do not always have access to a computer when you travel, is it also easy, cheap, and convenient (consider any time restrictions) to trade by phone?

- How is their customer service? Call the firm several times before opening an account. Do you have to wait? Look at the rating sites listed in this chapter and note investor comments. Check investment message boards at such places as the Motley Fool (*www.fool.com*) to see how many negative comments a firm has and how egregious the alleged offenses were.

- What are the costs? Check prices for the kind of trading you tend to do as well as for any additional fees. Many firms differentiate between costs for market and limit orders. Find out if there are any additional fees, often called handling charges, added to the cost of each order. Will it cost you to open an IRA, and more importantly, what is the annual fee? Is there a fee for dividend reinvestment? Find a written list of all fees you might be charged; then, unless your activity level makes it prohibitive, calculate how much you would have spent in fees had you been their customer last year.

- How reliable is the website? If you plan to do most of your trading online, find out about downtime and response time on the website, especially if you are an active trader. System downtime can cost you money as can slow response time. Gomez Advisors (*www.gomez.com*), a Massachusetts-based research firm, has a rating called the Performance Monitor in which it collects data about website response time every five minutes and compares it with an average and a top-10 list of other firms. The Monitor also includes an indicator of whether the broker's performance is getting better, worse, or is unchanged.

Several websites offer rankings of discount/online brokerage firms. The rankings rarely agree, but the information provided about each broker is generally valuable. Because every investor values different characteristics, performance in subcategories may be of more use than overall ratings. Several sites and their rankings follow in this section.

Gomez Advisors, Inc. at *www.gomez.com* ranks e-commerce providers in a multitude of industries. Their analysis of financial services includes a look at online banks, brokerage firms, insurance providers, and mortgage brokers. The Internet Broker Scorecard provides separate rankings for overall score and each of the component categories:[1] ease of use, customer confidence, on-site resources, relationship services, and overall cost. In addition, they match ranking for investors who fit the following profiles: hyper-active trader, serious investor, life goal planner, and one-stop shopper. Each of the firms listed has a one-page review which describes key benefits and shortfalls as well as each category rating.

The top 10 positions on the Internet Broker Scorecard in the summer of 2000 for overall score were as follows:[2]

1. Charles Schwab
   www.schwab.com or 800-435-4000

2. E*Trade
   www.etrade.com or 800-786-2572

3. Fidelity Investments
   www.fidelity.com or 800-544-7272

4. DLJdirect
   www.dljdirect.com or 800-825-5732

---

[1]Gomez Advisors, Inc. "The Internet Broker Scorecard, Summer 2000," *www.gomez.com*.
[2]Ibid.

5. Merrill Lynch & Co.
   www.mldirect.ml.com or 888-ML-ONLINE

6. TD Waterhouse
   www.waterhouse.com or 800-934-4410

7. National Discount Brokers
   www.ndb.com or 888-302-7764

8. A.B. Watley
   www.abwatley.com or 800-229-2853

9. Muriel Siebert
   www.siebertnet.com or 800-872-0711

10. American Express Brokerage
    www.americanexpress.com or 800-297-8800

The *SmartMoney Magazine* website at *www.smartmoney.com* has a comprehensive ranking of 25 discount/online firms for three different types of investors: do-it-yourselfers, delegators, and navigators. The categories covered are: commissions and fees, ease and accuracy of trades, services, mutual fund offerings, number of online products, stock research, and staying out of trouble. Links are provided for the brokerage firms listed.

The SmartMoney 2000 Broker Survey top ten for the do-it-yourselfer category was:[3]

1. TD Waterhouse
   www.waterhouse.com or 800-934-4410

2. Muriel Siebert
   www.siebertnet.com or 800-872-0711

3. Charles Schwab
   www.schwab.com or 800-435-4000

4. DLJdirect
   www.dljdirect.com or 800-825-5732

5. National Discount Brokers
   www.ndb.com or 888-302-7764

6. Fidelity Investments
   www.fidelity.com or 800-544-7272

7. E*Trade
   www.etrade.com or 800-786-2572

---

[3]"2000 Broker Survey," *SmartMoney Magazine, www.smartmoney.com.*

8. Mydiscountbroker.com
   www.mydiscountbroker.com or 888-882-5600

9. Scottrade
   www.scottrade.com or 800-619-SAVE

10. Merrill Lynch Direct
    www.mldirect.ml.com or 888-ML-ONLINE

Kiplinger's Personal Finance Magazine and its website *wwa.kiplinger.com* rank 21 online brokers, giving them a rating from one to five stars. Categories include costs, quality measures, securities trading, and services. Payment for order flow is noted in *Kiplinger's* survey. A broker who receives a kickback for sending orders to a particular firm (sometimes $2 per trade) may not be shopping for the best price. This practice results in poor executions, which is one of the hidden costs of trading. This practice is legal, but often not in the customer's best interests. *Kiplinger's* combines payment for order flow, percentage of NYSE-listed stocks whose executions took place on the NYSE (where you typically get the most competitive price), and the number of different firms that execute orders to determine whether a broker is really shopping for the best price.

Results from the November 1999 survey provided the following top 10 firms.[4]

1. Discover Brokerage (now merged with Morgan Stanley Dean Witter Online)
   www.msdw.com or 800-58-INVEST

2. Muriel Siebert & Co.
   www.siebertnet.com or 800-872-0711

3. Mr. Stock
   www.mrstock.com or 800-470-1896

4. Mydiscountbroker.com
   www.mydiscountbroker.com or 888-882-5600

5. Wall Street Access
   www.wsaccess.com or 800-925-5781

6. Brown & Co.
   www.brownco.com or 800-822-2021

7. Datek Online
   www.datek.com or 800-823-2835

8. TD Waterhouse Group
   www.waterhouse.com or 800-934-4410

[4]"Rating the Brokers," *www.kiplinger.com.*

9. Ameritrade
   www.ameritrade.com or 800-454-9272

10. A.B. Watley
    www.abwatley.com or 800-229-2853

Several additional sources provide information about the performance of online brokers. Internet Investing provides a listing of brokers that offer after-hours trading and online brokers whose "special services or features make them stand out from the crowd."[5] The listing, with information about and a link to each site, can be found at *www.internetinvesting.com/brokers.htm*. The site at *www.sonic.net/donaldj/brokers.html* covers 93 online brokers. The ranking is written by an individual investor, Don Johnson, and is divided into three categories: deep discounters, middle-cost discounters, and high-cost discounters. Varying amounts of information for each firm are listed, with a link to each broker's website. The Keynote Web Broker Trading Index at *www.keynote.com/measures/brokers/* follows transaction time for 19 online brokers each week, ranking them according to speed. Robert's Online Commissions Pricer at *www.intrepid.com/~robertl/commissions-pricer1.html* provides commissions on stocks, options, mutual funds, and bonds for internet trades, touch-tone phone trades, and broker-assisted trades.

Comparison information compiled about some of the largest internet brokers follows in Table 17–1.

Settling a Dispute with a Broker

The vast majority of securities transactions are completed without a problem, but occasionally disputes arise. The best weapon in settling a problem to your satisfaction is prevention. Following these guidelines can help:

- Never give anyone, including your broker, trading authorization over your account.

- Always read your monthly statement carefully and question any unauthorized transactions immediately.

- When placing orders over the phone, state both the name of the stock and its symbol. The broker should always repeat your order back to you, indicating a clear understanding of what you said. Most brokerage firms tape telephone calls. Do not be offended; this is to everyone's advantage.

---

[5]"Online Brokers," *www.internetinvesting.com*.

Table 17–1. Internet Brokers Compared (January 24, 2000)

Broker	Costs for Online Stock Trades	IRA Fees Open/Annual/Close	Ways to Trade	Real-Time Quotes	Minimum to Open Account
Ameritrade www.ameritrade.com 800-454-9272	$8.00 market $13.00 limit	$0/$0/$25	Internet, touch-tone phone, live broker	$30/month or 100 free per online trade	$2,000
Charles Schwab www.schwab.com 800-435-4000	$29.95	$0/$29 for accts. under $10,000	Internet, touch-tone phone, live broker, branch office	100 free per trade	$2,500
Datek Online www.datek.com 800-823-2835	$9.99	$25/$40/$60	Internet, live broker	Free	$2,000
Discover Brokerage Direct www.discoverbrokerage.com 800-584-6837	$14.95 market $19.95 limit	$0/$0/$50	Internet, touch-tone phone, live broker	Free	$2,000
DLJdirect www.dljdirect.com 800-355-5678	$20.00	$0/$35 with fewer than 3 trades per year/$50	Internet, touch-tone phone, live broker	100 free per trade	none
E*Trade www.etrade.com 800-786-2572	$14.95 listed market $19.95 limit and NASDAQ	Not offered	Internet, touch-tone phone, live broker	Free	$1,000

Broker	Commission	Transfer/Close Fees	Access	Research	Minimum/Inactivity
Fidelity Investments *www.fidelity.com* 800-544-7272	$14.95 market with at least 12 trades/12 months $19.95 limit ($14.95 w/72 trades/12 months)	$0/$0/$50	Internet, touch-tone phone, live broker, branch office	Free	$5,000/fees for inactive accounts
National Discount Brokers *www.ndb.com* 800-888-3999	$14.75 market $19.75 limit	$0/$35 for accounts under $10,000/$50	Internet, touch-tone phone, live broker	Free	None
Quick & Reilly *www.quickwaynet.com* 800-837-7220	$14.95 market $19.95 limit	$0 + up to $50 credit for incoming transfer fees/$0/$50	Internet, touch-tone phone, live broker	Free	$500
Muriel Siebert *www.siebertnet.com* 800-872-0711	$14.95	$0/$30 under $10,000, $0 over/$50	Internet, touch-tone phone, live broker	Free	None
SureTrade *www.suretrade.com* 401-642-6900	$7.95 market $9.95 limit	$0/$0/$0	Internet, touch-tone phone, live broker	Free	None
TD Waterhouse *www.waterhouse.com* 800-934-4410	$12	$0/$0/$0 Free commission voucher for transfer in >$10,000	Internet, touch-tone phone, live broker, branch office	Free	$1,000 regular None for IRA

- Keep a running journal of dates, times, and subjects of conversations with your broker.

- Retain copies of all correspondence between you and your broker, including e-mails.

- Read all prospectuses before investing. Always ask about the downside.

- Do not rush into making an investment decision. If it is a good investment today, it will also be good tomorrow.

- Remember that risk and expected return go together. If it sounds too good to be true, it probably is.

- If you have a problem that has not been resolved to your satisfaction, write to your broker and send a copy to the branch manager. Many misunderstandings can be solved at this level.

- If the dispute continues, contact the appropriate regulatory agency.

Filing a Complaint

If you cannot resolve the problem through your broker, you may have to file a complaint. You can do this online at the National Association of Securities Dealers regulatory website at *www.nasdr.com* using an online complaint form. You may also contact the regulatory office nearest you. Addresses are available at the NASDR website as are phone numbers, if time is of the essence. You should also contact your state securities commission. Addresses and phone numbers are available at your state's website (general format is www.state two-letter abbreviation .us) or at the NASDR website. Investigations into a complaint of broker wrongdoing by the NASD are regulatory in nature and may result in sanctions against or even suspension of the offending broker. However, they may not result in getting money or securities returned. For that, you may need to seek arbitration.

Arbitration

Most brokerage account agreements include a paragraph in which the customer agrees to binding arbitration of a dispute rather than a court settlement process. In arbitration, which is generally quicker and less expensive than traditional legal procedures, impartial individuals with experience in the industry act to resolve disagreements. While you may have a lawyer represent you, agreeing to arbitration usually means you give up the right to pursue the matter through the court system.

Securities arbitrations are conducted based on a code developed by the Securities Industry Conference on Arbitration (SICA), a group composed of representatives of various self-regulatory organizations (SROs); the Securities Industry Association; and public members. According to the SICA, you should decide where to file your claim based on the SRO that supervises the markets where the transaction occurred or where the securities are listed. The list below provides contacts for dispute resolution offices.

NASD Regional Dispute Resolution Offices

Northeast Region

NASD Regulation, Inc.
125 Broad Street, 36th Floor
New York, NY 10004-2193
212-858-4400

Western Region

NASD Regulation, Inc.
525 Market Street, Suite 300
San Francisco, CA 94105
415-882-1234

Southeast Region

NASD Regulation, Inc.
Office of Dispute Resolution
Boca Center Tower 1
5200 Town Center Circle
Boca Raton, FL 33486
561-416-2267

Midwest Region

NASD Regulation, Inc.
10 S. LaSalle Street, Suite 1110
Chicago, IL 60603-1002
312-899-4440

Other Providers of Dispute Resolution

American Stock Exchange

Investor Inquiries, Arbitration
   Department
212-306-1427
Boston Stock Exchange
617-235-2000

Chicago Board of Trade

Legal Department, 6th Floor
312-435-3500
Chicago Board Options Exchange
Department of Arbitration, 7th Floor
312-786-7466

Chicago Mercantile Exchange

Compliance Department, 5th Floor
312-930-8525

New York Stock Exchange

Arbitration Department, 5th Floor
212-656-2772

Pacific Stock Exchange
415-393-4000

The Arbitration Process. An arbitration begins when a claimant files a statement of claim, which outlines the dispute, provides supporting documentation, and indicates what relief (amount of money, action, etc.) is desired. Once the respondent receives the claim from the director of arbitration, a response must be filed within 20 calendar days for small-claim arbitrations (under $10,000) and within 20 business days for all others. The respondent may file a counterclaim that must be answered by the claimant within 10 calendar days for small-claim arbitrations and 10 business days for all others.

Next, arbitrators are appointed and hearings plus any prehearing conferences are set. After the hearing in which each party states its case, arbitrators send their decision in writing to all parties involved. Arbitrators are not required to state their reasons but may be requested to do so no later than the hearing date. Once a decision has been made, it is binding on all parties and will not be reconsidered even if new evidence is found.

Summary

The one-size-fits-all full-service brokerage firm is a distant memory since the deregulation of commissions in 1975. Now investors can choose bare-bones services at minimal costs or full money management, often at the same brokerage firm. Though the surveys pretend to choose the best firms, choosing a firm depends on what products and features are important to you and how much you are willing to pay for them. Do your homework carefully and consider having several different accounts, especially if you trade on the technology-dependent internet.

18
Investment Strategies

Most great endeavors begin with a plan. Whether you are waging a war, building a car, or making a seafood gumbo, you must identify your objective and then decide upon the best method of attaining your goal.

Investing is no different. Your investment objective is your goal—your seafood gumbo—and your investing style is your recipe. Paul Prudhomme and Emeril Lagasse will never agree on the same recipe, but they will agree that success depends on sticking to the one that is chosen.

Investing styles can be divided into two main categories, fundamental and technical. Fundamental analysis, chosen by investment greats such as Warren Buffet and Peter Lynch, focus on the business prospects of a particular company. Depending on the specific approach, asset values, earnings growth, or performance ratios may be given the most weight in assessing a stock's value. Technical analysis, in its purest form, considers only price and volume movements and the charts that they create. The company, its business, and industry are of no consequence.

Fundamental Analysis

The fundamental method of evaluating stocks involves interpreting financial results in the context of business and competitive climates. Numbers are crunched and ratios computed, but nonquantitative issues such as management expertise and the potential for new products are also considered. Here is where the investor adds value. Financial information about companies is widely available; it is the interpretation of this information that brings success or failure.

The two most widely followed fundamental investment styles, value and growth investing, share the investment objective of capital appreciation but differ in their approaches to obtain it. Income investing, another fundamental approach, claims an investment objective of current income with capital preservation.

Value Investing

Value investors focus on what a business would be worth if it were sold tomorrow. Most value stocks have the following characteristics:

- Low valuation measures such as price/earnings, price/revenue, and price/book value ratios
- Dividends

The prospectus of the AIM Value Fund provides insight into the mind of a value investor. It states:[1]

> The portfolio managers focus on undervalued equity securities of
> (1) out-of-favor cyclical growth companies,
> (2) established growth companies that are undervalued compared to historical relative valuation parameters,
> (3) companies where there is early but tangible evidence of improving prospects that are not yet reflected in the price of the company's equity securities, and
> (4) companies whose equity securities are selling at prices that do not reflect the current market value of their assets and where there is reason to expect realization of this potential in the form of increased equity values.

In value investing, the investor analyzes the worth of a company and purchases those stocks believed to be undervalued, hoping to sell when they become fully valued.

Value Indicators. The following list of valuation ratios can be helpful in determining whether a company is worth more than its current stock price indicates.

- Price/earnings (P/E) ratio: The ratio of a stock's current price to its earnings per share. All else being equal, lower is better because it means you are paying fewer dollars in price for each dollar in earnings per share. Measure the P/E ratio against an industry peer group and the stock's own P/E range for the past five years. You may also want to compare the industry average with its historical range, and with an index such as the S&P 500 or the Wilshire 2000. In some cases, an entire industry is out of favor and thus undervalued.

- Price/book value (P/BV) ratio: The ratio of a stock's price to its book value per share. Book value is the theoretical liquidation value of the business, computed by subtracting liabilities from assets. Dividing by the number of shares outstanding provides book value per share. A

---

[1] "Investment Objectives and Strategies," *AIM Value Fund Prospectus* (May 3, 1999): 1.

value investor's dream is a P/BV ratio less than 1, meaning the stock's price is less than its liquidation value. As with the P/E ratio, compare with historic values, industry, and index averages.

- Price/revenue (P/R) ratio: The ratio of a stock's price to its net sales per share. Compare with past ratios and an industry average.

- Price/free cash flow (P/CF) ratio: The ratio of a stock's price to its free cash flow per share. Free cash flow is cash flow less required capital spending, interest, dividends, and working capital needs.

- Dividend yield: The ratio of a stock's dividend to its share price. The dividend yield does not relate to the value of the company if it were sold tomorrow, but to the value of a share of stock as an income-producing investment. If there is enough cash flow to easily cover the dividend (i.e., no danger of a dividend cut), the yield creates a floor on the stock price. As the stock price falls, the yield rises to the point where investors will buy for income, thereby creating enough demand to prevent the price from falling more.

Interpreting the Indicators. The general rule for P/E, P/BV, P/R, and P/FCF ratios is that lower is better. A lower ratio means an investor is paying less in terms of stock price for EPS, book value, revenues, or cash flow. A value investor expects that eventually the stock will trade at a more "normal" multiple, as measured by the firm's history, industry, or index averages. Assuming that the denominator in each ratio does not deteriorate, the stock's price must rise.

Consider CNF Transportation, an NYSE-traded trucking company, as an example. The current price of CNF is $40 per share. Its trailing 12 months (TTM) EPS is $2.86.

$$P/E = \frac{Price}{EPS} = \frac{\$40}{\$2.86} = 14$$

The five-year P/E range for CNF is a low of 13 and a high of 29. If CNF's P/E reaches just the midpoint of its historical range (21) without any increase in EPS, its price should rise to $60:

$$\frac{\$60}{\$2.86} = 21$$

At the high point of the range, a 29 P/E, CNF's price would be $83:

$$\frac{\$83}{\$2.86} = 29$$

Frequently, you will find that some indicators demonstrate that the stock is undervalued, but others do not fit the pattern. For example, a stock might have low P/R and P/BV ratios, but a high P/E ratio, which often indicates a problem with profit margins. If further investigation reveals a short-term cause, such as the introduction of a new product or a temporary supply glitch, try normalizing earnings, then recalculating the P/E ratio.

To normalize earnings, take an average net profit margin (EPS/revenues per share) from earlier periods and multiply this times revenue per share. Then use this normalized EPS in the P/E calculation.

Now consider Dole Food Company, with a price of $30 and an EPS of $0.44, as an example. At 68, Dole's P/E ratio is more than twice the industry average of 26. Its P/R is 0.40, compared with the industry's 1.72, and P/BV is 3, compared with the industry's 11. Further investigation reveals that newly acquired businesses and Hurricane Mitch have recently increased costs. Dole's current net profit margin is 0.59%, while its average net profit margin in the last 5 years was 2.22%.

If you multiply the average net profit margin of 2.22% by revenues per share of $77, normalized EPS is $1.70. Using normalized EPS in the P/E equation gives you the following P/E ratio:

$$\frac{\$30}{\$1.71} = 17.5$$

So, if you are correct in believing that current low margins are temporary, Dole's P/E is in line with a value stock.

It is rare to find all indicators low in a healthy company. In fact, one difficulty of value investing is that many stocks have low valuations because they have little potential. As a committed value investor, you must be prepared to weed through the dogs.

If you find a company whose valuation ratios are low relative to its history, industry, or the market, and whose dividend yield is high, then what is next? Find out the reasons why. Good answers include anything that appears to be short term or a one-time occurrence. An industry that is generally out of favor is fine; investor tastes change. Even if problems are serious, consider the stock if you see some of the following positive characteristics:

- Management change—It may take a completely new outlook to turn things around.

- Disclosure—Identifying and understanding the problem is half the battle. Management must do this and take responsibility for making changes.

- A narrow problem—Problems concentrated by division or product line are much easier to address than issues that affect the entire company or industry.

Table 18–1. Value Stock Lilly Industries

	NYSE: LI Current Price: $19.25		
Valuation Ratios	Company	Industry	S&P 500
P/E ratio (TTM)	14.20	32.32	36.26
P/E high—last 5 yrs.	27.34	52.46	43.99
P/E low—last 5 yrs.	10.55	11.96	14.67
Price to revenue (TTM)	0.73	2.17	4.98
Price to book value	2.61	4.56	8.15
Price to cash flow	8.68	22.90	25.65
Price to free cash flow	68.69	33.92	42.74
Dividend yield	1.65%	1.91%	1.58%

SOURCE: Market Guide, data from June 1999.

- Sale of assets—This often indicates that steps have already been taken to divest nonproductive divisions or products. The resulting infusion of cash may help as the company changes its focus.

Table 18–1 provides an example of a value stock called Lilly Industries, which makes industrial paints and coatings.

The P/E ratio is half that of the industry and is in the low end of its historical range. Price to revenue, book value, and cash flow are significantly under industry and index averages. A high P/CF warrants further investigation. A possible cause is found in the five-year growth rate in capital spending, because "free" cash flow is calculated after capital spending. Lilly's capital spending growth rate is 17.5% versus an industry rate of 4.78%, indicating that the company is committing a relatively large amount of cash flow to capital spending. The dividend yield, between industry and index averages, is neither a positive or negative factor.

The company recently announced that it will close three U.S. plants and cut 75 jobs, or about 3.3% of its workforce, an indication that management is committed to cutting costs. Combine this with low valuation ratios for a typical value stock.

Dogs of the Dow: A Popular Value Strategy. Value investors look for stocks that have been battered in price, a situation often identified by a stock's high dividend yield (current dividend/stock price). The Dogs of the Dow strategy instructs investors to buy the 10 highest-yielding stocks in the Dow Jones Industrial Average at year-end, hold the portfolio for a year, and then reset it at the following year-end with the current 10 highest-yielding stocks. To take an even more contrarian approach, choose the five that have the lowest price, a strategy called Small Dogs of the Dow or Puppies of the Dow.

Results of holding Dogs have been mixed, with an especially poor performance in 1999, when 20+% returns of Minnesota Mining & Manufacturing, DuPont, and J.P. Morgan were reduced by a 53.2% loss in Philip Morris and a 41.7% loss in Goodyear. Table 18–2 provides historical returns, with dividends reinvested.

For the year 2000, the Dogs of the Dow are listed in Table 18–3.

To follow the Dogs of the Dow, or to learn more about the strategy, try the Dogs of the Dow website at *www.dogsofthedow.com.*

Growth Investing

Investment styles, like fashion styles, tend to be "in" one year and "out" several years later. For the past few years, growth investing has definitely been "in." Growth stocks have been leaders, and value stocks have not participated in the 30+% annual gains of the general market.

Table 18–2. Relative Performance by the Dogs of the Dow

Year	Dow Dogs	DJIA	S&P 500
1990	–7.6%	–0.4%	–3.2%
1991	34.3	23.9	30.0
1992	7.9	7.4	7.6
1993	27.3	16.8	10.1
1994	4.1	4.9	1.3
1995	36.5	36.4	37.6
1996	27.9	28.6	23.0
1997	21.9	24.9	33.4
1998	10.6	18.1	28.6
1999	3.6	27.2	21.0

SOURCE: *Barron's.*

Table 18–3. Dogs of the Dow in 2000

Company	12/31/99 Price	Dividend Yield
Philip Morris	$23.00	8.3%
J.P. Morgan	126.63	3.1
Caterpillar	47.06	2.8
General Motors	72.69	2.8
Eastman Kodak	66.25	2.7
Minnesota Mining & Manf.	97.88	2.3
ExxonMobil	80.56	2.2
DuPont	65.88	2.1
SBC Communications	48.75	2.0
International Paper	56.44	1.8

SOURCE: *Barron's.*

Growth stocks generally have both of the following characteristics:

- Above-average increases in sales and earnings growth
- Higher than average profitability levels, as measured by returns on equity or profit margins

A good example of a growth outlook is found in a brochure for Janus Equity Funds. In it, the Janus Enterprise Fund is described as follows:

> This nondiversified fund looks for midsize companies that dominate their markets and can maintain solid earnings in the midst of rapid growth. Managed aggressively, the fund typically focuses on quality businesses with long product cycles and substantial pricing power that can perform independent of the economy.

Investors in growth stocks focus on the following measures of performance and profitability.

Growth Stock Indicators. Growth stock indicators are as follows:

- EPS growth: The year-to-year percentage change in earnings per share. EPS growth is the most important evaluation factor for a growth stock investor. EPS growth is generally measured on a quarterly, annual, and long-term (5 or 10 years) basis. Compute EPS on a continuing operations basis, throwing out the effects of accounting changes and discontinued operations. Compare growth rates to a firm's previous rate and to an industry average.

- Sales growth: The year-to-year increase in net sales. Over time, sales growth must be healthy to fuel EPS growth. Compare with past percentage increases, industry growth rates, and EPS growth rates.

- Gross margin: Net sales less cost of goods sold. This measure of profitability and the other margins (operating and net profit) offer excellent insight into whether a company is becoming more efficient in selling its goods or services. Comparisons to the industry indicate which companies are the low-cost producers and thus are more likely to generate cash for growth and easily weather business downturns.

- Return on equity: Net profit divided by shareholders equity. Return on equity (ROE) and return on assets (ROA) provide a percentage return figure. How much did the company make in profits given the amount of equity or assets invested? Compare with past figures and industry averages. Be aware that capital structure, or the amount of debt versus equity, will affect the ROE figure by rewarding companies with high debt.

- Price/earnings/growth (PEG) ratio: The P/E ratio divided by the annual EPS growth rate. A growth stock investor who is not willing to buy growth at any price looks for a PEG near 1, meaning that the P/E ratio is approximately equal to the growth rate in EPS.

Interpreting the Indicators. Look for growth and profitability ratios that are higher than industry averages and are increasing for the firm in question. Earnings growth is a product of sales growth or rising profit margins, or both. Beware when EPS growth is largely dependent on share repurchases.

Sales growth can result from a number of things. The most desirable factors are growth in unit sales of existing products and the introduction of new products. While price increases may add to net sales, competition can erode pricing gains unless the firm is in a monopoly position or has good patent protection.

Use the PEG ratio to evaluate whether a stock's high P/E ratio is warranted. For example, in June 1999, popular growth stocks Microsoft and Biogen both had P/E ratios nearly double that of the S&P 500, but PEGs of just over 1.

Microsoft:

$$\frac{P/E = 68}{EPS\ growth = 62\%}\quad PEG = 1.09$$

Biogen:

$$\frac{P/E = 58}{\text{EPS growth} = 54\%} \quad \text{PEG} = 1.07$$

In addition to using formulas to evaluate a growth stock, make sure the company has the following:

- A superior product or service. Is the product or service innovative (think internet companies) or part of the everyday lives of millions (think food)? What is the potential for long-term increases in sales?

- Sustainable profits. Is the company the most efficient producer in its industry? Does the firm have pricing flexibility due to brand loyalty, or technical expertise?

- Barriers to entry. Profits attract competition. Are there significant start-up costs, patents, or trade secrets which would discourage new entrants to the field?

- Management excellence. Has management shown the ability to spot new opportunities in times of change? Is there enough depth to prevent a crisis at the loss of a key person? Consider management ownership of stock and compensation programs which reward managers for increases in stock value.

A good growth stock example is the Wall Street darling of the 1990s, Dell Computer. Some of its key ratios are detailed in Table 18–4.

Phenomenal sales and earnings growth have fueled the rise in Dell Computer, which began the decade at a split-adjusted $0.0625 and trades at $40 today, making a $1,000 investment worth $640,000. The growth rates and performance ratios speak for themselves. You might pause at a gross margin that is lower than the industry if you do not know their business, which is selling computers at a low cost through the mail. A low retail cost drives a low gross profit margin [(revenues–cost of goods sold)/revenues], but the lack of store overhead contributes to a net profit margin (net profit/revenues) that is higher than its peers.

A recent drop in stock price has followed concerns that past growth rates are not sustainable and competition is high. Table 18–5 summarizes some of the philosophical differences between growth and value investing.

Income Investing

Investors choose a growth style with capital appreciation in mind and a value style with capital appreciation and possibly some income in mind. Income investors, on the other hand, strive to maximize current income.

Table 18–4. Growth Stock Dell Computer

NASDAQ: DELL

Current Price: $38

Performance Ratios	Company	Industry	S&P 500
EPS growth (MRQ)	46.79%	40.11%	14.92%
EPS growth (TTM)	56.91	24.28	13.15
EPS growth (5 yr.)	82.99	37.43	19.49
Sales growth (MRQ)	41.25	22.44	11.71
Sales growth (TTM)	45.40	16.75	11.67
Sales growth (5 yr.)	44.73	19.12	16.81
Gross margin (TTM)	22.51	32.68	48.76
Net profit margin (TTM)	8.01	6.36	11.00
Return on equity (TTM)	87.23	35.20	22.20
Return on assets	26.69	10.94	8.30
PEG ratio	1.04		

MRQ = Most Recent Quarter, TTM = Trailing 12 Months.
SOURCE: *Market Guide*, June 1999.

Table 18–5. Growth versus Value Investing

	Value Investing	Growth Investing
Focus	Companies which are undervalued as measured by price to earnings, book value, or dividends	Companies with rapid and expanding growth in sales and earnings
Characteristics	Low price to value measures, such as P/E, P/R, P/BV, and dividend yield	High sales and EPS growth with high price to value measures
Risks	Valuation measures are low for good reason. Turnaround may take a long time. Upside is only as high as fair value.	Earnings surprises can cause high price volatility. Growth rates may not be sustainable.
Return	Capital appreciation and dividend income	Capital appreciation with little or no dividend income

Their goal for principal historically has been to maintain the principal invested. This goal led most income investors into bonds and CDs, due to their promise to return exactly the dollars invested. Given the fluctuations in inflation over the last three decades, however, many investors have realized that maintaining principal values is not the same as maintaining purchasing power. As noted in Chapter 5, just 3% inflation reduces the purchasing power of $1.00 to $0.55 in 20 years. Many inflation-wary investors have turned to the stock market for income investing because income stocks offer the potential of a growing income stream and the possibility of capital appreciation.

Though income stocks can provide good long-term returns, over the short term, an investor can lose principal. For investors who have a very short-term time horizon or absolutely cannot tolerate any loss of principal, U.S. government securities, CDs, and money market mutual funds, discussed in Chapter 8, are the way to invest for income.

Buying Stocks for Income. The risk-return relationship is an important concept in choosing income stocks. Stocks with steady, but not rising, dividends are similar to bonds in their fixed income stream, but do not have the guarantee of principal and income that bonds have. To take on the additional risk of a stock, you should insist on additional return in the form of dividend growth. A simple formula takes the dividend growth rate into account when predicting total returns on investments not expected to show capital appreciation.

$$\text{Expected total return} = \frac{\text{Expected dividend growth rate}}{+ \text{Current dividend yield}}$$

Another aspect affected by the risk-return relationship is the tendency for an investor to choose the income-oriented stock with the highest current return. Efficient markets price stocks so that those with the highest risk have the highest current yield. Risk in these cases is often the risk that the dividend will soon be cut or omitted entirely.

When choosing stocks for income, consider the following financial measures:

- Dividend yield: Also called current yield, this is the dividend per share divided by the share price. In addition to the risk-reward trade-off mentioned already, consider that stocks which have lower current yields may provide the best long-term results if they have high rates of dividend growth. (Use the expected total return formula.)

- Dividend growth rate: Dividends should show annual increases at a steady or increasing rate of growth. Not only is this imperative in rewarding you for the risk of buying an investment without any guarantees, but also growth in dividends can forecast the financial outlook for the company. Directors who have inside information about the financial health of the business set dividends. If dividends are generally increased by 10% each year and suddenly a 5% increase is announced, there are thunderclouds on the horizon. Conversely, acceleration or resumption of dividend growth signals a positive forecast. Zero dividend growth that comes after a pattern of positive dividend growth is a negative signal. Often a flat dividend comes directly before a dividend cut.

- Dividend payout ratio: Dividends per share divided by earnings per share equals the dividend payout ratio. A lower ratio means there is less danger of cutting or omitting dividends during business downturns. Also consider dividends per share divided by cash flow per share. Cash flow is a truer measure of ability to pay dividends because EPS includes non-cash items such as depreciation.

- Short-term debt as a percentage of total debt or total capital: Companies that finance long-term assets with short-term debt (a high ratio) run the risk that changes in their financial outlook could prevent short-term debt from being rolled over into long-term debt. This situation would cause either a default or the extension of more short-term debt at very high interest rates. Companies that habitually finance in the short term run the risk of being caught refinancing during spiking interest rates.

- Debt to equity: High levels of debt mean high interest payments that can be a strain on cash flow. Interest payments take priority over dividends when funds are limited. Compare ratios over five or more years and compare with other companies in the same industry. A ratio that rises above its historical levels or above industry norms signals a company with reduced financial strength.

Two Types of Income Stocks

Utilities.   Utilities are generally purchased for their dividend yields, which may run 50% to 100% higher than the dividend yield of the average industrial stock. In the past, investing in utilities required little analysis. You could assume that electric, gas, telephone, and water services were essential and certain companies had monopolies on these services, which led them to be profitable, dividend-paying investments. Regulatory changes have weakened or wiped out former monopolies, leaving utilities to compete for profits on a more level playing field. This leaves investors with the responsibility of analyzing such stocks more carefully, as profits are no longer nearly guaranteed.

Major categories of utilities can be described as follows:

- Telephone: A crowded field of price-competitive players exists. Large outlays are required to upgrade systems and increase capacity. Mergers are common; for example, since the 1996 Telecommunications Act, SBC Communications (formerly Southwestern Bell, one of the seven Baby Bells) has acquired or merged with Pacific Telesis Group, Southern New England Telecommunications, and Ameritech.

- Electric: A newly competitive environment leaves open the possibility of write-offs for excess capacity. Small companies are merging to gain size efficiencies and high-cost producers are purchasing lower-cost producers, then selling excess power.

- Water: Costs are expected to increase due to regulatory changes. Margins and dividends may come under pressure in weaker companies.

- Gas: Deregulation has changed the monopoly model, reducing profits. Profits are highly dependent upon weather conditions, making them unpredictable.

Because they are mainly purchased for their dividend stream, the prices of income-oriented stocks will tend to behave like bond prices, moving in the opposite direction of interest rate changes. This is due to the pressure to equalize the stock's yield with competitive investments. Analyze utilities as you would any income-oriented stock, but be aware that they may be more sensitive to interest rate changes because their business is so capital intensive, often requiring high levels of debt. If interest rates rise, then the interest cost on variable rate debt rises, reducing profits and vice versa.

Real Estate Investment Trusts. Real estate investment trusts (REITS) are corporations that own, lease, or lend money for real estate. Through special treatment by the Internal Revenue Code, they are considered conduits of income for their shareholders and thus do not pay a corporate income tax. This allows shareholders to avoid the double taxation (tax at both the corporate and personal levels) levied on most stock investments. In the late 1990s, as REITs fell out of favor with investors, prices fell and yields rose. Income investors looking for cash flow turned to REITs with yields in the 7% to 9% range.

REITs can be divided into two main categories, equity and mortgage REITs. Equity REITs own real estate, such as apartment buildings, hotels, or shopping centers. Mortgage REITs own mortgages on real estate. The differences between the two types can be compared with the differences in owning stocks versus bonds. For the equity REIT, the downside is higher, as loss of major tenants or falling real estate prices can significantly affect profits. The mortgage REIT is somewhat insulated since the real estate owner will avoid defaulting at all costs, cutting dividends to owners before missing mortgage payments. Concurrently, the equity REIT has a higher upside, for successful real estate investments bring higher asset values and growing cash flow from rising rents. Mortgage REITs, while benefiting from secure interest payments, do not participate in these additional gains.

Other factors that differentiate REITs include geographic concentration or diversity, type of property (hotel, hospital, shopping center, etc.), tenant quality, and leverage. Investing in REITs is discussed further in Chapter 15.

Finding Income Stocks. Due to their somewhat unexciting nature, you will not read about many income-oriented stocks in the hottest financial newsletters. Several sources that include information on stocks with high yields and increasing dividends are

> *Moody's Handbook of Dividend Achievers,* by Moody's Investors Service ($29.95). Recommended by Peter Lynch in *Beating the Street*, this book profiles more than 350 companies that have paid increasing dividends for the past 10 years. Dividend growth rates are listed for the last 10 years.
>
> *Standard & Poor's 500 Guide: 1999* ($24.95)
>
> *Standard & Poor's Midcap 400 Guide: 1999* ($24.95)
>
> Both guides feature reports and analysis on the stocks in their respective indices. Both also include the list, "Higher Dividends for Ten Years," made up of companies whose dividend yield is at least 2% and have paid higher cash dividends in each of the past 10 years.

Technical Analysis

Technical analysis is a method of using past price and volume patterns to predict future price movements. Purists might choose stocks using only these patterns, but most who rely on technical analysis use it in conjunction with other analyses or to provide cues for timing purchases and sales of already identified stocks.

Many who argue in favor of technical analysis choose one of the following reasons:

- Chart patterns display the past behavior of investors in an auction market. The pool of players remains fairly constant, so it is logical that their behavior will repeat itself.
- Chart patterns appear repeatedly in unrelated stocks, industries, and indices. Although we cannot explain the phenomenon, it is foolish to fight it.

Those who disagree with using technical analysis generally state that, if patterns are more than simple coincidences, then the causal relationship is not strong enough to justify making investment decisions from them.

Technical analysis looks for signs that a stock or index will move in a certain direction. Components that help shape these indicators are price, time, volume, and market breadth. Price reflects changes in supply and demand, which are dictated by investor attitudes. Time measures the period over which a change takes place. Volume measures the intensity of the change and thus its staying power. Breadth reflects the strength of market trends, as measured by the number of individual stocks that participate in a move.

Price Charting

The most popular charts for technical analysis are bar charts, which record the stock's high, low, and close for the time period. A volume chart is usually directly below the price chart so that the relative intensity of price moves can be calculated. Moves on higher than average volume are considered more important than moves on low volume. Figure 18–1 is a bar

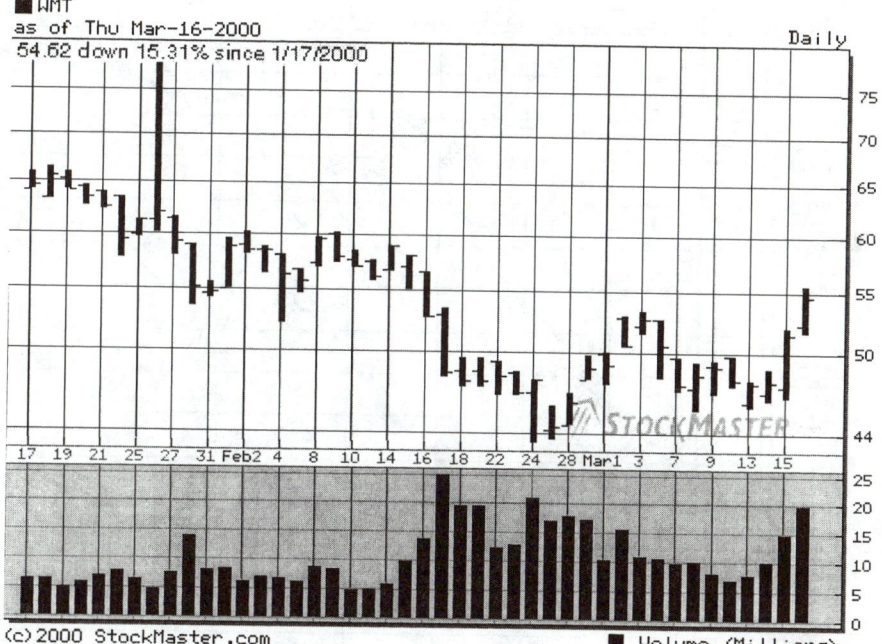

Figure 18–1. Bar Chart of Wal-Mart
SOURCE: *Stockmaster.com.*

chart for WalMart. For more information about bar charts, see *Technical Analysis of Stock Trends*, by Robert D. Edwards and John Magee (721 pages, $75); Amacom, 800-262-9699, *www.amanet.org*.

Point and figure charts are made up of *x*s and *o*s, in which an *x* is entered for a unit of price increase and an *o* for a unit of price decrease. Prices shown are only closing prices, and entries are made only if the stock's price changes. Point and figure charting focuses on reversal patterns, in which a buy is signaled when an X column rises above a previous X column. A sell is signaled when an O column falls below a previous O column. An example of a point and figure chart is shown in Figure 18–2. Read more about point and figure charting in *Point and Figure Charting: The Essential Application for Forecasting and Tracking Market Prices*, by Thomas J. Dorsey (256 pages, $59.95); John Wiley and Sons, 800-225-5945, *www.wiley.com*.

Candlestick charts date back to the 1600s when they were used by the Japanese to analyze the prices of rice contracts. These charts use high, low,

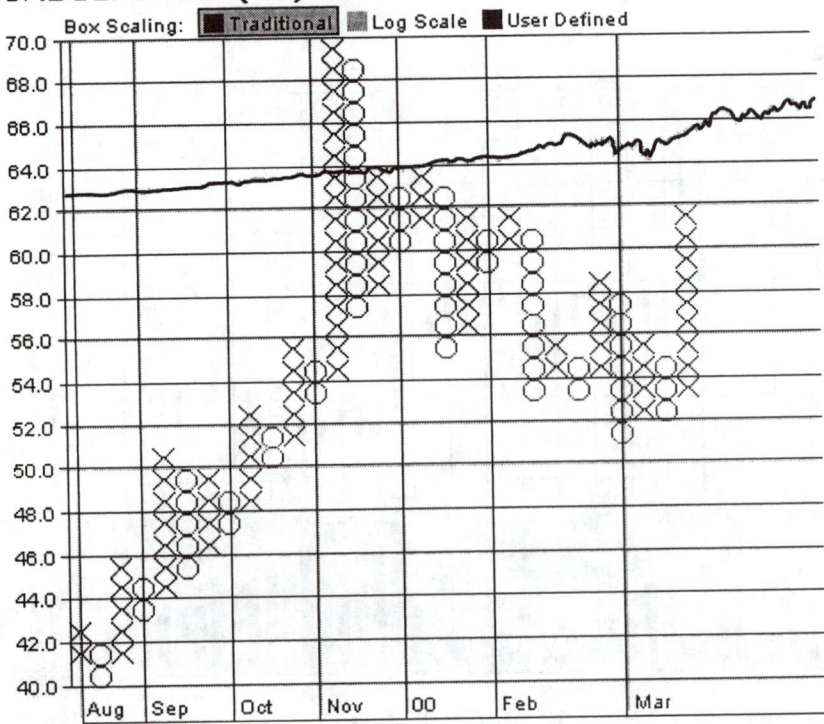

Figure 18–2. Point and Figure Chart of Home Depot, Inc.
Source: *Stockcharts.com*. Used with permission.

open, and closing prices. The body of the candlestick reflects the range between the open and close. The candlestick is black if the open was higher than the close and white if the open was lower than the close. Thin lines above and below the body (the wicks) represent high and low for the session. Figure 18–3 provides an example of a candlestick chart. Learn more in *Beyond Candlesticks*, by Steven Nison (282 pages, $65); John Wiley and Sons, 800-225-5945, *www.wiley.com*.

The equivolume system combines high and low prices and volume into a single chart. The chart looks much like a bar chart, except that the width of each bar indicates trading volume. You can read about equivolume in *Volume Cycles in the Stock Market*, by Richard W. Arms Jr. (143 pages, $39.95); Equis International, 800-882-3040, *www.equis.com*.

Price Patterns. Most charting services and the books mentioned here offer patterns specific to their charts. The patterns are too numerous to cover them all, so we provide an example to show you how they work. A common bar chart pattern is the "cup with handle." Think of the shape of a coffee cup, with its handle on the right. The left side of the cup is the stock's correction, which is often in line with a general market correction. The

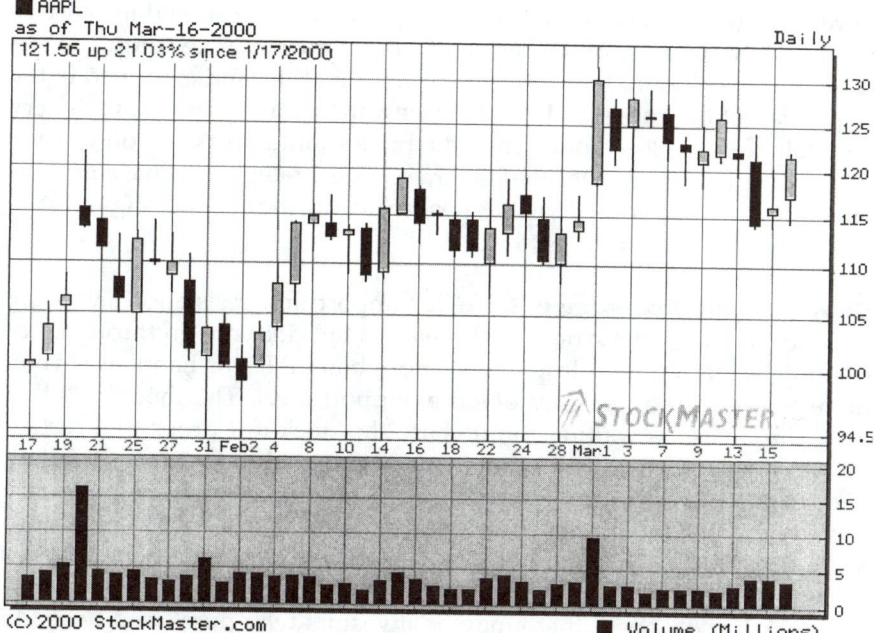

Figure 18–3. Candlestick Chart of Apple Computer
SOURCE: *Stockmaster.com.*

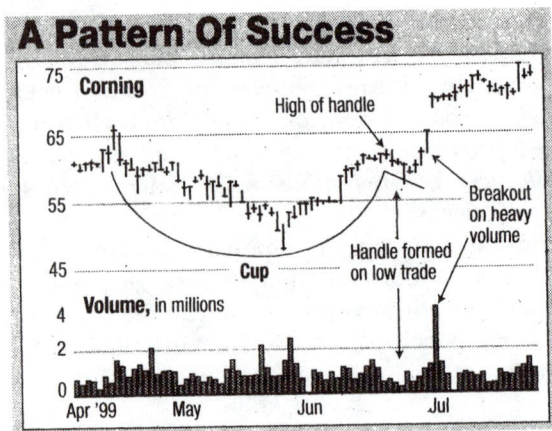

Figure 18–4. Cup-with-Handle Pattern—Chart of Corning
SOURCE: *Investor's Business Daily*, March 13, 2000.

stock may decline from 20% to 30% or 1.5 to 2 times as much as the market. Trading volume should slow at the bottom of the cup, indicating that selling has dried up. A spike in volume here without the stock moving any lower is also a good sign, as it shows support. Volume should increase as the stock rebounds, forming the right side of the cup. The completion of the whole cup should take three to six months. The handle, formed in the upper half of the cup, should drift downward for a few weeks, with very low volume at its low point. Then the price should break out on volume that is at least 50% greater than average. The strategic purchase point is one-eighth of a point above the peak price in the handle. Figure 18–4 shows a cup-with-handle pattern.

Support and Resistance Levels. Support and resistance levels are price levels that a stock repeatedly reaches but does not go through. For example, a stock might drop to $30 and rebound. If this happens several more times, $30 can be considered a support level. The thought is that there are investors waiting to purchase the stock if it drops to a certain price. When it does, their buying demand causes the stock to stop falling and rebound. By the same token, if the stock repeatedly rises to $45 and each time experiences a pullback to lower prices, it has found a resistance level. If the stock is on an upward trajectory, investors who bought lower may consider the stock overvalued at $45 and ripe for profit-taking. Or, if the stock has dropped, there may be investors who purchased near $45 and are waiting to get out even. In either case, their selling causes a pullback each time the stock hits their target price.

One strategy using support and resistance levels is to buy near support levels and take profits near resistance levels. Another strategy is to watch for breakouts, in which the stock moves through support or resistance levels on above-average volume. An upside breakout, through resistance levels, signals a stock that is trending upward. A penetration of support, or breakdown, is a negative signal. Once a stock has broken through a resistance level, that price often becomes the stock's new support level. The same happens on the downside, in which a support level becomes the new resistance level.

Moving Averages

The moving average of a stock's price can be charted over a week, month, or year, but two commonly used time frames are 50 and 200 days. The simple or arithmetic average takes the sum of the stock's closing prices on each of the last (for example) 200 days and divides this number by 200. Each day, the oldest price is dropped from the numerator as the most recent price is added. The exponential moving average, or EMA, is computed with a formula that gives more weight to more recent prices and less weight to older prices.

Moving averages are generally drawn on top of price charts to show the relationship between a stock's current price and its moving average. Crossing and remaining above a moving average is considered positive whereas crossing below an average is negative. The more sensitive 50-day average is useful for short-term price fluctuations, while the 200-day average is more geared toward the long-term trend. Note the predictive value of the 50-day average (the higher of the two lines) in Figure 18–5. In several instances, profitable trades would have been made by buying Microsoft when the stock price moved above the 50-day moving average and selling when it fell below.

The Market

A technically healthy market is not required for but certainly favors advancing stocks. Entire markets, as measured by stock indices, can be charted the same as individual stocks. Charting market trends can provide valuable insight into the direction of a bull or bear market. A lesson that most traders learn early when working with a market that seems to have unstoppable momentum is, "don't fight the tape." The tape refers to the ticker tapes used long ago to record stock prices.

Measuring market breadth is a way to take the temperature of the market, and it can be done in several ways. One of the most popular measures

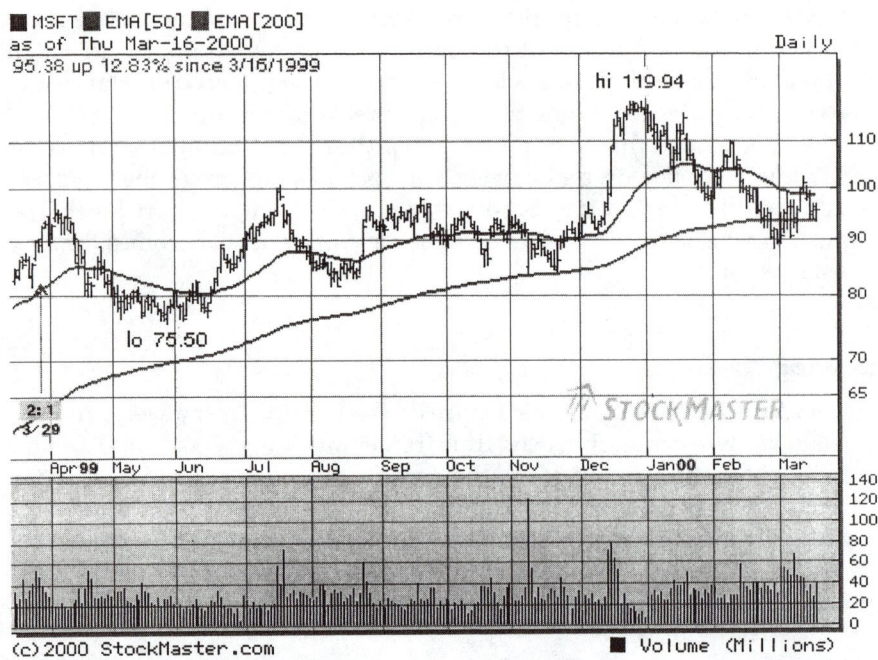

Figure 18–5. Moving Averages—Microsoft with 50-Day and 200-Day Moving Averages.
Source: *Stockmaster.com.*

of overall market strength is the advance/decline line (A/D line). The A/D line is a graphic depiction of the number of NYSE-listed stocks that declined for the day, subtracted from those that advanced, plus a cumulative total. When more stocks are advancing than declining, the line slopes upward and vice versa. By itself, the A/D line provides insight into market strength through its slope and pattern. Additionally, charting divergences between the A/D line and an index such as the DJIA or S&P 500 can forecast changes in market direction. A divergence between the two, where the A/D line loses its upward slope while the DJIA is still positive, generally signals a market top and the DJIA is seen following the A/D line downward shortly thereafter. In *Technical Analysis from A to Z*, Steven B. Achelis describes this relationship using the military analogy that trouble looms when the generals lead (e.g., the DJIA is making new highs) and the troops refuse to follow (e.g., the A/D line fails to make new highs).[2]

Other measures of market breadth look at the number of stocks in an index that are above their 200-day average or compare small indices such as

[2]Steven Achelis, *Technical Analysis from A to Z*, 2nd ed. (New York: McGraw-Hill, 2001). Check out his website at *www.equis.com.*

the DJIA with larger ones such as the S&P 500, or the NYSE composite. Divergences between blue-chip and broad averages may signal changes in market direction. For example, at a market bottom you might expect to see blue-chip averages turn around first as wary investors step in first with quality. Divergences between a particular sector and the market—for example, the high-tech sector which significantly outperformed all market indices in 1999—can create concern about market bubbles. Figure 18–6 is a chart of the S&P 500, its 200-day moving average, and the NYSE advance/decline line.

Popular Technical Analysis Theories

Dow Theory. Charles Dow first published his views on finance in *The Wall Street Journal*. They were compiled into what is now known as the Dow theory, the earliest technical analysis. Dow was interested in the direction of the general market and believed that most actively traded stocks reflect the movement of market averages. He created the Dow Jones Industrial Average (DJIA) and the Dow Jones Railroad Average (which would later become the Dow Jones Transportation Average, DJTA) with the idea that the industrials must rely on the transports to get their products to their customers. Therefore, when the industrials are doing well, the transports should too. These two averages must move in the same direction to provide a reliable market indicator.

Dow theory indicates three types of stock movements. Primary trends, either bullish or bearish, take place over several years. Secondary movements, which run counter to the primary trend, happen over the course of weeks or months. Daily movements are of no real importance other than their part in creating the overall trend.

When the averages' movements are confined to a range of about 5% for several weeks or longer, accumulation or distribution is occurring and an imaginary line is drawn. If both averages break out above the line, it was accumulation and prices are expected to advance. If they break out below the line, it was distribution and prices should head lower. Both averages must cross the line to provide a signal.

Dow theory subdivides bull and bear markets into phases marked by typical activity. Bull markets have two phases, the first of which is the accumulation phase. During this time, prices are depressed but farsighted investors buy low. The second phase, during which most of the profits are made, includes higher volume, rising prices, and growing corporate profits. At the end of this phase, the market becomes vulnerable to a reversal.

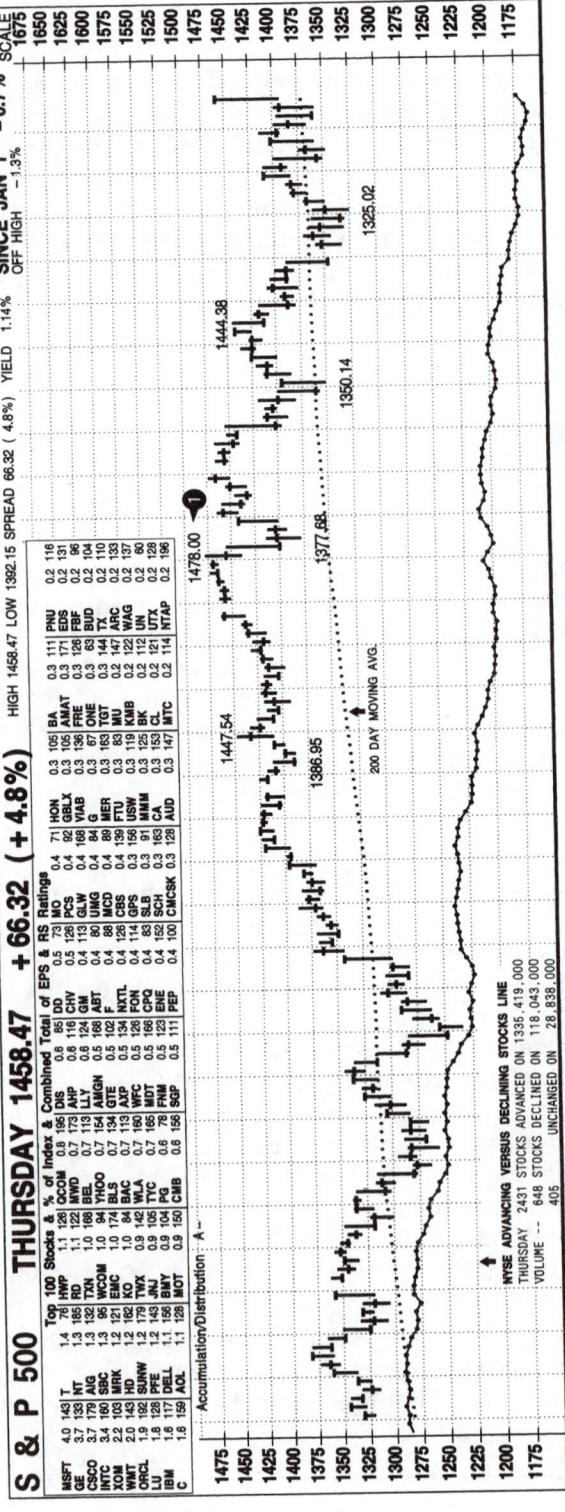

Figure 18–6. The S&P 500, Its 200-Day Moving Average, and the NYSE A/D Line

SOURCE: *Investor's Business Daily*, March 17, 2000.

Bear markets begin with distribution, in which astute investors start to sell as the masses are still rushing in to buy. Supply weakens prices, leading to the panic selling of the second phase in which prices drop drastically. In the third phase, prices continue to drop as all available news is bad.

Stage Analysis. *Stan Weinstein's Secrets for Profiting in Bull and Bear Markets* outlines Weinstein's theory known as stage analysis, which says that stocks follow four stages in a particular order.[3] In stage 1, called base building, a stock's price fluctuates in a fairly narrow range and may move back and forth across its 200-day moving average. In stage 2, the stock price advances past its 50-day and 200-day moving averages, though it may drop below the 50-day average during stage 2. In stage 3, the stock price peaks and may drop below the 200-day moving average, which has begun to slope downward. This is a sell signal. In stage 4, the stock price drops below both the 50-day and 200-day moving averages and continues its decline until it begins a new stage 1.

Elliot Wave Theory. Elliot wave theory was developed by R.N. Elliot in 1934 and popularized by A.J. Frost and Robert Prechter in a later book, *The Elliot Wave Principle.*[4] Underlying the theory is the assumption that, contrary to the efficient market hypothesis, financial markets are inefficient and controlled by the emotions of the investing public, who consistently overreact. Elliot's theory measures the effect that sociological functions, such as fear and greed, have on stock prices. According to the Elliot wave theory, these emotions are so ingrained that the most difficult part of using it is separating your own emotions from the analysis and this difficulty is what prevents the majority of investors from acting on the strategy provided.

Elliot waves are patterns of stock price movement. In general, there are five waves in one direction followed by one or more ABC corrections and then five waves in either the same or the opposite direction. The following waves describe an upward move.

Wave 1: A small number of investors buy because they suddenly believe that the stock is cheap, and thus cause an initial upward movement of the stock.

Wave 2: The stock begins to go down because investors in the initial wave consider it overvalued and take profits. It usually does not get back down to its former lows before being considered undervalued again.

---

[3]Stan Weinstein, *Stan Weinstein's Secrets for Profiting in Bull and Bear Markets.*
[4]A.J. Frost and Robert Prechter, *The Elliot Wave Principle.*

Wave 3: The stock becomes popular as more investors find out about it and bid the price up. Usually the longest and strongest, wave 3 generally exceeds the top prices of wave 1.

Wave 4: Profit-taking occurs in this wave. It is similar to wave 2, but weaker because there is still a strong bullish group.

Wave 5: Unbridled enthusiasm causes numerous investors to buy the stock in this phase, leading to the stock's overvaluation. At this point, the stock will either start over with wave 1 or go into one or more ABC corrections.

ABC correction: This correction involves lower volatility than the five-wave cycle, during which the stock will go down/up/down. It is a pause for the stock's fundamentals to catch up. If they catch up, it is simply a preparation for another five-wave cycle upward. If they do not, you may see a second ABC correction and five waves down. Several ABC corrections can occur. An odd number leads to a subsequent upward move and an even number leads to a downward move.

Charting Services

For the serious technical investor who is in search of detailed charts, the following services provide them on a subscription basis.

Daily Graphs
  William O'Neil & Co.
  12655 Beatrice St.
  Los Angeles, CA 90066
  310-448-6843
  16,000 NYSE stocks, 404 Amex stocks, and 620 OTC stocks are covered in two books. Available on a weekly or monthly basis. Price range: $386 to $745/year.

Mansfield Stock Chart Service
  2973 Kennedy Boulevard
  Jersey City, NJ 07306
  201-795-0629
  Separate books covering all NYSE, Amex, and OTC stocks for each exchange are available on a weekly, biweekly, or monthly basis. Price range: $217 to $1,727/year.

S&P Trendline
  65 Broadway, 8th Floor
  New York, NY 10006
  212-438-2000

Four publications offer a varying number of stocks plotted on a daily or weekly basis. Available weekly or monthly. Price range: $145 to $625/year.

Securities Research Chart Publications
Securities Research Company
400 Talcott Avenue
Watertown, MA 02472
781-235-0900
Covered are 1,100 exchange-listed stocks and 1,000 OTC stocks in various publications. Available monthly or quarterly; an annual issue covers 400 stocks going back 35 years. Price range: $104 to $154/year.

Charting Websites

Several websites provide extensive technical charts and data. Big Charts at *www.bigcharts.com* has an interactive charting feature that allows you to change variables and compare results with other stocks, indices, and indicators. Once you have decided on your settings, you can save them for future visits. ClearStation at *www.clearstation.com* has a daily "A-list" for stocks whose charts show buy signals. You can compare up to 100 stocks on one chart and each chart has a message board of comments from other ClearStation devotees. For newcomers to charting, the education center provides a tutorial. Stockcharts at *www.stockcharts.com* has an extensive list of interactive charts, including candlestick and point and figure, as well as preset industry, intermarket, and sentiment charts. Stockmaster at *www.stockmaster.com* has the most user-friendly interactive charting feature, designed not for the serious technical investor, but for anyone who wants to check stock charts against different stocks, indices, or moving averages.

Passive Investing Using Index Mutual Funds

Index mutual funds have gained tremendous popularity in recent years as frustrated investors have given up trying to beat the market with individual stocks or mutual funds. While individual actively managed funds may beat market averages in a given year or years, it is exceedingly difficult to do this over the long term. Why? The increasing availability of financial information makes it difficult to get an edge on other investors. Management fees and expenses such as transaction costs also add up to expense ratios ranging from 1% to 2%.

Choosing specific index mutual funds is discussed in depth in Chapter 12. What remains is how to use them as part of an investment strategy. Few investors place all their money in index funds; however, they can be used effectively in a portfolio that is split into passively and actively managed portions. This method, called the core portfolio approach, is commonly used by institutional investors.

The passively managed (index) portion of the portfolio acts as the portfolio's base and accounts for more than 40% of invested funds. It should track a broad index, such as the S&P 500, to ensure a market return for the majority of the portfolio. The actively managed portion can invest in funds or individual stocks concentrated by sectors (e.g., high tech) or styles (e.g., value) which you believe will do well under current economic conditions.

Beware of closet indexing with the actively managed portion of your portfolio. This occurs when the sum of targeted investments mirrors the composition of an index. For example, the components of growth and value funds that invest in midcap and largecap stocks, when combined, may resemble the S&P 500. Owning these gives you the expenses of actively managed funds with results similar to an index.

If you are inclined to invest exclusively in index funds, try an adaptation of the core portfolio approach. Make your core investment a broad market index, such as the S&P 500, and your actively managed funds specialized index funds in which you change weightings or indices based on current market conditions.

The Internet Phenomenon

The internet has turned the investment world upside down in more ways than one. In the beginning, it leveled the playing field by providing information access and cheap commissions. Then the stocks of internet companies formed an entirely new investment sector with rules of its own. Internet stocks fueled much of the 1999 gain in the NASDAQ, reaching stratospheric valuations by early 2000 only to come crashing down to earth in the spring. Before providing the arguments for and against and the postmortem, we will touch on what internet stocks are.

What Is an Internet Stock?

Before buying anything that ends in ".com," take a moment to understand the concept (because it isn't earnings) that drives the valuations of internet stocks. The internet is a means of linking computer networks and individual computers using a standard protocol that will allow communications among various types of networks. International Data Corporation (IDC) estimates that 160 million people around the world currently use the internet. IDC expects that number to reach 500 million by 2003, and predicts that those businesses and consumers will spend $1.3 trillion.

Internet stocks can be divided into two primary subsets: those that operate over the internet, such as retailer Amazon.com, and those that provide products or services that maintain the internet infrastructure, such as Akamai. A related group of stocks includes those whose primary business is not part of the internet, but who expect to derive significant revenues from either expanding their service onto the Internet, such as Barnes and Noble, or participating in the whole computer/internet boom, such as Intel.

The Argument for Internet Stocks

Those who buy internet stocks fall into two very different camps. Both camps have members who have made fortunes. The first group, most active during the wild ride of 1999/2000, trades internet stocks on momentum. Buy into a hot stock as the price is rising and don't be the last one to turn the lights out. Sell on the first sign of weakness to protect your profit. Don't get attached to your stocks; another will come along tomorrow, or later today. These are the traders, seeking to make fast money. They sell out quickly if a stock drops, creating downward momentum as perilous as the upward momentum is exhilarating.

The second group is the investors. They look at the data of IDC and other research companies and conclude that there is a New Economy, the internet is here to stay, and worldwide use will continue to grow exponentially. As long-term growth investors, they want to be in the fastest growing industry around. They cite the operating leverage of internet companies whose infrastructures are such that they require very little in additional manpower as their business grows. Most long-term internet buyers focus on market leaders, figuring that small companies will burn through their cash, leaving a small group of players with a reduced requirement for huge marketing expenditures.

The Argument against Internet Stocks

The argument against internet stocks is not one against the internet itself, just a friendly disagreement about what these companies are worth. Those who stayed away from the sector paid dearly in performance terms as the technology-laden NASDAQ screamed past other market indices in 1999.

The naysayers cited ridiculous valuations, such as this comparison of Amazon.com and Walmart in March 2000. Amazon.com, the internet retailer, had a market capitalization (stock price times shares outstanding) of $23 billion and annual revenues of $1.6 billion, with a loss per share of $2.175. Walmart, a brick-and-mortar retailer, had a market capitalization of $245 billion and annual revenues of $166 billion, with earnings per share of $1.25. Under this scenario, investors valued each dollar of Amazon.com's revenue at $14.37, while Walmart's revenues were valued at $1.47, a tenfold difference. Nevermind the earnings issue.

The Crash

In the Nifty Fifty fiasco of the early 1970s, a group of growth stocks, led by IBM, Xerox, Polaroid, and Coca Cola, sold at P/E ratios over twice the S&P 500 and outperformed value stocks by 30%. Their prices came crashing down in the 1973–74 bear market, some losing as much as 90% of their value. In a similar fashion, internet stocks came falling to earth beginning in late March and early April 2000.

Before the bubble burst, eBay, the online auctioneer, boasted a price/earnings ratio of 1,970, given its EPS of $.10 and mid-March 2000 price of $197. Yahoo, the internet portal,s had the same reported earnings and a price of $175, making its P/E 1,750. Inktomi, a company in the internet infrastructure business, was one of many internet stocks with P/Es of a mathematical infinity. Its price was $202 with EPS of –$.21 in March 2000.

By August 2000, eBay's price, at $50, was one-fourth its March valuation, Yahoo was down 26% to $130, and Inktomi had dropped in half to $100. The internet and technology sector woes dragged the NASDAQ down from its high above 5000 in March to just above 3000 in May. It subsequently rebounded to above 4000 before dropping below that mark in late summer 2000.

Summary

Few nonprofessional investors pick an investment style and use it exclusively, because many different styles have merit and there are benefits to using them in combination or in changing styles over time. For example, you can be a fundamental investor who uses technical analysis to time market purchases and sales. William O'Neil, founder of *Investor's Business Daily* and the CANSLIM system of investing, sings the praises of combining styles in this way (see Chapter 19 for more on O'Neil and CANSLIM). You might be a growth investor as a young person and shift some of your funds into income investing during retirement. Or you might lean toward either growth or value investing when the markets show an obvious bias. Beware that this strategy is tricky, as the bias may only become apparent after a market move, when the particular type of stock is ready to cycle out of favor. Whatever your choice of styles or combinations, the key is to invest with a plan, rather than haphazardly, to bring discipline into your decisions and remove some of your emotion. Additionally, a structure for decision making is key to learning from the past. Both successful and unsuccessful investments can become valuable learning experiences when you can track the reasons for making the investment. Being able to duplicate a winner or avoid a loser is much easier when you can spot its characteristics.

19
Following the Investment Experts

The world of investing has changed dramatically in the last 25 years as deregulated commissions, no-load mutual funds, online brokers, and online research and quotes have made it easy and inexpensive for investors to manage their own portfolios. A problem that remains for many investors suffering from an onslaught of investment information is picking a strategy or discipline to follow.

This chapter outlines the time-tested investment approaches of some seasoned investment professionals.[1] Though there is not enough room for every investment guru here, you will find a mix of pioneers and contemporary investors as well as a variety of different philosophies.

These successful investors, many of whom are household names, may not agree on their particular theories but they share the ability to clearly define their investment objectives and the criteria that make investments attractive to them. Most philosophies lean toward a categorization of either growth or value, but the overriding theme is that there is some gray area. Growth investors will not pay any price for growth, and the value investors realize that growth is necessary for a value stock to rise to a market valuation.

Peter Lynch, Story Investor

Peter Lynch is best known for his 13-year tenure at the helm of the Fidelity Magellan Fund, during which time assets grew from $20 million to $13 billion and his average annualized return was a remarkable 29.2%. In his

[1] The investor profiles in this chapter draw on books written by and about investment professionals; a series of articles by Maria Crawford Scott published in the *American Association of Individual Investors Journal;* and *The Money Masters* by John Train. For a complete listing of books and other sources, see the bibliography at the back of the book.

book, *One Up on Wall Street*, Lynch champions the idea of investing in what you know. He recounts stories such as his discovery of Hanes, when his wife brought a L'eggs pantyhose egg home from the grocery store. It was the first time that pantyhose had been available outside of a department store, the package was innovative, and the price was right. No matter what the company or the product (the more mundane the better), it must have a "story" like this one. The story is how the company expects to increase its earnings. Analysis of that potential is what uncovers exciting investment opportunities.

Before applying quantitative criteria, he categorizes companies by story line, dividing companies into the following types:

- Slow growers: These tend to be large, mature companies whose growth rates are simply average. Though they often pay good dividends, their lack of growth makes them unattractive.

- Stalwarts: These are large companies with a rate of earnings growth that exceeds 10%. While potential returns from these stocks are not stellar (at most 50% in two years), they are expected to hold up well during a recession.

- Fast growers: These stocks, which have earnings growth rates of 20% to 25%, provide the most potential for gains and the most risk. They are generally small, new firms, ideally growing fast in an industry that is not.

- Cyclicals: These are companies whose fortunes rise and fall with the business cycle, such as automobile manufacturers and those in the steel or homebuilding industries. Because they may be large and well known, it is possible to confuse these stocks with stalwarts. Timing is very important when investing in cyclicals because their prices can fall precipitously at the first sign of recession.

- Turnarounds: These are companies that have been battered by bad news. If a turnaround is successful in changing directions, its price can move up very quickly.

- Asset opportunities: Typical value plays, these are companies whose assets are worth more than the current stock price reflects. Screens for book value may be of limited help here, as knowledge about the industry and the assets in question is what provides the investor an edge.

Quantitative Criteria

After identifying a stock's story, Lynch applies some quantitative measures to the company's financials to further evaluate growth. He also seeks to determine relative value, reasoning that even a great story stock will not be profitable if it is too richly priced. He considers the following:

- Earnings growth: Earnings growth rates should be consistent with the company's story. For example, fast growers should have earnings growth of at least 20%.

- Year to year earnings: The pattern, stability, and ability to maintain earnings growth can be revealed by studying year-to-year earnings changes. Ideally, these changes should always be positive, without huge fluctuations in percentage terms.

- Price/earnings ratio: Using this common measure of value, Lynch compares a firm's P/E ratio to its historical average, its industry average, and its earnings growth rate (PEG). A study of historical P/E averages generally reveals a normal range for the company, providing insight into when a stock's P/E is at the high end (too expensive) or low end (relatively cheap) of its range. Comparing the stock's P/E with the industry can be valuable in identifying stocks that are neglected within their field. In comparing P/E ratios to growth, Lynch modifies the usual PEG (P/E ratio divided by EPS growth rate) to include the dividend yield. The calculation adds the dividend yield to the EPS growth rate in the divisor, making the adjusted formula:

$$\frac{\text{Price / earnings per share}}{\text{EPS growth rate + Dividend yield}}$$

Stocks with an adjusted PEG ratio (using this formula) greater than 1.0 are too expensive whereas ratios of 0.5 or less identify attractively valued stocks.

- Debt to equity ratio: A measure of financial strength, this ratio provides insight into staying power during difficult times. Lynch prefers bonds to bank debt, as some bank debt may be called upon demand.

- Net cash per share: The sum of cash and cash equivalents, less long-term debt, is net cash. Dividing by the number of shares outstanding provides a per share number which is often quoted by value investors. If net cash per share is high enough, it creates a floor for the stock price.

- Dividends and payout ratio: Dividend-paying stocks should have a history of steadily increasing dividends. Payout ratios (dividend per share divided by earnings per share) should be low enough to give the dividend security in a poor earnings environment.

- Inventories: Inventories can provide insight into changes in the rate of sales before that data is announced. Growing inventories signal slowing sales; depleted inventories are often the first sign of a sales recovery.

Qualitative Criteria

The following characteristics are attractive in a stock.

- It is an ugly duckling, meaning investors neglect the stock because the product or service is unexciting or even disagreeable.
- It is a spin-off that is receiving little attention from institutional investors.
- It is a fast growing company in a no-growth industry. Popular growth industries attract competitors who put pressure on profit margins and investors who bid prices up.
- The firm controls a market segment or is in an area that has high barriers to entry.
- The company is in an industry that would typically be termed *defensive.* Its product—often a consumer good such as beer, soft drinks, or toothpaste—sees little demand contraction during a recession.
- The company uses but does not produce technology. Firms that produce technology generally have high valuations. Firms that use technology to reduce their costs or improve their distribution can see higher profits as a result, without the high technology valuation.
- Institutional ownership and analyst coverage are low. The greatest gains are to be found in stocks that are yet undiscovered by Wall Street.
- Insiders are buying shares. This signals confidence in the company's prospects by those who have nonpublic information.
- The firm is repurchasing shares. Buybacks are often performed when management believes that the stock is undervalued. When a company has excess cash, share repurchases are preferable to spending cash on diversifying acquisitions, a term Lynch calls "diworsification."

When to Sell

Lynch's sell signals are more often related to the stock's story than its price. If the story does not develop as expected or there is an abrupt change in the story, it may be time to sell. If the price drops, but the story remains the same, it may be an opportunity to buy more of an undiscovered gem at even lower prices. If the price rises, he depends on initial expectations. If the story has played out as expected and the stock has reached a price level that leaves little hope for further large increases, sell it. If the price has risen but a fast grower's story is still the same, hold on to the winner. Lynch repeatedly says that "ten-baggers," stocks whose prices increase tenfold or more, are the key to high investment performance. You must be careful not to sell ten-baggers on their way up, just because you have made a nice profit so far.

Warren Buffet, Franchise Investor

Warren Buffet, whose investing prowess has made him one of the world's richest people, is probably the most well-known investor of our time. He practices his art through management of Berkshire Hathaway, a publicly traded investment holding company. Buffet is one of the few investment professionals who has not outlined his strategy in a book, but much can be gleaned from his annual letter to the shareholders of Berkshire Hathaway and from the numerous books written about him.

Warren Buffet's philosophy can be described as that of buying an entire business, which in fact he does, through his holding company. His holding period is so long term that he often calls it permanent, and he is known for saying that you should only buy a stock if you would be happy if the stock market closed down for the next 10 years. Buffet holds relatively few securities, generally under 20. His opinion on diversification can be summed up in what he calls the Noah's Ark approach: If you buy two of everything in sight, you end up with a zoo instead of a portfolio.

At the beginning of his career, Buffet followed Benjamin Graham's strictly quantitative, value-oriented approach. Later he modified this style to include qualitative issues, primarily the concept of the "franchise value" of a business. A company with strong franchise value has loyal customers for a unique product or service due to a strong brand name or a patent. Ideally, it is in an industry with significant barriers to entry. In the best cases, the company has a lock on its market and the ability to raise prices.

Businesses with a franchise or consumer monopoly fall into three categories.

1. Businesses with strong brand-name loyalty whose products are consumed or wear out quickly. Their consumer appeal is strong enough that merchandisers absolutely must carry their products. Examples include brand name drugs, or Coca-Cola, a Buffet favorite.

2. Communications firms that businesses must use to reach their customers. Examples include magazines such as *TV Guide* or *Racing Form*, newspapers such as *The Wall Street Journal*, and telecommunications networks.

3. Businesses whose consumer services are always in demand. Examples include companies that provide cleaning or lawn care and financial services firms such as Buffet's investments in American Express and GEICO.

Quantitative Criteria

Buffet looks for the following quantitative character sites in a stock:

- Earnings growth: A long trend of earnings per share growth and consistent year-to-year increases make a stock attractive.

- High cash flow and low-cost current operations: A company with high cash flow and a low level of spending required for daily operations requires little debt and can use excess cash flow for expansion or reinvestment in the business.

- Conservative use of debt: Buffet prefers companies that have little need for long-term debt. However, he does not object if debt is acquired to purchase a business with a similar consumer monopoly.

- High return on equity and assets: A company's ROE should be 15% or higher. Buffet's return on fixed assets calculation, called return on total inventories plus plant, uses a more conservative denominator than most, adding fixed assets and inventories together.

- High level and profitable use of retained earnings: What companies do with retained earnings signals management expertise. He looks for companies to reinvest earnings rather than pay a high dividend. If investment opportunities are not profitable, earnings should be used to repurchase shares.

- A low price relative to its valuation: Buffet analyzes a firm's financial operations to identify what he believes it is worth and what it will be worth in the future. Two of his valuation techniques follow.

   1. Divide a firm's trailing 12 month's earnings per share by the current rate on long-term government bonds to determine its worth relative to government bonds. For example, a stock with EPS of $5.00 per share would be worth $79.92 when long-term bonds yield 6.5% ($5.00/0.065 = $79.92). If you paid more than that, your initial return would be lower than government bonds. For example, if the stock was trading at $90, your initial return would be $5 divided by $90 = 5.5%. Because a stock's earnings per share are expected to grow, a stock whose value is comparable to a government bond on a return basis is more attractive than the bond, because future returns are expected to increase.

2. Project future earnings per share using past earnings per share growth, then multiply by the normal price/earnings ratio range to predict a price range. Consider a stock whose EPS over the last 10 years grew at an annualized rate of 10% and current EPS is $3.00. If the EPS growth rate continues to be 10% per year, then in 10 years EPS will be $7.78. Multiply this times an average high and low P/E ratio for the stock to find an expected price range. Estimated dividends paid over the period should be added to the resulting stock price. After the future stock price has been determined, compute an annualized rate of return based on the increase in stock price. Buffet's hurdle rate is 15%.

Qualitative Criteria

Buffet also searches for the following qualitative characteristics in a stock:

- It has a strong franchise or some sort of consumer monopoly due to brand names, patents, or regulatory licenses.
- The business is understandable. Buffet is famous for avoiding technology companies because he does not understand how their products work.
- Although he looks for capable management, in an often repeated quote Buffet says he buys "businesses that any idiot can run, because sooner or later one will."
- The business is a royalty on the growth of others. For example, the business of top advertising firms naturally grows as their clients grow.

When to Sell

Buffet buys stocks with the idea that he is purchasing a consistently growing company whose management will operate in the best interests of shareholders. As long as this is true, there is never a need to sell. However, if the nature of the business changes or another investment offers a better potential return, it is time to sell.

Benjamin Graham, Value Investor

Benjamin Graham is often called the father of value investing. His books, *Security Analysis*, a textbook written with David L. Dodd, and *The Intelligent Investor*, a guide for the lay investor, outlined an investment philosophy that is still used some 65 years later.

Graham's approach is to identify the intrinsic value of a business using primarily quantitative factors such as earnings growth, dividends, financial strength, and capital structure. Graham recommends that investors limit themselves to buying stocks selling near their tangible net asset value. Although he concedes that many growth companies are worth several times net assets, he recommends avoiding them because their market prices can be highly dependent on the fluctuations of the stock market. In looking at a stock's price to value relationship, he notes that the chief hazard confronting an investor is not the risk of paying too high a price for a good-quality stock, but of paying what seems to be a reasonable price for a low-quality stock.

Recognizing that all investors are not the same, Graham divides them into two groups, based not upon age or risk tolerance as is common, but upon the amount of time and effort the investor is willing to expend on the process. The defensive investor is concerned with avoiding losses and with being free from the necessity to make frequent decisions. The enterprising or aggressive investor chooses to spend more time and effort on investments and expects additional profits in return.

The approach to screening stocks for the defensive investor is stricter than the approach for the enterprising investor and therefore provides for fewer surprises, both upside and down. For example, Graham indicates that a defensive investor should only choose from stocks with a record of dividend payments that go uninterrupted for 20 years. For enterprising investors, the only dividend requirement is that some dividend be paid.

Quantitative Criteria

Graham recommends stocks with the following quantitative characteristics:

- Adequate size: In 1972, Graham excluded industrial companies with sales less than $100 million and public utilities with assets less than $50 million. Using the 5% growth rate applied by Maria Crawford Scott in the *American Association of Individual Investors Journal,* this roughly translates into current sales of $340 million for industrial companies or assets of $170 million for public utilities.

- Strong financial condition: A 2:1 current ratio (current assets to current liabilities) is needed for the defensive investor and a 1.5:1 ratio for the enterprising investor. Long-term debt to current assets should not exceed 1:1 for the defensive investor, but could reach 1.1:1 for the enterprising investor. For public utilities, long-term debt should not exceed twice stockholders' equity.

- Dividends: Uninterrupted dividends for the last 20 years (defensive) or some current dividend (enterprising) are a requirement.

- Earnings stability: A company must show positive earnings for each of the past 10 years (defensive) or 5 years (enterprising).

- Earnings growth: A company must show a minimum increase in earnings per share of one-third over a 10-year period (defensive), and past year's earnings per share greater than those of the period from 3 years previous (enterprising).

- Moderate price/earnings ratio: Current price should not be greater than 15 times the average earnings of the past three years. The inverse, earnings/price should not be more than the yield on a AA corporate bond.

- Moderate price/book value ratio: Current price should not be more than 1.5 times book value. A higher ratio is allowed in cases when the P/E ratio is lower than 15. The relationship between the P/E and P/BV should be such that their product is not greater than 22.5.

Qualitative Criteria

Benjamin Graham's value philosophy rests entirely on quantitative measures of value. He cautioned that quantitative measures must be used together when searching for stocks of high-quality companies and there is little room for subjective analysis.

When to Sell

Graham discouraged investors from paying attention to stock market fluctuations. In a statement often quoted by Warren Buffet, he said, "You are neither right nor wrong because the crowd disagrees with you. You are right because your data and reasoning are right." He recommended periodically evaluating holdings relative to their intrinsic value and selling when prices rise well above intrinsic value or when values deteriorate significantly.

William O'Neil, Fundamental and Technical Investor

William O'Neil's investment philosophy combines a growth-oriented fundamental analysis with technical analysis. His research firm, William

O'Neil & Co., publishes *Daily Graphs,* a chart service favored by many technical investors, and *Investor's Business Daily,* a business newspaper known for the valuable information provided in its stock tables. O'Neil's book, *How to Make Money in Stocks: A Winning System in Good Times and Bad,* outlines his investment philosophy, and 24 *Essential Lessons for Investment Success* further applies the principles.

O'Neil believes that stock markets are efficient and that most stock prices reflect their current worth. Rather than conclude that a stock with a low price/earnings ratio is undervalued, he believes it has a low price for a reason. O'Neil states that markets are rarely wrong on individual issues or the general market direction.

The system that O'Neil uses can be described by the acronym CANSLIM, which combines factors he deems important in choosing a stock. These factors include quantitative and qualitative criteria from both the fundamental and technical camps. Each component is reviewed in the following section.

CANSLIM Investment Criteria

C = Current quarterly earnings per share: Stocks that are poised to increase in price consistently show a major increase in current quarterly earnings per share as compared with the prior year's same quarter. The minimum increase acceptable is 18% to 20%, with 25% to 30% preferable, and during bull markets O'Neil recommends 40% to 50%. In addition to growth in the current quarter's EPS, look for an increase in the rate of quarterly EPS growth.

A = Annual earnings increases: Annual compounded growth in earnings per share should exceed 25% for the last five years. A single year's underperformance may be overlooked if the following year's earnings reached new highs. The EPS rating in the stock tables of *Investor's Business Daily* assists investors in evaluating the CA of CANSLIM. This rating compares a firm's two most recent quarter's earnings with the same two quarters a year ago. Then the long-term (three to five years) growth and stability of EPS are examined. The results are compared with all other companies and ranked from 1 to 99, with a 90 meaning that the firm outperformed 90% of other companies in earnings growth. Companies with superior earnings records have EPS ratings of 75 or better.

N = New products, new management, new highs: Companies that have exciting new products, new management, or whose industries are changing are often at the beginning of a price advance. Stocks that have risen, then spent a period of seven weeks to 15 months in a price consolidation are ready for a new move upward when the stock price reaches a new high on strong volume.

S = Supply and demand: When comparing two companies, the one with a smaller number of shares outstanding can have bigger price movements due to a limited amount of supply. Stocks with a large percentage of management ownership are valuable because management rarely sells, resulting in a reduction of liquid supply, and because management with an ownership interest is more likely to innovate and keep pace with changing times.

L = Leader or laggard: Buy stocks that are industry and market leaders in industries that are outperforming. Relative price strength, found in the *IBD* stock tables, is helpful in identifying leaders. This rating compares a stock's price performance with all other stocks over the previous 12 months, using a rating from 1 to 99. A 90 rating means the stock outperformed 90% of other stocks in the previous year. Choose stocks with a relative price strength rating of 70 or above. A rating below 70 indicates a laggard. In addition to individual price strength, check the industry's price performance with the industry group relative strength rating. This rating compares an industry's price performance with 196 other industry groups. An "A" rating places the industry in the top 20%.

I = Institutional sponsorship: Institutional sponsorship means institutional ownership by mutual funds, pension funds, large money managers, and so forth. Sponsorship is a balancing act in which neither too much nor too little is good. A complete lack of institutional ownership often means that professional investors looked at the stock and decided to pass. Very high institutional ownership may mean that all the good news is out and it is already reflected in the stock's price. Ideally, a stock will have 3 to 10 institutional owners with good track records. Demand from institutions who discover the stock later provide fuel for the stock price. *IBD*'s sponsorship rating combines the three-year performance of mutual funds owning the stock with the recent trend in number of funds owning the stock. Ratings are from A to E, with A being the highest.

M = Market direction: Even if you choose good stocks using the first six factors of CANSLIM, you are likely to lose money in a bear market. O'Neil recommends immediate action when market indices peak and begin reversals, suggesting selling 25% or more of stock portfolios. Helpful indicators in identifying market tops include heavy volume without further price increases; tops in individual market leaders; divergence of key market averages such as the DJIA, the S&P 500, and the NASDAQ Composite; and three successive discount rate increases by the Federal Reserve.

When to Sell

O'Neil's philosophy on selling a stock that has increased in price is to sell as it is rising, before it reaches a top and falls. He likens this to hopping off an elevator on the way up and reminds readers that "to retain profits, you must sell and take them."

O'Neil suggests that you make a plan as soon as you buy a stock; outline your goal price and how much of a decline you will withstand. He recommends a plan to cut losses at 8% and sell all but the strongest stocks when you have a 20% gain. He suggests "pyramiding up" by buying more of a stock that has advanced 2% to 3% so that you end up owning more of a stock with good performance. Stocks with losses should be pruned periodically and you should never carry a losing stock for more than six months.

Philip Fisher, Qualitative Investor

Philip Fisher began his investment career in 1951. The author of *Common Stocks and Uncommon Profits* (1958), Fisher is widely regarded as a leader in the focus on qualitative issues when choosing stocks for investment. A theme throughout his books, including two later writings, *Conservative Investors Sleep Well* and *Developing an Investment Philosophy*, is the value of "scuttlebutt" or "the business grapevine." Loosely defined, this is information that may be gleaned from conversations with a firm's customers, competitors, employees, and other sources such as industry and government officials.

This is not to say Fisher ignores traditional quantitative analysis of financial statements, because it is the first step in his three phases of analyzing a company. The three steps are as follows:

1. Analyze printed material. All public financial documents, such as the annual and 10-K reports, SEC filings, and interim financial reports, should be analyzed for growth in sales and profits. High profit margins are not always desirable, as they may attract competition. Wall Street research reports can be especially valuable, not for their information content, but to gain insight into the investment community's perception of a stock. Fisher notes that investment opportunity exists when there is a difference between that perception and reality.

2. Obtain additional information from business sources. This is where Fisher's approach becomes difficult for the ordinary investor to implement as it involves cultivating industry contacts and may include some

travel. He recommends trade shows as a rich source of scuttlebutt, noting that it is convenient to have so many industry resources in one place and that representatives are usually quite willing to talk about themselves and their competitors. Fisher also likes to get an inside view from industry association executives and government researchers, as well as a company's suppliers and customers.

3. Visit the company to talk with management. Fisher's stated goal in visiting management is to evaluate its business policies, whether the policies are being implemented, and the intelligence and honesty of the officers.

One difficulty in following Fisher's approach is that he does not use a screen to narrow the universe of potential stocks, but rather a 15-point system (in his first book), in which a stock either passes or fails each criterion. He does offer hints on timing purchases, indicating that good times to buy include:

- During the start-up period for a new plant. As earnings are temporarily depressed due to start-up costs, weaker investors will be driven out, providing a buying opportunity.

- Immediately following the announcement of bad news. The market generally overreacts to temporary bad news.

- When small investments of capital could produce big economies. Capital-intensive businesses can often benefit greatly from new technology, with little money expended.

He cautions against using economic data to time investment purchases, likening economists' ability to forecast to alchemists' knowledge of chemistry during the Middle Ages.

Fisher's 15-Point System

Because Fisher's system is so qualitative, a quantitative/qualitative delineation of the points is not particularly helpful. In his later writings, he separated the 15 points into three categories he deemed necessary for long-term growth.

Business Characteristics

1. Profitability: Here is one of the few places that Fisher recommends analysis of financial statements. Profit margins are important, though he does not use a strict screen for high margins, as they invite competi-

tion. Low margins can be acceptable if spending on research or sales is the cause.

2. Franchise value: Companies with brand-name loyalty, patent protections, barriers to entry, or other similar attributes have a competitive edge.

Functional Factors

3. Sales growth: Be wary of one-time spurts in sales but permit some fluctuation. Sales growth should be studied over the long term and the market size should be such to allow growth in the future.

4. Leading industry position: This position translates into superiority in production and low costs to produce or operate. Companies with low-cost structures can better survive economic downturns and better fund their growth internally.

5. Superior sales organization: Look for a broad organization, responsiveness, advertising, and efficient product distribution.

6. Research and development: Research is required for product innovation and technological advances that reduce costs. Rather than compare strict dollars spent, measure the effectiveness of those dollars by assessing how much in recent profits is the result of past research.

7. Financial controls: This point is two-pronged. Managers can only manage well if they have excellent financial information, and managers with integrity will set up systems that provide investors with accurate information.

8. Financial strength: Companies with sufficient capital will not need to dilute investor ownership by selling more shares.

Management and Labor Relations

9. Leadership skills: Management needs the leadership and foresight to steer a company into the future, as well as the industry-specific skills necessary to develop new products and services.

10. Teamwork: The ability for management to work together is crucial. Clues are the accessibility of upper management and the practice of promoting from within.

11. Depth of management: Companies with one or two key officers are at great risk should one depart.

12. Labor relations: Poor labor relations result in costly employee turnover and reduced workforce efficiency.

13. Long-range outlook: Management should have the foresight to look long term, rather than buckle to the what-have-you-done-for-me-lately attitude of the stock market.

14. Investor relations: Good investor relations are apparent in times of trouble. Good management will be honest about problems, while weak management will be evasive and avoid taking responsibility.

15. Integrity: Good management will operate honestly, putting shareholder interests ahead of their own.

When to Sell

In a philosophy echoed by Warren Buffet, Fisher claims that if you choose stocks correctly there is never a need to sell; however, he concedes a few exceptions. The first is that you made a mistake in your original appraisal. In that instance, sell immediately. The second exception is when a fundamental change occurs in the company and it no longer qualifies under your original appraisal method. Lastly, he recommends a three-year time frame for stocks that are underperforming but have not changed otherwise. Fisher discourages investors from selling a stock because its price has gotten too high, saying truly great companies, and their stocks, can continue to grow indefinitely.

T. Rowe Price, Growth Investor

Younger investors may equate the name T. Rowe Price with the successful family of mutual funds; however, he was a fixture on the investment scene for many years before his namesake fund family and is considered one of the pioneers of growth investing. Price, who died in 1983, did not write a book about his philosophies, but was a frequent contributor to financial periodicals such as *Forbes* and *Barron's*, and his approach is apparent in the history of the funds he managed.

At the beginning of his career, Price was a growth stock investor when most stocks were purchased for the stability of their dividends. His philosophy is that only real growth in earnings creates enough growth in dividends and market value to beat inflation over the long term. He believes that both industries and companies have a life cycle and that the most profitable and least risky time to invest is during the early stages of growth in companies that experience both earnings and sales volume growth.

In looking for growth stocks, he identifies several "fertile fields" for growth:

- New industries
- Existing industries whose new products were experiencing significant volume growth
- Niche industries whose markets are expanding

Quantitative Criteria

Price screened potential stock purchases for the following quantitative characteristics:

- Earnings per share growth: EPS should reach a new high at the peak of each succeeding business cycle. Some decline during the business cycle is acceptable, but the general trend must be upward, to rule out non-growth cyclical stocks.
- Earnings per share growth must exceed the rate of inflation.
- Price/earnings ratio: Do not buy growth at any price. P/E ratios must be in line with historical averages for the firm.
- A minimum 10% return on invested capital: Return on invested capital is computed as earnings before interest, taxes, and dividends (EBITD) divided by total capital, which is stockholders' equity plus preferred stock and long-term debt. In addition to meeting the 10% hurdle, the rate should not be declining.
- Profit margins: Growth in profit margins is a reflection of good management, and high margins relative to the industry are indicative of a good competitive position.
- Low payroll: Individual employees should be well paid, but total payroll should not be large in relation to total revenue.

Qualitative Criteria

Price also required the following qualitative characteristics in a stock:

- Management: Superior management is active in the business, exhibits an understanding of their markets, has a good relationship with employees, and owns stock in the company.
- Research: The future of the company depends on developing new products and new markets for existing products.

- Market protection: Look for firms whose market position is protected by patents and that are not subject to government regulation.
- Competition: Seek industries without intense competition.

When to Sell

Price's advice on selling is to sell when a company's growth period is coming to an end. He admits that this is difficult to spot, especially in times of recession when general economic malaise affects individual firms. One trigger that he uses is a decline in return on invested capital, which is a warning of maturity in a company. In excessively high prices or bull markets, Price might begin what he calls scale selling. In this process, he sells 10% of his position when a stock's price rises 30% over his highest purchase price. Each time it advances another 10% he sells an additional 10%. If a bull market appears to be peaking, the stock's price is collapsing, or the firm issues bad news, he sells out immediately.

David Dreman,
Contrarian Investor

David Dreman is an investment advisor and author of *Contrarian Investment Strategy—The Psychology of Stock Market Success* and *Contrarian Investment Strategies: The Next Generation*. He also writes a column in *Forbes* called "The Contrarian."

The cornerstone of David Dreman's contrarian strategy is the philosophy that the crowd is generally wrong. In contrast to William O'Neil's belief that the market price of a stock accurately reflects its current worth, Dreman is sure that psychological biases interfere with sound investment decisions and that the best approach is to buy stocks that are out of favor. If the crowd is wrong, then taking the opposite position of the majority makes their biases work for you. In some respects the result of a contrarian philosophy is similar to that of a value investor, because avoiding investment fads and market overreactions tends to direct the emphasis to stocks with low valuations relative to the average.

Dreman looks at history to prove his strategy, citing the Nifty Fifty mania from 1971 to 1972, during which time popular growth stocks outperformed value stocks by 30%, only to lose 90% of their value in 18 months during 1973 to 1974. While there was little fundamental change in these issues, investor perceptions changed, resulting in financial disaster for stockholders who followed the crowd.

According to Dreman there are many reasons that the majority is generally wrong. He believes that most investors draw on information that is insufficient, either by using too small a representative sample or by looking only at recent data. Investors, especially institutions whose performance is measured on a short-term basis, tend to be drawn to stocks with the highest performance and then feel justified when the market confirms their position. The contrarian philosophy on stocks that are outperforming is that they will always regress to the mean, meaning no one investment can deviate from the average over the long term.

Dreman offers five rules for the contrarian investor:

1. Do not be seduced by hot stocks with rapidly rising prices.

2. Look at probabilities of similar situations to help you assess the specific issue at hand.

3. Rates of return that differ sharply from the norm are doomed to return to it over the long term.

4. Do not expect immediate success; instead opt for a long-term view as it may take time for overblown investor emotions to play out.

5. Use price/earnings ratios to find stocks that are out of favor with the market.

Quantitative Criteria

Dreman uses the following quantitative criteria when screening for stock purchases:

- Company size: Medium and large companies offer more stability and less financial risk.

- Price/earnings ratio: Screen for a P/E in the lower 40% of the universe of stocks.

- Dividends: Insist on a high dividend that is at least stable, preferably growing. In addition to adding to total return, a good dividend provides some downside price protection. The payout ratio (dividends per share divided by earnings per share) should be low, indicating that the dividend can be maintained.

- Financial position: Look for a strong financial position, as indicated by standard measures such as high current ratio (current assets to current liabilities) and low debt to equity.

- Profitability: Measure profitability in several ways, including return on equity and pretax profit margins.

- Earnings per share growth: EPS growth should be higher than the S&P 500 for both the most recent year and projected one year into the future. Use very conservative projections to provide a margin of safety. According to Dreman, one mistake of crowd investing is believing inflated, long-term earnings estimates for which there is very little basis.

Qualitative Criteria

Dreman also provides the following qualitative recommendations:

- Avoid hot stocks in hot industries.
- Do not overreact to either good news or bad news.
- Expect unusual performance to regress to the mean for both in-favor and out-of-favor stocks.

When to Sell

Generally, a contrarian investor should sell a stock when its price/earnings ratio approaches that of the market average. However, if the increase in P/E is due to a drop in earnings, the market has probably overreacted to the earnings drop and it is not time to sell. Dreman recommends allowing two years for a stock to begin to move. Those that do not move, as well as any that have underperformed the market over two years, should be sold.

Screening for Stocks that Fit Investment Criteria

Once you have decided upon a methodology, nearly any financial website with a good interactive screening function can help you find stocks of interest. However, if you follow an expert's approach fairly closely, try the screening functions provided by the American Association of Individual Investors at *www.aaii.com* or Reesegroup.com at *www.reesegroup.com*. Both will screen according to the criteria of a selected professional, making the winnowing process much easier. Screens for each of the experts discussed here, as conducted by AAII can be found in the appendix.

Summary

Each of the professionals who were profiled in this chapter has a unique style; however, certain ideas overlap. Though not mentioned in each profile, all the experts except T. Rowe Price recommend small portfolios. Because diversification is one of the grounding principles of mutual funds, it is probably not surprising that Price suggests as many as 60.

Similarities abound, providing fuel to the theory that you can take a little from several investment approaches to create your own successful philosophy. Warren Buffet, who began as a disciple of Benjamin Graham's strictly quantitative value approach, was later known to quote Philip Fisher's qualitative approach. He developed his own distinct and highly successful style that draws from each.

Perhaps the most notable commonality is the ability each expert has to clearly articulate his theories. Nearly every successful investor, whether a day-trader or a long-term stock-picker will count discipline and planning as important parts of the game. Whether you use parts of these philosophies or create your own, know exactly what you are looking for, what makes a stock an attractive value, what your price goals are, and how much you are willing to lose.

Appendix: Applying the Methodologies of Investment Experts

The following stock screens provide lists of stocks that meet the investment criteria of the experts listed in Chapter 19. Stock screens are from *AAII.com*, the website of the American Association of Individual Investors.

Lynch's Passing Companies (Data as of June 30, 2000)

Company Name	Ticker	Exchange	Price	PE Ratio	PE Average 5 yr	PE to Div Adj EPS Growth 5 yr	Market Capitalization	Total Liabilities to Assets	EPS Growth 5 yr	Dividend Yield	Dividend Yield-Average 5 yr	Institutional Ownership %	Insider Ownership %	Cash
Bio-Logic Systems Corp.	BLSC	M - Nasdaq	6.1	11.3	26.1	0.5	25.5	21.4	24.6	0.0		8.7	40.1	5.0
Chicago Rivet & Machine	CVR	A - American	21.1	7.5	9.3	0.5	24.0	26.2	13.0	3.4	4.5	15.6	29.7	2.0
Herbalife International	HERBA	M - Nasdaq	8.8	5.3	13.4	0.5	250.7	47.6	5.8	6.9	3.8	11.1	76.3	98.3
Northern Tech. Int'l	NTI	A - American	6.3	9.1	12.9	0.5	24.2	5.9	16.7	2.6	1.7	16.8	32.8	3.2
Systemax Inc.	SYX	N - New York	3.9	4.7	23.7	0.5	132.7	45.9	9.2	0.0		14.7	83.9	8.3
Vitran Corporation, Inc.	VVN	A - American	3.7	6.4	31.3	0.5	36.7	65.3	12.8	0.0	1.0	16.9	57.8	
Westerbeke Corporation	WTBK	M - Nasdaq	2.9	7.4	9.5	0.5	5.5	40.5	7.7	0.0		0.6	68.7	0.1
Benihana, Inc.	BNHN	M - Nasdaq	14.0	10.7	15.5	0.4	86.3	44.3	28.7	0.0		6.8	88.6	1.5
CAM Commerce Solutions	CADA	M - Nasdaq	6.6	15.1	26.7	0.4	18.3	20.5	37.6	0.0		5.3	20.3	9.1
Delhaize America, Inc.	DZB	N - New York	15.4	8.0	17.6	0.4	2389.2	56.0	15.0	3.7	1.6	4.3	79.1	100.2
Great Northern Iron Ore	GNI	N - New York	50.4	8.5	9.0	0.4	75.6	11.6	8.6	11.9	10.9	2.6	6.7	1.2
Key Technology, Inc.	KTEC	M - Nasdaq	8.5	11.5	57.6	0.4	40.1	27.8	30.3	0.0		15.9	28.0	6.4
Taylor Devices, Inc.	TAYD	M - Nasdaq	3.1	11.6	19.8	0.4	8.7	42.3	21.1	0.0		0.0	45.9	0.4

(Continued)

Lynch's Passing Companies (Data as of June 30, 2000) *(Continued)*

Company Name	Ticker	Exchange	Price	PE Ratio	PE Average 5 yr	PE to Div Adj EPS Growth 5 yr	Market Capitalization	Total Liabilities to Assets	EPS Growth 5 yr	Dividend Yield	Dividend Yield-Average 5 yr	Institutional Ownership %	Insider Ownership %	Cash
UFP Technologies, Inc.	UFPT	M - Nasdaq	2.9	8.5	14.5	0.4	12.6	61.3	21.4	0.0		14.7	70.3	0.3
Air Methods Corporation	AIRM	M - Nasdaq	3.2	7.9	53.0	0.3	26.2	59.7	30.8	0.0		12.9	22.9	3.5
Baltek Corporation	BTEK	M - Nasdaq	7.1	6.0	17.4	0.3	18.0	28.6	18.5	0.0		10.3	52.4	2.3
Interlott Technologies	ILI	A - American	6.3	10.8	17.5	0.3	20.1	58.5	32.2	0.0		2.7	59.5	0.1
Lifschultz Industries Inc	LIFF	M - Nasdaq	14.4	7.8	12.9	0.3	16.1	27.8	24.0	0.0		0.1	64.3	0.5
Napco Security Systems	NSSC	M - Nasdaq	3.7	6.1	14.7	0.3	12.9	41.9	19.6	0.0		11.7	39.9	1.5
National Beverage Corp.	FIZ	A - American	8.1	11.6	12.2	0.3	147.8	49.7	0.6	0.0		5.2	79.1	33.6
ATS Money Systems, Inc.	ATSM	O - Over the counter	1.3	6.3	12.3	0.2	7.1	30.9	30.8	0.0		0.2	66.3	0.8
Ballantyne of Omaha, Inc.	BTN	N - New York	2.2	5.6	15.5	0.2	27.3	35.3	26.7	0.0		14.4	29.4	0.4
Chase Corporation	CCF	A - American	10.5	7.7	10.6	0.2	41.7	47.2	30.1	3.0	1.7	12.7	62.2	0.2
Emons Transportation Grp.	EMON	M - Nasdaq	1.5	6.0	34.1	0.2	11.3	57.1	28.3	0.0		12.6	53.7	1.5
Escalade, Inc.	ESCA	M - Nasdaq	17.1	7.7	13.7	0.2	37.0	45.6	40.5	0.0		4.0	58.3	0.0
Flamemaster Corporation	FAME	M - Nasdaq	7.4	11.2	16.5	0.2	11.9	5.7	68.3	1.8	2.8	0.8	37.9	2.1

General Employment Ent.	JOB	A - American	3.8	6.6	15.5	0.2	19.4	25.0	33.8	1.3		5.1	35.1	11.1
P & F Industries	PFIN	M - Nasdaq	8.5	6.7	7.2	0.2	30.4	46.4	35.1	0.0		11.5	72.0	0.3
Radica Games Limited	RADA	M - Nasdaq	3.1	5.0	19.0	0.2	55.1	23.7	24.5	0.0		5.4	51.8	30.5
Pubco Corporation	PUBO	M - Nasdaq	7.8	3.5	5.1	0.1	29.0	44.5	22.1	0.0		9.7	75.9	3.8
Village Super Market, Inc	VLGEA	M - Nasdaq	12.8	5.5	17.0	0.1	38.4	56.3	50.3	0.0		14.2	66.8	19.5

Buffett's Passing Companies (Data as of August 2, 2000)

Company Name	Ticker	Exchange	Price	EPS Cont–Growth 3yr	EPS Cont–Growth 7yr	EPS Growth Estimate	Return on Equity 12m	Return on Equity 7 year Average	Earnings Yield 12m	P/E Ratio	P/E Ratio Average 7yr	Buffett Price Growth–EPS Growth	Sustainable Growth Rate	Buffett Price Growth–Sust. Growth
Buffett Sustainable Growth Model Screen														
Theragenics Corporation	TGX	N – New York	7.23	53.3	45	27.5	15.7	16	8.16	12.5	61.1	70.3	16.03	36.3
MGI Properties	MGI	N – New York	2.31	74.7	46.7		185.6	35.7	466.06	0.2	11.6	119.1	3.22	35.5
Micros Systems, Inc.	MCRS	M – Nasdaq	22.25	124.2	30.7	22	20.1	19.1	9.21	11.6	40	48.9	19.09	34.6
Crossmann Communities	CROS	M – Nasdaq	14.75	27.7	27.2	13.8	21.7	24.7	23.66	4.1	7.8	35.2	24.66	34.5
Tofutti Brands, Inc.	TOF	A – American	2.13	91.3	45.8		22.9	21.3	6.59	19.3	43.2	61.9	21.29	32.5
Fossil, Inc.	FOSL	M – Nasdaq	17.13	52.5	28.6	20.4	26.7	25	9.81	10.6	15.6	34.2	24.97	29.6
Pre–Paid Legal Services	PPD	N – New York	30.06	54.3	33	40	33.1	21.6	6.09	15.5	46.8	47.7	21.63	29.5
Microsoft Corporation	MSFT	M – Nasdaq	69.69	36.2	36.1	22.6	23.2	28.6	2.61	40.8	31.3	33.4	28.56	28.5
Monaco Coach Corporation	MNC	N – New York	14.38	81.5	36.1	14.5	29.9	17.9	17.25	6	15.8	50.5	17.94	23.8
Fairfield Communities	FFD	N – New York	7.06	32.9	27.8	22	21.4	16.5	19.11	5.4	12.3	39.2	16.49	23.6
Craftmade International	CRFT	M – Nasdaq	8.25	44.9	27.3	27	23.2	21.7	6.55	15.3	17.4	29.7	20.21	22.8
Black Hawk Gaming & Dvlp.	BHWK	M – Nasdaq	6.5	47.7	31.9		16.2	12.8	23.54	4.3	12.2	46.6	12.77	22.3
K–Swiss Inc.	KSWS	M – Nasdaq	16.63	273.6	22.9	10.3	22	13	14.26	7.3	29.5	41.9	10.83	22
T. Rowe Price Associates	TROW	M – Nasdaq	40.38	32.3	31	15.4	30.8	28.3	5.67	18.8	19.5	32.8	21.2	22
Tellabs, Inc.	TLAB	M – Nasdaq	63.94	61.5	60.8	28.8	26.7	24.6	2.38	42.9	33.3	57.1	24.57	20.6

On Assignment, Inc.	ASGN	M – Nasdaq	25.06	33.1	30.9	23.4	21.7	22.5	2.83	33.4	27.2	27.5	22.49	19.9
KEMET Corporation	KEM	N – New York	24.06	21.9	21.7	14.3	12.8	15.6	3.66	28.3	28.9	22.4	15.63	18.4
Swift Transportation Co.	SWFT	M – Nasdaq	16	28.5	27.5	16	16.7	16.1	6.38	16	18.8	29.8	16.06	18
Chico's FAS, Inc.	CHCS	M – Nasdaq	29	108.8	27.1	23.8	31	22.5	3.79	27.6	23.7	25.8	22.5	17.3
Pacific Sunwear of CA	PSUN	M – Nasdaq	14.75	59.7	31.2	25.2	21.7	14.4	8	12.8	20.8	38.1	14.43	15.5
Buffett EPS Growth Model Screen														
MGI Properties	MGI	N – New York	2.31	74.7	46.7		185.6	35.7	466.06	0.2	11.6	119.1	3.22	35.5
Theragenics Corporation	TGX	N – New York	7.23	53.3	45	27.5	15.7	16	8.16	12.5	61.1	70.3	16.03	36.3
Tofutti Brands, Inc.	TOF	A – American	2.13	91.3	45.8		22.9	21.3	6.59	19.3	43.2	61.9	21.29	32.5
Tellabs, Inc.	TLAB	M – Nasdaq	63.94	61.5	60.8	28.8	26.7	24.6	2.38	42.9	33.3	57.1	24.57	20.6
Monaco Coach Corporation	MNC	N – New York	14.38	81.5	36.1	14.5	29.9	17.9	17.25	6	15.8	50.5	17.94	23.8
Micros Systems, Inc.	MCRS	M – Nasdaq	22.25	124.2	30.7	22	20.1	19.1	9.21	11.6	40	48.9	19.09	34.6
Xilinx, Incorporated	XLNX	M – Nasdaq	71.81	75.7	54.1	27.6	36.7	24.2	2.87	36.1	24.2	48.6	24.24	14.9
Pre-Paid Legal Services	PPD	N – New York	30.06	54.3	33	40	33.1	21.6	6.09	15.5	46.8	47.7	21.63	29.5
Black Hawk Gaming & Dvlp.	BHWK	M – Nasdaq	6.5	47.7	31.9		16.2	12.8	23.54	4.3	12.2	46.6	12.77	22.3
K-Swiss Inc.	KSWS	M – Nasdaq	16.63	273.6	22.9	10.3	22	13	14.26	7.3	29.5	41.9	10.83	22
Fairfield Communities	FFD	N – New York	7.06	32.9	27.8	22	21.4	16.5	19.11	5.4	12.3	39.2	16.49	23.6

Buffett's Passing Companies (Data as of August 2, 2000) *(Continued)*

Company Name	Ticker	Exchange	Price	EPS Cont-Growth 3yr	EPS Cont-Growth 7yr	EPS Growth Estimate	Return on Equity 12m	Return on Equity 7 year Average	Earnings Yield 12m	P/E Ratio	P/E Ratio Average 7yr	Buffett Price Growth-EPS Growth	Sustainable Growth Rate	Buffett Price Growth-Sust. Growth
Pacific Sunwear of CA	PSUN	M – Nasdaq	14.75	59.7	31.2	25.2	21.7	14.4	8	12.8	20.8	38.1	14.43	15.5
JONES PHARMA, Inc.	JMED	M – Nasdaq	32.31	58	37.7	22.2	19.5	17.4	2.75	32.6	35.6	37.5	15.55	14.3
Crossmann Communities	CROS	M – Nasdaq	14.75	27.7	27.2	13.8	21.7	24.7	23.66	4.1	7.8	35.2	24.66	34.5
Fossil, Inc.	FOSL	M – Nasdaq	17.13	52.5	28.6	20.4	26.7	25	9.81	10.6	15.6	34.2	24.97	29.6
Microsoft Corporation	MSFT	M – Nasdaq	69.69	36.2	36.1	22.6	23.2	28.6	2.61	40.8	31.3	33.4	28.56	28.5
T. Rowe Price Associates	TROW	M – Nasdaq	40.38	32.3	31	15.4	30.8	28.3	5.67	18.8	19.5	32.8	21.2	22
Swift Transportation Co.	SWFT	M – Nasdaq	16	28.5	27.5	16	16.7	16.1	6.38	16	18.8	29.8	16.06	18
Craftmade International	CRFT	M – Nasdaq	8.25	44.9	27.3	27	23.2	21.7	6.55	15.3	17.4	29.7	20.21	22.8
Alliance Capital Mgt Hldg	AC	N – New York	47.25	31.4	25.6	16	140	55.7	6.24	15.4	15.1	27.5	-7.41	
On Assignment, Inc.	ASGN	M – Nasdaq	25.06	33.1	30.9	23.4	21.7	22.5	2.83	33.4	27.2	27.5	22.49	19.9
Chico's FAS, Inc.	CHCS	M – Nasdaq	29	108.8	27.1	23.8	31	22.5	3.79	27.6	23.7	25.8	22.5	17.3
Home Depot, Inc.	HD	N – New York	52.69	32.8	28.3	23.4	18.9	16.9	2.07	49.7	35.9	24.7	14.94	10.4
Forward Air Corporation	FWRD	M – Nasdaq	43.63	41.9	34.6	22.5	29.2	20.2	1.95	47.4	22.9	24.2	20.2	6.8
Southwest Airlines Co.	LUV	N – New York	22.38	30.8	23.9	15.3	16.1	15.2	4.51	23.3	19.8	22.6	14.87	12.5
KEMET Corporation	KEM	N – New York	24.06	21.9	21.7	14.3	12.8	15.6	3.66	28.3	28.9	22.4	15.63	18.4

Graham's Passing Companies (Data as of June 30, 2000)

Company Name	Ticker	Exchange	PE	PE Using Average EPS 3 yr	PE Average 5 yr	Sales	Current Ratio	Long Term Debt to Equity	EPS Growth 5 yr	Dividend Yield	Dividend Yield Average 5 yr	Price to Book Value	Price to Book Value Average 5 yr
Graham Enterprising Screen													
Friedman's Inc.	FRDM	M - Nasdaq	3.8	4.7	16.2	353.4	4.3	21.9	12.4	1.2		0.34	1.61
Atlantic Tele-Network, Inc	ANK	A - American	4.3	4.1	9.0	82.4	2.3	9.3	13.9	7.4		0.59	1.14
Butler Manufacturing	BBR	N - New York	4.3	5.7	13.3	989.0	1.5	36.8	11.9	3.8	1.7	0.74	1.72
Federal Screw Works	FSCR	M - Nasdaq	4.5	5.8	6.5	121.6	2.0	0.0	24.8	1.0	3.8	0.81	1.01
Standard Commercial Corp	STW	N - New York	5.7	3.9		1105.8	1.5	133.9	17.5	4.4		0.40	1.16
Pitt-Des Moines, Inc.	PDM	A - American	5.8	7.1	8.7	664.9	2.2	8.4	14.4	4.2	2.7	0.78	1.06
Fleetwood Enterprises	FLE	N - New York	5.9	5.2	14.0	3766.9	1.6	13.8	17.2	5.3	2.2	0.80	2.36
PrimeSource Corporation	PSRC	M - Nasdaq	6.3	6.8	15.6	546.8	2.4	104.8	1.9	3.8	2.8	0.55	1.00
Roanoke Electric Steel	RESC	M - Nasdaq	6.3	7.1	7.7	389.3	2.9	81.7	15.7	3.2	2.6	0.96	1.32
Graham Defensive Investor Screen--Non-Utility													
Pitt-Des Moines, Inc.	PDM	A - American	5.8	7.1	8.7	664.9	2.2	8.4	14.4	4.2	2.7	0.78	1.06
Oxford Industries, Inc.	OXM	N - New York	6.4	6.7	25.2	818.4	2.3	25.6	7.2	4.7	3.4	0.87	1.49
Noland Company	NOLD	M - Nasdaq	6.5	9.6	13.8	489.6	2.1	20.8	5.5	1.9	1.4	0.46	0.67
Hughes Supply, Inc.	HUG	N - New York	6.9	7.7	10.7	3114.8	2.9	104.9	13.3	1.7	1.2	0.86	1.33

(Continued)

Graham's Passing Companies (Data as of June 30, 2000) *(Continued)*

Company Name	Ticker	Exchange	PE	PE Using Average EPS 3 yr	PE Average 5 yr	Sales	Current Ratio	Long Term Debt to Equity	EPS Growth 5 yr	Dividend Yield	Dividend Yield Average 5 yr	Price to Book Value	Price to Book Value Average 5 yr
Haverty Furniture Cos.	HVT	N - New York	7.0	10.3	11.9	632.7	2.4	81.9	17.5	2.4	2.1	1.11	1.22
Wabash National Corp.	WNC	N - New York	7.0	10.8	38.2	1465.7	2.6	69.1	3.9	1.3	0.6	0.71	1.97
Coachmen Industries	COA	N - New York	7.1	6.7	11.7	831.2	3.2	3.2	12.5	1.7	1.0	0.82	1.77
Tecumseh Products Company	TECUA	M - Nasdaq	7.1	7.6	10.7	1801.1	2.9	1.5	4.9	3.4	2.6	0.75	1.16
Thor Industries, Inc.	THO	N - New York	7.1	11.6	13.0	886.0	2.5	0.0	16.1	0.4	0.4	1.34	1.85
Lancaster Colony Corp.	LANC	M - Nasdaq	7.8	9.0	15.0	1101.4	3.7	0.7	11.6	3.3	1.7	1.79	3.58
A. Schulman, Inc.	SHLM	M - Nasdaq	7.8	8.3	15.9	1019.6	3.5	24.7	4.9	4.5	2.0	1.09	1.99
Cato Corporation	CACOA	M - Nasdaq	8.7	12.8	16.4	614.4	2.3	0.0	15.6	3.4	2.1	1.58	1.54
La-Z-Boy Incorporated	LZB	N - New York	8.8	11.1	13.3	1717.5	2.9	35.6	19.2	2.3	2.1	1.29	1.76
Genuine Parts Company	GPC	N - New York	9.3	10.0	15.8	8158.3	3.0	32.8	6.4	5.5	3.2	1.60	2.87
Superior Industries Int'l	SUP	N - New York	9.3	12.0	13.9	590.2	2.9	0.1	7.3	1.6	1.0	1.87	2.72
AAR Corp.	AIR	N - New York	9.4	9.8	21.4	996.2	3.0	52.7	30.4	2.8	1.9	0.94	1.84
Standard Register Company	SR	N - New York	10.0	6.9	13.6	1313.9	4.0	37.6	10.6	6.5	3.0	0.72	1.61
Skyline Corporation	SKY	N - New York	10.4	9.3	12.6	617.8	3.8	0.0	15.9	3.3	2.3	0.99	1.38
Liz Claiborne, Inc.	LIZ	N - New York	10.7	12.7	15.0	2915.3	2.8	34.9	24.2	1.3	1.3	2.20	2.59

Company	Ticker	Exchange											
Parker-Hannifin Corp.	PH	N - New York	10.8	12.6	13.4	5160.5	2.4	34.7	45.3	2.0	1.7	1.84	2.38
Kimball International	KBALB	M - Nasdaq	11.3	10.6	14.2	1156.4	2.2	0.5	11.6	4.3	3.1	1.24	1.74
Benjamin Moore & Co.	MBEN	O - Over the counter	11.3	11.9		791.9	3.1	7.6	15.4	7.0		2.06	
Pioneer-Standard Electr.	PIOS	M - Nasdaq	11.5	14.0	12.2	2434.9	2.9	115.2	6.1	0.8	0.9	1.27	1.69
Applied Industrial Tech.	APZ	N - New York	12.0	13.1	16.3	1557.2	2.5	31.1	4.4	2.9	2.2	1.13	1.70
Avnet, Inc.	AVT	N - New York	12.0	13.8	12.7	8085.6	2.2	77.6	18.6	1.0	1.2	1.42	1.52
Watsco, Incorporated	WSO	N - New York	12.1	14.2	20.8	1272.2	3.6	65.7	21.1	0.8	0.8	1.17	1.82
Wolverine World Wide	WWW	N - New York	12.2	10.9	19.6	676.8	8.6	43.1	12.2	1.4	0.6	1.19	2.46
ABM Industries, Inc.	ABM	N - New York	13.2	16.0	17.5	1708.2	2.1	14.9	16.6	2.7	1.9	1.79	2.20
Graham Defensive Investor Screen--Utility													
GPU, Inc.	GPU	N - New York	8.4	8.6	11.6	4864.8	0.5	155.6	20.8	8.1	5.6	0.91	1.26
RGS Energy Group, Inc.	RGS	N - New York	8.8	9.5	11.5	1267.4	1.4	104.0	6.3	8.1	7.3	1.01	1.23
Energy East Corporation	NEG	N - New York	8.9	11.8	11.4	2308.5	1.6	79.7	9.8	4.6	4.8	1.31	1.34
DTE Energy Company	DTE	N - New York	9.1	9.9	12.3	4886.0	0.9	109.0	4.5	6.7	6.1	1.14	1.38

(Continued)

Graham's Passing Companies (Data as of June 30, 2000) *(Continued)*

Company Name	Ticker	Exchange	PE	PE Using Average EPS 3 yr	PE Average 5 yr	Sales	Current Ratio	Long Term Debt to Equity	EPS Growth 5 yr	Dividend Yield	Dividend Yield Average 5 yr	Price to Book Value	Price to Book Value Average 5 yr
IPALCO Enterprises	IPL	N - New York	9.1	15.4	15.0	844.9	0.8	121.4	12.8	3.2	4.0	2.65	2.61
FirstEnergy Corp.	FE	N - New York	9.2	11.0		6505.0	0.6	131.9	4.9	6.4		1.14	
Cinergy Corp.	CIN	N - New York	9.8	11.8	15.3	6118.7	0.7	109.6	14.3	7.1	5.7	1.48	1.94
Puget Sound Energy, Inc.	PSD	N - New York	10.0	12.4	15.7	2138.4	0.6	134.3	4.7	8.6	7.5	1.28	1.57
OGE Energy Corp.	OGE	N - New York	10.2	9.9	13.1	2375.8	0.9	166.0	5.1	7.2	5.9	1.45	1.85
United Illuminating Co.	UIL	N - New York	10.4	13.1	12.1	692.3	1.1	115.7	3.7	6.6	7.4	1.32	1.25
Cascade Natural Gas Corp.	CGC	N - New York	11.2	16.8	25.4	237.2	1.4	98.7	15.4	5.8	5.6	1.46	1.56
UtiliCorp United Inc.	UCU	N - New York	11.2	11.8	14.0	19570.2	1.0	125.6	4.8	6.0	5.7	1.07	1.29
Entergy Corporation	ETR	N - New York	11.3	13.0	14.8	8944.8	1.5	101.1	8.4	4.4	6.0	0.92	0.94
Otter Tail Power Company	OTTR	M - Nasdaq	11.4	14.7	13.7	487.9	1.4	76.4	8.9	4.9	5.2	2.01	1.98
SCANA Corporation	SCG	N - New York	11.5	12.2	14.3	1925.0	0.7	112.2	7.2	4.8	5.3	1.17	1.60
IdaCorp, Inc.	IDA	N - New York	11.6	13.6	13.6	650.5	1.1	106.0	6.2	5.8	6.0	1.56	1.64
Alliant Energy Corp.	LNT	N - New York	11.7	13.8	16.0	2272.0	0.5	83.5	3.3	7.7	6.6	0.85	1.85
Southern Company	SO	N - New York	12.1	14.9	15.6	11716.0	0.5	137.8	4.1	5.7	5.2	1.73	1.80

NICOR Inc.	GAS	N - New York	12.4	12.8	14.2	1698.1	0.7	54.6	4.8	5.1	4.2	1.91	2.24
Central Vermont Public	CV	N - New York	12.6	11.9	21.3	421.0	1.7	89.2	3.5	8.0	6.6	0.66	0.82
Peoples Energy Corp.	PGL	N - New York	12.7	12.7	13.9	1327.1	0.7	39.1	4.1	6.2	5.6	1.41	1.67
South Jersey Industries	SJI	N - New York	12.7	15.7	15.5	413.2	0.6	88.9	10.5	5.6	6.0	1.44	1.52
CP & L Energy, Inc.	CPL	N - New York	12.9	12.0	14.2	3471.8	1.1	88.3	4.7	6.5	5.1	1.43	1.89
Piedmont Natural Gas Co.	PNY	N - New York	13.0	14.2	15.8	743.1	1.2	75.5	6.8	5.5	4.5	1.49	1.94
CLECO Corporation	CNL	N - New York	13.7	14.8	13.2	787.5	0.8	130.8	4.8	5.1	5.4	1.70	1.60
FPL Group, Inc.	FPL	N - New York	13.9	12.9	14.0	6494.0	0.6	64.5	7.0	4.4	3.9	1.56	1.79

CANSLIM Passing Companies (Data as of June 30, 2000)

Company Name	Ticker	Exchange	EPS Cont-Growth from Q5 to Q1	EPS Cont-Growth from Q6 to Q2	EPS Growth Estimate	EPS Cont-Growth 5yr	Float	Shares Outstanding	% Rank-Rel Strength 52 Week	Price as % of 52 Week High	Institutional Shareholders	Institutional Ownership %
Anaren Microwave, Inc.	ANEN	M - Nasdaq	36.8	35.3		43.1	8.4	8.46	99	94	134	51.9
PC Connection, Inc.	PCCC	M - Nasdaq	57.9	45.5	26.8	61.0	4.8	23.68	98	97	75	16.3
SERENA Software, Inc.	SRNA	M - Nasdaq	100.0	60.0	30.0	109.1	15.3	37.97	97	97	107	25.9
Techne Corporation	TECH	M - Nasdaq	65.2	55.6	25.0	25.2	10.5	20.37	97	92	233	67.8
Hall, Kinion & Associates	HAKI	M - Nasdaq	78.6	71.4	28.3	137.1	3.6	10.48	97	94	61	33.2
Braun's Fashions Corp.	BFCI	M - Nasdaq	213.0	160.0	20.0	114.8	5.4	6.8	95	94	68	57.8
Excel Technology, Inc.	XLTC	M - Nasdaq	50.0	-12.1		36.4	7.0	11.33	95	95	63	39.9
Technitrol, Inc.	TNL	N - New York	90.9	58.8	15.0	36.6	13.8	16.1	93	98	225	49.3
Direct Focus, Inc.	DFXI	M - Nasdaq	80.9	59.3	22.0	104.0	8.6	10.49	91	98	40	13.7
Syncor International Corp	SCOR	M - Nasdaq	43.2	25.8	24.6	66.2	4.8	11.86	87	97	168	54.4
Plantronics, Inc.	PLT	N - New York	41.5	8.0	22.7	26.9	7.5	16.25	82	97	260	89.6
Greater Bay Bancorp	GBBK	M - Nasdaq	92.0	54.4	16.5	34.0	11.5	14.03	78	94	129	24.2
GBC Bancorp.	GBCB	M - Nasdaq	95.8	61.2		33.4	8.5	11.52	78	98	95	33.7
Kewaunee Scientific Corp.	KEQU	M - Nasdaq	38.5	20.0		77.4	1.4	2.46	73	95	17	12.0

Fisher's Passing Companies (Data as of June 30, 2000)

Company Name	Ticker	Exchange	Price	Price-high 52 week	Price-low 52 week	Market Cap Q1	Net Margin 12m	Total Liabilities to Assets Q1	PE to EPS Est Growth 5yr	PE Ratio	EPS Cont-Growth 3yr	EPS Growth Est	Sales-Growth 3yr
Consolidated Graphics	CGX	N - New York	9.38	49.75	8.50	128.8	6.2	59.8	0.1	3.7	45.2	25.0	63.1
Formula Systems (1985)	FORTY	M - Nasdaq	53.00	92.19	22.38	497.1	16.4	60.8	0.1	4.3	72.5	30.0	49.1
TrueTime, Inc.	TRUE	M - Nasdaq	2.94	15.50	2.75	17.5	10.1	10.2	0.1	4.3	39.5	35.0	22.2
Deltek Systems, Inc.	DLTK	M - Nasdaq	5.91	21.00	5.88	98.8	17.4	19.3	0.2	5.9	34.6	27.5	33.0
Display Technologies, Inc	DTEK	M - Nasdaq	2.94	5.00	2.38	23.8	2.7	59.3	0.2	10.9	8.2	45.0	70.7
ePlus, Inc.	PLUS	M - Nasdaq	26.44	74.63	7.00	254.4	3.3	83.1	0.2	26.4	50.9	20.0	39.3
National RV Holdings, Inc	NVH	N - New York	10.50	27.31	8.13	101.4	7.6	22.3	0.2	3.6	18.8	160.0	45.2
Travis Boats& Motors, Inc.	TRVS	M - Nasdaq	5.50	16.25	5.00	24.3	2.6	77.6	0.2	4.6	25.2	20.0	41.3
Abercrombie & Fitch Co.	ANF	N - New York	12.19	49.69	8.00	1228.1	14.2	27.5	0.3	8.6	75.1	25.2	45.9
Avant! Corporation	AVNT	M - Nasdaq	18.73	25.25	8.91	728.8	19.4	30.8	0.3	12.1	44.9	35.5	34.8
Covenant Transport, Inc.	CVTI	M - Nasdaq	8.00	18.94	7.56	119.3	4.2	57.1	0.3	5.6	30.5	17.8	26.0
Crossmann Communities	CROS	M - Nasdaq	16.50	33.63	14.19	175.2	6.4	45.5	0.3	4.8	27.7	13.8	38.5
Cutter & Buck Inc.	CBUK	M - Nasdaq	7.94	19.75	6.31	82.1	7.0	25.0	0.3	7.6	25.2	26.0	48.5
Perry Ellis International	PERY	M - Nasdaq	8.00	13.63	7.16	53.9	4.2	67.8	0.3	4.7	22.1	18.0	16.7
JAKKS Pacific, Inc.	JAKK	M - Nasdaq	14.75	29.33	13.25	285.6	12.6	16.9	0.3	10.0	86.2	28.8	147.6

(Continued)

Fisher's Passing Companies (Data as of June 30, 2000) (Continued)

Company Name	Ticker	Exchange	Price	Price--high 52 week	Price--low 52 week	Market Cap Q1	Net Margin 12m	Total Liabilities to Assets Q1	PE to EPS Est Growth 5yr	PE Ratio	EPS Cont-Growth 3yr	EPS Growth Est	Sales-Growth 3yr
Matrix Bancorp, Inc.	MTXC	M - Nasdaq	6.75	16.06	6.75	45.6	12.5	95.2	0.3	4.7	31.1	17.5	64.8
Paxar Corporation	PXR	N - New York	11.50	11.94	8.00	524.6	11.8	45.9	0.3	6.8	1.4	20.0	26.6
Pomeroy Computer Resource	PMRY	M - Nasdaq	14.75	21.75	9.56	178.4	3.2	53.4	0.3	6.7	38.4	20.0	31.0
Stoneridge, Inc.	SRI	N - New York	8.75	19.50	8.69	196.0	6.3	66.1	0.3	4.6	40.7	15.5	22.9
Transport Corp. of Amer.	TCAM	M - Nasdaq	6.50	17.19	4.75	46.6	2.5	72.9	0.3	7.9	1.3	25.0	20.1
Wackenhut Correction Corp	WHC	N - New York	7.50	21.00	6.25	167.9	4.7	44.8	0.3	7.5	37.3	26.3	47.1
Tommy Hilfiger, Inc.	TOM	N - New York	7.50	41.00	6.31	711.2	11.4	46.1	0.3	4.2	29.8	13.9	50.7
A.C. Moore Arts & Crafts	ACMR	M - Nasdaq	6.38	7.94	4.00	47.2	2.3	31.1	0.4	8.9	-4.7	20.0	26.8
CAM Commerce Solutions	CADA	M - Nasdaq	6.63	28.88	4.94	18.3	4.0	20.5	0.4	15.1	17.1	35.0	20.8
Compuware Corporation	CPWR	M - Nasdaq	10.38	40.00	9.25	3766.3	15.8	50.2	0.4	11.3	50.1	26.9	40.0
Dave & Buster's, Inc.	DAB	N - New York	6.25	29.06	5.06	81.0	3.4	45.1	0.4	9.1	9.4	21.3	40.7
Discount Auto Parts	DAP	N - New York	10.00	23.81	8.50	167.0	4.7	56.9	0.4	6.2	4.2	14.4	18.5
Gehl Company	GEHL	M - Nasdaq	14.25	23.50	13.50	79.3	7.2	55.7	0.4	4.3	28.4	10.0	21.4
Healthcare Recoveries	HCRI	M - Nasdaq	3.56	5.56	2.56	38.9	7.5	48.6	0.4	8.1	-4.0	22.5	25.0
Immucor, Inc.	BLUD	M - Nasdaq	5.63	18.88	4.19	44.3	6.0	55.8	0.4	9.7	10.3	25.0	24.3

Company	Symbol	Exchange	Col4	Col5	Col6	Col7	Col8	Col9	Col10	Col11	Col12	Col13	Col14
NBTY, Inc.	NBTY	M - Nasdaq	6.38	19.06	5.81	428.4	6.3	56.6	0.4	10.1	3.7	24.5	33.4
Natrol, Inc.	NTOL	M - Nasdaq	3.25	9.50	3.25	43.9	9.0	26.8	0.4	5.6	-9.4	15.0	26.0
Northwest Pipe Company	NWPX	M - Nasdaq	11.88	18.50	11.13	76.8	5.3	62.9	0.4	6.0	2.4	17.0	21.1
Ocular Sciences, Inc.	OCLR	M - Nasdaq	11.75	23.44	11.63	270.9	20.2	16.8	0.4	7.4	37.9	20.8	24.8
P.A.M. Transportation	PTSI	M - Nasdaq	9.50	12.88	8.00	80.2	5.0	68.8	0.4	7.6	26.6	17.0	22.4
Pre-Paid Legal Services	PPD	N - New York	29.88	39.94	19.88	674.0	19.9	40.1	0.4	16.6	54.3	40.0	31.8
Tower Automotive, Inc.	TWR	N - New York	12.52	28.25	11.31	588.5	5.4	72.8	0.4	5.6	45.8	15.7	75.7
Tractor Supply Company	TSCO	M - Nasdaq	16.56	28.00	12.00	145.4	2.5	63.8	0.4	8.2	10.8	18.5	15.3
Urban Outfitters, Inc.	URBN	M - Nasdaq	8.81	31.06	8.56	152.1	6.6	21.3	0.4	8.4	12.1	19.0	20.9
AmeriPath, Inc.	PATH	M - Nasdaq	8.88	10.69	7.00	191.7	9.6	54.4	0.5	8.1	70.0	16.3	76.1
DVI, Incorporated	DVI	N - New York	16.00	18.06	11.25	227.6	13.9	83.7	0.5	10.7	19.2	20.0	32.8
Express Scripts, Inc.	ESRX	M - Nasdaq	62.13	92.38	28.50	2351.4	3.2	71.4	0.5	14.7	75.3	28.1	77.0
FPIC Insurance Group, Inc	FPIC	M - Nasdaq	15.69	50.88	10.38	148.1	11.1	73.5	0.5	8.2	12.8	15.0	30.4
Gametech International	GMTC	M - Nasdaq	4.63	9.50	3.38	52.2	14.4	11.2	0.5	7.7	41.2	15.0	97.7
M.S. Carriers, Inc.	MSCA	M - Nasdaq	17.63	32.44	16.13	206.4	4.6	63.9	0.5	7.6	34.2	15.8	22.2

(Continued)

Fisher's Passing Companies (Data as of June 30, 2000) *(Continued)*

Company Name	Ticker	Exchange	Price	Price--high 52 week	Price--low 52 week	Market Cap Q1	Net Margin 12m	Total Liabilities to Assets Q1	PE to EPS Est Growth 5yr	PE Ratio	EPS Cont-Growth 3yr	EPS Growth Est	Sales-Growth 3yr
MAXIMUS, Inc.	MMS	N - New York	22.14	38.94	20.00	466.6	9.0	20.9	0.5	15.0	12.8	27.7	33.0
NCI Building Systems, Inc	NCS	N - New York	20.23	23.19	14.50	361.8	5.0	67.2	0.5	7.7	16.8	15.0	41.2
Pediatrix Medical Group	PDX	N - New York	11.63	20.94	6.00	183.4	9.1	32.3	0.5	8.5	19.2	18.7	41.1
PJ America, Inc.	PJAM	M - Nasdaq	9.75	25.63	8.75	48.8	5.4	13.2	0.5	10.4	17.1	23.1	57.2
RSA Security Inc.	RSAS	M - Nasdaq	69.25	93.06	15.88	2734.8	71.9	49.9	0.5	17.4	133.2	32.3	36.2
SOS Staffing Services	SOSS	M - Nasdaq	3.06	7.00	2.63	38.9	1.3	39.1	0.5	8.1	-10.7	17.3	39.7
SanDisk Corporation	SNDK	M - Nasdaq	61.19	169.63	18.88	4072.6	77.4	21.9	0.5	18.2	13.3	34.3	36.3
Supreme Industries, Inc.	STS	A - American	4.50	8.84	4.05	47.9	3.3	58.9	0.5	6.0	19.3	12.0	15.4
Theragenics Corporation	TGX	N - New York	8.55	16.63	6.94	252.4	37.5	7.3	0.5	14.7	53.3	27.5	52.2
Toll Brothers, Inc.	TOL	N - New York	20.50	23.06	15.56	743.7	7.2	62.5	0.5	6.7	20.9	14.6	24.4
US Oncology, Inc.	USON	M - Nasdaq	5.00	12.81	3.03	455.1	5.3	42.6	0.5	8.2	3.7	16.1	36.2
USFreightways Corp.	USFC	M - Nasdaq	24.56	52.00	23.75	653.5	4.7	54.2	0.5	6.2	40.6	12.9	18.6

T. Rowe Price's Passing Companies (Data as of June 30, 2000)

Company Name	Ticker	Exchange	Price	Price--High 52 Week	Price--Low 52 Week	EPS--Growth 3yr	EPS--Growth 7yr	PE	PE--Average 5yr	Insider Ownership %	Institutional Ownership %	Return on Assets 12m	Net Margin 12m	Gross Margin 12m
T. Rowe Price Screen														
Consolidated Graphics	CGX	N - New York	9.38	49.75	8.50	45.2	31.7	3.7	23.2	33.7	40.9	5.7	6.2	30.0
Centex Construction Prod.	CXP	N - New York	22.69	41.81	21.75	44.1	69.6	4.0	8.6	61.8	33.5	24.7	25.9	40.9
MascoTech, Inc.	MSX	N - New York	10.81	17.69	10.63	43.0	24.7	5.7	14.1	43.0	30.1	4.4	5.6	25.8
NVR, Inc.	NVR	A - American	57.00	65.00	38.00	82.5	95.4	5.9	7.3	30.5	53.3	14.5	5.5	19.8
Genlyte Group Inc.	GLYT	M - Nasdaq	21.06	26.13	17.75	32.9	55.1	8.7	10.2	66.8	59.6	5.8	3.4	33.9
Control Chief Holdings	DIGM	M - Nasdaq	4.88	5.63	3.97	65.1	25.5	8.9	12.1	49.7	0.0	13.6	7.9	53.9
Pre-Paid Legal Services	PPD	N - New York	29.88	39.94	19.88	54.3	33.0	16.6	27.8	22.9	35.3	19.8	19.9	63.3
Credo Petroleum Corp.	CRED	M - Nasdaq	5.88	5.94	3.06	37.9	32.7	17.3	20.5	26.2	2.9	8.3	27.0	75.7
Sonic Corporation	SONC	M - Nasdaq	29.38	33.88	22.81	36.5	20.6	17.8	18.9	35.3	83.7	11.1	11.2	63.6
United States Cellular	USM	A - American	63.00	125.75	52.56	31.6	63.5	18.1	22.2	88.9	17.8	9.0	22.1	77.2

Dreman's Passing Companies (Data as of June 30, 2000)

Company Name	Ticker	Exchange	PE Ratio	%–Rank PE	PE Average 5yr	Dividend Yield	Div Yield Average 5yr	Dividend Growth 3yr	Market Capitalization	%–Rank Market Cap	Total Liab to Assets	EPS Cont– Growth 5yr	EPS Growth Estimate
Banco Latinoamer. De Exp.	BLX	N - New York	5.5	8	9.8	4.5	2.5	4.6	553.5	74	85.3	14.3	8.0
Greenpoint Financial Corp	GPT	N - New York	7.5	16	14.0	5.3	2.4	30.1	1933.6	87	86.7	15.4	13.1
Springs Industries, Inc.	SMI	N - New York	7.9	18	13.7	4.1	3.1	0.0	573.2	74	52.1	2.0	11.8
Royal Caribbean Cruises	RCL	N - New York	8.7	21	15.2	2.4	1.5	10.1	3345.2	91	48.1	14.0	17.4
A.G. Edwards, Inc.	AGE	N - New York	8.8	22	9.6	1.6	2.0	11.5	3401.2	91	67.9	25.2	
La-Z-Boy Incorporated	LZB	N - New York	8.8	22	13.3	2.3	2.1	7.2	859.6	79	45.6	19.2	11.8
Energy East Corporation	NEG	N - New York	8.9	23	11.4	4.6	4.8	6.3	2164.1	88	60.9	11.5	9.1
RenaissanceRe Holdings	RNR	N - New York	8.9	23	7.2	3.4	2.4	20.5	846.1	79	63.9	3.8	4.0
CNA Surety Corporation	SUR	N - New York	9.1	24	20.3	2.7			512.1	72	62.5		12.5
FirstEnergy Corp.	FE	N - New York	9.2	25		6.4		0.0	5388.0	93	69.6	4.9	5.5
Superior Industries Int'l	SUP	N - New York	9.3	26	13.9	1.6	1.0	15.0	672.4	76	24.7	7.3	10.6
Jefferies Group, Inc.	JEF	N - New York	9.4	26	18.7	2.0	0.5	30.5	492.9	72	86.3	19.5	12.0
Willamette Industries	WLL	N - New York	9.7	28	27.4	3.1	1.9	4.1	3018.1	90	53.7	7.8	17.0
Pinnacle West Capital	PNW	N - New York	9.8	28	12.6	4.1	3.4	8.9	2870.3	90	66.6	6.7	6.5
Worthington Industries	WOR	N - New York	9.8	28	21.4	5.7	3.1	7.0	905.1	79	59.8	-3.7	12.8

Company	Symbol	Exchange										
Lubrizol Corporation	LZ	N - New York	10.1	30	14.8	5.0	3.3	2.3	1126.4	82	52.5	-3.4	7.0
John H. Harland Company	JH	N - New York	10.2	30		2.0	2.7	-33.5	423.6	70	55.5	-3.7	11.0
Leggett & Platt, Inc.	LEG	N - New York	11.1	36	16.8	2.4	1.5	16.1	3241.5	91	48.4	16.5	14.0
Sherwin-Williams Co.	SHW	N - New York	11.3	37	17.1	2.5	1.6	11.1	3469.6	91	59.8	11.1	12.8
Weyerhaeuser Company	WY	N - New York	11.3	37	23.1	3.7	3.2	0.0	10017.0	96	60.0	0.9	16.1
Alcan Aluminium Ltd.	AL	N - New York	11.4	38	15.3	1.9	1.9	0.0	6779.3	94	42.8	24.6	10.0
BancWest Corporation	BWE	N - New York	11.5	38	14.2	4.1	3.5	1.1	2050.8	87	89.3	4.4	9.0
Carnival Corporation	CCL	N - New York	11.5	38	20.2	2.2	1.1	26.0	11786.9	96	27.7	19.8	15.1
Northwest Natural Gas	NWNG	M - Nasdaq	11.9	40		5.5	5.0	0.8	563.2	74	59.4	0.8	4.0

Part 5

The Investor's Resource Guide

The investor's resource guide is a key part of making this book a valuable addition to your investing library. In a comprehensive reference guide, there are limits to the details provided about each subject. The resources provided in the final chapters, whether the newspapers, magazines, and books in Chapter 20 or the websites in Chapter 21, provide further information and up-to-date data for the investor who actively manages a portfolio. The glossaries in Chapters 22 and 23 offer a quick reference for definitions to common investing acronyms and terms.

20

The Financial Media

It may be the age of the internet, but you will find few investing professionals who do not have a subscription to either *The Wall Street Journal* or *Investor's Business Daily*, perhaps both, and possibly *Financial Times* as well. Add to that a number of financial magazines and trade journals plus CNN or CNBC as background noise in the office. Yes, printed news is a day late, but old habits die hard, traditional publications can be easier to read, and a newspaper is very portable. In a situation that is the best of both worlds, most traditional publications now have websites that do not always offer the entire publication online, but have added features, current news, and an ability to search the archives for the article you remember reading six months ago but cannot find now.

Periodicals

The following list is a sampling of popular investment periodicals. There is something for everyone here, from the novice to the experienced investor.

Barron's

200 Liberty Street

New York, NY 10281

212-416-2700

www.dowjones.com

52 issues at $145 per year

Barron's, published every Monday by Dow Jones & Co., publishers of *The Wall Street Journal*, is best described as a cross between a newspaper and a magazine in both content and format, which is tabloid style. Each week's issue is full of news from the previous week, including comprehensive stock, mutual fund, bond, and commodities tables. Alan Abelson's dry wit in the page-three column, "Up & Down on Wall Street," is not to be missed, and pull-out sections make this lengthy periodical easy to navigate. Heavy on news, but with plenty of feature articles, *Barron's* is geared toward the experienced investor.

Bloomberg Personal Finance

P.O. Box 888

Princeton, NJ 08542-0888

888-432-5820

www.bloomberg.com

10 issues for $14.95 per year

Not surprising, coming from a magazine run by the financial data–delivery firm of Bloomberg, *Bloomberg Personal Finance* contains not only investment ideas, but also a good mix of news, financial data, and current features. The magazine and website are well integrated, with a recent issue providing a synopsis of interviews with market experts then sending the reader to the website for a download of the full discussions. Inside are also plenty of educational articles.

Forbes

60 Fifth Avenue

New York, NY 10011

800-416-9136

www.forbes.com

26 issues for $59.95 per year

Forbes is a financial magazine—part business, part investing—aimed at the experienced reader. The magazine begins with the "Fact and Commentary" section, which provides the views of Steve Forbes and Caspar Weinberger on politics, business, and world events. The meat of the magazine is one- to three-page articles on companies, industries, and the people that make them run. Toward the back, "Money and Investing" contains one-page columns on investing. There is little investment how-to, but lots of information about companies, markets, and strategies plus periodic ratings of mutual funds, corporations, and people (Forbes 400). *Forbes* was out front on the importance of the technology industry several years ago, when it began an add-on, technology-centered magazine called *Forbes ASAP*. Another add-on is *Forbes FYI*, a lifestyle magazine. (Both arrive free every few months with a subscription.)

Fortune

Time & Life Building

Rockefeller Center

New York, NY 10020

800-621-8000

www.fortune.com

26 issues for $60.06 per year

Like *Forbes, Fortune* is a business and investing magazine as opposed to the strictly investing perspective of some periodicals. Articles on companies and industries are in-depth, often running four pages or more. *Fortune* is well known for its company rankings, which include the Fortune 500. The "Investor" section is full of short articles about investing strategies and companies; "Money Manager" offers financial planning advice for the less-experienced investor.

Individual Investor

P.O. Box 37289

Boone, IA 50037-0289

888-616-7677

www.individualinvestor.com

12 issues for $22.95 per year

Individual Investor is an easy read for new investors. The articles are brief, yet informative; dealing mostly with contemporary news. The educational section titled "Investor University" covers several topics each month. Beware of the advertisements set up to look like articles.

Kiplinger's Personal Finance

P.O Box 3293

Harlan, IA 51593-2473

800-544-0155

www.kiplinger.com

12 issues for $14.97 per year

Kiplinger's Personal Finance is designed for the investor seeking well-presented investment ideas. News and general education topics take a back seat. The magazine is laid out in four conveniently color-coded sections: "Ahead" (short news briefs), "Investing" (stock, mutual fund, and industry ideas and profiles), "Managing" (financial planning topics), and "Spending" (the latest tech-toys and office equipment).

Money Magazine

P.O. Box 60001

Tampa, FL 33660

800-633-9970

www.money.com

12 issues for $19.95 per year

One of the most comprehensive personal finance periodicals, *Money Magazine* offers coverage of all areas of personal finance including investing, effective saving, retirement planning, spending, and tax preparation. Most articles are concise, easy-to-read snapshots into the current world of investment. *Money* also includes "Investing 101" for the less seasoned investor, plus frequent lists- of top-performing stocks, funds, and money managers.

Mutual Funds

P.O. Box 61591

Tampa, FL 33661-1591

800-421-6691

www.mfmag.com

10 issues for $9.97 per year

Mutual Funds is full of short articles and tips, a Q&A column, and one-page profiles of individual funds. "Portfolio Strategy" covers educational ideas and "Undiscovered Fund" seeks out lesser-known funds with star-quality performance.

SmartMoney

P.O Box 7536

Red Oak, IA 51591

800-444-4204

www.smartmoney.com

12 issues for $15 per year

SmartMoney offers a consistent array of compact, news-oriented columns such as "Update," "Model Portfolios," "Stockscreen," "Capitol Gains," and "Your Taxes." Feature articles provide a mix of investment ideas, market analysis, business, and lifestyle topics.

The Wall Street Transcript

67 Wall Street, 16th Floor

New York, NY 10005

212-952-7400

www.twst.com

52 issues for $1,890 per year, single issues $175, TWST Online $2,290 per year

The Wall Street Transcript is a weekly paper for serious investors. Each week, in-depth articles in a mostly Q&A format let the reader interpret the views of analysts, CEOs, and money managers. Sections include "Sector Roundtables," a panel of analysts reviewing a sector and naming specific recommended stocks; "Off the Record," a confidential survey of analysts on management performance of companies in a sector; "Money Manager Interviews," discussions with professional money managers; "Research Analysts," top analysts providing views on a particular sector and its stocks; and "CEO Interviews," in-depth interviews with company CEOs.

Worth

575 Lexington Avenue

New York, NY 10022

800-777-1851

www.worth.com

10 issues for $11.97 per year

Worth is strictly an investment magazine, geared more to providing ideas to the intermediate investor than education to the beginner. Several things make it stand out from the crowd; the most notable in a recent issue was the in-depth coverage of an industry: six articles covering 25 pages. The standard index of companies and funds mentioned has an unusual and useful twist. With each reference, it includes an up arrow (positive mention), down arrow (negative mention), or square (neutral or mixed mention).

Subscription Research

A multitude of subscription research services are available on the internet; many of these are reviewed in Chapter 21. Several paper-based research services also remain popular, however. Most are available at major libraries or by personal subscription. Charting subscription services are not listed here, since they can be found with the discussion on technical analysis in Chapter 18.

The big names in subscription investor research are Morningstar, Value Line, and Standard & Poor's. Though Morningstar is known for its mutual fund analysis and Value Line for its stock reports, each company offers additional research products. Standard & Poor's is known for its massive *Corporation Records* found in most libraries, but it also provides publications for individual subscription. Subscriptions are relatively expensive and data can become outdated quickly, compared with what is available over the internet. However, if you like the convenience of a paper copy delivered to your door, consider these services. Both researchers offer trial subscriptions at a greatly reduced price.

Morningstar

225 W. Wacker Drive

Chicago, IL 60606

800-735-0700

www.morningstar.com

Morningstar FundInvestor
12 issues for $99 per year

A 44-page newsletter full of mutual fund articles, industry news, and performance data on 500 mutual funds.

Morningstar Mutual Funds

24 updates, $495 per year; three-month trial, $55

Provides a full-page report on more than 1,700 mutual funds, with star ratings, performance and fee data, style boxes, and analyst commentary. Includes 160 closed-end funds. See a sample report in Figure 12–1 on page 277.

Morningstar StockInvestor

12 issues for $149 per year

This 32-page monthly newsletter features stock profiles from the Morningstar Select 300, a list of undervalued stocks; blue chips and popular stocks, a list of 150 widely followed stocks; and Microcaps, a list of 50 attractive small stocks.

Morningstar Variable Annuity Performance Report

Monthly updates, $695 per year; quarterly updates, $415 per year; one report, $135

Provides month-end returns for more than 8,000 variable annuity subaccounts, plus rankings of the 20 highest- and lowest-returning subaccounts in 27 Morningstar categories. Includes policy fees and features; and A.M. Best and Duff & Phelps ratings of issuing insurance companies.

Value Line

220 East 42nd Street

New York, NY 10017

800-535-8760

www.valueline.com

Value Line Convertibles Survey

$525 per year; eight-week trial for $65

Provides information and rankings on nearly 600 different convertible bonds. Rankings assess performance and potential for risk and return.

Value Line Investment Survey

Weekly updates, $570 per year; ten-week trial for $55

Offers one-page, information-packed summary research sheets on approximately 1,700 different stocks. Each stock is given a timeliness, safety, and technical ranking. Key financial data is provided on an annual basis, and rates of change are computed for important measures such as revenues, profits, and dividends. An analyst commentary and estimates for future performance are included. Stocks are arranged by industry, with an industry summary for each category, thus making comparisons easy.

Value Line Investment Survey—Expanded Edition

$249 per year without the standard *Investment Survey*; with it, $125 for the first year and $175 thereafter

The *Expanded Edition* picks up where the standard *Investment Survey* leaves off, adding 1,800 mostly smallcap stocks to the database.

Value Line Mutual Fund Survey

$345 per year; 10-week trial for $50

Provides performance data and rankings for 1,500 different mutual funds in a one-page format similar to the *Investment Survey's* stock data. Includes an additional monthly newsletter, *The Value Line Mutual Fund Advisor,* which analyzes mutual fund and market trends.

Value Line No-Load Fund Advisor

12 issues for $58 per year

This monthly newsletter is for investors who manage portfolios of no-load and low-load mutual funds. Each issue contains industry news, fund recommendations and data on more than 600 mutual funds. Funds are ranked against their peers with overall, risk, and five-year growth persistence rankings.

Value Line OTC Special Situations Service

24 issues for $495 per year; three-month trial for $39

This newsletter concentrates on emerging growth companies that Value Line analysts deem capable of providing unusual long-term capital gains potential irrespective of economic conditions. Though not all included in each issue, newsletter sections include "New Recommendation," a four-page report presenting a new, special situation for purchase; "Summary Index," recommendations on all stocks followed by the newsletter, with summary performance data on each; "Supervisory Reviews," update reports on stocks previously recommended; and "Performance Record," a complete listing of every stock recommended and its performance.

Standard & Poor's Corporation

65 Broadway, 8th Floor

New York, NY 10006

800-221-5277

www.standardandpoors.com

Standard & Poor's is probably best known for its deep red *Corporation Records,* a compilation of the public filings of 12,600 companies, found in nearly every public library. Most S&P products are designed for institutional investors, but a few appeal to the individual as well.

Stock Guide

12 issues for $182 per year

The 5″ × 8″ *Stock Guide* is a quick reference for more than 5,000 stocks. It includes ticker symbols, price ranges, dividends, total returns, balance sheet data, capitalization figures, and earnings per share for the current and previous four years, as well as interim earnings for the current year. In addition, there is limited information on open- and closed-end mutual funds and variable annuities.

The Outlook

51 issues for $298 per year

In existence since 1924, this weekly investment advisory letter provides 12 pages of varied investment information, including sections on "Asset Allocation," "The Economy," "Stocks in the Limelight," and "Start Status." Of special interest are periodic forecasts for the year, which include market projections, industries with superior potential, recommended portfolio sector weightings, and lists of recommended stocks and mutual funds.

Newsletters

Investment newsletters are available in so many different specialized areas that an attempt to profile the best would invariably omit many good ones. Two resources can help you weed through the masses.

Newsletter Access

www.newsletteraccess.com

Newsletter Access is a newsletter directory that outlines more than 5,000 newsletters on various topics. On a recent day, a search for stock newsletters turned up 157 titles, mutual fund newsletters returned 76 titles, and investment newsletters returned 595 titles. Each newsletter listing contains a description, address, and price plus a website link, if available. You may also register for free investment newsletter trial subscriptions.

The Hulbert Financial Digest

5051 B Backlick Road

Annandale, VA 22003

888-HULBERT

www.hulbertdigest.com

12 issues for $59 per year

Mark Hulbert, editor of *The Hulbert Financial Digest* and columnist at *Forbes,* has created a newsletter that rates newsletters. Each monthly newsletter reports the five top-performing newsletters from a list of more than 160 and profiles four top performers in an in-depth report of their long-term track records, strategies, and techniques. (Custom profiles can be ordered from the website for $25 each.) The "Stock Mutual Fund Page" lists stocks and funds that are heavily recommended as buys and sells by newsletters. "Long-Term Performance Ratings," updated twice a year, reports gains and losses and risk-adjusted ratings on 500 portfolios from more than 160 newsletters.

Newspapers

Your local newspaper probably prints stock and mutual fund tables, a sampling of interest rates, and a few pages of business news. This information is enough for many long-term investors, whose philosophy is to research investments carefully, then buy good companies or funds and ride out the daily fluctuations. If you are a more active investor and need more current information on markets, investments, and the economy, then a financial newspaper may be for you. Descriptions of the three big papers follow.

Investor's Business Daily

P.O. Box 66370

Los Angeles, CA 90066-0370

800-831-2525

www.investorsbusinessdaily.com

Weekdays, $197 per year

Investor's Business Daily (IBD), established in 1994, is a newcomer to the field of financial newspapers. The newspaper's style reflects the philosophies of its founder (William O'Neil) throughout. *IBD*'s stock tables provide all the data you will need to follow his CANSLIM approach to investing, as explained in Chapter 19. The first two pages are filled with short takes on current news stories, but the rest of the paper is devoted to assisting the reader in making better investment decisions. For example, "General Markets and Sectors" charts the NASDAQ Composite, the S&P 500, the DJIA, the IBD Mutual Fund Index, leading market sectors, and psychological market indicators. On the same page, "The Big Picture" describes the previous day's market activity, then interprets it, showing the reader certain points on each chart that led to the interpretation.

Financial Times

P.O. Box 1329

Newburgh, NY 12251

800-628-8088

www.financialtimes.com

Monday through Saturday, $368 per year

Known for its salmon-colored paper, *Financial Times (FT)* is a global financial newspaper that offers extensive coverage of international affairs, world news, and financial events. It is organized into three sections: Section I contains regional news coverage of the entire globe, plus people and management profiles and technology features. Section II covers world financial market activity. Section III, titled "Special Reports," contains industry, country, and management features. On Saturdays, the "Weekend FT" summarizes the week's business news and addresses lifestyle issues.

The Wall Street Journal

200 Burnett Road

Chicopee, MA 01020

800-568-7625

www.wsj.service@dowjones.com

Weekdays, $174.72 per year

The *Wall Street Journal (WSJ)* is the undisputed leader in investment news and information. The paper is organized into three sections: the cover section is devoted to financial, political, and world news; "Marketplace" contains features on corporations and industries; and "Money & Investing" contains the previous day's market action, stock tables, and the popular "Heard on the Street" column, which has been known to have an immediate impact on the price of stocks mentioned.

Television

Television's financial news is dominated by a few players exclusively devoted to delivering breaking news on financial markets. While the internet can duplicate the speed with which news is delivered, it cannot replicate the hands-free, audio ease of television, which can be left on in the background until something of interest catches the viewer/listener's attention. Another advantage of television is its ease of use, requiring no special equipment when traveling. For those who tune in when out of town in hopes of hearing prices on a few favorite stocks, the following paragraphs explain the ticker tape, which is a running list of stock transactions often shown at the bottom of the television screen during programming.

Ticker Tape

A ticker is a moving band of characters which reports the prices of stock transactions using abbreviations, called ticker symbols, for company names. Given what the human eye can read, the scrolling tape usually reports about 50 transactions per minute. Due to the tremendous trading volume on stock exchanges, only some data is reported on a ticker. This process is referred to as filtering. Depending on the broadcaster, filters generally include the highest-volume stocks and those with big changes in price, often eliminating multiple trades at the same price or within a tight range. The broadcaster can change the filter at any time. For example, during *Digital Jam*, CNNfn's technology program, the filter screens for tech stocks.

A transaction on the ticker might read, " DIS 32½ + ½." DIS is the stock symbol for Disney, 32½ is the price of the transaction ($32.50), and + ½ means the stock is up $0.50 from the previous day's close. When a transaction's volume is less than 5,000 shares, volume is not indicated on the ticker. When volume is between 5,000 and 10,000 shares, it is indicated, but the last two zeros are dropped. For example, "DIS 50s32½ + ½" means 5,000 shares changed hands (*s* stands for *shares*). When volume is above 10,000, the zeros are not dropped, so a transaction for 20,000 shares would read, "DIS 20.000s32½ + ½."

Broadcasters often run two tickers together, separating NYSE- and NASDAQ-listed stocks. Market summaries are shown periodically, and color coding helps to quickly identify whether a stock is up or down from the previous day's close.

Bloomberg Morning News

A partnership between Bloomberg Television and Maryland Public Television produces the half-hour show, *Bloomberg Morning News*, which airs each weekday morning on major public television stations. Topics include the previous day's market activity, interviews with money managers and analysts, reports from foreign markets, and stock recommendations. Bloomberg's website at *www.bloomberg.com/tv/public.html* provides a listing of stations and showtimes. For cable viewers, entering your zip code at *http://tvqc.bloomberg.com/zipcode/bloombergusa.asp* will help you locate a local channel. Bloomberg TV, a 24-hour financial station, airs on satellite television. The DIRECTV channel is 353. The EchoStar DISH Network channel is 207.

CEO Exchange

Jeff Greenfield, CNN's senior analyst, hosts *CEO Exchange*, a monthly Public Television program. Each one-hour show features in-depth interviews with two CEOs. Discussions include management issues, technology, business strategies, and values. To find channels, times, and guest lists, visit PBS Online at *www.pbs.org*.

CNBC

CNBC is a 24-hour business news cable channel. One of its most popular shows is *Squawk Box*, aired from 7:00 to 10:00 A.M. EST and 4:00 to 7:00 A.M. PT. This program aims to prepare investors for the trading day by taking them to the trading rooms of major brokerage firms and onto the floor of the New York Stock Exchange, where investment professionals are interviewed about their strategies. Another favorite is *Power Lunch*, the 12:00 noon to 2:00 P.M. EST and 9:00 to 11:00 A.M. PT program, which takes live viewer questions via phone and e-mail. For a full schedule, including weekend programming and a guest list, visit the CNBC website at *www.cnbc.com*.

CNNfn

CNNfn is a cable news channel devoted exclusively to financial programming. From 8:00 to 9:30 A.M. EST, *Before Hours* addresses overnight happenings in international markets and their potential effect on U.S. markets. From 11:00 A.M. to 12:00 noon EST, *In the Money* tracks investment ideas from market professionals; and *Street Sweep*, aired from 4:00 to 5:00 P.M. EST, provides a market wrap-up for the day. For a complete listing of programs and their descriptions, visit the CNNfn website at *www.cnnfn.com/services/fnonair/whatson/*.

Wall $treet Week with Louis Rukeyser

Each week, Louis Rukeyser sets the tone for *Wall $treet Week* with an opening commentary that is generously sprinkled with puns. In a crowded field, he has been successful in creating a half-hour program that is both informative and entertaining. Rukeyser is joined by a rotating group of panelists, which includes such well-known names as Ralph Acampora, Lazlo Birinyi, Frank Cappiello, and Martin Zweig. Together they answer viewers' questions and interview the week's guest—a money management professional. Ten of the regular panelists are designated as elves and weekly they vote as to whether they believe the DJIA will be at least 5% higher (bullish), at least 5% lower (bearish), or somewhere in between (neutral), in three months. For program channels and times, visit PBS Online at *www.pbs.org*, where you can also find information about future panelists, guests, and the elves' forecast.

Books

Among the thousands of great investment books available, only a small group stands well above the rest as a must-read list. Some are hot off the press and others have been in print since the 1920s, proving that while much has changed, much has stayed the same.

***Bogle on Mutual Funds*, by John C. Bogle.** John Bogle, the founder of the Vanguard Group of mutual funds, has written a comprehensive guide to investing in mutual funds. An excellent read for the new fund investor, there is also plenty for seasoned investors here. The book is readable and liberally sprinkled with graphs and boxes labeled "Caveat Emptor," which is Latin for "buyer beware."

***Common Stocks and Uncommon Profits and Other Writings by Philip A. Fisher*, by Philip A. Fisher.** The investment theory in this book is as qualitative as Benjamin Graham's is quantitative. Seven of Fisher's 15 characteristics necessary for growth focus on management issues such as teamwork, leadership skills, integrity, and labor relations. Fisher recommends thoroughly understanding the business in addition to analyzing the profit figures. He urges investors to visit trade shows to find out what competitors say about a company.

***Extraordinary Popular Delusions & the Madness of Crowds*, by Charles Mackay.** An interesting read for anyone who invests in internet stocks, this 16th-century classic addresses the crowd psychology at work in investment manias such as the 17th-century tulip bubble.

***How to Make Money in Stocks: A Winning System in Good Times and Bad*, by William O'Neil.** In his book, O'Neil outlines his CANSLIM philosophy, a combination of fundamental analysis for choosing stocks and technical analysis for timing purchases and sales. Though not necessarily limited to the experienced investor, this clearly written book is for those who are serious about their stock analysis. To use his system most effectively, you should subscribe to the newspaper he founded, *Investor's Business Daily*.

***The Greenspan Effect*, by David B. Sicilia and Jeffrey L Cruikshank.** This book offers a peek into the mind of Alan Greenspan, one of the greatest economists of our time, through careful analysis of his speeches and writings. The authors have created a very readable book by grouping discussion into logical topics, then interspersing Greenspan's words with explanations or the appropriate context.

***The Intelligent Investor*, by Benjamin Graham.** Written by the father of value investing in 1949, this book is the classic manual for finding a stock's intrinsic value and is recommended by investment legends such as Warren Buffet. It is heavy on quantitative analysis. An excellent book, but only for the serious investor.

***Market Wizards*, by Jack D. Schwager.** This book is a compilation of interviews with top Wall Street traders. Schwager asks specific questions about strategy and more general questions that help the reader understand how these successful moneymakers think and what makes them so good at what they do. An interesting book for any level of investor.

***McMillan on Options*, by Lawrence G. McMillan.** This book of practical demonstrations shows how to make money using options trading strategies. Trading tactics are illustrated with real trading situations, many from McMillan's own experience.

***The Motley Fool Investment Guide*, by David and Tom Gardner.** A good book for the novice investor, this guide is written in signature Motley Fool style, with an irreverent sense of humor. For anyone who finds investing intimidating, the easy manner makes it less so. It is full of practical ideas and help for getting started.

***One Up on Wall Street*, by Peter Lynch.** Peter Lynch writes in a clear, easy-to-read style that makes you think his "ten-bagger" stock picks were obvious choices. He recommends using what you know to choose companies that will prosper, a format anyone can follow. This is for both the new and experienced investor.

***A Random Walk down Wall Street*, by Burton G. Malkiel.** Burton Malkiel was one of the first to espouse the efficient market theory, which maintains that, given publicly available information, all stocks are efficiently priced. As such, it is nearly impossible to outperform the market over time.

***Technical Analysis of Stock Trends*, by Robert D. Edwards and John F. Magee.** This book, in its seventh edition with more than 850,000 sold, is the classic guide to technical analysis. In 700 pages, the reader will learn about all aspects of stock and index charting: what to buy, when to buy it, and when to sell.

21

Internet Resources

The internet has leveled the playing field for individual investors. The advantage that institutional investors once had was information—delivered immediately. Now rather than reading about it in *The Wall Street Journal* tomorrow, you have access to breaking news, such as earnings announcements and interest rate changes, as it is reported. You can learn about investment techniques, find financial data on public companies, and price your portfolio in real time. However, there are literally thousands of websites from which to choose. Finding the right resources for the information that you need can make the process much easier and less time consuming. The following lists, presented in alphabetical order, contain some of the best websites for investment information.

Financial Megasites

Financial megasites are comprehensive sites and are often a good place to start your search. Consider making one of them your home page—the first thing you see when you log on the net. They offer investment research, quotes, educational articles, and much more.

Subscription—America Online

Though often considered a place to get your feet wet on the internet and then move on, America Online (AOL) has a financial area that appeals to both novice and experienced investors. For new investors, the portfolio tools are easy to use and educational articles with links to Motley Fool are helpful. For the more experienced, the investment research area provides Hoover company profiles, Zack's earnings estimates, Market Guide Reports, and SEC filings. You can set your own stock screens or use one of 18 preset screens, such as Profitable Internets or Big Caps with Insider Buying. Broker research is available for a fee.

CBS MarketWatch
cbsmarketwatch.com

This site is one of the best for current financial news. Regular columns plus breaking features make it easy to stay abreast of the financial world. Set up portfolios and search through a library of articles using either symbols or keywords.

The Financial Center
www.tfc.com

Though not as comprehensive as some others, The Financial Center has excellent columns. A highlight is its Market Mavens radio show, which interviews experts on a variety of topics. Interviews are posted daily and users have access to archives.

FinancialWeb
www.financialweb.com

A complex of free financial sites, including Stock Detective, whose weekly Stinky Stocks Roundup seeks to expose stocks that are mostly hype. FinancialWeb is a good all-around financial site and offers up to 100 free real-time quotes per day. Registering at the site means you will be sent a daily e-mail full of advertising and little content; however, you can easily unsubscribe.

Invest-O-Rama
www.investorama.com

The biggest financial web directory, Invest-O-Rama, links to more than 14,000 financial sites. Enter a stock into the Stock Power Search to get a quote, chart and a list of links in the following categories: featured research, company background, earnings estimates and reports, message boards, stock quotes, stock charts, company news, corporate SEC filings, industry reports/competitors, insider trading, and other web links. Touching on a link takes you to the desired page, with your stock already entered.

MoneyCentral Investor
http://investor.msn.com

A comprehensive financial site run by Microsoft, MoneyCentral is easy to navigate and provides good research. For those seeking news, a bonus is the link with MSNBC News and a synopsis of important *Wall Street Journal* articles for the day. The Market Report may not be updated often enough for the active investor.

The Motley Fool
www.fool.com

A good place for beginning to intermediate investors, this website is packed full of educational articles. Try Fool's School and Personal Finance. The Fool's signature editorial style is a common sense, sometimes irreverent look at investing. Bulletin boards at this site are very popular.

Quicken.com
www.quicken.com

Sponsored by the software company of the same name, Quicken.com provides a wide variety of financial information, from household issues such as mortgages, taxes, and insurance to investing in stocks and mutual funds. This is a good place to go if you want to learn about a particular topic.

Charles Schwab
www.myschwab.com

This partnership between Charles Schwab and Excite offers a home page that may be customized for anyone, not only Schwab customers. It provides good general news and financial information. A highlight for beginning and intermediate investors is the Stock Analysis section, which allows the user to enter a symbol and receive a fundamental and price history analysis. Commentary is included to aid in interpreting results and a comparison with other stocks is also available. Unlike most other sites, but not surprising, there are no direct links to online brokers (other than Schwab) for placing trades.

Smart Money
www.smartmoney.com

This site, part of *Smart Money Magazine,* offers a good mix of current news, columns, financial data, and education. Proprietary features, such as Map of the Market, a green and red heat map of the daily performance in industries and individual stocks, make it worth the trip to this site.

StockMaster.com
www.stockmaster.com

With each quote at StockMaster.com, a one-year price chart is displayed, which offers adjustable settings for time frame, moving averages, and index comparisons. A comprehensive markets page provides access to performance of all the major indices, plus currency rates, market sector, and geographic indices, in quote and graph form. Guru analysis uses the methodology of eight different investment experts (several of whom are profiled in Chapter 19) to give an overall interest level for each stock, with a pass or fail rating on individual criteria.

Stockpoint
www.stockpoint.com

An uncluttered site that is easy to navigate, Stockpoint's best feature is its multitude of screening tools. The StockFinder Pro allows you to customize 26 data fields to sort through more than 10,000 stocks for those that meet your investment criteria. The site also offers free real-time quotes.

Stocksite
www.stocksite.com

Stocksite is run by Silicon Investor, which is known for its investor message boards. The site has good articles and useful tools such as an Expected EPS calendar, with companies expected to announce earnings and the consensus estimates. From there you can go to quotes, charts, and message boards on the company. The stock screen feature is not very comprehensive.

Wall Street City
www.wallstreetcity.com

Wall Street City is one of the best sites on the internet for stock research, packed full of information to screen stocks and find out about those you have. A great section (13 different categories) of financial calculators includes the usual home mortgage and retirement calculators, plus less common finds such as bond yield to maturity. Much of the site is accessible for no cost. Two subscription levels at $9.95 or $34.95 per month offer additional services.

Yahoo!Finance
http://quote.yahoo.com

Yahoo!Finance is one of the most popular financial portals. Quote pages are not easy on the eye, but functional and full of information. From a quote you can go to many different research pages, including a company profile with a link to the company's own home page.

Quotes

Nearly all financial sites offer quotes, usually with a disclaimer that they are delayed by at least 15 or 20 minutes. The following sites currently offer free real-time quotes.

America-iNvest.com
www.america-invest.com

America-iNvest.com offers free real-time quotes with registration. This site offers good, general financial information, with news and columns such as Ask the Expert and CEO Says.

FinancialWeb
www.financialweb.com

Financial Web offers up to 100 free real-time quotes per day. Registration is required. The site offers good, general financial information.

Fox Marketwire
http://invest.foxmarketwire.com

Fox Marketwire offers free real-time quotes for stocks and options plus Live Ticker for monitoring your portfolio.

Freerealtime.com
www.freerealtime.com

This site offers free unlimited real-time quotes. Registration is required.

Info Space
www.infospace.com

Info Space offers up to 50 free real-time quotes per day. Registration is required.

Stockpoint
www.stockpoint.com

Stockpoint offers free real-time quotes. Registration is required. This is a good financial megasite with an excellent stock screening tool called Stock-Finder Pro.

Thomson Real-Time Quotes
http://rtq.thomsoninvest.net/index.sht

This site offers up to 100 free real-time quotes per day. Registration is required.

Wall Street City by Telescan
www.tscn.com/wsc/free_RT_Quotes.html

Part of the free services offered by Wall Street City, free real-time quotes are available with registration.

Other sites offer real-time quotes for a subscription price. They generally have several levels of services, including NASDAQ level II quotes and real time charts. Check the following sites if you trade daily and need a high level of information. Exchange fees may be charged in addition to subscription prices.

Data Broadcasting Corporation—eSignal
www.esignal.com

This site offers 500 symbols of equities futures and options for $150 per month, prepaid annually. Equities only for 50 symbols is $79 per month, prepaid annually. An Excel link is offered.

DTN IQ
www.dtniq.com

Prices begin at $89 per month for equities. Annual subscribers get three months free. Add $20 per month for options. Comtex news service is included (many others charge extra).

PC Quote
www.pcquote.com

Prices begin at $55 per month and increase with a cafeteria of choices. Options and commodities are available. Charting is extra here, while it is included on most other providers. The program includes an Excel link for those who want to manipulate data on their PC.

Real Time Quotes
www.rtquotes.com

Prices begin at $75 per month for 20 hours. Unlimited use is $200 per month.

Quote.com
www.quote.com

Technical traders should visit Quote.com's Qcharts, either through the parent website or at *www.qcharts.com*. A monthly subscription of $79.95 gives you real-time data in charts.

4anything.com
www.4anything.com/stock.shtml

Check 4anything.com's quote area for links to quote providers, but plan to spend a little time. Many are listed but the sites are in no particular order and are not grouped according to free versus subscription or real-time versus delayed.

Stock Research

American Association of Individual Investors (AAII)
www.aaii.com

The AAII website is the cyber alternative to a paper subscription of the *AAII Journal.* An e-membership is $39 versus the *Journal*'s $49 per year, $64 if you want its Computerized Investing option. This site offers advanced, in-depth articles on investing techniques as well as a good amount of basic information. The stock screening tool can use preset parameters based on respected investment gurus to offer up lists of stocks that fit the investment criteria.

Ask Jeeves
www.ask.com

Named after the indispensable English butler, this is not a financial site, but a search site that allows you to ask questions in natural language. This method of questioning often provides much narrower results than keyword searches. If you cannot find the information you need at one of your regular sites, try Ask Jeeves, which can usually either answer your question or point you to the place to find it.

Best Calls
www.bestcalls.com

A real niche site, Best Calls provides a calendar of company to analyst conference calls. While much of the information in these calls is already public, occasionally a company spokesperson will throw in something interesting and new. You can search by company name or symbol for a calendar of calls, which gives phone numbers and any necessary passwords. You may also register for free e-mail reminders on your favorite stocks.

Big Charts
www.bigcharts.com

Self-proclaimed as "The world's coolest investment charting and research site," Big Charts has both quick (preset) and interactive charting. The interactive charting allows you to change variables and compare results to other stocks, indices, and indicators. Once you have decided on your settings, you can save them for future visits. Other good research includes loads of industry data and Big Reports, which sorts a chosen market for price or volume movements.

Briefing.com
www.briefing.com

Popular for its market commentaries, which are part of the free package along with standard fare such as quotes and portfolios, Briefing.com offers three levels of service. The Stock Analysis package ($9.95 per month) provides information on upgrades and downgrades, company reports, and splits and earnings calendars. The Professional package, ($25 per month) is for bond traders, with yield curves, bond quotes, and fixed income market analysis.

ClearStation
www.clearstation.com

Investors and traders using technical analysis will like this site. Charts are extensive and each day's "A-list" has stocks with notations such as "MACD bullish" or "Stochastic bullish." Below each chart is a message board of comments from other ClearStation devotees. You can compare up to 100 stocks on one chart. For newcomers to charting, the education center provides a tutorial.

Company Sleuth
www.companysleuth.com

Calling itself a source of free legal inside information, Company Sleuth combs the web for valuable information on up to 10 public companies, then e-mails you a report of its findings. Topics include patent and trademark filings, insider trades, short interest, and tidbits from message boards.

Daily Graphs Online
www.dailygraphs.com

This site was developed by William O'Neil, founder of *Investor's Business Daily* and author of *How to Make Money in Stocks: A Winning System in Good Times or Bad*. His CANSLIM method of investing uses a combination of fundamental analysis to choose companies and technical analysis to time purchases and sales. Daily Graphs Online provides fundamental and technical data on more than 11,000 stocks. Subscriptions run $66.58 monthly or $720 annually. CANSLIM enthusiasts who are active traders might want to try the seven-day trial for $19.95 (applicable to the first month's subscription).

Earnings Whispers.com
www.earningswhisper.com

A resource for the "whisper number" that you often hear about in statements, such as "XYZ company reported fourth quarter earnings of $1.20 a share. That was a penny above the whisper number and eight cents above consensus estimates." About three to four weeks before earnings announcements, this site publishes estimates alleged to be from inside sources. Enter the symbol for more than 4,000 stocks to see the whisper estimate, consensus estimates from investment analysts, earnings dates, and a bulletin board for each stock.

FreeEDGAR
www.freeedgar.com

Find SEC filings for publicly held corporations here. You can search by ticker, company name and, for filings after April 1, 1999, by specified text. Register for the FreeEDGAR Watchlist to be notified by e-mail when companies on your watchlist file new documents.

Hoover's Online
www.hoovers.com

Hoover is a well-known industry provider of detailed company financial profiles; in fact, much of the corporate financial information at other sites is provided by Hoover. The site provides a free synopsis of each company, and for $14.95 a month ($9.16 a month if you prepay for a year) you can get the full report. Hoover's IPO Central has a calendar of upcoming IPOs and a Red Hot Chili Rating for those expected to have a big first day. This, as well as quotes and basic investor education, is free.

The Internet Analyst
www.theinternetanalyst.com

If you are trying to find an undiscovered internet stock, look here. This online newsletter, published weekly (subscriptions are free), combs the web for information about the industry. The Unusual Suspects column covers little-known internet plays, Executive Zero interviews internet company executives, and Strong Buys covers companies getting "strong buy" recommendations from Wall Street firms.

IPO.com
www.ipo.com

This site provides news and educational articles about IPOs as well as a weekly calendar of upcoming offerings. Each stock on the calendar links to a several-page profile of the company and its offering, which in turn links you to SEC filings through EDGAR.

Market Guide
www.marketguide.com

A good place to find new investment ideas, this site is known for its powerful stock screening abilities. NetScreen, available online, and StockQuest, available free for download, screen more than 10,000 stocks using 20 or 75 variables, respectively. Other tools, such as the What's Hot/What's Not page, provide lists of stocks whose prices have increased the most in one- and five-day periods.

Multex Investor Network
www.multexinvestor.com

This site is one-stop shopping for professional research reports from more than 500 providers, including Morgan Stanley Dean Witter, Goldman Sachs, and Merrill Lynch. Reports are available for download, ranging in price from $5 to $150. Most are $5 to $10.

Reesegroup.com
www.reesegroup.com

This site is an interesting place to screen for stocks or find out what the experts think about yours. Idea Engines screens for stocks that meet the criteria of several investment gurus, including Peter Lynch, William O'Neil, Benjamin Graham, and David Dreman, all of whom are profiled in Chapter 19. The Research Wizard function reports whether one of the gurus would be interested in the stock entered. A ratio analysis shows which ratios pass or fail each guru's test.

Worldly Investor.com
www.worldlyinvestor.com

This site is dedicated to the international investor. An extensive list of columnists provides articles from different areas and points of view. The ADR Screener allows you to screen ADRs according to performance, country, and sector; the Offshore Fund Screener allows you to screen by country, asset type, investment objective, and currency.

Wright Investors
www.wisi.com

This site has an incredible database of international stocks in its Research Center area. Reports on more than 18,000 companies in 50 countries provide a Wright Quality Rating, a company profile, research report, analysis summary, sales analysis, and earnings analysis. To make comparisons easier, there is a feature that will change all figures into the currency of your choice.

Zacks Investment Research
www.zacks.com

Research reports from a variety of investment firms are available here for download, at prices that commonly range from $5 to $25. Some research reports listed here are only available from the source firms. Zacks will forward your request for these, but notes that delivery to you is up to the individual firm. Free on the site are Portfolio Tracker and Stockscreener, which provide daily e-mail alerts for revisions to earnings estimates and allow you to screen stocks using 96 different investment criteria. The Dawn Patrol column gives daily insight into where the market might be headed, based on early futures trading and news or government reports already issued. It also notes the time of day that reports are expected.

Mutual Funds

Sifting through the attributes of the thousands of mutual funds available is exponentially easier with a website search than flipping through pages of research reports. The sites noted here are not related to mutual fund providers, though most have links to them. A list of mutual fund providers and their websites, which are often very educational, can be found in Chapter 12.

Brill's Mutual Funds Interactive
www.brill.com

This site is full of links to providers of useful mutual fund information, as well as to the funds themselves. The Funds 101 contains general articles about mutual funds, plus the Experts area has articles written by a variety of mutual fund experts. Money Manager Profiles gives insight into the thought processes of your favorite fund managers.

Find a Fund
www.findafund.com

This mutual funds reference site offers few frills but basic fund reports sorted by name, investment category, or ticker symbol. Reports include links to fund websites. The similarity portfolio analysis calculation allows you to compare two mutual funds to see how well you are diversified.

Results are provided for style diversity, sector diversity, and holding similarity. Each category is given a score from 1 to 100, and underlying data is also provided.

Fund Alarm
www.fundalarm.com

This site does not list the best mutual funds, but the worst. Three-alarm funds, which have underperformed their appropriate benchmark for the past 12 months, three years, and five years, comprise a good sell list. The Fund Alarm Honor Roll is a list of funds with no alarms. Data is updated monthly.

IndexFunds.com
www.indexfunds.com

This site provides a comprehensive listing of index funds. Funds are listed by investment category, and links to Morningstar, Quicken, Stockpoint, and the funds' own websites provide detailed information. Funds are supposedly ranked by three-year performance, though many index funds have not been in operation that long and sometimes there appears to be no particular order.

Morningstar
www.morningstar.com

Morningstar is a good, all-around financial website from one of the leaders in mutual fund analysis. It includes stock and current market information as well as mutual fund articles and performance data. Basic interactive screens and preset screens are free. Advanced screens and other, more in-depth information is available for a membership fee ($9.95 per month or $99 per year).

Mutual Fund Education Alliance
www.mfea.com

Here is a nonprofit website with good general mutual fund investing articles. It provides bare-bones performance data and links to all the major mutual fund families. Useful searches include Funds for Fifty Dollars, a search for funds whose minimum investment is $50 or less. The screening feature is limited to no-load funds.

Bonds

Stocks have been getting all the space in the financial news lately and the internet is no different. A few sites are dedicated to bonds, but not nearly the variety and quality that can be found for stocks.

Bonds Online
www.bondsonline.com

This site has limited basic information on bond investing and links to other sites, such as rating agencies. The most valuable part of the site is its pricing area, which covers more than 12,000 bonds. Prices and yields for Treasuries are real time and offerings for other bonds are updated throughout the day.

BradyNet
www.bradynet.com

This site is the definitive net resource for information about Brady bonds, the Third World debt backed by the U.S. government. Discussion boards, news items, and market commentary are free, but the portfolio analyzer, interactive charting, and access to the full database are found in BradyNet Pro. Basic service is $99.95 per month. Add real-time quotes and charts to BradyNet Pro premium service for $199.95 per month.

Bureau of the Public Debt
www.publicdebt.treas.gov

Look no further for basic education about U.S. Treasury securities. Find the latest auction results and current savings bond yields. You can even buy Treasuries online through the TreasuryDirect service.

ConvertBond.com
www.convertbond.com

Operated by Morgan Stanley Dean Witter, this specialized site focuses only on convertible bonds and notes. For $120 per year (there is a two-week free trial), you may view 50 securities descriptions or charts per month and 10 prospectuses from more than 700 securities.

Investing in Bonds
www.investinginbonds.com

Produced by the Bond Market Association, an industry trade group, this site is the best place for the beginner to learn about bonds and the bond markets. The municipal bond pricing area provides the previous day's transactions for the state chosen, sorted by any one of seven variables (rating, volume, etc.). Individual transaction details are then available from the results page. Corporate bond transactions are available in a similar fashion.

Retirement

Many of the large financial sites, especially those of mutual fund companies, offer excellent retirement information. To avoid many duplicate listings, we include only a few of the very best general sites with retirement-specific sites within this section. For calculators that compare ordinary IRAs to Roth IRAs, try any of the following: Fidelity Investments at *www.fidelity.com,* Strong Funds at *www.strong-funds.com,* Vanguard Funds at *www.vanguard.com,* or T. Rowe Price at *www.troweprice.com.*

401Kafe'
www.401kafe.com

This site is an excellent source for information about 401(k) plan rules and regulations. Begin with Frequently Asked Questions and if you cannot find what you need there, search the archives of articles or ask Ted Benna. Benna, creator of the 401(k) plan, writes a plain-English column every week in which he answers questions submitted to the site. There is little discussion of how to invest your plan.

Fidelity Investments
www.fidelity.com

Fidelity's site has a comprehensive retirement area, which includes information about employer-sponsored retirement plans and retirement plans for small businesses, in addition to IRAs and Roth IRAs. Each question in the retirement planning calculator provides helpful tips on estimating figures, and a section called "Finding the Money to Invest" offers ideas for budget cuts with the resulting long-term effect on a savings plan.

Financial Engines
www.financialengines.com

A free financial forecast will show you what will happen to your current investments under different scenarios, plus information about the ins and outs of 401(k) plans. A $14.95 three-month subscription gives you specific advice on how to invest your retirement plan. You can adjust variables such as retirement age, risk tolerance, and savings rate to see what effect they will have on your nest egg.

Putnam Investments
www.putnaminv.com

The retirement planning calculator at Putnam's site provides an illustration of total retirement savings and how long they will last in both graphic and numeric form. If you are not happy with the results, you can change variables at the end to meet your goal.

Quicken
www.quicken.com

Quicken's website provides good education about different retirement plans plus one of the best calculators for finding out how much you will need. The calculator considers taxes paid on funds withdrawn from retirement accounts, which can be a big issue for assets in 401(k) plans, ordinary IRAs, and annuities. The results page allows you to solve for variables, such as a realistic retirement age, given the other data entered.

Roth IRA Website
www.rothira.com

This site compiles articles about the Roth IRA. Much of it is designated for financial planning professionals, meaning it can get pretty technical. If you need specific, technical information, this is a good place, though it is a little difficult to read and determine links since most of the text is blue.

Tim Younkin
www.timyounkin.com

This site, run by pharmacist and individual investor, Tim Younkin, offers comprehensive coverage of news, rules, and legal aspects of 401(k) plans, 403(b) plans, and IRAs. It includes recommended readings and a host of links to other sites.

News

Nearly all financial websites have some sort of market commentary and recent news articles; however, the sites whose primary focus is news are much more comprehensive and are generally updated more frequently.

Bloomberg
www.bloomberg.com

Bloomberg is a cluttered but valuable source of breaking news and financial articles. Follow your favorite columnist or choose by topic. The site includes key currency, bond, and commodity rates and prices.

CNBC.com
www.cnbc.com

This is an easy-to-navigate financial news site with proprietary news stories plus stories from MSNBC and *The Wall Street Journal.* Find schedules for CNBC television plus lists of appearing guests here. CNBC 101 gives a good explanation on reading a ticker tape for those who watch the television programs. With registration, you get access to portfolio tracking, a personalized ticker, and 25 free real-time quotes per day.

CNNfn
www.cnnfn.com

This site is packed with information in a layout that can make the numerous headlines and categories overwhelming. Once you take time to hit your areas of interest, it becomes easy to navigate. Coverage of international markets is extensive. You can find a detailed schedule of television programs on CNNfn's cable station.

Internet News.com
www.internetnews.com

This site is busy and not always easy to navigate, but if you are looking for one-stop shopping for news about the internet, visit Internet News.com. The home page is general news, but head down to The Internet Stock Report for a link to *internetstockreport.com.* Once there, see Chris Nerney's in-depth daily analysis of an internet stock in StockTracker.

The Street.com
www.street.com

A news site for the active trader, market commentary at The Street.com is updated frequently throughout the day. James Cramer, an opinionated hedge fund manager on Wall Street, is the most popular and prolific columnist. Articles are easy to find and you may search the archives by topic or columnist. The twice daily e-mail updates and annual price of $99.95 (or $9.95, monthly) make this a news site only for those who spend much of their time each day on trading.

Wall Street Journal
www.wsj.com

This site provides all the information in the print version plus updates throughout the day. The full database of Dow Jones publications, including *Barron's,* is available for searching. A year's subscription is $59, or $29 for those already receiving the print version. Daily rates are $0.75, a great option for anyone who is too busy to read on a daily basis.

Banking

Online banking has been somewhat slower to catch on than online investing, but is picking up speed as more brick-and-mortar banks begin to offer the service. The benefits of online banking include being able to view your account balance and transaction history, automatic bill paying, and the interface with financial software such as Quicken or Microsoft Money. The drawbacks include setup time and the sometimes complicated schedule of fees that may be charged.

To find comparisons of banks, their services, and fees, try the following websites.

Gomez Advisors
www.gomez.com

The Internet Banking Scorecard rates internet-only banks and banks with more than $2 billion in deposits on ease of use, customer confidence, on-site resources, relationship services, and overall cost. They also provide rankings for four types of banking customers: the internet transactor, the saver, the borrower, and the one-stop shopper.

The top 10 for Overall Score on the Spring 2000 Scorecard were:[1]

1. Security First Network Bank
   www.sfnb.com or 800-736-2321

2. Bank One
   www.bankone.com or 800-482-3675

3. Wingspan bank.com
   www.wingspanbank.com or 888-736-8611

4. Wells Fargo
   www.wellsfargo.com or 800-956-4442

[1]Gomez Advisors.

5. CompuBank
   www.compubank.com or 888-479-9292

6. First Internet bank of Indiana
   www.firstib.com or 888-873-3424

7. Citibank
   www.citibank.com or 800-285-3000

8. The Huntington Bank
   www.huntington.com or 888-351-6400

9. Citi f/I
   www.citifi.com or 800-2-citifi

10. Everbank.com
    www.everbank.com or 888-882-EVER

CyberInvest.com
www.cyberinvest.com/guide/bankonl.bankonl.guide.html

The CyberInvest site reviews many aspects of online investing and will take you to a comparison of online banks, their fees, and characteristics. The list is updated monthly. From the home page at *www.cyberinvest.com,* you can also find several helpful articles about banking and investing online.

Bankrate.com
www.bankrate.com

For the longest list (more than 120), but the least information about each bank, check Bankrate.com.

Internet Banking Dangers

The internet is an easy place for con artists to set up shop. Before sending your money to any organization that calls itself a bank, make sure that it is by way of the Federal Deposit Insurance Corporation (FDIC) search engine at *www.fdic.gov* or the FDIC Consumer Call Center at 800-934-FDIC (3342). The FDIC requests that you report any suspicious site using the suspicious internet banking site report form at *www.fdic.gov/bank/individual/online/sspcious.html.*

Government Resources

The Internal Revenue Service
www.irs.gov

If you can stand the pretend-newspaper format, the IRS website is worth a look. At the bottom of the home page are the necessary categories of information. Although the topics are certainly not comprehensive, this site is a quick and easy way to get basic information. The best area is Forms and Publications, where you can download tax forms and IRS publications and find links to obtain state tax forms.

Social Security Administration
www.ssa.gov

Check this site for general information about Social Security. The Frequently Asked Questions (FAQ) area is good and you can conduct some SSA business online. Try getting an estimate of your Social Security benefits with an online request for a Social Security Statement. You may be familiar with this form by its former name: Request for Personal Earnings and Benefits Estimate Statement. The results will be mailed to you in two to three weeks.

Bureau of the Public Debt
www.publicdebt.treas.gov

This site is the home of TreasuryDirect, a service of the government that allows you to purchase U.S. Treasury securities online. The Savings Bond Connection, also located here, allows online purchases of U.S. savings bonds. In addition to transaction capabilities, this site is full of educational material concerning savings bonds and Treasury securities.

Miscellaneous

Habib Bank AG Zurich
www.habibbank.com/xfcc.htm

This part of Habib Bank's website is a foreign currency calculator. Enter an amount into any of 26 currencies, press Calculate, and the table will translate the currency into the 25 others.

Investopedia
www.investopedia.com

For quick definitions on investing terms, look here. You can search by word or by topic.

National Association of Investors Corporation (NAIC)
www.better-investing.com

This is the website for the NAIC, an organization devoted to investment clubs. You will find information about how to start a club, sample partnership agreements, and recommended IRS filings. The site also includes education based on NAIC investment principles, and access to *Better Investing*, the NAIC newsletter, for members of the organization.

TaxPlanet
www.taxplanet.com

A good site for tax information, Tax Planet is strongest on current news and legislation and weakest on actual tax rules, making it a good complementary site to the IRS site. An interesting feature is the proposed tax plans of political candidates.

22
Acronyms

ACRS   Accelerated Cost Recovery System

ADR   American Depository Receipt

AGI   Adjusted Gross Income

AMBAC   American Municipal Bond Assurance Corporation

AMEX   American Stock Exchange

AMT   Alternative Minimum Tax

AON   All Or Nothing

ARM   Adjustable Rate Mortgage

ASE   American Stock Exchange

ATM   Automated Teller Machine

BAN   Bond Anticipation Note

BP   Basis Point

CAES   Computer-Assisted Execution System

CAPM   Capital Asset Pricing Model

CATS   Certificate of Accrual on Treasury Securities

CAV   Current Accreted Value

CBOE   Chicago Board Options Exchange

CD   Certificate of Deposit

CDSC   Contingent Deferred Sales Charge

CEO   Chief Executive Officer

CFA   Chartered Financial Analyst

CFP   Certified Financial Planner

CFTC   Commodity Futures Trading Commission

CIC   Chartered Investment Counselor

CMA   Cash Management Account (® Merrill Lynch)

CME   Chicago Mercantile Exchange

CMO   Collateralized Mortgage Obligation

COMEX or CMX   Commodity Exchange of New York

COO   Chief Operating Officer

CPA   Certified Public Accountant

CPI   Consumer Price Index

CPI-U   Consumer Price Index—Urban

CUSIP   Committee on Uniform Security Identification Procedures

DJIA   Dow Jones Industrial Average

DJTA   Dow Jones Transportation Average

DJUA   Dow Jones Utilities Average

DNR   Do Not Reduce

DOT   Designated Order Turnaround

DRIP   Dividend Reinvestment Plan

DTC   Depository Trust Company

DVP   Delivery Versus Payment

EBIT   Earnings Before Interest and Taxes

EBITDA   Earnings Before Interest, Taxes, Depreciation, and Amortization

EC   European Community

ECU   European Currency Unit

EDGAR   Electronic Data Gathering, Analysis, and Retrieval

EFTS   Electronic Funds Transfer System

EPS   Earnings Per Share

ERISA   Employee Retirement Security Act

EU   European Union

FASB   Federal Accounting Standards Bureau

FFO   Funds From Operations

FDIC   Federal Deposit Insurance Corporation

FGIC   Financial Guaranty Insurance Corporation

FHA   Federal Housing Administration

FHLMC   Federal Home Loan Mortgage Corporation

FIFO   First-In, First-Out

FNMA   Federal National Mortgage Association

FOMC   Federal Open Market Committee

FSLIC   Federal Savings and Loan Insurance Corporation

GAAP   Generally Accepted Accounting Principles

GDP   Gross Domestic Product

GNMA   Government National Mortgage Association

GNP   Gross National Product

GO   General Obligation (municipal bond)

GTC   Good-Till-Canceled

IPO   Initial Public Offering

IRA   Individual Retirement Account

IRR   Internal Rate of Return

IRS   Internal Revenue Service

ISP   Internet Service Provider

LBO   Leveraged Buyout

LEAPSR   Long-term Equity AnticiPation Securities

LIBOR   London InterBank Offering Rate

LIFO   Last-In, First-Out

LOC   Letter of Credit

MAGI   Modified Adjusted Gross Income

MBIA   Municipal Bond Insurance Association

MBS   Mortgage-Backed Securities

MLP   Master Limited Partnership

MMDA   Money Market Deposit Account

MMMF   Money Market Mutual Fund

MSCI   Morgan Stanley Capital International

NASD   National Association of Securities Dealers

NASDAQ   National Association of Securities Dealers Automated Quotation system

NAV   Net Asset Value

NCUSIF National Credit Union Share Insurance Fund

NIM Net Interest Margin

NMF No Meaningful Figure

NOW Negotiable Order of Withdrawal

NR Not Rated

NYCE New York Cotton Exchange

NYFE New York Futures Exchange

NYM or NYMEX/COMEX New York Mercantile Exchange

NYSE New York Stock Exchange

OCC Options Clearing Corporation

OID Original Issue Discount

OTC Over-The-Counter market

OTS Office of Thrift Supervision

PAC Planned Amortization Classes

P/E Price/Earnings ratio

PEG Price Earnings Growth ratio

PSE Pacific Stock Exchange

PSR Price to Sales Ratio

REIT Real Estate Investment Trust

RHS Rural Housing Service

ROA Return On Assets

ROE Return On Equity

ROI Return On Investment

RVP Receive Versus Payment

SARSEP-IRA Salary Reduction Simplified Employee Pension—Individual Retirement Account

SEC Securities and Exchange Commission

SEP-IRA Simplified Employee Pension—Individual Retirement Account

SIMPLE-IRA Savings Incentive Match Plan for Employees Individual Retirement Account

SIPC Securities Investor Protection Corporation

S&P Standard and Poor's Corporation

SOES Small Order Execution System

STRIPS Separate Trading of Registered Interest and Principal of Securities

TAC Targeted Amortization Classes

TEY Taxable Equivalent Yield

TSE Toronto Stock Exchange

VA United States Department of Veterans Affairs

VDB Variable Death Benefit

WTO World Trade Organization

www world wide web

YTC Yield To Call

YTM Yield To Maturity

ZBA Zero Balance Account

23
Glossary

Understanding investment terminology is key to assessing the risks and potential rewards of securities. As Mark Twain aptly put it, "The difference between the right word and the almost right word is the difference between lightning and the lightning bug."

10-K report: The financial report that companies are required to file with the SEC each year. The 10-K includes details not found in the shareholders' annual report.

1099-INT/1099-DIV: Payers of dividends and interest issue 1099s to the IRS and investors, which detail the amount of dividends or interest paid during the year.

1099-OID: The 1099 form issued to owners of taxable original-issue discount securities for the amount of implied interest received during the year. Dictated by formula, the amount is roughly comparable to the amount by which a discounted security increases in value each year as it nears maturity.

accrued interest: Interest owed but not yet paid. If a bond is sold between semiannual interest payments, the buyer must pay the seller for the interest accrued from the last interest payment through the purchase date. The buyer will be reimbursed at the next interest date when he receives interest for the entire six months, as if he had owned it the entire time.

advance/decline index: The cumulative total of the daily number of stocks advancing in price less the daily number of stocks declining. It is used by technical analysts as a measure of market breadth. When graphically presented, it is called the advance/decline line.

after-tax return: The return on an investment calculated after payment of required income and capital gains taxes.

all or none order: An order to purchase or sell a security which should only be executed if the entire order can be filled.

alpha: The mathematical estimate of the return on a security when the return on the market is zero.

alternative minimum tax (AMT): An alternative method of computing taxable income which includes items normally excluded from the computation, specifically losses from passive investments and interest paid on some municipal bonds.

American depositary receipt (ADR): A certificate that represents ownership in a foreign stock. ADRs are traded on U.S. stock exchanges.

annual report: The annual financial statement issued by a corporation. Annual reports generally contain a balance sheet, income statement, cash flow statement, and statement of changes in shareholder equity, as well as supporting documentation.

annuity: 1. A stream of equal payments made at regular intervals. 2. A life insurance product that provides tax-deferred investment growth before retirement and a series of payments after retirement. Annuities may be fixed, with a set rate of return, or variable, with returns based on underlying investments.

arbitrage: The simultaneous purchase and sale of the same asset in two different markets or two substantially similar assets in the same or different markets in order to profit from their price differences.

arbitration: Settling a dispute by agreeing to the decision of an impartial third party. Most securities firms require clients to agree to arbitration rather than settle disputes through the court system.

asked price: The lowest price at which a dealer will sell a security.

assay: A test to determine the purity of a precious metal.

asset: Anything of monetary value owned by an individual, business, or organization. A corporation's balance sheet lists the firm's assets and liabilities (debts).

asset allocation: The investment strategy of diversifying among asset types, such as cash, stocks, bonds, and real estate in order to reduce risk.

at the money: A put or call option whose strike price is equal to the price of the underlying stock.

back-end load: The common name for a contingent deferred sales charge, this is a commission charged when mutual fund or annuity shares are sold.

balance of payments: A measure of cash flows between countries. It includes imports and exports plus foreign investment and loans. A country's balance of payments plays a significant role in currency exchange rates.

basic shares outstanding: The actual number of a corporation's shares that are held by the public.

basis point: One hundredth of 1% or 0.01%, the unit of measure used to differentiate bond yields. A bond yield that changes from 7.25% to 7.5% has risen 25 basis points.

bear market: A period of time in which securities prices decline.

beta: A statistical measure of the price volatility of a stock relative to market averages. A beta of 1.00 connotes volatility equal to that of the market. A beta of 1.5 predicts a 1.5% change in the stock's price for every 1% change in the market.

blue chip: A stock with a long history of stability in earnings and dividends.

bond: A debt security which allows the issuer to borrow the face value of the bond while promising to repay it upon maturity, plus periodic interest until that time. Bonds may be issued by corporations, the U.S. government, or state and local municipalities. A bond owner is a creditor of the issuer and has no ownership rights.

bond rating: A rating for creditworthiness as determined by a rating service, such as Standard & Poor's, Moody's, or Fitch. Ratings assess the issuer's ability to pay interest and repay principal and range from AAA or Aaa to D.

book-entry security: A security which is not issued in paper form, but is held in an account for the owner, who receives a receipt or confirmation. U.S. Treasury bills are book-entry securities.

book value/book value per share: The book value of a corporation is the liquidation value of the business according to the financial statements. Subtracting all liabilities from assets results in book value. Dividing book value by the shares outstanding gives book value per share.

Brady bonds: The restructured debt of emerging markets whose principal is collateralized by U.S. Treasury securities.

breakpoints: The dollar amounts that must be invested for a mutual fund commission rate to be reduced.

breakup value: The sum of the market values of the individual parts of a corporation when valued as independent businesses. Firms may spin off divisions to shareholders when the breakup value exceeds current market value. Takeovers commonly occur when breakup values are high relative to current market values because the buying corporation can profit by selling divisions.

bull market: A period of time in which securities prices are rising.

buyback: A company's repurchase of its own shares of stock.

buying power: The dollar value of securities that may be purchased in an investor's account without requiring additional cash to be deposited. This is the sum of cash in the account and the amount that can be borrowed on securities held.

call: 1. A contract that gives its owner the right, but not the obligation, to purchase 100 shares of the underlying security for a specified price until its expiration date. The seller of the call has the obligation to sell 100 shares of the security if the call owner chooses to exercise the contract. 2. The right of a bond issuer to repay principal before a bond's maturity date. The call price is the price that must be paid. The call premium is the excess of the call price over the bond's face value. Call protection describes the period before the issuer can call the bond.

capital gain: The profit derived from selling an asset for more than its cost basis. Capital gains on assets held for more than one year are considered long term and are taxable at a 20% rate. Short-term capital gains on assets held for less than one year are taxable as ordinary income.

capitalization: 1. A term that refers to the market value of a corporation. It is computed by multiplying the current share price by the number of shares outstanding. 2. Capitalization also refers to the methods of financing used by a corporation.

cash flow: The amount of cash generated by a business, generally calculated as net income plus depreciation.

certificate of deposit (CD): A deposit held by a financial institution that promises to pay interest to the investor and repay principal upon maturity. Withdrawing principal before maturity results in a penalty.

churning: Excessive trading by a broker in order to generate commissions.

closed-end mutual fund: A mutual fund with a limited number of shares outstanding. Shares of closed-end funds trade on exchanges or in the over-the-counter market as opposed to shares of open-end funds, which are purchased from and redeemed by the fund.

collateral: Assets pledged as security for a loan. Collateral may be sold to repay the loan if the borrower defaults.

commission: The fee charged by a brokerage firm for executing a transaction on behalf of a customer.

commodity: Industrial and agricultural goods that are traded in bulk, such as grains, metals, lumber, coffee, and beef.

common stock: The class of corporate ownership which is entitled to voting rights and the residual value of the corporation after all obligations have been paid.

compound interest: A method of computing interest in which interest earned in previous periods is added to principal before computing the current period's interest.

consumer price index (CPI): A measure of inflation based on price increases for a basket of commonly purchased goods.

contingent deferred sales charge (CDSC): A commission charged on some mutual funds and annuities at redemption. Schedules generally decline over time, beginning at 5% or 6% and falling by 1% each year that the asset is owned.

contrarian investing: A strategy of investing in securities that are out of favor with most investors under the theory that most investors overreact to bad news.

convertible bond: A bond that is convertible into the common stock of the issuing corporation at the choice of the bondholder. The conversion ratio is the number of shares that may be exchanged for each bond. The conversion price is the common stock price at which conversion is a break-even proposition.

correction: A sharp, relatively short price decline in a security or an index that occurs in the middle of a general upward trend in prices.

correlation: A statistical measure of the tendency of two variables, usually the prices of securities classes, to move together. High correlation means they tend to move together. Low correlation means they do not. Negative correlation means they move in opposite directions.

cost basis: Also called *basis,* this is the amount that an investor paid for a security. The cost basis is subtracted from sales proceeds to determine a capital gain or loss.

coupon: The stated interest rate on a bond.

cross rate: The exchange rate between two currencies when neither are the trader's home currency.

current ratio: A measure of the liquidity of a corporation and its ability to meet short-term obligations. Current ratio = current assets/current liabilities. Current assets are those expected to be used within one year and current liabilities are debts due within one year.

current yield: The annual interest or dividend paid on an investment divided by its current price.

day order: An order that expires at the end of the trading day if it is not executed.

day-trader: A speculator who buys and sells securities for short-term profits. The term is derived from the fact that many do not hold their positions overnight.

debenture: An unsecured bond, backed only by the financial strength of the issuing corporation.

debt to equity ratio: The amount of long-term debt owed by a corporation as a percentage of shareholder's equity. The measure is used to gauge risk due to high debt.

default: Failure to perform under the terms of a contract. The term usually refers to the failure to pay interest or principal on a bond. Bonds termed "in default" are those upon which interest is not being paid.

deferred annuity: An annuity purchased with the expectation that annuity payments will not begin until some time in the future.

depreciation: An accounting method that allows the expense of an asset to be taken over its depreciable life. Depreciation expense is a noncash charge.

devaluation: A reduction in the value of a currency relative to other currencies.

diluted shares outstanding: The total number of a corporation's shares that would be outstanding if all convertible securities were converted into stock and all stock options were exercised.

direct transfer: The custodian-to-custodian transfer of a qualified retirement plan. The plan owner never has possession of the funds and the event is not taxable.

discount rate: The interest rate that the Federal Reserve charges on loans to member banks. This is one of the Fed's policymaking tools.

diversification: The practice of investing in many different securities in order to limit the risk of any one security. To maximize risk reduction, diversification should occur across industries and asset classes.

dividend: Distribution of a portion of a corporation's profits to it shareholders. Most dividends are paid in cash, but they may also be paid in stock. Dividends are generally paid quarterly.

dividend coverage ratio: Earnings per share or cash flow per share divided by dividends per share. Measures the ability of a firm to continue paying its dividend.

dividend payout ratio: Dividends per share divided by earnings per share or cash flow per share; measures what portion of EPS or cash flow is paid out as a dividend.

dividend reinvestment plan (DRIP): A plan offered by some corporations and some brokerage firms in which cash dividends are automatically reinvested in the issuing firm's stock. Commissions are generally low or nonexistent.

dividend yield: The most recent 12 months' dividend on a stock divided by the current share price.

dollar cost averaging: Investing an equal amount of money at regular intervals so that more shares are purchased when prices are low and fewer shares are purchased when prices are high.

downtick: A security transaction at a price lower than the previous transaction in the same security.

earnings per share (EPS): Net income divided by shares outstanding. EPS may be basic or diluted depending on whether the basic or diluted number of shares is used in the formula.

emerging markets: Countries in the midst of high economic growth; usually lesser-developed countries sometimes emerging from communist rule.

euro: The recently created currency of Europe.

exchange rate: The price of one currency in terms of another.

ex-dividend date: The first trading day upon which the seller of a security is entitled to an upcoming dividend. The opening price of the stock is generally lower by the amount of the dividend on this date.

exercise price: The price at which a call owner has the right to buy the underlying security or the put owner has the right to sell.

expense ratio: The ratio of a mutual fund's expenses to its assets, expressed as a percent. Expenses include management fees, 12b-1 fees, and general operating expenses of the fund.

face value: Usually in reference to a bond, this is the value stated on a certificate, which is payable upon maturity. A bond may be sold for more (a premium) or less (a discount) than face value during its life.

Fannie Mae: The common name for Federal National Mortgage Association (FNMA) securities. They are backed by pools of mortgages and the issuing institution passes through payments of principal and interest.

Federal Deposit Insurance Corporation (FDIC): A government agency that insures deposits at member banks. Each account that is separate by FDIC definition is insured for up to $100,000.

federal funds rate: The rate of interest that banks charge each other on overnight loans. Also called the fed funds rate.

Federal Reserve System: A system of 12 reserve banks with responsibility for overseeing the banking system. Through the Federal Open Market Committee (FOMC), it establishes monetary policy and carries out open market operations to reach desired policy goals. Also called the Fed.

fixed annuity: An annuity whose returns are fixed and do not vary with the stock market or other investment returns.

float: The number of shares of a company's stock that are held by the investing public. A low float often means higher price volatility.

forward contract: A contract for a currency, commodity, or security transaction to take place on a specified date in the future.

front-end load: A commission charged upon the purchase of a security, usually a mutual fund.

fundamental investing: Investing strategies based on the viability of a company as an ongoing business and on its value relative to its stock price.

futures contract: A contract that binds both the buyer and the seller of a commodity or financial asset to a transaction at a later date, at an agreed-upon price. A futures contract is different from a forward contract in that the contract is easily marketable, and different from an option in which only the seller is obligated.

general obligation bond: A municipal bond that is backed by the full faith and credit and taxing power of the issuer.

Ginnie Mae: The common name for the Government National Mortgage Association (GNMA). These securities are "pass through" pools of mortgages, in which the issuer passes interest and principal payments through to the GNMA owner.

going public: The process of selling ownership of a privately held company to public investors in a stock offering.

good 'till canceled (GTC): An order to buy or sell a security that remains in place until it is either executed or canceled by the investor. Also called an open order.

gross domestic product (GDP): The total dollar value of goods and services produced within the country. The level of output is measured from quarter to quarter or year to year to determine whether the economy is growing at increasing rates (expansion) or growing at decreasing rates (recession).

growth stock: The stock of a company whose sales and earnings are growing at an exceptionally fast pace. Often growth stocks do not pay dividends due to the need to reinvest the profits in the business. Stockholders expect their returns to come from stock price appreciation.

hedge: A securities transaction designed to lessen the risk of an existing or planned position. For example, an investor might hedge a stock position by buying a put, which gives that investor the right to sell the stock at a specified price.

immediate annuity: An annuity set to begin payments immediately after the initial deposit.

income statement: A financial statement that outlines a firm's revenues, expenses, and net income over a period of time. Also called a profit and loss statement or P&L.

index: A group of securities whose values, and sometimes income, are tracked in order to provide a benchmark for the performance of a particular market. Popular indices include the Dow Jones Industrial Average, Standard & Poor's 500 Index, and NASDAQ Composite Index.

index fund: A mutual fund that buys the securities listed in an index, or a representative sample of them, to mirror the performance of the index. Because these funds only trade when an index changes, transaction costs and turnover are very low.

indication: An expectation of the opening price of a stock, usually within a range. Indications are usually given when a stock is expected to open at a price very different from its previous day's closing price, due to news announced after the close.

individual retirement account (IRA): A retirement account to which individuals can contribute the lesser of $2,000 per year or their earned income. Nonworking spouses can also contribute if a working spouse's earnings exceed the combined contributions. Contributions may be tax deductible, depending on income levels and the availability of an employer-sponsored retirement plan. Investments in an IRA grow tax-deferred until withdrawn, at which time they are taxable as ordinary income. See *Roth IRA*.

inflation: A general increase in the prices of goods and services. The level of inflation is often measured by changes in the consumer price index.

initial public offering (IPO): The initial sale of the stock of a privately held company to the public.

inside information: Information about a company that is not available to the public but is known by the officers and directors of a company, who are called insiders.

institutional ownership: The percentage of a stock's outstanding shares that is owned by mutual funds, pension funds, large money managers, and the like.

interest: Payment for the use of borrowed money.

interim report: A financial statement issued by a company between annual reports. Interim reports are generally unaudited and not as comprehensive as annual reports.

International Monetary Fund (IMF): An organization created by the United Nations to oversee international exchange rates and aid countries with short-term balance of payment problems.

in the money: A term for a call option whose strike price is below the market price of the underlying security, or a put option whose strike price is above the market price of the underlying security.

intrinsic value: 1. The value of a stock calculated using quantifiable factors such as assets, earnings, and dividends. 2. The value of an option if it were immediately exercised. For a call: market price of the stock minus strike price. For a put: strike price minus market price.

inventory: The amount of goods held for sale plus work in progress at a business. Rising inventory levels predict falling revenues, and falling inventory levels indicate rising revenues.

inverted yield curve: A yield curve in which short-term interest rates are higher than long-term interest rates.

January effect: The tendency of stocks which have fallen in the previous year to rise in price in January. Because investors sell losing stocks at year-end to take tax losses, these stocks often become oversold and are ripe for a rebound.

joint tenancy with right of survivorship (JTWROS): A type of ownership in which each owner holds an equal share and upon the death of any owner his share is divided equally among the others.

junk bond: Any bond whose rating is lower than BBB or Baa by a rating agency such as Standard & Poor's, Moody's, or Fitch. Such a rating denotes high risk; accordingly, the expected yield to maturity is high.

letter of intent (LOI): An agreement with a mutual fund company to invest a certain amount over a specified time period to qualify for a reduced sales charge.

leverage: 1. Using investment methods that increase potential returns by requiring small amounts of capital to be invested. These methods include borrowing funds (margin) to purchase securities and buying options or futures whose cost is relatively small in relationship to the underlying investment controlled by the contract. 2. Refers to the relative amount of debt carried by a corporation. Higher leverage may be a sign of higher risk.

leveraged buyout: The takeover of a company in which the buyers borrow to buy outstanding shares, using the firm's assets as collateral. The new management often either uses the company's own cash or sells pieces of the company to pay down debt.

limit order: An order to buy or sell a security with a limit placed on the price you are willing to accept.

liquidity: Refers to the ability to sell an investment without incurring a loss. Investments with penalties for early withdrawal are not liquid. Stocks that trade with very small volume may not be liquid since a large order to sell can cause the price to drop.

load: The commission charged on a mutual fund or annuity.

lockup: The period of time, usually six months, after an initial public offering during which certain insiders may not sell their stock.

long: When you own a security, you are said to be "long" the security.

long bond: The 30-year U.S. Treasury bond.

lump-sum distribution: A distribution from a retirement plan, such as a 401(k), that is paid in one lump sum, rather than in a series of payments.

management fee: The fee charged by investment advisors to manage the investments in an individual account or large investment fund, such as a mutual fund or annuity. Management fees are levied as a percentage of assets under management. The expense ratio of a mutual fund includes the management fee.

margin: Borrowing money to buy securities. The initial margin requirement is the minimum amount that must be deposited for a transaction. Maintenance margin is the minimum percentage of equity that must be maintained in the account.

margin call: The request to deposit additional cash or securities into a margin account because equity in the account has fallen below the minimum maintenance requirement. Also called a *maintenance call.*

market maker: An individual or firm that makes a market in a particular security by buying from sellers and selling to buyers. Market makers profit from the spread, which is the difference between the price at which they buy and sell to the public.

market order: An order to buy or sell a security at the best price currently available.

market timing: An investment strategy in which investors move in and out of a security or all securities frequently, on the basis of technical, economic, or interest rate indicators.

mark to the market: Adjusting a futures trading account for losses or gains based on the difference in current market prices and futures contracts.

markup: A commission that is charged as part of the price of an investment. The dealer or broker buys a security at wholesale and sells it at retail. The difference is the commission or markup.

monetary policy: The policies of the Federal Reserve designed to smooth economic volatility and control inflation through the money supply. Tools of monetary policy include the discount rate, the federal funds rate, and bank reserve requirements.

money market deposit account: An interest-bearing account at a bank, savings and loan, or credit union. There are limitations on the number of transactions that may take place in these accounts.

money market mutual fund: A mutual fund that is invested in short-term interest-bearing securities. Shares are priced at $1 and interest rates paid will fluctuate.

moving average: An average of successive prices in which as each new price is added, the oldest is dropped. The arithmetic moving average is a simple average in which, for the 50-day average, the last 50 days' prices are divided by 50. The exponential moving average (EMA) places more weight on recent prices.

municipal bond: A bond issued by a city, state, or government body other than the U.S. government or its agencies. Interest on municipal bonds is not federally taxable and is generally not taxable at the state and local level for investors who live in the municipality.

mutual fund: An investment company that operates a portfolio of securities and sells shares of the portfolio to investors. Advantages of investing in mutual funds include diversification, professional management, liquidity, and small minimum investments.

National Association of Securities Dealers (NASD): The self-governing body of brokers and dealers of securities. Violation of NASD rules can result in an individual broker or firm being fined, censured, or expelled from the industry.

National Association of Securities Dealers Automated Quotation System (NASDAQ or Nasdaq): A computerized system that displays quotes and transactions for securities traded over the counter.

net asset value (NAV): The per share value of a mutual fund computed by taking the closing market value of all securities in the portfolio and dividing it by the number of shares outstanding. The NAV of a mutual fund will change daily as the values of the securities held in its portfolio change.

net income: The profit of a business, computed by subtracting expenses from revenues.

new issue: A stock that has recently completed its initial public offering.

New York Stock Exchange (NYSE): The oldest and largest organized stock exchange in the United States.

Nifty Fifty: Fifty large growth stocks that were investor favorites during the early 1970s. In a bubble that later crashed, investors seemed willing to pay almost any price for these companies.

no-load fund: A mutual fund that does not charge a commission for purchasing or redeeming shares. These funds still charge a management fee and may charge an additional annual fee, called a 12b-1 fee.

nominal interest rate: 1. The rate of interest stated on the face of a security. The nominal rate can differ from the effective rate of interest received due to compounding or purchasing the investment at a price other than face value. 2. The stated interest rate on an investment as opposed to the real interest rate. Nominal interest rate − inflation rate = real interest rate.

not held: An instruction on a purchase or sale order for the broker to use personal judgment in executing the order.

not rated: A bond that has not been rated by one of the large bond-rating agencies such as Moody's or Standard and Poor's. This does not necessarily mean that the issue is of poor quality.

odd lot: A stock trade for fewer than 100 shares. Odd lot theory says that investors who trade in odd lots are unsophisticated, so odd-lot volume is a contrarian indicator. When odd-lot volume is up, investors should sell, and when odd-lot volume is down, they should buy.

odd-lot tender: A tender offer by a company for holders of fewer than 100 shares to sell their shares back to the firm. Odd-lot tenders are designed to reduce the number of small shareholders and the accompanying cost of issuing dividend checks and annual reports. They are beneficial to the shareholders who do not wish to incur a commission for selling a few shares. These tenders are common after a spin-off, which may result in many odd-lot shareholders.

offer price: The best price at which other investors or market makers are willing to sell. Also called offer, asked price, or ask.

open-end mutual fund: A mutual fund that sells new shares to investors daily and redeems any shares that investors want to sell. Redemptions occur at net asset value (NAV), and sales to investors occur either at NAV or NAV plus a commission.

open interest: The number of options or futures contracts in existence for a particular security. High open interest means more active trading and liquidity.

open market operations: The purchase and sale of government securities by the Federal Open Market Committee (FOMC), designed to affect interest rates and the economy by fine-tuning the money supply.

open order: A securities order that is good until executed or canceled by the investor. Also called a good-till-canceled (GTC) order.

option: A security that gives its holder the right, but not the obligation, to buy (call option) or sell (put option) 100 shares of an underlying security at a designated price through its expiration date.

option premium: A term for the market price of an option.

ordinary income: Income that does not qualify for special tax treatment and is taxed at the marginal income tax rate. Wages, dividends, and interest are taxable as ordinary income.

original issue discount (OID): The difference between the face value of a bond and the price at which it is originally sold or issued. A common example of a bond with an OID is a zero coupon bond. Each year a portion of the OID is considered income, due to the nature of discounted bonds to rise in value as they near maturity and return their full face amount.

out of the money: A term for a put option whose strike price is below the market price of the underlying security, or a call option whose strike price is above the market price of the underlying security. An out-of-the-money option has no intrinsic value.

overbought: A term for a stock or a market that has risen rapidly to the point where it is considered overvalued.

oversold: A term for a stock or a market that has dropped rapidly to the point where it is considered undervalued.

oversubscribed: The term for an initial public offering in which there are more orders to buy shares than shares available for sale.

over the counter (OTC): Securities that are not listed on an exchange are traded in the OTC market by telephone or computer rather than on an exchange floor.

paid-in capital: The amount of capital generated in a stock offering.

paper gain or loss: The amount of gain or loss that would be realized if the investor chose to sell an investment. Also called unrealized gain or loss.

par value: The face value of a bond; the amount it will pay upon maturity and the amount upon which interest is calculated. For a common stock, par value is an arbitrary amount of no real significance.

penny stock: A low-priced stock, usually under $5 per share. Penny stocks are considered risky because they are often new, unproven companies, their markets may be very illiquid, and they are easily manipulated.

point: A $1 change in a stock's price or a 1% ($10) change in a bond's price.

poison pill: A tactic designed to ward off hostile takeovers. Stockholders are given warrants that allow them to purchase stock at below-market prices in the event that a hostile suitor acquires a certain percentage of the company's stock. The tactic's intent is to make the takeover prohibitively expensive.

positive yield curve: A yield curve in which short-term interest rates are lower than long-term interest rates.

preferred stock: A stock that has preference over common stock in the payment of dividends and in liquidation of the company. Unless designated as participating, preferred stock dividends do not change as a firm's earnings grow. Cumulative preferred stock must have all missed dividends paid before any dividends may be paid to common stockholders.

price/earnings (P/E) ratio: The current market price of a stock divided by its most recent 12 months' earnings per share (EPS). The P/E ratio is a valuation ratio designed to indicate whether a stock is too richly or too cheaply priced given its EPS.

price/earnings/growth (PEG) ratio: The ratio of a stock's P/E to its EPS growth rate. A PEG near 1 is said to be a fair value, a PEG much over 1 indicates an overvalued stock, and a PEG much under 1 indicates an undervalued stock.

prime rate: The rate that banks charge to lend to their most creditworthy customers.

privately held company: A business whose stock is not traded publicly.

producer price index (PPI): An economic indicator which tracks changing prices at the producer or wholesale level. The PPI is thought to be an inflation forecaster because increases in raw material prices often cause manufacturers to raise consumer prices.

productivity: A key in evaluating the inflationary momentum of an expansion, this term measures output per hour of employment. The economy can sustain increases in output without the corresponding inflationary increases in employment if productivity per employment hour rises.

program trading: Sophisticated, computer-driven arbitrage trading strategies, which involve taking simultaneous but opposite positions in stock index futures and their respective lists of stocks. Profits are made on market inefficiencies. Due to the sheer volume of transactions (an index may have 100 or 500 stocks), program trading may add to market volatility, though proponents say it increases market efficiency because trades are only made when markets are out of balance.

proxy: A shareholder's assignment of the right to vote shares at a shareholder's meeting. Proxies are mailed to shareholders before annual meetings because most are unable to attend.

publicly held company: A company whose stock is traded on public markets.

put: A contract that gives its owner the right, but not the obligation, to sell 100 shares of the underlying security for a specified price until its expiration date. The seller of the put has the obligation to buy 100 shares of the security if the put owner chooses to exercise the contract.

quick ratio: A liquidity measure for a firm that takes current assets less inventory and divides this by current liabilities. A higher ratio implies an ability to meet short-term obligations. Also called an acid test ratio.

quiet period: The period of time preceding an initial public offering when the stock issue is in registration and the company may not make any promotional statements.

real estate investment trust (REIT): An investment company that purchases real estate property or real estate loans. Shares of the company are sold to investors and traded like a stock.

real interest rate: The nominal or stated rate on an investment less the rate of inflation. The real interest rate is the return after taking into account the loss of purchasing power from inflation. In times of high inflation, the real interest rate on an investment may be negative.

recession: A period of declining growth in output, formally defined as six successive months of slowing growth in gross domestic product (GDP).

record date: The date upon which all owners of a security are entitled to receive an upcoming dividend.

red herring: The name for a preliminary prospectus given to potential investors in an initial public offering before the registration has been approved by the SEC.

registered securities: Securities held in certificate form which are registered with the company as to their ownership.

relative strength: The relationship of an individual stock's price movement to a market index. High relative strength means the stock is performing better than market averages. This is considered bullish for the stock.

reserve requirement: A percentage of customers' deposits that banks are required to hold in cash or on deposit at the Federal Reserve.

resistance level: The price at which a security encounters selling pressure, causing it to repeatedly move up to, but not pass, the price level.

return on assets (ROA): The ratio of a company's profit to total assets. This measures how much profit a firm makes given the amount of assets it has available.

return on equity (ROE): The ratio of profit to stockholders' equity; it measures the efficiency of a firm's operations. Note that high levels of debt relative to equity can inflate ROE, making a firm appear financially strong when it is the opposite.

revenue bond: A municipal bond associated with a particular project, such as an airport or toll bridge, whose revenues will support payment of interest and repayment of principal. Revenue bonds are considered more risky than general obligation bonds, which are supported by the taxing authority of the municipality.

reverse mortgage: A mortgage in which the bank makes monthly payments to the homeowner. With each successive payment, the homeowner's equity is reduced. It can be used by elderly homeowners to convert the equity in their homes to monthly retirement income.

reverse stock split: A method of reducing the number of shares of stock that a company has outstanding in order to increase the stock's price. For example, a stock undergoing a 1-for-10 reverse split would have its number of shares outstanding divided by 10 and its share price multiplied by 10.

rollover: The process of withdrawing funds from a qualified retirement plan—IRA, 401(k), etc.—taking possession of the funds and then depositing them into the same or another qualified retirement plan. To avoid income taxes and any applicable penalties, a rollover must be accomplished within 60 days.

Roth IRA: An individual retirement account in which contributions are never tax deductible, but withdrawals are tax-exempt if certain conditions are met. Income limits apply for eligibility to contribute to a Roth IRA.

round lot: The normal trading unit for a security. A round lot for stock is 100 shares; for bonds, it may be 10 or 100 bonds, depending on the market.

Sallie Mae: The Student Loan Marketing Association (SLMA), or Sallie Mae, is a government-chartered corporation that makes a secondary market in government-guaranteed student loans. Sallie Mae bonds are sold to investors as a means to purchase student loans from financial institutions.

savings bond: A bond issued by the U.S. government in small denominations. Series EE savings bonds are issued at a 50% discount to their face value. Series HH bonds pay interest semiannually. Interest on savings bonds is not taxable at the state or local level. They can be purchased from most banks or from offices of the Federal Reserve.

Securities and Exchange Commission (SEC): The federal agency that oversees securities trading and administers U.S. securities laws.

Securities Investor Protection Corporation (SIPC): Similar in concept to the FDIC, the SIPC covers customers of brokerage firms in the event of fraud or insolvency. Up to $500,000 in securities are covered per account, $100,000 of which can be cash. For SIPC purposes, a money market mutual fund is considered a security.

Separate Trading of Registered Interest and Principal on Securities (STRIPS): Zero coupon U.S. Treasury bonds created by separating the interest and principal portions of Treasury bonds.

settlement date: The date upon which a buyer must present cash to pay for a security and the seller must present the security sold. The standard time frame between a stock transaction and its settlement date is three business days. Options trade with next-day settlement, and bonds can be settled next-day or standard.

short interest: The number of shares of a stock that have been sold short. High short interest can be a bullish sign, because it indicates pent-up demand for the security when short sellers buy in order to replace the shares they borrowed.

short interest ratio: A stock's short interest divided by its average daily trading volume.

short sale: A strategy that profits from falling stock prices, short selling involves selling stock that is not owned. To sell, the investor must borrow shares so that they may be delivered to the buyer. Eventually the position must be covered, because the borrowed shares must be returned to the lender. The short seller's plan is to buy the shares back at a price lower than the sale price. The risk in short selling is very high, as there is no limit to how far the stock's price can rise.

short squeeze: A type of self-fulfilling prophecy in which a rising stock price pressures those who have sold short to cover their positions in order to limit their losses. The demand created by short sellers' covering causes additional price increases, which in turn pressures remaining short sellers even more.

single premium deferred annuity (SPDA): A deferred annuity purchased with a lump-sum payment. The amount deposited grows tax-deferred until withdrawn.

socially responsible investments: Investments or mutual funds that avoid industries considered to be environmentally unfriendly. Industries avoided may also include alcohol and tobacco.

spin-off: The distribution to a company's shareholders of the stock of one of the company's subsidiaries. A spin-off reduces the investor's basis in the parent company's shares by the amount designated for the spin-off's basis. No taxes are due until shares are sold.

spot rate: The cash price of a currency, metal, or other commodity.

spread: 1. The difference between the bid and asked prices of a security. 2. An options or futures strategy in which opposite put and call positions are taken with differences in expiration date or exercise price.

stock power: A form similar to the back of a stock certificate that can be completed in order to transfer the certificate. A stock power can be sent separately through the mail to avoid sending a signed stock certificate, which is negotiable.

stock split: A practice that increases the number of shares of stock a company has outstanding and decreases share price. A split is usually announced when a company wants to make its stock more affordable, since the stock's price, EPS, dividends, and any other per share data are decreased proportionately. For example, a 2-for-1 split would double the number of shares outstanding but cut the stock price in half. Because everything is adjusted, a stock split has no intrinsic value.

stop-limit order: Similar to a stop order, except that a limit price is set. When the designated price is reached, the order becomes a limit order, rather than a market order. There is no guarantee that an order will be executed if the market price gaps through (trades above and below, but not at) the limit price.

stop order: An order that becomes a market order when the stop price is reached. A buy stop order becomes a market order when the stock trades at or above the designated price. A sell stop order becomes a market order when the stock trades at or below the designated price. A stop order does not guarantee execution at the stop price.

straddle: An options strategy in which the investor buys a put and a call on a security, and the investor profits if the security is highly volatile. In a short straddle, the investor sells both a put and a call and profits if the security is not volatile.

street name: The term for securities held at a brokerage firm in a customer's account. Holding securities in street name alleviates the problem of keeping them in a safe deposit box and delivering them to the broker after a sale. Dividends and interest on securities held in street name are paid into the brokerage account on the payable date.

strike price: The price at which an option or futures contract may be exercised.

support level: The price at which a security encounters considerable buying activity, resulting in the security falling to this price but not going below it.

taxable equivalent yield (TEY): A yield calculation used to compare tax-exempt securities such as municipal bonds with taxable securities. TEY = tax-exempt yield / (1 – investor's marginal tax rate). The TEY shows how much a taxable investment would have to yield in order to provide the same after-tax return as the tax-exempt investment.

tax deferred: Refers to an investment upon which taxes are deferred until a later date. Examples include 401(k) plans, IRAs, and annuities. Taxes are not due on income and capital gains from the investment in a tax-deferred account until the funds are withdrawn.

tax-efficient fund: A mutual fund whose investment strategy is designed to minimize the investor's taxes. The strategy entails buying securities with little or no interest or dividends and trading infrequently so as to minimize the realization of capital gains.

tax exempt: Refers to an investment whose interest payments are not taxable at a particular level. For example, municipal bonds are not taxable by the federal government. Most states do not tax investors who reside in the state in which a municipal bond was issued.

technical investing: Investing strategies that depend on changes in price and volume for an individual stock or market index.

telephone switching: The agreement between an investor and a mutual fund that the investor may move from one fund to another by giving instructions over the telephone.

tenancy by the entirety: A form of ownership limited to married couples in which each spouse owns one-half of the asset but neither can give or sell his or her portion without the permission of the other. At the death of one spouse, the surviving spouse automatically receives the deceased spouse's share.

tenancy in common: A type of ownership in which the share of each owner passes to his estate or heirs upon his death, not to the other owners.

tender offer: An offer to buy some or all of a corporation's stock. The offer may be made by another company that wishes to perform a takeover or by the company itself. See *odd-lot tender.*

thinly traded security: A security that is not actively traded. A small number of bids and offers means that large trades may move the market price.

ticker symbol: The initials that designate a stock for trading purposes. Ticker symbols for NYSE- and AMEX-listed stocks have three or fewer letters. For example, the symbol for AT&T is T. Ticker symbols for NASDAQ stocks have four or more letters. For example, the symbol for Sun Microsystems is SUNW. A stock's ticker symbol is not necessarily the same abbreviation used in the newspaper.

time value: The amount by which an option's price exceeds its intrinsic value. For an out-of-the-money option, the entire premium represents time value.

trade date: The date upon which a transaction takes place.

trade deficit/surplus: The balance between goods and services exported and those imported. A surplus exists when exports exceed imports and a deficit exists when imports exceed exports. A surplus fuels the domestic economy and a deficit dampens it.

transfer agent: The agent of a corporation that is responsible for keeping stock and bond ownership records, sending dividend and interest payments, and transferring stock and bond certificates. Transfer agents are usually banks.

Treasury bills, notes, and bonds: Debt issued by the U.S. government. Bills mature in one year or less and are issued at a discount. Notes have maturities between one and five years, and bonds mature in as many as 30 years.

treasury stock: Stock that a corporation has issued, subsequently repurchased, and now holds in its treasury. It may be eventually reissued or retired. Dividends are not paid on treasury stock, and the number of shares are not included in shares outstanding for computing per share data such as earnings per share.

triple tax exempt: The term for a municipal bond that is free of federal, state, and local income tax for investors living within the municipality.

Uniform Gift to Minors Act (UGMA)/Uniform Transfers to Minors Act (UTMA): An act whose name differs by state, but which allows the establishment of investment accounts for minors. An adult, who may or may not be the donor, must act as custodian. Gifts are irrevocable and become the property of the child at the age of majority. The first $700 of income earned in a custodial account is not taxable. The next $700 is taxed at the child's rate of 15%. Any income in excess of $1,400 is taxable at the parents' rate (1999 rules).

unit investment trust (UIT): A portfolio of investments sold in shares to investors. UITs differ from mutual funds in that they are not actively managed. The investments held generally do not change over the life of the trust.

unrealized gain or loss: The amount of gain or loss that would be realized if the investor chose to sell an investment. Also called a paper gain or loss.

uptick: A transaction whose price is greater than the price on the transaction immediately preceding it.

variable annuity: An annuity whose return depends upon the performance of securities in investment accounts.

venture capital: Investor pools that provide capital for start-up companies, generally before they have a track record. Because new companies often fail, venture capital investing is very risky; however, the potential returns are very high, should a start-up turn into the next Dell Computer, for example. Typically, venture capital investing is available only to sophisticated investors with large amounts of money; however, several internet venture capital firms, such as Internet Capital Group and CMGI, are publicly traded.

volume: The number of shares or face value of securities traded over a particular period, usually one trading day.

warrant: A security that conveys the right to purchase a specified number of shares of stock at a particular price. Warrants are often issued with another security, such as a stock or bond, but may trade separately after their issuance. They usually have an expiration date.

wash sale: Selling a stock in order to take a tax loss and purchasing the same stock or a substantially similar security (e.g., a convertible bond) within 30 days before or after the sale. In this case, the loss is not tax deductible.

when issued (wi): A security that has not yet been issued. Trading in when issued stocks often occurs between the announcement of a split and the payment date of the split.

window dressing: The practice by a portfolio manager of selling losing stocks and buying stocks that have performed well near the end of a quarter, when portfolio reports are made public. This can create the appearance of successful management.

yield: The return on an investment, which can be calculated in several different ways. See *current yield, yield to maturity, yield to call,* and *dividend yield.*

yield curve: A graph of yields on the same security (usually U.S. Treasuries) at different maturities.

yield to call (YTC): The yield on a bond that is callable before it matures. This yield calculation combines interest received with any capital gain or loss on the difference between the purchase price and the first call price.

yield to maturity (YTM): The yield on a bond that is held to maturity. This yield calculation combines interest received with any capital gain or loss on the difference between the purchase price and the face value received at maturity.

zero coupon bond: A bond that does not make interest payments to the bondholder. Zero coupon bonds are sold at a discount from their face value. The difference between the purchase price and the maturity value constitutes interest.

Bibliography

Books

Beckner, Steven K. *Back from the Brink: The Greenspan Years.* New York: John Wiley & Sons, 1996.

Brealey, Richard, and Stewart Myers. *Principles of Corporate Finance.* New York: McGraw-Hill, 1981.

Bryant, Linda, Diane Pearl, and Ellie Williams. *99 Great Answers to Everyone's Investment Questions.* Franklin Lakes, N.J.: Career Press, 1993.

Chabot, Christian N. *Understanding the Euro: The Clear and Concise Guide to the New Trans-European Currency.* New York: McGraw-Hill, 1998.

Clinton, Ellie Williams, and Diane Pearl. *All About Your 401K Plan.* Chicago: Probus Publishing, 1995.

Dornbusch, Rudiger, and Stanley Fischer. *Macroeconomics.* New York: McGraw-Hill, 1984.

Dreman, David. *The New Contrarian Investment Strategy.* New York: Random House, 1982.

Fisher, Philip A. *Common Stocks and Uncommon Profits and Other Writings by Philip A. Fisher.* New York: John Wiley & Sons, 1996.

Graham, Benjamin. *The Intelligent Investor.* New York: Harper & Row, 1973.

Ibbotson Associates. *Stocks, Bonds, Bills, and Inflation 1999 Yearbook.* Chicago: Ibbotson Associates, 1999.

Kehrer, Daniel M. *The Cautious Investor's Guide to Profits in Precious Metals.* New York: Random House, 1986.

Lowenstein, Roger. *Buffet: The Making of an American Capitalist.* New York: Doubleday, 1995.

Lynch, Peter, with John Rothchild. *One Up on Wall Street.* New York: Simon & Schuster, 2000.

O'Neil, William J. *24 Essential Lessons for Investment Success.* New York: McGraw-Hill, 1999.

O'Shaughnessey, James. *What Works on Wall Street: A Guide to the Best Performing Investment Strategies of All Time.* New York: McGraw-Hill, 1998.

Palmer, Ralph A. *Real Estate Principles and Practices.* 4th ed. Revision authors: Joyce Thayer-Sword, Randall S. van Reken. Scottsdale, Ariz.: Holcomb Hathaway, 1996.

Prechter, Robert R. Jr. *At the Crest of the Tidal Wave.* New Classics Library, 1995.

Sicilia, David B. and Jeffrey L. Cruikshank. *The Greenspan Effect.* New York: McGraw-Hill, 2000.

Train, John. *The Money Masters.* New York: Harper & Row, 1980.

Wanger, Ralph A., with Mattlin, Everett. *A Zebra in Lion Country, Ralph Wagner's Investment Survival Guide.* New York: Simon & Schuster, 1997.

Wasendorf, Russell R. Sr. and Russell R. Wasendorf Jr. *Foreign Currency Trading from the Fundamentals to the Fine Points.* New York: McGraw-Hill, 1997.

Weisweller, Rudi. *How the Foreign Exchange Market Works.* New York: Simon & Schuster, 1990.

Periodicals and Newspapers

American Association of Individual Investors Journal
Appraisal Journal
Bloomberg Personal Finance
Barron's
Financial Times
Forbes
Fortune
Hulbert Financial Digest
Individual Investor
Investor's Business Daily
Kiplinger's Personal Finance
Money Magazine
Mutual Funds
Smart Money
The Wall Street Journal
The Wall Street Transcript
Worth

Websites

401 Kafe' *www.401kafe.com*
A.M. Best *www.ambest.com*
America-iNvest.com *www.america-invest.com*
America Online—Subscription
American Association of Individual Investors (AAII) *www.aaii.com*
American Institute of Certified Public Accountants (AICPA) *www.aicpa.org*
American Numismatic Association *www.money.org*
American Stock Exchange *www.amex.com*
Ameritrade *www.ameritrade.com*
AnnuityNet.com *www.annuitynet.com*
Ask Jeeves *www.ask.com*
Bankrate.com *www.bankrate.com*

Bear Tracker *www.beartracker.com*
Berkshire Hathaway Corp. *www.berkshirehathaway.com*
Best Calls *www.bestcalls.com*
Big Charts *www.bigcharts.com*
Bloomberg *www.bloomberg.com*
Bonds Online *www.bondsonline.com*
BradyNet *www.bradynet.com*
Briefing.com *www.briefing.com*
Brill's Mutual Funds Interactive *www.brill.com*
Bureau of the Public Debt *www.publicdebt.treas.gov*
CBS MarketWatch *www.cbsmarketwatch.com*
Certified Financial Planner Board of Standards *www.cfp-board.org*
Chicago Board of Trade *www.cbot.com*
Chicago Board Options Exchange *www.cboe.com*
Charles Schwab *www.schwab.com*
ClearStation *www.clearstation.com*
CNBC.com *www.cnbc.com*
CNNfn *www.cnnfn.com*
The College Board *www.collegeboard.org*
College Savings Plan Network *www.collegesavings.org*
Company Sleuth *www.companysleuth.com*
ConvertBond.com *www.convertbond.com*
CyberInvest.com *www.cyberinvest.com*
Daily Graphs Online *www.dailygraphs.com*
Data Broadcasting Corporation–eSignal *www.esignal.com*
Datek Online *www.datek.com*
Discover Brokerage Direct *www.discoverbrokerage.com*
DLJ Direct *www.dljdirect.com*
Dogs of the Dow *www.dogsofthedow.com*
Don Johnson's Discount Stock Brokers Ranked *www.sonic.net/donaldj/brokers.html*
Directory of Registered Investment Advisors *www.mmdaccess.com*
Drip Advisor *www.dripadvisor.com*
DTN IQ *www.dtniq.com*
Duff & Phelps Credit Rating Co. *www.dcrco.com*
E*Trade *www.etrade.com*
Earnings Whispers.com *www.earningswhisper.com*
European Investor.com *www.europeaninvestor.com*
Everbank *www.everbank.com*
Federal Deposit Insurance Corporation (FDIC) Institutions Search Engine *www.fdic.gov*
Federal Reserve Bank of New York *www.ny.frb.org*
Federal Reserve Bank of St. Louis *www.stls.frb.org*
Fidelity Investments *www.fidelity.com*

The Financial Center *www.tfc.com*
Financial Engines *www.financialengines.com*
Financial Planning Association *www.iafp.org*
Financial Times *www.financialtimes.com*
Financial Web *www.financialweb.com*
Find a Fund *www.findafund.com*
First Share *www.firstshare.com*
Fox Marketwire *http://invest.foxmarketwire.com*
FreeEDGAR *www.freeedgar.com*
Freerealtime.com *www.freerealtime.com*
Fund Alarm *www.fundalarm.com*
Futures Industry Institute *www.fiafii.org*
Goldsheet *http://goldsheet.simplenet.com*
Gomez Advisors *www.gomez.com*
Habib Bank AG Zurich *www.habibbank.com/xfcc.htm*
Hoover's Online *www.hoovers.com*
Hulbert Financial Digest *www.hulbertdigest.com*
IndexFunds.com *www.indexfunds.com*
Info Space *www.infospace.com*
InsiderSCORES.com *www.insiderscores.com*
Insider Trader *www.insidertrader.com*
The Internal Revenue Service (IRS) *www.irs.gov*
The Internet Analyst *www.theinternetanalyst.com*
Internet News.com *www.internetnews.com*
Investment Company Institute *www.ici.org*
INVESTools *www.investools.com*
Investopedia *www.investopedia.com*
Invest-O-Rama *www.investorama.com*
Investors Business Daily *www.investorsbusinessdaily.com*
Investing in Bonds *www.investinginbonds.com*
IPO.Com *www.ipo.com*
IPO Central *www.ipocentral.com*
IPO express *www.ipoexpress.com*
J.P.Morgan's ADR.com *www.adr.com*
Kiplinger's Personal Finance *www.kiplinger.com*
Keynote Web Broker Trading Index *www.keynote.com/measures/brokers/*
Market Guide *www.marketguide.com*
MaxEMG *www.maxemg.com*
Moloney Securities, Inc. *www.stocktrader.com*
MoneyCentral Investor *http://investor.msn.com*
Money Manager Review Online *www.slip.net/~mmreview*
Moody's Investors Service *www.moodys.com*

Morningstar *www.morningstar.com*
The Motley Fool *www.fool.com*
Muriel Siebert *www.siebertnet.com*
Multex Investor Network *www.multexinvestor.com*
Mutual Fund Education Alliance *www.mfea.com*
National Association of Securities Dealers (NASD) *www.nasd.com*
NASDAQ stock market *www.nasdaq.com*
National Association of Investors Corporation (NAIC) *www.better-investing.com*
National Association of Personal Financial Advisors *www.napfa.org.*
National Association of Real Estate Investment Trusts *www.nareit.org*
National Center for Home Equity Conversion *www.reverse.org*
National Discount Brokers *www.ndb.com*
National Futures Association *www.nfa.futures.org*
Nelson's World's Best Money Managers *www.nelnet.com*
Netstock Direct *www.netstockdirect.com*
Newsletter Access *www.newsletteraccess.com*
New York Stock Exchange *www.nyse.com*
PBS *www.pbs.org*
PC Quote *www.pcquote.com*
Philadelphia Stock Exchange *www.phlx.com*
The Public Register's Annual Report *www.prars.com*
Putnam Investments *www.putnaminv.com*
Quick & Reilly *www.quickwaynet.com*
Quicken.com *www.quicken.com*
Quote.com *www.quote.com*
Real Time Quotes *www.rtquotes.com*
Reesegroup.com *www.reesegroup.com*
The RightLine Report *www.rightline.net*
Robert's Online Commissions Pricer *www.intrepid.com/~robert1/*
    commissionspricer1.html
Roth IRA Website *www.rothira.com*
Securities and Exchange Commission *www.sec.gov*
Smart Money *www.smartmoney.com*
Social Security Administration *www.ssa.gov*
Standard and Poor's *www.standardandpoors.com*
Stockpoint *www.stockpoint.com*
Stockmaster *www.stockmaster.com*
Stocksite *www.stocksite.com*
The Street.com *www.street.com*
Suretrade *www.suretrade.com*
TaxPlanet *www.taxplanet.com*
TD Waterhouse *www.waterhouse.com*

Thomson Real-Time Quotes *http://rtq.thomsoninvest.net/index.sht*
Tim Younkin *www.timyounkin.com*
Value Line *www.valueline.com*
Wall Street City *www.wallstreetcity.com*
Wall Street City by Telescan *www.tscn.com/wsc/free_RT_Quotes.html*
Wall Street Journal *www.wsj.com*
Weiss Ratings Hotline *www.weissratings.com*
Worldly Investor.Com *www.worldlyinvestor.com*
WR Hambrect & Co. *www.openipo.com*
Wright Investors *www.wisi.com*
Yahoo!Finance *http://quote.yahoo.com*
Zacks Investment Research *www.zacks.com*

Index

About the Author

Ellie Williams is a former brokerage firm manager with over 15 years of banking and brokerage experience. She has coauthored a number of books on finance, including *99 Great Answers to Everyone's Investment Questions, All About Your 401(k) Plan, The Smart Woman's Guide to Spending, Saving, and Managing Money*, and *101 Great Answers to the Toughest Financial Questions*. The holder of six securities licenses, Williams owns MONEYWISE, a financial training and education firm. Dedicated to helping investors make educated financial decisions, MONEYWISE teaches the importance of knowing the right questions to ask.